*The publisher gratefully acknowledges
the generous contribution to this book provided by
the Simpson Humanities Endowment Fund
of the University of California Press
Foundation.*

THE ANIMATED MAN

The Animated Man

A LIFE OF WALT DISNEY

MICHAEL BARRIER

UNIVERSITY OF CALIFORNIA PRESS

BERKELEY   LOS ANGELES   LONDON

Frontispiece. Disney draws Mickey Mouse at a reception at the Savoy Hotel in London in 1946. Quigley Photographic Collection, Walt Disney File, Georgetown University Library, Special Collections Division, Washington, D.C.

University of California Press, one of the most distinguished university presses in the United States, enriches lives around the world by advancing scholarship in the humanities, social sciences, and natural sciences. Its activities are supported by the UC Press Foundation and by philanthropic contributions from individuals and institutions. For more information, visit www.ucpress.edu.

University of California Press
Berkeley and Los Angeles, California

University of California Press, Ltd.
London, England

Library of Congress Cataloging-in-Publication Data

Barrier, J. Michael.
    The animated man : a life of Walt Disney / Michael Barrier.
        p. cm.
    Includes bibliographical references and index.
    ISBN: 978-0-520-24117-6 (cloth : alk. paper)
    1. Disney, Walt, 1901–1966.   2. Animators—United States—Biography.   I. Title.
NC1766.U52D53155   2007
791.43092—dc22
[B]   2006025506

Manufactured in the United States of America

16   15   14   13   12   11   10   09   08   07
10   9   8   7   6   5   4   3   2   1

This book is printed on Natures Book, which contains 50% post-consumer waste and meets the minimum requirements of ANSI/NISO Z39.48-1992 (R 1997) (*Permanence of Paper*).

To my parents

CONTENTS

Plates follow pages 140 and 236

PREFACE   *ix*

ACKNOWLEDGMENTS   *xv*

INTRODUCTION: "It's All Me"   *1*

1   "The Pet in the Family"
    On the Farm and in the City, 1901–1923   *9*

2   "A Cute Idea"
    The Self-Taught Filmmaker, 1923–1928   *39*

3   "You've Got to Really Be Minnie"
    Building a Better Mouse, 1928–1933   *68*

4   "This Character Was a Live Person"
    The Leap to Feature Films, 1934–1938   *100*

5   "A Drawing Factory"
    Ambition's Price, 1938–1941   *134*

6   "A Queer, Quick, Delightful Gink"
    On a Treadmill, 1941–1947   *168*

7   "Caprices and Spurts of Childishness"
    Escaping from Animation, 1947–1953   *200*

8   "He Was Interested in Something Else"
    Escaping from Film, 1953–1959   *235*

9 "Where I Am *Happy*"
   Restless in the Magic Kingdom, 1959–1965   *270*

10 "He Drove Himself Right Up to the End"
    Dreaming of a Nightmare City, 1965–1966   *301*

AFTERWORD: "Let's Never Not Be a Silly Company"   *319*

NOTES   *327*

INDEX   *379*

PREFACE

Anyone who writes a biography of Walt Disney is obliged to explain what he is up to, given that a dozen or more biographies of Disney have already been published. It is not enough to say that most of those books are not very good. The question is whether a new biography can avoid the pitfalls that have doomed the earlier ones.

Most Disney biographies have portrayed either a man who fell short of perfection only in a few venial ways (he smoked way too much and used a great deal of profanity), or one who was personally odious (anti-Semitism being the sin of choice) and the products of whose labors are a stain on American culture.

I have found few signs of either Disney in my own research into his life, which began in 1969 with my first trip to California and interviews with Ward Kimball, one of his best animators, and Carl Stalling, the first composer for his sound cartoons. Disney was, in my reckoning, a stunted but fascinating artist, and a generally admirable but less interesting entrepreneur. The trick, I think, is to wind those strands of his life together, along with a few strands from his private life, in a way that yields something close to the whole man; and that is what I have tried to do in this book.

I have concentrated my attention on his work, his animated films in particular, because that is where I have found his life story most compelling. He was, from all I can tell, a good husband and a devoted father, but he was indistinguishable in those and other respects from a great many men of his generation. The Disneyland park was, and remains, an entrepreneurial marvel, but it was much more a product of its times than Disney's films, and its impact on American culture, for good or ill, has been exaggerated. Thomas Edison and Henry Ford may have transformed their country, but Walt Disney only helped to shape economic and demographic changes that would have occurred without him. It is his animated films of the 1930s and early 1940s that make him uniquely interesting.

My great advantage in writing this book is that I have already written a history of Hollywood animation (*Hollywood Cartoons: American Animation in Its Golden Age*) that includes a history of Walt Disney's studio in those years. In writing this book, I have been particularly fortunate in being able to draw on the interviews that Milton Gray and I recorded as part of my research for *Hollywood Cartoons*. Most of the people we interviewed who knew Walt Disney—some of them as long ago as the early 1920s—were rarely if ever interviewed otherwise, and almost all of them have since died. No one undertaking a Disney biography now can draw on a richer store of memories of Disney and his studio than the interviews for *Hollywood Cartoons*. Not all those memories are of equal value, of course, but Disney was a volatile and demanding boss, and his employees had every incentive to observe him closely and remember what they saw and heard.

For this book, I have interviewed a few more people who knew Walt Disney, mostly in connection with his live-action films. Regrettably, most of the people who worked alongside Disney on Disneyland are gone now. Milt Gray and I interviewed some of the park's most important ride designers—people like Marc Davis, Ken Anderson, Claude Coats, and Herb Ryman—but they worked first on cartoons, and our interviews for *Hollywood Cartoons* dealt almost entirely with their work in animation. Fortunately, however, there is no shortage of documentation in this area. Disneyland and related subjects, like Walt Disney's passion for railroads, have been the subjects of several well-researched books, notably *Walt Disney's Railroad Story*, by Michael Broggie, and an occasional memoir. *The "E" Ticket* (P. O. Box 8597, Mission Hills CA 91346-8597; *www.the-e-ticket.com*), a magazine devoted to Disneyland's history founded by Jack E. Janzen and his late brother, Leon J. Janzen, has included a valuable and often unique interview with a Disneyland veteran in almost every issue.

Walt Disney never wrote an autobiography, but he came reasonably close in 1956 when he sat for a series of interviews with Pete Martin, who interviewed celebrities for the *Saturday Evening Post* and had already ghostwritten books with Arthur Godfrey and Bing Crosby. As Disney's daughter Diane Miller explained in 2001, the original idea was that Disney's ghostwritten autobiography would be serialized in the *Post*, but he was not interested. Disney suggested instead that "they change their concept and have his story told by me, his eldest daughter. My sister and I would be paid for it and, although it would be about half of what they'd offered him, it was still a lot of money." That was Disney's way of helping his daughter and son-in-law and their two children get a financial foothold. As Diane Miller wrote, "I was always uncomfortable with assuming credit for authorship of the ensuing book [*The Story of Walt Disney* by Diane Disney Miller as told to Pete Martin (New York, 1957)], because I had very little to do with it, save for attending, with great delight, all of Pete's interviews with Dad. . . . The result is hours of taped interviews, which have been a wonderful resource for subsequent researchers."[1]

Internal evidence—like references to Jean Hersholt's death and a forthcoming Disney TV show—indicates that the interviews were recorded in May and June 1956 (not July, as Diane Miller remembered). Extensive excerpts from the interviews have been published on the Walt Disney Family Museum Web site and in many Disney-sanctioned books, sometimes in modified or paraphrased form. Copies of the complete transcripts (and the transcript of a 1961 Martin interview with Disney) are held by the Walt Disney Archives in Burbank and as part of the Richard G. Hubler Collection at the Howard Gotlieb Archival Research Center at Boston University. I have quoted from the transcripts rather than their published equivalents, correcting only misspellings and other obvious errors.

Hubler was a freelance writer who wrote many magazine pieces and was the as-told-to coauthor of Ronald Reagan's memoir *Where's the Rest of Me?* He was the first author commissioned by Walt Disney Productions and the Disney family to write a biography of Walt Disney, less than a year after Disney's death. In late 1967 and 1968 Hubler interviewed many Disney employees and members of Disney's family, some of whom were never interviewed otherwise. His book was never published. "Turned it in for corrections and/or defections in fact—and got a blank wall," he told me in 1969. "No comment, no reasons, no nothing at all. . . . They paid the considerable contractual penalty and let it drop dead."[2] Hubler retained drafts of his manuscript, complete and partial transcripts of dozens of interviews, and a wealth of other material, all of which he donated to Boston University and much of which I consulted in the course of writing my own book. Transcripts of a number of Hubler's interviews are also held at the Walt Disney Archives, and they have been quoted extensively in subsequent Disney-authorized books like Bob Thomas's biographies of Walt Disney and his brother Roy.

In all these interviews—my own, Martin's with Disney, Hubler's, and others with Disney's friends and employees—there are no gaping chasms of fact, few if any irreconcilable disagreements. (In my research, I have encountered starkly different versions of events only for the filming of *Swiss Family Robinson* on the island of Tobago. Disney never visited the island during shooting, so those disagreements were of limited importance to this book.) Disney himself, from the time in the early 1930s when he began revisiting his personal history for interviewers and approving press releases about it, was remarkably consistent in what he said. When he smudged or passed over episodes in his life, it was usually for readily discernible reasons, like his continuing resentment of what he saw as a former employee's disloyalty.

The greatest obstacle to writing an accurate Disney biography is not deliberate falsehood but the lapses of earlier writers. No writer wants to repeat research that other people have already done well, but a great deal of what has been published about Walt Disney's life incorporates small, avoidable errors. As reflected in the endnotes, I have tried to avoid such errors, especially by relying on primary materials whenever possible. Errors are inevitable, though, and as they surface I will post corrections on my Web site, *www .michaelbarrier.com.*

Some primary materials are more accessible than others. As part of my research for *Hollywood Cartoons,* I saw almost all of the theatrical sound cartoons that Walt Disney produced, as well as almost all of the surviving silent cartoons and a great many of the sponsored films like those made for the military. Thanks especially to the Library of Congress's collection, I have since seen all the live-action features made during Disney's lifetime, as well as almost all the live-action shorts, along with dozens of the Disney television shows. (I have seen only a sampling of the *Mickey Mouse Club,* however; you have to draw the line someplace.)

Although I enjoyed years of access to the Disney Archives during my work on *Hollywood Cartoons,* the rules have tightened since then, and I did not do any on-site research at the archives for this book—a minor inconvenience, fortunately, considering the research I had already done and the other sources available. Some primary materials are not yet available even to researchers who have the company's blessing. Roy Disney's papers, made available to Bob Thomas for his biography, remain closed to most writers, as do materials with continuing legal significance (in what are called the "main files"). If such a thing as a "definitive" biography of Walt Disney is even possible, it will be decades before it can be written. I make no such claim for this book. But I know that it is far more accurate than most books about Walt Disney, and I hope that it also offers a strong sense of what the man Disney was like and why he still commands our attention today. If I have succeeded in those aims,

I will be more than happy to let someone else aspire to write the definitive biography much later in this century.

Little Rock, Arkansas
August 1, 2006

ACKNOWLEDGMENTS

This book draws heavily on research I conducted for *Hollywood Cartoons: American Animation in Its Golden Age,* my history of Hollywood studio animation. Milton Gray, the animator who provided me with invaluable assistance during my work on that book, deserves just as much thanks for his contribution to *The Animated Man: A Life of Walt Disney,* even though I did not impose on him nearly as much this time around. I could use only a small part of the valuable information he gathered for me in the first book, and with this book I have made only another small dent in the accumulation.

I am grateful for the same reason to Mark Kausler, the greatest student of Hollywood animation. Without all the help he gave me in writing the first book, I could never have written this one. In writing about Walt Disney I have also received valuable help from my friends Robin Allan and J. B. Kaufman, two of the people most deserving of the much-abused title "animation historian."

Kaye Malins, the greatest booster for Marceline, Missouri, the little railroad town where Walt grew up, gave my wife, Phyllis, and me a wonderful tour on a rainy morning in March 2005, and she has been a great help in other ways. Michael Danley helped me locate many rare documents. Paul F. Anderson provided me with missing issues of *The "E" Ticket* and his own excellent magazine about Disney, *Persistence of Vision.* Keith Scott, the greatest authority on cartoon voices, sent rare audiotapes of Walt Disney's radio performances in the 1930s and 1940s. Gail Fines, May Couch, and Craig Pfannkuche were of invaluable help in finding markers of the Disney family's life in the public records of Kansas City, Marceline, and Chicago, respectively.

I have enjoyed assistance from dedicated people at many libraries, archives, and other organizations, but especially the following:

David R. Smith and Robert Tieman of the Walt Disney Archives; Rosemary C. Hanes of the Motion Picture, Broadcasting and Recorded Sound

Division of the Library of Congress, Washington; Ned Comstock of the Archives of Performing Arts and Dace Taube of the Regional History Collections at the University of Southern California, Los Angeles; Howard Prouty, Barbara Hall, and Faye Thompson of the Margaret Herrick Library, Academy of Motion Picture Arts and Sciences, Beverly Hills; Maria Morelli of the Howard Gotlieb Archival Research Center at Boston University; Carol Neyer, Lynn Rosenfeld, and Coco Halverson of the California Institute of the Arts, Valencia; Stine Lolk and Sven Hansen of Tivoli Gardens, Copenhagen; Sally McManus and Jeri Vogelsang of the Palm Springs Historical Society; Joan Blocher of Chicago Theological Seminary; Elizabeth Konzak of the University of Central Florida Libraries, Orlando; Carol Merrill-Mersky and Julio Gonzalez of the Hollywood Bowl Museum, Los Angeles; Fred Deaton of the Marshall Space Flight Center, Huntsville, Alabama; Janet Moat of the British Film Institute, London; Lillian Hess of the Danish Tourist Board, New York; Elaine Doak of the Picker Memorial Library at Truman State University, Kirksville, Missouri; Sara Nyman of the Kansas City, Missouri, Public Library; Eric Lupfer of the Harry Ransom Humanities Research Center, University of Texas at Austin; Michelle Kopfer of the Dwight D. Eisenhower Library, Abilene; Carol Martin of the Harry S. Truman Library, Independence; Lisa L. Bell of Smoke Tree Ranch, Palm Springs; Martha Shahlari of the Jannes Library at the Kansas City Art Institute; Por Hsyu of the Burbank Public Library; and the interlibrary loan staff of the Central Arkansas Library System.

Phyllis Barrier, Milton Gray, J. B. Kaufman, and Mark Kausler read the manuscript and made many helpful suggestions.

During my work on *Hollywood Cartoons*, around 150 people who worked for Walt Disney or knew him in other settings sat for interviews with me or Milton Gray, or with both of us, mostly in person but sometimes by telephone. Others provided full tape-recorded responses to my written questions. Many of the people who sat for interviews also answered my questions in letters and provided me with documents of various kinds. It is a source of deep regret that so many of the people on the following list are no longer here to read this book. I regret too that not everyone on the list is represented in the text, but they all contributed to my understanding of Walt Disney and his work. I am grateful to:

Edwin Aardal, Ray Abrams, Kenneth Anderson, Michael Arens, Arthur Babbitt, Carl Barks, Aurelius Battaglia, Ed Benedict, Lee Blair, Mary Blair, Preston Blair, Billy Bletcher, James Bodrero, Stephen Bosustow, Jack Boyd, Jack Bradbury, Jameson Brewer (known in the 1930s as Jerry), Homer Brightman, Bob Broughton, Jack Bruner, Robert Carlson, Jim Carmichael, Marge Champion, Donald Christensen, Ivy Carol Christensen, Bob Clampett, Les Clark, Claude Coats, William Cottrell, Chuck Couch, Jack Cutting, Arthur Davis, Marc Davis, Robert De Grasse, Eldon Dedini, Nelson Demorest, Philip Dike, Eyvind Earle, Mary Eastman, Phil Eastman, Jules Engel, Al Eugster, Carl Fallberg, Paul Fennell, Marceil Clark Ferguson, Eugene Fleury, Hugh Fraser, John Freeman, Friz Freleng, Gerry Geronimi, Merle Gilson, George Goepper, Morris Gollub, Campbell Grant, Joe Grant, Richard Hall (known in the 1930s as Dick Marion), David Hand, Jack Hannah, Hugh Harman, Jerry Hathcock, Gene Hazelton, T. Hee, John Hench, David Hilberman, Cal Howard, John Hubley, Richard Huemer, William Hurtz, Rudolph Ising, Willie Ito, Wilfred Jackson, Ollie Johnston, Chuck Jones, Volus Jones, Milt Kahl, Lynn Karp, Van Kaufman, Lew Keller, Hank Ketcham, Betty Kimball, Ward Kimball, Jack Kinney, Earl Klein, Phil Klein, Fred Kopietz, Eric Larson, Gordon Legg, Fini Rudiger Littlejohn, Hicks Lokey, Ed Love, Richard Lundy, Eustace Lycett, James Macdonald, Daniel MacManus, C. G. "Max" Maxwell, Helen Nerbovig McIntosh, Robert McIntosh, Robert McKimson, J. C. "Bill" Melendez, John P. Miller, Dodie Monahan, Kenneth Muse, Clarence Nash, Grim Natwick, Maurice Noble, Dan Noonan, Cliff Nordberg, Les Novros, Edwin Parks, Don Patterson, Bill Peet, Hawley Pratt, Martin Provensen, Thor Putnam, Willis Pyle, John Rose, George Rowley, Herb Ryman, Leo Salkin, Paul Satterfield, Milt Schaffer, Zack Schwartz, Ben Sharpsteen, Mel Shaw (known in the 1930s as Mel Schwartzman), Charlie Shows, Larry Silverman, Joe Smith, Margaret Smith, Carl Stalling, McLaren Stewart, Robert Stokes, John Sutherland, Howard Swift, Frank Tashlin, Frank Thomas, Richard Thomas, Clair Weeks, Don Williams, Bern Wolf, Tyrus Wong, Cornett Wood, Adrian Woolery, Ralph Wright, Rudy Zamora, and Jack Zander.

In addition, Marcellite Garner Lincoln, Tom McKimson, and Claude Smith provided helpful information through letters, and Fred Niemann shared his correspondence with Frank Tashlin.

After I began work on this book, I interviewed fifteen more people whose paths crossed Walt Disney's. I am grateful to:

Ken Annakin, Kathryn Beaumont, Frank Bogert, Jim Fletcher, Sven Hansen, Richard Jenkins, James MacArthur, Floyd Norman, Fess Parker, Harrison "Buzz" Price, Maurice Rapf, Norman Tate, Dee Vaughan Taylor, Richard Todd, and Gus Walker.

As indicated in the notes, I have been granted access over the years to the personal papers of a number of people who worked on the Disney films. I am indebted to the following people for that access: to Nick and Tee Bosustow, for items from the papers of their late father, Stephen Bosustow; to Mrs. David Hand, for items from her late husband's papers; and to the late Polly Huemer, for items from her late husband's papers, in addition to those that Dick Huemer himself permitted me to copy.

At the University of California Press, Mary Francis, Rachel Berchten, and Kalicia Pivirotto have made transforming my manuscript into a book an exceptionally pleasant experience. And thanks also to Edith Gladstone for her scrupulous, attentive editing.

Finally, I am especially grateful to my agent, Jake Elwell, who guided me through many revisions of my proposal for this book. I think he believed even more than I did that I could write a Disney biography significantly different—and significantly better—than those that had come before.

INTRODUCTION

"It's All Me"

Walt Disney was angry. Very angry. A few years later, when he talked about this time in his life, tears would come, but on February 10, 1941, his eyes were dry, and his voice had a hard edge.

He was speaking late that Monday afternoon in the theater at Walt Disney Productions' sparkling new studio in Burbank, in the San Fernando Valley just north of Los Angeles. That studio had cost more than three million dollars, and an experienced Hollywood journalist wrote after a visit that it compared with any other film studio "as a model dairy to an old-fashioned cow shed."[1] Disney was standing before several hundred of his employees, most of them artists of various kinds. Some directed his animated films, others wrote them. Still others—the Disney studio's true aristocrats—were animators, the artists who brought the Disney characters to life on the screen.

Walt Disney had nurtured his young animators throughout the previous decade, with spectacular results. In 1941, Disney could still lay claim to being a young man himself—he was not yet forty, slender and dark-haired, with a mustache and prominent nose that gave him a passing resemblance, especially when his face was in repose, to the actor William Powell—but he had been a filmmaker for almost twenty years. His earliest cartoons were lightweight novelties, just like almost everyone else's silent cartoons, but Disney stepped out of the pack when he began making sound cartoons in 1928. Over the next few years, he carried audiences with him into new territory, again and again, until, triumphantly, he made a feature-length cartoon, *Snow White and the Seven Dwarfs,* that was enormously popular with both critics and audiences. By the spring of 1938, little more than a year after it was released, that film had already returned to Disney and his distributor RKO almost seven million dollars—much more than any other sound film, and probably more than any other film ever released.[2] Its record was short-lived—*Gone with the*

1

Wind surpassed it the next year—but *Snow White*'s audiences may have been larger, because so many of its tickets were sold to children.

Disney had used much of his profit from *Snow White* not to enrich himself but to build the new studio. Its construction was a carefully planned undertaking, in contrast to the haphazard growth of the old Disney studio on Hyperion Avenue in Los Angeles. Everything—north light, recreation facilities, air-conditioning—had been conceived with the artists' comfort in mind. Some of the artists found the new plant inhumanly perfect and preferred the old studio's jumble of buildings, but no one doubted that Disney had tried to construct an ideal environment for his staff.

The splendid new physical plant spoke of Disney's self-confidence and his mastery of a difficult medium, but by early 1941—less than a year after his employees moved into their new quarters—everything was turning to ashes in his mouth. By then, it was clear that *Pinocchio* and *Fantasia,* the two costly features that followed *Snow White* into theaters in 1940, were not going to recover their costs at the box office. Along with the new studio, they had drained away all the money Disney made from *Snow White.* The war in Europe had cut off the major part of overseas revenues, and now Disney was being squeezed by fickle audiences, anxious bankers, and, most of all, the contradictions that had emerged in his own ambitions.

Disney's aims, when he was starting out as a filmmaker, were almost entirely those of a businessman—he wanted to own an animation studio that cranked out a cartoon a week. He had achieved extraordinary business success not by compromising his artistic ambitions but by expanding them. The 1930s were one of those rare periods when artistic quality and broad public acceptance coincided much more closely than usual. Jazz musicians like Duke Ellington might play one-night stands for dancers who were indifferent to art of any kind, but their music also had many sophisticated admirers. Movies that embodied the unique visions of such creators as John Ford and Howard Hawks drew large crowds. No one thrived more in that environment than Walt Disney. *Snow White and the Seven Dwarfs* is as intensely personal as any film ever made.

Disney had shrugged off many business decisions, leaving them to his long-suffering brother Roy. The two brothers (and their wives) owned all of the business, but Walt and his wife owned 60 percent of it. Roy's task was to find the money for Walt to spend. But with twelve hundred people on the payroll, and multiple features and short cartoons in production at the same time, Walt Disney had no choice but to think harder about what had been receiving only his spasmodic attention. He had to balance the demands of art and business with much more adroitness than had been required of him before.

By early 1941, as his financial difficulties worsened, Disney was finally thinking more and more like a businessman. For him to approach his employees in that role was problematic, though, because they were accustomed to him in his role as an artist. He could not lay off a large part of his staff—and save badly needed money—without jeopardizing much of what he still hoped to accomplish. If Disney reduced his staff, he would be dismantling a structure that was uniquely suited to making the kinds of films he wanted to make.

War-related prosperity had touched off a wave of union organizing efforts and strikes across the country. At the Disney studio, union organizers—spurned a few years before—had found newly sympathetic ears. In January 1941, a few weeks before Disney's speech, a union called the Screen Cartoonists Guild asked the federal government's National Labor Relations Board to designate it the bargaining agent for the studio's artists.[3]

The many members of Disney's staff who were still intensely sympathetic to their boss were troubled by the gulf they saw growing between him and them. On February 4, one of them, George Goepper, wrote a memorandum to Disney about the studio's difficulties. Goepper was an experienced assistant animator—one of the people who followed behind the animators, completing their drawings and adding new drawings to fill out a character's movements—but he was also a highly respected manager. In early 1941, he was supervising other assistants who were working on a new feature, *Bambi*. Morale was poor, Goepper wrote to Disney, especially among the animators and their assistants, and production was suffering as a result. He said that it would help if Disney himself "would personally talk to the group of men most involved with these situations." Such a speech, he suggested, "would throw a different light on this 'Union business.'"[4]

On Thursday, February 6, before Goepper sent his memo, Disney himself circulated a memo throughout the studio. Production had dropped 50 percent, he complained: "It is obvious that a great deal of valuable studio time is being consumed in discussing union matters that should be taken care of on free time." His memo was brusque and condescending: "Due to world conditions, the studio is facing a crisis about which a lot of you are evidently unaware. It can be solved by your undivided attention to production matters."[5]

The next day, Goepper sent his original memo to Disney, but he added another one in which he suggested that the sharp drop in production had to be "a product of a state of low morale, which caused discussions of a Union to become started among certain groups." As Goepper said many years later, he did not expect Disney to respond, "but he called me, and he was upset. It was about four o'clock, and I didn't get out of [Disney's office] until about six, just he and I talking. He said, 'I don't know about talking to these guys. They always twist things around. . . . ' I said . . . '*You,* who own the place, telling what your problems are, might have an effect and straighten up some of these guys.'"

As Goepper correctly remembered, "it was the following Monday we all got called out in the theater, and Walt got up there to read a speech. He gave a pep talk, sort of, but it was a little too late, I thought."[6]

Walt Disney's growing friction with his artists in early 1941 presaged struggles that would occupy him for more than a decade. Speaking to his artists on that February afternoon, Disney stood at the very fulcrum of his own life.

He insisted as he began his speech that he was addressing himself only to the studio's financial crisis, even though everyone knew that it was the union that was really on his mind. He had written his remarks himself, he said— "It's all me"—and, as if to prove the point, he peppered them with his customary profanity. (Someone removed the cursing from a mimeographed version of the speech that was later distributed to the staff.) The speech was being recorded on acetate discs to forestall any legal difficulties.[7]

Disney painted a dramatic picture of his own past:

> In the twenty years I have spent in this business, I have weathered many storms. It has been far from easy sailing. It has required a great deal of hard work, struggle, determination, confidence, faith, and above all, unselfishness. Perhaps the greatest single factor has been our unselfish attitude toward our work.
>
> I have had a stubborn, blind confidence in the cartoon medium, a determination to show the skeptics that the animated cartoon was deserving of a better place; that it was more than a mere "filler" on a program; that it was more than a novelty; that it could be one of the greatest mediums of fantasy and entertainment yet developed. That faith, confidence and determination and unselfish attitude has brought the cartoon to the place that it now occupies in the entertainment world.

As if he were a much older man—not thirty-nine, barely older than many of his employees, whose average age was twenty-seven[8]—Disney reminisced about the days when he had to scratch and fight to get a few hundred dollars more from the distributors of his short cartoons. As archaic as such battles must have sounded to many of his listeners, they were a good measure of how much Disney had accomplished. Only a few years before, a success like *Snow White*—or even a prestigious failure like *Fantasia*—had been unimaginable.

Disney was not particularly concerned, though, with the struggles he had gone through to make better films. Instead, he revisited hard times of a sort endured by many other small businessmen, especially during the Depression.

He spoke not of battles that he had fought alongside the artists who shared his ambitions for the "cartoon medium," but of battles that, he clearly believed, he had fought and won alone (with some help from Roy). As he spoke, his voice hardened even further. Genuine outrage threatened to break through.

> I have been flat broke twice in this twenty years. Once in 1923 before I came to Hollywood I was so broke I went three days without eating a meal, and I slept on some old canvas and chair cushions in an old rat-trap of a studio for which I hadn't paid any rent for months.
>
> Again in 1928 my brother Roy and myself had everything we owned at that time mortgaged. It wasn't much, but it was all we had. Our cars had been sold to meet payrolls. Our personal insurance was borrowed on to the limit to keep the business going. . . .
>
> It was over a year after Mickey Mouse was a success before we owned another car, and that was a truck that we used in our business on weekdays and for pleasure on Sundays.

As for what had emerged from those early struggles, Disney painted a picture that day of a happy studio where faithful employees, grateful for their boss's sacrifices, got regular bonuses. It was an idealized picture, but it was largely accurate. What had kept many of his employees satisfied, though, was not money so much as the sense that they had embarked together on a great adventure, the creation of a new art form—character animation. Artists who were working at other cartoon studios routinely accepted large pay cuts and took lesser jobs when they went to work for Disney. They came to learn.

Disney had nothing to say about such sacrifices, however, as he praised his own benevolence while the studio was passing through its financial crisis: "There was one thing uppermost in my mind while trying to solve this problem. And that was, I did not want to spread panic among the employees. I kept the true conditions from them, feeling that if they didn't thoroughly understand things, it might work against us instead of for us."

As Disney's ambitions had expanded in the years just after *Snow White*'s success, his concern for his employees had gradually metamorphosed into a suffocating paternalism. Now he was refusing to accept any responsibility for the studio's difficulties, even while taking credit for its successes. He congratulated himself for rejecting "obvious easy ways" to deal with the financial crisis. Drastic salary cuts "might have caused panic and lowered morale." Limiting production to "proven money-makers . . . would have meant the laying off of possibly half our studio staff," turning them loose on a cartoon industry that could not absorb them.

Worst of all, Disney said, would have been selling "a controlling interest" to another company or a wealthy individual.

> I made up my mind that if this business was ever to get anywhere, if this business was ever to have a chance to grow, it could never do it by having to answer . . . to someone with only one thought or interest—namely profits. . . . For I have had a blind faith in the policy that quality, tempered with good judgment and showmanship, will win against all odds.

Such indifference to profit and scorn for outside financing were tenable, though, only when money was rolling in. Already, in 1940, the Disneys had been forced to sell preferred stock in their company to outsiders—and they had started paying bonuses to employees in preferred stock, too. In his speech, Walt Disney's choice of words—"blind faith," "tempered with good judgment"—was telling. What he had achieved with *Snow White* had in fact unbalanced his judgment. He was not the first entrepreneur to misread the permanence of a single great success.

It was, however, as he attempted to "set to rest" various gripes and rumors that Disney signaled most clearly his estrangement from his staff. He showed no understanding, for one thing, of the discontent that a new regime of status symbols had created.

> Some people think that we have class distinctions in this place. They wonder why some get better seats in the theater than others. They wonder why some men get spaces in the parking lot and others can't. I have always felt, and always will feel, that the men who are contributing the most to the organization should, out of respect alone, enjoy some privileges. . . .
> Definitely there is no "closed circle." Those men who have worked closely with me in trying to organize and keep this studio rolling, and keep its chin above water, should not be envied. Frankly, those fellows catch plenty of hell, and a lot of you can feel lucky that you don't have too much contact with me.

Disney went on to address directly the subject of his own growing remoteness, the chasm that Goepper hoped such an appearance would close.

> Here is a question that is asked many times, and about which I think a complete misunderstanding exists. . . . The question is: "Why can't Walt see more of the fellows? Why can't there be less supervisors and more Walt?"

The real issue was one of artistic control, and whether Disney was willing to surrender any of it, now that the company had grown too large for him to supervise everything himself. If Disney insisted on retaining control—if his decisions were to be, as always in the past, the only ones that mattered—his employees would naturally seek to involve him in their work as much as possible. They would want "more Walt."

Again, Disney refused to give any ground. He rationalized his refusal to give his employees either more power or more of himself. He had realized "in the early days," he said, that it was "very dangerous and unfair" for him to get too close to any of his employees:

> This was especially true of new men. You all know that there are always those who try to polish the apple. . . . This is definitely unfair to the conscientious, hard-working individual who is not good at apple-polishing. I . . . am well aware of the progress of all the men after they reach a certain spot in this organization. Some of them I might not recognize when I meet them, but I know them by name and reputation. Believe me, when a fellow shows something, I hear about it; and not through my central source but by a general contact with all the key men in the organization.

If he was not to blame for the studio's difficulties, Disney knew who was. His powerful ego, so vital to his studio's artistic and business success in earlier years, was now driving him into open warfare with many of the people who should have been his strongest allies.

> The stumbling and fumbling around of green, inexperienced people has cost this studio millions of dollars. . . .
> My first recommendation to a lot of you is this: put your own house in order; put your own mind in order. . . . You can't accomplish a damn thing by sitting around and waiting to be told everything. . . . Too many fellows are willing to blame their own stupidity on other people.

Because he could not deal with the contradictions he had generated as he built his company, Disney had set up a test of strength with his own employees—and thus with animation itself, the medium he loved and had served so well. He had in effect called a halt to artistic growth in the animated films released under his name, locking in place a limited, and limiting, conception of what character animation was capable of.

Disney's own tremendous energies, devoted to animation for twenty years, would seek a new outlet in the years ahead. He would make a growing number of live-action features, some with animation and some without. He would make exploratory forays into television. He would dabble in miniatures, including a miniature railroad, and toy with the idea of building a children's park of some kind across the street from his studio. Then, quite suddenly, he would assemble elements from his work life and his hobbies in a "theme park" called Disneyland, a park given enormous impetus by its association with a new Disney television show.

His park would be fundamentally juvenile in the way that the best Disney films never were, but that limitation would turn out to be its greatest strength. Disneyland would be perfectly timed to capture the fancy of a country newly awash in both children and wealth, and its association with Disney's films would give it an emotional resonance that traditional amusement parks lacked.

In the decades after it opened in 1955, Disneyland would become the engine for the growth of Disney's company, spawning a host of imitations (some of them Disney properties) that in their collective weight would transform the American public's conception of leisure and entertainment. Disneyland's success would also, as an incidental effect, seal character animation's identity as a children's medium and thus make it more difficult to produce films comparable to those that had made Disney himself famous.

The echoes from Walt Disney's speech that day would be heard throughout Disney's company, and in much of American popular culture as well, for decades afterward.

CHAPTER I

"The Pet in the Family"

On the Farm and in the City

1901–1923

Marceline, Missouri, was a creature of the Atchison, Topeka and Santa Fe Railroad Company. In 1886, when the railroad planned a direct line between Chicago and Kansas City, it needed a town a hundred miles northeast of Kansas City as a "division point" where its trains could take on fuel, water, and fresh crews. There was no town there—that part of Missouri was sparsely settled prairie—and so the Santa Fe created one. The first town lot was sold on January 28, 1888, and Marceline was incorporated on March 6. It was in its early years a rowdy sort of frontier town, but by the turn of the twentieth century it had become more settled and respectable.[1]

When the town was laid out, its broad main street—called Santa Fe Avenue, naturally enough—intersected the railroad tracks alongside the depot. Dozens of trains passed through Marceline every day, and the townspeople, sensible of how those trains would disrupt a commercial street, built their businesses and homes not along Santa Fe Avenue, but along a street called Kansas Avenue. That street ran parallel to the rail line, always a city block or two away, veering north-northeast with the tracks until it ended at Missouri Street. From that intersection, Missouri Street ran due north, quickly turning into a country road.

Less than a quarter-mile north on that road, a mile from the Marceline depot and just outside the town limits, a two-story frame house a few years older than Marceline itself sat at the southeastern corner of a forty-five-acre farm. Early in the last century, that farm was home for a few years to a family named Disney—Elias, the husband; Flora, his wife; four sons, Herbert, Raymond, Roy, and Walter; and a daughter, Ruth.

The Disneys moved to Marceline from Chicago in April 1906, drawn away from the city by Elias's fear that its crime and corruption would taint his children. He had chosen Marceline, readily accessible from Chicago, for its rural setting and because of a family connection. Robert Disney, Elias's younger brother and one of his ten siblings, was co-owner of a farm of 440 acres, less than a mile west of Marceline.[2] Elias visited Marceline early in February 1906, just before he sold his house in Chicago.[3] A month later, on March 5, 1906, he bought a forty-acre farm that had been owned by William E. Crane, a Civil War veteran who had died the previous November.[4] The price was three thousand dollars, or seventy-five dollars an acre. A month later, on April 3, he paid four hundred fifty dollars for an adjoining tract, a little over five acres, that Crane's widow owned in her own name.[5]

The Disneys lived on Chicago's West Side, at 1249 Tripp Avenue.[6] Elias and Flora and their first child, Herbert, had moved to Chicago by 1890. They were living then at 3515 South Vernon Avenue in the Fourth Ward, just south of downtown and less than a mile from Lake Michigan. Their second son, Raymond Arnold, was born there on December 30, 1890. Chicago was growing rapidly—an 1889 annexation had added 125 square miles and 225,000 people—and there was plenty of work for carpenters; Elias Disney identified himself as one in the 1891 city directory.[7]

On October 31, 1891, Elias bought a lot at 1249 Tripp. By sometime in 1892 he had built a house on it.[8] Roy Oliver Disney, the third son, was born there on June 24, 1893, followed by Walter Elias on December 5, 1901, and, on December 6, 1903, the Disneys' youngest child and only daughter, Ruth Flora. The neighborhood, called Hermosa (for reasons that are unclear), was new and raw in the early 1890s, settled only a few years before by Scottish, German, and Scandinavian immigrants. It had been added to the city in the 1889 annexation.[9]

"A neighboring family just like ours was very close to us," Roy Disney told Richard Hubler in 1967. "We woke up one morning and two of their boys were involved in a car barn robbery. . . . Shot it out with the cops, killed a cop. One of them went to Joliet [Prison] for life and the other got twenty years. These kids were just the same age as my older brother and my second brother [that is, in their midteens]. We had a nice neighborhood. A lot of good Irish and Poles and Swedes around there, but it was a rough neighborhood, too, in a way." There were saloons on three corners where the Disneys bought their newspaper.[10]

Elias and the two older boys, Herbert and Raymond, escorted "a box car full of our household furniture and two horses that dad bought in Chicago," Roy recalled.[11] Flora traveled separately with the two younger boys and Ruth, evidently arriving ahead of her husband. Walt Disney was only four years old then, but he wrote more than thirty years later: "I clearly remember the day we arrived there on the train. A Mr. Coffman met us in the wagon and we rode out to our house in the country just outside the city limits. I believe it was called the Crane Farm. My first impression of it was that it had a beautiful front yard with lots of weeping willow trees."[12]

Roy remembered their new home as "a very cute, sweet little farm, if you can describe a farm that way." The forty-five acres included orchards of apples, peaches, and plums, as well as fields of grain, and the farm was home to dozens of animals—hogs, chickens, horses, and cows. "Of course," Roy said, "it was just heaven for city kids."[13]

Almost fifty years after leaving it, Walt Disney also spoke warmly of the farm. "It had two orchards, one called the old and one called the new. We had every kind of an apple growing in that orchard. We had what we called Wolf River apples. They were that big. . . . People came from miles around to see our orchard. To see these big things."[14]

(Disney's affectionate memories of his childhood on the farm, like anyone's childhood memories, may not be entirely trustworthy. On a return visit to Marceline in July 1956, he spoke to a welcoming crowd of his exploits as a "hog rider."[15] Then, as on other occasions, he said he rode atop sows until they plunged into what he variously called a "pig pond" or mud puddles. Roy Disney dismissed that story as "some of his ebullience. . . . There never were any mud puddles.")[16]

Marceline's population had risen to more than twenty-five hundred by 1900, and it peaked at around four thousand while the Disneys lived there. Marceline was just large enough—at a time when the majority of Americans lived in even smaller places[17]—and just close enough to the Disney farm, to hold a certain urban allure, at least for a boy who was too young to remember much about living in Chicago, as the older Disney brothers did. Walt Disney's strongest nostalgia in later years was less for farm life than for the busy life of a prosperous small town.

In the first decade of the twentieth century, Marceline was not some isolated, impoverished rural outpost. Kansas Avenue was lined with shops, and for most if not all of their Marceline stay, the Disneys had a telephone (their name is in a 1907 directory).[18] It was, however, the trains that kept Marceline in touch constantly with the wider world. In those days—with the automobile in its infancy and the roads for horse-drawn vehicles mostly poor—trains dominated freight and passenger service to an extent hardly conceivable a century later.

Walt Disney remembered the scarcity of automobiles in the Marceline he knew. In a May 15, 1952, meeting during work on *Lady and the Tramp,* an animated feature set at the turn of the twentieth century, he said: "In this period—I can remember those days, you know—I lived in a little town in Missouri, and there were only two automobiles. It was 1908. They began to come in then."[19]

The trains were, besides, daily reminders that much larger cities were only a few hours away. Combining speed, power, and the romance of faraway places, the railroads had few competitors for the imaginations of millions of people, boys especially. In the decades that followed, even as the railroads slowly gave up their position atop the American economy, model railroads thrived, their elaborate layouts built by middle-aged men who had fallen under trains' spell when they were children. As a train fancier in later years, Walt Disney would be one among many.

For the Disney children, a family connection enhanced the trains' appeal: their mother's older sister Alice (who had died in 1905) was married to Mike Martin, a Santa Fe engineer. The Martins lived a little more than a hundred miles up the line, in Fort Madison, Iowa, near the Mississippi River, and Martin's work took him through Marceline. As Roy Disney recalled, "We used to ride in the cab with him once in a while."[20]

Elias Disney had been modestly successful in Chicago, but he was not a man for whom success of any kind was a natural fit. Before moving to Chicago, he had failed as an orange grower in Florida. For him to return to farming of any kind was tempting fate, however unselfish his motives.

Elias was a Canadian, born in rural Ontario in 1859. He was the eldest of the eleven children of Kepple Disney and his wife, Mary Richardson, both of whom had immigrated to Canada from Ireland as children, with their parents. Kepple and Mary lived after their marriage on a farm about a mile from the village of Bluevale.[21] Official Disney biographies suggest that the Disney name is a corruption of a French original, and that the first Disneys came to England in the eleventh century with the Norman invaders, but, as traced through census records, the family tree's roots dwindle to invisibility in eighteenth-century Ireland.

Kepple Disney and his family moved to a farm at Ellis, Kansas, in 1878, and it was from there that Elias moved to Florida and undertook his failed venture as an orange grower. In Florida on January 1, 1888, he married Flora

Call, sixth of eight daughters (there were two sons) in a family he had known in Kansas. Flora, born in 1868, was nine years Elias's junior. Their first child, Herbert Arthur, was born in Florida on December 8, 1888.

After the family moved to Chicago, Elias found work as a carpenter at the World's Columbian Exposition of 1893.[22] The skimpy record of building permits issued around the turn of the twentieth century suggests that he had by then become an active contractor, building houses that he owned for resale.[23] When his father was a Chicago contractor, Roy Disney said, Elias "built the Congregational church in our neighborhood."[24] That was Saint Paul Congregational, at the intersection of Keeler and Belden Avenues, two blocks from the Disneys' home. The church was organized in 1898, and its newly constructed building was dedicated on October 14, 1900.[25]

"We belonged there," Roy said. "Dad used to sub for the preacher when he was away. All us kids went to Sunday school and church."[26] Elias was one of the church's trustees, Flora its treasurer. Walter Elias Disney was named for his father and for Walter Robinson Parr, the English-born minister of Saint Paul Congregational from 1900 to 1905. Walt Disney was baptized at the church on June 8, 1902. Parr gave the name Walter Elias to a son of his own in 1904.[27]

Elias Disney was a highly religious man, "a strict, hard guy with a great sense of honesty and decency," in Roy Disney's words. "He never drank. I rarely ever saw him smoke."[28] Elias was not just a Christian of a flinty sort, but also a socialist, a follower of Eugene V. Debs. Walt Disney remembered copying the cartoons by Ryan Walker in the Kansas-based socialist newspaper, the *Appeal to Reason,* which came to the Disney household every week: "They always had a front-page cartoon, of capital and labor, and when I was . . . trying to draw . . . I had them all down pat."

In 1894, when the Disneys were living in Chicago and the United States was suffering through a severe depression, capital and labor collided in the most traumatic fashion. The Pullman strike, which began in a company town south of Chicago, spread throughout the country when the American Railway Union, whose president was Debs, declared a boycott of trains that included Pullman sleeping cars. The strike ended only after President Grover Cleveland sent federal troops to Chicago and other cities in July; Debs was jailed for disobeying an injunction against the boycott. Elias Disney's socialist beliefs undoubtedly owed something to what he saw of the Pullman strike and its outcome.

Many people have found socialist and Christian beliefs compatible, and that was certainly true at the turn of the last century, but their juxtaposition was particularly unfortunate in Elias's case. His allegiances encouraged him to see his failures as evidence that he was in thrall to grim, implacable forces, either his own weakness and sin or an increasingly impersonal and machinelike economy. Elias had an entrepreneurial temperament, as evidenced by his repeated attempts to go into business for himself, but all signs are that his beliefs pushed him toward stoic persistence and away from the nimbleness and opportunism that have always marked successful entrepreneurs.

Elias's sons responded in different ways to their father's demands. The two oldest boys, Herbert and Raymond, shared a bedroom on the first floor of the Marceline house. "They didn't like the farm," Roy said, "and after about two years [probably in the fall of 1908] they went out the window one night and went back to Chicago."[29] Both soon wound up working in Kansas City as clerks.

The older sons apparently never talked on the record about their father, but Roy Disney did, at one point recalling an episode that would not seem to reflect well on Elias, whatever the transgression that provoked him:

"I remember in Chicago we had an apple tree in the back yard. He'd send me to my room where I could see down over the backyard. And he'd wait a half hour; then he'd casually walk out there and eye the tree and go over to it . . . making an impression on me . . . select a switch and cut it off, feel it, test it out like a little whip. All the time I'm in torture up there thinking about my licking. When he came up there he'd have a little switch and the biggest part of it would [be] no bigger than your finger. And you had to take your pants down and you got a switching. That was Dad."[30]

Both Walt and Roy Disney remembered their father's quick temper, which found a mirror in their own impatience with him. "He knew what he wanted to do," Walt Disney said, "and he expected you to know just what he wanted to do. . . . I'd say, 'And how can I read your mind? . . . I'd come right back at him. He'd get mad . . . and he'd start after me. And my dad was the kind of guy who'd pick up anything near him"—even a hammer or a saw, although Elias retained enough self-possession that he attacked his sons only with the handle of the hammer or the side of the saw. Walt's defense was to run away until his mother had restored calm.

Elias "had a peculiar way of talking," Walt said. "I could never figure some of the expressions he used. He'd get mad at me and call me a little scud. He says, 'You little scud, I'll take a gad to you,' and I found out later, when I was digging into Irish law and things, that a scud is equivalent to a little squirt . . . and a gad is something they used to sort of flail, you know, they used to beat the grain with it."*

---

* Disney's "digging" was probably to prepare for his 1959 live-action feature *Darby O'Gill and the Little People,* a film rich in Irish atmosphere but shot entirely in California.

The two younger Disney brothers remembered their father not as the forbidding man such anecdotes suggest, but with obvious fondness and unforced compassion. Elias was, they recognized, a decent man caged by harsh ideas. "A good dad," Roy said. "So I don't like him put in the light of being a brutal or mean dad. That he was not."[31]

Elias had no gift for small talk, even with his sons. He was, after all, past forty when his two youngest children were born. "Yet he was the kindest fellow," Walt said, "and he thought of nothing but his family." Walt spoke of his father "constantly," his daughter Diane said in 1956. "I think Dad had a very strong family feeling. He loved his dad. He thought he was tough. But he did love him. He loved that old man."[32] Strip away the crippling dogmas that Elias embraced, and a far more appealing figure emerges, a vigorous risk taker who was not afraid to take chances even when he was well into middle age—a figure with more than a passing resemblance to his youngest son.

Elias "loved to talk to people," Walt Disney said. "He believed people. He thought everybody was as honest as he was. He got taken many times because of that." Elias had a winning streak of eccentricity, as Walt recalled: "Dad was always meeting up with strange characters to talk socialism. . . . He'd bring them home! . . . And anybody who could play an instrument. . . . They were tramps, you know? They weren't even clean. But he'd want to bring them into the dinner table, and my mother would have nothing of it. She'd feed them out on the steps."

In a clear break with his astringent principles, Elias was "an old-time fiddler," as Don Taylor, the Disneys' Marceline neighbor as a teenager, remembered more than sixty-five years later; "and many Sundays he would harness the old buckskin mare to the family buggy, and while Ruth and Walt sat in the back with their feet hanging out, Mr. and Mrs. Disney put the violin in the buggy and drove to my parents' home. Here he was joined by another fiddler [while] my sister . . . would play the piano. . . . I still can see Walt and Ruth sitting in straight-back chairs listening to the music which would generally last about an hour or so. To me, Walt was a very quiet, unassuming lad; and in addressing me, he would always say, 'Hello, Dawn [sic].'"[33]

Flora Disney also softened the sternness of Elias's rule. "We had a wonderful mother that could kid the life out of my dad when he was in his peevishness," Roy said.[34] When the family was scraping by, selling butter and eggs, she put extra butter on the children's bread, turning the slices over so that Elias would not see that she was giving them butter he could have sold. "So," Walt Disney said, "we'd say to Dad, 'Look, there's no butter on the bread.' And it was just loaded underneath, you know?"

Walt escaped the worst of his father's wrath. "He was a pet around the house," Roy said. "Us older kids said that he got off easy with Dad because by the time Dad got around to him he'd worn himself out chasing us, so Walt had an easy time. Walt would get a chair between [himself] and Dad and just argue the dickens out of Dad. Dad couldn't get ahold of him."[35] Walt Disney used a phrase like Roy's to describe his role on the farm. "I just played," he said. "I was sort of the pet in the family."

Roy was a benevolent big brother to Walt and Ruth. "Roy was the one who would always see that Ruth and I had a toy," Walt said in 1956. "Roy didn't have much money, but by gosh he always saw we had a toy."

Marceline's new Park School opened in 1908, but Walt's parents did not send him there until the fall of 1909, when he was almost eight years old; he and Ruth, two years younger, started school together. Until then, "I had leisure time," he said. He spent much of it with his "pals" who lived on adjoining properties, the older men he identified as "Doc Sherwood" (Leighton I. Sherwood, who was in his seventies then) and "Grandpa Taylor" (probably E. H. Taylor, who was around seventy). For a time, he also enjoyed the company of his father's widowed mother, Mary Richardson Disney, who was, unlike her straitlaced son, "always into mischief." She aroused Elias's ire, Walt Disney said, by sending her grandson onto a neighbor's property to steal turnips.[36]

Disney remembered receiving encouragement to draw from some of his adult companions. Sherwood gave him "a nickel or something" to draw a picture of his horse, and his aunt Margaret—Robert Disney's wife—brought him pads of paper and crayons and praised his drawings ("stick things," Disney called them) extravagantly.[37] In one oft-repeated family anecdote, the young Walt drew what Roy called "his ideas of animals" on the side of the Disney house with soft tar that Elias had used to seal a barrel that caught rainwater.

The Disneys would need that rainwater if drought dried up their wells, and there are echoes in Walt's and Roy's memories of how hard and practical their farm life really was. The Disneys stored apples after the harvest, Roy said, then sold them "in March and April, when you could get a respectable amount of money for a bucket of apples. We did that two years, and then Dad and I and Walt—he was big enough then to tag along but he wasn't really much help—would go downtown and go door to door and peddle our apples. We really got good money out of it. In those days you could sell a bucket of apples for a quarter."[38]

Elias induced at least some of his fellow farmers to join a sort of union called the American Society of Equity, founded a few years earlier to consolidate farmers' buying power. In Don Taylor's recollection, Elias hosted an oyster supper at the Knights of Pythias Hall, on the second floor above Zurcher's jewelry store on Kansas Avenue. "Farmers came from all over with their families" to eat the soup made from five gallons of raw oysters. Writing in the 1970s, Taylor said that "never have I ever tasted oyster soup quite as good as that served at Elias Disney's in 1907."[39]

The Disneys lived on their farm for about four and a half years, until Elias sold it on November 28, 1910. "My dad had a sickness," Walt Disney said—Roy identified it as diphtheria, but it was evidently typhoid fever, followed by pneumonia[40]—"and they decided to sell the farm. So my dad . . . he had to auction all the stock and things. And it was in the cold of the winter and I remember Roy and myself . . . going all around to the different little towns and places, tacking up these posters of the auction. And I remember my mother heating these bricks in the oven, we put the bricks in the floor of the buggy and a robe over us and we went around, all around tacking up these posters."

As idyllic as life on the farm had been for the boys, Walt especially, leaving it was correspondingly painful. Roy Disney remembered "distinctly" that when the farm was sold, "we had a little six-month-old colt [that] was sold and tied up to a buggy and taken away, and Walt and I both cried. Later on that day . . . we were down in town and here was this farmer and his rig hitched up to the hitching rack and our little colt tied on behind . . . and the damn little colt saw us when we were across the street and he whinnied and whinnied and reared back on his tie-down, and we went over and hugged him and cried over him. . . . That was the last we saw of him."[41]

The Disneys moved into Marceline for the remainder of the 1910–11 school year, most of that time renting a house, probably at 508 North Kansas Avenue.[42] Then, on May 17, 1911, they left for Kansas City, Missouri, about 120 miles away.[43] (Robert Disney lived in Kansas City then and may have encouraged his brother to move there.) They lived first in a rented house at 2706 East Thirty-first Street.[44] Walt entered the Benton School at 3004 Benton Boulevard, barely two blocks from his new home, in September 1911. Although he had completed the second grade at Marceline, the Kansas City schools required him take that grade over. In September 1914, the Disneys bought a modest frame house at 3028 Bellefontaine Street, a few steps north of Thirty-first and about four blocks east of their first Kansas City home.[45]

Kansas City was vast compared with Marceline. The Missouri side alone was a city of more than a quarter million people. Add Kansas City, Kansas, and other surrounding towns, and the total was well above a half million. Since the Civil War, Kansas City had grown steadily by serving as a vital hub for western settlement, for cattle drives, and for barge and rail traffic in agricultural products and manufactured goods from throughout the Midwest. By early in the twentieth century, its remaining frontier rawness was retreating rapidly in the face of such refinements as broad, landscaped boulevards. In 1911, Kansas City was not just bigger than Marceline, it was truly different, a real city.

Marceline and Kansas City were, however, similar in some fundamentals. Disney cheerfully associated outhouses only with Marceline when he spoke to the crowd there in July 1956, but he had remembered differently just a few weeks earlier, when he was interviewed by Pete Martin, a writer for the *Saturday Evening Post*. He said then, no doubt correctly, that the Disney family relied on an outhouse at its Bellefontaine address until he and his carpenter father enlarged the house one summer, adding a kitchen, bedroom, and bathroom.

For the senior Disneys, who had lived in Chicago a few years before, the move to Kansas City may have been disheartening, one more setback to absorb, but the city cannot have been as startling a change for them as it must have been for their nine-year-old son. Yet unlike other children in such situations, Walt Disney seems not to have been thrilled or cowed by the city's crowds and bustle. He rarely if ever spoke of Kansas City with the nostalgic fondness he felt for Marceline. That was surely because—in contrast to his life on the farm—he had so little free time. From the time the Disneys moved to Kansas City, Walt was put to work.

As of July 1, 1911, Elias bought (for twenty-one hundred dollars) a *Kansas City Star* delivery route that extended from Twenty-seventh Street to Thirty-first Street, and from Prospect Avenue to Indiana Avenue, on the city's southeast side. Curiously, the route was in Roy's name, rather than Elias's, evidently because Elias, at fifty-one, was so much older than the typical *Star* route owner. Elias, Roy, and Walt delivered the morning *Times* to almost seven hundred customers and the afternoon and Sunday *Star* to more than six hundred, figures that increased over time.[46]

"It was a big load," Roy said. "And Sunday was a big work day. . . . We got out of the church habit because of that. That'll break your church, you know."[47] The "church habit" had probably begun to fade even in Marceline, where there was no Congregational church. Like his brother, Walt Disney noticed a falling away in the family's religious observances. The Disneys asked grace over dinner, he said, "but later on that kind of disappeared."

Disney spoke of the newspaper route's demands in 1955: "When I was nine, my brother Roy and I were already businessmen. We had a newspaper route . . . delivering papers in a residence area every morning and evening of the year, rain, shine, or snow. We got up at 4:30 A.M., worked until the school bell rang and did the same thing again from four o'clock in the afternoon until supper time. Often I dozed at my desk, and my report card told the story."[48]

Forty years afterward, he still dreamed that he had missed customers on his route. "I remember those icy cold days of crawling up these icy steps" to put the newspaper inside a storm door, he said in 1956. Elias insisted that the papers not be thrown on porches or in yards, but carried to the front door. "I was so darn cold I'd slip, and I could cry, so I cried." The Disneys' route encompassed grander homes than their own, and Walt said the "wealthy kids" on his route often left "wonderful toys" outside. He sometimes paused in his deliveries to play "with these electric trains or wind-up trains."

Roy Disney delivered newspapers for his father only until he graduated from Manual Training High School in 1912.[49] He then worked on an uncle's farm for a summer before taking a job as a clerk at the First National Bank of Kansas City. Walt Disney continued to deliver papers, for a total of more than six years. In the winter when snow was on the ground, said the Disneys' next-door neighbor Meyer Minda, Elias and Walt loaded their newspapers onto bobsleds. On summer mornings, the Mindas were awakened by the clanking iron wheels of the Disneys' delivery cart.[50]

When Elias hired other boys to help with the route he paid them three or four dollars a week, Walt Disney said, but he would not pay his son. "He said that it was part of my job. I was part of the family. He said, 'I clothe and feed you.' . . . So he wouldn't pay me." Walt began to find ways to make— and keep—money behind Elias's back, first by delivering medicine for a drug-store while he was delivering papers, and then by ordering and selling extra papers that Elias did not know about.

Meyer Minda, two years Walt's senior, remembered that the two boys "opened a pop stand together at the corner of Thirty-first Street and Mont-gall," near the Disneys' first Kansas City home, when Walt was ten, in the summer of 1912. "It ran about three weeks and we drank up all the profits."[51] Walt later drew cartoons for a barber named Bert Hudson, proprietor of the Benton Barber Shop on Thirty-first Street near the Benton School. He car-icatured "all the critters that hung out there," Disney said, and got haircuts in return.[52]

"The upshot of it was," he said in 1956, "I was working all the time."

So was his father. In addition to the *Star* route, Elias imported butter and eggs from a dairy in Marceline—"I think every week or two weeks," Walt said—and sold them to his newspaper customers. Sometimes Elias was ill when it came time to deliver the butter and eggs, and on those days his parents took Walt out of school so that he could help his mother make deliveries. Disney remembered his embarrassment at having to push the delivery cart through the neighborhood where his schoolmates lived.

As Walt grew up and Elias grew older, the weight in their relationship began to shift. Walt Disney recalled an incident when his father, angry because Walt had talked back, ordered him to the basement for a whipping. As Walt started down, Roy told him, "Don't take it." In the basement, when Walt again responded sharply to something his father said, Elias raised a hammer, "and he started to hit me, and I took the hammer out of his hand. He raised his other arm and I held both of his hands. And I just held them there. I was stronger than he was. I just held them. And he cried. He never touched me after that."

Walt and Ruth graduated from the seventh grade at Benton School on June 8, 1917.[53] Elias had sold the paper route on March 17, 1917, and it was apparently soon after graduation that he and Flora, and Ruth with them, moved back to Chicago. Elias had been investing in a Chicago jelly concern called the O-Zell Company at least since 1912, and the limited available evidence suggests that he moved in order to take a more active role in the company's management.[54] Walt stayed behind, continuing to work on the paper route for its new owner while living in the family home with Roy, their older married brother, Herbert, and Herbert's wife and baby daughter.

Roy had worked two summers for the Fred Harvey Company as what was called a news butcher, a vendor of candy, fruit, and soft drinks, on some of the many Santa Fe trains passing through Kansas City.[55] After graduation, Walt followed Roy into such a job for the Kansas City–based Van Noy Interstate Company, which owned the concessions on much of the country's railroad network (but not the Santa Fe). Walt lied about his age, not for the last time, since he would not turn sixteen until December.

Although Walt had been working almost all the time since his family had moved to Kansas City, he had always been under Elias's thumb; but now his father was in Chicago. As a news butcher Walt Disney was for the first time completely on his own, a fledgling businessman. By his own account, he fared badly at the hands of his customers. He was the repeated victim of cruel jokes that robbed him of empty soda bottles and thus of his profits. His co-workers treated him no better, pretending to help him while stuffing his hamper with rotten fruit—and Disney himself, attracted by the candy bars he was selling, "couldn't resist eating my own stock," in a repetition of what had happened with the pop stand. (He suffered in another way as well: almost forty years later, he vividly remembered being snubbed by a pretty classmate—"I had always had an eye on her at school"—who was a passenger.)

At the end of the summer, when he left to join his parents in Chicago, Disney was in debt to his employer. Roy said many years later that his brother "just wasn't attending to business. So he'd come in and he couldn't account for all that merchandise he took out so he'd run into a loss and who do you think paid his losses? . . . He was always that way. He never had any knack for business"—that is, business conceived in terms of the careful, precise accounting that Roy found congenial. "It just annoyed him."[56]

For all the disappointments associated with it, Disney remembered "this news butchering chore" as a "very exciting thing." Since he was very small, his life had been confined to Marceline and Kansas City; as a news butcher, he rode different lines' trains to surrounding states. For him, as for so many of his contemporaries, railroads opened up the world as nothing else could. "I loved them," he said of the trains he rode.

In Chicago, the Disneys rented a flat in a two-flat building at 1523 Ogden Avenue on the Near West Side, about five miles closer to the downtown Loop than their old Tripp Avenue address.[57] Walt enrolled in the eighth grade at McKinley High School at 2040 West Adams Street—and, as always, he worked, this time in the jelly factory of which Elias was part owner, in the 1300 block of West Fifteenth Street.[58] He washed bottles, crushed apples, and once carried a pistol as a very nervous sixteen-year-old night watchman. He also took classes three nights a week at an art school, the Chicago Academy of Fine Arts.[59] That was his only formal art training of any kind, apart from some children's classes that he attended "two winters, three nights a week" in Kansas City, sponsored by the school then called the Fine Arts Institute.[60]

At McKinley he was a typical high school cartoonist, displaying in his stiff, awkward drawings such limited artistic ability that most others would have shed any ambitions of that kind in favor of more mundane employment. The characters in Disney's cartoons for the monthly high school magazine, *The Voice*—pug-nosed and vaguely Irish—owe a great deal to the cast of George McManus's comic strip *Bringing Up Father*.[61]

While he was in school in Kansas City and Chicago, Disney said, "I was quite a ham. . . . I loved this drawing business but everything was a means to an end. When I put on a stage play I would make my own scenery. . . . I was putting on these little plays at school where I was always staging 'em, directing 'em, acting in 'em. . . . I always got something where I could fit the kids, because the kids would always laugh at the other kids." In Kansas City, he and his neighbor Walt Pfeiffer presented skits on amateur nights at local theaters, with Pfeiffer's mother accompanying them on the piano.

Disney performed at home, too—"I'd do anything to attract attention"—

with the help of hoary magic tricks like a "plate lifter," a bladder that he put under a plate or pan and then pumped full of air when he squeezed a rubber bulb attached to a tube running from it. His mother "got a big kick out of it" when he put the bladder under some kitchen pans, he said, and at her urging he put it under his father's soup plate. "Every time my dad would go down to get a spoonful of soup my mother would rock the plate. . . . My mother was just killing herself laughing." Elias noticed her laughter, but not the animated plate.

Walt Disney's capacity for hard work was enormous. From July to September 1918, he went to work at the Chicago post office around seven in the morning as a mail sorter and substitute carrier.[62] (The post office hired him, Disney said, only because he wore his father's clothes and lied about his age after he had been turned down as too young.) When he finished with that job in midafternoon, he sought out other work at the post office—carrying special-delivery letters or picking up mail from boxes—for an hour or so, until he rode the elevated line to the South Side to work as a "gate man," loading the trains during rush hour.

Roy Disney had joined the navy on June 22, 1917, soon after the United States entered the First World War. He was called up in the fall of that year, and after leaving Kansas City he passed through Chicago with other recruits on their way to Great Lakes Naval Training Station.[63] Walt met Roy at the rail terminal, where Walt was briefly mistaken for one of the recruits. "It put a bee in my bonnet," he said. When Roy came down from Great Lakes to visit the family, "he looked swell in that sailor's uniform," Disney said. "So I wanted to join him."

He was too young, but in the summer of 1918, when he was working in the Chicago post office, he signed up with "a private subscription deal forming for the Red Cross," as a driver in the American Ambulance Corps. "I was still a year too young," he said, and his father balked at signing the required affidavit, so his mother signed for both of them. Disney then altered his birth date on the affidavit, changing "1901" to "1900," so that he would appear to be seventeen, rather than sixteen, and thus old enough to get the required passport.

Disney was sick for weeks in the great flu epidemic of 1918, and so his departure for Europe was delayed. The war had ended by the time his Red Cross unit reached France on December 4, but he spent almost a year in a motor pool there before returning to Chicago early in the fall of 1919. His time in France was, in Disney's account, much like a greatly enlarged version of his summer as a news butcher. (In one echo of that earlier experience, his comrades surprised him immediately after their arrival in France with a seventeenth-birthday celebration at a French bar—they drank cognac, he drank grenadine—and left him to pick up the tab.) He was grateful, Disney said many years later, that he was so young then, "because I did things that I know when I got up to my twenties that it would be an ordeal for me to do. I'd sleep on the floor of my truck and never thought anything about it. I didn't need a cushion or a big featherbed. . . . And I didn't care where I ate. . . . Everything was an experience to me then."

There is nothing in Disney's history, or his memories of it, to suggest that he ever resented working so hard, starting so early. Disney himself professed to see continuity between his work for Elias and his work as a news butcher and as a driver in France, when Elias was far away. "I don't regret having worked like I've worked," he said. "I can't even remember that it ever bothered me. I mean, I have no recollection of ever being unhappy in my life. I look back and I worked from way back there and I was happy all the time. I was excited. I was doing things."

That was a remarkable statement, considering what Disney said about the miserable winter mornings when he was delivering newspapers, but it was no doubt how he preferred to remember even that part of his life. Neither did he express regret that his formal education ended after the eighth grade. "I don't know how kids can stand four years of college," he said many years later. "I should think they'd get so darn restless and tired, and I don't know how they can stay in college for four years without wanting to try to apply some of what they've learned."

Despite his enthusiasm for work, Disney wanted a job that would not entail the hard physical labor that had been a constant in his life since his family moved to Kansas City. In France, while his buddies were shooting craps, Disney was usually drawing cartoons that he submitted to humor magazines like *Life* and *Judge*. "I remember those damn rejection slips," he said. But he picked up money by drawing "special things for the guys"—caricatures and decorations.

By the time Disney returned to Chicago, he had determined on a career as an artist of some kind. Not only did he turn down an offer of twenty-five dollars a week to work at the jelly factory, he turned his back firmly on the kind of physically demanding work Elias had always done—"I didn't want any part of it"—and headed for Kansas City. "It was a smaller town," he said. "I sort of felt more at home." Moreover, Roy had been discharged from the navy in February 1919 and was in Kansas City working as a bank teller. Walt moved into the family home on Bellefontaine, sharing it again with Roy, Herbert, and Herbert's wife and daughter.[64]

As soon as he returned to Kansas City, Disney applied for a job at the *Star*, the newspaper he had delivered for years. He had hung around the paper's cartoonists when he was a delivery boy—"they'd give me old drawings I could take home"—but now there were no jobs open in the art department. He was "pretty husky" after his year of "manual labor" in France, and when he applied for a job as an office boy the *Star* turned him down again because he seemed too mature.

In October 1919, in Walt Disney's recollection, one of Roy's colleagues at the bank told him about an opening as an apprentice at a shop called the Pesmen-Rubin Commercial Art Studio.[65] Walt showed Louis A. Pesmen and Bill Rubin samples of his work—"they were all these corny things I'd done in France about the fellows finding cooties"—and he got the job. What he would be paid was left to be decided later.

"I worked at this drawing board and during the day I never left it," he said in 1956. "If I had to go to the toilet I just held it until noon." When Rubin approached him at the end of the first week, Disney was sure he was going to be fired. Instead, Rubin, after some hemming and hawing, offered him fifty dollars a month. "I could have kissed the guy," Disney said. It was not the first time he had been paid for drawings, but, for the first time, he had a real job making them.

Disney's new job did not last long, probably not much more than a month. It ended when Pesmen and Rubin ran short of work after a rush to prepare illustrations for catalogs. But, Disney said, his time at that studio was immensely valuable because he learned so many "tricks of the commercial [art] business." A striving for perfection was an unaffordable luxury in commercial art, he found: "When you get into the commercial art shop you cut things out and paste over and scratch out with razor blades. . . . Cutting corners. Moving. . . . That's what I learned in six weeks."

After he was laid off, in late November or early December 1919, he quickly found work with the post office, carrying mail during the Christmas rush. At home on Bellefontaine, using his newly acquired commercial art skills, he began working up samples with the idea of going into business for himself. Then Ubbe Iwwerks (known later as Ub Iwerks; the name is Dutch) called him, probably in early January 1920. A colleague at Pesmen-Rubin, he had been laid off, too. Iwerks, who in Disney's recollection did "mainly lettering" for Pesmen-Rubin, came to see Disney. He was distressed because he had lost the modest salary he was using to support his mother, who had been deserted by Iwerks's father. Disney told him, "'Let's go into business.' And he couldn't quite fathom that." But Iwerks went along, probably because the new business's capital would come entirely from Disney's savings, money he had left with his parents in Chicago.

Disney's parents reluctantly sent him only half the five hundred dollars he had left with them, but that was enough for Disney to buy two desks, an airbrush and tank of air, drawing boards, and supplies. The new firm—called Iwerks-Disney because, in Disney's words, Disney-Iwerks "sounded like an optical firm or something"—grossed what Disney remembered as $135 in its first month, a respectable figure measured against what the two young men had been earning at Pesmen-Rubin.

Disney had clearly inherited his father's entrepreneurial temperament, but as he entered business for himself for the first time, he enjoyed a great advantage: he was free of his father's rigid, debilitating beliefs. He was neither particularly religious nor strongly attached to any political persuasion. As for his field of endeavor, he had become a commercial artist in the first place because that was one area where he had identifiable if modest talents. He lacked education or background for any other pursuit. When he decided to go into business for himself, commercial art was again readiest at hand.

Disney's desire for independence was still half-formed. When the Kansas City Slide Company advertised in the *Times* and *Star* of January 29–31, 1920, for a cartoonist,[66] Disney tried to recruit the company as a client. Its proprietor, A. Verne Cauger, offered him a job at forty dollars a week instead. After conferring with Iwerks, Disney took the job.

Kansas City Slide made slides for local merchants—advertisements that were shown in movie theaters throughout much of the Midwest. Soon after Disney joined the staff, the company moved from 1015 Central Street to new quarters at 2449–51 Charlotte Street and took a new name, Kansas City Film Ad Company, an acknowledgment that short filmed advertisements—the equivalent of today's television commercials—had displaced slides as its principal product. Disney dated the start of his career in motion pictures to February 1920, the month he became a Film Ad employee.[67]

Iwerks stayed behind at Iwerks-Disney, but he was much quieter than Disney—much less adept at winning and keeping customers—and by March he had joined Disney at Kansas City Film Ad.[68]

As an animator for Film Ad, Disney worked with cutout figures, their movable joints riveted with a device that the brother of another animator called "this little gun."[69] Those figures could be manipulated under the camera, their position changing each time a frame of film was shot—an arm could be raised frame by frame, say—so that when the film was projected the figure seemed to move. The films were shot as negatives and projected as if they were positive prints, which meant that everything that was supposed to be black on the screen had to be white when it was photographed, and vice versa. That method saved the expense of making a positive print of a film that would be shown only briefly and then discarded.

Animation itself could not have been new to Disney. Animated cartoons—short films made with drawings, rather than cutout figures—had been commonplace on theater programs since 1915 or so. Those cartoons, made by New York studios, were at a peak of popularity—or at least visibility—in early 1920, to the point that Paramount, the largest distributor, felt obliged to launch a weekly cartoon package of its own after losing the cartoons made by John R. Bray's studio to a rival.[70] It was not until he went to work for Kansas City Film Ad, though, that Disney saw how such films were made.

Disney was intrigued by animation's possibilities and by what he called "the mechanics of the whole thing." He was essentially self-taught as an animator; he wrote to an admirer many years later, "I gained my first information on animation from a book . . . which I procured from the Kansas City Public Library."[71] That book was *Animated Cartoons: How They Are Made, Their Origin and Development* by Edwin G. Lutz. According to its copyright page, Lutz's book was published in New York in February 1920, the same month Disney joined Kansas City Film Ad, so he must have read it very soon after it was added to the library's collection. He said of the book in 1956: "Now, it was not very profound; it was just something the guy had put together to make a buck. But, still, there are ideas in there."

As elementary as the Lutz book was, it still offered a vision of a kind of animation far more advanced than the Film Ad cutouts. Lutz wrote at a time when animators commonly worked entirely on paper. They made a series of drawings, each different from the one before, that were traced in ink and photographed in sequence to produce the same illusion of movement that Film Ad achieved by manipulating cutouts under the camera. Lutz advocated the use of celluloid sheets to cut down on the animator's labor—the parts of a character's body that were not moving could be traced on a single sheet and placed over the paper drawings of the moving parts. Such an expedient (and Lutz recommended others) would have resonated with Disney, who had been so impressed by commercial art's shortcuts when he worked for Pesmen-Rubin.

On a more rarefied level, Disney also learned from one of the books composed of Eadweard Muybridge's nineteenth-century photographs, taken in rapid succession and showing people and animals in motion. He had Photostats made from the pages of the book. The Photostat paper was thin, he recalled, and so he could put his copies of a series of photographs one on top of another, "and I could get the phases of action."

Fortified with such knowledge, Disney "worked out tricks that they hadn't done" at Film Ad, he said. The exact nature of those "tricks" is hard to determine—Disney's descriptions were cryptic, and the films have long since disappeared—but it seems clear that he wanted to steer Film Ad toward drawn animation and more natural-looking movement.

Disney also found the advertising copy itself "a little stiff." As he saw orders for ads coming in, he went to the copywriters with catch lines that would be easier to illustrate, so that, for example, a bank's admonition not to drift through life might be illustrated with "this guy on a boat drifting down river somewhere." He "doubled in brass," Disney said, by posing for still pictures and acting in live action when a film ad required an actor. He pressed, with eventual success, to be allowed to shoot his own films "because I would plan things with my drawings and I couldn't get those guys [the regular camera operators] to do it. . . . The cameramen weren't doing half of what you prepared."

Verne Cauger responded favorably to his innovations, Disney said, and there is no reason to doubt that. From all appearances, Disney made incremental improvements—distinct, but not disruptive—of the sort most likely to be accepted by any but the most hidebound management. Even so, he said, his immediate superior, the manager of the art department, found him "a little too inquisitive and maybe a little too curious. . . . He was kind of sore at me, because I think he felt the boss paid me too much"—five dollars a week more than Ub Iwerks, and ten dollars a week more than some of the other artists.

Lower-level supervisors at resolutely mundane places like the Film Ad Company, protective of their own positions, usually regard bright ideas of any kind with suspicion, particularly if they call into question established methods. Disney did not describe his Film Ad experience in somber terms—that would have been inconsistent with his resolutely optimistic temperament—but it sounds in his recollection like one long narrow escape. However pleased Cauger may have been with what Disney did, the shelter of his patronage was not really very large; he balked at going beyond the jointed cutouts. Early in 1921, after about a year on the Film Ad staff, Disney talked Cauger into letting him borrow an old, unused Film Ad camera so that he could experiment at home on Bellefontaine, in the family garage, but even then Cauger was wary: "He kept saying, 'What are you going to do with it?'"

Elias built that garage after he and Flora returned to Kansas City, probably in mid-1920. The conventional story is that Elias had failed yet again, this time through the jelly company's bankruptcy, but there is no record at Chicago of O-Zell's bankruptcy, and Elias, by then in his early sixties, may simply have sold his interest and retired (his occupation in Chicago in 1920, according to the federal census, was again "carpenter"). Roy Disney remembered that even though the Disneys didn't own an automobile, Elias built a garage at the Bellefontaine house "for income. He was a carpenter and he wasn't working at the time, kind of retired then. . . . So he gets the garage started and talking about renting it and Walt said, 'You've got a customer. It's rented.' . . . I don't recall him ever paying rent, but he set up a cartoon shop in there. He'd come home long after everyone else was in bed and be out there still puttering away, working, experimenting, trying this and that. That's when he'd borrow Cauger's equipment, bring it out, use it at night."[72]

Disney said in 1956 that he "wanted to experiment with this other method, which is the method that was then being employed by the theatrical cartoonists," but what has survived of his experimental work differs sharply from the entertainment cartoons of 1921. It is a filmed editorial cartoon, the sort of thing familiar to audiences from newsreels that incorporated drawings by caricaturists like Hy Mayer. The very young Disney himself appears on-screen at the beginning of the film, as a lightning sketch artist. He had made a drawing in blue pencil—which would not photograph—and he then inked a part of the drawing before photographing it, one frame at a time, so that the drawing seems to materialize on the screen, emerging from the pen in Disney's hand (or, more precisely, from a cutout photograph of his hand holding a pen, which he moved under the camera to match up with the inked lines).

In another segment, to evoke the turmoil in the Kansas City police department in February 1921,[73] Disney shows policemen being thrown out of a station, as cutouts of the kind he had been using at Kansas City Film Ad. Just before that, he shows the policemen walking into the station in a few repeated drawings representing a step. This may have been his entry into "real" animation.

This sole surviving example of Disney's filmed editorial cartoons has been plausibly identified by Russell Merritt and J. B. Kaufman, authors of a book on Disney's silent cartoons, as a "sample reel" that he used to sell a series.[74] But it may have been a sample reel of another kind, one Disney took with him to California as a sample of his work more than two years later; that may be the only reason it survived. It is impossible to be sure; new titles were added by someone at the Disney studio decades ago, and the reel itself may have been reworked.[75]

Disney made his first film, whatever was in it, not just as an experiment in animation but as a speculative business venture. He titled the reel "Newman Laugh-O-grams," using the name of the Newman Theatre, one of Kansas City's grandest movie houses, in the hope that he could sell the reel as a regular feature. "So they looked at it," he said in 1956. "The fellow who was running the theater, Milton Feld . . . was very interested in it and he said, 'Send that kid up to see me.' So I was scared to death." So frightened, he said, that when Feld asked him about the cost of the reel—the cost to the theater, that is—Disney blurted out his own out-of-pocket cost. When Feld agreed to that figure, Disney was stuck with making his films at no profit.

"But I didn't care," he said, speaking still as a man who, as Roy Disney said, had no patience with "business." The money he would get "was paying for my experiment." In his indifference to money Walt Disney stood in sharp contrast not just to his brother but to his father, whose parsimony was of a piece with his grim persistence. "He was very thrifty," Walt said of Elias. "He wouldn't spend anything on himself. . . . I didn't inherit any of that thrift."

The first Newman Laugh-O-gram probably debuted at that theater (in the company of a number of newsreel segments) on March 20, 1921, on the bill with a Constance Talmadge feature called *Mamma's Affair.*[76] Disney remembered making one Laugh-O-gram a week—highly unlikely but not impossible, considering his work habits—at night while he was still an employee of the Film Ad Company. He enjoyed modest local fame as the films' creator, and Cauger made a point of exhibiting the young animator to his visitors. Even so, Cauger remained cautious about moving in the direction that Disney wanted to go. He approved buying only a few sheets of celluloid, and those turned out to be scratched discards. "We made a few things for him," Disney said, "but he never went for it too much. . . . He just didn't want to do it."

Disney eventually saved enough money (from his Film Ad job, where his salary had risen to sixty dollars a week) to buy a Universal camera and rent "this little shop" where he worked on his own films at night. "Then I put an ad in the paper, any boys wanting to learn the cartoon business and things, so they came up and they worked with me at night."

At this point, in the fall of 1921, tracking Disney's career becomes more difficult and his own memories more questionable. Who those "boys" were—Disney spoke of "two or three"—and how much they contributed to Disney's film, a version of *Little Red Riding Hood,* is a mystery. It seems unlikely that any of them worked for Disney on any of his later films. He spoke of Rudolph Ising as one of the "boys," but Ising almost certainly was not one.

It was an unsettled time for Walt Disney. Herbert, a mail carrier, moved his young family to Oregon in July 1921, and Elias and Flora followed them to Portland, probably in the fall, although once again there is a cloud of uncertainty about just what happened.[77] There is not even a record that Elias ever sold the Bellefontaine house, although city directories suggest that Walt moved by late in 1921 to the first of a series of rented rooms. He probably rented his "little shop" around the same time, since the family garage was presumably no longer available.

Disney spoke in 1956 of grooming Fred Harman as his replacement before he left the Film Ad Company ("They brought this young fellow in to take my place. . . . I had quite a time with him. He didn't know proportions and everything"). But in Harman's recollection, the two young men went into business together, as Disney and Iwerks had earlier, while they were both still working for Verne Cauger. Harman's younger brother Hugh remembered their collaboration in the same terms. "They were determined they were going to quit as employees and become their own Paul Terrys," he said.[78] Terry was an animation pioneer—still a young one, only thirty-four, when his weekly *Aesop's Fables* cartoons began appearing in theaters in June 1921, just a few months before the ostensible Disney-Harman partnership came into being.

Hugh Harman, a high school student then, spent afternoons and evenings at the new Kaycee Studios. As he remembered it, Fred Harman and Disney set up their first studio—this may have been the shop that Disney spoke of renting—in office space over Kansas City's streetcar barn. They soon moved to at least two other locations, the last in the 3200 block of Troost Avenue. Hugh remembered Fred and Walt working together on a cartoon, probably never finished, in which an artist's painting came to life on his easel.[79]

Fred Harman wrote many years later that he and Disney "secretly rented a studio, bought a used Universal movie camera and tripod and a second-hand Model T Ford coupe," and tried to shoot film for Pathé News of the first American Legion convention, held in Kansas City in October 1921.[80] In 1932, Harman wrote to Disney himself about that venture: "You can imagine the kick I get from seeing your films and news strip [the *Mickey Mouse* comic strip] and never loose [sic] an opportunity to stretch my suspenders when telling some of my friends about you. In fact, I've told them all of our ventures and never omitting the air flight with Cauger's camera."[81]

Disney also remembered the "air flight," describing it in 1956. He and Harman went up together during the legion convention, he said, Harman holding the tripod while Disney operated the camera. The pilot "had a hell of a time because of the two of us in the back there," but Disney was sure he had some wonderful shots. He had taken bad advice, though, and his camera settings were such that none of his film turned out.

Fred Harman, who gained his own measure of fame as the creator of the *Red Ryder* comic strip, wrote in 1968 that he and Disney "quit our jobs at the Film Ad Company. . . . We had been working very hard, traveling all around the neighboring towns in Missouri and Kansas signing up movie theaters for film ads we hoped to make, but we just couldn't swing it. Our rent was due and finally the Ford was repossessed." Harman's account is problematic on several counts—for one thing, Disney probably did not quit his Film Ad job until the spring of 1922—but Roy Disney also spoke about Walt's efforts to sell his own film ads: "In fact, the old man [Cauger] had a lot of theaters lined up for his slide films and Walt figured, 'Well, they're not selling to this theater over here so I can sell 'em over here,' so he bought a car, hit these little towns, little theaters, and tried to sell stuff he made." At that point, Roy said, "Cauger sensed he was his competitor" as well as his employee.[82]

Whatever its exact form, this was another Disney partnership, like the 1920 Iwerks-Disney combination, that was very short-lived, probably lasting no more than a few months in late 1921. By 1956, Disney had long since soured on partnerships of any kind, except for the one with Roy, and that may account for the way he brushed past his collaboration with Harman.

Kaycee Studios' last location, as Hugh Harman and Rudolph Ising remembered it, was on the upper floor of a two-story building at 3239 Troost Avenue, above a restaurant called Peiser's.[83] "For the most part," Hugh Harman said, "it was just bare floor—just a couple of cubicles partitioned off for their desks." By the time the eighteen-year-old Ising answered a newspaper ad for work as an artist there, probably in early 1922, Fred Harman was no longer involved. As Ising told J. B. Kaufman in 1988, "Walt had a little art studio . . . . He was doing sort of a newsreel insert for Newman theaters. . . . The only guys in the studio were Walt and myself. Red Lyon was probably also there at that time. He was the cameraman at Film Ad. Walt was working at Film Ad too, during the day. . . . I would go to the studio during the day, built some of the equipment or helped Red with the stuff, but mostly it was at night. That went on for three or four months."[84] Ising traced Disney's drawings in ink and operated the camera after Lyon quit. Disney was still shooting film "on spec" for Pathé News.

On May 18, 1922, Disney incorporated Laugh-O-gram Films. He probably left his job at Kansas City Film Ad around the same time. Laugh-O-gram was capitalized at $15,000, divided into three hundred shares of stock at a par value of fifty dollars each. At the time of incorporation, 51 percent of the stock issue was subscribed, giving the company assets of $7,700. Only $2,700 was in cash, though, with the remaining $5,000 in physical assets: equipment that Disney had bought—a camera and camera stand, three animating stands, seven chairs, and so on—plus one completed short cartoon and a few even shorter *Lafflets,* animated jokes. Oddly, the completed cartoon—which with the *Lafflets* was valued at $3,000—was identified in the incorporation papers not as *Little Red Riding Hood,* but as *The Four Musicians.* Disney was the largest stockholder, with seventy shares.[85]

Laugh-O-gram Films moved into the new McConahy Building at 1127 East Thirty-first Street, just one block east of Troost Avenue in the heart of an outlying commercial center a couple of miles south-southeast of downtown Kansas City. Laugh-O-gram occupied a suite on the two-story brick building's upper floor.

Disney was becoming a filmmaker and entrepreneur on the Elias Disney model. That is to say, he had created a business even though he had limited experience and limited capital, trusting to the strength of his desire for independence to make up for those shortcomings. That any investors should have been attracted to the new venture may seem surprising, but Disney had already enjoyed modest success as a filmmaker, thanks to the Newman Laugh-O-grams, and he had shown by making *Little Red Riding Hood* that he could produce a longer film as presentable as many of the short cartoons being made in the East. Add to that record the young Disney's enthusiasm and self-confidence, and investors could reasonably conclude that the risks attending a small investment in Laugh-O-gram Films were acceptable.

The new cartoon producer announced its birth in the trade press in June 1922. Supposedly, six films had already been completed, but that was not true. "They will be released one every two weeks," one article said. "Announcement of a plan of distribution will be made shortly." That plan had still not been announced in August, when Leslie Mace, the sales manager, and J. V. Cowles—a Kansas City physician and "well-known figure in the oil business" who was now Laugh-O-gram's treasurer and had presumably become an investor in the company—were in New York, as another article said, "arranging for distribution of a series of twelve Laugh-O-grams." The idea was still to release a cartoon every two weeks.[86]

Disney, a green animator himself, shepherded his very small, very young, and even greener staff through the production of his first few cartoons, rapidly burning through his capital as he did. He showed himself still hungry for instruction. C. G. "Max" Maxwell recalled that when he went to Kansas City to attend junior college and wound up taking a job at Laugh-O-gram, "I had a little portfolio of the [W.] L. Evans School of Cartooning on animation that had come with my correspondence course in cartooning, and when Disney saw this little portfolio that Bill Nolan [a leading New York animator] had got out for Evans, he grabbed that thing, and that was the last I ever saw of it."[87]

Hugh Harman, not long out of high school, became an animator on Disney's staff. "Our only study was the Lutz book," he said. "That, plus Paul Terry's films."[88] Terry was Disney's unmistakable model in one major respect because Disney's cartoons were modernized fairy tales, just as Terry's were modernized versions of the ancient fables. But Disney and his artists borrowed from Terry's cartoons on a more intimate level, too.

Disney knew Nadine Simpson, who worked at a local film exchange, and she let Disney, Ising, and others on the Laugh-O-gram staff borrow Terry's *Aesop's Fables* to study "over a light," Ising said. "A lion or something was always chasing [Farmer Al Falfa, a continuing character in the *Fables*]. We never could figure out how they did that sudden twist-around. Then we found out these were cycles"—short pieces of animation that could be repeated endlessly, seeming to form continuous actions—"and we could cut out a cycle; they never missed it."[89] Harman remembered clipping "maybe fifty or seventy-five feet" from the Terry cartoons. "They needed editing, anyway." Simpson joined the Laugh-O-gram staff in the fall of 1922 as its bookkeeper.

Although Harman and Ising remembered the Laugh-O-grams as being photographed mostly as inked lines on paper, with what Hugh Harman called "just occasional" use of celluloid,[90] only the first one, *Red Riding Hood,* is unmistakably of that type. The other surviving examples appear to rely heavily on celluloid—the drawings have been traced in ink on the celluloid sheets, painted, and photographed over background drawings. Using *cels* gave an animator much more freedom than working on paper, but it was not a step to be taken lightly in Kansas City. Celluloid had to be bought in large sheets and cut to the right dimensions, then punched with holes for the pegs that assured the proper alignment of the drawings.[91] Disney's use of cels was probably another sign of Terry's influence—the *Fables* were made with cels from the start—as well as Disney's ambition.

Four of the six completed Laugh-O-gram fairy tales have survived, and the cartoons are notable mainly for their strained efforts to be "modern." Cinderella, a little girl with dark hair fashionably cut, goes to the ball in a big car, with her pet cat as her chauffeur, and Red Riding Hood's "wolf" is a lupine predator of the human kind. The cartoons make heavy use of animation-saving devices, especially cycles. The drawing is invariably crude, too, even measured against the heavily formulaic drawing that dominated most cartoons made in the early 1920s. Cartoonists who could draw well while cranking out enough drawings to fill a one-reel cartoon were not plentiful in 1922, and on the evidence of the Laugh-O-gram fairy tales, none of them lived in Kansas City.

However lacking their cartoons, the Laugh-O-gram staff had a good time making them. "Walt was very much one of the boys," Maxwell wrote in 1973. Disney and his crew "would often get together on Sundays, to pretend we were shooting Hollywood type movies." Photos survive of such mock shooting on the roof of the McConahy Building. "Hugh Harman and a friend of his, Ray Friedman, had built a tiny log cabin in Swope Park," south of Kansas City, Maxwell said, "and that was a favorite rendezvous. . . . The movie camera used on these outings was a phony, built by Ub out of a box, a crank, and two film cans on top to represent magazines."[92]

It was not until September 16, 1922, that Laugh-O-gram finally signed a contract with a distributor for its cartoons. That company, Pictorial Clubs, distributed films to schools and churches, rather than theaters. Pictorial Clubs obligated itself to make only a hundred-dollar down payment for six cartoons, with a balance of eleven thousand dollars not due until January 1, 1924[93]—an astonishing arrangement that could not possibly make sense unless Disney had other sources of cash, as he did not. In accepting such a contract, he was amplifying the mistake he had made by selling his original Newman Laugh-O-grams at cost.

By October, Disney was completing *Puss in Boots,* the fifth of the six cartoons covered by the contract, but Laugh-O-gram's money was gone, and the company was rapidly descending into debt. Red Lyon, Laugh-O-gram's cameraman (or "technical engineer," as his business card had it) wrote to his mother in mid-October that the company was "worse than broke" and going into debt "about four hundred more each week."[94]

The search for additional sources of income began late in October. Laugh-O-gram announced then that the company had, in the words of a *Kansas City Star* report, "added the feature of photographing youngsters to its regular business of making animated cartoons. An admiring parent wishing to preserve the native graces of his progeny's actions" had only to get in touch with Disney and Lyon. "Then comes the stalking of the baby." A private screening in the parents' home was part of the package. Few if any doting parents took the bait.[95]

For reasons never explained, Ub Iwerks left his job at Kansas City Film Ad and came aboard Laugh-O-gram's sinking ship early in November 1922.

Max Maxwell remembered that after Iwerks came to Laugh-O-gram he invented what came to be called the "biff-sniff," a device for reducing or enlarging animation drawings: "He put the film in the projector, at the back of the machine, projected it up onto the glass, where the pegs were, and we could make it bigger or smaller."[96]

By the end of the year, after delivering *Cinderella,* the last of its cartoons for Pictorial Clubs, Laugh-O-gram had stopped paying its employees.

Laugh-O-gram did make a few more films, some for money and some as samples that went unsold. Around the end of 1922, Disney made an educational film on dental care, *Tommy Tucker's Tooth,* for which a local dentist paid five hundred dollars. In March 1923, Laugh-O-gram tried unsuccessfully to interest Universal in a sample reel of *Lafflets,* the very short comic films; none of them have survived. Around that time, Laugh-O-gram also made a "Song-O-Reel" called *Martha,* a sing-along film in which Ub Iwerks appeared in live action.

Disney was shameless in other efforts to keep Laugh-O-gram afloat. At one point, he offered a mail-order course in animated cartooning, using the letterhead "Animated Cartooning Studios" and listing himself as general manager and Ising as educational director. A promotional piece dangled the lure of "large earnings," saying: "The remuneration to be derived from taking this training will amaze you."[97] That was undoubtedly true.

Throughout the late fall and winter of 1922–23, and on into the spring, Laugh-O-gram survived, barely, on small loans, the first (twenty-five hundred dollars on November 30, 1922) from its treasurer, J. V. Cowles, who was presumably reluctant to see his initial investment turn sour. The next lender, Fred Schmeltz, owner of a hardware store, made loans totaling more than two thousand dollars between February and June 1923. Schmeltz, as a member of Laugh-O-Gram's board, had good reason to know how desperate the company's situation was, and he tried to protect himself—his loans were secured by all the company's equipment. On June 2, 1923, Disney assigned the Pictorial Clubs contract to Schmeltz as security not just for his loans but also Cowles's, as well as the unpaid salary owed to two employees.[98]

Disney's personal lifeline was an occasional check from his brother. Roy had been diagnosed with tuberculosis in the fall of 1920, and he moved from one government sanatorium to another—from the first, in New Mexico, to another in Arizona, and finally to one in Sawtelle, California, now a part of the city of Los Angeles abutting Santa Monica. Disney remembered that Roy sent him blank checks with instructions to fill them out for any amount up to thirty dollars, "so I'd always put thirty dollars." He scraped by on those small checks and the generosity of the Greek owners of the Forest Inn Café on the first floor of the McConahy Building. He also imposed on Edna Francis, Roy's girlfriend, who remembered that Walt "used to come over to my house and talk and talk till almost midnight. He was having a kind of a struggle and when he'd get hungry he'd come over to our house and we'd feed him a good meal and he'd just talk and talk."[99]

Disney said in 1956: "I was desperately trying to get something that would take hold, catch on. So I thought of a reversal. They had had the cartoons working with the humans, which was originated by Max Fleischer. I said, well, maybe I'll pull a reversal on that, I'll put the human in with the cartoons. . . . The [Fleischer] cartoon would always come off the drawing board and run around in a real room and work with a real person. I took a real person and put 'em into the drawing."

On April 13, 1923, Disney, for Laugh-O-gram, signed a contract with the parents of Virginia Davis, a four-year-old Mary Pickford look-alike with blonde curls who had already performed in at least one Kansas City Film Ad commercial. He hired Virginia to appear in a new film called *Alice's Wonderland;* her payment was to be 5 percent of the film's proceeds.[100] After the live action was shot, Disney and a few other members of his original staff worked on the film in the late spring and early summer of 1923. Hugh Harman, who was on Laugh-O-gram's payroll throughout May and June, claimed to have animated most of it.[101]

In the midst of production, probably in mid-June, Laugh-O-gram moved from the McConahy Building to less expensive quarters, the same space above Peiser's restaurant that had housed Disney's Kaycee Studios. "The studio was then in financial trouble," Rudy Ising wrote in 1979, "and Walt, Hugh, Maxwell, and I secretly moved all our equipment back to the original building . . . one night, leaving McConahy with some unpaid back rent."[102] Starting in July, Fred Schmeltz paid the monthly rent (seventy-five dollars) for the space above Peiser's. Maxwell remembered "taking turns with Walt on the camera stand for a long session shooting a circus parade"—a cartoon parade welcoming the live-action Alice to cartoonland—after the move.[103]

In May 1923, while *Alice's Wonderland* was still being animated, Disney wrote about it to potential distributors, offering to send them a print when it was finished. But, he said in 1956, "I couldn't get anywhere with it." Actually, his letter of May 14 to Margaret J. Winkler, a New York–based distributor, brought an immediate response. "I shall, indeed, be very pleased to have you send me a print of the new animated cartoon you are talking about," she wrote to Disney on May 16. "If it is what you say, I shall be interested in contracting for a series of them."[104]

Disney wrote to Winkler again more than a month later. "Owing to numerous delays and backsets we have encountered in moving into our new studio," he wrote on June 18, "we will not be able to complete the first picture of our new series by the time we expected." He planned to be in New York around July 1 with a print and "an outline of our future program."[105] Winkler replied that she would be happy to see him.[106] When Disney spoke of "backsets," he may have had in mind what happened after the animation for *Alice's Wonderland* was photographed. When the film was developed, the emulsion on the negative ran in the summer heat; at least part of the animation had to be reshot.[107]

In the film, Alice visits the Laugh-O-gram studio to see how cartoons are made, watches an animated cat and dog box on a drawing board, and that night dreams she is in a cartoon herself. The novelty is all in the combination work, which, as Rudy Ising explained, "was bi-packed, that is, the live-action print was run through the camera operation along with the unexposed negative film, thus being superimposed on the film at the same time as the cartoon was being photographed."[108] *Alice's Wonderland* otherwise suffers from some of the same disabilities as the Laugh-O-gram fairy tales, especially their repetitiveness, aggravated in this case by *four* off-screen fights that include three involving Alice and some escaped lions.

Regardless, by midsummer 1923 Disney had a finished film in hand and a New York distributor who was eager to see it. He probably could not afford a trip to New York, but he could have followed through in other ways, and he did not. The fate of the six modernized fairy tales may have had something to do with his failure to act.

In his first letter to Winkler, Disney invited her to get in touch with W. R. Kelley of Pictorial Clubs' New York office, "and he will gladly screen several of our subjects"—the fairy-tale cartoons—"for you."[109] It was around this time that Pictorial Clubs, a Tennessee corporation, went out of business. The films—but not the obligation to pay for them—wound up in the hands of a New York corporation also called Pictorial Clubs. Disney had been swindled, and Laugh-O-gram would not see the eleven thousand dollars it was supposed to receive the following New Year's Day.[110] That disagreeable experience with one distributor may have left him less than eager, for a time, to pursue a contract with another. Rudy Ising remembered that in the summer of 1923, after the move back to the original studio above Peiser's, "Walt was seriously considering going back to New York" to seek work as an animator on the *Felix the Cat* cartoons.[111]

In later years, Disney may not have wanted to remember this episode, perhaps the only time after he left Kansas City Film Ad that he was on the verge of going to work for someone else and giving up the idea of running his own business. Just as the memory of his failed partnerships seemed to annoy him, so the very idea that he might have spent his life working for someone else may have been too unpleasant to contemplate. He was by nature a man who wanted to be in charge, in undisputed control, and so he could tolerate neither sharing power with a partner (other than Roy) nor surrendering it to a boss.

With *Alice's Wonderland* finished and his hopes for a new series in abeyance, Disney returned to the kind of cartoon that had first brought him modest success. "I spent a number of weeks working on a plan to make a weekly newsreel for the *Kansas City Post*," he said in 1935, "but that deal fell through, too. That seemed to wash up all the prospects in Kansas City, so I decided to go to Hollywood."[112]

As Disney recalled in his 1941 speech to his employees, he passed through one true starving-artist phase in Kansas City, apparently when the studio was in the McConahy Building (although his reference to an "an old rat-trap of a studio" wouldn't seem to fit that place). His business a shambles, he was living at his studio and bathing once a week at Kansas City's new Union Station. He had nothing to eat but beans from a can and scraps of bread from a picnic. Characteristically, though, Disney refused to take a romantic, languishing view of his predicament when he talked about it again in 1956. Whenever he spoke of his hardships and how he overcame them, his voice was usually that of a rigorously optimistic entrepreneur. He loved beans, he said—"I was actually enjoying this meal."

CHAPTER 2

"A Cute Idea"

The Self-Taught Filmmaker
1923–1928

As his father had on several occasions, Walt Disney responded to defeat by pulling up stakes. When bankruptcy arrived for Laugh-O-gram Films in October 1923, he had already decamped for California, probably in late July. As had been the case with Elias in 1906, Robert Disney was part of the lure—he had moved to Southern California in 1922 and gone into the real estate business[1]—but so was Roy, since he was still hospitalized at Sawtelle.

Los Angeles itself was a natural destination for a midwesterner like Disney, more so than New York. In the Los Angeles of the early 1920s, the big movie studios were starting to introduce an exotic immigrant seasoning of the sort that was already part of life in the Northeast, but many residents were uneasy with the newcomers. Los Angeles was still in its prevailing mores a transplanted midwestern city.

"I'd failed," Disney said of his Laugh-O-grams venture—but, he added, that was a good thing. "I think it's important to have a good hard failure when you're young. . . . I learned a lot out of that." He came away from his failure buoyed by the entrepreneur's conviction that he would always land on his feet, and so "I never felt sorry for myself."

Disney said in 1961 that by the time he arrived in Los Angeles "I was fed up with cartoons. I was discouraged and everything. My ambition at that time was to be a director."[2] He said he would have taken any job at a live-action studio—"Anything. Anything. Get in. . . . Be a part of it and then move up." Roy Disney, speaking in 1967, had his doubts: "I kept saying to him, 'Why aren't you gonna get a job? Why don't you get a job?' He could have got a job, I'm sure, but he didn't want a job. But he'd get into Universal, for example, on the strength of applying for a job and then . . . he'd just hang around the studio lot all day . . . watching sets and what was going on. . . . And MGM was another favorite spot where he could work that gag."[3] Walt Disney said forty years later, "I couldn't get a job, so I went into business for myself" by returning to cartoons and building a camera stand in his uncle's garage.[4] Again, though, the documentary record indicates that his state of mind differed from what he chose to remember, and that he always intended to go into business for himself—making cartoons.

Soon after arriving in Los Angeles, he had a letterhead printed—"Walt Disney, Cartoonist"—with his Uncle Robert's address, 4406 Kingswell Avenue in Hollywood. He wrote to Margaret Winkler in New York on August 25, telling her that he was no longer associated with Laugh-O-gram and was setting up a new studio. "I am taking with me a select number of my former staff," he wrote, "and will in a very short time be producing at regular intervals. It is my intention of securing working space with one of the studios, that I may better study technical detail and comedy situations and combine these with my cartoons."[5] In other words, Roy was right—Walt was insinuating himself onto the big-studio lots not in search of a job but to "study technical detail and comedy situations."

When Winkler replied on September 7, she was clearly getting impatient. "If your comedies are what you say they are and what I think they should be, we can do business," she wrote. "If you can spare a couple of them long enough to send to me so that I can screen them and see just what they are, please do so at once."[6]

By then, Winkler had special reasons to be interested in Disney's film. She had been distributing Max Fleischer's *Out of the Inkwell* cartoons, but Fleischer was about to leave her and distribute his cartoons through his own company, Red Seal. Another cartoon-producer client, Pat Sullivan, wanted to take his popular *Felix the Cat* cartoons elsewhere for more money. Winkler was a states-rights distributor who marketed films to subdistributors who paid for the right to sell them for a limited time in one or more states; she was on the fringes of the business, compared with the big film companies like Paramount and Universal. She needed a new cartoon series, quickly, and *Alice's Wonderland*— Disney apparently sent her a print he had brought with him to California— persuaded her that Disney could meet that need. He was in the midst of making a sample "joke reel" for the Pantages theater chain—a new version of his Newman reels—when Winkler sent him a telegram on October 15, 1923, offering a contract for a series of six *Alice* films, with an option for two more sets of six.[7] Disney returned the signed contract on October 24.[8]

(Winkler wanted to buy *Alice's Wonderland* as an emergency backup reel, but Disney could not sell it because he did not own it—it belonged to Laugh-O-gram and ultimately passed into other hands during Laugh-O-gram's bankruptcy proceedings. Winkler offered only three hundred dollars for the film, a price that Disney was able to dismiss, no doubt with considerable relief, as simply too low.)[9]

At his brother's urging, Roy left the Sawtelle sanatorium to join Walt in a new Disney Brothers Studio. "One night," Roy said, "he found his way to my bed at eleven or twelve o'clock at night and showed me the telegram of acceptance of his offer and said, 'What do I do now . . . can you come out of here and help me get this started?' I left the hospital the next day and have never been back since."[10]

With characteristic optimism, Walt had already rented space (for ten dollars a month) on October 8, at the rear of a real estate office at 4651 Kingswell,[11] a couple of blocks west of Robert Disney's home and just around the corner from Vermont Avenue, a major north-south Hollywood artery that was home to many film exchanges. Instantly, when Roy joined him, Walt had a balance wheel of the kind he had lacked in Kansas City. Said Wilfred Jackson, who worked alongside both Disneys for thirty years: "Everybody thinks of Walt Disney as one person. He was really two people, he was Walt Disney and Roy Disney."[12] In 1961, Walt summarized the difference that Roy made, in this way: "Roy is basically a banker. He's pretty shrewd on the money."

Roy was also Walt's big brother, and the family ties that bound the brothers not just to each other but to Elias were as much in evidence in Hollywood as in Marceline. "When we were just getting started down here," Roy told Richard Hubler in 1968, "our folks put a mortgage on their house in Portland and loaned us twenty-five hundred dollars. In our family we all helped each other. I got that paid off just as quick as possible." Apparently, Elias's grudging way with a dollar no longer ruled when his sons were pursuing an entrepreneurial path of the sort he had taken so often himself. Roy himself put "a few hundred dollars" into the new business, and Robert Disney lent them five hundred dollars.[13]

"By Christmas we delivered our first picture," Roy said in 1967. "We got twelve hundred dollars. Thought we were rich."[14] (Roy's figures were a little off, in both directions. Margaret Winkler offered fifteen hundred dollars per cartoon. The first one, *Alice's Day at Sea,* was due January 1, 1924, but Winkler received it the day after Christmas.)

Roy remembered Walt at this time as "always worried, but always enthusiastic. Tomorrow was always going to answer all of his problems." Walt still bore the marks of his last few months in Kansas City, when he camped out in his studio and ate very little. He was "skinny as a rail," Roy said, and "looked like the devil. . . . I remember he had a hacking cough and I used to tell him, 'For Christ's sake don't you get TB.'"[15] (Walt was a heavy cigarette smoker by then; he most likely picked up the habit during his year in France.)

Walt Disney had embarked on his Laugh-O-grams with money in the bank and a small but adequate staff, but without Roy at his side. When Disney Brothers Studio opened for business on October 16, 1923—the day after Walt got Margaret Winkler's offer—he and Roy and Kathleen Dollard, whom they hired to ink and paint the animation cels, made up the entire staff. Margaret Winkler wanted Virginia Davis to star in the new series of *Alice Comedies,* and Disney wrote to her mother, Margaret Davis, that same day, offering the role.[16] In testimony to the power of Hollywood's glamour, the whole Davis family moved west in a matter of weeks.

The earliest *Alice Comedies* are not really cartoons at all, but are instead live-action shorts—strongly resembling Hal Roach's *Our Gang* series—with animated inserts. They could hardly be anything else, since Walt Disney himself was the only animator (and Roy his cameraman). Disney's animation is painfully weak even set against the Laugh-O-grams, burdened as it is by poor drawing and a desperate use of every conceivable kind of shortcut.

"In the very early days of making these pictures," Disney said in 1956, "it was a fight to survive. It was a fight first to get in, to crack the ice. So you used to do desperate things. I used to throw gags and things in because I was desperate." In a speech to his fellow producers in 1957, he remembered shooting live action in Griffith Park and narrowly escaping arrest "for not having a license. We couldn't afford one. So we used to keep an eye out for the park policeman, and then run like mad before he got to us. We would then try another part of the park, and another."[17]

As the Disneys settled into a production routine, they slowly added staff—first a cel painter, Lillian Bounds, on January 14, 1924 ("They tried to use me as a secretary, but I wasn't very good at it," she said more than sixty years later).[18] They hired a cartoonist, Rollin Hamilton, who at twenty-five was three years Walt's senior, on February 11. That same month, they moved to larger quarters, a storefront next door at 4649 Kingswell. Now they had a plate-glass window on which to emblazon "Disney Bros. Studio." The Disneys shared one large room with their employees; a smaller room housed the animation camera stand.[19]

In May 1924, Ub Iwerks wrote to Disney telling him he was ready to leave his Film Ad job a second time and join the Disney staff as an animator. Disney was delighted, and he encouraged Iwerks to come to Los Angeles as quickly as possible ("I wouldn't live in K.C. now if you gave me the place").[20] With Iwerks on his staff, Disney could finally cut back on the live action in his films, first making it a true framing device—short segments before and after the animation—and then getting rid of it altogether, except for increasingly brief appearances by Alice. Iwerks was now a more accomplished animator than Disney himself, and his technical skills were immediately useful, too. The Disneys' camera had to be hand-cranked to shoot the animation frame by frame, but Iwerks converted it to a motor drive, so that each frame could be photographed by pressing a telegraph key. He also drew the posters and lettered the titles and intertitles (the title cards in the body of the film) for the *Alice Comedies*.[21]

While their business was getting under way, the Disney brothers lived together nearby for more than a year. "First," Roy said in 1968, "we had just a single room in a house"—this was across the street from Uncle Robert at 4409 Kingswell, the home of Charles and Nettie Schneider, where the brothers probably moved in the fall of 1923 around the time they started their company. Later, Roy said, "we got an apartment"—the address is unknown—"and I used to go home in the afternoon and take a sleep because I was convalescing." Roy returned to the studio for a couple of hours before going home again to prepare dinner.

One night Walt "just walked out on my meal," Roy said, "and I said, 'Okay, to hell with you. If you don't like my cooking let's quit this business.' So I wrote my girl in Kansas City"—Edna Francis, to whom he had been more or less engaged since before he entered the navy—"and suggested she come out and we get married, which she did, and she and I were married on April 11, 1925. So that left Walt alone. So apparently he didn't like living alone, even though he didn't like my cooking."[22] Shortly afterward, Walt Disney proposed to Lillian Bounds, and she accepted.

Lillian Marie Bounds was from Idaho, where her father had worked as a blacksmith. She had followed her older sister Hazel Sewell to Los Angeles and taken a job at the Disney studio soon after she arrived. The studio was close to her sister's home, and she could walk to work. She was a slender, dark-haired girl, a head shorter than her boss and future husband. He stood around five feet, ten inches, and his slicked-back hair was light brown. Disney was slender himself then, so much so that in photos from the time his features seem sharper and his nose more prominent than in later years.

Disney's wardrobe was extremely limited when she first knew him, Lillian said. "He didn't even have a suit."[23] He wore a tan gabardine raincoat, a brownish gray cardigan, and a pair of black-and-white checked pants. He did not own a car, either, until sometime after Lillian was hired.

"We used to work nights," Lillian told Richard Hubler in 1968. "By that time he had a Ford roadster with one seat and an open back. He used to take us home after work. He took the other girl home first. When he got to my sister's he was embarrassed to stop in front of the house. One night he asked me, 'If I get a suit can I come and see you?'" The Disney brothers both bought suits at the same time, but Walt's had two pairs of pants to Roy's one. "Walt always got the best," Lillian said.[24]

"He just had no inhibitions," Lillian said of Walt. "He was completely natural. . . . He was fun. Even if he didn't have a nickel. . . . We would go to see a picture show or take a drive"—Disney had graduated to a Moon roadster by then. "We would drive up to Santa Barbara sometimes." On their dates, she said, "He was always talking about what he was going to do. He always wanted to do the talking."[25]

Although Disney was making films that were seen throughout the nation, he was well short of being any sort of celebrity.[26] An article about her marriage, ghostwritten from Lillian Disney's point of view, was published in *McCall's* almost thirty years later. Although bearing a title—"I Live with a Genius"—that inspires skepticism, the article is persuasive in many of its details, as in this account:

> The first time Walt ever saw one of his cartoon shorts in a theater was [in 1925], just before we were married. My sister and I were visiting a friend that night, so Walt decided to go to the movies. A cartoon short by a competitor was advertised outside, but suddenly, as he sat in the darkened theater, his own picture came on. Walt was so excited he rushed down to the manager's office. The manager, misunderstanding, began to apologize for not showing the advertised film. Walt hurried over to my sister's house to break his exciting news, but we weren't home yet. Then he tried to find Roy, but he was out too. Finally, he went home alone.[27]

Disney was not a prepossessing figure financially or otherwise in 1924 and 1925, and he was still very young. He was twenty-three when he and Lillian married, almost three years younger than his wife. The mustache he added by the spring of 1925 (he is wearing it in home movies from Roy's wedding) may have been in part a means of closing that gap, although Lillian said many years later that he had grown it when he and members of his staff "made a bet. They all grew mustaches. Walt wanted to shave it off later, but we didn't let him."[28]

Disney's optimism and charm were sufficient to overcome any reservations Lillian may have felt. "He said he married me because he got so far in debt to me," Lillian said in 1956. "He'd come around and say, 'Hold your check, again.' . . . Roy would tell him, 'Now don't let Lilly cash her checks.'"[29] As evidenced by Roy Disney's account book, it was very common during this period for members of the animation staff to take salary advances. Walt and Roy, on the other hand, often took less money out of the company than their salaries entitled them to, and they sometimes took their salaries a week or more late—three weeks late in May 1926—because of cash-flow problems like those that led to their pleas to Lillian.[30]

Walt and Lillian were married in her brother's home in Lewiston, Idaho, on July 13, 1925. On their return to Los Angeles by train, the newlyweds stopped in Portland, Oregon, where Lillian met Walt's parents for the first time. "They were just ordinary people," she said in 1986. "Very warm and very friendly and they loved him very much."[31] Disney, as a newly married man whose wife had left the payroll June 1, gave himself a twenty-five-dollar raise, effective July 3, to seventy-five dollars a week. Roy's salary remained at fifty dollars.[32]

Although Lillian had known her new husband as her boss, she was still jarred by his work habits. "When we were first married," she said in 1956, "my gosh, he didn't know what it was to go to sleep until two or three in the morning. I used to get so mad at him because he was in the habit of working so late at night." Invariably, she said, they wound up back at the studio in the evening. "We'd go out for a ride, we'd go any place—he'd say, 'Well, I've got just one little thing I want to do.'" She often slept on a couch until Disney was ready to leave, sometimes after midnight.[33]

Before they married, Walt and Lillian looked for a home to buy, and Walt recalled in 1956 that they had found a house they liked and were trying to estimate what the costs of home ownership would be. Lillian said that Walt could care for the yard himself, eliminating the need for a gardener, but he rejected the idea, clearly in the voice of Elias's son, the boy who had delivered newspapers in the snow and otherwise had his fill of manual labor: "I said, 'I've done too much of that all my life, hauling ashes, cutting lawns, doing things. . . . I'll never cut another lawn.' And I haven't."

Instead of buying a house, the newlyweds moved into rented quarters, first at 4637 North Melbourne Avenue, one street up from Kingswell and just a block away from the studio, and later at 1307 North Commonwealth Avenue.[34] They did not move into a home of their own until 1927. Walt's hacking cough was again a cause of alarm, this time to a landlady: she thought his coughing so severe that he must have tuberculosis.[35]

Two of Disney's former colleagues at Laugh-O-gram joined his staff in Hollywood on June 22, 1925, shortly before he left for his wedding in Idaho, bringing the total on the staff to a dozen. Hugh Harman and Rudy Ising had found other work after Laugh-O-gram's collapse; Ising had a photofinishing business, and Harman animated at Kansas City Film Ad. At night, though, they worked on a film of their own with Max Maxwell, who was still attending college in Kansas City.[36] They used Laugh-O-gram's camera stand and other equipment that Fred Schmeltz had taken as collateral for his loans. Their cartoon, *Sinbad the Sailor,* enjoyed only one theatrical showing, in October 1924 at the Isis Theatre at Thirty-first and Troost, a block away from Laugh-O-gram's old quarters in the McConahy Building. Disney knew what they were doing and encouraged his own distributor to look favorably on their efforts. "They are three very clever, clean-cut, young fellows," he wrote to Margaret Winkler, "and I would like very much to have them out here with me."[37] But no distributors were interested.

Their own hopes in abeyance, Harman and Ising were receptive to Disney's offer to join his staff as animators (and, in Ising's case, as a camera operator). Hugh's younger brother Walker came with them to work as an inker. Hugh Harman's and Ising's memories, and Ising's correspondence from the 1920s, are among the most reliable windows into what the Disney studio was like at the time.

"When we first came out here," Hugh Harman said, "nearly every evening we were at Roy's house, with Walt and his wife, and the three of us, Walker and Rudy and I. Or they were at our apartment; or we were at Walt's apartment. . . . We used to play tennis in those early days, every morning, including Saturdays and Sundays. Every morning, up at six, playing tennis." When everyone was together in the evening, Harman said, "we would do nothing after dinner but start thinking of stories and acting them out. We got to thinking to ourselves, well, here are cartoons, they've never acted. We resolved we were going to make them act."[38] Ising also remembered being with the Disneys "practically every night of the week. He was either at our place or we were at their place. This was when he first got married, for a couple of years."[39]

Not that long, surely—Disney fired Ising in March 1927 (he tended to fall asleep while operating the animation camera), and the studio had changed in other ways by then. But in 1925, there was still a chummy atmosphere very much reminiscent of the Kansas City days. So small was the staff, and so undifferentiated their duties, that Roy Disney washed cels for reuse until a janitor was hired in November 1925.[40] (Roy no longer photographed the live action of *Alice,* though—a professional cameraman was hired for the few days of shooting necessary.)

By the time Harman and Ising moved to Los Angeles, Walt Disney had stopped animating,[41] and his drawings were not much in evidence otherwise. As a guide for the animators on the *Alice Comedies,* Disney projected the live-action film of the girl through the animation camera and made rough sketches of her key positions in the scenes that would combine live action and animation.[42] "Maybe he had made a drawing showing her positions as they varied every three feet [of exposed film] or so—just high spots," Harman said.[43] Disney had probably drawn the model sheets for the Laugh-O-gram characters in Kansas City, but in Hollywood such drawings were most likely by Iwerks. As Ising said, those sheets showed "the walk, and the run, and the head and the body in a complete turn."[44] The drawings were reproduced in three different sizes so that the animators could trace them—as most of them did, although tracing gradually diminished.[45]

After he stopped animating, Disney assumed more control over the animation done by others. In Kansas City, the animators had written on the bottom of their drawings what the cameraman should do. For example, an animator might specify how many times a cycle was to be repeated. Ising, as the camera operator, might accept or amend such decisions: "If I thought a thing was good, and [the animator] said, 'Repeat two times,' I might repeat it four times. Or, if he said, 'Repeat eight times,' and I might think it was not that good, I'd cut it down."[46] In Hollywood, Disney began making what came to be called *exposure sheets,* which amounted to more formal instructions to the camera operator. "He would take the animator's drawings and time them," Ising said, "whether it was to be shot on one turn or two turns, or how many times a cycle was to be repeated."[47] Disney altered the drawings themselves "very, very little," Harman said, except to add "flicker marks"—a burst of six to eight drawings around a character's head that represented surprise or distress or inspiration.[48] "We got so we put them in to save him the trouble," Ising said.[49]

Disney also devoted more of his time to stories—"he was the one who really sort of put the story together" and assigned sequences to the animators, Ising said[50]—but shooting the live action first for the *Alice Comedies* did not mean that stories had to be planned in any detail. As the series advanced, Alice (three other girls succeeded Virginia Davis in that role) became more and more superfluous, her scenes fewer and fewer, and her filmed actions more and more generic, so that the live action could be combined with animation of almost any kind. Disney continued to trace the live action, providing rough sketches of the girl's position, but that task made fewer demands on his time as Alice's role in the films shrank.[51]

Gradually, as Disney added more animators and his animators gained more experience, the *Alice Comedies* looked better, with fewer obvious shortcuts, but they still suffered by comparison with some of their competitors. The level of invention in the *Felix the Cat* and *Out of the Inkwell* cartoons was simply higher—more interesting things happened than in Disney's. But even the characters in those cartoons had only traces of individuality; they were mostly vehicles for gags that took advantage of the characters' unreality. Felix's body, like everything else in his universe, was infinitely plastic, and KoKo, the clown star of the *Inkwell* cartoons, always materialized on the screen as a drawing on paper, one that could be crumpled or erased. For the most part, animators relied heavily on characters whose simply designed black-and-white bodies (Felix the Cat was typical) stood out clearly on the screen. The gags usually just piled up, instead of telling a coherent story.

The *Alice Comedies* offered few witty transmutations like those in the *Felix* and *Inkwell* cartoons. What happened much more often was that a body came apart and reassembled itself with remarkable ease. In *Alice Picks the Champ* (1925), a bear boxer's hand literally shatters on the head of a turtle sparring partner; the bear scoops up the pieces and clumps them together on the stump, as a fist again.

Occasionally, though, Disney's story ideas clothed themselves in more promising expression. In *Alice's Balloon Race,* released in January 1926, a hippopotamus, as he sits and smokes his pipe and spits, misses a spittoon; the spittoon grows legs and moves to where the spit fell. The hippo spits again, and again he misses. This time the spittoon grows arms as well as legs and points to its opening—and the hippo finally hits it, on his third try. Such a situation was as fanciful as anything in the *Felix* cartoons, but there was something real about it, something that originated not so much in the characters themselves or in what they did as in how they responded to each other. There was no playing to the audience, as Felix did so often: instead, the hippo looked perturbed as the spittoon dressed him down, then brightened as he assured the spittoon that *this* time he'd hit it. Here was a thread that Disney was just starting to pick up: when the characters on the screen seemed to believe they were real, the audience might be encouraged to accept their reality, too.

By the summer of 1925, Disney felt secure enough in his new situation not only to hire more animators and get married but also to build a new studio. On July 6, shortly before he left for Idaho, he and Roy deposited four hundred dollars toward the purchase of a vacant lot on Hyperion Avenue in the Los Feliz district east of Hollywood, roughly a mile from the Kingswell studio.[52] By early in 1926 the new Disney studio building at 2719 Hyperion Avenue was ready for occupancy. "They rented an old Ford truck," Hugh Harman said, "and we moved the stuff in that."[53] The Disney staff moved to its new quarters in a mid-February rainstorm, the rain so heavy that the studio's furnishings got soaked and stubbornly refused to dry.[54]

At the old studio, the Disneys had rented a vacant lot about three blocks away to shoot the live action for the *Alice Comedies* against white canvas strung up on the backs of billboards. At the Hyperion studio, the new prosperity asserted itself in the construction of an actual outdoor set. "We had to white-wash it every time we used it," Rudy Ising said.[55]

Walt Disney's new office impressed Ising, who wrote to his family that it "looks like a bank president's loafing room. Desk and chairs in walnut, large overstuffed divan and chair, floor lamp etc."[56] The Disneys' growing prosperity also permitted them to build new homes of their own, twin houses side by side on Lyric Avenue where that street ended at Saint George Street in the Los Feliz district. Construction began in August 1926 and ended in December.[57] Early in 1927, Walt and Lillian moved into 2495, on the more desirable corner lot, while Roy and Edna moved into 2491. Roy Disney put the cost of the land and the two "kit" houses, from Pacific Ready-Cut Homes, at sixteen thousand dollars.[58] Lyric is a narrow, winding street that leads southeast down a hill to Hyperion Avenue, just a few blocks from the studio's new location. The shorter (a half mile) and more direct route, though, and the one that the Disneys probably drove most often, took them northeast on Saint George to Griffith Park Boulevard; the studio was a right turn and a long block away.

If there was a cloud over the Disneys' success, it arose from their relations with their distributor. From the beginning, it is clear from Margaret Winkler's early letters to Disney, the final cut on the *Alice Comedies* was to be hers; she told Disney to send her "all the film you make, both negative and positive."[59] In 1924, her brother George went to the Disney studio to edit the films there. Starting in August of that year, Disney's dealings with Winkler Pictures were mainly through Margaret's new husband, Charles Mintz, who adopted a brusque, condescending tone in his letters. He often sounded wounded and indignant where money was concerned, in the manner that immediately raises suspicion about a correspondent's motives.

At first, though, Disney groveled. When he wrote to Mintz on November 3, 1924, he praised George Winkler's work as an editor, saying he had cut one film "down to its proper length." He even credited George with help on gags. Disney's tone in this letter is almost shockingly pitiable, particularly his constant invocations of George Winkler's name as protection against Mintz's aggressive demands—for example, that Disney include more live action, at the beginning and end of his films, and use a gang of kids instead of Alice alone. Disney protested that he wanted to add another cartoonist instead.[60] Mintz, in a letter of October 6, 1925, contended that it was only because he had sent his brother-in-law to Disney's studio that Disney was able to continue making films.[61]

Winkler Pictures had increased Disney's payment for each *Alice Comedy* after the first six—he got eighteen hundred dollars instead of the original fifteen hundred—and by 1925, in Roy Disney's accounting, each film typically showed a profit of more than six hundred dollars. Mintz wanted to shift to a profit-sharing arrangement for the third season, starting in 1926. In their correspondence in the fall of 1925 and winter of 1926, he and Disney wrangled over when and how they would share the rentals of their films, once Disney had received a reduced advance from Mintz (fifteen hundred dollars again, in two installments) and Mintz had covered that advance and the cost of making prints of the films. This was the sort of question on which disagreement and compromise were all but inevitable, but Mintz's rhetoric was extreme, haggling taken to the point of caricature. In his letter of November 17, 1925, he lectured Disney about how single-reel subjects were failing.[62] A week later, he took exactly the opposite tack, trying to talk Disney into waiting for his share of the box-office proceeds from the *Alice Comedies*— which would be substantial, he insisted—until Mintz had received fifteen hundred dollars in addition to all his costs.[63] It was only through protracted effort that Disney was ever able to wring any concessions out of him.

In these dealings with Mintz, it was always Walt Disney himself who jousted with his prickly distributor. There is no sign of Roy Disney in this correspondence, even though he and Walt surely conferred on how to respond. When the Disney Brothers Studio became Walt Disney Productions in 1926, that change of name was a simple acknowledgment that in business decisions, as in the making of the cartoons, Walt Disney's was the voice that mattered.

Disney's position in his dealings with Mintz—and his posture in his letters—gradually grew stronger as his cartoons got better. By late 1926, Disney had made forty *Alice Comedies,* and everything about the few surviving cartoons from that period—animation, drawing, character design—is noticeably more polished than what Disney and his crew could do a year or two earlier. The shortcuts, if still plentiful, are no longer quite so blatant. In *Alice's Brown Derby* (1926), Alice's cat sidekick Julius rides his horse into the lead in a race, in cycle animation of the usual kind—but as he does that, in a side view, he passes between other horses, creating a fleeting three-dimensional effect. (There are three levels of cels, with Julius in the middle between two cels of the other horses.)

The improved quality of Disney's films permitted Mintz to abandon states-rights distribution for the 1926–27 releasing season and sign up with a minor distributor called Film Booking Offices (FBO). A much bigger step forward was in store for the 1927–28 season. In January 1927, Mintz asked Disney to come up with a rabbit character—"I am negotiating with a national organization and they seem to think that there are too many cats on the market."[64] On March 4, 1927, Mintz signed a contract with Universal, one of Hollywood's major studios, for a series of twenty-six cartoons starring, as Universal had specified, a new character called Oswald the Lucky Rabbit. Disney would now receive an advance of $2,250 for each cartoon.[65]

At the Disney studio, Hugh Harman said, the switch from *Alice* to *Oswald* came without warning. "It was announced to us one morning, when we went in, that we were starting Oswalds," he said. "So the time was right now to think of an Oswald story. We all got together in Walt's little office . . . and dreamed up this first story [*Poor Papa*]. . . . We began to build on it, and about eleven o'clock, Walt said, 'Why don't we start animating?' He said, 'Hugh, the first part of that is pretty well worked out; you know what it is, don't you?' I said, 'Yeah, that's enough to start on.' So I went in and started Oswald pacing up and down on the ridge of this roof."[66]

Although Universal and Mintz were unhappy with that first *Oswald* cartoon (it was not released until 1928), subsequent cartoons in the series got warm reviews in exhibitors' trade papers like *Motion Picture News.* Those reviews were not meaningless puffs; the reviewers panned later *Oswalds*, made after Disney had left the series. New York animators liked Disney's cartoons, too, the Fleischer animator Dick Huemer said: "We used to seek them out and study them."[67]

Story work on the later *Oswald* cartoons was not as casual as it had been for *Poor Papa.* Disney had started preparing brief scenarios during the last year or so of the *Alice Comedies,* and the surviving scenarios for the *Oswald* cartoons are more detailed. Sketches, six to a page, often accompany the scenarios, showing in general terms how the animator should stage the action in each scene. Despite such increased preparation, though, the Disney cartoons were in something of a rut, and it was Disney himself, more than anyone else, who was keeping them there, through his increasingly strong control of what got onto the screen.

A majority of Disney's twenty-six *Oswald* cartoons have not survived, so generalizations are risky, but the sense from nine of the *Oswald*s is that Disney was slow to pick up on the possibilities for character comedy that he had opened up in some of the *Alice Comedies*. The problem was certainly not a lack of interest on his part. "Walt Disney just lived cartoons, that was his whole life," said Paul Smith, who joined the staff in December 1926 as a cel painter (then the first stage in an apprenticeship that led to work as an animator). "He talked of nothing else, ever."[68] But it was simply too easy to seek laughs by breaking cartoon characters into pieces—exploiting their impossibility, instead of encouraging audiences to accept their reality—and so, in *Oh Teacher* (1927), Oswald removes his own foot, kisses it for luck, and rubs it on the brick he plans to throw at a cat rival during school recess.

This was besides, as Max Maxwell said, "the period when Walt was very intrigued with off-color gags, such as cows with swinging udders and little characters running into outhouses."[69] Disney had grown up as a farm boy, after all, and in the late 1920s his earthy sense of humor was as much a legacy of his years at Marceline as his nostalgia for small-town life would be in later years.

Paul Smith remembered the story meetings during the *Oswald* period: "We'd all be called into Walt's office and hash over notes that he had made on the next picture. What did we think of this gag, was it too risqué . . . he was always putting in gags where a cow would get her udder caught in something."[70]

Around this time, if only briefly, Hugh Harman may have passed Disney in his sensitivity to animation's possibilities. Harman described an occasion in 1926 when Disney spoke of wishing he had the money to get out of animation and go into real estate. Harman responded by saying he wanted to stay in animation and eventually animate Shakespeare. "He looked at me," Harman said, "as if I had a hole in my head."[71]

Harman always spoke of his aspirations for his medium in such grand terms. Although he later produced many popular cartoons for Warner Brothers and Metro-Goldwyn-Mayer (MGM), most in partnership with Ising, he resented Disney's much greater success, and he invariably placed the least flattering gloss on Disney's words and actions. It is certainly true, though, that in the 1920s Disney conceived his future in animation mainly in business terms, so it is not at all unlikely that Harman's artistic goals were loftier then. *Bright Lights,* which Harman animated in 1927 with Rollin Hamilton, has glimpses of an Oswald with an inner life, a character whose emotions are mirrored in his actions. It is much harder to find anything of the kind in the surviving *Oswald* cartoons dominated by Ub Iwerks, whose mechanical proficiency was reflected in his animation's smooth clockwork quality. In the late 1920s it was Iwerks's kind of animation, more than Harman's, that was most in tune with Disney's ambitions.

Harman complained that Disney pressed his animators to turn out more footage—more animation—and to simplify their drawings. Iwerks contributed to such pressure, no doubt unintentionally, through his great facility. Paul Smith remembered an Iwerks who "never sketched anything roughly in his life. He would write his drawings out, with no preliminary sketches. . . . That's why he didn't want to work with an assistant. He wanted to make all the drawings himself. He'd work clean, straight ahead."[72]

As different as they were, Disney's animators felt a common itch to break away. In September 1926, when the studio was closed for two weeks of vacation, Harman and Ising, joined by Iwerks and Rollin Hamilton, made another cartoon of their own, this time without Disney's knowledge. They were again unsuccessful in finding a release, but they did not give up. On January 29, 1927, Ising wrote to his sister Adele in Kansas City: "We have a secret shop all equipped and can start immediate production on our own pictures in event of obtaining a contract. I hope this will be soon as we shall not make a name and fortune for ourselves working for Walt."[73]

The Disney studio was not a happy place in 1927. Animators who knew Disney as "very much one of the boys" in Kansas City had come to resent him in his new role, as what they saw as an overbearing boss. The studio's growth had given Disney no choice, however—he had to become more of a boss. Each contract with Mintz had brought a significant increase in the number of *Alice Comedies* he was obligated to produce, from twelve in 1924 to eighteen in 1925 to twenty-six in 1926. The *Oswald* contract covered twenty-six cartoons again, but for a more prominent and demanding national distributor. Disney's staff had grown along with his output, until by 1927 he and Roy employed roughly two dozen people, most of whom had not known him in Kansas City. Delivery schedules could generate cash crises; that happened in 1926, when Disney had to build up a backlog of *Alice Comedies* to meet the heavier FBO schedule. He dueled continually with Charles Mintz, who despite occasional truces could never accept Disney's insistence on behaving like an independent businessman, rather than an employee.

Disney was a successful filmmaker—his profit on each cartoon had risen to as much as a thousand dollars—but his success came at a price, part of which was estrangement from people who had been his friends, or might have been. On one occasion in 1927, Disney even reacted angrily to the caricatures that the animators drew of one another and pinned up for their amusement, a common pastime in cartoon studios. "One of the few times I ever saw Walt angry was one day when he got tired of seeing us waste time over those cartoons," Max Maxwell wrote in 1973. "He stalked through the studio and tore them all off the walls."[74] Maxwell, another veteran of Laugh-O-gram, joined the Disney staff in May 1927, but he left after only nine months in this bruising new environment.

Isadore "Friz" Freleng, who joined the staff on January 15, 1927, lasted less than eight months, leaving on September 1. At Kansas City Film Ad, Maxwell said, Freleng was "this little red-headed Jewish guy, everybody picked on him."[75] Freleng was a year younger than Harman and Ising, who were both born in August 1903, and three years younger than Disney; he had not known Disney in Kansas City. Freleng himself told Joe Adamson: "I'd become very sensitive as a child, because I was much smaller than other kids, and I was always defending myself, because they'd pick on me. Walt picked this up, and he used to rib me quite a bit, maybe size, or whatever it was, I don't think he really meant any harm. [But] when he'd make a remark, I'd take exception, and I'd make a nasty remark back to him."[76]

One evening, Freleng called Disney at home, "telling him I had something on my mind which bothered me. . . . It took him just a few minutes to drive over to where I was living in a boarding house. He wouldn't let me say a word until he arrived at the studio and opened the door. He got behind his desk and took out a cigar. He asked me to sit opposite to him, and said, 'Now start talking.' I told him how much he upset me emotionally, and reminded him of his letters to me expressing his patience in my learning animation. He apologized, and complimented me for having the nerve to speak my mind. He said he had a great respect for me, but I don't think really, truthfully he did, because after that, things became somewhat more unbearable." Finally, another confrontation led to Freleng's leaving the staff.[77]

The limited evidence suggests that Freleng's animation for Disney was in the same vein as Hugh Harman's. Freleng later worked in animation for many years, mostly as a director at the Warner Brothers cartoon studio. There is no reason to believe that Disney singled him out for attack because his performance was lacking (or, for that matter, because he was Jewish). The growth of his studio and his battles with Mintz had put Disney under a strain, and he was responding to difficulty as he would in other circumstances, by turning on his employees.

Their growing bitterness over such encounters made a number of Disney's employees receptive when Charles Mintz approached them in the summer of 1927 about setting up a new studio to make the *Oswald* cartoons. Ising wrote in August to his and Harman's friend Ray Friedman in Kansas City:

"Winklers have made us a definite offer for a next years [sic] release. Winklers are thoroughly disgusted with the Disneys and with the expiration of their present contract will have no more dealings with them. Their present contract expires in April, 1928." Iwerks was also planning to leave, Ising said, "to engage in a private enterprise."[78]

While they talked with Mintz and George Winkler, Harman and Ising continued to pursue a release of their own, all of this without Disney's knowledge. In November 1927, Ray Friedman was in Los Angeles. Ising wrote to Freleng, who was back in Kansas City, that Friedman was "at present working on the general manager of Cecil DeMille Studios. . . . Ray is putting all of his time towards the securing of a contract and getting everything in shape for starting production. It shouldn't be long now."[79]

Mintz, who visited Los Angeles occasionally in the 1920s, met and talked personally with the members of the Disney staff he was trying to lure away. "We met him at various places," Paul Smith said. "He made telephone calls and arrangements to talk with us."[80] But Mintz and the disgruntled Disney people were stringing each other along, each side hoping a better deal would turn up—in Mintz's case, with Walt Disney himself.

After months of meetings and calls, Mintz had not signed contracts with any of the Disney animators, but in February 1928, everyone was ready to move. On February 10, Ising wrote to Freleng: "Our plans to get a contract to make our own pictures this year fell through, so we are taking the next best thing. Hugh, Max, Ham [Hamilton] and I are signing a one-year employment contract with George Winkler to make 'Oswald the Lucky Rabbit.'"[81] Iwerks would not be leaving the Disney studio with them; his "private enterprise," whatever it was, had fallen through.

Ten days later, Disney arrived in New York, making what was apparently his first visit to the city since he passed through on his way to and from France, ten years earlier. He was there to negotiate a renewal of his contract with Winkler Pictures, but Mintz insisted that he renew on terms that amounted to a surrender of his independence. As Disney summarized their negotiations in a letter to Roy, "Charlie is very determined to get absolute control of everything and will do everything in his power to gain his end."[82] Disney, for his part, was determined "that if we did any business that it would have to be on a more equal basis."[83]

Disney stalled, talking with Mintz—they saw each other repeatedly, by themselves and with their wives, at Mintz's office on West Forty-second Street and over lunch and dinner (once at the Mintzes' home), and always on friendly terms—while he scouted for another distributor. There were no takers. The market for short subjects was weak, he was told, and Fred Quimby of MGM warned him that cartoons especially were in decline.[84]

It is not clear how explicitly Mintz threatened Disney with the loss of key members of his staff, but Disney was concerned enough that he wired Roy on March 1 to sign the "boys" to "ironclad" contracts. The "boys" refused to sign, and as Disney wrote to Roy on March 2, that meant "only one thing—they are hooked up with Charlie, because I know how the rest of the market is and they haven't a smell."[85] Disney wavered briefly; after talking with executives at Universal he considered signing up with Mintz for another year, in the hope that Universal would deal with him directly in 1929. But when he talked with Mintz again, he "found it impossible" to do business with him because Mintz's demands were so unyielding.[86] After three weeks in New York, he broke off negotiations and left for Los Angeles on March 13, 1928.

Universal owned the Oswald character, so Disney had no choice but to come up with a new one. Returning home on the train from New York, Lillian Disney said in 1956, "he was talking about different things, kittens and cats and this and that. Well, a mouse is awful cute, and he just kept talking about a mouse. So that's where he originated Mickey Mouse, was on the train coming home all by himself without asking anybody. He just decided that was a cute idea."[87]

Disney spoke later of the affection for mice he developed in Kansas City: "I used to find them in my waste basket in the mornings. I kept several in a cage on my drawing board and enjoyed watching their antics."[88] There was, however, nothing unusual in the choice of a mouse cartoon character. There were plenty of mice in cartoons in the 1920s. The very crude and simple drawing in most cartoons could make it hard to tell one animal from another, so a mouse's large ears, rendered as black circles or ovals, were a godsend. Paul Terry used a mouse couple—both apparently several feet high, like Disney's Mickey and Minnie Mouse—in several cartoons released in late 1927 and early 1928.

A fuller account of the return trip from Lillian Disney's point of view is part of that ghostwritten article in *McCall's*, and what it says about the naming of Disney's new mouse character—and, especially, Lillian's state of mind in 1928—is wholly plausible:

> I remembered the early Hollywood days when Walt and Roy were so broke that they would go to a restaurant and order one dinner, splitting the courses between them. I knew I wouldn't care much for that. I couldn't believe that my husband meant to produce and distribute pictures himself, like the big

companies. He and Roy had only a few thousand dollars between them. Pictures needed a lot of financing, even in 1927 *[sic]*. And what if Walt failed? He had insulted his distributor and hadn't even looked for a new connection.

By the time Walt finished the scenario [for *Plane Crazy*, the first *Mickey Mouse* cartoon] I was practically in a state of shock. He read it to me, and suddenly all my personal anguish focused on one violent objection to the script. "'Mortimer' is a horrible name for a mouse!" I exclaimed.

Walt argued—he can be very persuasive—but I stood firm. Finally, to placate his stubborn wife, Walt came up with a substitute: "Mickey Mouse." At this late date I have no idea whether it is a better name than "Mortimer." Nobody will ever know. I only feel a special affinity to Mickey because I helped name him. And besides, Mickey taught me a lot about what it was going to be like married to Walt Disney. We've never been so broke since—at least quite so visibly. But I have been plenty worried on occasion. It has often helped to look back on that period.[89]

The defecting animators remained at the studio for a few weeks after Disney returned, completing the last five of the *Oswald*s due under his contract with Mintz. Starting in late April, Iwerks animated the first *Mickey Mouse* cartoon in a back room, with Ben Clopton assisting him in some fashion. Harman remembered work proceeding behind a curtain, but that may have been only temporary.[90] Lillian Disney, her sister Hazel Sewell, and Roy's wife, Edna, inked and painted the cels in a garage at the Disney homes on Lyric Avenue (Lillian returned to the Disney payroll from April 28 to June 16, 1928). The animators who were leaving for Winkler's were not supposed to know what Iwerks was doing, but Harman told Paul Smith then that "Ub was animating a picture with a Mickey Mouse character in it."[91] Clopton was probably the source of Harman's information; he left the Disney payroll on May 12, 1928, a week after Harman, Smith, and Hamilton.

That first *Mickey Mouse* cartoon, *Plane Crazy*, was completed and previewed by May 15, 1928.[92] In it, Disney tried to exploit public interest in Charles Lindbergh in the wake of his transatlantic flight a year earlier. A second cartoon, *The Gallopin' Gaucho*, which Iwerks animated in June and early July, echoed the adventure films of Douglas Fairbanks, particularly *The Gaucho* (1927). The animation for the new cartoons, in Iwerks's clockwork manner, was arguably retrograde when set beside the subtler Harman-Hamilton animation in an *Oswald* cartoon like *Bright Lights*, but that was probably not why Disney got no offers from the distributors who saw the print of *Plane Crazy* that he sent to a film storage company in New York in mid-May. As Harman and Ising had already learned—and Disney himself had reason to know, after his unsuccessful efforts in New York earlier in 1928—new cartoon series were simply not very attractive to most distributors. Cartoons' brief burst of popularity in the early 1920s was long past; of the major distributors, only Paramount and Universal now offered cartoons to theaters.

In the spring of 1928 the film industry was still absorbing the impact of the first few features made with sound. The first "all-talking" feature, *Lights of New York,* would not open in New York until July. Disney realized that adding sound to his cartoons would be one way to make them stand out, but it was still not obvious then that sound features, much less sound cartoons, would completely supplant silent films. Neither was it at all obvious how best to add sound to a cartoon, except perhaps as Warner Brothers had done with silent features like *Don Juan,* starting in 1926, by recording an orchestra whose music could take the place of a theater's own musicians.

Musical sound tracks had been recorded for a few of Max Fleischer's cartoons earlier in the 1920s with the De Forest process. Sound had also occasionally accompanied silent cartoons in more inventive ways. Frank Goldman of the Bray studio told of how a New York theater's orchestra vocalized "ah-ah-ah" during a showing of a Bray educational cartoon on the human voice and thus gave an "unexpected lift" to the film.[93] But it was a long leap from such limited uses of sound to a cartoon with a fully integrated sound track, one in which animation was synchronized with music and sound effects. Disney's key insight was that such integration, and not sound alone, would be essential to a sound cartoon's success. By the end of June, he was writing to New York companies about what it would cost to add synchronized sound to a cartoon. On July 14, Roy Disney entered a charge of three dollars and five cents for "Sheet Music for Pic" in his account book.

Wilfred Jackson joined the Disney staff on April 16, 1928, just in time to see Disney and Iwerks make the first two *Mickey Mouse* cartoons. Thanks to his musical knowledge—limited but greater than that of other members of the Disney staff—he was intimately involved in making the third *Mickey Mouse* cartoon, *Steamboat Willie,* the first with sound, in the summer of 1928. He left this account:

> The story work [for *Steamboat Willie*] began with a "gag meeting" at either Walt's or Roy's home. The entire animation crew: Ub Iwerks, Les Clark, Johnny Cannon, and even me, although I was just beginning to learn how to [animate], were there with Walt and Roy. The concept of the story—a situation, or perhaps just a locale, or take-off on a well-known person—was usually all Walt had in mind to start the meeting going on these early Mickeys. On *Steam-*

boat Willie, it was just the idea of the song, "Steamboat Bill," and the Mississippi riverboat locale. Everyone came out with any ideas he could think of on the subject, especially funny business that might get a laugh. I don't recall that many sketches were made of the ideas. I think, mostly, we just talked. Nor do I believe anything like a story line, or continuity, was developed at this preliminary meeting.

Ub left his animation desk and spent the next few days after this meeting working with Walt in his office. The next thing I saw on the picture was some sketches of Ub's on animation paper. . . . When Walt was ready to time the action and make out the exposure sheets he had these sketches on his desk, but didn't refer to them very much. He seemed to have the story line for the whole picture clearly in mind, as well as the details of each piece of business, and knew exactly what he was after without any reminders.

I helped Walt as he timed the action the best I could with my mouth organ and a metronome—performing the function that was done for later pictures by a musician playing a piano—and I was able to observe how he tried out parts of the action this way and that, discarding something here, trying some new thing there, rearranging the order of other pieces of business, until the whole thing seemed to work with the tunes he had selected and finally suited him as a workable cartoon continuity. When he was done, each last little thing that was to happen all through the entire short had been visualized in complete detail and the length of time each action was to take on the screen had been determined. Thus, while he was timing the action, Walt was also doing the final part of the story work, and the way it ended up was changed quite a bit from how it was when he started to time it—but, later, when the picture was all finished, it came out very much like what he now had in mind.[94]

Jackson came up with the way to knit the music and the animation together, so that there was true synchronization. Using a metronome, he prepared "a little rudimentary bar sheet"—a sort of primitive score. "In the places where we had definite pieces of music in mind, the name of the music was there, and the melody was crudely indicated, not with a staff, but just with notes that would go higher and lower . . . so that I could follow it, in my mind."[95] Jackson prepared the bar sheet "almost simultaneously" with Disney's preparation of exposure sheets for the animators. For the silent *Alice*s and *Oswald*s, Disney had made the exposure sheets after the animators did their work, but now it was the other way around, because the animators' timing had to be more precise. Jackson laid out a bar sheet for each tune Disney wanted to use; Disney used the bar sheet to indicate measures and beats on the exposure sheets.[96] He did not describe the action in detail on the exposure sheets. Instead, a detailed synopsis of each scene was typewritten—almost certainly by Disney himself—alongside Iwerks's sketches, each synopsis describing how music and action were to fit together ("Close up of Mickey in cabin of wheel'-house [sic], keeping time to last two measures of verse of 'steamboat Bill.' With gesture he starts whistling the chorus in perfect time to music").[97] Iwerks was going to animate most of the film, and those synopses, combined with the exposure sheets, told him what he needed to know.

"When the picture was half finished," Disney wrote years later, "we had a showing with sound." (The best guess for a date for that showing is July 29, 1928, when Roy Disney noted a two-dollar charge for a "preview" of the unfinished film.)[98] "A couple of my boys could read music and one of them [Jackson] could play a mouth organ. We put them in a room where they could not see the screen and arranged to pipe their sound into the room where our wives and friends were going to see the picture. The boys worked from a music and sound-effects score. After several false starts, sound and action got off with the gun. The mouth-organist played the tune, the rest of us in the sound department bammed tin pans and blew slide whistles on the beat. The synchronism was pretty close. The effect on our little audience was nothing less than electric. They responded almost instinctively to this union of sound and motion. I thought they were kidding me. So they put me in the audience and ran the action again. It was terrible, but it was wonderful! And it was something new!"[99]

There is present in that account "some of his ebullience"—Wilfred Jackson remembered that the two Disney wives and Iwerks's wife and his own girlfriend "weren't particularly impressed; they were all talking about sewing, and knitting, and the things that girls talk about." It also seems likely that Disney was wrong in remembering that his "musicians" could not see the cartoon as they played. Jackson said that Roy Disney projected the film onto a bedsheet hung in front of a glass pane in Walt Disney's office door, so that he and his colleagues could see the cartoon in reverse, through the glass, as they played inside the office.[100] But Jackson did remember that Iwerks "rigged up a little microphone and speaker"; and there is no reason to doubt that Disney and his crew were elated by what they saw and heard.

Steamboat Willie was complete in silent form by late August, when Disney took the train to New York to try to get his sound track recorded. Lillian was not with him this time. He stopped in Kansas City to see Carl Stalling, the organist at the Isis Theatre, whom Disney had known since he was working at Kansas City Film Ad in the early 1920s. "Walt was making short commercials at that time," Stalling said in 1969, "and he'd have us run them for him. We got acquainted, and I had him make several song films"[101]—that is, sing-along films, like the later *Martha,* that showed the lyrics on the screen while the theater musician played the song. After Disney moved to Los Angeles, Stalling lent him $250 (which Disney repaid). Disney left the two silent *Mickey Mouse* cartoons with Stalling so that he could begin writing scores for them.

Disney arrived in New York on September 4, 1928, the day after Labor Day; he remembered the crowds returning from the holiday. As he made the rounds of recording studios, he saw one cartoon, an *Aesop's Fable* called *Dinner Time,* with a sound track that engineers for Radio Corporation of America (RCA) had added as an experiment. The *Fables* remained silent otherwise. So did Mintz's cartoons, not just the *Oswalds* but also the *Krazy Kat* cartoons that Mintz was making in New York. Disney heard of an effort to make a *Krazy Kat* cartoon in sound, with results so poor that the cartoon went unreleased, at least in its sound version.

Disney was not deterred by what he saw of this clumsy experimenting. Writing to Roy and Ub Iwerks three days after his arrival in New York, he embraced sound as a spur to growth: "It is not at all impossible for us to develop in this sound field the same as [short-comedy producers Hal Roach and Mack Sennett] and the others did in the silent."[102] A week later, he wrote again of his strong belief in the future of sound cartoons and the importance of quality—a belief he was going to back up by paying for a seventeen-piece orchestra (plus three effects men) for the recording of *Steamboat Willie's* score.[103]

Within a week of his arrival in New York, Disney had decided to record *Steamboat Willie's* sound track with Powers Cinephone, a sound system of dubious legality that had somehow managed not to run afoul of larger companies' patents (Disney noted, in a letter written shortly after his arrival, that "the Powers method is absolutely interchangeable" with the competing RCA and Movietone systems).[104] Powers Cinephone took its name from Patrick A. Powers, a colorful Irish rogue who had been an important figure in the film industry early in the century, when he and Carl Laemmle battled for control of Universal. Disney was impressed by Powers's wealth and apparent influence in the industry and swept up by his charm—"He is a dandy. . . . He is a fine fellow"[105]—but he also had very little choice. He had determined almost immediately that only Powers and RCA were good candidates for the kind of recording he had in mind, and RCA would have charged him far more than he could afford. The Disneys were by no means poverty stricken in 1928, but their assets were mainly their studio building and its equipment, rather than cash. They were not liquid enough to spend thousands of dollars on recording sessions.

The first recording session ran from 11:30 on the evening of Saturday, September 15, until 4:00 the next morning.[106] Disney himself provided the voice of a parrot. He recalled in 1956: "I had to yell 'Man overboard! Man overboard!' And I got so excited and I was right in the microphone and I coughed in it right in one of the takes. And that blew that take up and then they all turned to me and said, 'Now who did that?'"

The results of the first recording session were unsatisfactory, for reasons other than Disney's performance as the parrot. He had brought with him to that session a film a theatrical-trailer company had made for him, showing a ball bouncing in the musical tempo. He knew that some such device was needed during the actual recording if the synchronization was to be as tight as the bar-sheet system permitted. The conductor, Carl Edouarde, was apparently reluctant to pay strict attention to the ball, and as a result synchronization suffered. There were problems with some of the sound effects, too, and so a second recording session was scheduled for September 30.

Disney was strikingly cavalier about costs in a September 23 letter to Roy and Iwerks: "Why should we let a few little dollars [jeopardize] our chances. . . . We can lick them all with Quality."[107] Two days later, he wrote to Roy of pouring money back into the cartoons and making them as good as possible: "God help us put this thing over—we are sincere and deserve it."[108] On September 28, he brushed aside Roy's concern about expenses connected with the second recording for *Steamboat Willie:* "Forget these little details and concentrate on some good GAGS. . . . GAGS are going to do more to put us over than all the little figures you could ever think of."[109] He had by then already given Pat Powers two checks for a total of fifteen hundred dollars. His letters to his brother and his friend were long and rambling—intense, but rambling, reflecting his frustration at having "absolutely no one here to talk to. . . . I feel lots of times like dragging a bell boy in and paying him to listen to me."[110]

The second recording session, which began at ten on a Sunday morning, was successful, with much better synchronization of sound and image. The bouncing ball had been superimposed on a print of *Steamboat Willie,* in the space for the sound track alongside the frames of film, and this time Edouarde took it seriously. The musicians played with their backs to the screen—only Edouarde saw the bouncing ball, but so tight was the synchronization that there was no need, for example, for the piccolo player who provided Mickey Mouse's whistling to see the character or the ball on the screen.[111]

"The only thing we lacked," Disney wrote, "was the complete Orchestra score with all the effects written out accurately"—that is, sound effects that were integrated with the music. He was not completely satisfied with some of the effects, he said, but *Steamboat Willie* succeeded where it was most important: "It proves one thing to me, 'It can be done perfectly' and this is the one thing that they all have been stumped on."[112]

The orchestra was smaller, too, and, as Disney had written a few days earlier, the score itself had been "all rewritten to fit the action" by "the arranger," an important but apparently never identified figure in the *Steamboat Willie* episode.[113] Wilfred Jackson's bar sheet would not have sufficed as a recording score, so someone had to translate what he and Disney had done into real music. Carl Stalling did not do it—he was in Kansas City, working on scores for the two silent cartoons—and there is nothing in Disney's letters that says who did. Disney credited the arranger with "a completely original score" that included no "taxable" music—that is, music under copyright: "The parts for Steamboat bill *[sic]* were all written by the arranger." "Steamboat Bill" was still under copyright in 1928, however, and that song is a prominent element in the score. Disney's use of the song was not licensed by the copyright holder until 1931.[114]

After several weeks in Powers's intoxicating company, Disney was thinking in rather grandiose terms of making fifty-two *Mickey Mouse* cartoons a year—one a week, the same schedule that Paul Terry was meeting with his *Aesop's Fables*. "I think we have the basis of a good [organization] by just adding a few good animators and [systematizing] everything," he wrote to Roy and Iwerks—this at a time when he had lost most of his staff and had only one experienced animator.[115]

In the weeks that followed, Disney showed *Steamboat Willie* to potential distributors in New York. "By gosh, it got laughs . . . but I was gettin' the brushoff," he said in 1956.

Throughout the fall, in letters to his brother and Iwerks, Disney was unfailingly positive, writing enthusiastically about their chances for a major release even as one possibility after another withered away. He pounded on Iwerks, at great length and in near-manic tones, to finish animating a new *Mickey Mouse* cartoon, *The Barn Dance,* as quickly as possible—"Listen Ub— Show some of your old Speed. . . . Work like hell BOY. . . . It is our one BIG CHANCE to make a real killing"—so that he and Carl Stalling could record the score along with the scores for *Plane Crazy* and *The Gallopin' Gaucho.*[116] He was trying to compensate for his absence, since he certainly would have been egging Iwerks on if he had been in Los Angeles. His letters were typewritten now—in contrast to his handwritten letters on earlier visits to New York—and the greater speed the typewriter made possible encouraged the flow of his words. When Disney received a print of the first half of *The Barn*

Dance on October 22, he was predictably disappointed—this was, after all, the first of his cartoons to get this far in production with so little input from Disney himself.[117]

On other occasions, when Disney wrote to Roy and Iwerks about Powers and other film executives, he was so enthusiastic that he sounded a little ingenuous; there was scarcely a trace of cynicism, even though he sometimes expressed a wariness born of his experience with Mintz. He was franker in his letters to Lillian, but even when writing to her, as he did on October 20, he regarded Powers as different from the rest:

> I have certainly learned a lot about this game all ready *[sic]*. . . . It is the damndest mixed up affair I have ever heard of. . . . It sure demands a shrewd and thoroughly trained mind to properly handle it. . . . There are so damn many angles that continually come up that if a person hasn't the experience etc. it would completely lick one. They are all a bunch of schemers and just full of tricks that would fool a green horn. I am sure glad I got someone to fall back on for advice. . . . I would be like a sheep amongst' a pack of wolves. . . . I have utmost confidence and faith in Powers and believe that if we don't try to rush things too fast that we will get a good deal out of this.[118]

Stalling joined Disney in New York on October 26, 1928. "It sure seems nice to have someone near me that I know," Disney wrote to his wife that evening.[119] He and Stalling shared a two-room suite at the Knickerbocker Hotel—"we both washed our socks in the same bathroom sink," Stalling said—and worked together on the scores for *Plane Crazy, The Gallopin' Gaucho,* and *The Barn Dance.*[120] They viewed the films on a Moviola, a machine used in editing film that back-projected the picture onto a tiny screen. Disney was impressed by the machine: "We will have to get one to use at the studio."[121]

Disney was not paying Stalling any salary yet, only his hotel and living expenses, but the hotel suite alone was going to cost Disney a hundred dollars a week. "Be sure and have Roy look into the matter of selling my car and getting set for an additional Loan on our property," Disney wrote to Lillian on October 27. Disney's car was, he said in 1956, "a beautiful Moon roadster that I was so proud of"—presumably the car that Lillian remembered. "Cabriolet with the top that went down." Disney had bought it secondhand: "I never owned a new car until way after Mickey Mouse. I always would buy a second hand one . . . then I'd trade my old second hand one in on a new second hand one." But he had to sacrifice the Moon: "I had them send the pink slip [registration] to me. . . . They'd sold my car to meet payrolls before I ever got out of [New York]."

Harry Reichenbach, best known as a colorful press agent, was in Disney's recollection managing the Colony Theatre on Broadway. He was among the many people in the film industry who saw and liked *Steamboat Willie.* "He came to me," Disney remembered in 1956, "and he said, 'I want to put that on.' . . . I said, 'Well, I'm afraid that if I run it somewhere on Broadway that it'll take the edge off of my selling it and getting the distribution.' . . . He said, 'These guys don't know until the public finds out. . . . Let me have it for two weeks.' . . . Finally, he said, 'I'll give you five hundred for two weeks.' And we needed money like what and I said, 'Five hundred a week.' And finally he said, 'O.K., five hundred a week.' They gave me a thousand bucks to run it. And that was the highest price that anybody's ever paid, up to that time, for a cartoon on Broadway."

However much Reichenbach paid to exhibit *Steamboat Willie,* it was probably not a thousand dollars.[122] Disney later spoke of receiving half as much: "We didn't yet have a release for Mickey but Harry wanted to book him in the Colony regardless," he said in 1966. "At the time, we were in desperate need of five hundred dollars. To put it briefly, everything owned by Roy and me was mortgaged to the hilt. So I asked Harry for five hundred dollars for exhibiting the first Mickey Mouse one week. I knew that the price was pretty steep. So did Harry. But fortunately for us, he said, 'Let's compromise. I'll give you 250 dollars a week—and run the cartoon for two weeks.'"[123]

Disney may even have let the Colony show his cartoon without paying him anything at all. That is what Universal—which had been leasing the Colony for about two years[124]—was asking of him in October.[125] Since Disney's *Oswald* cartoons were Universal releases and were shown at the Colony, Universal's executives and the theater's management had good reason to think that a new Disney cartoon would be well received there. Universal's argument to Disney was that he would benefit so much from a Broadway showcase that he should let the Colony run the cartoon for free. (Universal itself was probably precluded under its contract with Mintz from signing a deal with Disney for a series of cartoons.)[126]

In any case, Disney had agreed by early in November to let the Colony have *Steamboat Willie.*[127] After the long slow month of October, matters were now moving much more rapidly. On November 13 and 14, in the week before the premiere, Disney and Stalling oversaw the recording of the sound tracks for *Plane Crazy, The Gallopin' Gaucho,* and *The Barn Dance.* In California, Iwerks had done preliminary work on the story for the fifth *Mickey Mouse* cartoon, *The Opry House,* and Disney was anxious to get back before work on it went much further.

Steamboat Willie premiered at the Colony on Sunday, November 18, 1928, and ran for thirteen days, sharing the bill with an early sound feature called *Gang War* and live stage acts. An opening-day advertisement in the *New York Times* proclaimed Disney's film the "first and only synchronized-sound animated cartoon comedy."[128] Carl Stalling remembered seeing it the first day, sitting "on almost the last row and [hearing] laughs and snickers all around us."[129] *Steamboat Willie* got excellent reviews (*Film Daily* called it "a real tidbit of diversion")[130] as well as enthusiastic audience response. When his cartoon was showing at the Colony, Disney said in 1956, "I was there every day."

Steamboat Willie was in some respects a curious breakthrough. Its comedy was as rough-hewn as almost anything in the *Alices* and the *Oswalds*, and the animation, almost entirely by Iwerks, was just as backward-looking. Near the start of the film, the steamboat's cat captain stretches Mickey himself wildly out of shape. The captain subsequently spits tobacco after one of his teeth rises like a window shade, only to have the wind blow the blob back in his face. The story is minimal, merely an excuse for gags that rely overwhelmingly on the crude manipulation of some animal's body. Mickey cranks a goat's tail, turning it into a sort of hurdy-gurdy after it has eaten some sheet music; he picks up a nursing mother pig and plays her teats as if he were playing an accordion. But all of this rude action was synchronized with music and sound effects, its precision entirely novel in the fall of 1928, not just for cartoons but for films of all kinds. This Disney cartoon combined sound and pictures with a seeming effortlessness that no other sound film matched. It was no wonder that critics and audiences alike loved it.

Pat Powers had broached the idea of representing Disney immediately after the September 30 recording session, and Disney had signed a two-year letter agreement with him on October 15, the idea being that Powers would help Disney find an outlet for his cartoons.[131] When he talked to distributors after *Steamboat Willie*'s successful Colony debut, Disney said in 1956, they wanted to make a deal—to hire him, not to make a contract that would leave him independent. There was irony here, because Disney's association with the legally dubious Cinephone system quite likely made some distributors reluctant to sign with him.

After Disney had spent about three months in New York, he and Stalling finally left for Los Angeles. At that point, Disney still hoped that Powers could make a deal for him with a national distributor. Instead, Powers quickly made a deal with the Stanley Fabian Warner chain of theaters wired for sound.[132] Charles J. Giegerich, who dealt with the Disneys for Powers, told Walt on December 31: "The prospects of making national distributing arrangements for any of the big companies at the present time were so doubtful that we considered it best to make arrangements for state right distribution."[133] Disney's new sound cartoons were being distributed just as his *Alice Comedies* had been—not just a less prestigious method of distribution, but one with problems of its own. With states-rights distribution there could be no nationwide release date. If Disney was eventually successful in finding a national distributor, there was the risk that its releases of his new cartoons would collide with states-rights releases of cartoons he had made a year or two earlier. The older cartoons would dilute the market for the new ones.

Disney's immediate challenge was to find ways to put his powerful new tool, synchronized sound, to its most effective use. Even Wilfred Jackson, new to animation, was aware of how hard that might be. "For most of us . . . when I first came to the studio," he said, "if it seemed to move it was animation— and if it looked funny to us when it moved, that was good enough." Disney, he said, was "not . . . so far ahead of the rest of us in knowing how to achieve convincing action and characterization with animation." The studio's "library" reflected Disney's lag. It consisted of a folder of clippings of magazine and newspaper cartoons, along with two books—Lutz and Muybridge, or something very similar—like those that had been his instructors almost a decade earlier.[134]

Just how limited Disney's horizons were at this time was revealed in a remark he made "sometime in 1928 . . . after viewing one of his last Oswald cartoons or one of his first Mickeys," Jackson recalled. Disney said to Jackson: "Some day I'm going to make a cartoon as good as a Fable."[135] That was not much of an ambition. Paul Terry's *Fables* were furiously busy cartoons, but that was about all. As animation's equivalents of the most brutal slapstick live-action comedies, they were populated by characters distinguishable from one another not by how they moved or what they did, but mainly through their starkly simple designs. There is, however, no reason to doubt Jackson's memory on this point, or to believe that Disney was being facetious. More than ten years later, Disney himself wrote: "Even as late as 1930, my ambition was to be able to make cartoons as good as the Aesop's Fables series."[136]

CHAPTER 3

"You've Got to Really Be Minnie"

Building a Better Mouse
1928–1933

Walt Disney and Carl Stalling disagreed over the music for the Disney cartoons almost from the day they began working together in Los Angeles in December 1928. "Walt was a person with no musical background at all," Wilfred Jackson said. "He was also not a person to recognize any limitation as to what could be done. When he thought a piece of action should be extended or shortened somewhat beyond what would fit with some certain part of a piece of music, he expected his musician to just simply find some way or other to expand or shorten that part of his music."[1]

Jackson remembered "a tremendous outburst of bickering" between Stalling and Disney "about whether some music should be changed; and it's my recollection that a kind of compromise was arrived at, in that if Carl would make his damned music fit the action Walt wanted in this Mickey, Walt would make a whole series . . . where the music would have its way."[2] The *Mickey Mouse* cartoon in question was almost certainly *The Opry House*, the first cartoon that Stalling scored in Los Angeles. *The Skeleton Dance*, the first cartoon in the new music-dominated series called *Silly Symphonies*, went into production next, before *The Opry House* was finished.

Disney later spoke of the *Silly Symphonies* as if those cartoons had been more his own idea—"We wanted a series which would let us go in for more of the fantastic and fabulous and lyric stuff"[3]—but Stalling had suggested such a series months earlier, probably when Disney stopped in Kansas City around the first of September on his way to New York. Disney told Roy and Iwerks about three weeks later that there was "a damn good chance to put over a series of Musical novelties such as [Stalling] had in mind. . . . We will have to make one and show it before we can talk business. . . . We have in mind something that will not cost much to make. . . . It would only be good in Sound Houses and the field is limited. . . . Therefore it would have to be inexpensive to make—What he has in mind sounds like it wouldn't cost much to make."[4]

(Disney's words might seem to apply to *Steamboat Willie,* too, but he prepared a silent version of that cartoon that differed a little from the sound version. He also prepared silent versions of the next few *Mickey Mouse* cartoons.)

Disney wrote to Roy on September 28: "Carl's idea of the 'Skeleton Dance' for a Musical Novelty has been growing on me . . . I think it has dandy possibilities . . . It would be dandy with all the different effects in it." The eccentric punctuation here is Disney's. He used strings of dots freely, but not carelessly, as an aid to a kind of free associating. He let his mind roam as he thought about what might go into a "Skeleton Dance" short: "I think we could Cartoon the Skeletons—and double print over a real background . . . Also used Stuffed OWELS [sic] . . . BATS . . . and other spooky things . . . Weird music . . . The Skeletons playing a tune on their ribs . . . Playing a tune on different sized Tombstones . . . Dancing and rattling of bones . . . Some of them playing instruments and all kinds of goofy gags. It wouldn't be so terribly hard to make if we made use of repeats . . . and music is full of repeats."[5]

He talked as well as wrote about story ideas in much the same way. There is abundant evidence of that in the transcripts from meetings later in his career.

Disney and Stalling returned to New York late in January 1929 to record the sound for both *The Opry House* and *Skeleton Dance.* Iwerks animated almost the entire *Skeleton Dance* while they were gone. Thanks to the system that Disney and Jackson had devised for *Steamboat Willie,* there was no need to complete the animation before the music was recorded. All that was needed was for the musician's bar sheet and the animator's exposure sheet to align, so that music and drawings were synchronized when combined in the finished film. Disney left Iwerks a highly detailed, single-spaced, typewritten scenario for *The Skeleton Dance* that covered seven pages.[6]

While Disney was in New York, he was in no position to supervise Iwerks's animation closely, but an ongoing conflict between them festered even while they were a continent apart. Their continuing disagreement was over whether Iwerks would animate "straight ahead"—leaving to an assistant only details like the skeletons' ribs—or as Disney wanted him to, with what were called *extremes* and *inbetweens,* the latter provided by an assistant called an *inbetweener.*

When animators first began using inbetweeners in the 1920s, the idea was that they could increase their output by delegating the less important drawings to less-experienced artists. The animators would draw the extremes, the key drawings that defined movement, while the inbetweener made the drawings needed to fill out the animation so it did not look jerky on the screen. That potential increase in productivity was an important consideration at a studio that relied so heavily on one animator, Iwerks, even though he already animated so rapidly. For Iwerks, though, the costs of the change were unacceptably great. His objections were summarized in notes from an interview with him around 1956: "Ub said he'd lose direction of action—he got better feeling of action [when] he animated straight ahead and left details to be filled in. Walt could never see this method."[7]

It was only when Iwerks's drawings were tightly synchronized with music that the dominant characteristics of his animation—smooth and regular and impersonal—became unmistakable virtues. What might have seemed merely mechanical was instead precise and pointed. *The Skeleton Dance* had no plot and few real gags, only simple and repetitive dances by skeletons with rubbery limbs, but so closely did the skeletons' actions mirror the music that they tracked not just the beat but the individual notes.

Disney said in 1956 that he had considerable difficulty getting *The Skeleton Dance* into theaters, citing one theater manager's complaint: "It's too gruesome." He spoke of tracking down "a film salesman" in a pool hall and, through him, getting the cartoon seen by the manager of the prestigious Carthay Circle Theatre in Los Angeles. In early May, Disney let the Carthay Circle book *The Skeleton Dance* for what he called "an extended pre-release showing." Disney wrote to Charles Giegerich of the Powers organization about the "unusual amount of attention" the cartoon was receiving during this run and urged him to "close a national release" for the *Silly Symphonies* "on the strength of this one subject, plus the reputation that we have created with the quality of our 'Mickey Mouse' series."[8] A second showing, in New York at the Roxy on Broadway, was equally successful. In August, Giegerich signed a contract with Columbia Pictures Corporation for thirteen *Silly Symphonies*.[9]

Although the *Mickey Mouse* cartoons and the *Silly Symphonies* were supposed to differ in their emphasis on music, the two series quickly became alike in their reliance on tight synchronization. (In the summer of 1929, Disney said he had "decided upon a policy that from now on all the action [in the *Mickey Mouse* cartoons] will be set to a definite [rhythm] and we will have no more straight action to a mere musical background"—that is, the *Mickey Mouse* cartoons would be as thoroughly synchronized as the *Silly Symphonies*.)[10] None of the earliest Disney sound cartoons were overwhelmingly superior to competitors' cartoons except in their use of sound, but that made all the difference. As other cartoon makers, ignorant of Disney's system, scrambled to add sound tracks, the results were invariably noisy and distracting. Disney's seamless synchronization was all the more impressive in contrast.

Disney knew from the beginning that he was in a strong position, and he was eager to exploit it. Writing to Roy and Iwerks from New York in February 1929, he was encouraged by the favorable response to *The Opry House* and by what he had heard about Charles Mintz's troubles (Universal was not renewing its contract with Mintz but was going to make the *Oswald* cartoons at a studio of its own instead). "Now is our chance to get a hold on the industry," he wrote. He was buying sound equipment from Powers so he could set up his own recording studio in Los Angeles, and he was seriously thinking about making a series of live-action shorts—"dialogue comedies"—in addition to his cartoons.[11] Those live-action comedies never happened, although the Disneys did set up a short-lived Disney Film Recording Company at 5360 Melrose Avenue after Walt returned to Los Angeles.

Disney also knew he needed more help, since Iwerks was the only experienced animator on his staff, backed up by several novices—Wilfred Jackson, Les Clark, John Cannon. As he had in 1928, Disney talked with animators in New York about coming to work for him. (There was no place else Disney could have found experienced animators, apart from the few who had already left him to work for Mintz.) In March, after Disney and Stalling returned to Los Angeles, the Disney staff "heard that some *real* animators were going to be brought out from New York," Jackson said. The first new hire was Ben Sharpsteen, a veteran of several New York studios, notably Max Fleischer's.

"He came in," Jackson said, "and was given his place to work, and given a scene to do, and he spent the whole morning working on it. We were real curious to see what he had done, and so when lunchtime came, none of us wanted to go to lunch, we wanted to see what he'd done. And Ben was a new guy there, he didn't want to be the first guy to go to lunch. So we were all there working, twenty minutes after our lunch hour, before Ben finally said, 'Hey, don't you guys ever go to lunch around here?' And we all pretended, 'Oh, my goodness, yes, it's lunchtime.'

"And Ben went out, and so we all went over to Ben's desk to see what he had done. Ub took the drawings and flipped them, and we all stood respectfully back to see what Ub's opinion would be. After he flipped them, Ub said, 'Huh! They look just like the clown'"—that is, like the Fleischer cartoons. "Ben did draw Mickey with funny little eyes that were like the clown, and a kind of a pinched little nose, at first."[12]

When he was in New York, Disney had visited Pat Sullivan's *Felix the Cat* studio, which was, thanks to Sullivan's stubbornness, as committed to silence as Disney was to sound—and thus was the kind of studio that an animator with an eye on the future would try to escape. "I think he wanted to hire Otto [Messmer]," said Al Eugster, a young animator on the Sullivan staff—Messmer actually made the cartoons that appeared under Sullivan's name—"and he took Burt Gillett with him."[13] Gillett, who had been animating for more than a decade, started work for Disney in April 1929 as the second New York animator to join the staff.

Roles began to change in response to the Disney cartoons' success. After the first few *Mickey Mouse* sound cartoons, Iwerks animated less, working instead with Disney and Stalling in the office called the "music room" because Stalling's piano was there (that term was later applied to a Disney director's room even after a musician no longer shared it). Iwerks's principal duty now was to make sketches that showed the growing staff of animators how to stage their scenes. "Walt still handed out the scenes to the animators for the most part," Jackson said, "but I believe Ub occasionally did this for him at this time."[14]

Disney had always been the de facto director of his cartoons—no one used that exact title—but sound had strengthened him in that role by giving him more control over the timing of the animation. His animators had to adhere to the timing on the exposure sheets, which Disney and Stalling wrote as they planned the music. Now, though, Disney was actually pulling back. Burt Gillett "moved into Walt's music room to help prepare the shorts for animation very soon after he came out from New York," Jackson said.[15]

The division of responsibility between Gillett and Disney was indistinct, Ben Sharpsteen said: "There wasn't anything formal in the division there, and Walt wouldn't hesitate to criticize Gillett in front of one of us. . . . Nothing was sacred to anybody then."[16] All the lines between jobs were fluid in the late 1920s, as Jackson explained: "Each animator drew his own layout [a drawing that showed the staging of a scene], working from Ub's little thumbnail sketch, each time he started to animate a scene—and the first animator, or inbetweener, who ran out of work as a cartoon was nearing completion was likely to be given the task of painting the backgrounds for the picture."[17] As the staff filled out with experienced New York animators, the animators' responsibilities in particular came to be better defined. Carlos Manriquez, who had started in ink and paint, became the first full-time background painter, probably sometime in 1929.[18]

The writing of the cartoons continued much as before. Sharpsteen remembered night meetings "for each new story concept. That's how Walt would get going on a new picture. He'd let us know what he had in mind, and the possibilities he saw in it. We were privileged to sit there and make sketches of ideas as they came to us. Otherwise, we'd turn in something at a later date."[19] Dick Lundy, who joined the staff as an assistant in July 1929, remembered that Disney called such meetings "a 'round table.' We had it in the director's room when we were small, but later on . . . they would have it in the sound stage, and the whole group would get a synopsis of . . . a story idea. 'Now, what gags can you think of?'"[20] As in the *Oswald* period, some gags came perhaps too easily. "In the early days," Wilfred Jackson said, "we always figured that we had three laughs that were free, and we had to work for the other ones. One was the drop-seat gag, two the thundermug [chamber pot] under the bed, and three the outhouse."[21]

The Plowboy, from June 1929, is filled with just that sort of cheerful farmyard ribaldry. A cow's udder is animated with great plasticity as Mickey milks it, and two of the cow's teeth move up and down like window shades to let out a stream of tobacco juice. The cow literally licks Mickey's eye shut—twice. The first time, he squirts milk from the cow's own udder in its face; the second time, he pulls the cow's tongue out to great length and wraps it around its muzzle. There's an undercurrent of lasciviousness, too. When Minnie calls to Mickey and his horse, both wave back—then the horse hitches up his chest and starts to swagger over, until Mickey orders him back. When Minnie is singing, wordlessly, she puckers, her eyes closed, and Mickey, drooling with desire, seizes the opportunity to kiss her (she smashes him over the head with a bucket). The cow laughs at Mickey—a trombone provides the laughter—he gives the cow the razzberry, and she stalks away, first flipping her udder at him in disdain.

The Plowboy ran afoul of a few censors, as did a couple of other 1929 cartoons. Disney expressed mystification that "anyone could take offense at any of the 'stuff' contained in our pictures; especially how anyone could be offended at anything pertaining to the milking of a cow."[22] Coarse, exuberant comedy of that kind was just what could be expected from a studio whose staff was made up largely of young men, most of whom, like Disney himself, had almost no formal art training, and limited formal education of any kind. Like so many schoolboys, the Disney animators ate their sack lunches behind the stage where Disney had filmed the live action for the *Alice* comedies. They also played horseshoes there—"Ub was the best," Jackson recalled.[23]

Some of Disney's animators had fallen in love with the medium when they were children, seeing what must have been some of the earliest series cartoons, like those of J. R. Bray. Jackson remembered growing up in Glendale, California:

We lived near the [trolley] tracks . . . and the conductors would tear all the transfers off, and they'd have a little stub left, about, oh, three quarters of an inch thick and half an inch wide, with a rivet through the middle, or a staple. But the ends you could flip, and so you could make any kind of a little drawing there, and make it move. So I used to walk up and down the car tracks, finding the stubs where they'd thrown them, and make my animation on those.[24]

In the expansive atmosphere created by the Disney cartoons' success and the growth of the staff, some of Disney's young animators tinkered with ways to improve their work—for example, by shooting some of their pencil animation on film to see if it was turning out the way they hoped. The animators made such *pencil tests* of "isolated actions within a scene when the animator came up against some new problem and wanted to see how effectively—or otherwise—he was handling it before going ahead," Jackson said.[25] In addition, Dick Lundy said, the animators tested cycles; it was particularly important to catch any mistakes in cycle animation, because the same mistake would be seen on the screen over and over again.[26] Walt Disney neither encouraged nor discouraged such tests. "We were allowed to use short ends of film that weren't long enough to shoot a scene with . . . if we wanted to come back at night and develop them ourselves," Jackson said.[27]

By the late summer of 1929, both Iwerks and Gillett were performing all the functions of directors, Iwerks for the *Silly Symphonies* and Gillett for the *Mickey Mouse* cartoons. Disney called them "story men" because they were responsible for their cartoons' stories, although that was the area where Disney himself continued to be most heavily involved. The two directors now made the layout drawings that showed the animators how to stage their scenes, and they worked with Stalling to prepare the bar sheets and exposure sheets.[28]

As Disney's involvement in the details of production receded, he began paying more attention to how he might improve his cartoons and achieve more of the "quality" he had fastened on as a crucial asset in the competition for audiences. Since the Laugh-O-gram days, he had been concerned with the poor drawing skills so evident in his cartoons and in most others, and in late 1929 he struck a deal with the Chouinard Art Institute, a school in downtown Los Angeles, to admit his employees to Friday-night classes.

That arrangement continued for several years. Disney's interest in the classes was no doubt sincere—he drove some of his employees to and from the school—but here, just as much as when he was a fledgling animator at Kansas City Film Ad, inertia was a powerful foe. Jack Zander, a Chouinard student in the late 1920s and early 1930s, remembered that as a duty under his working scholarship—this was probably in 1930, a year or so after the Disney people started attending Friday-night classes—"I had to walk around and monitor the classes and be sure everybody was there. It was my job to stay there at night and check on the Disney guys. He had about twenty guys there, and nobody wanted to go to the goddamn art classes. . . . I'd go into a class, and there'd be eight or ten guys standing around. I'd read off the list of twenty names, and every one would answer 'here.' We'd send a report back to Walt that twenty guys showed up to get their art instruction."[29]

In early 1930, Walt and Roy Disney had a far more pressing problem than animators' reluctance to attend art classes. They had been increasingly unhappy with Pat Powers, who wanted Walt to make the cartoons more cheaply (a lower negative cost would mean that Powers could pay Disney less and keep more of the advances from distributors). Powers's wounded tone in a rare letter—usually it was Giegerich who wrote to the Disneys—at the end of 1929 was remarkably similar to Charles Mintz's in many of his letters to Walt. Powers wrote of "the financial risk and burden of exploitation" he had assumed "after every distributor in the business had refused to handle the product under any kind of a basis which would enable us to get even the cost of it back. I know of no instance (and you, yourself, canvassed the entire trade) where they were even receptive or seriously considered handling the product."[30]

The Disneys wanted Powers to pay them money they believed he owed them from rentals of the cartoons. Powers did not want to open his books until the Disneys had signed a stronger contract with him than their two letter agreements for the distribution of the *Mickey Mouse* and *Silly Symphonies* series. Ultimately, on January 17, 1930, Walt and Lillian Disney and the Disneys' attorney, Gunther Lessing, took the train to New York to confront Powers directly. They arrived in New York on the morning of January 21—just about the time that Ub Iwerks walked into Roy Disney's office and told Roy he was quitting. "Speed in getting away seemed to be the main consideration," Roy wrote to Walt three days later.

Iwerks's defection was especially shocking and painful not only because of his ten-year association with Walt Disney but also because he was a partner in the Disney studio.[31] He had begun buying a 20 percent interest on March 24, 1928—that is, just after the blowup with Mintz, when the Disneys were especially grateful for his loyalty—through the deduction of twenty dollars each week from his salary. He began contributing thirty-five dollars a week as of May 19, 1928—an increase that probably reflected the Disneys' in-

creasingly difficult circumstances and was further evidence of Iwerks's friend-
ship. By the time he walked into Roy's office, he had applied $2,920 toward
his 20 percent share.

When Iwerks told Roy he was leaving, Roy asked him if Powers or
Giegerich—or Hugh Harman—had anything to do with his departure. "Ub
looked me straight in the face," Roy wrote, and told him that none of them
"had anything to do with it." Roy asked him, "On your honor?" Iwerks replied:
"Absolutely." The next morning, Roy received a telegram from Walt telling him
that Powers was indeed behind Iwerks's move. Confronted with this, Iwerks
"looked awfully sheepish," Roy wrote, and told him, "I didn't want to tell you."[32]

Under his earlier agreement with the Disney brothers, Iwerks could not
remain a partner after he left the studio. In a release dated January 22, 1930,
the Disneys agreed to pay him exactly as much as they had withheld from
his salary, in exchange for his complete surrender of any interest in the Disney studio. In a separate document bearing the same date, Roy (for himself
and as attorney in fact for Walt) undertook to pay the $2,920 within a year,
plus interest accruing at an annual rate of 7 percent.[33]

Iwerks remained on the payroll through Saturday, January 25 (he told Roy
Disney that he would come back to the studio the following week to finish
a *Silly Symphony* called *Autumn,* but he failed to show up).[34] That Saturday
morning, he and Roy had what Roy described, in a letter to Walt written
later that day, as a "very calm, quiet" talk. "I told him frankly that the worst
feature of this whole affair was the fact that a fellow as close to us as he had
been should turn on us at a time like this." Iwerks had begun negotiating for
his own producing deal the previous September, Roy wrote, and "did not
even know until two days before he received his contract that [Powers] was
behind it. . . . We know how gullible and easily [led] Ub is, and we have a
good dose of how two-faced Charlie Giegerich and P. A. [Powers] are. Not
trying to excuse Ub, but just trying to size it up all the way around, I believe
Ub at the start meant O.K., and I am sure that right now, even though he
won't admit it, he regrets very much the outcome."[35]

Powers had made a fatal misjudgment, since Iwerks was simply too re-
served a personality—especially compared with Walt Disney—to succeed
for very long as the head of a cartoon studio.* "Ub shunned responsibility,"

---

* Iwerks began the 1930s releasing his *Flip the Frog* cartoons through MGM, the biggest
and most powerful major studio, but then saw his fortunes decline. He rejoined the Disney
staff in 1940—as an employee, not a partner. He specialized in solving difficult technical
problems.

Ben Sharpsteen said. "He'd be kind of generous on being solicited and he'd give all the advice he knew how, but he didn't put himself ahead."[36]

Like the Mintz recruits in 1928, Iwerks cited his arguments with Walt Disney as his motivating force. Roy wrote: "Ub said when first approached, you and he had been having considerable friction and that he made up his mind it was best to step out."[37] For his part, Disney said in 1956 that he thought Iwerks had nursed a lingering sense of injustice. Disney believed that Iwerks was always troubled because he was far more experienced as a commercial artist—and surely more skilled—but was paid less than Disney after they both went to work for the Kansas City Film Ad Company.

Carl Stalling also resigned from the Disney staff, the day after Iwerks did. "I thought something was wrong," Stalling said many years later. "When Roy Disney told me that Ub was leaving, I told him, 'Well, I guess I'll be leaving, too.'"[38] In Stalling's case, as in Iwerks's, arguments with Walt had made him eager to leave. Stalling had accepted Walt's offer of a one-third interest in the *Silly Symphonies*—twenty-five dollars a week had been withheld from his salary since December 31, 1928—but as in Iwerks's case, leaving the studio voided the agreement.[39] Stalling had also invested two thousand dollars in the Disney Film Recording Company early in 1929, when Walt was trying to raise enough money to pay for the Cinephone equipment he needed on the West Coast. The Disneys repaid that money.

More acrimony surrounded Stalling's departure than Iwerks's. When Stalling returned to the studio to remove his sheet music, on the same day that Iwerks said his farewell, Roy refused to let him take all of it. "He showed a disposition to get nasty and take it in spite of me," Roy wrote to Walt, "and I thought I was going to have to resort to throwing him out!"[40]

Walt Disney had now been in two partnerships with Ub Iwerks, one rather more nebulous partnership with Fred Harman, and a semipartnership with Carl Stalling. Two of those partnerships, the first with Iwerks and the one with Harman, had fizzled quickly, and the other two had ended in the rupture of long friendships. There would be no more partnerships. Although the Disneys seriously considered sharing ownership with outside investors in 1932, only Walt and Roy and their wives would own the company as long as it remained privately held.[41] Disney spoke guardedly or misleadingly of all his former partners in future years (in 1956, he referred to Stalling as "the organist"), and, as one new employee learned in 1930, he was particularly bitter about the most important one, Ub Iwerks.

David Hand, an animator from New York, accepted a job on the Disney studio's staff on his thirtieth birthday, January 23, 1930. Unlike the New York animators who preceded him, Hand had not been lured west by an offer from Walt Disney. Instead, he moved to Hollywood in the hope of making a career in live action. "But you couldn't get a job," he said many years later, "so I went to Disney's." Hand was hired on a Thursday—probably by Burt Gillett, who had known him in New York, since Walt Disney himself was not around to do any hiring.

When Hand finally met Disney, he said, "Walt was awful mad at Ub, because he didn't talk about anything else to me." Disney complained to Hand—in an echo of his petulance in the 1920s—that Iwerks would not stay at his drawing board. Instead, he parked his car in the driveway beside the studio building and spent the day there, working on the car and ignoring Disney's plea that he animate and let a mechanic do the work.[42]

None of Disney's other employees followed Iwerks out the door. The New York animators had been recruited by Walt Disney himself and had relocated because of him. Like Ben Sharpsteen, who turned down a job offer from Iwerks, they may have felt justified skepticism about their former colleague's ability to run a successful studio. Sharpsteen summed up their attitude a couple of days after Iwerks announced he was leaving; as quoted by Roy Disney in a letter to Walt, he said, "We know that the difference of these cartoons over the average run is nothing more or less than Walt's personality, along with cooperation from his fellows."[43]

The net effect of Iwerks's and Stalling's departures was to leave the Disney brothers in a stronger position, personally and financially, than ever before. What Walt heard in New York must have given him added confidence that he had outgrown a parsimonious, small-scale distributor like Pat Powers. "From what Dick [Huemer] and Jack Carr [another veteran New York animator] told us," Lillian Disney wrote to Roy on January 30, "[the Fleischer and Mintz studios] get everyone [sic] of our pictures and run them for the crews over and over again."[44]

The break with Powers was messy, to the point that Disney changed hotels and registered under an assumed name, the better to elude process servers, after he wrote to Roy on February 7, "Have definitely broke [sic] with Powers. Will deliver no more pictures."[45] On February 19, he signed his own contract with Columbia, which had been distributing the *Silly Symphonies* under its contract with Powers, and left for Los Angeles, ending yet another protracted stay in New York.

Although Walt had until this point taken the lead in business matters, it fell to Roy to go to New York in April 1930 to work on the settlement with Powers. Their correspondence makes clear that Walt still called the shots, but

Roy's background as a "money man" was finally being put to productive use. The three-sided negotiations, involving Columbia as well as the Disneys and Powers, had actually begun by early March, and Roy took part only for the last couple of weeks. What he saw left him skeptical about Columbia, which he described to Walt as not "overburdened with good intentions."[46] The settlement, signed on April 22, was expensive—the Disneys not only gave up their claims against Powers but had to give him fifty thousand dollars, money they borrowed from Columbia and would have to repay from their films' profits before they saw any profits themselves. But Columbia would advance the Disneys seven thousand dollars upon the delivery of each film—they would actually be able to spend more on each cartoon than they could when they were getting smaller advances from Powers and seeing none of the profits. "I honestly feel elated over everything," Roy wrote to Walt on May 6. "Settlement going to work out good and future very bright."[47]

At this point, Walt Disney may not have been ready to take full advantage of his improved situation. In the early 1930s, he could be strikingly conservative when he spoke for publication about cartoons. In a statement for *Film Daily* in April 1930, he was cautious about both color and the wide screen: "After all, in a cartoon comedy it is laughs and personality that count. Color alone will not sustain public interest."[48] About a year later, *American Magazine* quoted him as saying that it was a "mistake" to think "that American audiences always want brand-new gags—surprises and cute turns. We have found out that they want most to laugh. They easily forget the original turns, but if a picture has given them a good laugh, whether by old gags or new, they always remember it."[49]

Disney remembered all the gags in his silent cartoons, or so it seems, because gags from *Alice* comedies like *Alice's Fishy Story, Alice's Orphan,* and *Alice's Brown Derby* can be identified in cartoons made years later—reworked and improved, to be sure, but still the same gags. "The best gag men are those with the best memories," David Hand said in 1946, two years after he left the Disney studio. "Disney has the most marvelous memory—like an elephant he never forgets, and he remembers all the awful animation you ever did."[50]

Disney's model for the "laughs and personality" he sought was not any new talkie star, but the greatest star of the silents, Charlie Chaplin. In 1931, Disney cited Chaplin as a principal source for Mickey Mouse: "We thought of a tiny bit of a mouse that would have something of the wistfulness of Chaplin . . . a little fellow trying to do the best he could."[51]

In the first few months of 1930, after Iwerks's departure, the Disney staff continued to gather at night once a week or so—in Walt's office, or in the adjacent music room—to talk about gag ideas. No one on the staff devoted full time to writing. No one had devoted full time to writing for Disney's silent cartoons, either, but in their last year or two—if the surviving examples are a fair measure—he had still been able to fill at least some of those cartoons with comic business that was dense and complex. When Disney was making his early sound cartoons, though, the greatest challenge they posed was essentially technical—sound and images had to fit together in a pleasing way.

Iwerks had met that challenge adroitly, after hitting his stride with *Skeleton Dance,* and that is why so many of the early Disney sound cartoons seem more his creations than Disney's own. Iwerks's kind of animation, ticking away with mechanical precision, could not have been better suited to the demands of early sound cartoons. By 1930, though, Disney and other members of his staff had absorbed the basics of making cartoons with sound, and the loss of Iwerks's expertise could actually be seen as a blessing. The Disney cartoons could now recoup some of their pre–*Steamboat Willie* vitality, but with sound as a fillip.

How to do that was the problem. Disney in the early 1930s was not some visionary leader, trying to inculcate in his followers what he had already grasped himself, but was instead groping toward some better kind of cartoon alongside his animators. He was notoriously inarticulate. "In the real early days," Ben Sharpsteen said, "Walt didn't seem to have the command of ways of expressing himself for the benefit of the animator, and I would say that most of the progress was made among the animators themselves, in pinpointing faults."[52] Les Clark remembered a Disney who "talked a lot and sometimes you didn't understand what he wanted. . . . Maybe he didn't, either, until he saw something he liked."[53]

Disney was never ambiguous about what he liked or, more often, disliked—"Walt was much less easily satisfied with whatever we did than any of the rest of us," Wilfred Jackson said—but it was frequently difficult for him to translate his ideas into guidance for his animators. It was only after he had worked with people for some time that a simple expression of approval or disapproval told them what they needed to know.

Even in the early 1930s, Jackson said, "Walt already did have his fast eye and quick overall comprehension of whatever he put his attention on, so he would usually be first to detect what it was that made [the animation in a competitor's cartoon] more effective than ours." Jackson cited as examples of the "little things that would make a big difference": "Varying the spacing of the inbetweens so as to slow out of a hold before moving full speed toward the next one, and then slow to a stop to avoid . . . abrupt, jerky motion. Or spreading out, then condensing the spacing to get an accent in the action."[54]

The "big difference" produced by such "little things" was to make the animated characters on the screen seem a little more real. This was the thread that kept surfacing in Disney's films in the 1920s—in the repentant hippo in an *Alice* comedy, in bits and pieces of the *Oswald* cartoons—but had been mostly absent from his first year and a half of sound cartoons, dominated as they were by coarse gags and synchronized sound. Now it was slowly coming to the fore again, but in a different way at first, through movement that seemed worthy of belief even when the characters were wholly fanciful.

In a *Silly Symphony* called *Frolicking Fish,* released in May 1930, an animator named Norman Ferguson introduced what his colleagues called "moving holds," breaking with the sharply defined poses that were characteristic of much other animation, like Ub Iwerks's. Ferguson, one of the New York animators hired the previous year (he had worked at Paul Terry's *Aesop's Fables* studio), animated a fish trio that moved with a new freedom and naturalness. As Wilfred Jackson put it, "He slowed in, moved through. If one part moved, some other thing moved. Before that time, we'd get into a pose and hold it; we'd move into another pose and hold it."[55] Ferguson gave to his colleagues a tool they could use in animating many different kinds of characters.

When Ferguson animated his fish, Disney was still expanding his use of assistants and inbetweeners in order to increase the more experienced animators' output. "I kind of think it was the nicest thing I ever did for this business when I realized that it was not like the old art of painting and things, that it was a new art," Disney said in 1956. "That it was a mass production for survival. . . . Of course, the industry was set up that way . . . before I came into it. But I think I organized more mass production things"—that is, a more refined division of labor—"than had ever been used in the industry before."

The gains were slow in coming. Sometimes the animator might turn to an assistant for help in providing inbetweens, Dave Hand said, but "at other times when there was a difficult bit to do, we did our own inbetweening."[56] The animator's assistant might be no more than "an apprentice inbetweener"— the term Ed Benedict applied to himself when he recalled his work as an assistant to Wilfred Jackson in 1930—whose inexperience left the animator no choice but to do most of the work himself.[57]

Disney's 1956 remarks echoed the work of Frederick W. Taylor, whose *Principles of Scientific Management* (1919) was a classic argument for the benefits of the division of labor. In the eighteenth century, Adam Smith pointed out the advantages of breaking production down into discrete tasks and assigning each to a specialist. Taylor carried that idea further, dividing tasks into simple components that required little or no specialized knowledge or skill. But what happened at Disney's bore no resemblance to what Taylor had in mind, or, probably, to what Disney himself had in mind at first. Instead, the division of labor was increasingly pursued—at least at the levels above those of inbetweeners and inkers and painters—as a means of artistic collaboration.

Around 1930, a few assistants began to improve their animators' drawings as well as make inbetweens. Some animators may have produced a few more drawings than they did before, thanks to that change; they no longer had to struggle with their shortcomings as draftsmen. But the gains came less in increased output than in better-looking cartoons. This was a countercurrent in the Disney studio's use of assistants and inbetweeners, one that worked against the higher output that such a division of labor could be expected to bring.

Increasingly, the pattern at the Disney studio in the early 1930s was not that Disney himself introduced stunning advances, but that he recognized, accepted, and often encouraged the improvements that his people were coming up with on their own. When the animators began shooting pencil tests, for example, "we got to shooting more and more tests," Wilfred Jackson said, "and Walt rather encouraged us to, because we would often make good improvements."[58] It was because he was so receptive to such changes that Disney stood apart from the proprietors of other cartoon studios, most of whom attempted comparable improvements only because their cartoons were suffering by comparison with Disney's.

It was probably not until 1931 that animators began shooting complete scenes as pencil tests, and again this was an idea that Disney endorsed but did not originate. Shooting complete scenes had conspicuous advantages for all concerned—Disney, the director, and the animator—as compared with what Jackson called the "primitive, laborious, makeshift" alternative of shooting only parts of scenes and judging the rest of the animation solely by how it looked on paper, "flipping the drawings to see portions of the action a bit at a time."[59] Small wonder that Disney should decide that shooting complete scenes was a good idea.

Throughout 1930 and 1931, even as pencil tests came into general use and made it easier to spot mistakes, the cartoons that emerged from the Disney studio suffered from glitches—as when a character departed sharply from its standardized appearance for a scene or two—that must have been obvious but were not repaired, probably because repairing them would have been too expensive. In *Midnight in a Toy Shop* (1930), for example, a spider is simply enormous just after it enters the toy shop of the title; it has supposedly entered the shop through a keyhole, but it is far too big to have done that.

In those years, Disney was working within the limitations imposed on each cartoon by Columbia's advance of seven thousand dollars—a figure that was liberating at first, but quickly became a straitjacket. Disney expanded the studio's physical plant significantly between February and July 1931, at a cost of a quarter of a million dollars,[60] but much of that construction—of a sound stage, in particular—as well as much of the studio's hiring, was dictated by the complications created by sound, and the need to have more people on hand to deal with them. The cash available to spend on any one cartoon was still tight.

Disney was keenly interested in licensing Mickey Mouse merchandise as early as 1929, when he wrote to Powers's man Charles Giegerich: "I should think that there would be a big market for MICKEY dolls, toys and novelties for the coming season and it may not be a bad idea to feel out the possibilities along these lines as these things are also considered very good publicity."[61] He said in 1956 that he began licensing merchandise when he was in New York "and we needed money and a fellow kept hanging around the hotel with three hundred dollars cash waving at me all the time and I finally signed a deal" to put Mickey Mouse on writing tablets. That must have been in 1929—and may have been a handshake agreement—since the Disneys signed the first contract of which there is a record early in 1930. That first contract, dated January 24, 1930, was with King Features Syndicate for a *Mickey Mouse* comic strip that had actually started running eleven days earlier. Walt Disney and Gunther Lessing sealed the deal while they were in New York to confront Pat Powers.[62]

Once the licensing of toys, novelties, and books was under way—it began with a February 3, 1930, contract with Geo. Borgfeldt & Co.—Walt Disney played almost no role in it. He left that side of the business to Roy, although he showed a continuing interest in the comic strip; it was drawn at the studio by Ub Iwerks at first, and later by Floyd Gottfredson.[63]

The revenue from such licensing was still small in the early 1930s, however, and the staff's limitations were a continuing handicap, too. An advance like Ferguson's on *Frolicking Fish* occurred in the context of work that was typically much cruder (and Ferguson himself was notoriously weak as a draftsman). At Disney's in the early 1930s, the animator Ed Love said, "We were all pretty lousy artists. I remember one time they were doing a scene in a *Silly Symphony*, of a guy playing a xylophone [with a bone], and nobody could figure out how to draw a hand, holding the bone. Dave Hand, who was then starting to direct, said, 'Oh, just make a black circle and put a bump on it.'"[64]

Even in the early years of the Great Depression, such untutored artists (Love had no formal art training) still made up most of the pool of talent available to Disney. When Love applied for a job at the Disney studio in 1931, he was hired personally by Walt Disney. "I showed him probably three quarters of an inch of drawings that he flipped. Mickey Mouse came out on a stage, played a violin, made a sour note, got embarrassed, started to go off, tripped and fell. . . . [Disney] said, 'Come to work.'"[65]

Disney's animators seized upon various expedients when they tried to dress up their animation. *Rubber-hose* animation, for example, was basically action that curved excessively in the direction of the movement. This device suppressed the jitter that was always a hazard when a stiff vertical line animated across the screen, but, Wilfred Jackson said, it was overdone "tremendously" in the early 1930s until Disney cracked down.[66]

Animators might achieve something lifelike, and take pride in the result, but such occasions were still scattered and rare. Ed Benedict, who assisted Rudy Zamora, spoke of Zamora's pleasure in one scene in *The China Plate*, a *Silly Symphony* with Chinese characters that Zamora was animating in March 1931: "Rudy had this scene and he was quite delighted to have thought to do this himself; I remember him leaning over to me, flipping the animated drawings [and] saying, 'Hey, how do you like this?' . . . This little girl was to turn from left to right—but when she turned, the hair trailed across her face. That had never been done before. That's a first—beginning to loosen up things."[67]

Zamora was, however, famously casual about his work, and he lasted at the Disney studio only about a year, from January 1931 until early in 1932. He was at one point a victim of Disney's habit—familiar to his employees since the 1920s—of roaming through the studio after hours. Dave Hand, who described Disney's nocturnal visits as "a little sneaky," remembered when Disney—finding that Zamora had done no work on a scene—trapped him into bringing him a stack of blank paper with only a few drawings on top. Disney peeled off those drawings, revealing the blank paper beneath.[68]

There was, in short, no smooth upward trajectory at the Disney studio, but more of a stuttering pace.

Sometime in 1931, Disney said twenty-five years later, "I had a hell of a breakdown. I went all to pieces. . . . As we got going along I kept expecting more from the artists and when they let me down and things, I got worried. Just pound, pound, pound. Costs were going up and I was always way over what they figured the pictures would bring in. . . . I just got very irritable. I got to a point that I couldn't talk on the telephone. I'd begin to cry." He spoke again of weeping in a 1963 interview: "Things had gone wrong. I had trouble with a picture. I worried and worried. I had a nervous breakdown. I kept crying."[69]

Disney left with Lillian on a cross-country trip in October 1931 after he "finished a picture that I was so sick of. Oh gosh, I was so sick of it. So many things went wrong with it. And I went away 'til that picture turned over"—completed its initial theatrical runs, presumably. On that trip, Disney said, "I was a new man. . . . I had the time of my life. It was actually the first time we had ever been away on anything like that since we were married."

When he returned, "I started going to the athletic club. I went down religiously two or three times a week. I started in with just general calisthenics. Then I tried wrestling, but I didn't like it because I'd get down there in somebody's crotch and sweaty old sweatshirt." Disney moved on to boxing and then to golf and horseback riding. He showed up at the golf course at 5:30 in the morning, played five holes, then cut across the course to the eighteenth hole. "Eat breakfast fit for a harvest hand and then go up to the studio just full of pep," he said. Starting in 1932, Disney played what Les Clark called "sandlot polo" with Clark, Norm Ferguson, Dick Lundy, Gunther Lessing, and Jack Cutting of the animation staff; they rode horses rented from a riding stable.[70]

There is no way to know which cartoon Disney found so distracting, and it is not even clear how long he was gone on his restorative vacation—probably four to six weeks, but in any case not so long that his absence troubled the people who worked for him. None of his employees at the time ever cited his "breakdown" as a major event in the studio's life. As closely as some of them observed their boss and tried to anticipate his wishes, his "breakdown" seems to have made no impression on them. Disney's emphasis on his tears smacks of the self-dramatization—the obverse of "some of his ebullience"—that he sometimes lapsed into, but there is no reason to doubt that he was truly distressed.

Roy was aware that something was wrong. He wrote to their parents on December 30, 1931, that "Walt is feeling much better than he was before his vacation, but is not back to his old self." Roy wrote of a physical cause of Walt's "trouble," however—"some sort of parasitic growth in his intestines of a vegetable nature"—even though he added, "Things are going much better at the studio so it is much less of a nerve-wracking job for him than before."[71] Whatever the nature of that "parasitic growth," it seems not have made any lasting impact on Walt's health.

There is little direct evidence of Disney's thinking in the early 1930s—nothing much in the way of memoranda, transcripts, or letters that speak to his state of mind—but this was the time when his role in the studio changed decisively. His distress probably arose from that circumstance, and it may have been building for years, contributing to his repeated arguments with his closest associates.

By 1931, Disney's involvement even in story, the area where he concentrated his efforts after he surrendered the director's duties to Iwerks and Gillett, had diminished with the hiring early that year of two full-time gag men, Ted Sears and Webb Smith. After so many years of animating and then directing—and, before that, years of other kinds of jobs that required working with his hands, and before that, years of manual labor, all the way back to his newspaper-delivery days—Disney now had to persuade himself of the legitimacy of purely mental work.

He was still trying to persuade himself, a quarter century later. "People don't . . . attach any importance to the coordinating of all the talents that go into these things," he complained in 1956. "The vital part I played is coordinating these talents. And encouraging these talents. . . . I have an organization over there of people who are really specialists. You can't match them anywhere in the world for what they can do. But they all need to be pulled together."

For Disney to be a coordinator in 1931 was especially hard because he was not leading his men toward some goal that only he could see. He was leading them toward something that even he had only a vague conception of. His new role—and his difficulties in adjusting to it—were making more complex what been a basically simple personality. Like his father, he had always been an entrepreneur by nature, with an entrepreneur's rather diffuse urge to dominate and control. Now he was on the verge of becoming an artist, too. With that change would come an impulse to control for increasingly distinct and ambitious purposes.

Disney passed through his crisis as the studio itself was becoming a somewhat different place, one where more of the people who worked there were taking their work seriously—not just feeling delight in the occasional well-executed scene, but striving for consistency at a higher level. There was still plenty wrong with the Disney cartoons. However much Disney may have wanted to ban rubber-hose animation, it still turned up, in quantity, in the *Mickey* called *Barnyard Olympics,* released in April 1932. More than one Disney cartoon from early 1932 brims over with obvious, cost-cutting cycles. But the tide was turning the other way.

"Everybody was enthused in those days," Ed Love said. "We'd have meetings, and Walt would talk, and everybody would yak. I remember they'd talk about simple things like how do you go from putting stuff on *twos* to on *ones*.

It was a big deal, and nobody could figure out what to do."[72] (The questions involved were when to use the same drawing for two successive exposures, or frames of film, as opposed to using a separate drawing for each frame, and how to manage the transition from one to the other.) Dick Marion (later known as Dick Hall), who worked as an inbetweener under the animator Jack King, was fired by Disney around the end of 1931 when it came out that he was looking for another job. "You had to be dedicated," he said, "and that was not being dedicated. I shouldn't have even thought about leaving."[73]

Around the beginning of 1932, in a step that speaks of Disney's new confidence in his role as coordinator, he ordered his animators to start making their animation drawings as rough sketches, rather than finished drawings, and to make pencil tests of the roughs. Until then, pencil tests were shot only after the animation was in finished form, ready to be inked on cels. In Wilfred Jackson's recollection, it was seeing some of Norm Ferguson's very rough animation in pencil test—animation that "read" clearly despite the sketchiness of the drawing—that spurred Disney to order the change.[74]

Kendall O'Connor, who as a Disney layout artist knew Ferguson a few years later, described him to Mark Langer as "a typical New Yorker, high pressure and very fast. I think he thought we were all too slow out here. . . . He twiddled his hair, a little forelock, with a finger all the time he talked to you. He was a very nervous chap."[75] That nervous energy probably found a readier outlet in rapid sketching than in finished drawings.

"By encouraging Fergy to concentrate on the *actions* with rough drawings and assigning to him an excellent draftsman to clean up his animation drawings," Jackson wrote, "Walt felt Fergy was able to produce better quality as well as great quantity of outstanding animation. Walt felt, also, that it should work this same way for his other animators and let them know he expected them to do their animation in the same way, too."[76]

Ferguson was possibly not the first Disney animator whose work was cleaned up by others, Jackson said. But "I do recall Fergy's use of a cleanup assistant being held up as *the* example of how he wanted all the other animators to work by Walt, when some of them were reluctant to adopt that method."[77] Before Disney's edict, by the time he saw a scene in pencil test it was so far along the road toward ink and paint that his criticisms must have frequently been more relevant to the animator's next assignment than to the scene at hand. But now he could use pencil tests of rough animation to get at his animators' work before it was too late to make major changes. "Walt felt that if you roughed out an action," Les Clark said, "you could see much faster whether it would turn out the way Walt wanted it to. If it didn't, discard it, and make changes. You didn't have to throw away a lot of cleaned-up work."[78]

By insisting that they draw their animation roughly, Disney was encouraging his animators to think in terms of movement, rather than individual drawings. "The hardest job," he said in 1956, "was to get the guys to quit fooling around with these individual drawings and to think of the group of drawings in an action. They couldn't resist when they had a drawing in front of them that they had to keep noodling."

Some among the New York animators, especially, showed a taste for essentially mechanical solutions to animation's problems. Dave Hand, when animating something like a flock of birds in *Flowers and Trees* (1932), "would chart it out," Dick Lundy said, so that the birds moved not in flowing, slightly irregular movements that would suggest real life, but in robotic patterns instead.[79] It was probably in Jack King's work that those old ways of animating collided most conspicuously with the new ways that Disney was cultivating.

Chuck Couch, one of the young Californians who began populating the Disney studio's lower ranks in the early 1930s, was King's assistant, and he remembered King as "a meticulous draftsman; he didn't rough stuff out very much. He'd always make very clean drawings."[80] When King joined the staff in 1929, such "clean drawings" were highly valued because the inkers had so little difficulty tracing them onto cels. Dick Lundy, who was also hired in 1929, remembered that one reason he got his job was that "they liked my line. I had a hard line, which was great for inking."[81] King's drawings, though, were not simply clean, but rigid. King traced one coin for Mickey Mouse's head and another for his belly—small coins for long shots, larger coins for closer shots—and, as Wilfred Jackson said, "that made a real stiff little character."[82] Les Clark saw Ben Sharpsteen, too, use coins to draw Mickey's head.[83] Such expedients weighed against moving the animation in the direction Disney wanted, and the animators who indulged in them felt his wrath whenever he learned what they were doing.

Since the construction of the 1931 additions to the studio, Disney had been watching pencil tests in a small windowless room that quickly came to be called the *sweatbox*. Before that, Disney had looked at pencil tests on a Moviola. According to Wilfred Jackson, Disney switched from Moviolas to the sweatbox in part for his own convenience—so he would not have to "respond to requests all through the day," from one animator after another, to look at tests on the Moviolas—but in large part so that the animators could keep in touch with what their colleagues at the rapidly growing studio were doing.

Once the sweatbox had been set up, Ben Sharpsteen said, "Walt devoted considerable time to sitting in" on pencil tests "with most of the animators concerned on the picture." Here again was the newly confident artist, or coordinator, at work, enlisting his animators in sustained scrutiny of their colleagues' work as well as their own.

The negotiations with Powers had left the Disneys cool to their new distributor, Columbia, and they wasted no time in signing with United Artists (UA) less than eight months later, in December 1930. That agreement was a striking advance over the Columbia deal, since it provided for an advance on each cartoon of fifteen thousand dollars. It took a year and half for the Disneys to work off their obligations to Columbia, however, and the first cartoons under the new agreement with UA did not appear until mid-1932. Early that year, the Disneys and UA began gingerly to explore the idea of making one or more of the *Silly Symphonies* in Technicolor. The idea originated with Walt Disney, but it was Roy Disney who exchanged letters with Al Lichtman, UA's vice president and general manager for distribution, at its New York headquarters. Moving to Technicolor was not to be undertaken lightly; earlier color films had neither looked good nor been accepted by audiences, and the additional cost for prints (twelve thousand dollars for two hundred prints, Lichtman said) would be substantial. Success might even be a bigger headache than failure, Lichtman suggested: if the exhibitors wanted color in all future *Silly Symphonies*, "could we get enough additional money [from the exhibitors] to pay for the extra cost of colored prints?"[84]

The Technicolor company itself was behind him, Walt Disney said in 1956, because "they were not quite far enough along with the color process to go into heavy production with any big live-action theatrical feature. A cartoon was ideal for their experimentation." The cartoon Disney had in mind for Technicolor treatment was called *Flowers and Trees*. He had completed it in black and white by early June 1932, when Lichtman told Roy that it was "one of the nicest Symphonies I have ever seen," so nice that UA was going to release it as its first *Silly Symphony*.[85] Roy asked him to hold off until the color version was completed—a version no doubt made with the same inked cels, but with the black-and-white paint washed off their backs.

The color version of *Flowers and Trees*—a fantasy in which two young trees are lovers menaced by a jealous stump—premiered on July 18, 1932, at Grauman's Chinese Theatre in Hollywood, accompanying MGM's pretentious feature *Strange Interlude*. It was a huge success, and when Lichtman wrote to Roy a few days later he joined in the applause but worried aloud about whether the Disneys should be sinking their money into such expensive films in the midst of a depression. Roy was clearly elated by the cartoon's reception, and he wrote in reply: "I realize that Walt and I do not run our business on a strictly 'business basis,' but honestly we have more concern over re-intrenching [sic] ourselves during these difficult times by making our product as desirable to the exhibitor as we possibly can, feeling that if we can only ride out these present times we are really doing well in the final analysis. Then when better times do return, we will still be in the front and be able to take care of the old family sock."[86] Roy, as much as Walt, wanted to go into color, and he was working hard to justify such a move, to himself as well as Lichtman. By November 1932, there was no longer any doubt—it would be wrong, Roy wrote to Lichtman, to do other than make all the *Silly Symphonies* in Technicolor.[87]

At first, when the Disney studio began making color cartoons, colors were set more in the story department than by the directors or layout men, but in this area, as in most others, the decisions were really being made by Walt Disney. Wilfred Jackson was a director then. "By the time I would talk to [Emil] Flohri [the principal background painter] about the backgrounds, Walt had been there," Jackson said. "Flohri was telling me what he was going to do in the way of coloring, I wasn't telling him."[88]

In the early 1930s, Disney was still close to the people who worked for him, literally so in some cases. He lived just a few blocks from the Hyperion Avenue studio and across the street from Don Patterson—an assistant animator at the studio (and formerly an animator for Charles Mintz).[89] But with the studio more prosperous thanks to the UA release, Disney was ready to move again.

In the spring and summer of 1932, Walt and Lillian Disney built their second new home, this one a twelve-room house described as "Norman-French" in style, at 4053 Woking Way in the Los Feliz Hills.[90] Like the Lyric Avenue house, it was on a winding street not far from the studio, but the new neighborhood, north of Los Feliz Boulevard, was, like the house itself, considerably grander than its predecessor. Roy Disney marveled in 1968 at the audacity of the construction: "He hung this swimming pool up on the corner of this darn thing. It's a granite hill and we were taking bets to see if it would stand. It's thirty-five years and it's still there."[91]

(Even in 1964, Disney was a little defensive about just how grand the house was. "Everybody gets mad at the rich for owning these big places," he told the Hollywood columnist Hedda Hopper, "but they forget how many jobs it creates. It takes a lot of people to run a big estate. I built a house in Los Feliz during the Depression. Men used to line up there in the morning hoping to get work. I found a graduate of the Vienna Academy of Fine Arts and had him paint my whole ceiling.")[92]

By mid-1932, the enthusiastic, cheerleading voice in Disney's 1928 letters from New York was being heard in the story outlines for new cartoons that were distributed throughout the studio with a request for help with gags. The outlines typically begin with a summary of the story—running as long as four pages—that was probably dictated by a member of the story crew, followed by notes that sound like Disney himself, right down to the profanity, as in the outline for *Mickey's Mechanical Man* ("This could lead to a helluva lot of gags and a new type of Mickey").[93]

In an outline distributed in July 1932, Disney scoffed at the doubters who said a *Mickey Mouse* cartoon called *Building a Building* could never be made: "Production has been started on it twice before, and it was side-tracked both times because it was thought to contain too much detail. I cannot agree with this. I believe it can be handled in a simplified manner and turn out to be very effective. . . . So let's go after it with a vengeance and make something very good out of it."[94] There was a disingenuous side to Disney's cheerleading—who else but Disney himself could have "side-tracked" a cartoon because "it was thought to contain too much detail"?—but his enthusiasm was genuine.

In his addenda, Disney always adopted a positive, can-do tone. In August 1932, he touted the possibilities of *Mickey's Good Deed,* a Christmas cartoon to be released at the end of 1932: "Here is a story that has everything necessary to make it a wow. A good plot—good atmosphere—personality—pathos—and plenty of opportunity for gags. There are seven major sequences to this story—each holds wonderful possibilities for good gags and bits of human action. I am expecting everyone to turn in at least one gag on each sequence."[95] (Disney was correct when he said that the story had a "plot." It does have one in the strict Aristotelian sense, with beginning, middle, and end—one of the first Disney cartoons of that kind.)

In November 1932, at the end of the outline for a *Mickey Mouse* cartoon, a burlesque of costume dramas set in medieval England to be called *Ye Olden Days,* Disney dwelled at length on the musical and comic potential in the story, and on how different characters could be portrayed: "I see this story as a wonderful possibility for a burlesque on a comic opera . . . For a change I would like to see us make a Mickey built around good musical angles . . . This is our first costume Mickey—think of gag possibilities with the King in his royal robes—his funny looking attendants—the court jester and the court musicians with quaint ruffled costumes with balloon trunks, etc. . . . Possible chance for a Zasu Pitts type in Clarabelle Cow as the lady-in-waiting—she could be the nervous type who doesn't know what to do to help yet is a very sympathetic type—when Minnie cries, she cries too, and when Minnie is in love, she feels it too . . . The King could be the type that is very blustery and excited over the least thing. I have in mind Mary Pickford's story *Dorothy Vernon of Haddon Hall* . . . Chance for some funny characters in the King's army. The soldiers could have guns of the blunderbuss type with forked stick to hold them up while they fire them—making noise like auto horns along with muffled explosions."[96]

These distinctive notes vanish from the outlines starting early in 1933; the closing notes from then on have a more functional, workmanlike quality, less concerned than before with the feeling behind the gags. Disney, the ever more confident coordinator, was stepping back still further from a day-to-day role in work on the films.

That work was becoming steadily more organized. Disney told Bob Thomas that Webb Smith devised what came to be called the *storyboard,* almost by accident: "We would sit in his office in the morning and think up gags. . . . After lunch I'd drop in Webb's office and he'd have the sequence sketched out on sheets of paper. They'd be scattered all over the room, on desks, on the floor, every place. It got too tough to follow them; we decided to pin all the sketches on the wall in sequence. That was the first storyboard."[97]

It probably did not happen quite that quickly and neatly. If, as seems likely, the first real storyboard was put up for a 1932 Technicolor *Silly Symphony* called *Babes in the Woods,* a retelling of "Hansel and Gretel," other cartoons came after it without the help of fully developed storyboards. Wilfred Jackson remembered that the storyboard for the *Silly Symphony* called *Father Noah's Ark* (1933) "was just a grouping of sketches here and there on the board with each group depicting a gag or a short continuity of business for an incident."[98] It may have taken a year or two before the idea of telling a complete story through sketches pinned to a large piece of corkboard really took hold. But even in embryonic form, the storyboard's efficiency must have appealed to Walt Disney himself, at a time when the pressures on his time were multiplying, along with the budgets of his cartoons and the size of his staff.

Art Babbitt, a former animator at Paul Terry's new Terrytoons studio in New York, was one of the many new members of the staff; he was hired in July 1932. The Friday-night classes at Chouinard had ended by then. As reflected in Jack Zander's anecdote, many of the Disney animators had been reluctant to attend such classes, but by the summer of 1932, with the cartoons changing rapidly and drawing skills in greater demand, interest in formal art instruction was quickening. When Babbitt organized classes of his own and hired a model, growing numbers of his colleagues turned up each week for three weeks.

Disney noticed that Babbitt was succeeding where he had not. At Disney's instigation, Babbitt moved the classes to the studio, where Disney picked up the tab. Babbitt said in 1973 that Disney "was quite upset. As he put it, it wouldn't be very nice if the newspapers ever came out with the story that a group of Disney artists were drawing naked women in a private house. . . . He thought it would look a lot better if these art classes were held on the sound stage."[99] Disney did not have to be persuaded of the value of such classes, of course. In November 1932, he hired a Chouinard instructor, Donald W. Graham, to teach life classes at the studio two nights a week.[100]

Phil Dike, who taught painting at Chouinard for four years before joining Graham at Disney's, said of his colleague that "he had a practical sense of what made things work, from his engineering background"—Graham had originally studied to be an engineer—"and also intuitively."[101] William Hurtz, who studied under Graham at Chouinard in the mid-1930s, said that Graham "was concerned with space, volume, movement—kind of a structural approach to drawing."[102] That approach was highly appropriate for animated characters of the kind that were emerging in the Disney films.

As the Disney animators learned from innovations like Ferguson's moving holds how they could produce more lifelike animation, the life classes forced them to look outward, to consider the life to which some of their animation now bore resemblance. From their earliest days, the Disney cartoons' characters had been flat and simple formula characters, most often animals whose faces were, like Mickey Mouse's, white masks on black bodies. By 1932, though, Disney's animators were drawing characters that looked more realistic (very generally speaking) and could move convincingly in what seemed to be three-dimensional space.

Once a formula has been established, it exerts a powerful gravitational pull on artists who have used it. Resisting it, and observing life directly with the idea of reproducing it more accurately, is hard work, as the Disney animators found. The effects on their drawings were sometimes awkward at first. "I'd go to this art class," Dick Lundy said, "and then I'd come back, and I would try to put bones in Mickey, and he wasn't built that way."[103]

Mickey Mouse was immutably a formula character, but human characters were troublesome, too. In assessing the plausibility of characters on the screen, audiences make increasingly rigorous judgments the more closely those characters resemble themselves. Working with animal characters, animators could improve their skills without exposing their weaknesses to withering scrutiny. It was in their animation of the animals in *Silly Symphonies* like *Birds in the Spring* and *Father Noah's Ark,* both released early in 1933, that the Disney animators showed most clearly just how rapidly their skills were improving.

By early that year, the Disney cartoons had changed so rapidly, in so many ways, that the timing was perfect for a cartoon that in its seven minutes summed up how far they had come—and how far they might go. Disney made just such a cartoon, *Three Little Pigs,* which was released in May 1933.

"I was told," Walt Disney later wrote, "that some exhibitors and even United Artists considered the *Pigs* a 'cheater' because it had only four characters in it."[104] *Father Noah's Ark,* by contrast, was overflowing with animals of all kinds, as well as human characters. But the small cast of *Three Little Pigs* was exactly what Disney needed at this point. He had been making cartoons, like *Santa's Workshop* (1932), that were as intricate and detailed as elaborate mechanical toys or department-store windows at Christmas. Their characters were more realistically drawn than earlier cartoon characters, but they were not much more than moving parts. In *Three Little Pigs,* Disney was making a cartoon where the audience's attention would be squarely on the characters.

In his addendum to the outline for *Three Little Pigs* that circulated in the studio in December 1932, Disney talked at length about how to make those characters appealing:

> These little pig characters look as if they would work up very cute and we should be able to develop quite a bit of personality in them. Use cute little voices that could work into harmony and chorus effects when they talk together and everything that they would say or do in the first part of the story, while they are building their houses, could be in rhythmical manner. Anything that they would say would be handled either in singing or rhyme. The old wolf could be the fourth in a quartette, the bass voice, growling snarling type. When he fools the little pigs, he raises his voice, into a high falsetto. All the wolf dialogue would also carry either in rhyme or song. . . .
>
> Might try to stress the angle of the little pig who worked the hardest, received the reward, or some little moral that would teach a story. Someone might have some angles on how we could bring this moral out in a direct way without having to go into too much detail. This angle might be given some careful consideration, for things of this sort woven into a story give it depth and feeling. . . .
>
> These little pigs will be dressed in clothes. They will also have household impliments *[sic]*, props, etc., to work with and not be kept in the natural state. They will be more like human characters.[105]

Only a few animators worked on the film, assigned carefully to characters, so that Norm Ferguson—the studio's pioneer in giving the semblance of life to animated characters—animated almost all of the Big Bad Wolf, whereas Dick Lundy and Fred Moore, an upcoming young animator, handled most of the pigs' scenes.

Moore was a small, compact man who survived in his colleagues' memories as something of a cartoon character himself. Although he was a superb athlete, "his proportions were cute . . . and it kind of tickled you to watch him move around imitating someone like Fred Astaire or Chaplin, or trying some fancy juggling act," the animators Frank Thomas and Ollie Johnston have written. "Even if the stuff dropped on the floor, Fred would always end up in a good pose—just like his drawings."[106]

Early in work on the story, Albert Hurter had drawn the pigs as idealized versions of real young pigs, smooth and pink and round. Moore animated those characters with the pleasing elasticity that animators call *stretch and squash*. There was nothing loose or sloppy about this stretching and squashing—instead, Moore animated his characters from one pleasing shape to another. There was no sense that their true form had been compromised just to inject a little life into the animation. Instead, whatever shape they assumed at any given moment had the same pleasing roundness and solidity.

Norm Ferguson had shown animators how to suggest that a character was alive. Now Moore showed them how to enhance that illusion, almost to the point that it seemed that the character had a personality. His animation in *Three Little Pigs*—he handled the scenes at the start of the cartoon when the pigs introduce themselves—was charm itself.

The real genius of the cartoon, though, was that all its action took place within the musical framework that Disney described. In *Three Little Pigs*, the pigs' expressions, if not their movements, were still formulaic—they struck attitudes, rather than revealed emotions. There was no confusing them with any kind of real creature. It was music that filled the gap. *Three Little Pigs* was the first cartoon to plunge wholeheartedly into the sort of operetta style that had been germinating in the *Silly Symphonies* almost from the beginning of the United Artists release. *King Neptune* (1932), scored by Bert Lewis, opened with the title character singing about himself, and the operetta flavor was even stronger in *Father Noah's Ark,* whose characters introduced themselves through song within Leigh Harline's classically oriented score.

Frank Churchill, who wrote the score for *Three Little Pigs,* had nothing like Harline's musical education—Harline majored in music at the University of Utah—but he was a highly adaptable musician with a skill common to musicians who worked in the silent-film era, the ability to improvise quickly to fit whatever was happening on the screen. Churchill was perfect as composer for *Three Little Pigs* because the cartoon's action required him to switch gears constantly. When the wolf pretends to give up his pursuit of the two foolish pigs, he goes into hiding to the accompaniment of what Ross Care has called "a charmingly bland 'wolf-trot.'" Later, the Practical Pig executes, in Care's words, "an imposing piano cadenza a la Rachmaninoff"—played on the sound track by Carl Stalling, Disney's original musician, who had returned to the studio briefly as a freelancer—"as the wolf literally blows himself blue in the face while vainly attempting to blow down the door of the brick house."[107] All of this takes place within a score dominated by "Who's Afraid of the Big Bad Wolf?" the song that Churchill wrote for the cartoon, but *Three Little Pigs* is so fragmented and musically demanding that the song is never heard in its entirety.

Since directors and musicians worked as teams in the early 1930s, assigning Churchill to *Three Little Pigs* meant assigning Burt Gillett to it, too. Gillett had been directing the *Mickey Mouse* cartoons, which by 1933 had become a series devoted mostly to comic adventures depicted in broad strokes. Even though Mickey Mouse and the other characters in those cartoons were little more than what Walt Disney later called "animated sticks," it made a strange sort of sense for him to assign Gillett to a cartoon like *Three Little Pigs*, in which the characters themselves were the center of attention.

Gillett "was quite talkative, and a pretty good salesman," Ben Sharpsteen said. "He'd act things out. It was pretty horrible, but that was what Walt wanted—it was stimulation."[108] Gillett was distinguished by his enthusiasm and energy and his small-boy liking for excitement, Wilfred Jackson said (Gillett chased fire trucks). He "visualized each thing with his whole body," Jackson said, and this made him a "noisy neighbor" to have in the music room above Jackson's.[109]

Gillett did not bring to his direction anything like the care and precision that Jackson brought to the *Silly Symphonies*. Dick Huemer recalled forty years later that he was "just floored by the perfectionism" when he picked up his first assignment from Jackson, on a 1933 *Silly Symphony* called *Lullaby Land*. "The fact that [Jackson] would hand me a scene, and all the [camera] fields would be marked, and the trucking [camera movements toward and away from the animation drawings] would be marked (I had never heard of cartoon trucking before), with a little red square indicating where the action would be in close-up. . . . This would be handed to me; and several action poses in that scene to boot."[110] As Huemer said, "All I had to do was just move [the characters] around"—and Jackson always conferred carefully with his animators about how they would do that, too. Gillett worked as a director much less precisely, exactly the right approach for the principal animators on *Three Little Pigs* (Moore and Ferguson rarely animated for Jackson). The important thing, with Gillett as director, was that animators who wished to bring more to the characters in *Three Little Pigs* could easily find room to do it, as Moore in particular did.

It was in such sensitive casting of director and animators, and in his understanding of how music could shore up half-grown character animation, that Walt Disney now made his ability as a coordinator felt, first in the studio and then beyond. "The main thing" about *Three Little Pigs,* Disney said in 1956, "was a certain recognition from the industry and the public that these things could be more than just a mouse hopping around."

In terms of that broader recognition, *Three Little Pigs* was indeed a breakthrough, especially where the public was concerned. It played for only a week (May 25–31, 1933) at Radio City Music Hall in New York, but as it spread to neighborhood theaters it aroused more and more enthusiasm. No short cartoon had ever been so popular; *Three Little Pigs* ran for weeks at some theaters, through one change of feature after another. "Who's Afraid of the Big Bad Wolf?" was the first hit song to come from a cartoon.

The timing of the cartoon, and especially the song, made a difference— *Three Little Pigs* was released in the depths of the Great Depression, and its song could be heard as an echo of Franklin Delano Roosevelt's first inaugural address, with the Big Bad Wolf a bogeyman no more to be feared than "fear itself." But other cartoons were just as cheerful, and scoffed at the Depression much more directly, without stimulating anything like the same response. It was, Disney said in 1941, because he and his animators were beginning "to put real feeling and charm in our characterization" that *Three Little Pigs* was so successful.

"Feeling" was the key word. There was nothing like real feeling in *Three Little Pigs,* but it was the first Disney cartoon that fully employed many of the elements—lifelike movement, rounded forms that seemed to move in three dimensions, characters whose appearance was realistic enough to invite a suspension of disbelief—that would be most useful if a cartoon were ever to make an emotional connection with its audience. And this, it was increasingly clear, was where Disney wanted his cartoons to go.

If in the 1920s Hugh Harman was most concerned with cartoon acting, Disney was now seizing on its possibilities. Her husband acted out scenes, Lillian Disney said, "always—to the sky, the birds, to anything. He was always making gestures—talking. . . . Laughing and acting out something he was working on. He was always doing that."[111]

It was hard to translate this interest in "feeling" into animation that embodied it, especially when human characters were involved. When animation of *The Pied Piper* began under Wilfred Jackson's direction in May 1933, just as *Three Little Pigs* was entering theaters, the key scenes of Hamelin's mayor and the piper himself went to two young animators, Hamilton Luske and Art Babbitt. More than any other animators on the Disney staff, they could bring to the animation of human figures not just a reasonably high level of draftsmanship, but also an intense, analytical interest in how the human body actually moved.

Their scenes should have been a big step forward from Norm Ferguson's animation of the Big Bad Wolf or Fred Moore's scenes with the pigs. Neither Ferguson nor Moore had studied real movement as Luske and Babbitt had. Yet there is nothing so deadly in an actor's performance as the sense of performing consciously actions that ordinary people perform without thinking about them, and this sense pervades Babbitt's and Luske's animation. However lifelike a character's individual movements might be, those movements could not in themselves make the character lifelike. In fact, the reverse was true: isolated by analytical animation, even the most carefully observed movements would seem shallow and counterfeit.

Norm Ferguson's and Fred Moore's animation had much more vitality but also lacked the particularity of real people. Thus the challenge before them and all the other Disney animators was one that artists working with more respectable materials had met and mastered many times before, going back to the Greek artists of the classic period. What those artists valued most, E. H. Gombrich has written, was that "the new-found freedom to represent the human body in any position or movement could be used to reflect the inner life of the figures represented. . . . This is what the great philosopher Socrates, who had himself been trained as a sculptor, urged artists to do. They should represent the 'workings of the soul' by accurately observing the way 'feelings affect the body in action.'"[112] Disney and the best of his animators, working in their own humble medium, were struggling to bring just such an emotional dimension to animation that represented the mechanics of movement with increasing accuracy. Theirs was not an easy task, considering animation's history of triviality and crude formulas.

In April 1933, shortly before the release of *Three Little Pigs,* Paul Fennell animated a scene for *Mickey's Mechanical Man,* a cartoon in which the robot of the title boxes a gorilla. "I had a test of Minnie, pounding the mat," Fennell said, and he showed it to Disney in the sweatbox next door to Wilfred Jackson's music room. "Walt looked at it, and ran it again, and he said, 'You know what's wrong with this? You don't know anything about psychology. You ought to go home and read a book on psychology. It's feeling. You've got to really be Minnie, you've got to be pulling for Mickey to beat that big lunkhead. You've got to hit that mat hard, you've got to stretch.' I got a good bawling out, but I didn't understand him. Later on, I knew what he was trying to tell me. We learned it: feeling."[113]

By 1933, Disney had caught up with his best animators, and his ambitions for the medium were surging ahead of theirs. Now there were fewer and fewer occasions when the churlish Disney of the 1920s, the Disney who had driven away Hugh Harman and Ub Iwerks and Carl Stalling, showed his face. The Disney in charge was once again the enthusiastic, ambitious Disney who had set up his own cartoon studio when he was just twenty years old—but armed now with more than a decade of experience making cartoons and, most important, with an artist's excitement about the possibilities he saw in his medium.

It was this combination, his powerful entrepreneurial drive combined with his new artist's sensibility, that made Disney so inspiring a figure to many of the people who worked for him in the middle 1930s. "Somehow," Wilfred Jackson said, "Walt always made it seem to me that the most important thing in the world was to help him make a picture look the way he wanted it to look. It was a lot of fun to feel I was doing the most important thing in the world, every day."[114]

CHAPTER 4

"This Character Was a Live Person"

The Leap to Feature Films
1934–1938

In March 1934, someone who signed himself "an animator" wrote to the *Hollywood Citizen-News:*

> Walt Disney's personal achievements, since the creation of Mickey, have been
> largely the use of his ability in the fields of production, business, publicity,
> and direction, rather than his actually doing any of the things to which his
> name is signed. He does not draw the newspaper strip, neither does he draw
> any of the movies. The entire operation is done by others under his direction.
> Although much credit is due Disney, a great deal must be given to the account
> of those who perform the actual work. After all, they make the pictures.[1]

The anonymous writer was pointing out that Disney did not draw the cartoons that bore his name; he had not done so for the better part of a decade. But in early 1934, Disney was about to make a picture himself, for the first time in several years—that is, he was going to direct one, a *Silly Symphony* called *The Golden Touch,* a retelling of the King Midas story.

Even though Disney had reconciled himself to his role as his studio's all-powerful coordinator—someone who never lifted a pencil himself but passed final judgment on the work of others who drew—he was never entirely comfortable with it. Over the years, he fell back on awkward analogies to explain just what he did. At one point, for example, he invoked a musical parallel: "I like our cartoons to be put together like a symphony. You know, there's a conductor—I guess I'm it—and then there are the solo violins, and the horn players, and the strings, and a lot of other fellows, and some of them are more stars than others, but every one has to work together, forgetting himself, in order to produce one whole thing which is beautiful."[2]

In early 1934, he had found a persuasive reason to depart from his role as "conductor": he had decided that his studio would make its first feature cartoon, *Snow White and the Seven Dwarfs,* and that he would direct it himself. By making *The Golden Touch* he would be warming up for that far more demanding job.

Disney had decided to move ahead with a feature by the fall of 1933, although there was no public announcement to that effect, and he may not even have settled yet on *Snow White* as its title. In November, the animator Art Babbitt wrote to his friend Bill Tytla in New York: "We're definitely going ahead with a feature length cartoon in color—they're planning the building for it now [a second animation building was added to the Hyperion plant in 1934] and the money has been appropriated. Walt has promised me a big hunk of the picture."[3]

The public's enthusiasm for *Three Little Pigs* encouraged Disney to believe that people would turn out for a feature, but cool business considerations pushed him in that direction, too. *Three Little Pigs* on the marquee might attract more customers than the feature it accompanied, but the increased traffic at the box office redounded to the benefit of the feature's producer, and not Disney. There was only so much Disney could accomplish in the short form, either artistically or financially.

Although he had turned to fairy tales when he first began making cartoons at Laugh-O-gram, there was nothing automatic about Disney's choice of a fairy tale as the subject of his first feature. Given the popularity of Mickey Mouse, he could easily have put his star into a feature-length comedy that would have been the equivalent of the features that the silent comedians made when they moved up from two-reel shorts. There is no indication that he ever considered doing that. For all of Disney's affinities with the silent comedians—particularly his intense exploration of gag possibilities—he had not created screen personalities strong enough to sustain a feature, as Chaplin, Keaton, and Lloyd had done. Mickey Mouse might echo Chaplin's Little Tramp, but the Tramp was a much richer character. And so, when Disney went into feature production, he turned to the fairy tales that were already giving him the narratives for some of his *Silly Symphonies.*

Disney remembered seeing the silent Marguerite Clark live-action version of *Snow White* when he was a fifteen-year-old newspaper carrier. The *Kansas City Star* sponsored five free showings of *Snow White* at Kansas City's Convention Hall on January 27–28, 1917. The film was shown on four screens hanging at right angles in the center of the hall, so that someone sitting at one of the angles could see the film on two different screens. "From the spot where I viewed the picture," Disney wrote in 1938, "I was able to watch two screens at the same time. I could look at one screen and tell what was going to happen on the next."[4]

Although the Clark *Snow White* seems clumsy now, its Kansas City show-ings were a huge event, attracting crowds that the newspaper sponsors claimed totaled sixty-seven thousand people. The film made an impression on Disney for more than one reason. Not only was it one of the first "big feature pictures" he had seen, but "I thought it was a perfect story."[5]

If nothing else, he knew from that film that the Grimms' story could be expanded without strain to feature length. Many other fairy tales, like the few he had already made into *Silly Symphonies,* could not. Fairy tales are as a rule rather stark. Disney's challenge in adapting one of them for an animated film was to enrich the characterizations without destroying the story's structure. The "Snow White" of the brothers Grimm was especially well suited to such expansion because its characters included seven undifferentiated dwarfs.

One of the earliest traces of work on *Snow White*—twenty-one pages of "Snowwhite [sic] Suggestions," dated August 9, 1934—includes a list of sug-gested names and traits for the dwarfs, who are unnamed in the Grimms' version of the story.[6] Giving the dwarfs distinct identities would permit shift-ing the weight of the story away from the lethal rivalry between Snow White and the queen, and toward Snow White's stay with the little men. The girl and the dwarfs could have a warmer relationship, to say the least, and one more congenial to animation as it was developing at Disney's studio. As much as Shakespeare or Verdi, Disney chose a subject that would take advantage of the abilities of the performers—that is, the animators—he was working with.

Disney's life was undergoing significant changes away from the studio, too. After more than eight years of marriage and two miscarriages, Lillian had given birth to a daughter, Diane Marie, on December 18, 1933. With a new home and a new daughter, Lillian now had strong competitors for whatever interest she felt in her husband's work.

Disney's prosperity showed itself not just in the new house on Woking Way but in other ways. "For a good many years after Mickey Mouse was a success," he said, "I still didn't have a new car. And I think the first new car that I actually bought, I bought for Mrs. Disney. I still drove around in a lit-tle second-hand one that I had. When I got my family, then I had to get a family car, so . . . I splurged, I got a Packard, a new one."

The scrappy clothes that Lillian remembered from the 1920s were now far in the past. "He was always a nice dresser," Roy Disney said in 1967. "He had a good taste for clothes, according to the styles at the time. . . . Walt always liked sports, he always liked the outside, he always liked . . . the dressy nice sides of life." His attire was almost always California casual—a 1935 interviewer found him wearing "a gray polo shirt, tieless and open at the neck, light gray slacks and brown suede sports oxfords"[7]—but in photos from the time, he is clearly a man who enjoys well-made clothes.

In the middle 1930s, the studio itself was, in the eyes of many of the people who worked there, a place made warm and inviting by its new prosperity. James Culhane, who worked for the Fleischer and Van Beuren studios in New York before joining the Disney staff in 1935, was struck by how different the Hyperion studio *looked:* "Everything was painted in bright tints of raspberry, light blue, and gleaming white, no institutional greens or bilious browns like the other studios."[8]

There was also, at least in the upper ranks of animators and assistants, much less of the brute pressure for footage that was so common at other studios. That is not to say that Disney's employees had no incentives to work hard. By 1934 he was paying semiannual bonuses, based on profits and on a rating determined by five factors, including "importance to the organization" and "production department rating as to footage and quality of work." But Disney "was the first one to introduce the idea of relaxing the grim grind on people," the animator Dick Huemer told Joe Adamson. "And as a result he got more work out of them, because they worked out of love for what they were doing. And the fact that they were doing something a lot of them thought would be imperishable."[9] So relaxed was the atmosphere in the middle 1930s, the animator Grim Natwick said, "at one time there was quite a lot of dice rolling in the animation rooms. We heard that it disturbed Walt, and Jack [Campbell], who was a rather astute fellow, came in one day with big rubber dice that you couldn't hear rolling."[10]

The studio, until then populated almost entirely by people with no more than high school educations, was beginning to see an influx of new employees with college degrees. They tended to arrive in small waves, as word spread among friends—at Stanford University, for example—about the opportunities at Disney's. In 1933 and 1934, beginners at Disney's—one small group at a time, perhaps three or four men—got a brief "trial without pay." They were trained to draw inbetweens by a man named George Drake, and at the end of a week, or perhaps two, were either dismissed or hired, at fifteen dollars a week.[11]

There were variations in this pattern. When he started on June 1, 1933, George Goepper said, "it was sort of a revolving door, hiring and firing. Ben Sharpsteen would say to George Drake, 'Who are we going to let go today?'" Goepper remembered Sharpsteen's telling him, "If you want to try it for nothing, we'll let you do that." Goepper "started on a Wednesday, and at that time they worked until noon on Saturday, and paid then. It surprised me when I got a Mickey Mouse check, for eight or nine dollars." When Sharpsteen asked him to work for nothing, Goepper concluded, "they were testing my attitude, too."[12]

The trainees were separated from the inbetweeners already on the payroll by what Eric Larson called "a little line of demarcation." Larson, who also started on June 1, 1933, remembered being one of a handful of inbetweeners in this "bullpen," "working like hell, waiting to be assigned to a unit, waiting for an animator to say, 'I want that guy.'"

It was during the "trial without pay"—and then in new hires' continuing work as inbetweeners under Drake—that the Disney studio adhered to something like the old "grim grind." Drake himself was disliked by most of his charges. As an inbetweener, "you'd be on the board with a drawing," Larson said of Drake, "and he'd sit down and make a correction for you, and he couldn't draw worth a damn. He'd make a correction—didn't like it—he'd erase it. He'd make another one—erase it. Pretty soon, everything was so black, you couldn't see what was on the board."[13]

Ben Sharpsteen described Drake—"a remote cousin-in-law from my mother's side of the family" and previously an assistant animator of limited talents—as a victim of Walt Disney's tendency to put people in jobs they were not capable of filling. As Sharpsteen put it, "Walt was often entirely too optimistic in the parceling out of responsibilities."[14] Said Ollie Johnston, one of the Stanford alumni who joined the Disney staff: "It was a strange thing about that studio. There were so many impossible people, and there was a genius like Walt who sometimes didn't recognize these problems."[15]

Disney's attitude was consistent with his entrepreneurial temperament: he was interested in what he wanted to do himself, not in assembling a management team, and he concerned himself with filling certain jobs only because someone had to be in them for the studio to function.

In the late spring of 1934, the *New York Times*'s Douglas Churchill reported on a visit to Disney's office, where he found an energetic man who was engrossed in his work. "Swimming, ice-skating, polo and riding are his diversions," Churchill wrote. "Seven of his studio associates play polo with him, but purely for recreation, unlike those actors and executives on other lots to whom the game is serious business. He mixes little in Hollywood night life, feeling that he cannot do good work if he loses sleep."[16]

In a curious comment, Disney spoke dismissively to Churchill of "a professor" he had brought in "to lecture the boys on the psychology of humor. . . . None of us knew what he was talking about." He was undoubtedly referring to Boris V. Morkovin of the University of Southern California, who in April 1933 opened a ten-part lecture series at the Disney studio. Morkovin survived in the memories of some of his auditors as a heavy-handed pedant; his lectures bore such numbing titles as (for the sixth one) "cinematic treatment of characterization and externalization of mental states—normal and by distortion, by means of acting, mannerisms, symbolism, of animate and inanimate objects, atmosphere, contrast and different means of cinematic emphasis." But Morkovin evidently impressed Disney. Later in 1933, at Disney's request, he prepared a formal critique in which he worried to death an innocuous *Mickey Mouse* cartoon, *The Steeplechase,* and he continued to work at the studio for several more years.[17]

Perhaps Disney was reluctant to admit to an outsider like Churchill just how seriously he was now approaching his work. He spoke to Churchill of making his first feature for only a quarter of a million dollars—that is, ten times the cost of a typical *Silly Symphony,* for a film about ten times as long—and, quite unbelievably, of destroying the feature if it didn't please him. He was just a few weeks away from handing out scenes for *The Golden Touch* to the two animators he had chosen to animate that entire cartoon—Fred Moore and Norm Ferguson, the most admired members of his staff.

It was those animators' breakthroughs that were making a feature cartoon conceivable not just as a business proposition but as a piece of animation. In *Three Little Pigs* and then in *The Flying Mouse*—not yet released when Churchill interviewed Disney—Moore had animated characters that were warm and appealing like none before them. Ferguson, in the March 1934 release *Playful Pluto,* had through pointed changes in expression and posture successfully represented the flow of emotions in the title character's dim canine brain as he struggled to free himself from flypaper. In other respects, too, the Disney films were advancing rapidly. By late 1933 and early 1934, production for some *Silly Symphonies*—*The Flying Mouse, The Big Bad Wolf*—was taking six to eight months, with the added time paying off in richer surfaces and finer details.[18]

But Disney's layer of first-rate talent was still thin. The *Mickey Mouse* cartoons that followed *Playful Pluto* in 1934 do not suggest that anyone learned very quickly from what Norm Ferguson had done. Only in *Mickey Plays Papa,* a September release, is there any animation that seems to take Ferguson's *Playful Pluto* animation as its model. In that animation, by Dick Lundy, Mickey struggles to remove a rubber nipple from his nose—but there is no sign of the clearly visible, rapidly changing mental states that distinguished Ferguson's animation. There is instead only an elaborate prop gag.

As the Disney animators struggled to absorb the techniques and insights that their most creative colleagues had come up with, they often had to apply those techniques and insights to stories that resisted them. The gap between what Ferguson had shown to be possible and what was actually being done was perhaps at its widest in the tableau that closes *Mickey's Steamroller,* released in June 1934. Two young mice have used a steamroller to wreak havoc, finally destroying a hotel. Mickey rises from the rubble with the little mice teeter-tottering on his head—and he grins witlessly. It is all too obvious that some imperative—for a "happy ending," perhaps—has overridden, easily, any faint impulse toward emotional plausibility.

Disney had shown some awareness of the problem. Early in 1934, he offered fifty dollars to anyone outside the story department who came up with a usable story idea. He was explicit in wanting more than just a title or a setting. "A story is not merely a bunch of situations thrown together in any form, just to allow an opportunity for action," he wrote in a memorandum distributed to the staff. "A good story should contain a lesson or have a moral—or it should definitely tell something interesting which leads up to a climax that will have a punch and impress an audience. . . . Your story should deal mostly with personalities." He offered *Three Little Pigs* as the prime example of what he was after: "The biggest hit to date in cartoon form and yet so simple that it only contains four characters, with no large objects"—that is, big machines like trains or boats—"to detract or take away from the personalities of these characters."[19]

By the time he wrote that memo, Disney had good reason to know how difficult it would be to adhere to its precepts. Toward the end of 1933, he had dictated a three-page outline for "A Silly Symphony Idea, Based on the Lives of the Little Penguins in the Far-Off Artic [sic] Land." That idea, as rewritten three times by Bill Cottrell, eventually resulted in *Peculiar Penguins,* a *Silly Symphony* released in September 1934. The film itself is an insipid romance, nothing but a more elaborate version of such very early *Silly Symphonies* as *Monkey Melodies* (1930)—boy and girl characters cuddle and dance in the first half of the cartoon and dispatch a menace of some kind in the second half—but Disney's outline was even worse, loading up the story with a rival to its hero, "Peter Penguin," and concluding with a wedding.[20]

There is no record of who worked with Disney on the story for *The Golden Touch* in the spring of 1934, but he clearly was deeply involved (his comments—in distinctive hand-blocked characters—show up on a heavily reworked treatment or preliminary script).[21] He began handing out animation for *The Golden Touch* in June 1934, and it was more than six months before Moore and Ferguson delivered their last scenes. The film itself reached theaters in March 1935.

Surprisingly, considering Disney's plans, the completed *Golden Touch* signals immediately that its director is recycling old ideas more than testing new ones. King Midas and his cat are indistinguishable from characters Ferguson animated in earlier films. The king tips his crown and winks at the camera before breaking into a very deliberately articulated song (this was one of the first *Silly Symphonies* with a lot of dialogue recorded in advance), accompanied by very broad, shallow, stagey gestures. Midas is an unattractive character because he is so greedy, but to make things worse, he performs in a highly artificial manner sharply at odds with the more realistic acting style that was emerging in live-action films. Whatever sympathy or interest an audience might want to feel is put to the test right away.

Neither is it easy to like Goldie, the elf who bestows the golden touch. Moore animated all of his scenes, just as Ferguson animated almost all of Midas's, but there is in the animation of Goldie none of Moore's vaunted charm. Goldie's gestures, like a waggling index finger, are as hackneyed as Midas's, and he responds to the distraught Midas's plea for a hamburger by asking, in a nasty tone of voice, "With or without onions?"

Disney struggled with his film. The animation of *The Golden Touch* bumped along slowly, with pauses and delays, and it stopped completely late in the summer while Disney reworked the middle of the story. It was apparently not until October 1934 that *The Golden Touch* was sufficiently under control that Disney could begin leading meetings devoted to *Snow White and the Seven Dwarfs*. Notes survive from four meetings held that month.

One artist, Albert Hurter, took part in at least one of the October meetings, but Disney was working mostly with writers who did not draw. Just as with the silent *Alice*s and *Oswald*s, there is nothing to indicate that sketches played a very important part in early story work. Most of the Disney cartoons made in 1934 still had very little dialogue, but *Snow White* in its early stages threatened to become a dialogue-heavy film, as if Disney and his writers could not help but measure themselves against live-action features. Dick Creedon in particular dictated many pages of dialogue in the days just after he circulated an eighteen-page outline dated October 22.[22] What Creedon wrote betrayed his origins as a radio writer, telling too much—as if the action the dialogue accompanied would not be visible—and revealing too little. Creedon's dialogue for a "lodge meeting" of the dwarfs even resembled an episode of *Amos 'n Andy,* complete with such ludicrous "lodge" titles as "the Much Most Exalted Mastodonic and Majestic Mammoth."

The dwarfs, readily imaginable as cartoon characters, were at the center of this early effort. Everyone had trouble getting a grip on the other characters, the queen in particular, and on the story as a whole. It demanded a serious approach that was alien to writers and artists who had always been concerned with gags and whose first impulse was to find ways to give *Snow White* a pervasive comic tone.

More outlines and a large meeting followed in November, but then the record trails away. Disney made several stabs at dictating a detailed continuity—essentially, a greatly expanded outline—in December, with the final twenty-six-page version dated December 26, 1934.[23] Insistent on simplicity and directness in his short cartoons, Disney now had trouble meeting the same demands in his *Snow White* continuity. This was especially evident in his handling of the scenes with the queen, which he saw as dominated by heavy-handed scare, and some of the sequences with the dwarfs, who were to eat soup and build a bed for Snow White in what looked like long digressions. His continuity was D.W. Griffith–inspired—in the worst melodramatic sense—in its handling of the prince, as it described him breaking out of the queen's dungeon and racing to Snow White's rescue.

By early 1935, Disney's confident predictions of a few months earlier about *Snow White*—he had foreseen release late in 1935 or early in 1936—had been called into question by events. The writing of the story was not proceeding smoothly, and Disney's own work as a director had disappointed him and his colleagues. And there was something else. While Disney was making *The Golden Touch,* Wilfred Jackson was directing *The Goddess of Spring,* a *Silly Symphony* whose cast was dominated by more or less realistically drawn human characters of exactly the sort that would be so important in *Snow White.*

Goddess was released in November 1934. That month, Jackson said in a studio publication that "the characters selected for the leading roles were not a definite enough type for the broad treatment which must be used in cartoon drawings."[24] Those characters, the goddess Persephone and the god Pluto, were spongy in appearance and movement, the drawing and the animation weak and tentative. Disney never explicitly identified *The Goddess of Spring* as a trial run for *Snow White,* but it could not have encouraged him to proceed with the feature.

Against these setbacks, Disney was making progress on other fronts. *The Tortoise and the Hare,* released in January 1935, took a long step forward in its animation, particularly the scenes of the hare animated by Hamilton Luske. An athlete himself, Luske did not just give the hare natural movements that recalled a real athlete's; he also edited those movements in a way that emphasized the hare's fantastic speed. He exaggerated the anticipation and the follow-through in the hare's swing, for example, as the hare played tennis with himself—but because the swing itself looks natural, the hare's speed wins acceptance on its own terms. This was not just comic exaggeration, but true caricature of movement.

Advances like Luske's may not have been immediately applicable to the challenges that *Snow White* posed, but they encouraged other advances. In mid-1935, an unsigned memo asked for "stronger and better gag situations" and offered rewards of twenty-five to fifty dollars for usable ideas. The "gag situations" the anonymous author had in mind were ones that animators could exploit effectively: "In many cases some impossible gag was made to look plausible. Audiences laugh at the Hare's one-man tennis game because it is made to look possible by exaggerated speed and realistic action."[25] A gag writer might ask for that "exaggerated speed and realistic action," but only the animator could provide it.

Where such animation advances were concerned, the Disney animators worked in an atmosphere that was strikingly generous and open, especially compared with those studios where animators jealously hoarded their bags of tricks. "It was not at all unusual for one animator to help another, or to tell him of a discovery," Art Babbitt said. "For instance, I learned of flexibility in the face when a character is speaking; the guys who hammered it home to me were Ham Luske and Freddie Moore. Before that, it was sort of hit and miss for me. Sometimes I did it right, and sometimes I didn't. But now I knew."[26]

Character animators like Luske and Moore had shed more and more routine duties as the years had gone by, passing them along to two or three layers of assistants. By 1935 the transition was complete. The character animators worked on only the most important drawings, and those "in the rough"—a procedure alien to most of the animation industry. As Disney methods changed, the studio's doors gradually closed to experienced animators from the outside, people steeped in other ways of making cartoons.

One of the few outside animators to win a place on the staff after the early 1930s was Bill Tytla, who followed his friend Babbitt from the Terrytoons studio in New York in November 1934. Tytla might have joined Disney a year earlier than he did, but for Disney's reluctance to pay Tytla as much as the studio's top animators were already making. He wanted Tytla to first prove himself on Disney films. (It is unclear who finally gave in.)[27] The dancer and actress Marge Champion—who as Marjorie Belcher married Babbitt in the summer of 1937—remembered Tytla as "this incredible Slavic creature" who cultivated a sort of peasant exterior: "It always surprised me that he was as sophisticated as he was," she said, "because his pretense was always [that he was] like the farmer, the working person, the immigrant." Tytla was "colorful," she said, "because he was so passionate."[28]

Tytla's was a passion so distinctively ethnic (he was the child of Ukrainian immigrants) that it may have made Walt Disney a little uneasy. Even as Tytla emerged as one of the studio's best animators, Disney's sympathies were clearly weighted toward the sort of animation Fred Moore was giving him— that is, animation that was immediately appealing, even if it purchased that appeal by sacrificing some of the complexity suggested in the best animation by Tytla and Babbitt.

Disney clearly admired Tytla, but "he and Tytla didn't fit together in the same way that he and Fred [Moore] did," Ollie Johnston said. "Walt and Fred didn't seem to have any problem communicating with each other," whereas Moore could be more difficult for others to understand. He talked in a sort of verbal shorthand that required a frame of reference to comprehend fully—and Disney obviously had it.[29]

Disney was now raising up animators to take the places that once would have been filled by older men who had worked at places like the Fleischer and Mintz studios. By 1935, the inbetween department had become a full-fledged training department, and, Don Graham said, "classes of a dozen or so new employees got six to eight weeks of instruction in drawing and animation," the first two weeks of it entirely in Graham's life classes. They were also encouraged to attend the night classes.[30]

As the studio grew—by 1935 it had more than 250 employees—Walt Disney himself became a remote and even intimidating figure to some of his employees. Eric Larson, as a junior animator in the middle 1930s, typically saw Disney only in the sweatbox: "He'd go in the sweatbox, and he'd tear things apart, and he'd go out, in a matter of a half hour. . . . I had some demoralizing experiences with him right off the bat, when I started animating. For instance, in *On Ice* [which was being animated in the spring of 1935], Mickey and Minnie were skating and had these big smiles on their faces— they were happy—and I didn't take them off. Walt was sitting there next to me, watching this, and he turned to me and said, 'Can't they ever shut their damned mouths?' . . . I bet I hadn't even gotten to my room when some-body stopped me on the way and said, 'I hear Walt wants you to shut Mickey and Minnie's mouths.'"[31]

Campbell Grant, who started as an inbetweener in 1934 after working in a federal arts project, recalled: "The whole philosophy at that time . . . was exemplified by Ben Sharpsteen, who once told me flat out, 'Listen, you artists are a dime a dozen, and don't forget it.' He was pretty close to it; there were a lot of guys, and some damned fine artists, that were having a hard time."[32]

With other jobs scarce, newer members of the staff had every incentive to try to find ways to catch Disney's attention. Thor Putnam, who joined the staff in 1934 and began working in layout the next year, remembered that one of the first things he learned was that "you always left a good drawing on your board" because Disney so often prowled the studio at night.[33] In the story department, Homer Brightman said, the office politics were fierce, with real danger that good gags would be stolen. The only sure way to get credit, he said, was "to pull a terrific gag in front of Walt."[34] Joe Grant attracted Disney's eye with story sketches that incorporated color and were sometimes more finished than the norm. "Your whole focus was appealing to Walt to stimulate him," he said. "And also to raise yourself in his esteem; after all, I was new."[35]

In the middle 1930s, Disney's relationships with those employees who had known him since the studio was much smaller began to change irrevocably. It was not that their affection or regard for Disney diminished. Wilfred Jackson even speculated that Disney's cigarette cough was in part genuine and in part "consideration": "I think he liked to let us know he was there. Anyway, there was that cough, and you'd always come to attention."[36] Grim Natwick recalled that when he came to the Disney studio in 1934, Disney "play[ed] handball with the guys, and even used to get out and play softball. . . . Walt was just like anybody else."[37] But Disney was becoming a celebrated man—he monopolized the Academy Awards for animated short subjects after the Academy of Motion Picture Arts and Sciences established that category in 1932—and his growing fame, along with his prosperity and his new baby, combined to make socializing with his employees increasingly what Dick Huemer called "an unnatural arrangement. . . . One by one everybody dropped out of the little coterie."[38] Disney did visit some of his employees' homes in later years (usually with a specific purpose in mind), and he occasionally recruited one of them as a traveling companion when Lillian was not available. But there was never any sense that he was "just like anybody else."

Disney's separation from his employees coincided with his emergence as an artist, and the two developments were closely related.

"Nobody took offense at the slightest criticism," Huemer told Joe Adamson. "We asked for it, we'd go to Walt and say, 'Walt, in the last picture, I wasn't satisfied with something. What was wrong?' And he would try to tell you. . . . We had that interest in our product. It was a like a crusade to do the best, and it never seemed good enough."[39] Such traffic was to be in one direction, of course. Disney was not interested in revisiting even his most recent failures. Early in March 1935, the veteran animator Johnny Cannon sent him two type-written pages on how *The Golden Touch* might have been improved—a gratuitous exercise, to say the least, but Disney responded graciously:

> Some of the thoughts expressed sound very good and might have helped considerably to pep up the picture. However, at this stage it is too late. I know the picture is not good, but it is impossible to make any radical changes in it at this time. It is unfortunate that we missed on MIDAS as I felt that it had possibilities of being a very good cartoon. About the best thing we can do at this stage is to profit by our mistakes in the making of future pictures.[40]

Not only was "the best" to be as Disney defined it, but by 1935 he was articulating what "the best" meant to him as he never had before, at least on the record. If in the early 1930s the cartoons had advanced mainly thanks to the trading of ideas among the animators themselves—exchanges that took place in an environment that Disney created, of course—he had now more than caught up. Disney was always a man who wanted to be in charge, even in someone else's home. "You tried to be the host—it was your house, and your food—and he made it impossible for you to be the host," said Kenneth Anderson, a highly versatile artist and trained architect who joined the staff in 1934. Instead, Disney took over and dictated how things should be done.[41] For him not to be taking the lead was, from his point of view, simply an unnatural situation.

On June 1, 1935, Disney sent memoranda to thirteen of his animators, criticizing their work individually. There is a tremendous gap between Disney's cheerleading of three years earlier and the cool, direct language he addressed to his troops in these memos. This paragraph preceded each memo: "The following suggestions are offered in the sense of constructive criticism only. In our apparent avoidence [sic] of your good points and stress on your weaknesses, we have not lost sight of any of your virtues. But praise accomplishes nothing but a feeling to a small extent of self-confidence. It is just as likely to be a dangerous factor and be of more harm than good to you. Therefore, take these in the sense in which they are offered, as constructive criticism and let's try to benefit by them."

There was not a memo for every animator—Ham Luske apparently did not get one—but of those who did, no one escaped unscathed. Dick Huemer was losing interest in his animation after the first pencil test. Dick Lundy was not drawing well enough. Bill Tytla and Grim Natwick were guilty of a lack of system. To Bob Wickersham he addressed these comments:

It has been observed that you lack an understanding of the proper portrayal of gags. The development of showmanship is a valuable thing and plays a great part in one's analytical ability. Your sense of timing is limited and needs to be developed. Likewise, your resourcefulness in handling a personality has need of improvement. There is an approaching danger of a laxity in the general systematic handling of your work. Be sure to watch for every opportunity of making your drawings foolproof, from the assistant's and inbetween's standpoint. Don't lose sight of the fact that confusion at any point in a scene's progress, be it on your board or the assistant's or the inkers, makes for loss of time and an increase in animation cost.[42]

The memo for Art Babbitt was unique in that Disney's comments were addressed mainly not to his animation, but to the way he conducted himself: "It is up to the animators to maintain the morale of the plant by setting the examples for the younger men. In your own case, it has been observed that you have set bad examples many times by maintaining social relations during business hours, that, though of a dignified nature, have a tendency to create a non-professional makeup in younger and less experienced men. I believe we can count on your cooperation in this respect if only [i]n appreciation of the recent evidence of our faith in your ability."[43]

When Disney wrote those memos, he was preparing to leave on a trip to Europe with Roy, Lillian, and Edna. He was not fleeing the studio in doubt and despair, as he had in 1931. There was a medical aspect to the trip—Roy said many years later that "Walt was having treatment for what the doctors said was a defective thyroid," and Roy thought that getting away from the studio would be better for his brother than the injections he was receiving—and there was a business side, too, since Walt would accept an award from the League of Nations in Paris. But otherwise it was to be a true vacation, a tenth wedding anniversary trip for both couples, with visits to a half dozen countries. It was the first time either Walt or Roy had been to Europe since just after the war, and neither of their wives had ever been.

The Disneys arrived in London on June 12, on the boat train from Plymouth, and the Associated Press reported that "a throng that included many children" greeted them so enthusiastically that "police had to intervene to protect them from the crush."[44] In the weeks afterward, they saw England, Scotland, France, Switzerland, Holland, and Italy, driving much of the time. "Walt was quite a tourist," Roy said. "One of the things at Strasbourg—the mechanical clock up there [in the cathedral]. . . . Walt was intrigued with that clock in Strasbourg and made sketches of it and went to quite a bit of effort to try to get up in the tower to try to see how it worked. He wasn't successful in that. But things like that intrigued him very much."

On July 20, the Disneys traveled from Venice to Rome, where they had audiences with Premier Benito Mussolini and the pope.[45] Roy spoke of Mussolini's office in terms that all but cry out for cartoon treatment: "You know, he had a real big office—real big. He was back in the corner. We had to walk across that. The fellow that was taking us in had the squeaky Italian shoes that you may have heard. So, down there, squeak, squeak, squeak, squeak all the way to Mussolini. He was sitting there and he has the spotlight on you and he sits in the relative shadow. You sat in the chair and you were right under a spotlight. But he was most pleasant, most cordial."[46]

On August 1, after six weeks in Europe, the Disneys arrived back in New York on the Italian liner *Rex*.[47] Four days later, they disembarked at the Santa Fe station in Pasadena, where, the *Los Angeles Examiner* reported, Walt was "immediately rushed by autograph seekers."[48]

Disney's absence from the studio did not mean that cartoons were released without his involvement. The production records indicate that the cartoons released during and just after his trip were far along in work before he left, so he could have seen and approved the rough animation, at least. As for the cartoons in production, when he returned, Bill Tytla wrote, "some of the pictures took a beating—some parts had to be done over," but Tytla himself managed "to get by with very little changes."[49]

Disney had been reassured by the success in Europe of programs made up of five or six of his shorts—their success boded well for *Snow White and the Seven Dwarfs*, and Disney's enthusiasm for the picture had been rekindled after a long dormant period. In an interview with Louella Parsons just after his return, he spoke in terms highly similar to those he had used with Douglas Churchill the year before. He expected to devote fifteen months to the production of *Snow White*—he was still thinking of having it ready for release at Christmas 1936, in other words—and to spend more on it "than we have ever spent on any four of our other pictures."[50]

On the evening of October 8, 1935, Don Graham held the first of a series of classes in "action analysis." The idea, Disney said in an October 17 memo, was to study the movements of the human body, and to hear at times from animators who would describe "any advancement or improvement that they have been able to make in the handling of their animation."[51] Observation of the real world, of how people and things actually looked and moved, had been a priority at the Disney studio since Graham's classes began in 1932, but now, with the feature in prospect, such study would become more intense.

As the animation changed, one casualty was the flicker marks around a character's head that Disney himself used to add. Such marks, Ham Luske wrote in 1935, "should no longer be used."[52]

In the run-up to the feature, Disney's key people were committing their thoughts to paper in a way that was new. In August, Ted Sears wrote a memo on "Disney Characters at Their Best" ("Mickey is most amusing when in a serious predicament trying to accomplish some purpose under difficulties or against time"), and at the end of the year Ferguson, Babbitt, and other animators described how they animated the characters Sears had discussed from a story point of view. Disney intended that such memoranda would guide those members of the staff left behind on the shorts when he put what he considered his best animators to work on the feature.

Toward the end of the year, Disney himself reduced his thoughts to paper in several long memoranda, extraordinarily detailed compared with anything of the kind he had written before.

Even though the memo titled "Production Notes—Shorts" is unsigned and undated, it clearly was written around the end of the year, and the "I" who speaks in it is unmistakably Disney. (Neither is there any indication to whom the memo is addressed, although its content suggests that it went to the directors and a few other members of the staff who worked closely with him.) Disney dismissed two of the more inventive cartoons of the preceding year: *Music Land,* a musical fantasy in which humanized musical instruments from the "Land of Symphony" war with their counterparts on the "Isle of Jazz," and *Cock o' the Walk,* in which barnyard fowl, in astonishing numbers, parody the elaborate Busby Berkeley dance numbers in such live-action musicals as *Gold Diggers of 1935.*

"True," Disney wrote of those cartoons, "a lot of people will like these pictures, but the vast public that we are appealing to will not like them as a whole. . . . They are not the type of picture that we want to make, because we are making . . . pictures to appeal to the masses." The best cartoons, he said, as if laying out a credo for his feature, appealed both to specialized tastes and to "the masses." Writing in terms that applied at least as much to his feature as to the shorts, he fastened on the importance of the animators to successful films: "An animator should not be allowed to start on a scene until he has not only the mechanics and routine of the business, but the feeling and the idea behind the scene thoroughly in mind." Animators' time in story meetings should be devoted "to finding out what possibilities the scene presents to the animator, stirring up his imagination, stirring up his vision, stimulating his thought regarding what can be done in the scene."[53]

In a December 20, 1935, memorandum evaluating Bill Tytla's animation in *Cock o' the Walk,* he emphasized caricature, calling it "the thing we are striving for." He offered this advice: "On any future stuff where we use human action, first, study it for the mechanics, then look at it from the angle of what these humans could do if they weren't held down by the limitations of the human body and gravity." He expressed a strong preference for "doing things . . . which humans are unable to do."[54]

Disney emphasized caricature again in a memo he wrote to Don Graham three days later, to lay the groundwork for more extensive training: "The first duty of the cartoon is not to picture or duplicate real action or things as they actually happen—but to give a caricature of life and action."[55]

There was, in short, a lot of intensive self-examination by Disney and his people, "with the thought in mind," as Disney said in his October 17 memo, "to prepare ourselves now for the future." The question was, as work on *Snow White and the Seven Dwarfs* began to pick up speed again, whether Walt Disney's stubbornly personal working methods were really compatible with the industrial apparatus he had assembled and would need now to make a feature.

As in previous years, the increase in employees' numbers did not bring a significant change in the number of releases; only eighteen Disney shorts came out in 1935, one more than the year before. New employees were further dividing work that was already being done, as with the animators who now specialized in "special effects" like rain and fire, or they were doing jobs that had not been done before, as with the sound-effects department that Disney set up in 1934. It started with two members and soon grew to five.

Inevitably, the studio was growing more bureaucratic as it grew larger, but Disney—like many an entrepreneur at the head of a rapidly growing small business—continued to regard the studio as an extension of himself. Wilfred Jackson explained how that worked: "When [Walt] got ideas, he visualized the whole thing, 100 percent. . . . He'd give you a little action, he'd describe something the Mouse should do, and you'd think you had the whole idea of what Mickey was supposed to do, and you'd show him the drawings, and he'd say, 'No, Jack, we talked this all over, his tail shouldn't be back there, it should be up like this.'"[56]

However problematical Disney's intensely personal approach to film-making may have been in some respects, it also contributed immensely to the success of his films, for reasons suggested by Douglas Churchill in his 1934 article. "When he talks of a picture or a plot," Churchill wrote of Disney, "he becomes animated, intense; his mimicry leaps out; he moves about impersonating the characters, making grotesque faces to stress his point."[57] This was a side of Disney's involvement that his animators found particularly appealing, and particularly helpful. Said Ward Kimball, who witnessed such performances in later years: "When he took the parts of . . . any of the people in the pictures, valets, anything—he all of a sudden was a valet, just as good, we said, as Chaplin, for that moment, in the room, showing us how it ought to be done."[58]

That side of Disney's involvement is also particularly hard to grasp now. The transcripts of story meetings rarely give any sense of how he might have been portraying a character. The closest thing to a window on Disney's performances is probably a radio program heard only on the West Coast, the *Hind's Hall of Fame* Christmas show of December 23, 1934.[59] At the time, he was wrestling with the continuity for *Snow White,* but the radio show is a romp, with Disney pretending to banter with his cartoon characters (all represented by the people who gave them their voices on the screen, like Clarence Nash, the voice of Donald Duck, and Pinto Colvig, the voice of Goofy).

Disney read scripts on any number of radio shows in the 1930s, always stiffly, but on the *Hall of Fame* he seems for once to lose himself in a role, that of the boss of a gang of unruly cartoon characters. Disney's sparring with Donald Duck and the others is not really acting so much as it is play-acting—enthusiastic and spontaneous make-believe. He is playing "Walt Disney," of course, but with striking emotional openness, and it was surely that openness, more than any acting skills, that made his performances so valuable to the animators and writers who watched him. There may be awkwardness in Disney's radio playacting, but there is no hesitation or embarrassment. Though Dolores Voght, Disney's secretary for many years, was not thinking of such performances when she said, "There was nothing subtle about that man at all, believe me,"[60] her words sum up their particular virtues.

By 1934, the Disney cartoons were relying increasingly on dialogue recorded before the animation began—an aid to more realistic acting, because now the animator could be stimulated by what he heard in the character's voice. Disney himself had recorded Mickey's falsetto dialogue for years (after a long struggle in the first year or two to come up with a suitable voice), and he was joined in voice recordings by Marcellite Garner, a member of the ink and paint staff who provided Minnie Mouse's voice. In recording sessions, Garner said, Disney "would go through a whole situation and act out all the characters and explain the mood, 'til I really felt the part. Burt Gillett did the same if it wasn't necessary for Walt to be there. However, no one else could just simply become all the characters as Walt did."[61]

In November 1935, Disney still intended to direct *Snow White* himself, but it is not clear just how much of the nuts-and-bolts work of a director he expected to do. A piece under his name that was published while *Snow White* was in production said that a cartoon director was "primarily an expert technician, versed in the mechanics of picture-making," and Disney looked upon much of the director's work as "pretty routine," Ben Sharpsteen said.[62] But Disney clearly thought that the studio could absorb work on *Snow White* without serious disruption. As of late 1935, he intended, as he wrote in his memorandum titled "Production Notes—Shorts," that "short subject directors and crews [that is, their layout artists and assistant directors] will remain practically as they are" during work on *Snow White*.[63]

In a November 25, 1935, memorandum, Disney listed how he expected to assign about a dozen of his animators to *Snow White*. He envisioned spreading the characters among the animators, so that Fred Moore, Bill Tytla, Bill Roberts, and Dick Lundy would all be animating the dwarfs. Likewise, although Ham Luske was to be in charge of Snow White herself, Disney planned to have Les Clark animating the girl, too, with Grim Natwick and another animator, Eddie Strickland, acting "in a way as assistants to Ham, handling [action] scenes under his direction, with Ham concentrating on personality entirely. I feel sure that both Natwick and Strickland will gain a great deal of knowledge by working this way with Ham."[64]

In other words, Disney planned to cast his animators in only the most general terms, departing from a pattern he had already established in his short subjects. From the start of the United Artists release, Disney had encouraged more sustained and thoughtful work by his animators, giving many of them sequences lasting a minute or so on the screen. With *Three Little Pigs* he had gone a step further, casting his animators not just by sequence but by character. He had continued casting them in that fashion on many of the cartoons that followed, the *Silly Symphonies* especially.

In *Broken Toys*, whose animation was completed just a few weeks before Disney wrote his November 25 memo, the animators were cast very thoroughly by character, to the point that most scenes have only one character in them. A girl doll was wholly Natwick's, just as other characters belonged to Bill Tytla, Art Babbitt, and Dick Huemer. The doll was convincingly feminine in both drawing and animation, like other characters Natwick had animated, and she could only have reinforced Disney's intention to assign Natwick to Snow White herself.

Other cartoons had been cast by character almost as thoroughly, and animators often shared scenes. But *Snow White* was going to be a much longer film, with many more characters, and Disney most likely shrugged off the idea of casting by character as hopelessly impractical, the sort of thing that might drag out production months longer. The alternative—smoothing out inconsistencies in the different animators' handling of the same character—must have seemed like the easier road to take.

Disney was, however, pitting his new film not against other short cartoons but against live-action features, with casts made up of real people. To hold an audience's attention, his characters' screen presence would have to be comparable to that of the live actors who would be their true competition. In a short cartoon, color and music and cleverness could easily outweigh minor differences in the way a character looked and moved after being drawn by several different animators. In a feature there was a much greater danger that such a character would seem superficial or even incoherent, a mere mannequin defined mostly by voice and design.

Even when he cast by character in the shorts, thereby making his animators the equivalents of live actors, Disney was not entirely successful. His most individual characters were always a little generalized compared with real people. The more naked a cartoon's plot, the more it magnified this shortcoming. A "story cartoon" like *Elmer Elephant*, with simple characters and simple plot, and music subordinate to both, was unmistakably juvenile, in a way that an intricate miniature operetta like *Three Little Pigs* was not, even though *Pigs* was based on a children's story. Disney's limited success with casting by character may have persuaded him that he had little to lose by taking a different approach.

The dwarfs in particular demanded a level of complexity that no earlier Disney characters had approached, and by 1935 they still existed mostly as vague story sketches. Audiences had to be able to tell them apart easily—they had to look alike, and yet different, but some elements of their appearance, like their clothes and beards, did not lend themselves to sharp differentiation. The vital task that Disney presented to Fred Moore and Bill Tytla at the beginning of 1936 was to make distinct everything about each dwarf that could be made distinct—eyes, noses, mouths, posture, waistlines. (The idea at first was to differentiate them even further by clothing them in what the color stylist Maurice Noble called "strong, simple colors.")[65]

For Snow White herself, Disney had an even more striking answer to the question of how to preserve consistency across the work of several animators. All of Snow White's scenes were to be photographed in live action first, and the animation would then be based on tracings of the frame blowups. Disney evidently had something like this procedure in mind from early in work on *Snow White*. A memorandum titled "Routine Procedure on Feature Production"—undated, but written in the fall of 1934—assigned to the writer Harold Helvenston responsibility for "stage settings, sets, props, costumes," and said that he "will be responsible for the setting of the stages, the production of all props and sets, and will see that the work on the stage progresses with a minimum time load."[66]

This was probably Disney's response to the inadequacies of the character animation he saw in *The Goddess of Spring*. Why struggle with the animation of the girl, he may have reasoned, when a solution (already used extensively by Disney's rival cartoon producer Max Fleischer) was close at hand? The dwarfs and not the girl were to be at the center of the film, in any case.

Filming began under Ham Luske's direction in November 1935, with Marjorie Belcher, the teenage daughter of a dance studio's owner, performing as Snow White. In the earliest days of the live-action filming, she wore what she later remembered as a sort of helmet, with Snow White's hair painted on it, in an extreme example of the effort to bring the live action as close as possible to the result desired in the animation. (Snow White's head was to be larger in proportion to her body than the real girl's.) The helmet was hot and uncomfortable, she said, "so I'm sure it restricted my movements a lot, and they soon gave that up." She always wore a Snow White costume during filming, however.[67]

By the time he wrote his November 25 memorandum, Disney had six story units, ranging in size from one to four men, working on *Snow White,* and he expected to shuffle those men around as they finished work on particular sequences. In the same spirit of confidence and command evident in so much of what he said in the last months of 1935, he clearly anticipated a steady flow of work from both animators and writers.

In one aspect of the production, he was not disappointed. There was friction between Ham Luske (who adhered to Disney's wish that Snow White be presented as a sweet child) and Grim Natwick (who wanted the girl to be more mature and knowing), but there was never any question who would prevail, and animation of many of the scenes devoted to Snow White herself proceeded smoothly. In other respects, though, work on *Snow White* was a steady slog, as Disney and his people struggled to recover from two fundamental errors.

For one thing, they had misjudged the nature of the story. The Grimms' version of "Snow White" is a serious fable about a girl—and about youth and age, and sexual maturity, and life and death—and not a vehicle for seven funny little men. Even the Marguerite Clark version, as clumsy as it was, assigned the dwarfs a strictly supporting role. But from the beginning, Disney had conceived his version of the story mainly in comic terms, with lots of gags for the dwarfs. It was taken for granted in various synopses and treatments that even the more menacing characters—the queen herself, especially in her disguise as an old hag, and the vultures that were to circle down after her fatal fall—would be treated as figures of fun. The story could not accommodate so radically different a point of view without being changed fundamentally, into something much less serious—not more comic, but trivial—than the Grimms' original.

(Some changes in the Grimms' story could be accommodated much more easily. The prince's kiss that awakens Disney's Snow White is borrowed from Perrault's "Sleeping Beauty." In the Grimms' original, the girl awakens when a piece of poisoned apple is dislodged from her throat.)

The dwarfs themselves were at the heart of the second mistake.

It was not until late in September 1936 that Fred Moore produced the final model sheets of the dwarfs, each specific enough to be used by the assistant animators who would clean up the animators' drawings. By then, he and Tytla had been working on the dwarfs—designs and two pilot sequences—for about nine months. Moore, the avatar of charm and cuteness, had so refined the dwarfs that the knobbiness and wiriness of the earliest storyboard drawings had been smoothed away. Beards, jowls, bellies, all were clearly different on each of the seven characters, who had names—Doc, Grumpy, Dopey, Happy, Sneezy, Bashful, and Sleepy—that fit some salient trait. The animators who followed after Moore and Tytla would be working with sturdy, all but foolproof designs.

Or so Disney must have hoped and expected. But even though Moore and Tytla had worked together for so long, there were already visible differences between their versions of some of the dwarfs. Tytla was a powerful draftsman whose work naturally veered away from Moore's softness and cuteness in favor of a more intense and muscular sort of animation. He had animated the dwarfs as they washed for supper after Snow White sent them outside, and his Grumpy and Doc, in particular, were vigorous physical presences in a way that Moore's were not.

By late October 1936, other animators had begun to work on scenes with the dwarfs, and as they did, such differences multiplied. For all the work that

Moore had put into his model sheets, it was not enough. The animators now trying to master the dwarfs had trouble keeping them distinct on the screen—it was not always clear which dwarf was which—and the same dwarf could look very different in different animators' hands.

Disney had stepped back from casting by character because of the difficulties it promised. Now reconciling so many different versions of so many different characters was proving to be even more difficult. As he recalled at a meeting almost two years after *Snow White* was finished: "We'd be in here with Marvin [Woodward] or [James] Culhane or one of those guys and in order to get it over, we used to have to call Fred [Moore] in."[68] Nothing could have seemed more natural than to deal with the dwarfs, and their animators, en masse; and yet, if Disney had assigned the dwarfs individually—one to an animator—he could scarcely have gone through more arduous struggles than those he endured as he tried to pull the other dwarf animators into line with the work of Moore and Tytla, as well as to reconcile the work of his two principal animators.

By the fall of 1936, Disney had abandoned any thought of being *Snow White*'s director, at least in the usual sense. Although he had planned to leave the shorts directors in place, he brought David Hand onto the film to badger and cajole the dwarf animators. (Hand ultimately became *Snow White*'s supervising director. The other two shorts directors, Ben Sharpsteen and Wilfred Jackson, also came onto the film to direct parts of it.)

In late 1936 and early 1937, Hand followed Ham Luske's example and began shooting live action that could guide the dwarf animators, as live action was guiding Luske and the animators working under him on Snow White. The use of live action for the dwarfs actually originated, Frank Thomas and Ollie Johnston have written, "during a discussion of how . . . Dopey should act in a particular situation" (this would have been in early 1936). Someone suggested Eddie Collins, a burlesque comic, as a model. A group went to the burlesque house to see him perform, he was invited to the studio, and "a film was shot of his innovative interpretations of Dopey's reaction—a completely new concept that began to breathe life into the little cartoon character," unformed till then. "Freddie Moore had the assignment of doing the experimental animation on Dopey, and he ran the Collins film over and over on his Moviola, searching not so much for specifics as for the overall concept of a character. Then he sat down at his desk and animated a couple of scenes that fairly sparkled with fresh ideas. Walt turned to the men gathered in the sweatbox and said, 'Why don't we do more of this?'"[69]

From all appearances, live action did prove genuinely useful on a number of occasions in 1937. The actor Roy Atwell was filmed as he delivered some of Doc's dialogue, for example, and Frank Thomas, when he animated that scene, successfully caricatured Atwell's nervous hand movements as he spoke. Thomas so well integrated those movements with the dialogue that the words seemed, as the writer and director Perce Pearce told a studio audience in 1939, to be really "coming out of that character. It wasn't just some funny dialogue that some dummy was rendering."[70]

Live-action filming for the dwarfs petered out quickly, though, until by July 1937 Don Graham was speaking of it as an abandoned effort.[71] Too much of what the dwarfs were supposed to do did not lend itself to live-action preparation. There was to be no easy answer to the quandary Disney had created when he chose not to cast by character.

Ultimately, the story of the production of *Snow White* is not a story of how Disney's men realized his conception of the film, but of how Disney himself recovered from such potentially fatal mistakes and wound up making a much better film than the one he had set out to make. In the fall of 1935, stenographers began making not just summaries or paraphrases but word-for-word transcripts of what was said in many of the meetings in which Disney took part. There is thus a remarkably comprehensive record of how *Snow White* was made—a record, in effect, of the ebb and flow of Walt Disney's thought, since everyone working on the film was responding to his wishes.

As Disney submerged himself in his film, scrutinizing the story over and over again in one meeting after another, he gradually surrendered the idea that he was making a gagged-up film centered on the dwarfs. As late as an October 19, 1936, meeting, he was still thinking of the queen's transformation into a hag as a semicomic scene ("she could holler for her wart, then as the wart appears she would cackle"), but retrogression of that kind occurred less and less often over the coming months.

Disney had to decide what to do with three whole sequences dominated by the dwarfs and what was supposed to be comic business: the dwarfs would sing as they ate Snow White's soup at the dinner table; they would hold a "lodge meeting" and decide to build her a bed; another comic sequence would show how they did it.

Disney conceived of his film as a Hollywood product. When he "talked" the general continuity at a meeting with more than two dozen members of his staff on December 22, 1936—it was the first time many of them had heard the story of the film as a whole—he invoked other Hollywood films: "This mirror is draped with curtains, like Dracula. . . . The Queen says a little hocus-pocus, and the mirror appears—sort of a Chandu thing."[72] His audiences expected comedy from him. The thought of abandoning any of those sequences and making the film's tone more serious could not have been pleasant.

There had already been expressions of discontent, even as the problematic sequences were polished and made ready for animation. The writer Dick Creedon, in a November 15, 1936, memo, made a powerful case for dropping the lodge-meeting and bed-building sequences, arguing that they would divert attention from the critically important encounter between Snow White and the queen (in her guise as an old peddler woman, offering Snow White the poisoned apple) without providing any compensating "entertainment value." There is no evidence that Disney took Creedon's objections seriously.[73]

The soup sequence in particular was redundant, in many ways simply echoing the sequence that preceded it, when the dwarfs washed for dinner. Snow White would try to teach the dwarfs how to eat soup, for one thing, and as Dave Hand remarked at a story meeting in November 1936, the pattern of her speech was "too similar to Doc's starting the group into washing."[74] Likewise, Dopey—who swallowed a bar of soap in the washing sequence—would swallow a spoon at the table, Grumpy would be surly and come last to the table in the same way he resisted washing, and so on.

The lodge-meeting and bed-building sequences suffered from similar defects, but the bed-building sequence was, besides, atavistic in the compressed, artificial construction envisioned for the bed. When, in a February 23, 1937, story meeting, Ham Luske remarked, "It's darn near a *Santa's Workshop*"—referring to the 1932 *Silly Symphony*, full of mechanical toys moving in tight synchronization with cheerful music—the writer Otto Englander replied: "That's what we're trying to get."[75] The artificiality of the sequence bothered even the layout men who were designing the bed itself: The bedposts were supposed to be four growing trees, but were those trees growing in a perfect rectangle by plan or by accident?[76]

By the summer of 1937, all three sequences had been wholly or partly animated, but Disney decided to scrap them anyway. By then, he knew that he could make those cuts without any damage to *Snow White* itself because what was left in the film was so concentrated. There was no need to tell more about the dwarfs through the soup-eating and bed-building sequences, in particular, because so much about them would have already been revealed in earlier sequences.

To achieve that result, Disney had no choice but to scrutinize the work of his animators intently in the sweatbox, ordering changes that were in many cases extraordinarily subtle. Such orders were not nitpicking. It is almost always clear from the sweatbox notes that Disney was asking for changes so that a character better conformed to his conception of that character as it was evolving in his work on the story.

On March 6, 1937, for example, he watched a Dick Lundy scene in which Happy approaches the kettle where Snow White has started soup cooking; Grumpy stops him, warning of poison. "The feeling was not that Happy was going to taste the soup," the sweatbox notes said, paraphrasing Disney's comments, "but that he expected Grumpy to interrupt him. This of course is not right. He should keep right on going as though he doesn't know Grumpy is coming." Happy was the fattest of the dwarfs; he would not have been easily distracted from the soup.

Moore and Tytla, who had first animated the dwarfs, were not immune from such detailed inspection of their work. On June 11, 1937, Disney sweatboxed a Tytla scene in which Grumpy takes offense and sticks out his tongue at Snow White. Disney asked for these changes: "Have Grumpy make his reaction . . . a few frames earlier and have him react a little slower. Don't have [the] reaction so extreme—it would be just sort of a stiffening before he turns around, it is sort of a little take—not violent."

The animators themselves caught the spirit of what Disney was doing. Lundy recalled animating "a walk that I think was the best walk I ever did; but when I got a test on it, it wasn't Happy. It was drawn and looked like Happy—but it wasn't the way Happy walked, so I had to throw it away and redo it, so it would be the way Happy walked. I had everything working . . . twist, and overlap, and all that sort of thing. But it wasn't Happy, so I just had to toss it. His personality wasn't there."[77]

As work on the film progressed, Disney became ever more absorbed in his characters and the story. Robert Stokes, one of the animators of the girl Snow White, spoke of observing him: "I can remember nights when I worked a little bit of overtime, say, and he'd come in and pull up a chair and we'd talk . . . until eleven o'clock, just his views on things. Animation, the character, the type of person this character was—he believed that this character was a live person, and he had a way of instilling that in you. . . . I'd hear him padding around in the various rooms, maybe run a Moviola or flip a few drawings and then go on to the next room."[78]

Dick Huemer remembered Disney's "utter dedication" during work on *Snow White*: "He used to come on like a madman, hair hanging down, perspiring . . . Christ, he was involved."[79]

Wilfred Jackson, who moved over from short subjects to direct part of

Snow White in 1937, said: "There is more of Walt Disney himself in that particular picture than in any other picture he made after the very first Mickeys. There wasn't anything about that picture—any character, any background, any scene, anything in it—that Walt wasn't right in, right up to the hilt. . . . I mean literally that he had his finger in every detail of that picture, including each line of dialogue, the appearance of each character, the animation that was in each scene . . . nothing was okayed except eventually through his having seen it."[80]

It was not just the animation of the dwarfs that caused headaches as production of *Snow White* spread beyond the small group that had worked on the film through much of 1936. On the shorts, a single layout man and a single background painter typically handled an entire film, assuring a consistency of treatment; but *Snow White* would, of necessity, be spread among dozens of artists. Here again it fell to Dave Hand to try to fit everyone into a single harness. As the layout artists for different sequences bumped against one another, it was all too easy to miss an opportunity to make what was on the screen seem more real. "There must have been at least fifty or sixty corners in the main room of the Dwarfs' house," the layout artist Tom Codrick lamented, "because different units were working on the same room and had basic thoughts about what the room was like or the shape of it."[81]

To further complicate matters, Disney planned to shoot parts of *Snow White* on the new multiplane camera, a gargantuan device his technicians had designed to enhance the illusion of three-dimensionality. For those scenes, the cels, background paintings, and overlay paintings might be on as many as six different levels, with the backgrounds and overlays painted on sheets of glass mounted several inches apart. As the camera moved—trucking in and out or panning—different levels would come in and out of focus, as if they were being photographed by a live-action camera. Hand worried aloud that multiplane scenes might stack up late in production.[82]

Disney's attention to detail extended to such matters as well as to the characters. In a September 3, 1936, story meeting on Snow White's encounter with the animals in the woods, a stenographer recorded these comments, probably directed mostly at the layout artist Charles Philippi, one of the participants: "In the long shots, work in the larger animals in the foreground. Also work in shadows of leaves against the trees wherever possible. Work in mushrooms through this sequence—different colored mushrooms that you see in Europe."[83]

A month later, talking about the dwarfs' march home from their mine, he said he wanted "different settings as they walk along—some trees that have lost part of their bark and stand out white in spots—have them go through a bunch of pines and come out in an aspen grove—or birches . . . and spots where there are big rocks with moss on them of different colors—young and green and old, dark and dried."[84]

Disney's conception of his film matured so remarkably over the two years of production that he was able to resist even the strong temptation to pump up the brief sequence in which the dwarfs mourn Snow White at her bedside. Almost a year after the film was finished, Dave Hand was still speculating about how, "had we been clever enough, and analyzed the situation more thoroughly, we could have obtained a stronger audience reaction." Hand pointed to the pies that Snow White was making when the queen interrupted her and tempted her into eating the poisoned apple: "Might we not have used these uneaten pies as a touch in there to draw a little more of a tear from the audience? By a deep analysis of our situation, might we not convey the idea to the audience a little stronger, instead of this crude way of presenting Snow White dead and the dwarfs around her crying?"

Hand was speaking to a studio audience, and some of his auditors got into the spirit of things, suggesting that the sequence could have been made even more affecting if the soup and bed-building sequences had been left in the film: "It would have been a touching thing to have shown Snow White on that bed—the dwarfs wanted to build it for her, then got it ready only in time for her death."[85]

That sort of overemphasis, so common in Hollywood live-action features, threatened to invade *Snow White and the Seven Dwarfs* throughout its production. Work on the film was less a search for such weak ideas—they were there from the start, as with the "tear-jerker" of a prayer that Disney himself initially thought that Doc should deliver—than a continuing struggle to keep them out. Disney not only had to work free of his own mistakes, but he also had to resist well-meant but potentially deadly suggestions from members of his staff. He had to exclude from his film anything that might amount to an expression of doubt that animated characters could ever command an audience's attention for the length of a feature film.

Disney's firmest expressions of confidence in his medium came during work on the grieving sequence, which was written and animated in the spring and summer of 1937, late in production of the film. He insisted, in effect, that the dwarfs could win the audience's sympathy without begging for it. "Each one should do a simple thing," he said. "If you try to do too much with the scene you will run into trouble." He wanted his audience to see his characters plain. When the layout artist Ken Anderson voiced concern that the dwarfs "might look funny crying," Disney replied, "I think you'll really feel for them. . . . You'll miss something if you don't show close-ups, I think."[86]

Disney never expressed any second thoughts about the deliberate pacing and tight framing of that sequence, but he did regret that he had not slowed the pace a little at other points in the film, as when Snow White prays for the "little men." "Before we finished *Snow White*," he said in 1938, "I was talking to Charlie Chaplin about it, and he said, 'Don't be afraid to let your audience wait for a few things in your picture—don't be afraid to let your tempo go slow here and there.' Well, I thought he did it too much, because I used to get itchy from watching his pictures. But it's the truth—they appreciate things more when you don't fire them too fast."[87]

In his memo to Don Graham, Disney had used the phrase "a caricature of life" to describe what he wanted from animation, but he dwelled mostly on the caricaturing of physical action. It was in work on *Snow White*, and particularly in his shaping of the animation of the dwarfs, that Disney embraced a broader conception of such caricature, one that encompassed the mind as well as the body. Bill Tytla's animation of Grumpy was the purest expression of such caricature. Tytla drew extraordinarily well, and he preserved in his animation the sense of a consistent character while representing accurately a tremendous fluidity of thoughts and emotions. "It is the change of shape that shows the character is thinking,"[88] Frank Thomas and Ollie Johnston have written—a point made especially clear by the changes in Grumpy's face in Tytla's animation. Grumpy was still a cartoon character, with a cartoon character's exaggerated features, a big nose especially, but Tytla took advantage of those features by using them to make the tumult inside Grumpy's head wholly visible.

Grumpy was the dwarf who at once most strongly resisted Snow White but also cared most for her. Tytla conveyed that mix of emotions with extraordinary vividness, so that, for example, when he sticks his tongue out, Grumpy is not so much hostile to Snow White as indignant and resentful that he cares about her. Tytla was, in effect, a "method actor" in animation. He owned Richard Boleslavsky's *Acting: The First Six Lessons,* the 1933 book that introduced to many Americans the Russian Konstantin Stanislavsky's ideas about acting, and he pursued Stanislavsky's goal of an emotional identification with his character—something that simply had not existed in animation before.

It was through such animation that Disney reconciled his impulse to make a comic film—one organized around gags, as his shorts had been—with the serious nature of the story itself. The dwarfs were, in their appearance and their actions, unmistakably comic characters, and *Snow White* itself had a clear comic structure, in a way that the original story did not. (In the film, Snow White's return to life is truly the happy ending, whereas the Grimms' story saves for the last the queen's gruesome death, the penalty she pays for trying to cling to youth and beauty.) But the film was also as serious, in its way, as a comic opera by Mozart, because the best animation of the dwarfs was so emotionally rich, the range of their emotions so persuasively broad. They were funny and endearing little men, not little men who did funny things.

Snow White was important to the studio, Don Graham said while work on the film was still under way, because it knocked down ideas about what could and could not be done in animation. Difficulties lay not in "the limitations of animation," he said, "but the inability of the animator to handle it or to understand the problem."[89] It was in Tytla's animation—which Graham admired tremendously—that animation's horizons opened widest, but others among the Disney animators were not far behind.

In the closing weeks of 1937, no one had time to consider the implications of what Tytla had done in his animation, and of what Disney had done in the entire film. Years later, Disney lamented *Snow White*'s rough edges. "We were really not ready," he said in 1956. "We needed another two or three years to do what we wanted to do on *Snow White*." Some shortcomings, like the weak rotoscoped animation of the prince, were beyond remedy, for lack of time, money, and adequate skills, but Disney could correct another mistake. In November, just weeks before the film's scheduled premiere, he cut two minutes from Moore's sequence—the first one he animated—in which the dwarfs confront Snow White in their bedroom. Perce Pearce, a writer and then a director of part of *Snow White,* suggested in 1939 that Disney paid a price for relying heavily on written scripts in the early work on *Snow White,* when the bedroom sequence was written. Because it is difficult to describe pantomime action adequately, but easy to get the same point across through dialogue, "you just naturally go after it [by] over-writing dialogue," Pearce said.[90] The deleted minutes were heavy with dialogue made superfluous by Moore's animation of the rest of the sequence.

In inking and painting, particularly, the pressure in the final weeks was intense, as some of the women who worked there remembered many years later. Toward the end of work on *Snow White,* Les Clark's sister Marceil said, "it was almost as if you were in a trance, all the time, like an automaton, getting the stuff out."[91] In the drive to finish the film on time, Mary Eastman said, "the girls almost got a little hysterical over it. It was this great community effort, and we were the ones who were putting it through—for Walt, who had such charisma. . . . The girls had a worshipful attitude toward him."[92] Said Margaret Smith: "We'd go in at seven and work until ten three days, and until five on the other two days. We worked all day Saturdays, and sometimes we'd work Sundays."[93] At the peak of work on *Snow White*, Dodie Monahan said, the inkers and painters were working "from seven in the morning until eleven at night. . . . I never heard anybody complaining; it was kind of a thrill to work there at that time, on the first feature."[94]

Women were restricted to such work as a matter of studio policy, as a 1938 handbook for potential employees made clear: "All inking and painting of celluloids, and all tracing done in the Studio, is performed exclusively by a large staff of girls known as Inkers and Painters. This work, exacting in character, calls for great skill in the handling of pen and brush. This is the only department in the Disney Studio open to women artists."[95] The boundaries were not as rigid as that statement might suggest—Dorothy Ann Blank received screen credit as one of *Snow White*'s writers, for example—but the assumption was widespread that women were suited only for "exacting" work, and not for animation.

Snow White's negative cost (the total cost before any release prints were made) grew ultimately to almost $1.5 million, just a little less than the Disney's studio's total revenues in 1937, the year the film was completed.[96] Disney liked to talk as if he were flirting with disaster in the last months *Snow White* was in production. "Roy has the greatest confidence in me, in our medium and in our future," he wrote in 1940, "but he is a business man and doesn't like to live dangerously twelve months out of the year."[97] Despite the scale of the borrowing required to finish the film, there was probably never any serious risk that the money would run out. When Roy Disney arranged for a Bank of America executive to see an incomplete version of *Snow White* on September 11, 1937, he told Walt the previous day: "The bank matter is all set." The banker was going to see the film with an executive from RKO Radio Pictures, Disney's new distributor, "purely for a little support of their own opinions and judgment," Roy told his brother.[98]

As to whether the studio could survive failure in the marketplace—that was another matter. "I recall the preview of *Snow White* [at a theater in Pomona]," Wilfred Jackson said, "the first time the picture was shown to an audience. About two-thirds of the way through the picture quite a number of people got up and walked out of the theater all at about the same time. It was an awful moment. We, all of us from the studio, just about died on the spot. But then, after this fairly large group had left, no one else walked out until the end of the picture. Afterward, we learned there had been a large number of students in the audience from some nearby school dormitory where they had a curfew, so they had to leave to keep out of trouble. But, for a few moments, it looked as though the people who had warned Walt, 'No one will sit through a feature-length cartoon' were right."[99]

Throughout the 1930s, critics commonly paired Disney with Chaplin as the two great motion-picture artists. By the time *Snow White and the Seven Dwarfs* opened at the Carthay Circle Theatre on December 21, 1937, it was perhaps the most widely anticipated film ever—not only because Disney had made it, but also because no one could be absolutely sure that the audiences that loved Disney's short cartoons would love a cartoon ten times as long.

As soon as the film opened, first in Los Angeles and then a few weeks later in New York and Miami, the answer was not in doubt. Critics as well as audiences adored *Snow White*, which was praised as much in intellectual journals as in the mainstream press. Disney had so thoroughly transformed animation in just a few years that sophisticates who would have yawned at the old silent cartoons found themselves weeping with the dwarfs at Snow White's bedside.

Disney had become a father again in the midst of work on *Snow White*. In January 1937, after Lillian—who was now approaching forty—had suffered another miscarriage, the Disneys adopted a two-week-old baby girl they named Sharon Mae. There would be no Walt Disney Jr. As the father of two young girls, Disney expressed a certain wry satisfaction in censors' occasional classification of *Snow White* as too intense for younger children. "Before seven or eight," he told a reporter, "a child shouldn't be in a theater at all. But I didn't make the picture for children. I made it for adults—for the child that exists in all adults."[100]

Snow White radically altered the Disney studio's financial status. In 1937, total income was $1.565 million, including $1.187 million in film rentals. In 1938, in the first nine months alone, total income was almost three times greater, at $4.346 million.[101]

The film's success, artistically and financially, altered Disney's own status as well. On successive days in June 1938, he received honorary degrees from Yale and Harvard Universities (neither degree a doctorate, but rather a master of arts).[102] Talking to reporters after the Harvard ceremony, Disney expressed uncharacteristic regret that he had never had a college education himself: "I'll always wish I'd had the chance to go through college in the regular way and earn a plain bachelor of arts like the thousands of kids nobody ever heard of who are being graduated today."[103]

Disney recalled in 1956 that when he was on the train to California in 1923—"in my pants and coat that didn't match but I was riding first class"—

he fell into conversation with some fellow passengers and told them that he made animated cartoons. "It was like saying 'I sweep up the latrines' or something, you know." As he acknowledged, those anonymous skeptics meant nothing to him; but remembering them contributed to the satisfaction he felt at the success of *Snow White*.

In a piece published under Disney's name in 1937—and that does seem to reflect his thought—he articulated his growing ambitions for animation, invoking "caricature" as his goal. "While we have improved greatly in our handling of human figures," he said, "it will be many years before we can draw them as convincingly as we can animals.... The audience knows exactly how a human character looks and acts, but is rather hazy regarding animals, and therefore accepts our caricatured interpretations of animals without reservation. Some day our medium will produce great artists capable of portraying all emotions through the human figure. But it will still be the art of caricature and not a mere imitation of great acting on stage or screen."[104]

In another interview with the *New York Times*'s Churchill, published early in March 1938, just as the dimensions of *Snow White*'s huge success were becoming apparent, Disney again used the crucial phase "a caricature of life": "Our most important aim is to develop definite personalities in our cartoon characters. We don't want them to be just shadows, for merely as moving figures they would provoke no emotional response from the public. Nor do we want them to parallel or assume the aspects of human beings or human actions. We invest them with life by endowing them with human weaknesses which we exaggerate in a humorous way. Rather than a caricature of individuals, our work is a caricature of life."[105]

"Caricature" has a parasitic sound, though, and by the time Disney was finishing *Snow White* he was actually up to something rather different. He was working his way through the artificial elements of animation—all its elements—so as to emerge with an art form that was unmistakably artificial, did not turn its back on animation's fundamental characteristics, but still had the breadth and impact of those rare live-action films—Jean Renoir's, say—that had fully captured life on film.

The subversive thought that *Snow White* encouraged was that hand-drawn animation's capacity for artistic expression might equal if not exceed that of live-action films. In live action, it is ultimately the actors who must win the audience's allegiance, by seeming to become the characters they portray. *Snow White* proved that on this ground the animators could compete as equals. There was no reason that animation as powerful as the best of that in *Snow White* had to be restricted to animal stories and fairy tales.

The critic Otis Ferguson, writing in the *New Republic,* was among the many who rejoiced in *Snow White,* but with this caveat: "There is this to be said of Disney, however: he is appreciated by all ages, but he is granted the license and simplification of those who tell tales for children, because that is his elected medium to start with. It is not easy to do amusing things for children, but the more complex field of adult relations is far severer in its demands."[106] By the time *Snow White* was released, Disney had already decided not to deal with such demands, at least not yet.

CHAPTER 5

"A Drawing Factory"

Ambition's Price

1938–1941

By 1938, Walt Disney's life resembled more closely the lives of other successful movie people. He and Lillian had begun visiting the desert resort of Palm Springs—he played polo there at first—and he was helping finance a ski resort, Sugar Bowl, near Lake Tahoe in Northern California. He was one of dozens of Hollywood celebrities who financed Hollywood Park, a new race track near Los Angeles.[1] From playing sandlot polo with members of his staff, he had graduated to playing the game with movie stars at the Riviera Country Club in Brentwood—at one point he owned nineteen polo ponies.[2] That figure may seem surprisingly large, but as the actor Robert Stack, one of Disney's fellow players, explained, "You have to have a lot of horses because if you play a lot, they get damaged a bit and they get tired."[3] Disney himself got "damaged a bit"; he had given up polo by early 1938, after injuring his neck in a match.[4] For exercise he turned to badminton.

He also continued to ride, and for several years starting in the late 1930s he rode with Los Rancheros Visitadores—"the visiting ranchers," a group composed of dozens of mostly wealthy and famous horsemen who made an annual weeklong trek through the Santa Ynez Valley, north of Santa Barbara, camping out each night. Frank Bogert, who played polo with Disney at Palm Springs and shared a camp with him on those rides, remembered him as a man who could give and take practical jokes:

> There was a guy named Clyde Forsythe, who was one of the leading Western artists. . . . We were riding way out, a whole bunch of guys, and Walt came

over and told me, "We're going to play a gag on Clyde." He said to Clyde, "There's a beautiful view over here. Come on out with us." So we went away from the ride, way out on a point. Clyde was stone deaf, and he had a great big battery hanging down on his chest. Walt and I started talking but never saying anything. Clyde said, "Oh, shit, I'm off the air." And he took out his battery and threw it down the hill.

The next year, Walt had a little pup tent he slept in, one of those little bitty things, and Clyde brought up a descented skunk and stuck it in Walt's tent. Walt knew something was in there. He got his flashlight and found out it was a skunk, and he ripped that tent apart trying to get out. He said, "The son of a bitch got even with me."[5]

Even on his rides with the Rancheros, Disney never left his work wholly behind. David Hand recalled that when he accompanied Disney on one such trip, Disney "would talk at me, all the time . . . what we should do on some picture or problem," thinking aloud until Hand got "so full and so confused, with his changing his mind," that he began avoiding his boss.[6]

Walt and Roy Disney shared their prosperity with their parents, who in early 1938 moved from Oregon to a new home their sons built for them in the Los Angeles suburb of Toluca Lake, near Roy's home. The new house had a defective gas furnace. On the morning of November 26, 1938, Bill Garity, the studio's chief engineer, noted in his "daily report": "George Morris called me to advise that Walt's and Roy's mother had passed away in the morning from gas poisoning of some kind."[7] Flora had been overcome by the concentration of gas in her bathroom. Elias too was rendered unconscious by the gas, but the elder Disneys' housekeeper found him in time to revive him. Flora was buried at Forest Lawn Cemetery on November 28.[8]

As deeply as both brothers were affected by their mother's death—years later, Walt Disney could not bring himself to speak of it—they could not pause in their work for long. Walt's success in the late 1930s meant that the demands his studio was imposing on him were actually growing, as he said in 1956: "As soon as *Snow White* hit, I said, 'Well, we've got to go into features. We've got to begin to make features.' And there was no denying it after it grossed eight million dollars." In the Hollywood of 1938 it was an all but inevitable step for Disney to make his studio into a feature-film factory, even though his first feature owed its distinctive character to its being nothing like the products of the MGM or Warner Brothers assembly lines. By 1938, almost none of Disney's Hollywood peers were making films one at a time, the way he had made *Snow White*. Chaplin worked that way, but Chaplin's films—still silent, with music tracks—were increasingly eccentric in the Hollywood scheme of things. His most recent one, *Modern Times,* had lost money in its domestic release in 1936.[9]

For five years, from 1932 to 1937, Disney's short cartoons were distributed by United Artists, a company founded by Chaplin, among others, as a distributor for films made by independent producers. When Disney went into feature production himself, he adhered not to Chaplin's model but to that of a United Artists producer of another kind—Samuel Goldwyn, who made a small number of relatively expensive and prestigious features each year.

Disney broke with UA over its insistence on controlling the television rights to his cartoons.[10] On March 2, 1936, he signed new distribution contracts for the short cartoons and *Snow White* with RKO Radio Pictures, not one of Hollywood's biggest major studios, but a major studio nevertheless. Both contracts—each of which Disney signed twice, as an individual and as president of Walt Disney Productions—reflected how much Disney's stature in the film industry had grown in just a few years. RKO would advance $43,500 for the production costs of each short and as much as $23,000 for prints and advertising, and split the revenue from distribution fifty-fifty after recovering its costs. The *Snow White* contract gave Disney 75 percent of domestic revenues, and smaller but still very high percentages of foreign revenues.[11] The financing for Disney's features would come not through advances from his distributor, but through a line of credit from the Bank of America.

Disney began work on two more features before he completed *Snow White.* Some of his writers were studying Felix Salten's novel *Bambi: A Life in the Woods* by the summer of 1937, and Disney attended a *Bambi* story meeting in August. The writing of a feature version of Carlo Collodi's *Pinocchio* was under way by late November 1937, a month before *Snow White*'s premiere.

Disney undertook this expanded schedule without making any corresponding changes in his own role, which was in critical respects more demanding than that of the typical producer of live-action films. He retained control of his films not just as an impresario, the ultimate authority, but as an artistic arbiter who could be, as in the case of *Snow White and the Seven Dwarfs,* even more intensely involved in day-to-day work than a film's nominal director. A live-action director like John Ford could make a film that was really his own even while he was working under the aegis of so assertive a producer as Darryl Zanuck. No Disney director could do that.

In speaking about the films he made during these years, Disney often slipped into the first person, saying of the multiplane camera, for instance, that he had made "very good use of it in *Bambi,* especially, where I had [the camera move] between the trees." Or on the origins of Donald Duck: "I put him in this picture where Mickey had a little amateur show to be presented. . . . The gag I worked there was the kids booed him off the stage and he never got to do his recitation, you know? And from there he evolved into a pal of Mickey's and I worked him in with Mickey in stories and eventually we decided to set him up in his own pictures."

In other words, he saw no real distinction between himself and his studio, even though it had grown to around 675 employees by February 1938, shortly after *Snow White* was released.[12] Given his intensely personal conception of his studio, as well as the realities of the motion picture industry in 1938— not to mention his desire to retain the staff he had assembled and trained— Disney had no obviously good choices other than to proceed as he did.

Even though Disney felt compelled to retain complete control over several new features, he could not give them anything like the attention he had given to *Snow White* and most of the shorts that preceded it. He did make one stab at delegating authority in 1938, by making Dave Hand, fresh from success as the supervising director of *Snow White,* the studio's general manager. Hand took charge of the short subjects—and Disney really did give him control, if only for a while—and tried to organize the rest of the studio along conventional lines of authority. Ben Sharpsteen remembered that Hand "had the attitude that [if] Walt gives me a job to do certain things, and outlines it that way, that's it—it's going to be that way. But Dave would no sooner turn his back than he'd find out Walt had given part of his job to somebody else. Walt had no regard for protocol."[13]

Hand said that Disney's violations of the chain of command came in the form of orders to people removed physically from the director who was nominally in charge of a particular film: "It would be an animator, or his assistant (most likely), or special effects, or maybe background. Or it could even be in the camera department—or in ink and paint, ordering a change of character color (and that could cause trouble). Walt's decisions would then have to move back up the chain of command, and word of the change get to everyone who needed to know."[14]

Disney's personality, so entrepreneurial at its core, made it difficult for him to delegate authority of any kind, particularly where the features were concerned. He complained at times that he did not have enough really good animators to go around, but by expanding his studio's output so rapidly, he all but guaranteed that he would be short of the help he most needed.

Even the best of Disney's animators were not equal to every possible challenge. In the wake of *Snow White*'s success, some members of the Disney staff were more acutely aware of the limitations of their medium as they had developed it to that point. Ham Luske listed such shortcomings in a lecture to members of the staff on October 6, 1938: "We can't manage slow movements, it's hard for us to handle long speeches, long holds are necessary but tough, trick camera angles and perspective problems are difficult to combine with drawn acting. Long shots are a problem. It's hard to make our transitions of thought subtle, easier to get broad transitions."[15]

In short, the Disney studio was a surprisingly perilous environment in late 1937 for the kind of character animation that Disney and some of his animators had pioneered. In mid-1937, Disney was speaking of *Bambi* as his second feature, evidently because he thought his animators would be more comfortable with animal characters than with the humans who would make up most of *Pinocchio*'s cast. Salten's *Bambi,* which dealt with the life of a deer, threatened to be difficult to adapt, though—it was grim and bloody over much of its length—and Disney had decided by the fall to push ahead with *Pinocchio*.

Beyond the narrow question of whether animals or humans would be easier to draw, both *Bambi* and *Pinocchio* were intimidating subjects for animation of the sort that Disney had nursed into existence in *Snow White*. There were no characters at the center of either story who could engage an audience's sympathies in the way that the dwarfs had, unless the stories were drastically rebuilt. Moreover, Collodi's *Pinocchio* was a picaresque tale, and such stories are intrinsically difficult to film. Episodes must be pared away if the resulting movie is not to be intolerably long; but editing can so compromise the episodic character of the story that organizing its remaining pieces into some kind of plot becomes unavoidable.

For all the challenges that both *Bambi* and *Pinocchio* posed, Disney may not have seen the alternative story possibilities as any less daunting. Few traditional fairy tales lent themselves to expansion in the way that the Grimms' "Snow White" did, and other classics of fantasy literature did not promise to pose fewer difficulties than *Bambi* and *Pinocchio* would.

In any case, Disney was in a hurry. When work on *Snow White* was all but finished, and a large crew was waiting, he was anxious to put his artists to work. On December 3, 1937, at what seems to have been the second story meeting on *Pinocchio* that Disney himself attended, Otto Englander, the "story supervisor," read aloud what was probably a very rough continuity for the entire film. Disney gave it his blessing and told his writers to break the story down into sequences.[16]

On December 11, 1937, at his third meeting on *Pinocchio*, Disney outlined a plan to move through the story sequence after sequence, developing material that could be used in a later sequence if not in the one at hand. He was concerned mainly with getting something ready to animate, but he presented his plan as a way to deal with the book's picaresque structure, too. "That way," he said, "we'll gradually arrive at a continuity as we work along. In a story like this it's impossible to complete a continuity before you work out a situation and its possibilities."[17]

Disney also began to sound a theme that would lead him away from the book's version of Pinocchio himself. That character, who is most definitely a puppet and not a boy, is a rather nasty little creature. It is thanks only to his misbehavior, though, that the book can lead the reader out into a world teeming with talking insects, enormous fish, and donkeys that once were children; and it is only because Pinocchio is so disagreeable at the start—and so firmly separated from humanity—that his eventual transformation into a real boy gives the rambling story a true resolution. The danger in such a character is that the audience will never grow to like him, and Disney did not care for such risks. In work on *Snow White,* he had shown a strong bias toward characters that were immediately appealing—like the dwarfs as designed by Fred Moore—and the same bias soon showed itself during work on *Pinocchio.*

On December 11, he spoke of an early scene in which Pinocchio would say bedtime prayers: "We ought to get all the comedy we can on the thing, because if he's cute and likable and full of little tricks, they're going to like him right away." And on January 6, 1938: "All this [opening] sequence should win the audience to the little guy. The audience should be right with him." He suggested in that meeting that Pinocchio pucker up to kiss the Blue Fairy who brought him to life, after she kissed him on the head. The dwarf Dopey had done the same thing in *Snow White,* but Disney identified Harpo Marx as his inspiration.[18]

It had been in work on *Snow White,* ironically, that Disney faced a challenge at least as great as the one he faced in work on *Pinocchio.* There was nothing automatically likable about the dwarf Grumpy, in appearance or personality; but as soon as Bill Tytla's scenes began to appear on the screen, Grumpy became intensely sympathetic. As a subject for filming, Collodi's Pinocchio was much the same kind of character.

Not only was Pinocchio impudent in his earliest Disney incarnations, he was also unmistakably a puppet, a creature drawn as if he were made of wood, and rather crudely at that. Fred Moore softened that design early in 1938, just before animation began. Moore was not animating at that point; instead, he and Ham Luske had become overseers of a sort, resources for the newer animators on the staff. Moore's influence, so strong during work on *Snow White,* was now pervasive throughout the studio. He had redesigned Mickey Mouse—making Disney's signature character rounder, softer, and, thanks to eyes that now had whites as well as pupils, more expressive—and Disney planned to make Moore one of the lead animators on *Bambi* when that film was finally ready to go into animation.

Even Moore's magic touch was not enough. Disney rushed *Pinocchio* into animation in mid-January 1938, about two months after story work began. When he saw the first animation of Pinocchio as a Moore-designed puppet, he immediately shut down production.

That animation was by Frank Thomas, who had come to the studio from Stanford and had apprenticed under Fred Moore before animating on a few shorts and then on *Snow White*. Thomas had very quickly become one of the studio's leading animators, and the difficult task of animating the grieving dwarfs fell to him. When animation of *Pinocchio* began, he and Ollie Johnston—his friend from Stanford and his successor as Fred Moore's assistant—shared the pilot scenes.

Dave Hand, speaking a few years later to a British audience, used Thomas as an example when he was explaining how such younger Disney animators differed from Norm Ferguson, one of the studio's stars in the middle 1930s. (Hand did not identify either animator by name, but Ferguson and Thomas were unmistakable from his references to their work.)

"[Ferguson's] mind was what I would call an elementary mind; he hardly went above the fifth grade in school, and [Thomas] was a college graduate," Hand said. "It was the refinement in [Thomas's background] that came out in his drawings, against [Ferguson's] heartier, cruder, if you will, representation."[19]

Ferguson was a comic actor through his animation. Frank Thomas, like Ollie Johnston and others among the newer animators, was more like a commercial artist of a highly responsive and intelligent kind. The difference lay not in talent—Thomas in particular had it in abundance—but in a cast of mind. Ferguson, and older animators like him, could not help but leave the impress of their own personalities on the characters they animated. Thomas and Johnston and others among the younger animators, most of whom had spent their entire professional lives at the Disney studio, were less distinctive but far more adaptable. They were prepared to be vehicles for whatever Walt Disney wanted to do.

After *Pinocchio*'s animation had been stalled for six months, Milt Kahl, another of these gifted young animators, came to the rescue by animating a scene with a Pinocchio who was even more of a Fred Moore character than those Moore himself had designed. This new Pinocchio was barely a puppet

Advertising Laugh-O-grams in a parade of the South Central Business Association of Kansas City, circa 1922. Walt Disney is seated in the back seat, Rudolph Ising is behind the car, and Leslie Mace has his foot on the running board. Courtesy Rudolph Ising.

Left to right: Rudolph Ising, Roy Disney, George Winkler, Margie Gay ("Alice"), and Walt Disney on the outdoor set where live action was shot for the *Alice* comedies, circa 1925. Courtesy C. G. Maxwell.

Walt and Lillian Disney outside the Disney Brothers Studio on Kingswell Avenue around the time of their marriage in 1925. Courtesy Rudolph Ising.

Disney holds a movie magazine's award for best short subject of 1933, won by *Three Little Pigs*. Quigley Photographic Collection, Walt Disney File, Georgetown University Library, Special Collections Division, Washington, D.C.

Disney played polo at the desert resort of Palm Springs in the 1930s. Courtesy Palm Springs Historical Society.

Lillian and Walt Disney disembark in New York from the Italian liner *Rex* on August 1, 1935, returning from their triumphant tour of Europe. Courtesy University of Southern California, on behalf of the USC Specialized Libraries and Archival Collections.

Disney and child star Shirley Temple admire the special Academy Award—with seven statuettes representing the Seven Dwarfs—he received in 1939 for *Snow White and the Seven Dwarfs*. Cliff Wesselmann Collection, Academy of Motion Pictures Arts and Sciences Library, Beverly Hills. Courtesy Gregory Paul Williams.

Lillian and Walt Disney arrive for the premiere of *Fantasia* at the Broadway Theatre in New York on November 13, 1940. The theater was known as the Colony when *Steamboat Willie* premiered there twelve years earlier. Courtesy University of Southern California, on behalf of the USC Specialized Libraries and Archival Collections.

The picket line at the Disney studio in 1941 often reflected the artistic ingenuity of the striking employees. Art Babbitt is standing at left. Courtesy Art Babbitt.

Lillian and Walt Disney, on the *Queen Elizabeth*'s sun deck, arrive in a rainy England in the fall of 1946. It was their first visit to Europe since the end of World War II. Quigley Photographic Collection, Walt Disney File, Georgetown University Library, Special Collections Division, Washington, D.C.

Disney testifies before the House Committee on Un-American Activities in October 1947. He condemned what he called the Communist role in the 1941 strike at his studio. AP Photo.

The Disneys—Lillian, Walt, Diane, and Sharon—return to Los Angeles from England on August 28, 1949. AP Photo.

at all, but rather what Thomas and Johnston later described as a "chubby, naive little boy in [a] Tyrolean hat."[20] When "the first model sheets were made of the new Pinocchio," Thomas said, "I was stunned, because no one had told me they weren't going to do a wooden puppet." Even though Thomas was in a sense a victim of Disney's decision, he defended it. Before the changes in Pinocchio's design, he said, "nobody [in the film's cast] was warm. . . . When he put [*Pinocchio*] back into work, [it] was because he'd found now a warm little boy character that could . . . hold his own with Shirley Temple, who was big at the time."[21]

By developing such animators, Disney had solved the worrisome question of how to assign them. Thomas, Johnston, and Kahl ultimately wound up animating many scenes apiece with Pinocchio, and there are no significant differences in how their work looks on the screen. That uniformity was owing not just to the animators' skills but also to the character himself. In his concern that Pinocchio be "warm," Disney had made him bland and passive, robbing him of anything that made him interesting. The same fretting over warmth and "cuteness" transformed another character, Pinocchio's "conscience," Jiminy Cricket, from a caricatured insect into a miniature man. "They call him a cricket, so he's a cricket," said Ward Kimball, who as another of the rising young animators struggled with the design for the character. "He's small, so I guess he can't be anything else."[22]

Even as he surrendered himself to the search for "cuteness," Disney acknowledged the value in leaving even a relatively minor character with the same director and animator who handled him in earlier sequences. "That keeps the coachman's personality the same," he said in a December 8, 1938, *Pinocchio* meeting.[23] But by then such considerations were shrinking rapidly in importance.

While Disney was struggling with *Pinocchio* and to a lesser extent with *Bambi*, plans for another feature were taking shape in his mind. The new feature was the outgrowth of his decision in 1937 to make a musically more ambitious short than any he had made before—a sort of super *Silly Symphony* based on Paul Dukas's symphonic poem *The Sorcerer's Apprentice*, with Mickey Mouse in the title role.

Dukas's music told a story, one that had itself originated in another medium; Disney's greatest challenge was thus to come up with images that were more than superfluous. That challenge must have seemed manageable for a cartoon studio that had already provided a striking visual complement to Rossini's *William Tell* overture in *The Band Concert*, a *Mickey Mouse* cartoon released almost three years earlier.

Soon after he bought the rights to the Dukas music in July 1937, Disney ran into Leopold Stokowski, the former conductor of the Philadelphia Orchestra and a Hollywood celebrity in his own right, at a Los Angeles restaurant. "I was alone having dinner at a table near him and he called across to me 'why don't we sit together,'" Stokowski wrote to Richard Hubler in 1967. "Then he began to tell me how he was interested in Dukas' Sorcerer's Apprentice as a possible short, and did I like the music. I said I liked it very much and would be happy to co-operate with him."[24] Disney may have been slow to follow up, but in October, Gregory Dickson, one of Disney's New York representatives, reported that he had run into Stokowski on the train to New York and had found him not only serious about working on *The Sorcerer's Apprentice* but also "a very charming person and not at all the 'prima donna' that various publicity stories have made him out to be."[25] Dickson's letter set Disney on fire: "I am greatly enthused over the idea and believe that the union of Stokowski and his music, together with the best of our medium, would be the means of a great success and should lead to a new style of motion picture presentation. . . . Through this combined medium, we could do things that would be impossible through any other form of motion picture now available."[26]

Stokowski conducted the music for the sound track with a Hollywood orchestra on January 10, 1938. The recording, at the David O. Selznick studio, began at midnight and ended a little over three hours later. Bill Garity was not impressed by Stokowski's performance: "My positive conclusion is that all we are getting for this very expensive work is Stokowski's name on the main title and that the musical results which may be spectacular and satisfactory to the average audience do not even approximate the perfection which we had expected would result from this effort and expense."[27]

As it turned out, Walt Disney did not share Garity's skepticism—quite the opposite. Work on the animated version of *The Sorcerer's Apprentice* proceeded slowly and expensively during 1938. It was not substantially complete until November 4, 1938, when a "rough preview" was held for studio employees.[28] By the time that preview was held, sketches for a whole feature made up of animation set to classical music were beginning to appear on storyboards. Over the course of 1938, Disney's ambitions had grown. He spoke early in that year of making a series of short cartoons based on classical pieces, but by the end of the summer he was planning a whole "concert feature" in which Stokowski would be heavily involved. Disney's "Apprentice" would not be released as a special short, but as a small part of the concert feature.

Disney had made few cartoons at all comparable to what he had in mind now. In 1937, though, shortly before the release of *Snow White and the Seven*

Dwarfs, he made a short called *The Old Mill.* Essentially plotless, it simply showed a storm's effects on an old windmill and the small animals and birds that lived in it. *The Old Mill* was the first Disney cartoon to be filmed in part with a multiplane camera, but Disney did not conceive of the film as a test of the camera. It was instead, its director Wilfred Jackson said, to be a cartoon "that depended more on the pictorial aspects of it than on characterization of personalities. . . . I was made to feel that there was more involved than just trying to see if a camera would work."[29]

Now the whole concert feature—or *Fantasia,* as it was being called by the fall of 1938—would depend on the "pictorial aspects." In September meetings on the new film, Disney was clearly much more excited by *Fantasia's* visual possibilities than he was by *Pinocchio's* nagging problems. He even foresaw the "pictorial aspects" being expanded to embrace manipulation of the sound track. "We can make a truck shot of that mountain and come right back," he said on September 14, 1938, talking about a closing sequence whose music would be Schubert's "Ave Maria." "At the same time the whole chorus comes right down the sides of the theater," seeming to enter a church just ahead of the camera.[30]

Disney relished the task of populating the miniature world of fairies, flowers, insects, and tiny animals that he envisioned for Tchaikovsky's *Nutcracker* Suite, at one point demonstrating how a Chinese turtle should dance by moving in a stiff-jointed way and jerking his head back and forth in what a stenographer described as a "wooden tempo."[31] He was even enthusiastic about Stravinsky's *Rite of Spring,* premiered barely twenty years before and still very much "modern music." But the violent music—which probably would have repelled him had he heard it for the first time in a concert hall—sounded altogether different when he was reading a continuity that envisioned it as the accompaniment to a screen full of animated volcanoes. "This fits right to a tee, doesn't it?" he said in an October 19, 1938, meeting. "Stravinsky will say: 'Jesus! I didn't know I wrote that music!'"[32]

While Disney was enjoying a sort of busman's holiday on *Fantasia, Pinocchio* suffered. His words about *Pinocchio* had a curiously distracted sound. On January 14, 1939, in one of the earliest story meetings on *Alice in Wonderland,* he spoke as someone who was already looking back ruefully at *Pinocchio*— even though the writing of the film was still not finished, and the animation of the principal character had resumed only a few months earlier. He expressed regret at not sticking closer to the Collodi book: "We didn't explore what was in *Pinocchio.*"[33]

Two days earlier, Ham Luske had gathered two dozen animators and layout men to go over extensive revisions in *Pinocchio*'s opening sequence—costly changes attributable only to how distracted and indecisive Disney had become in work on that film. Disney wanted some scenes added and others dropped, and many changes would have to be made in scenes that had already been committed to film, in pencil-test animation. Even though Disney had delayed much of the animation for seven months so that the story could be reworked, some aspects of it—specifically, the handling of Jiminy Cricket—remained so unsettled that weeks of work had to be discarded or redone when he finally made up his mind.[34]

Disney was not indifferent to costs but instead voiced concern about them repeatedly, as when he told Ben Sharpsteen, in regard to the preparation of what were called Leica reels—in effect, slide films made up of story sketches for *Pinocchio*, keyed to an accompanying sound track—not to let his artists "get too fancy. . . . I would rather see a good expressive sketch than an attempt at animation." Early in the writing of *Pinocchio*, he warned against ideas that would eat up running time and so raise costs.[35] But he had never shown comparable restraint when it came to elaborations that did not add to a film's length but made it look richer. The man who liked to dress well himself also liked to see his cartoons well dressed on the screen. When the effects animator Ugo D'Orsi hand-painted (in oils) the animation of a waterfall for the short cartoon *Little Hiawatha* (1937), "he was like one thousand percent over budget," the layout artist Gordon Legg said. "When Walt saw the stuff on the screen, he said, 'That's beautiful, that's terrific, give him a bonus.' And he got a big fat bonus. Walt was interested in results. . . . He was encouraging good work."[36]

Disney's concern with his cartoons' appearance extended to the inked lines on the cels. "Walt was very particular as to how the inking was done," Marcellite Garner said, "and we had to use [tapered] lines instead of the rather heavy lines used in other studios. He often said that people might not notice all the little details that he required, but would miss them if they were left out."[37]

In work on *Pinocchio*, Disney resorted repeatedly to the sort of "noodling" he had criticized in his animators' work—expensive embellishments, like the delicate rendering of the whale Monstro, that might conceal other problems. *Pinocchio*'s story weaknesses "did cause the overall costs to rise," said Ben Sharpsteen, Disney's straw boss for the film, and "encouraged more elaborate production methods and practices," like extensive use of the multiplane camera.[38]

The writing of *Pinocchio* suffered persistently from Disney's insistence that his leading character be so passive. As the story reached the screen, Pinocchio springs to active life only when he decides to rescue Geppetto from Monstro, more than an hour into the film. From all appearances, Pinocchio has spent only a single night on Pleasure Island, and yet when he returns to Geppetto's shop the cobwebs tell of a long absence—and Geppetto has in fact been gone long enough to be swallowed by Monstro and brought close to starvation. There is more fudging of this kind—the sort of thing that can subtly erode an audience's sympathy—throughout *Pinocchio*'s closing sequences.

In the atmosphere that surrounded work on *Pinocchio,* the merely painstaking could degenerate rapidly into nitpicking, or into something even more pernicious. There was, for example, the case of Hugh Fraser, who animated under Norm Ferguson and Thornton Hee (known, of course, as T. Hee) when they were directing part of *Pinocchio.* "I think I have the record on pencil tests," Fraser said. "I did forty-eight pencil tests on a six-foot scene"—one in which the villainous fox, Honest John, speaking to the coachman who is to carry Pinocchio to Pleasure Island, asks, "Now, coachman, what's your proposition?" "I did forty-eight different ways of saying that," Fraser said, "and they took the third one I did. T. Hee and Fergy would say, 'Well, let's try another one.' . . . They wanted the best there was."[39]

Using live action to guide the animation was part of the *Pinocchio* plan from the beginning—Thomas and Johnston used it for their pilot scenes in early 1938—and the animators wound up working with a great deal of it. Although he allowed the use of live action for *Snow White*'s animation, Disney had been cool to it, at least where the dwarfs were concerned; now he welcomed it as a crutch. When he spoke about live action at a *Bambi* meeting on September 1, 1939, his words echoed what Dave Hand had said at a meeting for the animators of the dwarfs, almost three years earlier. "The nice thing about it," Disney said, "is that it eliminates the back-breaking work in the sweatbox. There's so much done ahead of time that when an animator picks up, he's got hold of his character." In other words, if different animators were relying on live-action film of the same actor—Christian Rub, say, who portrayed Geppetto in live action as well as providing his voice—their work might have something like the same consistency that could have been gained by assigning one animator to the character.

By then, work on *Pinocchio* was winding down, and the animation of *Fantasia* was just getting under way. Disney dwelled in that *Bambi* meeting on the problems that had accompanied the production of *Pinocchio,* especially when he tried to push work through into the hands of his animators. "We've tried to take care of the whole plant in *Pinocchio,*" he said, "and there's where we got into trouble. Not having a thing prepared. Trying to build a story before we ever even knew it. . . . We didn't know the story. We had to live with it."[40]

His remarks about *Fantasia* were very different, and often far more ambitious, in keeping with the scale of what he and Stokowski were attempting. In a meeting on August 8, 1939, on the sequence based on Beethoven's *Pastoral* Symphony, Disney spoke of the power of the screen's giving visible form to what has only been imagined: "When it's common on up here ["indicating brain," the stenographer noted] but hasn't been seen on the screen, then you have something. Then it hits everybody in that audience. . . . You couldn't ask anybody these things, but the minute you see them on the screen, they know. There is some contact. Even an ignorant so-and-so like me—I get the idea."[41]

In May 1939, Stokowski recorded the rest of the music for *Fantasia* with his old orchestra, in Philadelphia; Disney attended the recording sessions. At a meeting on July 14, 1939, the artists working on each sequence listened to the new recordings and suggested adjustments in the sound—bringing it up or down, altering the emphasis given various instruments—so that it would work more effectively with the images.[42]

Musical comedies aside, music had always played a fundamentally supporting role in films of all kinds, even in *Snow White and the Seven Dwarfs,* whose songs were carefully integrated into the story. By elevating music to such importance in *Fantasia,* and suppressing sound of other kinds, Disney greatly aggravated the danger that the film would resemble nothing so much as a silent feature with orchestral accompaniment, except that most of *Fantasia* would lack a strong narrative. Let daylight slip between the music and the drawings on the screen, let there be lost the sense of what Disney had called "action controlled by a musical pattern," so that the audience became even dimly aware of sound and images as separate entities, and the results could be disastrous. As Stokowski said in one of the early *Fantasia* meetings, on September 26, 1938, "The big masses of people don't like concerts and they don't like lectures"—and, it could be assumed, they wouldn't care much for a concert accompanied by extraneous pictures.[43]

It was increasingly important to the Disney studio that *Pinocchio* be a hit. The studio's income went skidding down after *Snow White:* from $4.346 million in the first nine months of 1938, to $3.844 million in the next twelve months, to $272,000 in the last three months of 1939—lower even at an annual rate than in the pre–*Snow White* years. The studio showed a loss in that quarter.[44] In June 1938, Disney floated the idea of paying his employees a very large bonus from the profits of *Snow White*—as much as a million dollars, compared with around $120,000 that was actually paid that year in "salary adjustments"—but by the fall of 1939, he had spent the money *Snow White* had brought him.[45] Money was still pouring out—into *Pinocchio,* into *Fantasia,* and into a new studio in Burbank that was nearing completion.

Sharpsteen said many years later that Disney's unease about *Pinocchio,* voiced so often during production, had grown into distinct misgivings by the time the film was previewed in January 1940. The endless touching up continued even then, as Milt Kahl redrew the scenes at the end of the film showing Pinocchio as a "real boy." Frank Thomas and Ollie Johnston drew the inbetweens for Kahl's animation. "As I recall," Thomas said, "we had less than a full day to complete our drawings and get them over to ink and paint."[46]

In the meantime, as work continued on *Fantasia,* there was evident the same attention to detail, but from different motives, to burnish a jewel rather than rescue a mistake. Disney's commands "sometimes added hours to our work" in the inking and painting department, Marcellite Garner said, "as for instance in a scene from *Fantasia,* we did long sliding cels of mud bubbling up. Must have been hundreds on a cel, and we used about five different shades of colored ink, so close in hue that we could hardly tell them apart."[47]

Fantasia was the beneficiary—and the studio the victim—of a subtler form of extravagance. During work on the film, as the effects animator Cornett Wood said, "effects techniques were invented on the spot, scene by scene," the "effects" being things like the bubbles (for "The Rite of Spring"). "Everything depended on the needs of the scene," Wood said.[48] Sometimes this constant improvisation extended beyond the effects animator's own desk—the camera department and perhaps other members of the staff would be enlisted in the search for a certain effect, which might not be achieved until several tests had been shot. Once the desired effect was on film, no one bothered to write down the steps needed to produce it, except as a sort of personal reference, distinct from anything the studio required.[49] The prevailing attitude, the effects animator George Rowley said of this ad hoc process, was that "it's done and worked out all right, so that's that."[50]

Disney's attention in the late 1930s was splintered among not just *Pinocchio, Fantasia,* and *Bambi,* but also other features in earlier stages of development. The work on those embryonic features was dominated by written material, to the exclusion of drawings.

Al Perkins's highly detailed, 161-page "analysis" of *Alice in Wonderland,* dated September 6, 1938, is a particularly striking example. Perkins explains in a note at the front that his "chapter-by-chapter and scene-by-scene breakdown . . . has been prepared for the benefit of those in the Studio who may be called upon to work on the feature based on the book. Each scene or episode of the book has been summarized, and some preliminary exploration has been made into various ways in which the material might be treated. No attempt has been made to work out a story line, to find gags or amusing business, or to develop any of the many characters into real personalities."[51]

Stories were developed as continuities and even scripts before they were visualized as story sketches. In the case of *Alice,* no drawings of any kind went up until May 1939, about six months after story work started, and even then the artwork was blowups of the Tenniel illustrations.

Disney himself began to take part in meetings on *Alice* in December 1938, around the time that *Pinocchio's* most vexing story problems had been resolved. The meeting notes indicate that Disney did not read Lewis Carroll's book until March 1939, and they reflect a great deal of frustration, confusion, and ambivalence on his part. On September 20, 1939, at a showing of a Leica reel for *Alice,* he spoke like a man trapped inside a mechanism he had designed himself but had come to dislike: "I don't think the day will ever come when we can write our stories. Some of the best stuff comes after we get thoroughly acquainted with the characters."[52]

Features had generated writing problems as great as the animation problems—and those problems were magnified the more remote Disney was from the story work. That was true of no feature more than *Bambi.* In June 1938, Disney spoke as if *Bambi* would be ready for release a year later.[53] By the end of 1938, though, that timetable had slipped to the point that he was speaking of production taking another two years.[54]

From the start, the *Bambi* unit was at a distance from the rest of the Disney studio. It worked at first in the "annex," a building across the street from the main studio that also housed the training department. In October 1938, a little more than a year after story work began, the unit moved to a building at 861 Seward Street, several miles away. That building had housed the Harman-Ising studio run by Walt Disney's old colleagues Hugh Harman and Rudy Ising, who by then had given up independent production and were cartoon producers at MGM.

Disney himself, preoccupied with problems at the Hyperion Avenue plant, almost never visited the Seward Street operation. Since only he could make real decisions, work there proceeded at a snail's pace under the supervision of Perce Pearce, who had been a key writer of both *Snow White* and "Sorcerer's Apprentice." The unit was staffed mainly with strong draftsmen who knew how to draw animals. Drawing classes were held just for the *Bambi* unit, first at Seward Street and then over a cafeteria on Vine Street. Rico Lebrun, a Chouinard instructor and renowned animal artist, presided over classes in animal drawing for a year and a half.[55]

During story work, Carl Fallberg recalled, "we'd go out on field trips and look for animals and background material. It was all very, very scientific. . . . I even bought a pair of skunks from Minnesota and kept them over at Seward Street for a while." (There were live deer on the Hyperion Avenue premises for a year or so, too. The state of Maine sent them to Disney in the summer of 1938.)[56]

When Disney did make a rare visit, he "knew what he wanted generally," said Fallberg, who had worked under Pearce on "Sorcerer's Apprentice" and accompanied him to Seward Street. "But sometimes he couldn't put it into words and he'd have to see something, so there was a period when we'd try something out and be groping ourselves, and hoping that would be it. That was particularly true on *Bambi,* of course. . . . We were all a little bit in awe of it . . . it was so different from everything that had been done before."[57]

In August 1939, with work on *Pinocchio* winding down and the animation of *Fantasia* under way, Disney began tending to unfinished business. He put Dave Hand in charge of *Bambi,* with an unmistakable mandate to accelerate work on the story. At the end of the month, Disney attended his first *Bambi* story meeting in more than a year. He attended more meetings after that, and the detours that had multiplied under Perce Pearce were closed off.

The planning and construction of a new Disney studio in Burbank had been another demand on Disney's time (as well as the profits from *Snow White*). The *Bambi* group was the among the first to move to the Burbank studio, late in 1939, before the buildings were finished.[58] Frank Thomas and Milt Kahl began experimental animation of the deer around the same time. Clair Weeks recalled that the *Bambi* story crew—heavily influenced by the realistic sketches drawn by Bernard Garbutt, perhaps the strongest draftsman working on the film—felt some resentment when the animators took over. "I felt, well, now these guys are going to make cartoony figures out of all this research and all this drawing that we have been putting into the story," he said. "They're going to lose this."[59]

Frank Thomas and Ollie Johnston wrote years later as if the *Bambi* animators had done just that: "The more an animator goes toward caricaturing the animal, the more he seems to be capturing the essence of that animal, and the more he is creating possibilities of acting. . . . If we had drawn real deer in *Bambi* there would have been so little acting potential that no one would have believed the deer really existed as characters. But because we drew what people imagine a deer looks like, with a personality to match, the audience accepted our drawings as being completely real."[60]

The deer in *Bambi*—as designed by Milt Kahl—were, however, not "cartoony" at all. Neither is there anything about them that suggests "caricature" in the normal sense. Kahl did not exaggerate characteristics of real deer. Instead, he departed from the real mainly by giving the deer eyes and mouths that could be manipulated more freely. Crucially, he drew the fawn Bambi and other young animals—rabbits, skunk—in a way that maximized their cuteness, their resemblance to human children, by giving them large heads and wide eyes. Such designs would presumably enhance the characters' immediate appeal to the audience.

Bambi's deer wound up neither real nor unreal but stranded somewhere in between, and thus perfectly suited for a highly sentimental version of Salten's story, one in which death enters an idyllic forest only by way of hunters' guns. The Kahl-designed deer were also made to order for a kind of animation that departed fundamentally from the animation in *Snow White* but was a natural outgrowth of the way Disney had been building his studio. Kahl initiated the change by proposing at a *Bambi* meeting on September 9, 1939, that the animators be cast by sequence—becoming in effect sub-directors when *Bambi* went into animation.[61]

Kahl was one of the four animators whom Disney had already tabbed as his key animators on *Bambi*—the others were Frank Thomas, Eric Larson, and Fred Moore, all of whom were winding up assignments on *Pinocchio* (Moore animated the character Lampwick near the end of work on that film). In making his suggestion Kahl was motivated largely by boredom—as one of the principal animators of Pinocchio, he had gotten tired of the character. That was hardly surprising, since the puppet had been reduced to a neuter before animation began, thanks in part to Kahl himself.

Thomas and Ollie Johnston, in their book on Disney animation, single out a *Bambi* sequence on a frozen pond as one of the first to benefit from giving a supervising animator control over a sequence. That sequence echoed much earlier Disney animation, as Walt Disney himself recognized. In a 1939 story meeting he said of the *Bambi* sequence, "It is the same situation" as in a 1935 *Mickey Mouse* cartoon, *On Ice,* when the dog Pluto struggled to right himself on ice skates.[62] Norm Ferguson animated Pluto, who was alone on the screen. In the feature, though, there were two characters, the fawn Bambi and the young rabbit Thumper, on the ice. The feature sequence had "a character relationship with strong beginnings in the story department," Thomas and Johnston wrote, adding: "Developing this relationship . . . only could have been done by one person [Frank Thomas] handling both characters and completely controlling every single bit of action, timing, and cutting."[63]

Other films are persuasive evidence that control could be divided among a director and two or more animators with entirely satisfactory results, but younger animators like Thomas and Kahl could hardly be blamed for seeking more control for themselves. Walt Disney had cultivated these talented and highly flexible artists, but now he was spread so thin that he could not work with them as he had worked with his animators on *Snow White*.

More than that, he was recoiling from character animation's difficulties and seeking refuge in cinematic embellishments of many kinds. At a February 3, 1940, meeting on *Bambi*, Disney complained of "too literal" a handling of color in that film. He wanted something more subjective, color that strengthened a mood rather than copying nature.[64] In an April 19 meeting he talked about "road-showing" *Bambi*, presenting it in a limited number of performances each day and with the same sort of elaborate sound system he also envisioned for *Fantasia*.[65]

As in work on *Pinocchio*, the appetite for perfection seemed to know no limits in work on *Bambi*. "There was one scene in *Bambi* that I shot fourteen tests of," the effects animator Cornett Wood said. "They wanted Bambi to be scared, and he looks up, and it's starting to rain, with the thunder and everything, and he doesn't know what that is. He looks up, and there's this rain coming down at him. They wanted a shot [looking] up like that, of the rain coming down. Fourteen times we did it. That's the way they worked in the effects department, they really tried. I always had the feeling they tried too hard."[66]

There were experiments in giving more roundness to the characters, the layout artist Dave Hilberman recalled: "For a while, we were exposing the original hard character, and then double-exposing over that a second, softer treatment—the shadows, and color, and everything else, to get this softness. . . . This was a very expensive experiment—if they had tried to do the feature that way, it would have cost an enormous amount of money. It meant at least four times the normal amount of work, right down the line—inking, painting, camera, everything. Except for some of the romantic musical sequences, where some of it was carried on, we just had to settle for the simplest solution, putting airbrush [that is, spray paint using a compressed-air atomizer] on some of the lower parts."[67]

As work on *Fantasia* and *Bambi* proceeded, *Pinocchio*'s performance was a growing shadow over the studio. *Pinocchio* opened at the Center Theatre in New York on February 7, 1940, to favorable reviews but also to what soon proved to be disappointing results at the box office. RKO had wanted to show *Pinocchio* at Radio City Music Hall, but the music hall, in an act of foresight, would not guarantee an unprecedented ten-week run.[68] (The Center, a huge theater—thirty-two hundred seats—was also part of Rockefeller Center, but it was a decidedly less prestigious venue.)

The two fat years after *Snow White*'s release were now emphatically over—not only was the domestic audience lukewarm toward *Pinocchio,* but in the spring of 1940 European markets disappeared under the boots of the German army. By the fall, seven months after it was released, *Pinocchio* had returned to the studio less than a million dollars in rentals, and Disney was forced to write off a million dollars of its cost. His misgivings had hardened into a feeling that *Pinocchio* should never have been made, Ben Sharpsteen said. (Sharpsteen himself was the target of recriminations; Ham Luske, in a mid-1950s interview, blamed him for selling Disney on the idea of making the film.)[69]

In the fall of 1938, when the studio was flush with money from *Snow White,* Disney scorned the idea of sharing ownership through a public sale of stock. "You see," he told a *Los Angeles Times* reporter, "this isn't 'business' in the sense of primarily making money for shareholders who don't work at it. My brother and I own all the stock and I keep a controlling interest. We won't sell any to outsiders nor to employees. If either of them owned stock they might want the studio to make money first and good films would come second. We put the good films first."[70]

As late as January 1940, Disney still resisted selling stock—"I wanted to build this in a different way," he told some of his artists[71]—but by then his need for money was such that going public had become the lesser of evils. Preferred stock in Walt Disney Productions was offered to the public on April 2, 1940. The money raised helped pay for the Burbank studio ($1.6 million) and retired other debts (more than $2 million). The common stock remained in the Disneys' hands. The company took out a $1.5 million insurance policy on Walt's life.[72]

Disney remembered having lunch with Ford Motor Company executives a few days after the stock issue, when he passed through Detroit on his way back from New York. Henry Ford himself joined the group after lunch, and when Disney told the old autocrat about selling preferred stock, Ford said, "If you sell any of it, you should sell it all." That remark, Disney said, "kind of left me thinking and wondering for a while." Ford "wanted that control," Disney said. "That's what he meant by that." Disney shared the sentiment, even in relatively small matters. On July 1, 1940, he told the studio's publicity department: "From now on all publicity going out of this studio must have my O.K. before it is released. There shall be no exceptions to this rule."[73]

People who joined the Disney staff after work on *Snow White* began typically saw very little of Walt himself. "I met him on a couple of occasions, in story meetings and so forth," said Dan Noonan, who started as an inbetweener early in 1936 and eventually worked in the story department on *Bambi*. Said Marc Davis, who joined the staff in 1935: "Walt Disney was kind of an image; we might see him walking in or out. It was a long time before we got personal attention from him."[74]

Disney added around five hundred people to his staff in the two years after *Snow White*, increasing its size in 1940 to roughly twelve hundred, half the industry's total.[75] He became correspondingly more remote, having little or no contact even with people whose roles were such that they would certainly have seen much of him in earlier years. Norman Tate joined the Disney staff in July 1936 and rose through the studio's ranks to become an animator with screen credit on *Pinocchio* and a corresponding credit in the program book for *Fantasia*. But he never met Walt Disney, never spoke with him directly, until the two of them happened to be leaving the Burbank studio together—this was probably in the summer of 1940—and Disney, making conversation, showed Tate the script for the feature called *The Reluctant Dragon* and asked him how he liked the studio commissary's food.[76]

Even though many of the new employees barely knew Disney himself, Disney animation was for them a semimonastic vocation, and entering Walt Disney's employ was a veritable taking of orders. The 1938 booklet sent to prospective employees made such devotion all but mandatory: "Walt Disney assumes that every artist who enters the studio plans to make animation his life work." At the time of the early Disney features, the animator Howard Swift said, "animation to us was a religion. That's all we talked. If we went to somebody's house—a bunch of animators, we all had wives and we would have a little party, a barbecue—the guys, all they talked was animation."[77]

The Hyperion Avenue studio "was a drawing factory," said Martin Provensen, who worked in the model department. "Drawing was everywhere; the walls were plastered with drawings. . . . You developed a certain attitude toward drawing: You saw drawing as a way of talking, and a way of feeling. Instead of regarding an individual drawing as a sacred thing it was waste paper." At the studio, he said, "you had youth, and you had immense talent, all over the place—talent was taken for granted, no one thought much about it one way or the other."[78]

Some artists had trouble adjusting to life in the "drawing factory." "I worked very hard," said Herbert Ryman, whose first story work was on *Pinocchio*. "I'd try to do a piece of artwork. Of course, all that would happen would be, 'Ah, we can't use that.' These things were yanked off and fell on the floor."[79] But most members of the staff got caught up in the studio's rhythms.

"Every day was an excitement," Marc Davis said. "Whatever we were doing had never been done before. It was such a great thrill to go in there. . . . There was excitement and there was competition; everyone was young and everyone was doing something. We saw every ballet, we saw every film. If a film was good we would go and see it five times. . . . Everybody here was studying constantly. We had models at the studio and we'd go over and draw every night. . . . We would all study the acting of Charles Laughton. We all read Stanislavsky. . . . We tried to understand Matisse and Picasso and others, even though our end result shows very little of that literally. . . . It wasn't that you *had* to do these things—you *wanted* to do them."[80]

It was not artists alone who submerged themselves in their work. The camera operator Adrian Woolery recalled that in the late 1930s, "it was not unusual to put in close to thirty-hour, round-the-clock sessions shooting camera. All we got for it was a fifty-cent meal ticket, which we took over to the old SOS Cafe, on Sunset Boulevard."[81]

In only one part of the studio, the model department, was there drawing that came close to being drawing for its own sake, as opposed to drawing that was measured, like Ryman's rejected drawing, against its potential usefulness in making a film. Formed originally to design characters for *Pinocchio,* the model department eventually branched into story work, putting up many of the sketches for several parts of *Fantasia.* Those seductive drawings could be maddeningly difficult to translate into animated film. Joe Grant, the model department's head, dismissed the concern about costs Walt Disney repeatedly voiced in meetings in the late 1930s and early 1940s: "That was his way of getting out of it if he didn't like it. . . . When he liked the pastel drawings and the color stuff in the model department, he never made such a remark. All he did is call in the ink and paint department and ask them, 'Can you get that effect?'"[82]

The model department's principal members differed markedly from other members of the Disney staff. Several of them had never worked in the inbetween department. John P. Miller, for instance, grew up as a banker's son in Westchester County, outside New York City; he was "aimed at Princeton," he said, "and wouldn't go." Miller referred to the model department as "sort of a goldbricking department," used as a showpiece for prominent visitors because it looked like something creative was going on. His memories of his work there were "mostly social." Said Martin Provensen: "I'm sure the rest of the studio—we all knew it at the time, in fact—saw us as just ridiculous."[83]

Disney's principal role in the model department, as in other parts of the studio, was as an editor of ideas. That was what his "coordination" chiefly consisted of. He was very involved, said James Bodrero, another model-department artist, "in a critical sense."[84] However questionable the initial conception of a film might be, what wound up on the screen after Disney had gone to work was usually more economical and effective than the earlier versions of any given story that can be reconstructed from meeting notes and other sources. In work on *Pinocchio*, for example, he pruned away tedious exposition, and for *Bambi* he eliminated superfluous dialogue.

"He was very helpful," Carl Barks said of Disney's role in story meetings on the *Donald Duck* cartoons. "Very seldom did he ever say a real hurtful thing to any of the story men, something that would cause . . . great discouragement. If he turned down a story completely, he would do it as gently as he could. As he walked out the door he would say, 'Well, I think the best thing to do with that is just to shelve it for a while.' So you knew that was the end."[85]

Sometimes in notes from story meetings there is a particularly strong sense of Disney himself and how he worked. On August 8, 1939, he reviewed what had been done on a cartoon then called *Donald's Roadside Market* (it was eventually released as *Old MacDonald Duck*). This was one of his first meetings on a short cartoon after he had left the shorts in Dave Hand's care for more than a year. In the meeting, Disney impatiently rejected what he called "old stuff," thought aloud and at length, warmed up to an idea (making a full-fledged musical out of the story), and then got really involved in the possibilities ("Gee, I'd like to sit in with you and see what we could get on the start of that music").

"Musical things can't miss," he said (this was in the midst of work on *Fantasia*). "That is why you can sit and watch a tap dancer for ten minutes straight. . . . And then there is that old gag we used in a picture a long time ago and that is these hens laying eggs to music and it's funnier than hell." He seized on music as a way to rescue the struggling shorts and steered discussion toward basing *Roadside Market* on either swing or opera. "I think it wouldn't hurt for us to make some musical things," he said. (The finished cartoon, *Old MacDonald Duck*, is not a musical.)[86]

Those meeting notes also reflect Disney's abundant profanity, which everyone remembered, though the stenographers edited it out in many instances. The notes are sprinkled with hells and damns, and Disney sounds generally impatient and irascible—"Why do we have to have all these damn chases?"

Disney's most common expression—"Oh, shit"—survives in memoirs and interviews but apparently not in any meeting notes. That was probably because Disney censored himself in the presence of female stenographers—sometimes ostentatiously, as when he apologized so profusely to a stenographer for using the word "prat" (for buttocks) that "the gal started blushing," Gordon Legg said. To him, it appeared that Disney "was doing it purposely, to make her feel uneasy."[87] Disney was, however, notoriously and incongruously prudish in some respects—members of his staff learned quickly that he disliked jokes about sex—and it seems just as likely that he sincerely regretted what he regarded as a lapse in his deportment.

Disney's comments in meetings could be almost self-parodying in his repeated use of words like "fanny" and "cute," as during a 1937 meeting on *The Practical Pig:* "We can get cute actions on the fanny. Arrange it so that the little guy gets in cute poses with that fanny. That is what will strengthen this picture a lot—cute actions of the little fellows. With cute actions it will make a very interesting picture."[88]

As if harking back to the late 1920s, he frequently came up with mild bathroom gags, as in the August 3, 1937, meeting on a *Mickey Mouse* cartoon called *The Fox Hunt.* He suggested that the foxhounds plunge into a body of water, with only the tips of their tails showing as they sniff along vigorously underwater. "The funny part would be to have all the tails converging on one tree and then the duck comes up and yells at them to come on."[89] (That gag is in the finished film.) "In the minds of those making our pictures," Disney wrote in 1937, "there never have been any thoughts of vulgarity—merely humorous situations from life exaggerated—and, to me, dogs sniffing trees and fire plugs is very humorous."[90]

"He had a very earthy sense of humor," said Jack Cutting, who joined the Disney staff in 1929. "His humor was what I would call rural, or rustic. . . . It was an unsophisticated sense of humor, and because he had that, he instinctively sensed what might go over well with the average audience. Dick Huemer's sense of humor was sophisticated, and there were others there that had that sophisticated sense [of humor], but . . . Walt wouldn't try to step into the orbit of Dick's type of humor. Everything had to be basic, in Walt's way. He expected others to accommodate to him, but he wasn't going to accommodate to others."[91]

Many of the anecdotes about Disney from the years immediately following *Snow White* reflect attempts by his employees, the writers in particular, to manipulate him—usually for no more sinister purpose than self-promotion at a studio where the boss was increasingly worried and distracted and there were many more people, and thus more opportunities to lapse into invisibility, than there had been a year or two earlier. Some members of the staff, justly or not, came to be regarded as particularly cunning. Perce Pearce, for example—admired during work on *Snow White* for his ability to assume the dwarfs' personalities—was, after he moved on to supervising the writing of *Bambi,* dismissed by many as a con man. Wilfred Jackson recalled Pearce's catching Disney's attention in noisy meetings by speaking much more quietly than anyone else—perhaps getting Disney to move into the seat next to his, in the bargain.[92]

Some of Disney's habits of mind all but demanded manipulation. Members of his staff cited one in particular: he could be difficult in a story meeting, showing no interest in what he heard, and then, a week or so later, Campbell Grant said, "he'd come into your room all full of enthusiasm, and he'd sell you back your own idea."[93] Other times, in a variant on this pattern, Disney heard someone else's ideas and then offered them as his own a short while later in the same meeting.[94] "I've sat in story meetings with Walt," Dave Hand said, "and heard someone . . . bring up a spontaneous gag, to go in a certain place. Walt's sitting there, frowning, looking usually someplace else, and before the meeting is over, *he* gets the idea out of the air, excitedly explains it, and it goes in the picture. He never even heard it mentioned earlier, except that he *did* hear it."[95] Only a few people—Joe Grant was one—ever so captured Disney's attention that he did not absorb and play back their ideas as his own.[96]

The writers tried to read his moods and play to them as they presented their storyboards, sometimes straining in their search for subtle clues in his behavior. "When you [presented a storyboard] to Walt," Chuck Couch said, "it was grim. You'd have a story meeting set up, and you just got butterflies in your stomach. . . . You were always scared to death of him. . . . You'd start telling a story to Walt, and first of all, you'd look to see the expression he had on his face when he sat down in the chair; whether he was congenial to someone sitting next to him or just came in with a frown on his face. You'd start telling the story, and you'd always keep watching him. For one thing, if you saw his eyes go way ahead of you, that was all right, it caught his attention. But if he sat there and started drumming his fingers, you were in trouble."[97]

Most writers, like Couch, sensibly interpreted the tapping of Disney's fingers on the arm of his chair as a sign of impatience ("Oh, God," Jack Hannah said, "you'd have to go ahead and finish the story, hearing that rapping on the chair"),[98] but T. Hee found variations in the tapping. He claimed that only a slow, steady tempo spoke of unhappiness, and that Disney bounced his hand up and down in a faster, lighter tempo when he was pleased. And then there was the tapping of his ring. "He had this big ring on his finger," Leo Salkin said, "and when he got restless you could hear him tapping that goddamn ring on his chair, and it'd drive you right up the wall."[99] Disney might also slap the side of the chair with his hand, "which he did when he enjoyed something," T. Hee said.[100] Bill Peet interpreted that slapping differently: "When he slapped the arms of his chair lightly he was the least bit impatient. When the slapping became 'heavy-handed,' Walt was showing his irritation—ready to explode."[101]

Directors, too, tried to keep a step ahead of the boss. Dick Lundy, who was directing *Donald Duck* shorts by the time of the move to Burbank, said he "used an awful lot of psychology with Walt," specifically by deferring to Disney on which gags to cut from a story that was running too long. Lundy believed that if he suggested which gags to cut, Disney would go "against me, to put me in my place."[102]

Other employees, in other circumstances, believed they had experienced punishment of the same kind, for the same reason. During the planning for the Burbank studio, Ken Anderson wrote to Disney to remind him of his six years of education in architecture and to volunteer his services. "Boy, that was a death knell," he said. "I never should have done that." Anderson was excluded from any role in the design of the new studio.[103]

After *Snow White* demonstrated the viability of animated features, Disney at first considered expanding and remodeling the Hyperion plant.[104] Then, when the huge dimensions of *Snow White*'s success became apparent, he decided to build a new studio on a fifty-one-acre site in Burbank, in the San Fernando Valley, just over the Hollywood Hills from the Hyperion Avenue studio. Walt Disney Productions bought the property, until then used as a military academy's polo field, from the City of Los Angeles's Department of Power and Light in August 1938.[105]

"They thought they would be very happy if *Snow White* grossed three million," Disney said to a small group of his key artists in January 1940—"they" being his brother and others on the studio's business side—"so when it went over that I said . . . I want to build a new studio. . . . But really, I have a hard time getting money out of them."[106]

He succeeded, though, in extracting more than three million dollars for the new facility, at Buena Vista and Alameda Streets. Once some space in the new buildings could be occupied, the move from Hyperion took the better part of a year. Although the camera rooms at Burbank were in use by late August 1939, the inkers and painters and Roy Disney's offices still had not made the move by April 1940.[107]

At the heart of the new studio, whose resemblance to a college campus was widely noted, was the three-story animation building. Disney himself, his writers, and the model department were on the top floor. The directors and their layout artists were on the second floor, animators and their assistants on the first. A secretary was posted at the entrance to each wing, instructed to bar anyone from visiting the artists unless they had first been announced.[108]

Disney intended that the Burbank studio would be not just architecturally impressive—its sleek Art Deco styling extended all the way to the design of the animators' desks—but also uniquely well suited to the needs of people working in animation. For someone coming there after having worked at one of the other cartoon studios, as Fred Kopietz did in April 1940, the new plant could indeed seem heavenly, as Kopietz explained: "Everything was so relaxed by comparison with [the Walter Lantz studio], I couldn't believe it. . . . Everything was so easy-going, with no real push. . . . Here I was used to push, push, push, all the time." There was, besides, much better equipment—at Disney, in contrast to Lantz, an animator could have a Moviola in his room, and the entire studio was air-conditioned.[109]

(Kopietz had animated at Lantz for years, but by 1940 such outside animators could not expect to join the Disney staff at the same level. Kopietz started with Disney as an assistant in special effects animation, and at much lower pay than he had been making, before advancing to character animation on the *Donald Duck* cartoons.)

Even the animators already working for Disney found the change dramatic, Jack Bradbury said: "When we went to the new studio, we went from a room that we had worked in with several guys to rooms all by ourselves, with drapes on the windows, carpeting all over the floor, a nice easy chair to sit in." Each animator had a separate room, with two animators' assistants sharing a room in between. But the atmosphere was chilly, the writer Stephen Bosustow said. "It was cold, you didn't know who your boss was . . . it was just a cold-fish organization." He spoke of "the impersonal feeling that came over the whole studio after being what we thought was a warm, big, happy family."[110]

It was not just the size and complexity of the new plant that were alienating. Status symbols were more important at the new studio than they had been on Hyperion. "The animators had carpets on the floor," Ward Kimball said. "The assistants and inbetweeners had linoleum. Cold, hard, noisy linoleum." Status at the Hyperion studio was determined "more or less [by] what you were doing," Kimball said. "But when we got over to the Burbank studio, you acquired the status symbols—the car you drove, and so forth."[111]

In the new studio it was not as easy as it had been at Hyperion to move freely, the assistant animator Van Kaufman said, in words that summon up memories of hall monitors in high school. "We never walked down the hall unless we carried [the animation drawings for] a scene under our arms. If you were just screwing off, and you were going over to see a friend in another wing, you took a scene with you." Said Hawley Pratt, another assistant animator: "You'd get lost at Disney. You'd be down a corridor, in a little room, and nobody would ever know who you were or what you were doing. You didn't know what was going on—as we would say—upstairs. The second floor you would get to, once in a while, but the third floor—that was like going to heaven."[112]

The writer Carl Barks once recalled in a letter: "The physical layout of the Hyperion studio was very informal, and for that reason [it] was a more pleasant place to work. We Duck and Pluto crews got moved every few weeks into quarters that were still being hammered together by carpenters. At Burbank we were catalogued and classified and packaged like so many guinea pigs in quarters that seemed as friendly as hospital four-bed wards. Units lost personal contact with each other, and the only camaraderie was surreptitious sneaking back and forth with bets for the horse race pools."[113]

Disney's paternalism backfired comically in one instance described by Jack Hannah, Barks's partner as a *Donald Duck* writer. "He had a big soda fountain downstairs that catered room service to all units," Hannah told Jim Korkis. "All you had to do was pick up a phone and say, 'Send up a double chocolate malt and a tuna sandwich.' Any time of the day or night you could call and it would arrive with a cute little waitress in a fancy outfit. . . . It was just too good a thing. Walt would go by downstairs in the middle of the day and he would see the same people sitting there having a cup of coffee or whatever. They'd be sitting there half the day instead of working. Walt finally blew up and the whole thing was thrown out. The whole set-up. All those cute young things."[114]

The ironies were thick as Disney completed the move to his luxurious new studio in the spring of 1940. Instead of soaring aloft with grand new feature films, Disney was scrambling furiously to find some way to make less expensive features and bring in badly needed cash. His haste mirrored the haste he had shown in moving *Pinocchio* into animation early in 1938, but now his motives were radically different. At a National Labor Relations Board (NLRB) hearing in 1942, Disney broke into tears as he began talking about this period in his studio's life: "In the spring of 1940 I was about going crazy—pardon me, excuse me, please?" The NLRB trial examiner ordered a recess of five minutes.[115]

One project was *The Reluctant Dragon,* a live-action tour of the Disney studio itself (with animated inserts) that would tap the public's strong, or so Disney hoped, curiosity about how animated films were made. The live action was shot in the fall of 1940, with Robert Benchley as the star. Benchley told his wife he found the experience disagreeable: "I know I have had to do a lot of stuff I didn't like personally, and don't think I want to keep on in the cartoon business. . . . They play too comical in cartoons."[116] Disney had said at a *Pinocchio* meeting on December 8, 1938: "Certain actors who want to do voices for our characters, they look at it differently than they used to."[117] But now, with the public markedly cooler to that second Disney feature than it had been to *Snow White,* the prestige of a Disney association was starting to shrink, too.

Fantasia was Disney's most ambitious film by far. It reached the screen in New York on November 13, 1940, in a two-thousand-seat theater called the Broadway. Its earlier name was the Colony—it was the same theater where *Steamboat Willie* had premiered a dozen years earlier. Disney had leased the theater for a year and especially fitted it to reproduce *Fantasia*'s multichannel Fantasound.[118]

By then, Disney had so muddied and compromised his original vision of an equal partnership between music and images that the film defied admiration except as an exercise in a limited kind of virtuosity. Musically, *Fantasia* is false from the start. The musicians, as they take their seats in the introductory live action, are hopelessly misplaced, their instruments in positions that would never be duplicated in a real performance. Disney himself probably had little to do with the seating and lighting of the orchestra—Lee Blair, a color stylist, did most of the planning, working with miniature figures— but the introduction is in keeping with much of the rest of the film, where an enthusiasm for the purely pictorial overrode any musical considerations. If the idea originally was to integrate great music with pictures, by the time the film reached the screen the music was clearly subordinate to the cartoons— "Walt Disney plus Bach or Beethoven," as one reviewer put it, noting that the opening-night crowd "applauded exactly where it would have applauded if the score had been composed by a Hollywood musician."[119]

Deems Taylor, acting as *Fantasia*'s master of ceremonies, reveals how flimsy had become its rationale. Of the film's version of Bach's Toccata and Fugue in D Minor, he says: "What you will see on the screen is a picture of the various abstract images that might pass through your mind if you sat in a concert hall listening to this music." In other words, Disney's toccata and fugue— and, by extension, much of the rest of *Fantasia*—was a gratuitous exercise, since why should an audience want a film to do its daydreaming for it? The more difficult and potentially rewarding task, to mirror on film the formal structure of Bach's masterpiece and to make what was on the screen as powerful as the music—that task was not even attempted.

Disney himself regarded *Fantasia* as an unsatisfactory compromise: "I wanted a special show just like Cinerama plays today [in 1956]. . . . I had *Fantasia* set for a wide screen. I had dimensional sound. . . . To get that wide screen I had the projector running sideways. . . . I had the double frame. But I didn't get to building my cameras or my projectors because the money problem came in. . . . The compromise was that it finally went out standard [that is, standard screen dimensions] with dimensional sound. I think if I'd had the money and I could have gone ahead I'd have had a really sensational show at that time."

Fantasia got mixed reviews, but even admirers couldn't help but voice reservations that were sometimes telling. Hermine Rich Isaacs, writing in *Theatre Arts,* praised many of the film's segments, like "The Sorcerer's Apprentice" and the ballet parody "Dance of the Hours," as "pure Silly Symphonies," but some of them, like "The Rite of Spring," gave her pause:

> The moving celluloid picture can no longer be judged on its own merits; it is now successful only insofar as it is a successful complement to the music. Here then is the obstacle that *Fantasia*'s creators meet and do not entirely conquer in their pioneering effort: they are faced with an audience familiar with the musical score, and with many preconceived notions about it which *Fantasia,* with its own notions, cannot dispel. Every person who has heard the pieces has a definite idea of their interpretation, and although his conception sometimes coincides with Disney's, more often it does not. Where Stravinsky's *[Rite of Spring]* suggested the story of evolution to the filmmakers, to some of the listeners it is more suggestive of orgiastic dancing and festivals of springtime, and to others it is absolute music that cannot be interpreted in literal terms.[120]

Fantasia cost almost $2.3 million, and even uniformly glowing reviews could not have saved it. Its road-show engagements were limited by the unavailability of enough Fantasound equipment—defense orders were taking precedence—and the studio's receipts from the thirteen engagements were pitifully small, only about $325,000.[121]

Disney—the entrepreneur who had been so doggedly optimistic in the 1920s—adopted the same tone in late 1940, when he wrote: "Instead of one feature-length picture every two years which seemed the limit of our capacity two years ago, we are now reorganized and equipped to release nine features in the next two years, each at a fraction of *Pinocchio*'s cost."[122] The reality was that as of February 5, 1941, the Disney studio owed the Bank of America $2,781,737.92, and its loan agreement permitted it to borrow less than $20,000 more.[123] Simply completing the features then in production would be difficult enough.

Although Disney stubbornly adhered to the idea that *Fantasia* could be made new every year by replacing some of its segments with new ones, he now spoke constantly of the need to cut costs in meetings on two contemplated additions to *Fantasia*'s program, "The Ride of the Valkyries" and *The Swan of Tuonela*. He did not want "Valkyries" to be made with a flurry of short scenes. "Quick cuts are very expensive," he said in a meeting on January 27, 1941. "This thing depends on what it's going to cost us." He said of *Tuonela*: "You don't have to animate that swan. You just get a very good model [that is, single drawing] of it."[124]

Disney expressed similar urgency in meetings on a short subject, *Invitation to the Dance*, that was to star characters from *Fantasia*. "You're going to have to go through this stuff and see where you can get away from the two characters working together, because that's what runs your costs up," he said on April 24, 1941.[125] As early as March 1941, Disney contemplated making a wholly live-action film, based on Felix Salten's *The Hound of Florence*. He expected to make it for under $400,000—much less than he was spending on his animated features.[126]

It was in the midst of this turmoil that some of Disney's employees began thinking about how a labor union might protect them.

In early 1941, most Disney employees had been represented for three years by an independent union called the Federation of Screen Cartoonists. The federation was a company union, in fact if not in name, but it had been installed with overwhelming support. On February 11, 1938, when the federation filed its petition with the federal government's National Labor Relations Board, it submitted membership cards signed by 568 of the 601 employees in the bargaining unit it sought. Hearings were held in October 1938, and the NLRB certified the federation on July 22, 1939.[127]

Even though the federation was the Disneys' creature, they made no pretense of taking it seriously or even bargaining with it, and the union's officers did not force the issue. "It's maybe like some guys with their wives," Ollie Johnston told Bob Thomas. "They want to be the ones to decide when she's going to get a new dress instead of having her go out and buy it. I think that's the way he felt"—that is, Walt Disney wanted to decide when someone got a raise, rather than adhere to a union contract. And raises were plentiful. As

Jack Hannah put it, "every two and a half months, or something like that, you'd get a raise of two dollars a week. You always knew that you had a little raise ahead."[128]

New employees typically started their Disney careers by doing boring and repetitive work on the bottom rungs of animation's ladder, but always with the promise ahead of them that strong performance would soon be rewarded handsomely, with stimulating work and higher pay. Now they felt a cold wind on their necks. Gordon Legg recalled many years later that "the most militant union organizers" were found among the assistant animators and inbetweeners, those artists at the very bottom of the animation ladder. They were "newer guys who had never really known Walt," Legg said. "He didn't speak to them, unless he said, 'Hi, fellas,' because he didn't know them."

Even so, Legg believed that if Disney "had called the people together more often, and talked to them . . . I think he could have laid people off and they would have understood why."[129] This was a persistent theme not just in Legg's comments but in those of other employees: if Disney himself had known what was going on (and he did not, because the studio had gotten so much larger), he could somehow have made things right. "Guys who were working their tails off weren't getting paid any more than some of the older guys who were goldbricking," Legg said. "That wouldn't have happened when the studio was smaller."[130]

Around the end of 1940, Disney set up several committees to review the work of animators and their assistants. The animation board, made up of ten senior animators, was charged with scrutinizing the work of the character animators and their senior assistants.[131] Said Dick Lundy, a member of the animation board: "The place had gotten so big that management couldn't look and say, 'You're doing great, we'll see that you get a raise.' They didn't even know you."[132]

Disney often spoke as if he regarded his employees differently from outsiders like Charles Mintz and Pat Powers. In 1938 he told Douglas Churchill of the *New York Times:* "We don't have to answer to anyone. We don't have to make profits for any stockholders. New York investors can't tell us what kind of picture they want us to make or hold back. I get the boys together and we decide what we want to do next. It is my ambition to set the thing up so that it belongs to the people in the organization." Churchill noted that there were no time clocks in the Disney studio, thanks to Disney's own resentment of time clocks at one of the first places he worked. "He feels that a time clock places a premium on deception and that it is no bar to dishonesty."[133]

Actually, though, there was a sharp demarcation in Disney's mind between himself and Roy and the people who worked for them, as Churchill observed: "Disney's regard for his men is a peculiar combination of wide individual latitude and rigid organization demands. A rugged individualist himself, he requires that his staff mold itself to his individualism." Disney had no use for those who were reluctant to do so—especially those who expressed that reluctance by support for a truly independent union. "No matter who you were," Ward Kimball said, "and what he paid you, somewhere in the back of his mind he figured he was doing you a favor because he was paying you money."[134]

By late 1940, a truly independent union was making headway. Early in December, the Screen Cartoonists Guild,[135] which had already organized most of the other Hollywood cartoon studios, wrote to Disney telling him that it now represented a majority of his employees. On December 6, Disney hastily summoned the officers of the dormant federation and told them to "get busy . . . and we can stop this thing."[136]

By then, even employees who wanted no part of an adversarial union were growing discouraged. After their meeting with Disney, the federation's officers gathered on December 16, 1940. It was the first time they had met in a year or more, and they sounded gloomy. Said the background painter Brice Mack: "I think one thing, that the people we represent in the majority don't resent any of the pinching that we have had to take through salary"—salaries had already been cut—"or working harder but they do resent the attitude that they seem to get from the studio." The director Bill Roberts decried Disney's excessive interest "in what he calls the 'creative and inspirational help.' And he isn't interested and doesn't respect those jobs where there is tedious but absolutely necessary work and hard work."[137]

Art Babbitt, the highly regarded animator who was the federation's first president and then its vice president, had suffered through a bruising encounter after he suggested that the studio's lower-ranking employees deserved better pay. Many years later, Babbitt remembered meeting over lunch with Roy Disney and Bill Garity, the technical chief, and making "a pitch for a two-dollar raise for the inkers. Well, all hell broke loose, and that afternoon, Roy Disney called me on the phone. He said, 'Look, if you don't keep your goddamn nose out of our business, we're going to chop your nose off.' That sort of hastened my leanings toward a bona fide union."[138]

At the December 16 meeting, Babbitt lamented that Walt Disney shared his brother's hostility toward unions: "As swell as Walt has been in the past . . . he's never taken the trouble to see the other side. He's firmly convinced that all unions are stevedores and gangsters. It has never occurred to him that he might find a decent person to deal with."[139]

In other words, Disney's employees were already withdrawing from him when he delivered the speeches on February 10 and 11, 1941, that he hoped would turn them away from the Screen Cartoonists Guild. His speeches could not have been better drafted if the aim was to alienate as many workers as possible.

Disney concluded with a mixture of belligerence and bravado, and only a trace of the optimism that was usually so dominant in his personality. Mostly he insisted that his employees must accept responsibility for the future of a business over which he had exercised complete control since 1923:

> Now in conclusion, I want to say that I have given twenty years of hard work, I have battled against some very heavy odds, I have sacrificed and I have gambled to bring this business to the place where it is now, and believe me, I don't intend to do any differently now. To me, the future of the business has never looked better. The possibilities in this organization have never looked better. And I can assure you boys that I still have plenty of pep and fight left in me, and I have the utmost confidence in my ability to solve our problems and to run this business; and I want you to know that I am rarin' to go.
>
> Here is the answer to the crisis with which we're confronted. I'll put it in a nutshell. There are three things: quality production is number one; efficient operation is number two, which leads to the third—production turnover. That is the solution to this whole thing.
>
> Simplifying it down to the individual, I would say that . . . the whole thing, is this: *A good honest day's work.* Believe me, that will be a cure for all our problems. You can't deny that it is individual efficiency that leads to collective efficiency. . . .
>
> This business has been, and still is, a pioneering venture. Every one of you men here today are pioneers. Most of you are young, and a big percentage of you—a very large percentage of you—have been in this business less than five years. Regardless of what you think, you've got a hell of a lot to learn. Regardless of what you think about conditions, every one of you should feel lucky that you're in the business that you intend to make your career. We should all feel fortunate that we are here, that we have a chance, that we're in on the ground floor. Probably throughout the country there are many men who are more capable than any one of us who don't even have the chance to secure an art education, or even maybe a high school education. I honestly believe that instead of complaining, we should count our blessings.
>
> This business is ready to go ahead. If you want to go ahead with it, you've got to be prepared—you've got to be ready for some hard work—you've got to strengthen yourselves in every way—you've got to make yourselves strong. If the business is to survive the many storms that are ahead of it, it must be made strong; and that strength comes from the individual strength of the employees.

Disney ended his speech with yet another appeal for strength, this one barely distinguishable from a threat:

"Don't forget this—it's the law of the universe that the strong shall survive and the weak must fall by the way, and I don't give a damn what idealistic plan is cooked up, nothing can change that."

CHAPTER 6

"A Queer, Quick, Delightful Gink"

On a Treadmill

1941–1947

In the spring of 1941, under pressure from the Bank of America and the holders of preferred stock, Walt Disney Productions agreed to scale back its production costs to about fifteen thousand dollars a week. According to Walt Disney himself, that meant he had to hold the negative cost of new features to around $700,000, or one-third the cost of *Pinocchio* or *Fantasia*.[1] Since labor costs made up 85 to 90 percent of Disney's total costs, implementing such severe economies would mean laying off more than half the staff.

Disney loyalists later promoted the idea that the studio had been all but immune to layoffs until the 1941 crisis. "Employment by Disney was tantamount almost to a pension," Gunther Lessing said, "as it was almost impossible to get Walt to fire anybody who possessed the least promise."[2] Hal Adelquist, Disney's personnel manager, testified at a National Labor Relations Board hearing in 1942 that the layoffs in the spring of 1941 were the studio's first.[3]

That was not true. Low-key layoffs—not just individual firings, but small group layoffs that took place on what a 1951 union publication called "a fairly regular semi-annual 'ax-day'"[4]—were routine at Disney's in the 1930s. Isolated layoffs in response to the studio's financial crisis had begun in 1940. By the spring of 1941, the staff had already shrunk by more than a hundred people from its peak of more than twelve hundred. What was new in the spring of 1941 was the prospect of much larger layoffs than ever before, with employee performance only one of many factors in deciding who was to leave (although Lessing, for one, could not resist turning up his nose at the "dead wood" that was being eliminated "because of inferior ability in most cases").[5]

It did not help that the studio was much larger and seemed far more impersonal to many employees than it had a few years earlier. "When they did start laying off some guys," the animator Jack Bradbury said, "it seemed like the fellows up in the clerical type work, upstairs, never seemed to diminish at all. You'd see these guys running around with papers you'd have to fill out, duplicates for every bit of work you did, and they never seemed to cut down. There were always plenty of them."[6]

After Disney's speeches to his employees, sentiment swung sharply in the Screen Cartoonists Guild's direction. Art Babbitt epitomized the shift: not only did he leave the federation and join the guild on February 18, 1941—just a week after the second of Disney's two antiunion speeches—but in March he was elected chairman of the guild's Disney unit.[7]

The guild had presented Disney with membership cards signed by a majority of the employees in its proposed bargaining unit, but Disney insisted on a secret ballot. This was probably not a negotiating ploy. Disney quite likely believed that his employees would choose him over the union if they could make their choice in secret. "My boys have been there, have grown up in the business with me," he said in 1947, in a characteristic expression of his paternalism, "and I didn't feel like I could sign them over to anybody. They were vulnerable at that time. They were not organized."[8] But of course many of them *were* organized, only not in a way that Disney approved; and a high percentage of the people who worked for him had not "grown up in the business" with Disney but had instead been hired during his studio's furious expansion after the success of *Snow White.*

On May 20, 1941, Disney sent this memorandum to about twenty employees: "Will you please be in 3-C-12 [a projection room] at 5:15 this afternoon?" There, Disney fired them personally, reading aloud a statement in which he assured them, "This release is not based on unsatisfactory performance on your part." Steve Bosustow, one of those dismissed, remembered that another employee asked Disney, "What do we do now?" Disney replied: "I don't know. Start a hot-dog stand."[9]

It is not clear how many of the laid-off employees were guild members when Disney fired them (or exactly how many people were in the group). Lessing, the Disney attorney, contended later that only a half dozen were members but that many of the others joined the union after they were fired. Dave Hilberman, a leader of the guild as its secretary, said, to the contrary, that "eighteen or so" were members, and "that since the majority were union, we couldn't let it go."[10] In any case, the guild, no doubt correctly, believed that the layoffs, in combination with Disney's refusal to bargain, were a challenge it had to meet.

When the guild's membership voted on the following Monday, May 26, to strike unless Disney met with a union committee, Disney upped the ante. He fired Art Babbitt the next day, through a letter from Lessing that the studio's police chief hand-delivered as Babbitt left the studio restaurant. Lessing told Babbitt he was being fired because he had disregarded warnings against proselytizing for the union on company time. Babbitt had admitted to Adelquist in a transcribed conversation that he had done so, but that was in March, and the timing of Babbitt's firing was a thumb in the union's eye.[11] A picket line went up on May 28, 1941.

According to a memorandum by Lessing, 1,079 people were on the Disney payroll at the time of the strike; 294 employees within what he called the guild's "proper" jurisdiction went out on strike, 352 stayed in. Several employees—"perhaps five"—went out only one day; 37 others returned before the strike ended. Another hundred employees honored the guild's picket line.[12]

"When the strike was called," Hilberman said, "many of the people who had signed up stayed in, and many of the people who hadn't signed came out."[13] The sense that working in Disney animation was more a calling than a job had by no means been entirely lost. The effects animator Jack Boyd voiced an attitude typical of many nonstriking Disney employees: "I figured I got the job on my own. They didn't ask me to come there, I would have worked for free—which we practically did."[14]

Disney later described the strike as a turning point in his own thinking. His father was "a great friend of the working man," he said, "and yet he was a contractor and hired people. . . . I grew up believing a lot of that . . . but I was disillusioned. I found that you had to be very careful giving people anything. I feel that people must earn it. They must earn it. You can't give people anything." His own experiences as an employer were such, Disney said, that "a lot of my dad's socialistic ideas began to go out the window. . . . Gradually I became a Republican."

As the strike unfolded, the wounded feelings on both sides flared in outbursts like something out of divorce court, with Disney as the boorish husband and the union members his enraged spouse. Disney himself was a frequent target of taunts as he entered the studio ("Walt Disney, you ought to be ashamed," Babbitt called out to him one day).[15] Disney was, as the animator Preston Blair noted, "a great Chaplin imitator and student," and now he evoked Chaplin in confrontations with the strikers. One day, Blair recalled, Disney had driven through the picket line and was walking from his car to his office "when suddenly he cut loose with a wild Chaplin-like gesture of a man ripping off his coat to have a fist fight. Walt was suddenly the Tramp."[16]

Disney struggled to keep a feature schedule alive, but money was tight. By June 20, Roy Disney was in New York, trying to persuade not just RKO, the Disneys' current distributor, but also United Artists, their old distributor, to put more money into the Disney films. Roy told George Schaefer, RKO's president, that the Disney studio was planning three films—*Wind in the Willows, Bongo,* and *Uncle Remus*—to follow *Bambi* and an unnamed *Mickey Mouse* feature. Each film would cost $730,000 to $750,000, Roy said. But the Disneys were "without necessary finances to see this schedule through," Schaefer wrote to another RKO executive, and were seeking financial aid from RKO, to the tune of thirty thousand dollars a week for fifteen months.[17] Schaefer was skeptical.

Four days later, Roy had a different offer for Arthur W. Kelly, UA's vice president. He wanted UA to put up half the cost—which he now set at a million dollars each—of three features (the rest would come from a bank loan). The list of planned features he presented to Kelly included not just the three that Schaefer listed, but also *Peter Pan.* Kelly was not interested in an investment that large.[18]

The Disneys were in a bind. Even though they had planned to lay off many of their employees, they could not continue normal production with a reduced workforce during the strike. A critical factor was, ironically, that many strikers were from the studio's lower ranks—the very people, like the inkers and painters of cels, whose work was essential in the later stages of a film's production. The day before the strike, Disney had spoken to the inkers and painters to ask for their help in finishing *Bambi,* which by then was mainly in their department; he promised to support them if they crossed the picket line.[19] Every week of the strike pushed *Bambi*'s release date further into the future and denied the studio desperately needed revenue. By August the studio's bank debt had risen to $3.5 million—$300,000 above the ceiling the Disneys had accepted just a few months earlier.[20]

On July 1, Disney outraged the guild by welcoming the intervention of Willie Bioff, a notorious labor racketeer who had been indicted in May on federal extortion charges.[21] Bioff and George E. Browne, president of the International Alliance of Theatrical Stage Employees, which embraced many of the movie industry's craft unions, were charged with (and eventually convicted of) extorting more than a half million dollars from producers by threatening strikes if they were not paid off. Bioff's involvement in the Disney strike was significant because of the control he exercised over other unions; by withholding support from the guild, he could make its position more difficult. On July 8, after the guild refused to let him negotiate a settlement, Bioff ordered about a hundred union members who had been honoring the guild's picket lines to return to work.[22]

Roy Disney defended what he called "a lot of dealings with Bioff at that time. . . . As long as the guy's fighting with you, you welcome him on your side. Not to say that I was condoning Bioff. . . . But money was never the basic problem in this thing, as much as communism."[23] As far as the Disneys were concerned, Bioff's anti-Communist credentials were in order, whereas those of the strike's leaders definitely were not.

Dave Hilberman was a Communist Party member at the time of the strike,[24] and a few other strikers and guild officials were party members or sympathizers. The guild was affiliated with the union that represented the painters of movie sets, and Herbert Sorrell, the painters' business representative, was repeatedly accused of being a Communist. Sorrell consistently denied the charge, but, in any case, his gravest offense was probably his longstanding hostility to Bioff. There has never been any reason to believe that the strike itself was called to serve Communist Party purposes.

The result of the Disneys' flirtation with Bioff was, as the federal mediator Stanley White reported to Washington, to leave the strikers and the studio more antagonistic than ever.[25] In the wake of the Bioff episode, the federal government began pressing for arbitration to end the strike. The guild embraced the idea but the Disneys rejected arbitration until finally accepting, through a telegram from Gunther Lessing, on July 23. The strike ended on July 28 after the arrival in Burbank of James F. Dewey, described by *Daily Variety* as the labor department's "ace conciliator." He required the studio to reinstate all the strikers while arbitration hearings were under way. When almost three hundred strikers came to the studio the next day, fifty were given work, and the rest were to get work as it became available.[26] That layoffs would soon follow was a given; *Daily Variety* reported on July 31 that a large number of Disney employees would be laid off "under a retrenchment policy planned by the company" once an agreement with the union had been reached. The critical question was how the layoffs would be distributed among strikers and nonstrikers.[27]

Roy Disney, Gunther Lessing, and Bill Garity represented the Disney studio at the arbitration hearings; Walt Disney was not present. On the second day of the three days of hearings at the studio, the Disney executives agreed to recognize the guild and accept a closed shop—key elements of the award that Dewey and Stanley White, the other federal arbitrator, imposed on studio and union on August 2.

A "final report" bearing that date by the labor department's Conciliation

Service noted that, on August 1, Dewey had gone to the studio to "try to bring about a reconciliation between the inside 'independent' union [a new company union called Animated Cartoon Associates] and the returning strikers' Union. He addressed a large theatre gathering of all the Disney employees, and the process of restoring a measure of harmony was begun. It was a bitter conflict, with a great deal of personal vilification between the parties."

The strike's poisonous effects were felt in a more concrete form. When Roy Disney proposed on August 11 to lay off 207 strikers and only 49 non-strikers, the guild protested. On August 15, with studio and union at an impasse, Roy ordered the studio shut down for two weeks. It ultimately stayed closed until September 15, a few days after Dewey imposed a settlement that required the studio to lay off strikers and nonstrikers in line with their percentages in each department.

Art Babbitt returned to the studio with the other union members who had been laid off in May. By October 1941 he was animating on a *Donald Duck* cartoon called *The Flying Jalopy*.[28] Dave Hilberman, the other strike leader, gave up his job—because, he said, the union "offered my scalp in exchange for so many people to be returned. . . . Disney felt he was making a great deal, but I was a very willing sacrifice. It was a mistake; I should have gone back, simply to cement the victory and make sure that things went well." But he returned to art school instead.[29]

The Disney bonus plans, now relics of much happier days, officially ended on September 12.[30] The studio installed time clocks around the same time. Walt Disney had scorned such devices only a few years earlier, but he was not at the studio to see his opposition to them overturned. He and Lillian had flown out of Burbank August 11, leaving on an 11 P.M. flight for a trip to South America. He made the trip in the company of fifteen employees, a mixture of writers, artists, and other staff people—none of them strikers. Lillian's sister Hazel Sewell, who was by then married to Bill Cottrell of the Disney staff, also came along. (She had been the supervisor of Disney's ink and paint department until her marriage.)

On the day he left, Disney wrote a rambling, defiant three-page letter to the right-wing columnist Westbrook Pegler. In words that echoed his February speeches, he declared that "the entire situation is a catastrophe. The spirit that played such an important part in the building of the cartoon medium has been destroyed."

The strike had been "Communistically inspired and led," he said, and the strikers themselves were "the malcontents; the unsatisfactory ones who knew that their days were numbered and who had everything to gain by a strike. . . . I am thoroughly disgusted and would gladly quit and try to establish myself in another business if it were not for the loyal guys who believe in me—so, I guess I'm stuck with it."

Disney told Pegler that the South American trip was "a godsend. I am not so hot for it but it gives me a chance to get away from this God-awful nightmare and to bring back some extra work into the plant. I have a case of the D.D.'s—disillusionment and discouragement."[31]

As early as October 1940, before any Disney trip to Latin America was contemplated, the federal government, through John Hay Whitney, was encouraging Disney to add "some South American atmosphere in some of the short subjects to help the general cause along," as Roy Disney put it.[32] By June 1941, during the strike, Disney had agreed not only to make a trip but also to produce twelve shorts on South American themes.[33] The federal government would underwrite 25 percent of the cartoons' negative cost, as well as paying seventy thousand dollars of the expenses of the trip itself.[34]

Disney recalled years later that he had resisted making a mere goodwill tour of Latin America: "I said, 'I'd feel better about going down there and really doing something instead of going down there and shaking a hand.'" The 1941 trip was thus officially a "field survey" during which the Disney group would "make a study of local music, folklore, legends, scenes, characters and themes." The trip took the Disney group from Miami to Puerto Rico, and then on extended visits to Rio de Janeiro (from August 16 to September 8, with a side trip to São Paulo) and Buenos Aires (September 8 to September 25, with a side trip to Montevideo).

Leaving Buenos Aires, the group—"El Grupo," as its members called themselves—split up. Disney himself flew to Mendoza, in the foothills of the Andes, while others in the party scattered to points in Argentina, Chile, and Peru. After a few days in Chile, Disney, Lillian, the Cottrells, and seven other members of the group boarded the Grace liner *Santa Clara* in Valparaiso on October 4. The trip to the United States took more than two weeks, with stops along the way in Peru, Ecuador, and Panama.[35]

On September 13, while Disney was in Buenos Aires, his father died. Elias was buried next to Flora at Forest Lawn.

Whatever Disney's intentions when he set out, the trip's "survey" nature was mostly eclipsed by an unending round of cocktail parties, special screenings of Disney cartoons, interviews, public appearances, and meetings with politicians and other local luminaries. The artists in the group did make some sketches, and the Disney people even set up an impromptu studio on the roof of a Buenos Aires hotel, but the trip was in substance the goodwill tour Disney later said he had not wanted to make—even though, as it turned out, he was very good at it.

"Walt Disney is far more successful as an enterprise and as a person than we could have dreamed," Whitney reported to Nelson Rockefeller from Rio de Janeiro on August 29. "His public demeanor is flawless. He is unruffled by adulation and pressure—just signs every autograph and keeps smiling."[36] (Rockefeller was in overall charge of such activities as the government's co-ordinator of inter-American affairs; Whitney, another heir to a famous fortune, was director of the motion picture division of the coordinator's office.)

As noted in a detailed itinerary written after the trip, apparently by John Rose of the Disney staff, Disney entertained two thousand children at Mendoza not only by showing them cartoons, but also by literally standing on his head.[37]

Disney reached New York from his South American trip on October 20, 1941, and was interviewed soon thereafter by a writer for the *New Yorker*. Although he had previously explained his role at his studio by describing himself as a sort of an orchestra conductor, his experience with *Fantasia* may have made him uncomfortable with such an analogy. In any case, he now used a new one, one he invoked repeatedly in the years ahead. "In the studio," he said, "I'm the bee that carries the pollen." The *New Yorker* described Disney as he demonstrated: "Rising in illustration, he held out his two cupped hands, filled with invisible pollen, and walked across the room and stood in front of a chair. 'I've got to know whether an idea goes here,' he said, dumping some pollen into the chair, 'or here,' he went on, hurrying to our side of the room and dumping the rest of the pollen on our knees."

In that interview, Disney repeatedly disdained the "arty," using language strikingly different from the ambitious sentiments he had often voiced during work on *Fantasia*: "A man with a dramatic sense but no sense of humor is almost sure to go arty on you. But if he has a really *good* dramatic sense, he'll have a sense of humor along with. He'll give you a little gag when you need it. Sometimes, right in the middle of a dramatic scene, you've got to have a little gag. . . . I don't want any more headaches like the 'Nutcracker Suite' [in *Fantasia*]. In a thing like that, you got to animate all those flowers, boy, does that run into dough! All that shading. That damn thing cost two hundred thousand dollars—just the one 'Nutcracker Suite.'"[38]

Disney spoke of working "off the cuff. Don't have any script but just go along and nobody knows what's going to happen until it's happened." He had not made films in anything like that way since the 1920s, but he may have been measuring *Fantasia*, which required so much preparation, against the film he was then promoting; it had its premiere in New York on October 23, 1941, succeeding *Fantasia* at the Broadway Theatre. Fifteen years later, Disney described *Dumbo* as "the most spontaneous thing we've ever done. . . . It started with a little idea, and as we kept working with it we kept adding and before we knew it we had a feature."

Dumbo, the story of a baby circus elephant that learns to fly using its very large ears, originated as a very short children's book, which may never have been published in its original form (the Disney studio purchased "the name and basic story," apparently while the book was still in manuscript).[39] It was one of the dozens of properties the studio scooped up in 1938 and 1939, after *Snow White*'s success provided both the money and the incentive to acquire suitable stories. Although the idea at first was to make *Dumbo* as a short, in January 1940 Joe Grant and Dick Huemer, the team that had supervised the writing of *Fantasia*, began writing a feature treatment, a book-length version broken down into chapters. Disney was immediately enthusiastic, and by late in February 1940, with chapters of the treatment still arriving in his office, *Dumbo* had won a place on the feature schedule.[40]

From that point on, the film did indeed fly through production, especially as measured by the pace set by *Pinocchio* and *Bambi*. It took only about six months to put up storyboards for *Dumbo* and iron out a few kinks in the Grant-Huemer treatment, and animation was under way by October 1940. The film was finished, except for some rerecording of the sound track, when the strike began.[41]

By the time of *Dumbo*'s premiere, *Pinocchio* and then *Fantasia* had failed at the box office, the war in Europe had wiped out a large part of Disney's foreign market, and the studio had been roiled by Disney's standoff with the Screen Cartoonists Guild. *Dumbo*, with its modest budget—at around $786,000,[42] its cost was close to the $700,000 limit Disney had agreed to accept in the spring of 1941—had acquired an importance in the Disney scheme of things out of proportion not only to its cost but also to its length. It was sixty-eight minutes long, barely acceptable for a feature—but it was the only kind of feature that Disney's finances would permit him even to consider making in the fall of 1941.

Dumbo won uniformly favorable reviews and a warm reception in theaters. Not all was smooth sailing—a planned cover feature in *Time* in early December was bumped by the Japanese attack on Pearl Harbor—but it ultimately returned a profit to the Disney studio of about a half million dollars on its initial release. Here was a way for Disney to continue making features—and at the same time escape from the trap that has snared so many American popular artists.

Such artists have always found it difficult to sustain growth in their work for more than a few years without losing much of their audience. Most often they are trapped by their own success; the public demands repetition, not change. Film directors of whom the public was only half aware, like John Ford and Howard Hawks, could over a long span of years make films that satisfied both themselves and their audiences, but the more visible Frank Capra was not so lucky when he tried to advance beyond his huge popular successes of the 1930s. Disney had been nimbler than most, but, with *Fantasia* especially—two hours of animation set to classical music—he had run up against that seemingly iron law. Now, with *Dumbo,* he had begun winning his audience back.

There was a problem, though, one that Disney himself identified when he read the paean to *Dumbo* that ultimately appeared in *Time's* issue of December 29, 1941. Unusually, that article dwelled at length on the contributions of people like Grant, Huemer, and the animator Bill Tytla. Disney himself was mentioned relatively little. "Walt didn't like that writeup," Huemer said. "He said, 'Hell, it looks like I didn't do anything on this picture.'"[43]

Measuring Disney's contribution to *Dumbo* is harder than usual because the documentary record is scantier than usual. Although Disney's desk diary shows him attending dozens of meetings on *Dumbo* in 1940, none of those meetings were transcribed. In the increasingly harsh financial climate—and with a story that needed only minor adjustments—a stenographer's time was an expendable luxury. There are many hints in *Dumbo* itself, though, that other hands played a larger part in shaping it than was usually the case. Ben Sharpsteen supervised *Dumbo,* and in its economy and clarity, *Dumbo* recalls the best of the short cartoons (*Mickey's Circus, Moving Day, On Ice*) that Sharpsteen directed for Disney before he directed part of *Snow White* and supervised all of *Pinocchio*. Then there is the casting, with all that it implies about the animators' control over their characters.

As with no Disney film since the shorts that preceded *Snow White,* *Dumbo's* animators were cast by character, most notably Bill Tytla, who animated the title character. In many scenes one man animated several characters, but usually those were scenes like Tytla's of the circus elephants, or Ward Kimball's of the crows—tiny communities so tightly knit that sensible casting could mean, in those cases, giving a single animator the entire group. Only one major character—Timothy, the mouse who serves as Dumbo's faithful retainer—was divided between two animators, Wolfgang Reitherman and

Fred Moore. Timothy was a special case because Moore by then was sliding into full-blown alcoholism. Perhaps for that reason, Disney never followed through on his original plan to make Moore one of the principal animators of *Bambi;* Moore did not work on that film at all.

Moore had been one of the four "supervising animators" on *Snow White,* along with Tytla, Ham Luske, and Norm Ferguson. Together, they had been responsible for the film's principal characters. All four men suffered, Frank Thomas and Ollie Johnston wrote, because "animation took a direction that demanded a refinement no longer compatible with their styles. . . . Their work was easy to understand, to recognize, and to study. But as new men with formal art training came along, and Walt's thinking turned toward an increasingly sophisticated type of animation, a more subtle kind of action with more complex acting and more meaningful expressions developed."[44]

Thomas and Johnston were writing about *Bambi,* most of all. While work on *Dumbo* proceeded smoothly, *Bambi* lumbered toward the finish line. "Everybody [on *Dumbo*] was having fun," Eric Larson recalled, "and we were working our tails off to get deer walking around right."[45] By the time of *Dumbo*'s premiere, though, *Bambi* was, at long last, all but finished.

There was in *Dumbo* a strong sense of caricature, of exactly the kind that Walt Disney had once espoused but that was almost totally lacking in *Bambi.* The animators were different, too. Of the four supervising animators on *Snow White,* only Bill Tytla was still active as an animator, and his animation in *Dumbo*—devoted above all to giving Dumbo and his mother an emotional presence on the screen—was in striking contrast to the more "sophisticated" animation in *Bambi* by the younger animators, like Thomas and Milt Kahl.

The "subtlety" and "complexity" that *Bambi*'s animators embraced, and that required their control over sequences rather than characters, left no room for the identification between actor and character that occurs in the best acting on stage and in live-action films. "While the actor can rely on his inner feelings to build his portrayal," Thomas and Johnston wrote years later, "the animator must be objectively analytical if he is to reach out and touch the audience."[46] That had already been disproved by others among the Disney animators, and by Tytla, above all.

Tytla had animated large, powerful characters in *Pinocchio* (the puppet master Stromboli) and *Fantasia* (the demon Tchernabog, in "Night on Bald Mountain"), so the elephants were a natural fit—but not necessarily the baby elephant, Dumbo. Tytla had, however, based his animation of Dumbo not on his knowledge of elephants, but on what he knew about human children, especially his own two-year-old. "I've bawled my kid out for pestering me when I'm reading or something," he told *Time*, "and he doesn't know what to make of it. He'll just stand there and maybe grab my hand and cry. . . . I tried to put all those things in Dumbo."[47]

Through the animation of its characters, *Dumbo* validated and extended Walt Disney's own great central achievement in *Snow White*. The ideas that Disney had so often expressed and that had shaped the earlier film—the "caricature of life"—were even stronger in *Dumbo*. But success had come at a fatal cost. It was clear from *Dumbo*, as it had not been from *Snow White*, that vivid characterization could be achieved through intelligent casting and sensitive direction—but, as a result, Walt Disney's own close involvement had ceased to be essential, a development Disney could not have welcomed. Moreover, in *Pinocchio, Fantasia,* and *Bambi,* Disney had already embraced different ideas about his animated features. Other things were now more important than the immediacy of animation like Tytla's.

(Disney rewarded those animators whose work was most consistent with his new priorities. As of November 1941, when the dust from the strike was settling, he was paying Tytla $191.25 a week, but Frank Thomas and Milt Kahl, the principal animators of *Bambi,* were making $212.50 a week. Only Ham Luske and Fred Moore were paid more, at $255 a week, and their salaries reflected the wider responsibilities of each man in the years just after *Snow White*.)[48]

Disney had once been enthusiastic about low-budget projects like *Dumbo,* seeing in them a way to use characters like Mickey Mouse and Donald Duck in films that would be more profitable than short subjects. Low-budget features would also be good vehicles for staff artists who were not suited for Disney's more ambitious features, like *Fantasia* and *Bambi*. Story work on a version of "Jack and the Beanstalk" with Mickey and Donald was under way by late in 1939, around the time that *Dumbo,* too, emerged as a potential feature.[49]

In a February 27, 1940, meeting on *Bambi,* Disney spoke of *Dumbo*'s "great possibilities. . . . The personalities are the type of thing we can get hold of . . . that everybody can get hold of." He referred to *Dumbo* as "an obvious straight cartoon. I'll deliberately make it that way. It's the type to do that with. It's caricature all the way through. I've got the men for it. They don't fit here," that is, in work on *Bambi*.[50] He was still enthusiastic in an April 2, 1940, meeting on *Alice in Wonderland:* "If *Dumbo* can prove . . . that you don't have to have birds and bunnies and [a] wishing well, it would be *the* picture."[51]

By May 1940, with *Pinocchio* unquestionably a failure and Hitler's army wiping out European markets, movies of *Dumbo*'s dimensions were starting to look altogether different than they had a few months before: less like auxiliaries to the big-deal features like *Bambi* than like potential lifesavers. Disney still approached them with apparent enthusiasm. In meetings on "Jack and the Beanstalk" that month, he spilled out a stream of ideas, almost as if he found working on that story relaxing, a welcome change from more serious stories. But in a meeting on May 14, 1940, he was frank about the reasons for his intense interest: "The main idea is that we are trying to get a feature out of here in a hell of a hurry. . . . It's a long story but it can be told in a few words—mainly that our European market is shot—which you're all aware of, and we have to get something out of here that can go out and make some money on just the American market alone."[52]

Even though Disney spoke of completing the "Beanstalk" feature in four months, story work dragged, and the film did not go into animation until early in 1941. It was unfinished when the strike began. So was another low-budget feature, *The Wind in the Willows,* based on Kenneth Grahame's book; animation did not begin until April 1941. Neither film was ever released as a feature, although animation from both was salvaged and reused in postwar "package" features. "Jack and the Beanstalk" was the first casualty, shelved soon after Disney's return from South America in October 1941. RKO's reluctance to distribute the film was probably decisive, but Disney himself decided to halt production of *Wind in the Willows.* From all accounts, both films threatened to be fatally thin and dull if released as features.

(*The Reluctant Dragon,* the live-action studio tour with animated inserts, was completed before the strike and released in the summer of 1941, just in time for its portrait of a cheerful studio to collide with the reality of the strike. Even though its cost was lower even than *Dumbo*'s, around $635,000, rental receipts fell almost $100,000 short of covering that cost.)[53]

Bambi was finally released in August 1942—it opened at Radio City Music Hall in New York on August 13, after a premiere in London five days earlier. The Disney studio's share of the rental receipts ultimately fell short of the film's cost by about $60,000.[54] *Dumbo* did not return as much in rentals, about $400,000 less than *Bambi,* but its much lower cost made it highly profitable. In other words, the public would turn out for a *Bambi,* the kind of film that Disney now wanted to make, but not quite in numbers that were large enough. (*Bambi* played at Radio City for only two weeks.)

It was one thing to make low-budget features as part of a broader program, each "B" picture alongside a big-budget "A," but low-budget films were confining when there was nothing else. People who had been animating on more expensive films with what one of Disney's directors, Bill Roberts, called "straight drawing" were not necessarily well equipped to make the transition.

For instance, James Algar, who directed much of *Wind in the Willows,* came to that film after directing not only part of *Bambi* but also the extravagantly expensive "Sorcerer's Apprentice" in *Fantasia.* The artists Disney called "caricaturists"—the ones who dominated work on *Dumbo*—were better suited to making cartoons whose characters emerged as if in swift strokes, but by 1941 Disney's allegiance had shifted decisively toward artists of the "straight drawing" kind. What he saw on the screen in the two shelved cartoons, and in *Dumbo* itself, could only make him more aware of what was no longer possible for him.

Roy Disney met Walt in New York when he returned from South America in October 1941. Before the *Santa Clara* arrived he wrote a memorandum to his brother, to bring him up to date on what he would find when he returned to the studio. "You will possibly find a lot of things that will be very annoying to you," Roy wrote, "but please try to understand that we were facing a terrible situation and we did the best we could to make the best of it."[55]

One annoyance was the presence of Art Babbitt, back on the staff with other rehired strikers. Disney and Babbitt had never been friends, but in the years before the strike Babbitt had been a valued if willful and rather eccentric animator, one whose work Disney praised on more than one occasion. As late as March 3, 1941, Disney wrote to the director Wilfred Jackson about the need to help Babbitt get rid of the "stiff old-fashioned" quality that afflicted his animation in the short *Baggage Buster* of the dim-witted dog character Goofy—a character that had been defined largely by Babbitt in earlier cartoons. "Babbitt is capable of good results if you work very closely with him and not let him have his way too much," Disney wrote. "He's a very stubborn punk, but we've got to get him out of the groove he's in."[56]

In the months before the strike, though, Babbitt became the magnet for all of Disney's anger and frustration, which Babbitt himself did little to relieve. A few weeks before the strike, Babbitt called Disney to ask for a raise for one of his assistants, Chuck Shaw—hardly a sensible thing to do under the circumstances. Disney responded, in Babbitt's account (which neither Disney nor his attorneys challenged): "Why don't you mind your own goddamn business. . . . If you stopped messing around in other people's business and stopped carrying the torch for a bunch of guys who don't deserve to be fought for in the first place, you would be a hell of a lot better off." Disney said of Shaw: "Well, if he doesn't like it here he can go work in a service station."[57]

Babbitt also described a confrontation in a corridor of the animation building on the morning of May 5, 1941, with Disney again boiling with anger:

"If you don't cut out organizing my employees you are going to get yourself into trouble. . . . I don't care if you keep your goddamn nose glued to the board all day or how much work you turn out or what kind of work it is, if you don't stop organizing my employees I am going to throw you right the hell out of the front gate."[58]

Babbitt's accounts, even if not word for word accurate, certainly reflected the hostility to the union, and to Babbitt in particular, that Disney voiced on other occasions. A few weeks after Disney returned to the studio, Babbitt's work started to dry up. He spoke of "trying desperately to get some work" for about ten days, until finally he was laid off on November 24, 1941.[59] Babbitt immediately challenged his dismissal as unjustified. A year later, a trial examiner for the NLRB agreed. Babbitt himself wrote to a friend around that time that Disney had "lost his halo and tinsle [sic] as far as I'm concerned. I think he's a confused mixture of a country bumpkin and a 1st degree fascist."[60]

Disney's intense dislike for Babbitt, and for Dave Hilberman, the other leader of the strike, is one source of the persistent claims that he was anti-Semitic. (Although Babbitt questioned the characterization, both he and Hilberman were Jewish.) There is simply no persuasive evidence that Walt Disney was ever in thrall to such prejudices. Roy Disney expressed some wonder at his brother's tolerance in an interview with Richard Hubler not long after Walt's death: "For an artist that had delivered, Walt didn't care how he combed his hair, or how he lived his life or what color he was or anything. A good artist to Walt was just a good artist and invaluable."[61]

Whatever the exact motives for Babbitt's layoff, it was not an isolated event. The Disney studio announced the same day that it was laying off a total of two hundred employees, shrinking its staff to 530, less than half the prestrike total.[62] Although *Dumbo* was doing well and *Bambi* was all but ready for release, the studio's most substantial work on hand was the short cartoons on South American themes. Then, on December 7, the Japanese attacked Pearl Harbor, and everything changed.

The army moved hundreds of troops—Disney put the figure at more than seven hundred—into the studio. "These soldiers were part of the anti-aircraft force that were stationed all around," Disney said. "They had these guns all over the hills everywhere, because of the aircraft factories and things"—Burbank was home to Lockheed Aircraft. Disney remembered that soldiers began arriving uninvited on December 7, but *Variety* reported that troops did not move into the animation building until a week after Pearl Harbor, at the studio's invitation.[63] The army also occupied the studio's sound stage, Disney said, "because they could close the stage up and work in a blackout."

This impromptu conversion of part of the lot lasted for what Disney said was eight months, but his involvement with the war effort lasted much longer. Disney had begun seeking defense-related work in March 1941, but not too eagerly, and with only limited success. His most important commissions came from the National Film Board of Canada, which ordered four cartoons, all using old animation, to promote the sale of war bonds, as well as a training film on the Boys MK-1 antitank rifle. Production of those five films began on May 28, 1941, and continued until early in 1942,[64] by which time Disney's war work for his own government had increased dramatically.

As soon as the United States entered the war, the navy moved swiftly, commissioning Disney to make twenty films to help sailors identify enemy aircraft and ships. So closely did the navy and Disney work together that Captain Raymond F. Farwell, author of *Rules of the Nautical Road* (translated into film by the Disney artists), lived in Disney's office suite for months. "He did his washing in there and everything," Disney recalled.

With much of the Burbank studio empty, Disney leased space to Lockheed for use by production illustrators. As Robert Perine, who was one of them, later wrote, "Rows of animators were simply replaced by rows of technical artists, turning out complicated, two- and three-point perspective drawings of aircraft parts."[65]

In February 1942, at the annual Academy Awards ceremony, Disney received the Irving Thalberg Award, given not for a particular film but for a consistently high level of quality. The stress of the previous two years caught up with Disney as he accepted the award from the producer David O. Selznick, and he wept openly. "It was difficult for anyone to hear Disney clearly," *Daily Variety* reported. "He found it difficult to speak and was only able to say, with great emotion: 'I want to thank everybody here. This is a vote of confidence from the whole industry.'"[66]

In the spring of 1942, work on the twelve South American–themed shorts was moving forward rapidly—understandably so, since the writing of all those shorts began before the 1941 trip did, and the people who did most of the work on them were not part of El Grupo, the studio contingent that accompanied Disney to South America. Disney attributed to his distributor, RKO, the idea of combining four of the shorts into a sort of feature, to overcome the difficulty of selling a Brazilian-themed short in Argentina, and so on. "They said, 'You've got to put these together somehow. So I didn't know how to put 'em together but I had taken 16mm film of our trip. . . . I took the 16mm film, blew it up to 35, used it as connections between the four subjects and presented it as a tour of my artists around."

Saludos, as the forty-two-minute result was called for its release in Spanish-speaking Latin America, included cartoons that placed familiar Disney characters in South American settings (Donald Duck in Bolivia and Brazil, Goofy in Argentina) and introduced new Latin-flavored characters (José Carioca, a Brazilian parrot, and Pedro, an anthropomorphic mail plane). The film played to enthusiastic crowds throughout Latin America. In Buenos Aires, a representative of the coordinator's office reported, "the sequences, particularly those dealing with Argentina, amazed the audience with their authenticity, their charm and their humor. . . . There was little doubt that the Brazilian sequence and particularly José Carioca were considered [even] more enjoyable than the Argentine sequences—and this in Buenos Aires is news."[67] Retitled for its domestic release, *Saludos Amigos* opened in the United States in February 1943. It returned rentals to the studio of $623,000, more than twice its negative cost of less than $300,000.[68]

By the summer of 1942, the Disney studio still had only around 500 to 550 employees,[69] but war work was beginning to take up the slack left by the dormant feature program. That work accelerated the Disney studio's turn away from being strictly or even mainly a cartoon producer. By 1943, about half the film footage the studio produced was live action, most of it for defense series like *Aircraft Production Methods.*[70] In order to get his men who were making military films deferred, Disney brought members of draft boards to the studio—where, he said, they could not get security clearances to see some of the most sensitive work being done.

In the later months of 1942 and the early months of 1943, as war work ramped up, Disney somehow found time and money (receipts from *Bambi* no doubt helped) to make another feature, this one radically different from those he had made before the war. Although Disney is best remembered as a train enthusiast, he loved air travel, too, and in early 1942 his South American trip stimulated him to plan a bargain-basement feature on the history of aviation. Instead, that plan was subsumed in a largely animated version of *Victory Through Air Power,* Alexander de Seversky's 1942 book advocating a reliance on long-range bombers to defeat the Axis powers.

Disney's artists had adapted rapidly to the new demands of the military training films, so far removed, both in graphics and as narrative, from anything they had done before. The maps and diagrams and symbols that make up much of *Victory's* animation, illustrating Seversky's ideas, were a further challenge, especially combined with Disney's zeal for the subject matter. "I was confused" after a meeting on the film, said Herb Ryman, whose métier was the evocative sketch. "I could only see maps. Walt followed me out of

[the] room. He hit the jamb of the door with the flat of his hand. 'What's the matter, Herbie? Is that a bad idea?' 'No . . . no . . . no . . .' You couldn't say no to Walt."[71]

Disney remembered getting pressure from both naval and army air corps officers during work on *Victory Through Air Power*. He made *Victory*, after all, in the midst of making training films for the navy, and Seversky's book alarmed officers in both services, although its ultimate impact was slight. "It was just something that I believed in and for no other reason [than] that I did it," Disney said. "It was a stupid thing to do as a business venture." That was true. RKO sagely passed on the film, so in November 1942 Disney signed a distribution contract with United Artists instead. When *Victory Through Air Power* was released in July 1943, the Disney studio lost more than $450,000 on the film.[72]

In other respects, too, the war was a trying and difficult time for Disney. During the war, he complained more than ten years after it ended, "the theaters had no time for Disney . . . and all the little brats Disney attracted. . . . Wartime was a poor time for us." The theaters prospered without the "family trade," he said, because "they were doing such a business with any old piece of cheese they'd put in."

Disney did not enjoy working with many of the military officers and government officials who had to pass on his films. "Some of those people, when they got a uniform on, it was like a pinning a badge on somebody," he complained in 1956. "They just couldn't hold it." Frequent visits to Washington—he made five in 1942 alone—were a necessity but no pleasure. Sometimes, Disney said, he couldn't find a hotel room, so "I went and sat through a movie several times to have a place to sit down."

Joe Grant remembered hearing Disney talk about his studio, on one of those trips to Washington, in terms that were in striking contrast to the conditions that prevailed by then. Perhaps Disney was speculating about some ideal arrangement, or about what might have been if the strike had not intervened. "He wanted a dormitory on the lot, he wanted people to live there," Grant said. "I got that on a train ride back to Washington once. As [Henry] Ford did, when he had all of his employees living there; he had a perfect setup. He not only had a belt-line, but he had all the accessories to go with it, which were people."[73]

For all the jarring changes that Disney and his studio had endured in the last few years, outsiders could still find the man and the place refreshingly attractive compared with the rest of Hollywood.

The novelist and screenwriter Eric Knight worked at the Disney studio in

1942, as a major in the army, when Disney was making animated inserts for the *Why We Fight* series produced by Frank Capra's military film unit. Knight, in Hollywood since 1934, was by the time he met Disney disgusted with "the Hollywood idea . . . that a writer is the lowest form of life—a sort of stenographer." Jaded though he was, Knight liked the Disney studio, marveling at its "offhandedness," and, as he wrote to his wife on August 6, 1942, he found Walt himself "good fun. He is always trying to wangle an idea out of me. . . . He is a queer, quick, delightful gink with more capabilities rolled into one man than even me."

On August 17, 1942, Disney wanted to know what Knight thought of a possible film about "Gremlins and Fifinellas and Widgets. Gremlins ride on [Royal Air Force] planes with suction cup boots and drill holes in planes. Fifinellas are girl Gremlins—all cousins to a leprechaun. Widgets are young Gremlins born in a nest. . . . So we laugh at lunch and I can kid him any way I want. . . . Then back after lunch to maps and more maps . . . and Walt comes in popping open the door once in a while to give valuable technical suggestions."[74]

Disney no doubt found Knight unusually congenial company when so much of his time was taken up with far more mundane matters. During the war, "the technical films we were making didn't call for the type of meetings that Walt liked," the animator Ollie Johnston said.[75] Transcripts have survived from some of the meetings on "technical films" that Disney attended. For example, on April 15, 1942, he and members of his staff devoted most of the afternoon to two meetings with Earl Bressman, director of the agricultural division in the office of the coordinator of inter-American affairs. They reviewed storyboards for two of a series of 16mm educational films commissioned by the coordinator's office for showing in Latin America. One film, ultimately titled *The Grain That Built a Hemisphere* (1943), was about corn and corn products. The other film, *The Soy Bean,* was never completed. The tone of the meetings differed sharply from that of the meetings on the prewar features and shorts. Although Disney occasionally expanded on an idea, it was always Bressman's wishes that were paramount, rather than Disney's.[76]

It was through his association with the coordinator's office, though, that Disney kept a toehold in the market for entertainment features. Plans for a second feature combining four shorts on Latin American themes were under way by June 1942,[77] and the success of *Saludos Amigos* cemented those plans. Mexico was an obvious candidate for inclusion in the new film. (Six members of El Grupo had spent four days in Mexico City on the way back from South America, but none of the cartoons in *Saludos Amigos* had a Mexican theme.) The coordinator's office paid for a three-week trip to Mexico in December 1942 by Disney, his wife, and ten members of his staff.[78] By then, as a Mexican publication reported early in 1943, Disney already had "a new creation in mind, typifying the national character of Mexico. This is to be represented on the screen by a peripatetic, swaggering little rooster."[79] Members of the Disney staff made two more trips to Mexico by mid-1943. First referred to as *Surprise Package,* the film ultimately was named *The Three Caballeros,* the three being Donald Duck, José Carioca, and the new Mexican character, a rooster named Panchito.

By the time it was finished, in the fall of 1944, *The Three Caballeros* bore little resemblance to *Saludos Amigos.* It was almost a half hour longer. It included two short subjects that had always been planned as part of a second group of Latin American shorts, and most of the rest of the film was assigned two short-subject production numbers, but the newer "shorts" were much longer and more elaborate than the other two. Far more ambitious than *Saludos Amigos, Three Caballeros* was for much of its length a sort of travelogue in which Donald and José, and then Panchito, mingled with live-action performers from Brazil and Mexico. Disney had mixed animation and live action occasionally since his *Alice* comedies in the 1920s, but never so extensively as in *Caballeros,* and never before in Technicolor.

It was during the war that he got interested in combining live action and animation again, Disney said years later, because "we did not have enough artists and animators to work on the full-length subjects."[80] Of course, *Three Caballeros* in its genesis was not to be a "full-length subject," but a collection of shorts. By transforming such a modest idea into a film bursting with elaborate and frenzied combinations of live action and animation, Disney showed in *Three Caballeros* just how frustrating it was for him not to be making those "full-length subjects."

Three Caballeros premiered in Mexico City on December 21, 1944, and in New York on February 3, 1945. G. S. Eyssell, Radio City Music Hall's managing director—a former Kansas Citian whom Roy Disney had known as a schoolmate[81]—rejected *Three Caballeros* harshly as an attraction for that theater. "Of all the Disney feature length pictures," he wrote to Nelson Rockefeller on November 29, 1944, "this one I feel will have the most limited appeal. . . . It seems to me that aside from its lack of story and continuity, it is a boisterous bore. Even when it becomes an animated travelogue it misses its mark because one gets but a confused and sketchy picture of Latin America." He was not impressed by the film's pyrotechnics, dismissing them as "dull demonstrations of technical virtuosity."[82]

The Three Caballeros performed indifferently at the box office, its returns to the studio falling almost $200,000 short of its cost.[83] A third Latin American feature, *Cuban Carnival,* was in the works throughout 1944, but it fell out of the studio's plans after *Three Caballeros*'s disappointing results. Disney himself smarted under reviews that compared his new films unfavorably with the features he made before the United States entered the war. "I had a lot of people just hoping that it was the end" of the Disney studio, he said in 1956.

Throughout the war, Disney could do no better than assign a few people to work briefly on stories for possible films that had long figured in the studio's plans, like *Peter Pan, Cinderella,* and *Alice in Wonderland.* (Story work on *Peter Pan* was halted "to make room," an internal Disney publication said, for *Victory Through Air Power.*)[84] Of *Alice* in particular, Disney said in 1943 that production might be postponed until, in a contemporary report's paraphrase, "further development of methods which would sharply reduce" production time—and thus keep costs under control.[85]

Any return to full-length animated features of the *Pinocchio* or *Bambi* kind would require financial muscle that was simply not evident in the studio's annual reports to its stockholders. The idea of making cheaper features at the *Dumbo* level, with budgets under a million dollars, never quite died, but Disney continued to regard such projects with little enthusiasm. In May 1943, one possible cheap feature dropped away when Disney and RKO canceled the dormant distribution contract for the Mickey Mouse "beanstalk" feature.[86]

By 1945, the Disney studio had begun to devote "substantially all of its facilities to entertainment product," as the company's annual report for that year said, because of the "general lessening" of the government's demand for training films.[87] But, for the moment, Disney had embraced the idea that animated educational and training films could be a mainstay of his studio's operations in peacetime, too. Such films could speed up training, he said, and help trainees retain more of what they learned. "The screen cartoon," he told a writer for *Look* early in 1945, "has become so improved and refined that no technical problem is unsurmountable *[sic].*"[88] Disney had set up an industrial film division by November 1943, when he visited Owens-Illinois Glass Company in Toledo, Ohio, on what the *Wall Street Journal* called a "preliminary investigation . . . of the place of motion pictures in the post-war industrial world."[89] Five large corporations contracted for Disney training films by November 1944.[90]

In September 1945, as the Disneys emerged from the war's hard grind, they hired two professional managers to share some of their responsibilities. The move made sense, given the nature of the postwar studio as the Disneys envisioned it. John F. Reeder assumed Roy's titles of vice president and general manager. Reeder had been vice president of the Young & Rubicam advertising agency, and he was thus accustomed to dealing with big businesses of the kind that were the likeliest customers for the studio's industrial and educational films.

Fred Leahy, the new production manager, had worked in "production control" for eighteen years at MGM and Paramount, the biggest and most prestigious of the Hollywood studios. He would in effect serve as Walt's stand-in during work on films that inevitably would be, when measured against the prewar shorts and features, too dry and routine to absorb much of Walt's interest. Walt himself gave up his title of president, surrendering it to Roy.[91] He was going to devote himself to new features.

"Commercial work answered our prayers," wrote Harry Tytle, who managed Disney's short subjects, "as it not only supplied badly needed capital during the war, but also because the companies that were our clients gave us greater access to film and other rationed materials. . . . But while the studio made money with this type of product . . . it was not a field either Walt or Roy were happy to be in. Their reasoning was sound. We didn't own the product or the characters we produced for other companies; there was absolutely no residual value. If the picture was successful, the owners of the film got the rerun value. If the films were unsuccessful, it could be detrimental to our reputation. Worse, we were at the whim of the client; at each stage of production we had to twiddle our thumbs and await approval before we could venture on to the next step."[92]

Disney himself said years later that he rejected the idea of making "commercial pictures," saying to his investment bankers, "I think that doing that is a waste of the talent that I have here and I can put it to better purposes by building these features that in the long run pay off better." He made only a dozen commercial films, for clients like Westinghouse Electric (*The Dawn of Better Living*) and General Motors (*The ABC of Hand Tools*), before delivering the last of them in 1946.

The rationale for hiring Leahy and Reeder thus evaporated within months of their hiring. In early 1946, Harry Tytle has written, "Reeder wanted the [production schedule for a feature cartoon, apparently *Make Mine Music*] moved up so that it would fall on a more marketable release date, like Easter or Christmas. An earlier release date meant Walt would have less time to make what he felt was an acceptable picture. Reeder was circumventing Walt—and

Walt didn't like it. . . . Reeder, in a pattern that would repeat itself, was prov-ing inflexible, apparently intent on teaching Walt and Roy the ad business in-stead of learning the studio ropes."[93] (Reeder left the Disney staff in 1948.)

As it happened, *Make Mine Music* did have its premiere in New York on April 20, 1946, the Saturday before Easter, although it did not go into gen-eral release until August (possibly because of the difficulty in the immediate postwar years of getting enough Technicolor prints). Joe Grant, who super-vised production of the film for Disney, spoke of being with him in New York then: "Walking down a street once, during the Easter parade [on Sun-day, April 21, the day after the premiere], he demonstrated some story stuff by walking up and down the curb. People all dressed up for Easter were watch-ing this man wearing a crushed felt hat of some kind, explaining to me this gag, for a feature, I think, and going through all the crazy antics that he would do, with his eyebrow up and down, and so on, and then get back on the street and go on, and probably wind up at the automat for some beans. We stayed at the Sherry-Netherland, or the Pierre, one of those hotels, and instead of eating there, we'd go down to the automat and he'd order chili and beans."[94]

Disney had been thinking about making such package features for years; he brought up the idea during a September 9, 1939, story meeting on *Bambi*. Both *Saludos Amigos* and *The Three Caballeros* had been package features of a sort, but *Make Mine Music* differed from them in having only "music" as a very loose theme. Many of the short cartoons that made up the film were clever but also rather broad and obvious compared with Disney's prewar work, lacking both the emotional richness of a *Dumbo* and the sugared elegance of a *Bambi*. It was not a triumphant return to feature-length animation.

After the war, Disney said in 1956, "it kind of seemed like a hopeless thing to begin to pick up again," and even Roy "was kind of confused. He didn't know what to do. . . . I knew I must diversify. I knew the diversifying of the business would be the salvation of it. . . . I tried these package things, where I'd put five or six things together to make an eighty-minute subject. Because I had a lot of ideas I thought would be good in the cartoon form, if I could go to fifteen minutes with it."

Wilfred Jackson spoke sympathetically in 1973 of Disney's growing dis-engagement from what had been his passion: "Walt wanted so badly for each thing he did to top each thing that he had done before, and he didn't ever want anything to look like a repeat of anything he had done. This made things more and more difficult, as time went on, because there's really only so much you can do with cartoons"—at least, as Jackson wrote later, "along the lines that appealed to him."[95] The "lines that appealed to him" were, of course, those evident in early features like *Snow White* and *Bambi*—full-length stories, told through painstaking productions whose cost was now beyond the studio's reach.

"I think it was just after the war when nothing seemed to stimulate him," Disney's daughter Diane said in 1956. "I could sort of sense it. I could tell he wasn't pleased with anything he was doing."

Disney was, from all evidence, always a loving and attentive father, whose struggles and reverses rarely impinged on his daughters' lives unless they noticed that faint melancholy cast. In an August 1938 letter, Roy Disney mentioned to his mother, Flora, that he and Edna and their only child, Roy Edward, had met Walt and Lillian and the two girls at the merry-go-round in Griffith Park on a Sunday morning.[96] Such visits to the park were a regular thing in the late 1930s and early 1940s, Diane recalled in 1956: "Daddy took us to Sunday school and afterward around to . . . Griffith Park, usually, to the zoo or to amusement parks or something, and he would sit and watch us. . . . Every Sunday we used to go with him. Wherever we wanted to go he'd take us. . . . And then he'd take us over to the studio. And we'd wander around with him from room to room, or while he was in the studio we'd roller skate around the lot. And as we grew older we'd . . . drive around the lot. . . . We learned to drive that way and we had several little disasters."

The girls went to a Christian Science Sunday school for a while. In the fourth grade, Diane attended a Catholic school, and perhaps, from her father's point of view, liked it a little too much: "I wanted to become a nun. . . . I went around at my lunch hour saying prayers in front of statues and everything." Disney sent her to a public school the next two years. Her father believed in God, Diane said, but never went to church. "Not that I remember—ever. I think he had had it and he felt that he wanted us to sample and to make our own choice."[97] Walt and Lillian did not have either daughter baptized. "Dad thought we ought to have our own church. He didn't want anything in our early life to influence us."

The Disney girls remembered no playmates when they were children. On Woking Way, they lived "on the very top of a hill," Sharon said, "and there were no playmates around us." They had friends in school, but not in their own neighborhood, and so their father filled in as what Diane called "just a big playmate. I remember he could do anything. . . . He could throw us around by our heels, you know. I don't know how he did it." Sharon remembered her father as "a great rough-houser when we were little—tossing us up in the air and throwing us around. We loved it. Just loved it. Very patient in things like that."[98]

But not in everything. The temper he could show at work could flare at home, too. "He had quite a temper," Sharon said. "If he was upset about something, Diane or Mother or I could make some comment at the dinner table and set him off and he'd get mad at us. He'd blow up. He would just blow up. And he'd go on about the women in the house and he usually would digress quite a bit. . . . I can't quote him. But I just remember thinking, 'Oh, oh, he's in a bad mood tonight. Watch out.'"[99] Diane also remembered bursts of temper "when my sister and I would monopolize the conversation or fight or something and then he would get furious."[100]

Another source of strain was the presence of Lillian's older sister, Grace Papineau, after she was widowed. (Another sister, Hazel Sewell, and her daughter had lived with the Disneys in the early 1930s after Hazel's marriage to Glen Sewell ended.) Grace "lived with us for ages," Diane Miller told Richard Hubler in 1968. "And a lot of the tension in our home had to do with the fact that there was an outsider at the dinner table every night who couldn't help but pass judgment in family arguments."[101]

In the middle 1940s, around the time World War II ended, Disney installed a projection room in his home. "I used to bring the dailies home" from his earliest live-action productions, he said in 1956—referring to the *rushes,* or film shot the previous day—but he stopped because "my family would come in" and "they'd get so critical" after seeing several versions of a scene. Diane, who was eleven then, remembered that her father "was so excited. And I would sit there . . . and say, 'Oh, that's corny. I don't like that.' I think I was embarrassed by the sentimentality of the scene. And it infuriated him and upset him."[102]

Disney described his daughters—in a wry tone—as "very severe critics" on a radio show in 1946. "They have a favorite expression they use. They say, 'That's corny, Dad.'"[103] Their target was *Song of the South,* a film roughly two-thirds live action and one-third animation that was based on Joel Chandler Harris's Uncle Remus stories. It was the second of Disney's postwar features, released in November 1946. An Uncle Remus feature had been part of the studio's plans since the heady late 1930s; at least two research reports had been written by April 1938.[104] He would have made *Song of the South* as an entirely animated feature, Disney said in 1956, but he "filled in" with live action because "I didn't have enough talent."

Most of the writing of the film, live action and animation alike, took place in mid-1944. "When Walt started *Song of the South,*" the cartoon writer T. Hee said, "we thought he had guys there—including us [Hee and Ed Penner, who had both attended classes on play writing]—who could write the screenplay for it. . . . He said, 'Aw, hell, we've got to get some real writers. You guys aren't writers, you're just cartoonists.'"[105]

When Disney chose someone to write a treatment, though, it was not a seasoned Hollywood screenwriter but Dalton S. Reymond, a native Louisianan who since 1936 had served as a "technical adviser" and "dialogue director" for several films set in the South.[106] He was from all appearances a sort of professional Southerner, but he had no screenwriting credits. His treatment passed into the hands of two real screenwriters, first Maurice Rapf and then Morton Grant, but neither of them had imposing credentials, Grant especially (his career had been devoted mostly to "B" westerns for Warner Brothers).

As director of the live action, Disney chose H. C. Potter, who had directed the live-action portions of *Victory Through Air Power*—scenes shot on a sound stage, in which Alexander de Seversky expounded the ideas in his book. Potter was fired early in work on *Song of the South,* before location filming began—Hedda Hopper reported that "he and Walt couldn't see eye to eye on handling of the story"[107]—and Disney handed direction to Harve Foster. There was nothing especially distinguished about Potter's career, but he had directed a dozen features, whereas Foster had worked until then only as an assistant director. His elevation was clearly a matter of expediency.*

Probably without giving the matter much thought, Disney was transferring to live-action filming attitudes bred in work on his cartoons. In the writing of his animated shorts and features, Disney had arguably contributed more, as an editor, than any of his writers ever had, and his directors' decisions were likewise always subject to his extensive revisions. When he went into live action, he was not looking for writers or directors with strong ideas of their own. In any case, *Song of the South*'s live-action story—sentimental and patronizing toward its black characters, if not "racist" by any reasonable standard—was no more than a frame for the three animated segments based on Harris's Brer Rabbit stories. (Reviewers were much kinder to the brisk and lively cartoons than to the rest of the film.)

The animation got under way in October 1944. Disney was more involved in the details of *Song of the South* than he had been in work on some of the preceding films, said Wilfred Jackson, who directed the animation. "It was easier to get him in on meetings; he'd come in more times just on his own hook to see what was going on, and you had a chance to try things out on him instead of waiting until it was a stale thing and you couldn't bother to bring it up at a meeting."[108]

---

* After *Song of the South,* Foster directed just a few insignificant theatrical features.

The film's live-action exteriors were filmed in Arizona early in 1945; Disney was there for four weeks in February and March. The rest of the film was shot at the Samuel Goldwyn studio in Hollywood. Wilfred Jackson remembered an incident during the filming that gives a rare glimpse of Disney's mind at work in a more urgent circumstance than the transcribed story meetings. The scene involved was a central musical number in which Uncle Remus, played by James Baskett, would begin singing "Zip-A-Dee-Doo-Dah," as the background changed from the darkness of his cabin to a bright, rear-projected cartoon.

"We had painted two backgrounds," Jackson said, "and we had shot a rear-projection scene, which was timed, so that when you synchronized it with the clap-sticks and started the playback [the recording of the song] that Jim Baskett was to work to, it would have the last line of the story he was telling, and the beginning of the song. During the transition, we had a dissolve in the rear-projection background, from the background that was behind him, sitting in his cabin, talking to the little boy, and with the camera close on him, into this springtime scene. After the dissolve, the camera was to dolly back as Jim walked forward on the live-action set. We had the action all worked out so that the right things would be there, included in the camera, as it dollied back."

But there was a hitch:

The rear-projection scene didn't work because we couldn't get the right color balance on the print out of Technicolor on time. . . . The technicalities of it kept putting this scene off, until we were right down to the very end of the live-action shooting. There was no more time on the schedule; the crew was going to be dismissed. The night before, we went down to the [Goldwyn] studio, where we were doing the live-action photography, and in their projection room, we saw the print that we got from Technicolor. It wouldn't do. The cameraman, Gregg Toland, was going to go over to Technicolor to work with them to get a print that we could use the next day. I went home, and I didn't sleep well, because I didn't know just what we were going to do if that didn't come out right. I slept with fingers and toes crossed, hoping we'd have a print we could use. I couldn't think of a way out; I was cornered. . . .

The next day, we came down [to Goldwyn], and Perce Pearce was there—he was Walt's associate producer—and Walt was there. When I saw Walt, I thought, "There's trouble." And there was; the word was that the print wouldn't do. Walt called everybody on the set, and he had them all sit around in chairs, and he had coffee served, and he started talking. First of all, he turned to me and said, "Jack, the print won't do. What plans do you have to work this out, now that the print won't do?" I said, "Walt, I've thought about it, and thought about it, and I don't know what to do." He said, "Well, let's all talk about it, let's see what ideas anybody's got." He called on different people, and some of them had some sort of a notion of just making a scene cut. Of course, I could think of that, but it wasn't going to accomplish the purpose, it wouldn't have given a nice effect. I didn't have to tell Walt you could cut from one scene to another.

Finally, after Walt had asked everybody else, Walt sat back, waited a while, and we all started to sweat. Then Walt said, "Would it be possible, Gregg, to arrange your lights in such a way that you could shine a light up on Jim's face and it wouldn't show on the background, and would it also be possible to have other lights that would light the set up, on signal? When I drop my hand, would it be possible for them to turn on all the other lights and douse that light, simultaneously, so that just in a flash the whole set would light up and you'd find him in this background?" Of course, we had a backdrop that we could use there, to replace the cartoon, because that was going to be used for other scenes in the sequence. Gregg said, "Sure that could work." Walt said, "All right, when Jim sings 'Zip,' we'll change the lights." The thing was ten times as effective as what we had planned. This was Walt Disney at work.[109]

(A cut was necessary when Baskett started walking toward the camera, but only because the blue backdrop wasn't large enough to permit the camera to dolly back as planned. In addition, an animated sunburst was added around Baskett as the lights went up. But the basic effect is the one Disney proposed, and it is as striking and successful as Jackson said.)

One complication was that some of the live action had to allow for animation that would be added later, so that, for example, Uncle Remus and Brer Rabbit could appear on-screen together. During the live-action shooting, Jackson said, Disney "kicked Ken [Anderson] off the camera," because he "was just sure that we were wasting a lot of time." But since Anderson could not ride the camera boom, and give the operator a tap "at the right time to do certain things with the camera to make room for our cartoon character," the footage was unusable.[110] Disney, confined so tightly by his studio's precarious finances for the previous few years, could not have welcomed one more constraint. To plan the live-action filming so carefully was to acknowledge from the start that combination work was terribly confining; better to put off that acknowledgment until it could no longer be avoided.

Peacetime did not bring an improvement in the studio's finances. Without the prop of contracts for government and industrial films, and with foreign earnings once again possible but locked up by widespread embargoes on the export of currencies, the Disneys had to rely mainly on domestic receipts from their entertainment shorts and features. Only through reissues of *Snow White* and *Pinocchio* did the studio avoid showing losses in its 1945 and 1946 fiscal years (the Disney fiscal year ended around September 30). It was a measure of the Disneys' difficulties that in March 1946, Roy Disney asked RKO for a million-dollar advance on the earnings from foreign distribution of Disney films whose release overseas had been held up by the war, and whose release would now be complicated by currency restrictions like those that prevented the exchange of British pounds for dollars.[111] RKO's executives were taken aback by the request; Ned E. Depinet, RKO's executive vice president, wrote to N. Peter Rathvon, the company's president, that "Roy's proposal really baffles me . . . he is indeed asking us to assume a great burden."[112]

Harry Tytle wrote about that loan request in a diary entry of July 15, 1946, after Paul Pease, the studio's controller, came to see him. Tytle reproduced that entry in his autobiography fifty years later: "Paul's problem was money. It appears we are spending it much faster than we are getting it! Our salvation is a million dollar loan from R.K.O., and Paul indicates it is even possible for this loan not to go through. In that case, we are in bad straights *[sic]* and would have to cut [personnel] drastically. Also, the loan at the bank is $4,000,000 and his opinion is that it cannot be raised, and we are bouncing very close to that ceiling. Paul is scraping up all the possible funds in order to stall until the loan comes through. Two points that are making things increasingly difficult at this time (first) the live-action payrolls are very heavy and secondly, we may be forced to pay a large retroactive check, somewhere in the neighborhood of $200,000."

That "retroactive check" would go to members of the Screen Cartoonists Guild, which was insisting on a 25 percent increase in base pay, part of it retroactive, as a condition of continued negotiations. "The emotional climate at the studio during this time was extremely tense," Harry Tytle wrote. "I noted at the time that one of our cartoon directors 'almost poked someone' from the cartoonist's *[sic]* union who was talking strike."[113]

In August 1946, the Disney studio laid off 459 employees, leaving 614 on the staff. RKO eventually agreed to Roy's request, advancing the money on October 15, 1946, and getting in return expanded foreign distribution rights. Thanks presumably to this loan, by the end of the year the net reduction in the number of employees was smaller, but still more than three hundred. The total number on the staff was now under eight hundred, or about two-thirds the prewar total.[114] As employment bobbed up and down, an inevitable effect was to fray any ties of loyalty that many Disney employees may have felt to their employer. Such fluctuations banished remnants of the idea that employment at the Disney studio was a higher calling. For most of the people working there it was, by the mid-1940s, emphatically a job; to regard it as something more was to solicit disappointment.

In these difficult times, Walt Disney's habits of command were increasingly troublesome to some of those who worked for him. One "dilemma we faced with Walt," Tytle wrote, was that "for him, making the picture was 'job one'—the budget ran a distant second. But as we had seen with the shorts program, if the budgets were ignored long enough, we all suffered." The Disney shorts cost about twice as much as the shorts made by the other cartoon studios, and by 1946, both Disney brothers had concluded that short subjects were a losing proposition.[115]

There was a related problem. A number of times, as Harry Tytle wrote, Disney's "husbanding of authority proved to be an expensive bottleneck," in particular because of the "lack of story inventory."[116] If Disney would not make decisions and let stories move forward into animation, the people making his short cartoons would be left without work or would spend their time redoing what they had already done.

But Disney was, as always, the absolute ruler of his studio. Joe Grant spoke of what happened when he supervised *Make Mine Music* and tried to make his decisions stick: "On a picture like that, if there's something you don't like, you almost had to go in on Walt's coattails and put him in front of you. . . . There was only one authority in that studio: Walt. That was the final signature on everything."[117]

Periodic efforts, by Disney or members of his staff, to work around the consequences of his absolute rule almost invariably failed, and members of the staff were left, as before, trying to find ways to manipulate him so that production could move forward. Jack Kinney remembered writing the "All the Cats Join In" segment for *Make Mine Music* with Lance Nolley and Don DaGradi: "We did some very rough sketches—scratches. . . . We put them up for staging, and the business," using only one pushpin for each drawing. "He came in, and we went through the story, and he says, 'This needs tightening up. Tighten it up, and call me in'"—meaning, make the action itself more pointed and economical. "So we tightened it up," Kinney said. "We got Tom Oreb, and he took the same drawings, and put them underneath his drawing board [and made more polished versions of the same sketches]. This time we put two or three pushpins in each drawing. Walt came in and he said, 'Yeah, yeah, that's fine.'"[118]

It is easy to picture the Walt Disney of the middle and late 1940s: distracted, financially pressed, and impatient to put films into the marketplace and begin collecting rentals. It was in work on his short subjects that this Disney was most clearly visible. He now looked for nothing more in his short subjects than reassuring gestures—synthetic cuteness, perfunctory bows toward narrative logic. That such gestures were employed feebly mattered less than that a short cartoon was recognizably "Disney." Disney and his people were willing to settle for much less than they would have found acceptable a few years earlier. Exhibitors and theater audiences had responded. Whatever their residual fondness for Disney characters like Mickey Mouse and Donald Duck, they had by the middle 1940s transferred their loyalties to more aggressively comic rivals, particularly Bugs Bunny, from Warner Brothers, and Tom and Jerry, from MGM.

Except in 1938, when he assigned them to David Hand, Disney seems never to have delegated supervision of the shorts entirely to their directors, or to anyone else. Disney—so much the small businessman in other ways—was one here, too, retaining control even though he could no longer exercise it effectively. During story work on the shorts in the mid-1940s, the sketch artist Eldon Dedini said, "Walt Disney was there for the final meeting. Then there was a yes or no. When we had a meeting at 11 o'clock, from 8:30 till 11 we were going to the bathroom about every ten minutes."

Dedini, who had not worked at the Disney studio in earlier years, still found it an attractive and stimulating place to work. He recalled "great enthusiasm. . . . There was a lot of in-house foolishness—which I think was wonderful, because, after all, that's eventually what had to show up on the screen. You almost had to be it to do it."[119]

Other people, who had been on the staff in better times, measured the postwar atmosphere against those memories. The animator Marc Davis said of Disney: "I've heard Walt say that he liked to put people together who were in conflict with one another, because he probably got a better result. I never fully understood this, but I guess he was just putting another kind of pressure on you, the pressure of having a contest with the guy you're working with. . . . He felt that if any two guys got along too well, they became complacent." When Davis and Ken Anderson worked together briefly as a story team in the late 1940s, and Davis told Disney they had enjoyed the collaboration, Disney replied: "What do you guys want to do, sleep together?"[120]

There was friction throughout the studio. The writer Ralph Wright spoke of the story department: "The jealousy in that place, my God! You never heard anybody say . . . it was too bad somebody lost a story. There was kind of a sadistic delight in it: 'Walt kicked all his stuff out.'"[121] Said Homer Brightman, another writer: "Walt was a hard man to get on with, he really was, because he was very temperamental and changeable, and he was a perfectionist. He believed that if you can go this far you can go that far. Money didn't mean anything to him, and he didn't think that the fellows should really be interested in money. . . . He would take all the pains in the world to get a picture the way he thought it should be, but he didn't think about the people working on it, they didn't count, they were cogs in the machine. And he took all the bows."[122]

Brightman was a jaundiced witness—Disney eventually fired him—but his portrait is consistent with what others observed. For Disney, the muffled conflict that characterized his relations with his employees had become the natural state of affairs. There had been competition throughout the studio before the war, of course—the difference was that such competition was no longer secondary to making ever-better cartoons.

In mid-1946, Disney was still talking ambitiously of making three features a year, weighted toward combinations of animation and live action. He spoke to the Hollywood columnist Hedda Hopper of an *Alice in Wonderland* in which Alice would be a real girl, played by Luana Patten (one of the two child leads in *Song of the South*), of yet another Latin American feature, and of *The Little People,* a feature set in Ireland.[123] Disney visited England and Ireland in November 1946, his first trip to Europe since the end of the war.[124]

The big layoffs in August 1946 derailed some possible features. Jim Algar and Frank Thomas were codirecting *Wind in the Willows* until it was shelved again after the layoffs. But *Alice*—in its original form a loosely connected string of bizarre episodes—at least promised to lend itself to adaptation as one of the new combination features: it could easily be envisioned as a collection of animated short subjects, with a live-action Alice as the bridge connecting them. And about all that the Disney studio could now do reasonably well, it had become clear by the end of 1946, was make short cartoons— not traditional shorts, but the kind embedded in features as different as *Make Mine Music* and *Song of the South.*

CHAPTER 7

"Caprices and Spurts of Childishness"

Escaping from Animation
1947–1953

Walt Disney was a founding member of a conservative organization called the Motion Picture Alliance for the Preservation of American Ideals—others of its leaders included the directors Sam Wood, Norman Taurog, and Clarence Brown—which vowed its opposition to "the effort of Communist, Fascist, and other totalitarian-minded groups to pervert this powerful medium into an instrument for the dissemination of un-American ideas and beliefs."[1] At the alliance's first meeting at the Beverly Wilshire Hotel on February 4, 1944, most of the speakers attacked only the Communists. Disney was present—and was elected as the organization's first vice president—but did not speak.[2]

He was not an aggressive Red hunter; his conservatism had a strongly personal cast. An employee's politics were not of any particular concern to him if that employee was not challenging him as Art Babbitt and Dave Hilberman had. Some of Disney's employees, like Ward Kimball, flourished even though it was no secret that their politics were far more liberal than his. Maurice Rapf, who worked for Disney as a live-action screenwriter for two and a half years in the middle 1940s, was an extreme example. He wrote many years later that Disney "knew very well that I was a dedicated left-winger. He may even have known that I was a Communist. He certainly knew that I was Jewish."[3] When Rapf left the studio in 1947, it was not because of his politics but because Disney refused him a raise.

Rapf's politics were, however, not a matter of public record: "Whether I would have been fired later in the year when I was named as a Communist at the hearings of the [House Committee on Un-American Activities], where Disney appeared as a friendly witness, I will never know."[4]

Disney testified in Washington on October 24, 1947, during highly publicized hearings on Communist infiltration of the movie industry; he was the principal witness on that Friday. Speaking of the strike, he said, "I definitely feel it was a Communist group trying to take over my artists and they did take them over." He denounced Hilberman as the "real brains" behind the strike. "I believe he is a Communist. . . . I looked into his record and I found that, No. 1, that he had no religion and, No. 2, that he had spent considerable time at the Moscow Art Theater studying art direction or something."

(As vocal as he was in his dislike for Hilberman, nothing indicates that Disney pursued a vendetta against his old adversary. He held grudges, certainly, but he seems to have acted on them rarely. By 1947, Hilberman was in New York, as one of the proprietors of a new commercial animation studio called Tempo. "But we had just knocked on a couple of doors; nobody knew us, so [Disney's testimony] had no impact," he said in 1976. "We were able to grow without that affecting us at all."[5] It was in the early 1950s, long after Disney's testimony, that Hilberman and Tempo suffered for their Communist connections.)

Asked his opinion of the Communist Party, Disney replied: "The thing that I resent most is that they are able to get into these unions, take them over, and represent to the world that a group of people that are in my plant, that I know are good, 100-percent Americans, are trapped by this group, and they are represented to the world as supporting all of those ideologies, and it is not so, and I feel that they really ought to be smoked out and shown up for what they are, so that all of the good, free causes in this country, all the liberalisms that really are American, can go out without the taint of communism."[6]

As always, Disney was refusing to concede that the strike might have had causes other than the Communist affiliations of some of its leaders.

Harry Tytle contrasted Walt with his elder brother: "Roy relished the flexibility, the give-and-take approach in studio relationships . . . and he wanted others to be the same way. . . . Walt was not prone to praise people directly. Perhaps he was afraid it would prompt them to ask for an increase which they didn't deserve, maybe he thought it would make them overconfident. Roy, on the other hand, was effusive when he felt praise was due, and Roy was not only generous with praise but also with other, more tangible rewards. . . . Thus, while both Walt and Roy were truly family men, Roy's interest in the domestic side *included* those at work; for Walt, the two worlds were quite separate."[7]

Outside the studio, Disney certainly knew a great many people, but he was also a self-isolated figure. "He really didn't have time to make friends,"

Lillian Disney said. "Sam Goldwyn was one . . . but we very seldom saw him socially. Walt had too much to do. He had to have a clear mind for work the next day." Lillian herself rarely talked with her husband about his work. "As a rule I never paid much attention to the studio," she said. "Walt was all I had contact with."[8]

Sharon Disney Brown remembered that her father "never brought [studio business] home. If he was terribly enthused . . . he'd start talking about a funny scene or something. . . . But other than that he never really talked that much about it. . . . If he was enthusiastic he was just going to talk whether we listened or not. . . . Once in a while [her mother would] make some remark, something like, 'Well, I don't think that's too funny.' And he'd say, 'Well, you don't know anything about it anyway.' That would be the end of it."[9]

After dinner, Disney read scripts.

In the postwar years, live action—with its real scripts—was an increasingly large part of Disney's plans. In the spring of 1947, he envisioned several combination features, including *Treasure Island* and a Hans Christian Andersen feature.[10] One all-live-action feature was also held up by Roy Disney as a possibility in a letter to N. Peter Rathvon, RKO's president. *Children of the Covered Wagon,* based on a 1943 novel by Mary Jane Carr, would have been a vehicle for Disney's two child stars of *Song of the South,* Bobby Driscoll and Luana Patten.[11]

Disney had already begun work in 1946 on a combination feature called *How Dear to My Heart* (based on a Sterling North book called *Midnight and Jeremiah*); production eventually stretched well into 1948. The film was released early in 1949 as *So Dear to My Heart.* This was a film set at the turn of the century, around the time of Disney's own boyhood, in a small midwestern town that inevitably recalled Marceline, Missouri, and with a boy protagonist, Jeremiah (played by Bobby Driscoll), who loves a black lamb, just as Disney loved the animals on the Disney farm.

Animation was always part of the plan. Although some early reports suggested that Disney's original thought was to make a combination feature with an animated lamb, the idea was probably always to add animation as musical inserts, similar to those in *Song of the South.*[12] Contractually, Disney had little choice but to add animation in some form. His distribution contract with RKO for four features provided that each feature, *So Dear* one of them, "shall be an animated cartoon or may be part animated cartoon and part live action."[13] There was no provision for a feature wholly in live action.

Card Walker, then a rising young studio executive, remembered that the inserts, as brief as they are—about fifteen minutes in total—added a year to production (the animation was not completed until August 1948, well over a year after the live-action filming). "One picture he really spent a lot of time on was *So Dear to My Heart,*" Walker said. "Boy, he spent a lot of time. . . . He knew he had a problem. And that's when he went back and started building those little vignettes in there in animation. He was working to improve it, to make it better."[14]

Absent characters as strong as those in *Song of the South*'s cartoon sequences, there was no way that animated inserts could give more spine to a sweet-tempered, sentimental, and very slight story in which Disney had indulged his nostalgia for his childhood. *So Dear to My Heart,* like *Song of the South,* is a movie populated mostly by children and old people—like the childhood Disney remembered in Marceline, when he spent much of his time with Doc Sherwood and Grandpa Taylor—with no young adults in sight. The animation is superfluous at best.

In his work on the dominant live-action portions of *So Dear to My Heart,* Disney refined the pattern for his involvement in live action he had begun to establish in work on *Song of the South.* He would be heavily involved in the writing of the screenplay and the casting of the film; he would hire a reliable journeyman director—for *So Dear to My Heart* it was Harold D. Schuster, who had directed the horse picture *My Friend Flicka* not long before—to do the actual shooting, with limited input from Disney himself; and he would be heavily involved again in the final phases, like the editing and musical scoring.

Schuster, who filmed most of *So Dear to My Heart* in the summer of 1946 at Porterville, in the San Joaquin Valley in central California (a stand-in for the book's Indiana), told Leonard Maltin that "Walt would come up sometimes on weekends, we would have Sunday breakfast, and talk over the [film that Schuster had recently shot]. . . . His suggestions were always presented as suggestions only. He left the reins firmly in my hands."[15]

Disney never had any reason to believe that his director would use his grip on the "reins" to impose any distinctive ideas of his own on the film. He was making a trade-off. *So Dear to My Heart* and the live-action films that followed would lack the artistry that only a strong director could bring, but they would be more purely Walt Disney films. Since, as a practical matter, there was no way he could oversee most of the shooting of a live-action film, Disney would make his films his own by reducing the importance of what happened on the set as much as possible, and by elevating the importance of what happened before and after shooting. Whether such a trade-off would result in better films was very much in doubt, but Disney's preference for strengthening his control over his films was in keeping with his history.

So Dear to My Heart, if no disaster at the box office, was by no means a success either, earning $2.7 million in gross rentals (shared by Disney and RKO) against a negative cost of $2.1 million.

Animation was still the studio's lifeblood, and in early 1947, when live-action filming for *So Dear to My Heart* had resumed for another seven weeks, Disney was completing another animated package feature, *Fun and Fancy Free.* It was made up of what was usable from the scrapped "Jack and the Beanstalk" feature with Mickey Mouse, plus "Bongo," based on a Sinclair Lewis fantasy about a circus bear that had been published in *Cosmopolitan* in 1930. The two halves were stitched together with live action of Luana Patten, the ventriloquist Edgar Bergen, and Bergen's dummies Charlie McCarthy and Mortimer Snerd.

By then, two more package features, *All in Fun* (released in 1948 as *Melody Time*) and *Two Fabulous Characters* (released in 1949 as *The Adventures of Ichabod and Mr. Toad*), were on the schedule. It was clear from the middling performance of *Make Mine Music* that package features were a financial question mark—they might turn a small profit or at least recoup their costs, but they held the threat, too, of losses that the studio could not afford. There was no reason to hope that any of them would be a breakout hit and put the Disney studio on sound financial footing.

"I like our operation the way it is," Disney said in 1955. "I wouldn't want the responsibility of a big studio. We were asked to run RKO before Howard Hughes bought it [in May 1948], but I turned it down."[16] That was in all likelihood a fanciful interpretation of a desperate passage in the Disney studio's fortunes, in the spring of 1947; or Disney simply may not have been fully aware of what was going on around him.

Walt Disney Productions and RKO were in negotiations for two months, from April till June 1947, over a combination of some sort that almost certainly did not amount to Disney's being "asked to run RKO." Jonathan Bell Lovelace, a Los Angeles investment manager and a new member of the Disney board, was the lead negotiator on the Disney side. The idea seems to have been that the two studios would combine many overhead functions and perhaps share production facilities on the Disney lot.

At RKO's request, the Disney studio produced dozens of pages of detailed information about its financial status and production plans, a clear indication that Disney—which apparently initiated the talks—would have been the junior partner in such a combination. These negotiations took place, after all, only a few months after Disney was so desperate for cash that it pleaded with RKO for a million-dollar loan. Walt Disney was from all appearances only peripherally involved in the negotiations, but he was Walt Disney Productions' most important asset. Correspondence among the negotiators reflected concern that he not be distressed by the outcome.[17]

The negotiations apparently petered out in early June. It was around then that Floyd Odlum, RKO's principal owner through his Atlas Corporation, took the first steps toward the eventual sale of the studio to Howard Hughes. On Disney's side, receipts from *Make Mine Music* and *Song of the South* were providing a welcome breathing spell. Both films were modestly profitable, returning to the studio a total of more than a million dollars in rentals above their costs. In the fiscal year that ended in September 1947—the month that *Fun and Fancy Free* was released—Walt Disney Productions' bank debt fell from an intimidating $4.2 million to a more manageable $3 million.[18]

It was around this time—with the studio on reasonably solid financial footing but the prospects for its features dubious—that the Disney brothers had one of their loudest and most consequential disagreements. Even though Walt Disney Productions was now a public company and outsiders had been allowed to own common stock since June 1945—Odlum's Atlas Corporation was the first such buyer, in a special transaction, of shares representing about 7 percent of the total—Walt and Roy and their wives still owned more than half the common stock, and so arguments about the company's course had an intensely personal flavor.[19]

"I wanted to get back into the feature field," Walt Disney said in 1956—that is, he wanted to make more full-length features like *Snow White* and *Bambi*. "But it was a matter of investment and time. Now, to take and do a good cartoon feature takes a lot of time and a lot of money. But I wanted to get back. And my brother and I had quite a screamer. . . . It was one of my big upsets. . . . I said we're going to either go forward, we're going to get back in business, or I say let's liquidate or let's sell out. . . . I said, I can't run this plant without being able to make decisions. I said, I have to plan not a year ahead but two years ahead. I have to take care of these artists, and overlap between productions. I have to keep the whole thing going."

Roy Disney remembered that disagreement as "one of the biggest differences we had in our lives. . . . I remember one night he came down to my office, we sat here from quitting time to eight o'clock or so and I finally said, 'Look, you're letting this place drive you nuts, that's one place I'm not going with you.'

I walked out on him. So, I didn't sleep that night, and he didn't, either. So the next morning, I'm at my desk, wondering what the hell to do. . . . I heard his cough and footsteps coming down the hall. He came in and he was filled up, he could hardly talk. He says, 'Isn't it amazing what a horse's ass a fella can be sometimes? . . . That's how we settled our differences."[20]

By the beginning of 1948 the Disney studio was firmly on track to make its first full-length feature since *Bambi*. In Roy's recollection, though, the substance of his disagreement with Walt was not over making such a feature but over whether the studio should resume work on *Alice in Wonderland* and *Peter Pan*, two features that had been shelved during the war. Roy found both subjects unappealing as film properties. Walt won the argument—"Walt always had his way around here," Roy said—and *Alice* and *Peter Pan* remained on the schedule; yet the first full-length feature would be neither of those films, but *Cinderella*, another story that had been considered as a possible feature since 1938, at least.[21]

Cinderella was Disney's riskiest and most important—in terms of the studio's fate—feature since *Snow White and the Seven Dwarfs*. There was, however, no excitement surrounding the start of work on *Cinderella* to match the fever that had attended the writing and animation of *Snow White*. To thrive, the studio needed a success, but no one thought *Cinderella* would be an equivalent leap forward in the art of animation.

With his feature films a source of limited satisfaction, Disney had begun exploring other kinds of film—nature films, in particular. It was when he had live-action film of deer shot for his *Bambi* animators, Disney said, that he began thinking about the potential in nature films "because I did get some very unusual things. And I just had a feeling if we could get a cameraman out there to stay long enough we could really get some unusual things." Disney was intrigued by Alaska, too. He watched sixteen-millimeter film from that remote territory as early as February 14, 1946.[22] He had hired a husband-and-wife team to film Alaska, he said in 1956, to "see if I couldn't do something in an educational way. . . . During the war I ran into a lot of educators, and they kept talking of the need of good films and kept emphasizing the fact that we could do a lot in that field."

The studio had bought hundreds of hours of such sixteen-millimeter film; a May 1947 story inventory report said, "We have 482 rolls of Kodachrome shot in Alaska."[23] Disney's film editors were then making a "rough edit" of that film and blowing it up to the thirty-five-millimeter size used in theatrical projection. One appealing possibility was to use it in a film resembling *Saludos Amigos*, tying together cartoons set in Alaska with live action filmed there.[24] Any release made from this film would be a bargain; the studio had invested less than $75,000 in it.

In the summer of 1947, Disney seized an opportunity to indulge both his curiosity about Alaska and his enthusiasm for aviation. He left August 10 on a three-week flying trip to Alaska with Russell Havenstrite, an oilman and polo-playing friend. When Lillian bowed out, Sharon, then ten years old, went with her father.

"I enjoyed being with him and I was always game to go anyplace with him," Sharon said in 1968. "When he'd want to go up in the airplanes I'd always go to the airport with him, and sit there and watch the airplanes come in. . . . He wanted to fly. He wanted to fly very badly. . . . He constantly talked about it. . . . He always wanted to get in a plane and fly."

The Alaska trip as Sharon remembered it took them—first in Havenstrite's DC-3 and then in a smaller plane—from Juneau to Anchorage to Nome, and then to a tiny Inuit village "where we slept in an airplane hangar. . . . I thought it was all great fun, you know—it was filthy, but I thought it was great fun. And then from there to Kotzebue and Kobuk and we stayed in a camp at the base of Mount McKinley. . . . A lot of this was in single-engine planes, and it was quite a rough trip."

During the trip, she said, "Daddy was the picture of patience, really. I don't know how he did it. You know, braiding my hair every morning—long hair down the back. . . . He took care of me . . . he did more, I think, than most fathers would do just as far as being a mother and father."

Sharon recalled "one incident. When we flew from Nome to Candle [the Inuit village], we had two very small planes. I think there was the pilot and room for three passengers. We took off and we lost our radio. We were above the clouds and we didn't know where we were. Of course, I didn't know this . . . but Daddy and [Havenstrite] . . . knew we might crash into a mountain. . . . [Havenstrite] had just become a grandfather for the first time and on that premise they decided to get loaded. . . . We finally came out of the clouds and landed in Candle. They put the steps down and Daddy took one step down and landed flat on his face."[25]

In April 1948, Disney floated vague plans for films about Alaska—a possible feature with or without animation, a possible short subject devoted to seals in the Pribilof Islands.[26] Before long, "I abandoned the Alaskan [feature] project," Disney said—much of the footage was just plain dull, apparently—but he followed through with the short subject. "I took the film that I'd shot about the seals on this island," he said, and "wrapped it up and made it as an entertainment package." By June, that film, *Seal Island,* photographed by the husband-and-wife team of Alfred and Elma Milotte, was complete except for the narration, and Disney was calling it the first in a series of documentaries, *True-Life Adventures*.[27]

Seal Island won an Academy Award after it played for one week in December 1948 at a theater in Pasadena. Despite the Oscar, RKO resisted distributing the *True-Life Adventures* at first—*Seal Island*'s length, just under a half hour, was awkward at a time when many theaters showed double features—but finally agreed in May 1949 to distribute *Seal Island* and two more.[28] This time RKO's reluctance was misplaced: *Seal Island*, made at a cost of $86,000, grossed $434,000.

James Algar, *Seal Island*'s director, wrote the next year that the *True-Life Adventures* series was "based on the premise that information can be entertainment if interestingly presented. . . . Too many so-called educational films fall under the supervision of people who know their subject thoroughly but their medium very little. They remind us in the film business of some of the technical advisers assigned to training films during the war. A technical expert usually loves his subject. . . . So he makes a film which takes for granted that you are interested and want to learn. And sadly enough, the thing turns out dull and fails of its purpose. One of the first lessons of film making in the entertainment field is this: you must win your audience. All entertainers know this, instinctively. And it is a discipline that can well be carried over into the teaching film of the future. It is in this respect, perhaps, that *Seal Island* offers something new."[29]

In other words, the *True-Life Adventures* were another channel for the impulse that had briefly made Disney enthusiastic about the potential for sponsored films around the end of the war. Now, though, his films could be "educational" without being subject to constraints imposed by third parties. Disney made the connection himself in an interview that coincided with *Seal Island*'s Los Angeles debut. "I learned much during the war years," he said, "when we were making instruction and technological films in which abstract and obscure things had to be made plain and quickly for the boys in military services. . . . I began, with the return of peace, to plan the informative-entertainment series which now has jelled in the True-Life Adventures."[30]

The succeeding *True-Life Adventures* won more Oscars and a great deal of mostly favorable attention, as well as more than paying their way. *Seal Island* was no fluke: the second *True-Life Adventure*, *Beaver Valley*, cost only a little more, at $102,000, but grossed far more, at $664,000. Disney wrote in his company's annual report for 1950, after the release of *Beaver Valley*: "In my years in the motion picture business I never had more enjoyment than I am getting out of the production of our True Life Adventure series. They have completely fascinated me."[31] There is no reason to doubt him, even though making a *True-Life Adventure* was very different from making an animated feature, or a live-action feature of the usual kind. Disney sent photographers into the wild for months at a time, or sometimes longer. He also pieced together films—*Water Birds* (1952) was one—by buying film from "these naturalists who'd shoot birds." Although shooting would begin with a distinct end product in mind, Algar's principal role, as director, was to sort through hour after hour of film in search of some kind of narrative.

Disney found irresistible the temptation to manipulate film, as well as the animals themselves, to tell coherent stories. This is evident in *Seal Island* during an episode about a pup that cannot find its mother. Winston Hibler, who wrote the narration with Algar and then delivered it for the film itself, remembered that "we wrote the narration first and built the picture track afterwards."[32] The frequent cuts, the multitude of camera angles, the close-ups and long shots—all argue that the "story" has been at least as much manufactured as recorded, by taking advantage of how indistinguishable, to human eyes, at least, seals are one from the other. What is supposed to be one pup could just as well be several. There was more of the same in the *True-Life Adventures* that followed, and there was aggressive tinkering with the raw footage, too. Through optical printing, repeats and reverses and other patterns that had no parallels in nature could be imposed on animals' movements.

As much as he enjoyed working on the *True-Life Adventures,* their scale was too small to command Disney's full attention the way his early feature films did. Disney, a man always happiest when he was excited about some new project, was primed for a fresh enthusiasm. He found it in a new hobby. Trains were it.

It was sometime before Christmas 1947 that Ward Kimball alerted Ollie Johnston that Disney had a model train layout set up in his office suite. Disney wrote about the train layout to his sister, Ruth Beecher, on December 8, 1947: "I bought myself a birthday-Christmas present—something I've wanted all my life—an electric train. . . . What fun I'm having. I have it set up in one of the outer rooms adjoining my office so I can play with it in my spare moments. It's a freight train with a whistle, and real smoke comes out of the smokestack—there are switches, semaphores, station and everything. It's just wonderful!"[33]

While the men were looking at the layout, Johnston said, Disney "turned to me and said, 'I didn't know you were interested in trains.' I told him I was building a [miniature] steam engine. He said, 'You are? I always wanted a backyard railroad.' And so he came out to where we were building mine, out in Santa Monica, and looked at it. He came out two or three times, and he started getting his ideas on how he was going to build his."[34]

Not only had Disney bought a model railroad as a present for himself, but he had also bought three other Lionel train sets after asking Ruth, his brother Herbert, and Marjorie Davis, his sister-in-law Hazel's daughter, if children in their families would like a train set, too.[35] Roger Broggie, the head of the studio's machine shop, had joined the Disney staff in 1939, but he remembered that he first had "direct contact with Walt" in the weeks before that same Christmas, in 1947, when "he came down to the shop and he wanted to [do] an HO gauge [the standard track size for small electric trains] for a nephew. . . . So we put it together on a track about as big as this table, on a thing that was supposed to be hoisted up in the garage. We put the trains together and he worked on it, the landscaping, the whole bit. . . . We got through with that and then . . . he wanted to know—'This is an electric train, now what's for real?' So I looked into what we call 'Live Steam'"—that is, miniature trains that were functionally identical to real ones.

Disney and Broggie looked at the "equipment that was available," Broggie said, "and he didn't like it. The style was more or less a modern steam locomotive, and he wanted something earlier." Broggie showed Disney photographs of nineteenth-century locomotives, and Disney settled on Central Pacific Railroad no. 173, a locomotive built in 1864 (and rebuilt in 1873, after a fatal crash). "He liked the looks of the thing," Broggie said.

Broggie wrote to the Southern Pacific, which had absorbed the Central Pacific line, and "I asked them for any historical information about Locomotive no. 173 Central Pacific and we got a blueprint. And from that print and the photograph we then made drawings. The draftsman who did the job, Eddie Sargeant . . . was a very meticulous draftsman. With a glass, and the photograph and this blueprint, he made the drawings, then we made the patterns." Sargeant began making the drawings in September 1948.[36]

In the meantime, on June 1, 1948, Walt and Lillian Disney had bought a five-acre lot at 355 North Carolwood Drive in Holmby Hills, a luxury residential development next to Beverly Hills, northeast of the campus of the University of California at Los Angeles. Once again, as with his previous two homes, Disney was building rather than buying an existing home—a pattern he observed with his weekend homes at Palm Springs as well as his principal residence. One attraction of the Carolwood lot was that it had room enough for a layout designed for trains one-eighth real size. Lillian and Diane had found another site they liked, Lillian said in 1968, "but Walt said it was too close to Wilshire [Boulevard] and [had] no place for his train."[37]

In August, Disney attended the Chicago Railroad Fair of 1948, the single most important driver in his growing enthusiasm for miniature trains. "The stated reason for the celebration," Karal Ann Marling has written, "was the hundredth anniversary of the first steam locomotive to enter Chicago, the nation's greatest railroad center. The real reason was to revive an industry hard hit by competition and burdened with an inventory of rolling stock all but worn out by hard use during World War II. . . . Experts had put the number of railroad hobbyists and model makers at one hundred thousand; their total investment ran to some $10 million. Organizers of the Chicago fair of 1948 were eager to tap this reservoir of interest and goodwill. And so, with a perfunctory nod to tomorrow, they set out to indulge the growing American appetite for cow-catchers, pistons, smokestacks, old cabooses—and the fabled historical romance of the rails."[38]

Disney invited Kimball, the Disney studio's most advanced railroad buff, to make the trip to Chicago with him. (Kimball owned not miniatures but real locomotives, which Disney had seen, and operated on at least one occasion, on visits to the Kimball home in San Gabriel.) They left Los Angeles for Chicago by train—of course—on August 19 and spent several days at the fair. Its highlight was a huge pageant, "Wheels a-Rolling," that incorporated any number of historic steam locomotives as well as modern diesels. Pat Devlin, an actor in the pageant, remembered persuading Disney to perform on stage one night dressed in nineteenth-century costume (what Devlin called a "Diamond Jim Brady" outfit).[39]

Kimball's home movies from the trip "show Disney in a state of unrestrained bliss from the moment the Santa Fe Super Chief left the Pasadena station," Marling has written. "The railroad knew he was coming; the engineer let him ride in the cab and toot the whistle at level crossings. The fair had acres of famous engines and working replicas thereof and Kimball's film suggests that the pair inspected every last one of them. Disney caught Kimball at the throttle of an ancient engine; Kimball, in turn, took pictures of Disney, in a top hat and vest [evidently the Diamond Jim Brady costume], acting the part of a hungry passenger stopping to dine at a trackside Harvey House," in the eighth of the dozen scenes that made up the "Wheels a-Rolling" pageant.[40]

The fair included what the official guidebook called "fifty dramatized acres of exhibits"—"themed" exhibits, in fact, in which participating railroads recreated scenes that a rail traveler might see on their lines. The Santa Fe's exhibit was an Indian village where members of six southwestern tribes practiced traditional crafts and performed traditional dances. At a trading post run by the Fred Harvey Company, visitors could buy Indian curios as well as admire displays of them.[41]

Before returning to Los Angeles, Disney and Kimball also went to Dearborn, Michigan, outside Detroit, and visited a village of another kind—Henry Ford's Greenfield Village, a collection of old and reconstructed buildings that included the Wright brothers' bicycle shop and a replica of Thomas Edison's laboratory. Greenfield Village, which Ford established in 1929, had a strong autobiographical element: many of its buildings were there because they had been significant in Ford's life, as with the school he attended and the scaled-down replica of his first auto plant. Greenfield was, besides, a make-believe village, a mixture of buildings spanning centuries. There was no pretense, as at Colonial Williamsburg, of re-creating the past.

Disney had visited Greenfield Village at least once before, in April 1940, but this time he returned to Burbank with his imagination stimulated. He was thinking now beyond a miniature train for his own home. He drafted a memorandum on August 31, 1948, in which he set out in detail what might go into a "Mickey Mouse park" on the sixteen acres the studio owned across Riverside Drive. Ford's influence can be felt in Disney's description of an idyllic small town, anchored by a city hall and a railroad station. There would have been a specifically Disney presence in the park only through a toy store that sold Disney toys and books and a shop where Disney artists could sell their own work.[42]

Disney had been talking about a park of some kind, on the studio lot or adjacent to it, for years, perhaps since the late 1930s, the idea being to have something to entertain visitors to a studio that was otherwise very much a workaday place. For the studio to embark on such a project in 1948 was impractical, though, given its financial condition, and Disney's memo had no immediate consequences.

Eddie Sargeant had translated the original blueprints for no. 173 Central Pacific into drawings of the proper scale by January 1949. Roger Broggie then parceled the work out to the shop's machinists. When Disney implored Broggie to let him help, Broggie "cleared off one of the unused workbenches toward the rear of the shop," his son Michael Broggie has written. "He equipped it with an assortment of basic hand tools and placed a clean shop apron on a hook nearby. The next morning, Walt came in as usual, chatting with the machinists as he worked his way through the shop. Then he spotted a hand-lettered sign on a workbench: 'Walt's Workplace.'"

Roger Broggie himself wrote in 1952 of Disney's apprenticeship at the machine shop, which stretched into 1950, until Disney had set up a workshop at his home: "Walt Disney came into the shop and learned to operate all the machine tools by making some of the parts himself. He made the whistle, flag-stands and hand rails on the lathe. He learned sheet metal work by laying out and fabricating the headlamp and smoke stack. Then [he] made numerous parts in the milling machine and learned to silver solder and braze on many small fittings."[43] The work had to be fitted around the shop's regular maintenance of cameras and other photographic equipment. Diane Disney Miller remembered in 1956 that Disney "used to go over to the machine shop at the studio at night and work there on his train and on his little miniatures."[44]

Roger Broggie said in 1951 that he and his colleagues were surprised by Disney's aptitude for machine work. "In many ways, Walt's a temperamental guy. Lots of the boys didn't think he'd be much good in the shop."[45]

Seventeen years later, Broggie told Richard Hubler that teaching Disney how to run a lathe and drill press and other machinery was difficult "because he was impatient. So I'd make what we call a set-up in a lathe and turn out a piece and say, 'Well, that's how you do it.' . . . He would see part of it and he was impatient, so he would want to turn the wheels—and then something would happen. A piece might fly out of the chuck and he'd say, 'God-damn it, why didn't you tell me it was going to do this?' Well, you don't tell him, you know? It was a thing of—well—you learn it. He said one day, . . . 'You know, it does me some good sometimes to come down here to find out I don't know all about everything.' . . . How would you sharpen the drill if it was going to drill brass or steel? There's a difference. And he learned it. You only had to show him once and he got the picture."[46]

This was a characteristic that other people in the studio noticed. "He had a terrific memory," Marc Davis said. "He learned very quickly. . . . You only had to explain a thing once to him and he knew how to do it. Other people are not the same. I think this is a problem he had in respect to everybody . . . his tremendous memory and his tremendous capacity for learning. He wasn't book learned but he was the most fantastically well educated man in his own way. . . . He understood the mechanics of everything. . . . Everything was a new toy. And this also made him a very impatient man. He was as impatient as could be with whoever he worked with."[47]

Disney's lack of formal education manifested itself sometimes in jibes at his college-educated employees, but more often in the odd lapses—the mis-pronounced words, the grammatical slips—that can mark an autodidact. "For a guy who only went to the eighth grade," Ollie Johnston said, "Walt educated himself beautifully. His vocabulary was good. I only heard him get sore about a big word once in a story meeting. Everyone was sitting around talking and Ted Sears said, 'Well, I think that's a little too strident.' Walt said, 'What the hell are you trying to say, Ted?' He hadn't heard that word before."[48]

In the early months of 1949, Disney began exploring with increasing seriousness what building a miniature railroad might involve. He visited hobbyists who included not just Ollie Johnston but people more on a par with himself financially, like the film composer David Rose. Sharon Disney Brown remembered the intensity of his enthusiasm. "Mother didn't have his great love for trains and Diane was older by then and was interested in other things," she said in 1968. "So I was always getting to go along with him on these various odds and ends of junkets" in the late 1940s, like an overnight train to Los Gatos for a picnic with "a bunch of old crony-type train owners up there."[49]

(When the girls entered their teens, they became reluctant to spend their Sundays with their father, Diane said in 1956. "Sharon was his buddy for a longer time . . . but then there came a time when Shary left him. And that was the crushing blow, I think." After that, Disney took his poodle, Duchess Disney, with him for company.)[50]

As Disney got more into work on his own train layout, he quickly grew more confident in his own judgments on such matters. Johnston remembered a visit after Disney had started to lay track on his own property. "He started looking at my track, and he looked around for about three or four minutes, and then he hauled out this set of blueprints of how he was going to do his," Johnston said. "And he started telling me about how I could get a figure eight like he was going to have if I'd just change my plans, you know. He tried to get me to do it all the way he was going to do it. . . . He was kind of a benign dictator."[51]

As he learned to work with metal, Disney also started using woodworking tools. Here Disney, the son of a carpenter, was on familiar ground. "I never felt as an artist [that] I was a good artist," he said in 1956. "I was never happy with anything I ever did as an artist." By contrast, "I loved mechanics. I mean, I got to be a pretty good carpenter working under my dad. . . . I can still go and make anything in a cabinet shop."

Diane Disney Miller remembered that "this is when dinners started to be fun because he'd bring this little piece of wood he had turned and sit there all through dinner and be so proud of it. He'd pass it around for inspection. I remember one evening . . . he brought a piston to dinner from a locomotive and he sat this thing on the dinner table. He was being humorous about it but, also, he was awfully proud of this piston."[52]

(Disney stage-managed at least one display of uncharacteristic modesty in the face of machines' demands. In 1951, after attending a preview of *Alice in Wonderland* at the Disney studio, Hedda Hopper was escorted to the studio's machine shop, where she found Disney working on what she called a "toy train." She remembered Disney saying, "Hedda, every time I begin to think myself a big shot, I come to this shop, work with my hands, and learn humility.")[53]

Disney had passed through a crisis in the early 1930s when his work no longer required him to use his hands—to draw, or make out exposure sheets, or anything else. Now he was working with his hands again. This "work" was a hobby, but his history was that of a man who became intensely involved with whatever seized his interest, and who tried to harness the object of his interest to some larger purpose. There was simply no way that his new interest in trains and woodworking and related activities could remain a modest avocation.

Disney's locomotive, which he dubbed the *Lilly Belle* in honor of his wife, had its first "steam-up" on December 24, 1949, on three hundred feet of track on a studio sound stage.[54] But its eventual home was to be on a half-mile track encircling the Disneys' huge new home on Carolwood (more than five thousand square feet, plus a two-story building that housed a garage and a recreation room), which was then nearly finished.

Even though Sharon accompanied her father on train trips, the three Disney women regarded Walt Disney's enthusiasm for his new hobby skeptically. That was made clear in 1953, in the *McCall's* article that appeared under Lillian Disney's name (it speaks at one point, with chilling wifely condescension, of Walt's "caprices and spurts of childishness").

"I wasn't being entirely selfish when I argued against having the railroad on our grounds," the article's Lillian says. "In the first place, although Walt adores the train now, I am not sure his enthusiasm will continue after he has done everything possible to it. And putting up miniature tracks entails a formidable outlay of money, because there has to be so much expensive grading. In the second place our girls are growing up. When they marry we may not need or want such a big house. And if we should ever decide to sell our house there won't be many prospective buyers who'll want a place with a yard full of railroad track.

"So the girls and I, using our best female wiles, tried to persuade Father to keep his train at the studio, where he could play with it at noon and run it all over the lot to entertain visiting firemen." The Disney women admitted defeat after Walt brought home a "right-of-way contract for his railroad" and insisted they sign it as a condition of building the new house. "We were quite prepared to put our names on the dotted line, when Walt picked up the contract and said he'd trust us."[55]

The Disneys moved into their new home in February 1950,[56] but it was not until December, after months of grading, that the first track was laid—a total of about twelve hundred feet that "consisted of a complete loop with a figure 8 inside, one passing track, and one siding," Roger Broggie wrote in 1952. The balance of the track, about fourteen hundred feet, was laid in May 1951. This new and longer loop crossed a sixty-five-foot-long trestle, passing nine feet above another piece of track, and ran through a ninety-foot tunnel. There were other, shorter bridges, too. The combination of track, bridges, and tunnel was "necessary because of the contour of the land and to enable the train to run in either direction over any part of the track," Broggie wrote. Disney could ride for almost a mile "without going over the same track in the same direction twice."[57] The total cost, of layout and rolling stock, was around fifty thousand dollars—a huge investment in a hobby in 1950.[58] The size of the investment, coupled with Disney's celebrity, attracted a great deal of attention, especially among other railroad hobbyists, and Disney eventually recouped much of what he had spent by selling castings and construction drawings through advertisements in *Miniature Locomotive* magazine.[59]

Disney worked on a highly detailed, fully furnished caboose throughout 1950; it was the only car he intended as purely a display piece. He began working at home after equipping the "barn" that housed controls for his new railroad—which he dubbed the Carolwood Pacific (CP)—with woodworking and metalworking tools. Lillian said in the *McCall's* article: "Now Walt has something to interest him that doesn't drive him crazy. He stays home weekends. Once in a while he even comes home early to run the train a while before dinner."[60]

Once the train was operating, Roger Broggie said, "there was a thing of going out there on weekends and running the train for guests and so on."[61] Guests would ride the freight cars while the engineer, usually Disney himself, sat directly behind the locomotive, on the tender. The guests were plentiful, and Disney did his best to dazzle them. Ward Kimball remembered one striking feature of the new house: "He'd say, 'Let's put the train away and go up to the party house and I'll make chocolate ice cream sodas.' He'd get behind the counter of his soda fountain, which was his boyhood dream come true with all these different flavors of ice cream, and he'd make these long tall things with whipped cream and cherries. They'd be a mile high and he'd bring them to Jules Stein [founder of the MCA talent agency] or whoever his guests were. He was excited because he was doing something he liked to do."[62]

As Lillian had predicted, the CP did not have a long life. Although a miniature, the *Lilly Belle* was powerful enough—and its "live steam" hot enough—

to pose a hazard to the unwary. It was, in other words, a more dangerous toy than it appeared to be. Roger Broggie remembered "a few problems involved with, let's say, motion picture celebrities, being shown, well, 'you pull this lever and it makes you go forward; this is the throttle; this is what we call the junction bar; that's forward, this is reverse, this makes it go.' . . . But that thing is capable of about thirty miles an hour if you want to open it up. . . . No problem, except that there's some tight curves in the thing because it had twenty-six hundred feet of track, and a couple of times it turned over."

Broggie or another machinist was sometimes on hand to keep the train running properly, but on other occasions Disney "would fire it up himself [and end up] being, say, a combination of host, a bartender, an engineer, and a fireman, all at once. And it doesn't work. Because it's a little tricky to keep [the proper steam pressure] in a boiler and keep it fed with water and fire and either not let it blow up or not let it run out of fire. You can't do both, and he found this out. You can't be a host to a group of people and run a train at the same time."[63]

Wrecks didn't bother Disney himself, "for repairing wrecks is part of the fun," Lillian said in the *McCall's* article. "He came home from England last summer [1952] with two new engines—a ten-foot locomotive and a switch engine. I heard him enthusing to actor George Murphy, who loves to train too, 'Boy, we're sure to have wrecks now!'"[64] But wrecks in which guests were injured were another matter. One wreck in the spring of 1953 "knocked off the safety valve and it threw out a jet of steam and burned a kid's leg," Broggie said. "Walt said, 'Well, I can't tell these people that they don't know really what they're doing unless they have a lesson or two.' . . . At the last occurrence . . . when it dumped over, he said, 'This is the end of it.' . . . There were problems with kids, and some of the kids were his relatives. . . . What he finally realized was that the average person doesn't understand what a potential case of dynamite a locomotive boiler is."[65]

After less than three years, the CP was out of business. Disney ordered the damaged *Lilly Belle*—"the cabin was all broken up and the safety valve busted off," Broggie said—into storage. His interest in trains had not been extinguished, however. "His ideas always grew and grew," Ollie Johnston said of Disney's mushrooming interest in trains in the late 1940s and early 1950s. "He used to say, 'I've got to have a project all the time, something new to work on.'"[66]

In the late 1940s, Disney's interest in trains was growing alongside his work on *Cinderella,* a less satisfying project. The meeting notes for that film— usually, but not always, stenographic transcripts—show him filling his usual role, as a shrewd and decisive story editor, although that role was a little more ambiguous than usual. In a January 15, 1948, meeting, for example, Disney was responding to what was already up on the storyboards. The transcript shows him repeatedly identifying crucial story points and leading the way toward resolving problems satisfactorily. He seems to be going well beyond what was already on the storyboards, but it is impossible to be sure. (He also offered ideas that didn't wind up in the film, but they were not bad ideas, only superfluous.)

As the story moved toward animation, it became clear that *Cinderella* and Disney's role in it were both significantly different than anything that had come before. For one thing, Disney was using live action more extensively than ever to guide the animation of the human characters. Most of the film was shot in live action, on bare-bones sets, with actors playing the parts of Cinderella, her stepmother, the stepsisters, and other human characters. Disney had turned to live action as an aid to animation not only during work on *Snow White* but for *Pinocchio*, too, and for parts of *Fantasia*. In 1938, he had spoken of building a larger sound stage to shoot "more and more live action" for *Alice in Wonderland* and *Peter Pan*.[67] But now live action seemed less like a useful tool and more like an indispensable crutch.

Said Frank Thomas, who animated Cinderella's cruel stepmother: "I sensed this lack of confidence, lack of knowing where he was going, what he wanted to do with the picture. So, he relied heavily on live action to set his staging, his timing, and the business. . . . [The live action] looked pretty silly, you know, with no backgrounds, but you could follow it and say, 'Well, this is dragging, this is not.' . . . So, this helped him and it helped the story people immeasurably"[68]—even though it hobbled the animators. As Thomas and Ollie Johnston wrote: "Everyone's imagination as to how a scene might be staged was limited by the placement of the camera, for once a scene had been shot it was very hard to switch to a whole new point of view."[69]

Disney was uneasy with the results. He said in a December 13, 1948, meeting, after he saw animation of Cinderella for the start of the film: "I think the boys on Cinderella have to watch, as they go along, to take more freedom—they're all good animators and don't have to literally follow those Photostats" blown up from the frames of live-action film.[70]

Marc Davis, who animated much of the Cinderella character, said that if the animator participated in shooting the live action for his scenes, "it really amounted to doing your first rough animation through the performer."[71] That was exactly the purpose that the live action of Snow White had served, a dozen years earlier, but now the live action was more confining. "Cinderella was a real girl," Frank Thomas said, "and the stepsisters and everybody who worked with her, particularly the Prince and the stepmother, to my way of thinking had to be just as real as she was. You couldn't let up and have them half-cartoon."[72] There had been just such a gulf between Snow White—a "real girl"—and the dwarfs—who were considerably more than half cartoon—but Disney himself, in collaboration with animators like Bill Tytla, Fred Moore, and Ham Luske, had bridged it through a new kind of animation acting. In *Cinderella*, though, the "straight" characters, like Cinderella and her stepmother, rarely shared the screen with true cartoon characters that could pull them away from their live-action origins.

Instead, Disney cultivated a parallel conflict, between the stepmother's cat, Lucifer, and the mice that are Cinderella's friends, to match the conflict between Cinderella and her stepmother. The two essentially independent stories were expertly braided together, so that, for instance, the film's initial encounter between mice and cat nests snugly with the first humiliation of Cinderella by her stepmother and stepsisters. Gus the mouse has hidden from Lucifer under a teacup that Cinderella unwittingly delivers to the stepsisters, and they accuse her of a malicious trick.

There was only a hint of the cat-and-mouse conflict in a March 25, 1947, treatment, but it was emerging as an important element by the time of the January 15, 1948, meeting on *Cinderella*. Disney said that the story as it existed then "doesn't do justice to what we have. . . . We have to pull out a lot of gags that are just in as gags."[73] Shortly thereafter, he put Bill Peet—who was largely responsible for writing the animated segments in *Song of the South*—in charge of the cat-and-mouse segments.

It was as those segments took shape, on the storyboards and then in animation, principally by Ward Kimball, that Disney showed rare enthusiasm for what he was seeing. "Thing's looking awfully good," he said during a February 28, 1949, meeting, after seeing John Lounsbery's animation showing the mice as they elude Lucifer while gathering beads and buttons for Cinderella's dress. (That episode appeared on the storyboards relatively late, added probably in anticipation of the animals' audience appeal.)[74]

Otherwise, Disney was more often reacting cautiously to what his people did than prodding them to realize ideas of his own. He wanted Cinderella's fairy godmother to be a "tall, regal" type, Frank Thomas said—in effect, a new version of the fairy in *Pinocchio*—instead of a small, plump woman: "Boy, he wasn't sure of that. He just wasn't sure to the very end. But when he saw [Milt Kahl's] animation on it he finally bought it."[75]

There was a sort of casting by character on *Cinderella*, as with Thomas's animation of the stepmother and Johnston's animation of the stepsisters, but the heavy reliance on live action reduced the importance of such casting. When a character like Cinderella herself was parceled out among two or more animators, reconciling the different versions was less a matter of achieving consistent acting than of smoothing out variations in drawing. Eric Larson said that his and Marc Davis's versions of Cinderella herself weren't the same because "the character models hadn't been set. Usually, those things never get set until hundreds of feet of animation have been done."[76] Assistant animators were responsible for ironing out such differences, once there was a final version of a character.

By the late 1940s, Disney's role in feature production had shrunk noticeably. He no longer dropped in every day or two for brief, unannounced visits between more formal meetings, while the director was preparing his part of a cartoon for animation. The directors were left to exercise their own judgment more on details.[77] A director like Wilfred Jackson "would have noticed [Disney's] absence a lot more than [the animators] would," Ollie Johnston said, "because he was probably in and out of Jackson's room two or three times a week, while we might see him once every three or four weeks."[78] Jackson, one of *Cinderella*'s three directors, lamented the change. "Walt was a very inspiring person," he said, "and it was much more exciting and a lot more fun to work on a picture where I was in direct contact with him every few days than it was when he would let us go further ahead . . . and only check up on us at less frequent intervals."[79]

Jackson remarked on another change that was consistent with the greater reliance on live action: "*Cinderella* . . . was the first cartoon I worked on in which the musician, Ollie Wallace, composed his music for all the sequences I directed after the animation was finished and okayed for inking, with the exception, of course, of the 'musical sequences'"—that is, the songs. This was a shift toward the way scores for live-action films were composed, without the careful synchronization of music and action that had characterized the Disney features until then—even though conspicuous "mickey-mousing," as it was sometimes called, had all but disappeared by the time of the first Disney feature. For Jackson, the most musically involved of the directors, that change was occasion for regret: "It seemed to me that the time and effort I spent in pre-timing the action, working closely with the musician as he pre-composed the musical interpretation of it, was not only the very most delightful part of directing a cartoon, but also one of the most significant for [its] effectiveness."[80]

Cinderella lacks the lavish detail of *Pinocchio*, in particular, but it was through attention to detail that *Cinderella* most strongly echoed the earlier features, in methods if not in results. The effects animator Edwin Parks recalled that the stepmother

> had a cane, with a gold head on it, and there was a highlight that had to go down [the length of the gold head]. . . . We would have a conference about a thing like that. It would get into a quite detailed discussion, taking sometimes many hours, and tests, and color models—the whole works—on just whether this highlight should go from the top of the gold color down to where it ended, or maybe it should end just before it got to what would be a natural border. And those things always ended up that maybe it shouldn't quite touch. So then you had the problem of cutting this thing off so it wouldn't crawl back and forth [that is, so the bottom edge of the highlight wouldn't appear to move]. We might do it, and it might be shot in final, but then they'd find out there's too much crawling, and now we've got to go back and change them all and re-shoot the whole works—do it over in ink and paint. . . . We did it over [with the highlight still ending above the border], and it still crawled, and finally they just decided, well, why do it the hard way.[81]

Despite such occasional relapses into old ways, *Cinderella* still came in at a cost of $2.2 million—a full-length feature made for little more than the cost of each of the package features that preceded it. When the film opened in February 1950, it was greeted with a *Newsweek* cover and hailed almost universally as a return to form. *Cinderella* was Disney's greatest box-office success since *Snow White and the Seven Dwarfs,* with gross rentals of almost eight million dollars. The film's heroine and her prince, her lovable friends, the story's adroit expansion of its fairy-tale source—all of this recalled *Snow White* in the most satisfying way. Only a few critics discerned the troubling void at the center of the film, a void left by Disney's own limited involvement and his compensating reliance on live action. John Mason Brown, in an extended review of *Cinderella,* saw in it the bottom of a long decline and dismissed Disney's "heroes and heroines" as "bloodless transparencies cursed with wafer faces."[82]

It was not just trains that distracted Disney from *Cinderella.* On June 11, 1949, he and his wife and daughters left on a trip to England, Ireland, and France that would keep him away from his studio until August 29.[83] (On that Monday, his first day back, he sweatboxed the *Cinderella* sequences Ham Luske had directed and ordered many minor changes, as well as a significant reworking of the very end of the film.)[84] Disney himself flew back to London on October 13, when production of *Cinderella* was essentially finished. He was gone three weeks.

The immediate occasion for Disney's trips was the filming in England of his first wholly live-action film, *Treasure Island.* Making such a film was a way for Disney to use British earnings that he could not convert into dollars under postwar currency restrictions. Such an option was not available to him where animated features were concerned, since as a practical matter he could make those features only in Burbank. (David Hand had set up a British animation studio a few years earlier for the J. Arthur Rank organization, but despite Hand's best efforts the results fell short of Disney standards in every respect. Rank closed the studio after two years.) RKO, which had blocked sterling of its own, shared the production costs of *Treasure Island.*

Filming began in July 1949 at Bristol harbor.[85] Disney had hired an American director, Byron Haskin, another of the very ordinary, relatively inexpensive directors he was coming to rely on. Haskin's most valuable credential may have been his work in special effects on such 1930s swashbucklers as *Captain Blood.* The producer—Perce Pearce, from Disney's Burbank staff—was American, too, as was one of the stars, the boy Bobby Driscoll. The bulk of the cast was made up of veteran British character actors, most notably Robert Newton as Long John Silver. In the film, Newton makes an arresting John Silver, his face constantly in motion as if he were some sly animal. Haskin, in a book-length interview with Joe Adamson, complained that Newton's performances in rehearsal were more vivid, and that he throttled back during the actual filming, but if so, Newton knew what he was doing.[86]

In that interview, Haskin described a Disney almost wholly detached from the film, the writing and editing included. Such a Disney is radically at odds with the Disney seen by other people in work on other films, a Disney intensely concerned with details. It is thus easier to credit Gus Walker, the Scot who was in charge of building the sets for *Treasure Island.* He remembered that Disney had trouble believing that the tiles on a roof in the Bristol harbor set were painted, and not the real thing: "I had to get a ladder for Walt to go up . . . and have a look. . . . He hadn't had a lot of experience of construction for films. It was something new for him."[87]

Treasure Island differs strikingly from earlier Disney films in its matter-of-fact handling of the story's violence (at one point, the film follows the book by having Driscoll, as Jim Hawkins, shoot a pirate full in the face). For the most part the violence is neither glossed over nor dwelled upon, just as in the Robert Louis Stevenson novel itself. *Treasure Island*'s tone—serious and often foreboding—was new for a Disney feature, and it may be owing mainly either to Haskin or to Lawrence Edward Watkin, the former Virginia college professor who wrote the screenplay; but there is no reason to believe that Disney was not fully aware of it or that it did not have his approval.

Disney's attention to details was evident in his preparations for the 1949 trip itself, which reflected his concern about postwar shortages. "I remember Daddy sent over a whole lot of food," Sharon Disney Brown told Richard Hubler. "All this canned bacon and canned hamburgers. You just couldn't get meat. . . . We stayed in London the whole trip. . . . And we stayed at the Dorchester Hotel almost the whole time because Daddy was making a picture. I remember the waiter was so nice. Every so often he'd come over and say, 'Mr. Disney, I have two eggs.' And it was the biggest moment!"

The Disneys made driving or flying trips to northern England, Ireland, and the continent. But, Sharon said, "most of the trips were short ones. . . . He was there for a purpose and he didn't want to spend six months just traveling around. . . . We ate most of our meals at the hotel because he was tired at night and wanted to go to bed early. . . . He was an all day worker. He didn't slow down at all. But he wanted his sleep at night and he was always in bed early. He was always in bed by ten o'clock."[88]

Treasure Island was released in July 1950 to mixed reviews. It returned to the Disney studio and RKO gross rentals of $4.8 million, about two-thirds of *Cinderella*'s total, and almost three times its negative cost ($1.8 million). Making *Treasure Island* consumed all of Disney's blocked sterling,[89] but making films in Britain had proved its worth on other grounds, and Disney and RKO set out to make another in 1951.

For *The Story of Robin Hood and His Merrie Men*, Disney cut back the American contingent to three: the producer, Pearce; the writer, Watkin; and the studio's production manager, Fred Leahy, all of whom sailed to England on the *Queen Mary* in January 1951.[90] At first, Disney said later, the idea was to focus the story on Bobby Driscoll as "a young boy who hung around Robin's camp. . . . But the plan simply wouldn't jell."[91] (Legal considerations may have weighed against using Driscoll. In September 1949, deep into shooting of *Treasure Island,* the boy was fined a hundred pounds for working in England without a permit from the Ministry of Labor. By the time the fine was upheld on appeal, Driscoll had completed his role in the film.)[92]

By the fall of 1950, Disney had settled on Richard Todd, a young British star, as his Robin Hood. Todd remembered how Disney applied his charm when Todd visited the Burbank studio to talk about taking the role. "I didn't want to do Robin Hood; I thought it was rather beneath me," he said. "I didn't want to be an Errol Flynn—I couldn't be, anyway, physically. I wasn't up to it, at all. Walt himself persuaded me by saying he didn't want a heavyweight, he wanted a quick-witted, quick-moving welterweight, which is what I was."[93] After some hesitation, Todd accepted the role in January 1951.

When Pearce and Watkin arrived in London, Todd joined them in meetings to plan the film. "I was fascinated by the attention to detail," he wrote in his autobiography. "At each [meeting] a sketch artist was present, and as each camera set-up was worked out and agreed, he produced a pencil-and-wash picture of exactly what would be in the camera lens. These sketches were photo-copied and bound into folders, and all of us at these meetings were eventually issued with the bound volumes, showing every single shot."[94]

Here was how Disney could extend his control over live action into the actual shooting, through the planning of each shot on what amounted to storyboards similar to those he had used for almost twenty years in making his cartoons. Directors at other studios might prepare such storyboards themselves—Alfred Hitchcock was the most famous example—but on *The Story of Robin Hood* the director, Ken Annakin, found such preparation already completed when he came onto the film.

"Later," Annakin wrote in his autobiography, "I was to discover that at least fifty percent of the reason for working this way was to enable Walt to exercise control, and supply his creative input from six thousand miles away. Each week during pre-production, the continuity sketches had been shipped back to Burbank and returned with Walt's suggestions and corrections. Now, these were handed to me as the Bible—even more important perhaps than the script."[95]

Disney supervised preparation in other ways as well. On March 6, 1951, in a long, chatty memorandum to Perce Pearce and Fred Leahy, he responded to test footage of the film's principals. He was troubled by the costumes chosen for Joan Rice, who would play Maid Marian: "It seems that women of that period always have scarves up around their chins, but I think it does something to a woman's face. . . . Where we see Miss Rice disguised as page, this costume seemed bulky and heavy. The blouse or tunic was too long and hung too far down over her hips—it didn't show enough of her and I thought detracted from her femininity. I think a slight showing of the hips would help a lot."[96]

With his control so firmly established, Disney had no need to hover over the set. Filming of *The Story of Robin Hood* began on April 30, 1951, but Disney did not leave Burbank until June 11, and then he sailed to England on the *Queen Mary*. While he was in Britain he came onto the set "from time to time; not often," Richard Todd said. "He wouldn't linger all that much. . . . He wasn't obtrusive. He didn't discuss the picture, particularly, at least not with me. It was like a friend dropping in and having a chat, and that was that."[97]

The resulting film is low-key, lacking the excitement generated by the Errol Flynn version made in Hollywood and released in 1938. Disney had sought, in place of that excitement, a new authenticity, but the story of Robin Hood is inherently inauthentic because there is no historical record of such a person. The Disney film departs so far from any kind of authenticity that it offers Norman kings and queens who not only speak English instead of French but orate like Saxon patriots.

Disney financed a third British-based feature, *The Sword and the Rose,* a romance set in Tudor England, not in partnership with RKO but through a wholly owned subsidiary, Walt Disney British Films Limited.[98] He left Los Angeles for London on June 23, 1952, to, as *Daily Variety* put it, "supervise production," and returned to New York on September 3.[99] He arrived several weeks before shooting began in August and left before it ended. He also squeezed in visits with miniature-train enthusiasts in Britain and Switzerland.[100]

Ken Annakin was involved in the planning for the film from the first day. "As Larry [Watkin] fed us the script pages from Burbank, devised and approved by Walt," Annakin wrote, "I worked alongside Steven Grimes, a young British sketch artist. . . . For four months we broke down the scenes into setups and sketches." Richard Todd also remembered "frequent script conferences, in which every set-up was planned, sketched and photocopied into albums for each of us."[101]

There was, Todd wrote, a "special quality" of working on a Disney film, "quite unlike the atmosphere on any other production. There was very much a family ambiance, a feeling of harmony partly engendered by Perce Pearce's avuncular presence, partly arising from the fact that most of us had worked together and knew each other well—but mostly perhaps due to the smoothness with which the schedule rolled along as a result of the careful pre-planning of previous weeks." This atmosphere was particularly beneficial to Annakin, who was, Todd wrote, "the kind of quiet, coaxing director who understood his actors and gentled the best from them."[102]

It is not clear why Disney chose Annakin to direct his second and third British productions, although Annakin himself thought it likely that Disney had seen the short films he directed for two anthologies based on Somerset Maugham short stories.[103] Annakin was exceptional among the directors Disney hired, earlier and later, in his sensitivity to the actors working with him. *The Sword and the Rose* benefits immensely from his attention to the characters' relationships and from the nuanced acting by the three principals (Todd, Glynis Johns, and James Robertson Justice). Unfortunately, the film lacks a sense of scale. Even though the cast is full of kings and dukes and other such personages (Justice plays Henry VIII and Johns his sister Mary

Tudor), an appealing intimacy is not balanced by a sense that the love story is taking place in the context of great events. There is no blaming Annakin for this; the fault is in the story. Disney had become too much of an Anglophile for his films' good. *The Sword and the Rose* cost more than *Robin Hood* but grossed only $2.5 million, half as much as its predecessor.

Disney and Richard Todd hit it off during the production of *Robin Hood.* "We saw a lot of each other when he was in England," Todd said, "and then when I went to Hollywood, whether I was working for him or not, he just took me under his wing." Todd was an exceptionally attractive figure, a dashing and handsome movie star, an Oscar nominee in his first Hollywood role, in 1948, who was also a true war hero (he was the first British soldier to parachute into Normandy on D-Day). "I'm not easily intimidated by anybody, no matter what their standing," Todd said in 2004. "I mean, I had at that time—in the fifties, certainly—a lot of self-assurance. I think the war did that. You didn't stand any nonsense from anybody; you had a sort of authority about you."

Todd found Disney—his senior by almost eighteen years—"very kindly. I think he respected me because—well, little things, like I wouldn't have a double to do stunts. They were very worried about that, because of the insurance problem. I think that rather tickled him. And he was a bit of a social climber—in England. What he was in America, I don't know, but in England he liked to be amongst very high-ranking people, and I happened to have access to some of them. He was very happy to join in some of the gatherings."[104]

Disney planned to begin shooting a fourth British production, *Rob Roy the Highland Rogue,* in Scotland in the spring of 1953, with Todd as the title character. But however much he liked the country itself, he knew that shooting in Britain was only an expedient, and that a serious live-action program had to be based in Burbank. The question was, which feature would be his first domestic production entirely in live action?

The leading candidate was initially *The Great Locomotive Chase,* based on the same Civil War episode as Buster Keaton's silent feature comedy *The General.* In that episode, known as the "Andrews raid," Union spies almost succeeded in stealing a Confederate locomotive and wrecking a vital rail line. Since two vintage locomotives would necessarily play a prominent part, the story's appeal to Disney was obvious.

Harper Goff, a sketch artist for Warner Brothers, was in England in 1951—evidently when Disney was there for the filming of *Robin Hood*—and he encountered Disney at a store called Basset-Lowke, famous for its miniature locomotives. (Disney had just bought a locomotive that Goff, also a train fancier, coveted.) "He asked me what I did for a living," Goff said, "and I told him that I was an artist. . . . He said, 'When you get back to America, come and talk to me.' By the time I went to see him at the Studio, he was aware of my artwork in *Coronet* and *Esquire* magazines. . . . He explained that he was planning to go into live-action filming, and do motion pictures with actors and sets. This fit in with my experience at Warner Brothers."[105] Goff joined the Disney staff on October 22, 1951.

By February 1952, Goff—who identified himself in correspondence then as "director of production research for live-action pictures"—was scouting locations for *The Great Locomotive Chase* in Georgia. That project was still very much alive in October 1952, when the studio paid for Wilbur Kurtz, an Atlanta commercial artist and expert on the Andrews raid, to travel by train to Los Angeles. (Kurtz was the son-in-law of William Fuller, the Confederate conductor who foiled the Union spies' plans.)[106]

Locomotive Chase's rival for a place on the schedule was *20,000 Leagues Under the Sea*. Disney wrote of *20,000 Leagues* early in 1952: "We have added to our list of future productions Jules Verne's spectacular and adventuresome *20,000 Leagues Under the Sea*. We have acquired the rights to this story, which can make one of the all-time great motion pictures. Our production plans are tentative at this stage, but the knowledge we have acquired in developing our True Life Adventure series will be extremely valuable in filming the fantastic under-sea creatures depicted by Verne. This feature will be all live action and except for the underwater scenes, which will be filmed somewhere along the trail of the *Nautilus,* will be shot in Technicolor in our own studio."[107]

By the time Disney spoke about the film at a sales meeting at the studio in June 1952, the estimated budget was $3 million to $4 million.[108] By February 1953, *The Great Locomotive Chase* had been shouldered aside, and what the *Los Angeles Times* called "experimental underwater material" for *20,000 Leagues* was being shot off Catalina Island.[109] Disney began building a third sound stage specifically for *20,000 Leagues* in the spring of 1953.[110] The new stage held a water tank, measuring 60 by 125 feet, and 3 to 18 feet in depth, that could be used to film scenes supposedly taking place at sea.[111] In late August 1953, soon after his return from Europe, Disney announced that he would not make another feature in Britain in 1954, devoting his attention instead to *20,000 Leagues,* his first all-live-action feature made at the Burbank studio.[112]

The timing of Disney's decision to make his most ambitious—and expensive—live-action feature was significant. It came when all of the film industry was under the growing shadow of television.

The Disney brothers had been interested in television since the middle 1940s, at least. The *New York Times* reported in October 1945 that Walt Disney Productions had recently "applied to the Federal Communications Commission for a television and FM band in Southern California preliminary to the establishment of three to five television stations in various parts of the country. . . . Current plans call for the use of the cartoon medium and the 'live' action and cartoon combination in the Disney brand of television entertainment."[113]

Nothing came of that. Like most other Hollywood producers, Disney was not so much hostile to television as uncertain about how best to make use of the new medium. He was seriously considering entering television by the fall of 1948, although he worried about how to reconcile TV's demands for low costs with his own preferences where animation was concerned.[114] "When television hit," Disney said in 1956, "I went back to New York and spent a week in New York just to study television. . . . It was '48, '49, somewhere in there. . . . I saw it here [in Los Angeles] and they said, 'Well, you've got to see it in New York.' It was basically the same, only more of it. And I had the feeling then that it was important and that we ought to get in it."

Disney "got in it" on Christmas Day 1950, when the National Broadcasting Company (NBC) aired "One Hour in Wonderland," a show built around the forthcoming *Alice in Wonderland;* Disney appeared on camera, as did both of his daughters, Kathryn Beaumont (the voice of Alice), and even the *Lilly Belle.* Said Bill Walsh, the show's producer: "I think that was the first time Walt saw TV in its true light—as a promotion device for the studio."[115]

Writing shortly after "One Hour in Wonderland" aired, Disney said, "I regard television as one of our most important channels for the development of a new motion picture audience. Millions of televiewers never go to a picture theatre, and countless others infrequently. . . . In these highly competitive days, we must use the television screen along with every other promotion medium, to increase our potential audience."[116]

On March 30, 1951, Disney summoned four of his executives to talk about a possible half-hour show. "The plan of the program," Harry Tytle wrote in his diary, "is to boost our theatrical attendance, exploit merchandising, etc., along with the selling of television shows. We mainly discussed various items that would go into the format," like black-and-white cartoons, "very simple" animation done especially for TV, and "live-action subjects."[117]

Again, nothing came of such ideas at the time, but the Disney studio was nibbling around the edges of television in other ways. Throughout 1951, Roy Disney wrote at the end of that year, the studio engaged in "small-scale production of live action films for television, particularly spot announcements, through a controlled subsidiary, Hurrell Productions, Inc., which operates on our studio lot at Burbank. This subsidiary is exploring the possibilities of producing serialized dramatic and comedy shows on film for TV."[118] (George Hurrell was a fashion photographer who was married to Lillian Disney's niece, Phyllis Bounds.) The studio completed its first animated television commercials, for Mohawk Carpet Company, in September 1952.[119]

Disney's interest in TV waxed and waned throughout the early 1950s. "I'm in no hurry to get into television," he said in the spring of 1952, "although I do believe in cooperation with that medium. It's very valuable in advertising a film."[120] He made a second Christmas show in 1952, to promote *Peter Pan,* and in the summer of 1953, a three-year deal with General Foods appeared to be in the offing.[121] But still nothing jelled. (According to Bob Thomas, the General Foods deal foundered on the sponsor's insistence that Disney make a pilot program.)[122]

It was while peppered by distractions of many kinds that Disney made *Alice in Wonderland,* finally bringing to film his version of a classic that had been a nagging presence since 1938—a film Disney felt he *should* make but did not really want to. The film went into production in the summer of 1949, just after Disney left for London and *Treasure Island.* Like *Cinderella,* it was shot largely in live action on skeletal sets, to guide the animators' work. Shooting began on June 22, 1949, and continued until November 2, 1950. This time, many of the voice performers, like Kathryn Beaumont, the English girl who was Alice, and Ed Wynn, the veteran comedian who was the Mad Hatter, played the same characters in the live action, acting to playbacks of their voice recordings.[123]

In making *Cinderella,* Disney could use *Snow White and the Seven Dwarfs* as a sort of template, but he had no help of that kind with *Alice.* Like *Pinocchio,* it was an episodic story that went against the grain of straightforward narrative as Disney practiced it; and again like *Pinocchio,* it demanded imaginative handling that Disney had neither the time nor the inclination to give it. During work on *Alice,* Disney said in 1956, "we got in there and we just didn't feel a thing. But we were forcing ourselves to do it. . . . You're in so deep sometimes you've got to fight it through. You can't turn back." He summed up his problem this way, years later: "The picture was filled with weird characters."[124]

During work on *Alice,* Frank Thomas said, Disney "had trouble communicating to almost anybody what he really saw in the material. You could sense what it was, but every time you thought you had it, he would say, 'No, no, you don't want stuff like that in there,' or 'You're missing the boat,' or 'That's not what we want to do.'"[125]

In an interview with Christian Renaut, Thomas cited his difficult encounters with Disney over his animation of the Queen of Hearts: "He said, 'Try some stuff. What is she doing in the picture?' So I was supposed to take up a funny character and do some stuff that I needed to be kind of strong. He looked at it and said, 'You've lost your comedy.' So I tried it funny. 'You've lost your menace,' and I asked, 'Now what is she doing in the picture? Give me some business and I'll give you a character,' and he said, 'No, you give me a character and I'll give you some business.'"[126]

Such difficulties were reflected in the film's cost, which rose to more than three million dollars—almost a million more than *Cinderella*'s—before *Alice* was released in the summer of 1951. The film's box-office performance was disappointing, and the studio wrote off a million-dollar loss.

In the fall of 1951, shortly after *Alice* was released, Disney's writers finally nailed down an acceptable continuity for *Peter Pan,* another story that had been a nagging headache since before World War II. Disney had bought Paramount's rights to the James Barrie story in October 1938 and had signed a contract with the copyright owner, the Hospital for Sick Children in London, in January 1939.[127] Disney did not mean to dawdle; as early as May 1939, with story work in the most preliminary stages, he already had in mind animators for the pirates (Bill Tytla), the dog, Nana (Norm Ferguson, the animator of Pluto), and Tinker Bell, the fairy (Fred Moore).[128]

For more than a decade, though, Disney's writers generated huge quantities of paper—treatments and outlines, as well as storyboards—until the story was finally in a form that he could accept. Even then, Captain Hook, more so than the Queen of Hearts in *Alice,* was an unsettled character—alternately comedian and menace, his inconsistencies bridged only by Hans Conried's highly colored vocal performance—but in 1952, when animation was under way, Disney was content to leave the resolution of such issues to his animators. Making animated features was by now a reflex activity for him; his real interests were elsewhere.

By 1952, Disney was absorbed by a new passion for miniatures, a passion generated by his success in building a miniature train, especially the miniature caboose that he made himself in 1950. Said Roger Broggie: "We started to build what was to be an exhibit of Americana in the same scale [as the caboose], an inch and a half to the foot, or one-eighth the full size. That means the figure would be nine inches tall."[129]

Somewhere toward the end of 1950—probably after he finished his caboose—Disney had applied his new skills as a maker of miniatures to a diorama called "Granny's Cabin"; it reproduced a set from *So Dear to My Heart.* When Disney exhibited Granny's Cabin at the Festival of California Living at the Pan-Pacific Auditorium in Los Angeles two years later, in November and December 1952, the *Los Angeles Times* described it as "an eight-foot-long replica of a Midwest pioneer farm home, handicrafted [sic] by Disney in every minute detail of structure and the furniture supplemented by objects from historical collections."[130]

Granny herself was not represented in Granny's Cabin. At the festival, Beulah Bondi, who played Granny in the film, talked about pioneer life in a recording. Disney posed with Bondi and Kathryn Beaumont (who was the voice of Wendy in *Peter Pan* as well as the voice of Alice) in front of Granny's Cabin, which was recessed into a wall at eye level.

By then, Disney had been collecting miniatures for several years. His collection of miniatures had grown so large by early in 1951 that he was seriously considering sending it on tour.[131] It would go out as what Roger Broggie called "an exhibit of Americana"—that is, a set of dioramas, each furnished with Disney's miniatures. The *Times* described Granny's Cabin as "the first unit in [Disney's] miniature Americana."

Disney's ambitions increased with each succeeding diorama. For an "opera house" miniature, Disney wanted a tiny vaudevillian to perform on stage, and so in February 1951, the actor and dancer Buddy Ebsen was filmed performing in front of a grid that Roger Broggie and Wathel Rogers used as a guide in reproducing his movements through a system of cams and cables.[132] Although Disney himself built Granny's Cabin, his direct involvement seems to have diminished as each diorama became more mechanically elaborate. The initial sketches for the dioramas were made by Ken Anderson, whom Disney borrowed from the studio's staff for the purpose.

Work began on a third, still more ambitious diorama—a barbershop quartet—in June 1951. Actors were filmed in front of a grid, as Ebsen had been. After Harper Goff joined the Disney staff in October, he designed a tableau with five characters, a quartet whose mouths would be synchronized with their singing voices, and a fifth man who was getting a shave. "My wife Flossie made the clothes out of a very fine silk," Goff said in an interview with *The "E" Ticket,* a magazine devoted to the history of Disneyland, "and I applied a varnish to the moving areas so the material wouldn't wear out too quickly. . . . I made a little model of the scene . . . it wasn't a very careful model, but it was sized right. . . . The guys would sing, 'Down by the old mill stream . . . ' Their mouths didn't move in that first model I made. What I did was the setting . . . what the barber shop would look like, so you could visualize it. Walt then took it and had other people work on it."[133]

When *Popular Science* published photos of Granny's Cabin in its February 1953 issue, it described the diorama as part of "Disneyland, a miniature historic America that is to cover a 50-acre tract in Los Angeles. . . . Its purpose is to entertain people of all ages and also to teach them by means of tiny but exact models how life in the U.S. developed to its present level." The magazine reported that Disney had collected "miniature copies of antique furnishings from all over the country and built others in his studio workshops."[134]

Popular Science may have conflated two or more potential Disney projects, but that would have been easy to do, considering that Disney's plans were, to say the least, fluid in the early 1950s. He seems to have flitted restlessly from one idea to another, trying to find some way to put his enthusiasm for miniatures to work in an incongruously grand project. When he wrote to his sister, Ruth, about "my newest project"—the dioramas—on December 4, 1952, while the Festival of California Living was in progress, he wrote as if he thought a touring show of miniature Americana was a live possibility. He said he was "hoping it will become a reality, but at this point it's very much in the thinking and planning stage. . . . I've been collecting all sorts of miniature pieces for the past three or four years, with this project in mind. It's been a wonderful hobby for me and I find it is something very relaxing to turn to when studio problems become too hectic."[135]

By the time Disney wrote to Ruth, though, the original plan for a traveling show (which at one point was to be called "Disneylandia") was, if not yet dead, close to it. When he ultimately called a halt, only two members of the barbershop quartet had been built.

The problem was not the public's response. At the Pan-Pacific Auditorium, Harper Goff said, "people would watch and watch. They wouldn't go away. They saw the whole show and they stayed for the next one. So the show had to be stopped for 25 minutes to clear out the audience. Walt knew it was a success."[136] But the logistics and economics were another matter. "Walt envisioned a big long train which would go all over America," Goff said. In each city the train visited, "people would come and go through the railroad cars. They would start at the back of the train and all the cars would have these little animated things that you could watch. This is what caused Walt to choose the size he did for the displays. . . . He wanted to make sure he had an aisle [in each railroad car] with enough room. . . . This idea called for a

21-car train on a siding with public access. The railroad companies said they would put in a 'Disney line' with a rental of thirteen thousand dollars a month or something like that. And the word got around. I think that Walt, who was used to success on his terms, may have expected all these cities to say, 'Oh yes, Mr. Disney, please come to our town . . . ' But then everybody began planning to make a lot of money, just to let Disney in."

Putting the displays in railroad cars was going up in cost, Goff said: "Walt bought three old Pullman cars, just to kind of fool around with. Then, suddenly, when he wanted to get some more the price had gone up substantially." Disney learned that simply moving his special train around the country would be enormously complex and difficult: "In order to get to Denver, for instance, the train would first have to go to Cheyenne, Wyoming. Then it would have to turn around (on a different railroad, the Colorado and Southern) and go back south to Denver. And they didn't have tracks to accommodate the train."[137]

When Granny's Cabin went on display at the Festival of California Living, Disney was already exploring another outlet for his enthusiasm for miniatures. His plans for a park to be called "Disneyland" had been public knowledge for more than seven months—not the fifty-acre park that popped up in the *Popular Science* article, but a smaller park in Burbank. In March 1952, he got tentative approval from the Burbank Board of Parks and Recreation for a $1.5 million development on the sixteen studio-owned acres across Riverside Drive from the Disney plant. His Mickey Mouse Park of 1948 was within financial reach now that the studio's fortunes had improved. Disney's desire to put his miniatures to work as an attraction had breathed new life into the dormant idea for a park, as Michael Broggie has written: "Initial design drawings by Eddie Sargeant showed an elaborate 1/8th scale railroad layout, complete with roundhouse and covered rail equipment storage tracks; rails wound over bridges crossing a gravity-flow canal boat ride."[138]

On March 27, 1952, the *Burbank Daily Review* quoted Disney as saying that "Disneyland will be something of a fair, an exhibition, a playground, a community center, a museum of living facts and a showplace of beauty and magic."[139] The park was to include what the newspaper called "various scenes of Americana" and a "zoo of miniature animals," like two donkeys he had brought from Italy.

(Disney visited Italy in the summer of 1951, in an excursion during the filming of *The Story of Robin Hood*, and he was taken with the tiny Sardinian donkeys he saw there; he brought two to Los Angeles late that fall. Although he told a reporter that he hadn't decided whether to keep the donkeys at his home or at the studio—predictably, they wound up at the studio—he surely had his amusement park in mind when he made his purchase.)[140]

Disney said the park was to be home to a "complete television center," from which programs would be transmitted to the whole country. It would "focus a new interest upon Burbank, Los Angeles and Southern California through the medium of television and other exploitation," he said. Most curiously, Disney described the park not as a commercial venture, but rather as a facility that would be "instantly available" to civic groups. That idea fell by the wayside very quickly.

CHAPTER 8

"He Was Interested in Something Else"
Escaping from Film
1953–1959

For years, Disney had been visiting amusement parks and other attractions in the United States and Europe with at least half an eye toward what he could learn that would be useful in a park of his own. In the early 1950s, with a Disneyland on Riverside Drive a live possibility, he began looking more closely at such places.

Bud Hurlbut, who owned a small "kiddieland" amusement park in El Monte, a suburb northeast of Los Angeles, told Chris Merritt of seeing Disney "kind of looking around at my rides. . . . I saw this man come on my property, and by the time he was there the second or third time I decided he wasn't just a park customer"—that is, someone who wanted to buy rides that Hurlbut manufactured. "Walt was studying how things worked, and I just walked up to him and said, 'You look like you're interested in rides,' and he said he was 'kind of looking at them.' He was a really nice fellow, so I sat down with him and answered a lot of his questions." Disney wound up inviting Hurlbut "to his house to ride his miniature steam train. I spent several Saturdays over there, and it was just like being with a neighbor. He would sit on the floor and relax, and as we sat there, we talked about trains and rides."[1]

Disney was also taking more concrete steps, like commissioning a master plan from the architectural firm Pereira and Luckman. Charles Luckman, who had known Disney for years, remembered hearing him describe his conception of Disneyland over lunch in April 1952, just after Disney announced his plans for a Burbank park: "He had a vivid mental image of it all—the streets and stores from other eras, the parade of Disney characters led by Mickey

Mouse, the bright lights, the bands playing, the variety of restaurants, the scenes and sets of his cartoons to serve as backgrounds for the concessions, water rides through enchanted lands, the mechanized people who could speak, the birds who could sing, the monorail [sic] which he would drive on opening day." Disney apparently hoped that the architects would devise a plan that would permit him to pack as many attractions as possible into the small area across Riverside Drive. Luckman returned a month later with a "preliminary concept" for a seven-acre Disneyland, which Disney rejected as clearly too small. "As the weeks went by," Luckman wrote, "the proposed size went from ten to twenty acres, then to thirty. Walt was screaming."[2]

Perhaps aware of the ongoing discussions, a *Daily Variety* columnist reported on October 27, 1952, that "Disney is shopping for a big tract of land to build 'Disneyland'—a playground for kids and grownups with restaurant, theatre, miniature railway, etc."[3] Satisfying Disney's ambitions within the geographical constraints of the Riverside site was turning out to be beyond the abilities of an architectural firm.

"By the time we reached fifty acres," Luckman wrote—this was probably in late 1952 or early 1953, around the time *Popular Science* wrote of a park of that size—"I called a halt." Building a Disneyland that big, or bigger, would not only require a larger site than the one on Riverside, it would also require money that Walt Disney did not have. Disneyland was one of those rare Walt Disney projects that had run aground on Roy Disney's skepticism. Because Roy resisted making more than a small amount available for the planning and design of a park, Walt formed and funded a separate private company, Walt Disney Enterprises, to carry out those functions. It came into existence on December 16, 1952. He was the sole shareholder. The corporation changed its name to Walt Disney Incorporated in March 1953, shortly before Disney and Walt Disney Productions signed a new employment contract on April 6, 1953, that explicitly gave him the right to pursue outside projects. An entirely predictable (and ultimately unsuccessful) minority stockholder's suit followed in June, attacking the employment contract and Disney's relationship with the company generally.[4] Perhaps to put a little distance between Walt Disney Productions and his private company, Disney changed its name to WED Enterprises in November 1953.[5]

The line between the public and private companies was always blurry, but Disneyland, especially in its early stages, was a personal project of Walt Disney's, distinct from the studio as little else had been since Walt Disney Productions became a public company in 1940. Disney had already bought the rights to Johnston McCulley's Zorro stories as another personal project, with

Ned E. Depinet, RKO's president, shakes hands with Walt Disney in 1950 to mark the conclusion of a new distribution deal. Roy Disney is at left, the Disney attorney Gunther Lessing at right. Quigley Photographic Collection, Walt Disney File, Georgetown University Library, Special Collections Division, Washington, D.C.

Lillian and Walt Disney on a 1952 visit to the Swiss village of Zermatt, a favorite Disney summer vacation spot. This photo, by the Zermatt firm Perren-Barberini, was part of the collection of Paul and Andrée (Dédée) Tilmant-Jeghers of Belgium, who visited with the Disneys at Zermatt in 1952 and again in 1958. Courtesy Pierre Nicolaï.

Disney and Richard Todd, (center), the star of three of his British-based live-action films, enjoy cotton candy with an unidentified third man on a visit to Coney Island in August 1953. Courtesy Richard Todd.

Disney as he appeared on the first episode of the *Disneyland* television program on October 27, 1954. ABC Television photo.

Disney tours Sleeping Beauty Castle in Disneyland, under construction in 1955. Courtesy University of Southern California, on behalf of the USC Specialized Libraries and Archival Collections.

Disney plays with young admirers at Smoke Tree Ranch in Palm Springs in an undated photo probably taken around 1960, after the Disneys had built their second weekend home at Smoke Tree. Courtesy Palm Springs Historical Society.

Disney at the controls of Disneyland's monorail, which began operations in the summer of 1959 along with the Matterhorn bobsled ride and the submarine ride. Courtesy University of Southern California, on behalf of the USC Specialized Libraries and Archival Collections.

Disney, an increasingly committed Republican over time, attended the 1964 GOP convention in San Francisco and posed there with former president Eisenhower, a personal friend. Courtesy Dwight D. Eisenhower Library, Abilene, Kansas.

Disney visited Tivoli Gardens in Copenhagen frequently on his trips to Europe and acknowledged Disneyland's debt to its Danish predecessor. On this visit, on September 5, 1964, he posed with Sven Hansen, a member of Tivoli's Boys' Guard. Courtesy Tivoli Gardens.

Walt Disney, Florida governor Haydon Burns, and Roy Disney at the November 15, 1965, press conference at which the Disneys revealed some of their plans for the 27,000 acres Walt Disney Productions had bought near Orlando. Courtesy Florida State Archive.

Disney (with help from Mickey Mouse) was grand marshal of the Pasadena Tournament of Roses Parade on January 1, 1966. Courtesy Tournament of Roses Archive.

In his later years, Disney became a devotee of lawn bowling, both at Smoke Tree Ranch in Palm Springs and at a public park near his home in Holmby Hills. Here he is with an unidentified fellow bowler at the Smoke Tree bowling green. Courtesy Palm Springs Historical Society.

Disney signs autographs for admirers on an October 9, 1966, visit to the Kansas City Art Institute, the school whose Saturday classes he attended fifty years earlier. Courtesy Mark Kausler.

an eye toward making a television series. As a result, there was a Zorro building on the lot, and that was where the first employees of WED were housed.

There is apparently no way to determine the dates when Disney hired those earliest WED employees, since the company was separate from Walt Disney Productions at the time (and the employees themselves were vague or clearly incorrect when they spoke of dates). But it could have been no later than early 1953 that Disney hired Richard Irvine, an art director for Twentieth-Century Fox who had worked for him in the mid-1940s on the live-action portions of *Victory Through Air Power* and *The Three Caballeros*. (Disney called art directors—who design the physical settings of live-action films—"brick and mortar men.") "I think the reason that he called me was because I was the first one that built models of a set for him, and he could see immediately the flexibility by rearranging and changing, as to how we could plan the action," Irvine told Richard Hubler in 1968. Irvine's first assignment was to act as Disney's liaison with Pereira and Luckman, then still involved with the project and exploring the possibilities of a site in Palos Verdes, on the Pacific coast. At that point, Irvine said, Disney decided he needed a staff of his own to develop his ideas before turning them over to an architect. "And then finally when he started to jell the ideas the momentum started to build and he got excited about it and went ahead and did it in house, so to speak."[6]

Irvine brought over two other art directors from Fox, Bill Martin and Marvin Davis. They shared offices with Bill Cottrell, Disney's brother-in-law and longtime employee, and Nat Winecoff, a promoter who was playing an ill-defined role in getting the Disneyland park off the ground.[7] Davis remembered the Zorro building as "a ramshackle wallboard thing, very temporary, hot in the summer and cold in the winter. . . . Walt had bought some period furniture, a dining set and other stuff . . . heavy dark wood furniture that he had in mind to use on the Zorro set. Bill Cottrell . . . was in charge of Zorro at the time. He had some scripts and some writers, and he was looking around for a cast. It might have been a feature film, or maybe a series, but it was important to Walt."

Davis first met Disney when Irvine introduced them in the Zorro building. "Then he invited both Dick and I up to his house to take a ride on his train, which was impressive for me because it was Walt Disney," Davis said in an interview with *The "E" Ticket*. "I was pretty thrilled about all of this. I got the impression that he was trying to give us the idea of what he wanted for Disneyland. He used his Carolwood Pacific railroad as an example of what he wanted to do next. There was a definite link between Walt's train at his home and what he went on to do at Disneyland."

When Davis went to work for WED, Disney had not yet surrendered the idea of Disneyland as a park on the sixteen acres across Riverside Drive, "which at that time was a storage area for pieces of sets and props and things," Davis said. Harper Goff, who had joined the Disney staff a few months before the plans for a Riverside Drive park were announced in March 1952, had drawn what Davis called "a little schematic thing, drawing up what was mostly a kiddieland, because that was what the idea was at that time. He did a kind of aerial perspective of it, and it was filled with mostly Harper's ideas. He had a train going around it, and some other stuff, and from that, Dick Irvine and I got started."

Davis remembered producing "a hundred and thirty-three different drawings and designs, because we had no idea where the park was going to be or anything [else about it], to begin with. I just started out putting together the ideas that we had all talked about . . . the idea of the train circling everything, in a kind of oblong shape. Then we started using the pear shape, because it seemed to accommodate all the things we needed."[8]

Davis's job was to help Disney "see what the vague ideas in his mind would look like on paper"[9]—thus the constant flow of new plans for the park. It was not long, Davis said, before "we were planning something bigger, and we knew it wouldn't fit on the property there."[10]

Disney regularly visited the Zorro building, which was near the front gate to the studio, as he entered from the parking lot. "He would drop into my office every day and see what I was doing," Bill Martin told The "E" Ticket. "He didn't pressure you, and at first I wondered how you got a decision around there. Things just seemed to happen."[11]

Disney maintained that vagueness deliberately, Dick Irvine said: "We used to have storyboards, and we would make a list of ideas, concepts and nothing was really pinned down except that 'what would people need,' 'what would they do,' 'what kind of entertainment would they have.' All the needs for the public that would have to be contemplated going into this park. We would just take this and put up our ideas, write our ideas out on squares of paper, put them up on a board, and he'd come down in the afternoon and sit there and look at them and juggle them around. . . . And eventually it evolved."[12]

There were similarities between the Disney of the early 1930s and the Disney that Irvine, Davis, and Martin knew in the early 1950s. In the 1920s, Disney had first animated, then had written gags for others to draw as he directed their work. In the early 1930s he finally moved into a wholly supervisory role, and only then, after he assumed that role, did his films begin to change at an accelerated pace. In the late 1940s and early 1950s, likewise, Disney first worked with his own hands, using machines and woodworking tools to build miniatures of one kind or another. By 1953, he had realized that the park taking shape in his mind would be, in effect, a tabletop layout blown up almost (but not quite) to full size. Its trains would be small but indisputably real, and far more satisfying to own and run than his miniature *Lilly Belle*. And this time, Disney moved from a hands-on role to a supervisory role with no evidence of the distress he felt in the early 1930s.

It was instead his wife who felt distress as he poured their own money into planning for the park. "Before I got that park going, I spent over $100,000 that I borrowed on the insurance that I'd been paying on for thirty years," he said in 1956. When he did, Disney said years later, "my wife raised the dickens with me. She wanted to know what would happen to her if something happened to me."[13]

In Bob Thomas's words, "The stock [in Walt Disney Productions] was his principal asset, and although he lived well, by Hollywood standards he was not a rich man." Even in 1951, Disney responded to a friend's request for a loan by pleading that he had "borrowed close to the hilt on my insurance and on personal notes—am close to fifty thousand dollars in debt, which is the limit of my personal borrowing ability. The new house cost much more than I anticipated."[14] Said Lillian Disney in 1956: "I've always been worried. I never have felt secure. Never. . . . He's always telling us how wealthy we are, how much we've got, and we haven't got anything."[15]

The involvement of the studio—and, as it turned out, of other sources of money—would be essential when Disney was ready to move beyond planning and design to the purchase of land, the building of rides, and construction of the park itself. The first step, though, was to decide where the park was to go. To help make that decision, Disney turned to a consulting firm called Stanford Research Institute (SRI), which had a five-man Los Angeles office.

"Walt was at a cocktail party with Charles Luckman, the architect, and Luckman knew me," said Harrison "Buzz" Price, a member of SRI's Los Angeles staff. "Walt had been trying to get help from Luckman and [William] Pereira and [Welton] Becket; he had three buddies who were big-time architects in town. He was having a hard time articulating his idea in architectural terms so he could have a dialogue with guys like that. Luckman told him, 'Why don't you go to Stanford Research? They did a good job for us in Hawaii when we were building a new kind of stadium.' That's how I got the lead."[16]

Price's first meeting with Disney took place on June 3, 1953.[17] Writing about that meeting, Price said that what Disney described to him "sounded strange, unlike anything you would expect in an amusement park. . . . Walt's major investment would be committed to creating a storytelling environment. Rides would be subordinate to story and setting. Most shocking, there were no thrill rides, no roller coaster, no super fast fear of falling rides anywhere."[18] Moreover, Disney wanted to open his park in just two years, in 1955.

Disney was, in Price's description, coolly hardheaded when it came to finding the most desirable location for the new park in Southern California. He refused to point Price toward any desired outcome, deferring instead to the data that Price and his colleagues would assemble. "I asked him, 'There are four thousand square miles. Do you have any ideas of your own about where you think it should be?' He threw it right back at me: 'You tell me.' . . . So we did. We came back in twelve weeks and told him right where it ought to go."[19]

Two days after meeting with Disney, Price submitted his "Proposal for Research for Disneyland" dated June 5, 1953. A site study, titled "Analysis of Location Factors for Disneyland," was dated August 28, 1953, exactly twelve weeks later.[20] Roy, committed now to his brother's idea, paid Stanford Research a total of $32,000 for that site study and a four-month feasibility study.[21]

Price's analysis took into account a large number of factors, including likely population growth patterns, freeway construction, and "the effect of terrain on television transmission," since the idea was that TV "will play an important part in the promotion and development of Disneyland."[22] The study pointed toward a location southeast of Los Angeles in Anaheim, in Orange County just off the Santa Ana Freeway. That freeway was then under construction, but most of it between downtown Los Angeles and Orange County was scheduled for completion in 1954. It would be the main route to Disneyland.

"I had a precise assignment," Price said in 2003, "and I didn't burden myself with the idea, is this crazy? For example, how do you figure the location of this thing that's going to draw a lot of people and it's going to have worldwide interest. Where do you put it in southern California? There were ways to measure that, and we did it, and we put it in the right place."[23]

Disney's behavior in 1953 was as entrepreneurial as it had been thirty years earlier, but with a major difference. He now understood that he needed solid footing of some kind before he made a speculative leap. Even then, economic studies could not tell him whether an amusement park like Disneyland would be successful, but only how to improve the odds for success. Harper Goff remembered that Disney recoiled at first from the implications of Price's study, taking refuge again in the notion of a Riverside Drive park. "The Stanford Research people said that when Walt Disney puts in an amusement park, he's got to have a lot of space, but Walt was horrified," Goff said. "He said, 'They think I'm making a lot of money, and they're trying to get me to spend a lot. I can't go into a big thing like that.' But finally Walt was convinced when they said there wouldn't be enough space for parking" at the Riverside Drive site.[24]

Goff's own involvement with Disneyland was limited at the time because he was the de facto art director (a title that union rules denied him on the screen) of 20,000 Leagues Under the Sea. It was while Disney was ramping up his involvement with Disneyland that work on that film got under way. For the first time, Disney had signed top-rank movie stars—Kirk Douglas and James Mason—for one of his live-action films. Douglas's salary alone, for twelve weeks' work, was $175,000, which Douglas later claimed, probably correctly, was the most Disney had ever paid an actor in his live-action films.[25] Making 20,000 Leagues would entail other expenses exceeding any previously incurred on the studio's live-action films. The new sound stage was only the beginning; underwater filming off the Bahamas and abundant special effects still lay ahead. 20,000 Leagues was one of the first films made in the CinemaScope wide-screen process, a major weapon in Hollywood's effort to win back audiences lost to television.

Disney was making his entrance into real Hollywood filmmaking as flashy as possible, clearly with the idea of establishing himself immediately as something more than a producer of children's films. 20,000 Leagues was unusual, Disney said, in that Roy Disney had confidence in the film, even as the budget climbed past four million dollars. "For some reason, from the very start he believed in that picture. . . . I got worried then. I thought there was something wrong with him."

Harper Goff remembered that Disney himself could not suppress anxiety about the risks he and his brother were taking. Goff had designed the *Nautilus,* Captain Nemo's submarine, to suggest a sea beast, with prominent "eyes" and saw blades on the prow that could tear through the hulls of wooden ships. "I had to sell the features in my drawings of the *Nautilus* to Walt. He'd say, 'Do you think all of this is necessary? Do you know what all of this is going to cost? . . . ' Walt tried everything he could to keep things simple and keep things cheap because he hadn't made any money from these pictures yet. He once said to me, 'Harper, all the money that my brother and I have made in our lives is tied up in this one stupid picture.'"[26]

Other members of the Disney staff sensed in Disney—who was now in his early fifties—some of the same unease. "Walt Disney had to make a lot of difficult decisions in the 1950s," Frank Thomas said in an interview with *The "E" Ticket.* "He scaled back animation, increased his involvement with

Disneyland and live-action filming. I don't think he was that sure of himself on a lot of his decisions, at that point. I can remember the way he said things to us, and the way he acted, and the way he squirmed in his chair. I felt that he wasn't sure, but he didn't want to admit that he wasn't sure, because he was our leader."[27]

Whatever Disney's worries, they did not slow his improvised research for his park. In August 1953, when *The Sword and the Rose* was released, Richard Todd was in New York "doing a promotional thing for him—I was there damn near a month, and I was living at the Waldorf-Astoria in the Towers, being very well looked after." Disney had just returned to New York on August 9 from a month in Europe. "He rang me up one day and said, 'Come to Coney Island with me.' I could feel my face falling. It wasn't my ideal place, but, anyhow, I said, 'Yes, yes, thank you.' We had a hell of a good day, actually. That was the beginning of Disneyland. He was going to see what the things were that people liked doing. We did everything—the switchbacks [roller coasters], the horses, everything. We ate the fluffy stuff [cotton candy]. We had a lovely day, thoroughly enjoyed ourselves."[28]

In California a few days later, Todd and his wife spent a day with Walt and Lillian at their home in Holmby Hills, where Todd saw "cabinets full of the objects he loved: tiny things; miniatures of all sorts in china, wood or metal." Disney gave Todd a tiny potbellied stove that he had made himself, "a beautiful little thing about six inches high, painted in white, green and gold."[29]

With a site for his park chosen but his own resources exhausted, Disney needed the studio's help to buy the 160 acres Disneyland would require. On September 11, 1953, he won his board's support by arguing, in effect, that television could be used for more than promoting the studio's theatrical films, until then the prevailing rationale. He would use television as a lever to bring his park into existence, by making a network's investment in it a condition of his providing a program. Then he would use his TV show to promote the park itself.[30]

But first he had to find a willing partner. Although the park may have come up in discussions with networks and potential sponsors—as in the General Foods deal that fell through earlier in the year—only now did the Disneys begin seriously pushing to make support for it part of an agreement.

Walt Disney's own thinking about Disneyland had advanced past enthusiastic words to the point that it could be embodied in a drawing—not by him, but by Herb Ryman, who was no longer working at the Disney studio. Disney may have been reluctant to reduce his ideas to a drawing, even so.

"He had I think thirty-seven or forty ideas for different rides," Irvine said. "He had tried to lay out areas for different theme ideas [but] he wasn't anxious to get it to sketches and visualization." Disney was most concerned, instead, with "a plan for circulation," for people's movements within the park. "However," Irvine said, "we had to do a birds-eye view of it for Roy to take back to New York."[31]

Disney summoned Ryman—a highly facile illustrator who had a particular gift for romantic, atmospheric drawings of unusual places—over the weekend of September 23–24, 1953, to collaborate with him on an aerial rendering of the proposed park. This very large drawing—the image area is 39 inches high by 67 ½ inches wide on a slightly larger sheet—is one of the most celebrated relics from Disneyland's early history. It shows a park divided into various "lands" that open off a hub—Frontier Country, Fantasy Land, Lilliputian Land, True-Life Adventureland, and so on, all dominated by a castle at the end of Main Street. Visitors would enter through one entrance, under an elevated railway station; the tracks would encircle the park.[32]

A "pitch kit," prepared around the same time (it bears a 1953 copyright date), described Disneyland's "lands" in considerable detail, and the park itself in fulsome language:

> The idea of Disneyland is a simple one. It will be a place for people to find happiness and knowledge.
> It will be a place for parents and children to share pleasant times in one another's company, a place for teacher and pupils to discover greater ways of understanding and education. Here the older generation can recapture the nostalgia of days gone by, and the younger generation can savor the challenge of the future. Here will be the wonders of Nature and Man for all to see and understand.[33]

It is not clear what kinds of meetings Roy Disney held during his September trip to New York, but, in any case, there were no immediate takers for a Disney TV show with park attached. NBC and the Columbia Broadcasting System (CBS) were the dominant networks, with far more affiliates than the also-rans, the American Broadcasting Company (ABC) and DuMont. Neither of the two big networks was interested.

In November 1953, Roy was back in New York. He said in *Motion Picture Daily*'s paraphrase that "work is progressing on a format for a Disney television show to emanate from the studio. When the format is completed . . . network affiliation will be sought." As far as the Disneys were concerned, Roy said, TV would be what *Motion Picture Daily* called "an exploitation medium for theatrical pictures." The article made no mention of the Disneyland park.[34]

In the official Disney version, a frustrated Roy Disney, fed up with NBC's stalling, called ABC's president, Leonard Goldenson, and ABC leaped at the chance to strike a deal.[35] Goldenson's version differed. When the Disneys called him in late 1953, he wrote in his autobiography,

> ABC was really [Walt] Disney's last hope. He'd gone to the banks, and when he tried to explain what he wanted to build, they just couldn't grasp the concept. They kept thinking of a place like Coney Island. Very risky. They turned him down. . . .
>
> I offered to take the Disneys in to see our board. But as a condition, I said, "I want a one-hour program, every week." . . . At first my board opposed the deal. After all, they said, CBS had turned Disney down. NBC had turned him down. And the banks had said no. More to the point, where were *we* going to get financing? . . .
>
> Then I hammered out a deal with the Disneys. We would put in $500,000 and guarantee [bank] loans [of $4.5 million]. In exchange we took 35 percent [actually 34.48 percent] of Disneyland, and all profits from the food concessions for ten years. I knew that could be a gold mine.
>
> And of course there was programming. That's what I really wanted from them. We agreed to a seven-year deal, with an option for an eighth, at $5 million a year. At $40 million, it was then the biggest programming package in history.[36]

ABC and Disney were actually a good fit. ABC had been frozen in place for two years, until early in 1953, while the federal government scrutinized its merger with United Paramount Theaters. It desperately needed not just high-profile programming like a Disney show, but programming of any kind. Moreover, Goldenson was an early advocate of filmed programs—the Disney show would be one—at a time when most TV shows were "live." The Disneys needed a network that would put their show on the air, with minimal interference, and invest some money in the park, and ABC had every incentive to do both.

Even so, the negotiations evidently took several months. Finally, in March 1954, the Disneys signed a contract with ABC for an hour-long weekly series, starting in October. On April 5, immediately after both boards had approved the deal, Roy Disney said the TV show would be "made to serve our motion picture program."[37] Walt Disney spoke in similar terms near the end of his first season in TV: "We went into it in the belief it would help our [theatrical film] business."[38] Unquestionably, though, it was the opportunity the contract provided to build and promote his park that was most important to him.

The show, like the park, would be called *Disneyland,* and its four "lands" would mimic the four—Fantasyland, Frontierland, Tomorrowland, and Adventureland—into which the Anaheim park would be divided. "I had a contract that said I had complete say of what we produced," Disney said in 1956. "So I just sort of insisted that my Disneyland park be a part of my television."

In addition to the corporation that eventually became WED Enterprises, Disney had formed another corporation, Disneyland, by August 1953.[39] He was the owner of "substantially all" of the stock of Disneyland, Incorporated, and he transferred from WED to the new company what a corporate document called "the plans, models and other properties for the Park."[40] Disney probably set up the Disneyland corporation in anticipation of what happened in May 1954. It was then that it became a real company, with Disney as president and board chairman. His board was made up mostly of representatives of ABC and his other principal financial backer, Western Printing and Lithographing Company, which had been for more than twenty years the publisher of Disney books, comic books, puzzles, and games. Besides Disney himself, the only member of the board from Walt Disney Productions was Paul Pease, who had been the studio's treasurer since 1947.[41]

As ABC had, Walt Disney Productions bought 34.48 percent of Disneyland's stock. Western Printing bought 13.79 percent, and Disney himself, personally and through WED, retained ownership of 17.25 percent. The four owners invested almost $1.5 million in the park, providing leverage for the bank loans that would pay for most of its construction. So the deal with ABC did require a dilution of the control Disney valued so highly. He remained completely in control of WED Enterprises, which planned and designed the park under a July 1, 1954, agreement with Disneyland, Incorporated, but ownership of the park itself was divided.

As construction approached, Disney sent teams of his employees to inspect other attractions that might hold lessons of some kind for the Disney park. Such visits had been taking place at least since the previous fall, when Price explored sites in the United States as well as Tivoli Gardens in Copenhagen. "The highlight of our feasibility analysis," Price wrote many years later, "took place at the amusement park annual convention and trade show in November 1953 at the Sherman Hotel in Chicago. There we cornered four of the nation's leading amusement park owners and fed them Chivas Regal and caviar in our suite. Dick Irvine, Nat Winecoff, Bill Cottrell and I presented the concept of the park in a two-hour evening session," with Ryman's bird's-eye drawing as a visual aid. "The reaction was unanimous: *It would not work.*"[42]

Disney rejected the doubters' arguments—for example, that he was planning to spend too much on aspects of the park, like landscaping, that would produce no revenue—but not the doubters; he hired two of them as consultants. And as Randy Bright has written in his authorized history of the park, Disney took advice that he thought made sense: "One constructive point that Disney did pick up quickly from nearly all of the amusement park operators was the need for efficient high-capacity operations. It was very apparent that a few seconds lost in loading each ride vehicle translated into major attendance loss at the end of each day."[43]

Disney had an advantage in that his people were visiting more attractions, and scrutinizing them more carefully, than any operator, preoccupied with his own business, could hope to do. Harper Goff remembered that during the summer and fall of 1954, "Walt sent us all around to every amusement park in the country. We would take pictures and come back and tell Walt all about what they were doing. One of the main things we tried to get was their 'gate' . . . how much they charged, how many people came through, and how much they made. Also what kinds of operating problems they had, such as dishonesty."[44]

Borrowings from existing attractions were inevitable, given the tight schedule. Much of Disneyland's novelty would have to arise from how cleverly it combined such elements in a way that made sense for a park opening in 1955.

Roger Broggie was in charge of making a direct connection between Disney's backyard railroad and his new and much larger layout: "In 1954, when they said, 'we're now going to do Disneyland,' I pulled out all the drawings on this *Lilly Belle* and there were a very few modifications required to blow it up to a three-foot gauge," the standard for a narrow-gauge railroad. "All we actually did was take those drawings of the *Lilly Belle* and blow it up five times and it came out 36-inch gauge."[45]

After visiting Palm Springs for a decade or more, Disney had built a vacation home there in 1950, at a private development called Smoke Tree Ranch. It was to pay for two locomotives and the track surrounding the park that Disney sold his home at Smoke Tree in 1954. The railroad was the property not of Disneyland, Incorporated, but of his personal company, WED Enterprises.[46] The steam railroad would remain Walt Disney's property, through WED, even after he transferred his minority ownership in the park to Walt Disney Productions.

In 1950, when Disney built his Carolwood Pacific layout at Holmby Hills, "I got the power company and paid them a good price to remove or build a new power line behind me," he said, so that the lines would not interfere with the illusion he wanted to create. He linked that early effort to exclude the outside world to what he planned for Disneyland, where he would exclude the outside world with a berm. "It's like setting atmosphere," he said. "You're doing a mood. You don't see the city out there."

On-site construction began in July 1954, about a year before the opening date to which Disney had committed himself in his contract with ABC. Meanwhile, Disney was scrambling to fulfill another part of that contract, to deliver a weekly TV show. "When I went into television," Disney said in 1961, "it was a sudden thing, and I had to improvise. . . . I found myself with a contract and I had to start to deliver in October and it was April."

When the show was being put together, Disney said in 1956, "I know I was dying for somebody to suggest my doing the emceeing." That he would be the host seems never to have been seriously in doubt. He was not a neophyte; besides his frequent appearances on radio throughout the 1930s and 1940s, he had appeared on a few television shows in addition to his own two Christmas specials.

A crucial decision was that Disney would speak directly to his audience. As he said, the Christmas shows "were impersonal. We let the audience look in on something we were doing but we didn't talk to the audience. . . . I was talking with some friends in the advertising business and they . . . said, 'Look, Walt, you talk to them.' Television is a very intimate thing. So they said, 'Talk to them.'" He had done that on some radio broadcasts, but not on TV. For that reason, perhaps, Disney said he was "scared to death" when he was filmed for the first *Disneyland* shows; but he soon came to enjoy being his show's host. He acknowledged that "I have a nasal twang. It's a Missouri twang. And my diction—I get sloppy. . . . I say, 'Now we're gonna . . . '" His diction was in fact a little peculiar; he tended to drawl, stretching out words in no discernible pattern. But in his early appearances he never seemed stiff or nervous or tense. When he addressed his audience, it was as a relaxed, low-key camera subject who was especially suited to television, that "very intimate thing."

The first *Disneyland* show, on October 27, 1954, opened with a studio tour, the sort of amiable behind-the-scenes humbug that purports to show people at work when the only work they are doing is performing for the camera. The real business of the premiere was to cement the identification between the show and the park to come. Disney spoke of the park in the grandest terms, as "a fair, an amusement park, an exhibition, a city from the Arabian

Nights, a metropolis of the future—a place of hopes and dreams, fact and fancy, all in one." He said that in the future the TV show itself would originate "from this Disneyland"—which never happened—"but this year we want you to see and share with us the experience of building this dream into a reality."

Here, more successfully than ever before, Disney was transforming the promotion of his products into something else, an ostensible sharing of what would ordinarily be secret. He made it seem as if he were taking his viewers into his confidence. There was no sense in what he said that by revealing how his park was built—or his films made—he might prevent anyone from sharing the illusion, the "dream" or the "magic." Instead, what he showed of the park's construction would itself become part of the "magic."

Disneyland broadcast only two additional progress reports on the construction of the park before it opened in July 1955, but there were, besides, two shows promoting *20,000 Leagues Under the Sea* (which was released in December 1954), two promoting the *True-Life Adventures,* and one promoting *Lady and the Tramp,* an animated feature scheduled for release in the summer of 1955. In most cases, the full hour was not devoted to such previews—but each week's broadcast also ended with a trailer promoting a current Disney theatrical release.

Otherwise, *Disneyland* relied heavily on films from the studio's past, both animated and live action, including some features that had not done particularly well in theaters *(So Dear to My Heart, Alice in Wonderland).* The Disneys had always brushed aside suggestions that they might sell their older films for television showings—TV simply couldn't pay enough, Roy Disney said—and now their wisdom had been validated; they could show their films on TV without giving up ownership in any way. "When it came to television," Walt Disney said in 1956, "the one thing I wanted was to control my product. I didn't want anybody else to have it. I wanted to be able to control the format and what I did with it. Now I had complete control. There is nobody . . . that can tell me yes or no."

The timing for a show like *Disneyland* was uncannily good. The eldest children of the "baby boom" were only eight years old, but the young parents of 1954 had once been the children who in the midst of a long Depression delighted in the Disney shorts and *Snow White and the Seven Dwarfs* and all the merchandise and comic strips and books associated with them. Hence there was a double layer of affection and interest. Moreover, it was only in 1954 that television was becoming truly ubiquitous in the United States; a federal freeze on new licenses had left some parts of the country without any stations until 1952. Since there were only four networks (although DuMont was fading fast), and thus a limited choice of programs at any one time, there was a great opportunity for a successful program to reach a huge audience.

Disneyland did exactly that. In its first season, despite ABC's weak lineup of affiliates and against popular programs on CBS and NBC, it finished sixth overall in the Nielsen ratings, watched by 39.1 percent of all the households that owned a television set. Only one other ABC program finished in the top thirty.

Disney could not have been wholly surprised by such strong results, but he was certainly surprised by the public's response to the first *Frontierland* episode in *Disneyland's* 1954–55 season. On December 15, 1954, *Disneyland* aired "Davy Crockett, Indian Fighter." It was the first of three *Frontierland* installments about the legendary frontiersman.

Disney had been considering a film of some kind about Davy Crockett for almost a decade. A 1947 story inventory report listed a "roughout"—a rough outline for a Crockett-themed musical production—by the Missouri artist Thomas Hart Benton, who worked briefly at the Disney studio in 1946.[47] In the immediate postwar years, other celebrated writers and artists, like Salvador Dali and Aldous Huxley, also worked for Disney briefly. The reasons for their hiring varied from case to case—Disney hoped to incorporate an attention-getting Dali-designed segment, "Destino," into one of his package features, and Huxley, as an eminent English writer, was hired to work on that English classic *Alice in Wonderland*—but nothing came of any of those associations. In the spring of 1948, fresh from *Melody Time* with its folktale heroes Johnny Appleseed and Pecos Bill, Disney was speaking to the columnist Hedda Hopper about making a film of some kind based on Davy Crockett's life, but that idea too fell into abeyance, until the TV show revived it.[48]

Fess Parker, who was then thirty years old, was chosen by Walt Disney himself to play Crockett, under circumstances that the matte artist Peter Ellenshaw described: "I happened to be in the sweat box waiting for dailies, when Walt came in with a talent scout, he was looking for an actor to play the role of Davy. They screened some short scene from a film called *Them!*, with an actor in it by the name of Jim Arness. He was the man Walt was supposed to be considering, but when Walt asked who the actor was playing a small role in the scene, the talent scout didn't know, had to put in a phone call to find his name was Fess Parker!"[49]

Public enthusiasm for the Crockett shows was remarkably strong. The theme song by George Bruns and Tom Blackburn—simple but unforgettable—sat atop the hit parade for months. Huge crowds greeted Parker on a twenty-two-city publicity tour in the spring of 1955, and sales of coonskin caps and hundreds of other Crockett-labeled items rose into the many millions of dollars. It was a Texas exhibitor, Disney said, who suggested the highly unusual step of combining the three Crockett television shows into a feature film.[50] Released in color in the summer of 1955, *Davy Crockett, King of the Wild Frontier* grossed $2.5 million on the tickets of customers who had mostly seen the shows before, but only in black and white.

Disney spent more on the Crockett shows than other TV producers did on comparable fare, not just by shooting in color but also by shooting on location in North Carolina and Tennessee. There is, however, no confusing those shows with more polished Hollywood theatrical products. The climactic battle at the Alamo, in the third episode, was all too obviously shot on a confined sound stage. Writing about the Crockett craze more than thirty years later, the newspaper columnist Bob Greene was undoubtedly correct when he pointed to Fess Parker himself as the critical element in the TV shows' success: "In his portrayal of Crockett, Parker brought to the small screen a presence that was palpable; people looked at him, and they listened to him, and they tingled. The face and the voice combined to represent everything that was ideally male in the United States."[51]

Although he leaped to celebrity in a TV show, Parker's impact was that of a bona fide movie star. He was tall (six foot five) and handsome, but so were many other young leading men in the 1950s. Parker brought to the screen two priceless assets in addition to his good looks. For one thing, he was relaxed in front of the camera as few actors are, especially in TV, where the demands for speed and efficiency have always encouraged actors to be tight and guarded. For another, he could deliver dialogue with complete conviction, as in his stirring speech to Congress attacking President Andrew Jackson's treatment of the Indians in the second Crockett episode. Parker seemed emotionally open, as good actors must, but the emotions were those of a strong and even stoic man—one with a sly sense of humor, suited to "grinnin' down a bear."

Disney had gone into television expecting to manipulate it to his own ends, by promoting his park and his theatrical films, but television had demonstrated through the Crockett craze how unpredictable it really was; and it had bestowed on him a full-fledged star whom he had signed to a personal contract, rather than a contract with the studio, and whose career was in his hands. "We've had lots of offers from other studios wanting to borrow Fess Parker," Disney said in May 1955, "but we've got four Davy Crockett pictures to make, and they'll have to wait until next winter for Fess." The idea initially was to film four more Crockett episodes for *Disneyland*. The first two of the second batch were filmed on location, in Ohio and along the Mississippi River, starting in June 1955.[52]

In mid-July, Disney pulled Parker and his costar, Buddy Ebsen, away from location shooting and back to Los Angeles to sing at the Hollywood Bowl on a Thursday and Friday evening, July 14 and 15. Each evening's "Tribute to Walt Disney," made up of music associated with Disney films, concluded with "The Ballad of Davy Crockett," sung by Parker, Ebsen, and the Roger Wagner Chorale.[53] The occasion was the official opening of the Disneyland park the following Sunday, July 17, an event that would be nationally televised by ABC.

The park would not be completed on its opening day—and not just because Disney frequently emphasized that he considered it a work perpetually in progress, in language like this: "The park means a lot to me, in that it's something that will never be finished, something that I can keep developing, keep plussing and adding to." Disneyland was not finished in any sense, and not really ready for guests, but they were coming anyway. The construction schedule had proved to be difficult and finally impossible to meet.

Certain stories turn up in almost every account of Disneyland's construction, and sometimes they tell more than might first appear. Randy Bright wrote that Disney "found it very difficult to understand the necessity for certain costly building materials and methods. As a longtime filmmaker, Walt had imagined that Disneyland would be built more like a motion-picture set, on a temporary basis. He had to be introduced to the real world of occupancy regulations and building codes. One day, on a walk-through of the construction site with [Joe] Fowler [a retired navy admiral who supervised construction] and Dick Irvine, Disney became furious when he saw the amount of concrete that was being poured for the Main Street train station foundation. 'By the time Joe gets through burying all our money underground,' he snapped, 'we won't have a thing left for the show!'"[54]

Disney was similarly incensed by the excavation for a dry dock for the *Mark Twain*, a scaled-back stern-wheeler: "Joe Fowler viewed the hole, a dry dock-to-be for the Mark Twain during its important maintenance overhauls, as an operational necessity. To Walt Disney, it looked more like the excavation for King Tut's tomb. 'By the time you get through with that damn ditch, we won't have any land left!' exclaimed Disney. For a long time thereafter, he called it 'Joe's Ditch' and gave him, perhaps, one final sarcastic jab by officially dubbing it 'Fowler's Harbor.'"[55]

The extremely tight schedule virtually guaranteed that there would be cost overruns and that the park would not be ready on its opening day—both of which happened—but Disney, anticipating the construction of what he thought would be something like a huge movie set, may not have realized just how tight the schedule really was, or how ominous the threat of cost overruns. (For one thing, the schedule was an invitation to labor problems, which arrived in the form of a plumbers' strike shortly before the park opened.)

As it happened, the estimated cost of building the park roughly quadrupled in the year construction was under way, as Joe Fowler explained to Bright: "At ground-breaking, I had a budget of four and a half million dollars. That was before we had any plans at all. Two months later, in September, it went up to seven million dollars. In November, it was up to eleven million. We were still talking eleven million dollars in April [1955] when I was walking down Main Street with Roy and a representative from Bank of America who scanned the project and said it looked closer to fifteen million. But by the time opening day had arrived, we had spent seventeen million dollars."[56]

Ultimately, as money ran short, the financing for Disneyland was completed by what *Business Week* called "a special plan for concessionaires. The 32 of them paid the first and last year rent on a five-year lease. Then, with both ends anchored, the Disneys hocked the middle three-year lease expectations at the bank."[57]

Disney visited the construction site most often on Saturdays. Harper Goff told *The "E" Ticket* that "Walt would seem discouraged at the beginning because nothing seemed to be happening. I guess he thought he could just 'sneeze twice' and there would be work completed each time he went down there. They were just moving dirt . . . they weren't building anything that you could see. . . . He'd say, 'Will they ever get this so it looks something other than just a hole in the ground?' And a week later he'd say, 'I'd better go down there and see if I can stir them up a little bit,' and then, 'Not one goddamn thing's changed . . . are they working?' So I'd take him over and show him the concrete forms which were in place for the waterfall, and then we'd walk around and do 'questions and answers' on all the work going on."[58]

Sometimes Disney did get the quick results he wanted. "All through the construction phases," the landscape architect Morgan "Bill" Evans said, "Walt would be out there every weekend, and we would take a kind of ritual hike on Saturday. . . . Once in a while we'd be walking along with Joe Fowler and Dick Irvine and Walt, with all the troops strung along behind us, and Walt would turn to Joe Fowler and say, 'Joe, that tree looks a little close to the walkway, doesn't it?' And then he'd turn around and he'd say, 'How about moving that tree, Bill . . . ?' And this was maybe a fifteen-ton tree." But Evans would move it.[59]

Appropriately, it was the trains that were completed most quickly and easily. "We had a train running around Disneyland on the Fourth of July before the park opened," Roger Broggie said, "and had it well finished before that. . . . We never could close in the whole track because they took a section out to run big equipment through, because the park was under construction, up until midnight before they opened. But we had a running head start on the trains."[60] On the Fourth of July, at a small party for the members of the Penthouse Club, the studio's elite, Disney had his first opportunity to operate the park's two steam locomotives. It was, Ward Kimball told Leon Janzen, "a big day for Walt. . . . To the eighty or ninety people that were there that day, the park was basically a big empty place, with a lot of work going on. . . . But to Walt, the locomotives were under steam! . . . To him the Mark Twain and the Disneyland trains were like the seventh and eighth wonders of the world."[61]

In the feverish last days before the park opened, Walt and Lillian marked their thirtieth wedding anniversary with a private party at Frontierland's Golden Horseshoe Saloon on Wednesday, July 13. The celebratory Thursday and Friday nights at the Hollywood Bowl followed. Meanwhile, work continued furiously, at the studio and the park, to tie up as many loose ends as possible. Disney, who had been giddy with happiness at the anniversary party, and who appears to be in a similar state in photos from the Hollywood Bowl, was by the Saturday night before the opening immersed in the park's unfinished details. Work continued through the night.

Cash Shockey, who worked in the studio's machine shop on Disneyland attractions, wrote in 1968: "We had everything shipped for the grand opening except the cars for the railroad, which were to leave at 6 A.M. Every car was finished except the observation car, which lacked murals on either side." Around three in the morning, "Walt came by and said, 'Cash, where are the murals for the observation car?' I told him the plans didn't call any. In his quiet way he looked at me and said, 'This car leaves at 6 A.M. and they better be there at 6 A.M.' I had never painted a mountain or a river, but I did then. When Walt saw the murals he just smiled and shook his head—he had his murals not good but fast."[62]

When Disneyland opened on July 17, 1955, Main Street was finished and a half dozen Fantasyland rides were operating, but the other three "lands" offered only that many rides among them (a precise count being difficult because so many attractions broke down in the course of the day). "From a purely landscape standpoint," Bill Evans told *The "E" Ticket,* "I don't think that park was finished for about three years. We were striving to achieve an instant maturity—the appearance of full growth—within the constrictions of a meager budget. We had an acceptable maturity in the jungle, in Town Square and the hub, but . . . when you got out in Frontierland there was nothing but little tiny five-gallon trees."[63] Much of the park—this is visible in early photos and in the opening-day television show—was bare dirt and empty spaces.

Opening day was by general agreement a disaster, with the basic ingredients for trouble—blazing heat, water fountains that were not working, balky rides—magnified by the thousands of people who entered the park on counterfeit tickets. The TV show, rough-hewn like so much early live TV, gives only a hint of all the off-camera headaches.

Fess Parker and Buddy Ebsen appeared on the show, in their roles as Davy Crockett and his companion George Russel. They were victims of one of the many opening-day mistakes, soaked by accidentally triggered sprinklers.[64] Later, they joined Disney for a drink in his apartment above the firehouse, on the town square just off Main Street. "There wasn't any agenda," Parker recalled for *The "E" Ticket.* "We were just sort of his 'side men.' At that point he was wearing a sport shirt, and once in a while he'd put on his little hat and go out there. He would just stand and let people come up and speak to him. He really, truly was happy to see his hopes and beliefs succeeding right before his eyes. You know, we often see athletes when they've won an Olympics championship or some other tremendous athletic accomplishment . . . there's a way that people look when they've reached a certain goal. Walt was in that kind of elevated state on that day."[65]

Disney was still the host who reveled in entertaining riders on the Carolwood Pacific, but now he was entertaining on a vastly larger scale. "I think if you really look at Walt Disney's life," Michael Broggie said, "and what he took pleasure in . . . his miniatures, and what adults call 'scale models,' the truth is, Walt was playing with his toys."[66] Now Disney—the newspaper carrier who had played surreptitiously on his classmates' porches—was the kid with the best toys, the most popular kid in the neighborhood.

What really set the Disney park apart, as with the Disney TV show, was the way it evoked more distinctive Disney achievements, the early animated features especially. Disney's park designers had paid close attention to those films as they made their plans. Other operators were already opening parks like Storyland in New Jersey, with attractions based on fairy tales and nursery rhymes.[67] But such imitators could not duplicate the Disney characters, which were not only visible in some of the rides but also roamed the park, embodied by costumed Disney employees wearing gargantuan cartoon heads.

Wherever possible, Disney linked an attraction to a film, especially an animated film, however flimsily, so that the Frontierland theater became Slue-Foot Sue's Golden Horseshoe, named after a character in the Pecos Bill segment of the 1948 package feature *Melody Time*. Such connections were easiest to make in Fantasyland. That "land," the one that drew most heavily on Disney's films, was also the part of the park most nearly ready for visitors on opening day.

Fantasyland was dominated by "dark rides" with antecedents in the haunted houses and other attractions in older amusement parks that exploited the properties of "dark light." Disneyland's dark rides, however, presumed to tell stories of a sort—they were made up of tableaux from various Disney films *(Snow White, Pinocchio,* the toad half of *The Adventures of Ichabod and Mr. Toad, Peter Pan)*. Most of these potted stories made sense, though, only to people already familiar with the films; the rides were too brief for their tableaux to be experienced as stories independent of the films. At the very least, the stories being told in Fantasyland were impoverished compared with the rich narratives of the best Disney animated features. The rides resembled nothing so much as big-city department-store window displays that told a Christmas story, but with the difference that there was no opportunity for a Disneyland visitor to linger over any particular display. Where imagination was most apparent was not in the rides themselves, but in the ways Disney's people and their contractors made each ride system safe, workable, and appropriate to the attraction—so that the Peter Pan ride's passengers rode in sailing ships suspended from an overhead track, the passengers for Snow White's Adventures in mine cars, the passengers for Mr. Toad's Wild Ride in antique automobiles, and so on.

Even in Fantasyland, tight budgets meant that the rides had to squeeze into prefabricated buildings, rather than buildings designed to accommodate the rides. But it was in Tomorrowland—where there were no Disney characters to serve as window dressing—that Disney's haste and his financial strains were most evident. The sets from *20,000 Leagues Under the Sea* were plugged into Tomorrowland just to fill an empty building.

Each of Disneyland's "lands" was "themed," with every ride and store and restaurant keyed in some way to an overarching idea. Such environments had been around for a long time. The first real suburban shopping center, Country Club Plaza in Kansas City—a place that Disney surely visited after it was built in 1922—was themed in its evocation of Spain (and was, besides, groundbreaking in the way that it catered to the automobile). The great movie palaces of the 1920s were routinely themed; examples have survived in cities as diverse as Atlanta and Santa Barbara. Many great hotels have always been themed. Especially when his studio was still on Hyperion Avenue, Disney dined often at the Tam O'Shanter Inn, a thoroughly themed mock-Scottish restaurant a mile and a half away on Los Feliz Boulevard. That Disneyland's theming had the impact of something new was thanks mainly to its thoroughness— that is, to Walt Disney's characteristic attention to detail. (For example, Disney did not want the costumed employees from one part of the park blundering into other areas and confusing the theme.)

It was in the town square and Main Street and the central hub, through which all visitors passed as they entered the park, that Disneyland was most distinctive. As the British essayist Aubrey Menen wrote in 1963, "All fairgrounds have a central avenue which is usually a blaring catchpenny road designed to make the visitor join in the fun or feel a boor if he doesn't." At Disneyland there was no such midway: "Here all was tranquil and detached. The visitors were not belabored into enjoyment; on the contrary, it seemed as though they were forgotten. They appeared to have wandered, by chance or some spell, into the past."[68] It was, however, a peculiar past, much more serene and ordered than the real past ever was. In that respect, Main Street owed less to nostalgia—Marceline's Kansas Avenue never looked much like it— than to a foreign model, Tivoli Gardens in Copenhagen, which Disney visited multiple times, before and after he built his own park. "Architecturally and stylistically," Buzz Price said of Tivoli, "it was in harmony with a lot of what Walt was going to do."[69]

Tivoli has changed since Disney's day, but even now, at the center of that park, a vital similarity to Disneyland—as Walt Disney conceived it—is unmistakable. Dominated by flowers and elegant landscaping immediately reminiscent of Bill Evans's work for Disneyland, that part of Tivoli resembles a beautiful city park or public garden, but one that is free of the hint of menace that can shadow even the loveliest such places in the United States. The sense that Disneyland is completely *safe*—early guidebooks mention in passing that forty-five full-time security officers are on hand—has been a vital but unstressed part of its appeal. An admission charge always serves as a filter, but the landscaping at Disneyland, as at Tivoli, reinforced that effect by subtly imposing calm and order on an environment, the amusement park, that can be coarse and chaotic. As Walt Disney knew, such landscaping is anything but a cosmetic garnish—it encourages people to behave better. Disney acknowledged his debt to Tivoli in a July 4, 1961, speech, at Ålborg, Denmark. "Personally, I owe much to Denmark," he said, adding by way of explanation that Disneyland had been called "the Tivoli of the United States."[70]

Disney claimed, in an interview with Aubrey Menen, that he conceived his park with adults as much as children in mind, if not more so: "I noticed, in amusement parks for children, that the grownups were bored. So I wanted to give them something to do."[71] What he really did, though, was understand that adults, particularly the parents of very young children, would come to a park like his not for imaginative stimulus, but to be soothed by a perfectly orderly, predictable environment—especially one with such pleasant associations as those with the Disney films. "Something clean and respectable for all ages was what I was striving for," Disney told a *New York Times* reporter a few years after Disneyland opened. "Sort of nostalgic, but with the fun angle, the excitement."[72]

Disney's rethinking of the American amusement park had striking and immediate business consequences. Because his park was such a pleasant place, people stayed there longer, and because they stayed longer, they spent more. "Basically," Price said, "he tripled per-capita expenditures [because] he tripled stay time."[73] After Disneyland had been open only seven weeks, it had already received a million visitors, 50 percent more than projected.[74]

The rushed schedule left Disneyland with many rough edges beyond those that marred the opening day, not just physically but in the way the park operated. Disney had hired C. V. Wood, Price's boss at Stanford Research, as Disneyland's general manager. Wood was deeply involved in every aspect of Disneyland's birth, including crucial negotiations with the city of Anaheim and the multiple owners of the property chosen as the park's site; he was besides a flamboyant personality whom Disney may have regarded as a competitor for the spotlight. Wood was, in short, the natural scapegoat in the anxious circumstances that prevailed in Disneyland's earliest days, and Disney fired him a few months after the park opened.[75]

There is a sense, in accounts of the first harried months, that Disney and his people were in a constant race to fix problems, large and small—the shortage of rides, unpredictable live animals—before they soured the pleasant experience that visitors were eager to have. For example, when Disneyland opened, general admission was a dollar, and individual attractions were priced from ten to thirty-five cents. For visitors and employees alike, handling so many coins was an irritant. Late in 1955, Disneyland began selling ticket books. The ticket books, which included admission and tickets for eight rides, were priced (at $2.50) to approximate the total that the average visitor was already spending.[76]

The early rides suffered from one miscalculation after another. "One thing we intended," said Ken Anderson, who moved back and forth between films and Disneyland projects, "was that everybody on the [Snow White's Adventures] ride would understand that they were Snow White. As you rode the attraction, you were taking Snow White's place . . . you were the girl that was being threatened. And nobody got it. Nobody actually figured that they were Snow White. They just wondered where the hell Snow White was."[77]

Thanks to his abbreviated construction schedule, Disney had little choice but to hire outside contractors to perform many of the park's functions, like cleaning and security. "The custodial company's standards apparently stopped at cursory cleanliness," Randy Bright wrote. "The security guards evidently thought that they had been retained specifically to protect Disney property from thugs, a description they liberally applied to anyone who came through the gate."[78] Getting rid of such people quickly, and replacing them with Disney employees who had been trained to be customer-friendly, was vitally important to the park's success. No matter how good the park looked, surly employees could spoil the effect—and unlike a tabletop or backyard layout, Disneyland had to be filled with real people.

Even so, the presence of all those people could have worked against Disney's maintaining control: what if they didn't behave the way he wanted them to? It was here that Disney manifested true entrepreneurial savvy. He understood that it is easier to maintain control over customers if they think they are doing what *they* want to do, as opposed to what someone else wants them to do. To preserve that illusion of autonomy, Disney was more than willing to make countless small adjustments, like paving a shortcut that visitors were taking through a flower bed, rather than putting up a fence to keep them out.

John Hench, one of the studio artists who joined the park's design team, wrote years later: "To design most effectively for our guests, we learned that we had to observe them up close, waiting in lines with them, going on rides with them, eating with them. Walt insisted on this. . . . This was new to us; as filmmakers, we were used to sitting in our sweatboxes at the studio, passing judgment on our work without knowing how the public might actually respond to it. Going out into the park taught us how guests were being treated and how they responded to patterns of movement and the ways in which they expressed their emotions. We got an idea of what was going on in their minds."[79]

Once Disneyland was open, Disney continued his Saturday-morning visits in the company of a half dozen key people, now scrutinizing not the construction but the operation of the park. "He was always serious looking," Bill Martin said of a photo of Disney taken during one of those walkthroughs. "We'd take notes and refer later to [photographs taken during the walk-through], then start in on any modifications that came up as a result," Martin told *The "E" Ticket*. "We would take these ideas back and in the next day or two we would drum up some drawings. Then Walt would take a look at them and he'd say, 'Well, let's go a little farther with this,' or 'Let's change it to something like this.' . . . .About noon, we'd go to Harvey's Lunchwagon and have hamburgers. . . . Walt loved hamburgers . . . he didn't care about anything else. We'd eat there, and then we'd all go home. . . . He never complained [during the walks], as I recall, and he never complimented anybody either, to speak of."[80]

Some stories from Disneyland's early years turn up repeatedly in memoirs and official histories. Van Arsdale France, who was in charge of training Disneyland employees for many years, offered one version of a cherished anecdote in his memoir:

> A "trip time" of seven minutes had been established for the Jungle Cruise ride. . . . When there were hundreds of people lined up on a hot day, the operators tended to speed up the trip, and Walt was a passenger on one of these abbreviated trips. Dick [Nunis, then the manager of Adventureland] was standing on the dock when Walt steamed up with his eyebrows raised. "Dick, what is the trip time for this attraction?" "Well, sir, it is seven minutes," Dick responded. Mad as hell, Walt came back with, "Well, I just had a four-minute ride and went through the hippo pool so fast I couldn't tell if they were rhinos or hippos." After being completely chewed out by Walt, Dick made a very bright career decision. He asked Walt if he had time to ride with him and explain how he wanted the ride to work.
>
> Walt took the time. He spent an hour explaining how the sequences should work and how to play the show, because it is show business. "If the trip time is seven minutes, and you cut out three minutes, it's like going to a movie and having some important reels left out."
>
> Dick then instituted a concentrated training program. A week later, Walt came back for a review. Dick recalled, "Walt felt I might have stacked the deck with the best operator, so he went around with five different hosts." Dick continued, "When he finally left after his last trip, Walt gave me a smile and a 'thumbs up' sign."[81]

It is safe to assume that each of those rides took very close to seven minutes.

In this story, as in others, Disney is a model entrepreneur, acutely sensitive to how customers respond to his business. His attention to detail at the park extended to the sticks used in the ice cream bars—flat sticks, "nothing with round sticks, people trip on them." Probably because Disney's focus was so obviously and exclusively on the park and visitors' experience of it, he seems never to have become the target of fear or resentment from Disneyland's employees. "Nobody ever blamed Walt Disney for anything," France wrote.[82]

Disneyland did not get its first "thrill ride"—a roller coaster of sorts—until July 14, 1959, when two other major attractions, a submarine ride and a monorail, also opened. Although Disney had deliberately excluded thrill rides from Disneyland, he found a way in 1959 to introduce such a ride without obviously compromising the idea that the park's entertainment would be themed. The roller coaster came enclosed in a mountain, a miniature of the Matterhorn, and the ride itself was costumed as a bobsled run. The submarine ride, like many other Disney attractions, was a variant on a successful attraction elsewhere. It recalled the glass-bottom boats at Florida's Cypress Gardens, except that the boats had in effect been turned on their sides—passengers looked at an underwater show through portholes.

Once the park was open, Disney continued to use his weekly TV show to promote it; at least one program in each of the next three seasons was devoted in whole or in part to Disneyland, in addition to the programs devoted to new theatrical films. But whatever its promotional value, television was expensive, and Roy Disney voiced concern about TV's appetite for dollars a little more than a year after the first *Disneyland* show aired. He wrote in December 1955 that "our production costs to date have been substantially greater than the direct income. Fortunately we have been able to recover most of these excess costs from other revenue indirectly attributable to TV [the Davy Crockett movie would be an example]. However, with respect to future television production, unless we can realize a proper direct profit from television pictures our output in this medium will be greatly reduced."[83]

To complicate matters, Walt Disney had launched that fall on ABC a five-day-a-week, one-hour show aimed directly at children, *Mickey Mouse Club*. Disney had made notes of ideas for the show in the summer of 1954, linking it to his new park ("clubhouse at Disneyland"),[84] but in strict economic terms the new show made little sense. Like the weekly show, it would cost more than the studio could recoup from ABC—Walt Disney said in November 1955 that a year's programs would cost four million dollars, but that ABC was paying only $2.8 million for them[85]—with fewer promotional benefits. Disney had, however, been drawn to the idea of making a similar show since the late 1940s, and, as he had demonstrated, he rarely let go of an idea he liked.*

Roy's warning about reduced output was presumably a negotiating ploy directed at ABC (and perhaps his brother, too). Early in 1956 he negotiated new contracts with ABC for both *Disneyland* and *Mickey Mouse Club*. At the end of 1956, although he still expected "production costs for the current year's program . . . to exceed domestic income by about $269,000," Roy expressed confidence "that the programs will eventually return a good profit from subsequent uses at home and abroad."[86] One effect of the studio's increased activity was visible in its payroll: between October 1955 and October 1956, the number of employees increased from 855 to 1,271.

In the meantime, Walt Disney was proving less than sure-footed in live action, especially in the handling of his star, Fess Parker. In the two new Crockett episodes for the second season of *Disneyland* (down from the planned four, since the Crockett craze died rapidly in the fall of 1955), Disney and his director, Norman Foster, permitted Parker to be overshadowed by Jeff York, who played the boatman Mike Fink as the sort of crudely one-dimensional character already familiar from TV situation comedies.

After the Crockett episodes were finished, Parker moved on to *The Great Locomotive Chase,* the film that had been elbowed aside by *20,000 Leagues Under the Sea* a few years earlier. Filming began in Georgia on September 26, 1955.[87] Disney was on hand for the first few days. Two vintage locomotives (one from the Baltimore & Ohio Museum, the other owned by Paramount Pictures) were the true stars, with Parker cast in a terribly misconceived lead role, that of the leader of a group of Union spies. The screenplay, by Lawrence Watkin, invited a positive response not to Parker but to the Confederates pursuing him. Parker was a "hero" who failed in his mission and was hanged for his pains.

Shooting of *Westward Ho the Wagons!* Parker's next starring vehicle, began just three and a half months later, on January 16, 1956—but he was cast again in a puzzling role, in effect playing in support of several of the child actors from the *Mickey Mouse Club* show.[88] He did not have another feature assignment until *Old Yeller,* which was filmed in the first few months of 1957. Although he received star billing, Parker had been cast in a supporting role again, in a film whose real stars were two children and a dog.

In the summer of 1957, Parker joined the cast of *The Light in the Forest,*

---

* Another example was a weekly *Zorro* show—that unrealized project of Disney's private company—which began running on ABC in the fall of 1957.

another film in which he ostensibly starred but that had him, again, in a de facto supporting role. The film's true star was James MacArthur, the nineteen-year-old son of the actress Helen Hayes. When Disney tried to cast Parker in yet another supporting role with yet another very young actor—this time Sal Mineo, in a western called *Tonka*—Parker finally balked. He and Disney parted company in 1958. But the damage had been done. In four years, Disney had squandered Parker's popularity and effectively destroyed the possibility that he would ever enjoy a major film career. There was no trace in Disney's handling of Parker of the well-organized promotion of contract players into important stars that had been a hallmark of the big Hollywood studios in earlier decades.

In other ways, too, Disney was surrendering any claim to be taken seriously as a producer of live-action films. None of the features he made in the years just after *20,000 Leagues Under the Sea* was nearly as ambitious. That film, as written by Earl Felton and directed by Richard Fleischer, had emerged as a handsome and intelligent spectacle, even though weighted down by a host of liabilities: serious mistakes in casting (only James Mason as Captain Nemo is wholly plausible as his character), heavy-handed music, a seal that mugs almost as energetically as Kirk Douglas. *20,000 Leagues* was modestly successful, both critically and commercially—it earned $6.8 million in gross rentals—but not a hit big enough to justify the large amount (in proportion to the studio's revenues) that Disney had devoted to it.

By the mid-1950s, he understood that in contrast to his feature cartoons, many of his live-action films were likely to seem dated after a few years. "Live pictures are different," he said. Their reissue potential was correspondingly limited (*20,000 Leagues* was a rare exception, earning more than two million dollars in a 1963 reissue). But they could smooth out the studio's revenue stream, they could be recycled on the weekly TV series—and they gave the studio's new distribution apparatus something to sell.

Despite the success of the *True-Life Adventures,* RKO was cool to the idea of a *True-Life* feature, evidently for legal reasons. The Disneys wanted to package the feature with two short films, one of them a cartoon based on Robert Lawson's children's book *Ben and Me*, and RKO's lawyers believed that it could not sell the films as a package without violating the terms of the Supreme Court's 1948 antitrust decision, which had required the major studios to divorce production and exhibition.[89] Roy Disney decided that the studio would bypass RKO and distribute *The Living Desert,* the first feature-length *True-Life Adventure,* through a new Disney-owned distribution company named Buena Vista, after the Burbank street where the studio was located.[90] Released in November 1953, *The Living Desert* ultimately returned $6.8 million to the Disney studio on a negative cost of $293,000.

RKO had been run into the ground by its eccentric owner, Howard Hughes, and in September 1954 the Disneys broke with their longtime distributor over terms for *20,000 Leagues Under the Sea* and *Lady and the Tramp*. Roy Disney asked for a $3.5 million advance on those films and a reduction in RKO's fee from 22.5 percent to 20 percent of rental revenues; Hughes wanted an increase in the fee to 25 percent.[91] There was no animosity in the breakup—Roy subsequently made deals with RKO for the distribution of *20,000 Leagues* in Latin America and Asia—but *The Living Desert*'s success was powerful evidence that the Disneys did not need a middleman, especially at a time when Disneyland and the weekly TV show were imposing new demands on the studio's finances.

As for Walt Disney: his attention absorbed now by the Disneyland park; still determined that nothing of consequence should happen at the studio without his approval; and wary of high costs (except when he wanted to spend the money himself), he more than ever leaned toward live-action directors who would translate his wishes onto film quickly and efficiently, without leaving any traces of their own personalities. Directors who worked mostly in television were ideal for his purposes, and he watched television shows with that in mind.

By the mid-1950s, Walt and Lillian Disney were heading for bed by 9:30 or so, and they were usually asleep by 10:30. They watched little television together, although they both liked the Groucho Marx quiz show, *You Bet Your Life*. When the Disneys ate dinner alone together, they usually ate in front of the TV set, "and then he looks at everything," Lillian Disney said. He liked to "study" even bad programs, she said.[92]

One director whose work he liked was Robert Stevenson, who had directed theatrical features but by the 1950s was a TV regular. Disney hired him in 1956 to make *Johnny Tremain,* a film about the American Revolution that was originally conceived as a two-part television show but was released theatrically instead, in June 1957 (it wound up on the Disney TV show in 1958). "Directing for Walt was very interesting," Stevenson told Richard Hubler in 1968, "because, certainly the pictures I worked on, we worked much more thoroughly and much more creatively on the script than any other producer I've worked for. He would really be doing an awful lot of writing, even though he didn't put it onto paper."[93]

No transcripts were made of such meetings, but Disney himself provided a glimpse of his "writing." In 1956, the Texas novelist Fred Gipson came to the studio to collaborate with the screenwriter William Tunberg on a script based on his dog story *Old Yeller*, which was to be the second Disney feature Stevenson directed. After Gipson left the studio, Disney, Stevenson, and Tunberg made "a re-arrangement of the material to help out the production side of it," as Disney put it in a letter to Gipson. Disney described the changes as "straightening out the story from a shooting-continuity point of view. Certain transpositions in the early stages of the story were done to make it play a little better. I do not believe we have lost anything in doing this and I feel it will improve the finished effect when put on film."[94] Gipson gave his blessing to the revised script, suggesting only that one scene be omitted, and to the finished film.

Once a script was finished and shooting began, Stevenson said, "the extraordinary thing is . . . he would leave a director entirely alone. . . . He never gave any instructions during the shooting of a picture. . . . He would then come back very solidly in the editing."

Harry Tytle, who began supervising live-action films for the television show in the 1950s, concurred:

> Walt always insisted on plenty of coverage [that is, a great variety of shots that he could choose from in editing a film]. . . . He liked plenty of variety in the coverage of various actors, including listening and reaction shots of the other, non-speaking actors in a scene. . . .
>
> He was most interested in the editing of his pictures, that is, putting the film together to tell the story. Woe to the director who camera-cut a picture . . . converting the story directly to film so rigidly that there is no latitude for anyone to do other than just assemble the film. Such an approach gave Walt no room to get away from what he considered a poor performance, or to concentrate on a character who he thought was "coming off" well.[95]

The fruits of such an approach, one that shrugs off the actual shooting as of limited importance, can be seen in *Johnny Tremain*. The acting—and behind it the direction—make ready resort to the obvious (Johnny, played by Hal Stalmaster, hangs his head and slouches when he's rejected), and the actors themselves give every sign of being performers of the kind who are valued because they can master a role quickly, if superficially. Such filmmaking founders on anything the least complex or ambiguous. In *Tremain,* there is an unsettling contrast between the elevated sentiments expressed by James Otis (Jeff York), in particular, and the protracted ugliness of the colonists' guerrilla attacks on British troops. The emphasis on British restraint, pronounced throughout the film, makes the sniper attacks that kill ordinary soldiers exceptionally unpleasant to watch.

A creative director could have found any number of ways out of this box, even though the final cut remained in the producer's hands, as was ordinarily the case in Hollywood at the time. Disney was simply not interested in hiring such people, and he sometimes seemed to go out of his way to avoid them. To direct *The Great Locomotive Chase*, Fess Parker's first theatrical starring vehicle, Disney chose Francis Lyon, a film editor with no directing experience. (As Parker said, "There was more tender loving care of the locomotives than of their live asset.")[96] *Westward Ho the Wagons!* the next Parker film, was directed by William Beaudine, a veteran who cranked out dozens of low-budget westerns in the 1930s and 1940s and by the 1950s was working almost exclusively in television. Before and after his feature assignment, he directed—with blazing speed—the serials running on *Mickey Mouse Club*. A 1963 *TV Guide* article quoted Disney's admiring words about Beaudine: "When I came to Hollywood in 1923, I was wandering around the old Warners lot and I watched him shooting a picture with actor Wesley Barry. He's still tops on the low-budgeted type of thing. That sort of fits his temperament. He wants to move. That's why he's so good in television."[97]

It was in making the *True-Life Adventures* that the editor's role was particularly dominant, and that surely accounted for some of Disney's warm feelings for the series. He resisted making the *True-Life Adventures* longer than a half hour, he said in 1956, until he had made seven of them and felt confident that he could assemble enough material and present it properly. "The biggest problem [with the wildlife photographers] was getting them to keep shooting. . . . They would be too conservative with film because when they were working on their own they had to buy that film. . . . It got to the point they'd never dare come in and tell me something that they saw that they didn't photograph because I used to raise heck with them."

Notes from a screening for Disney of what was probably a rough cut of *The Living Desert* show him approaching the music for that *True-Life Adventure* as he would have approached the music for any other live-action film. He was telling the composer, Paul Smith, what he wanted in the score.

> In sequence where tortoises are courting, . . . they look like knights in armor, old knights in battle. Give the audience a music cue, a tongue-in-cheek fanfare. The winner will claim his lady fair. . . .
> *Pepsis* wasp and tarantula sequence: Our heavy is the tarantula. Odd that the wasp is decreed by nature to conquer the tarantula. When her time comes to lay eggs, she must go out and find a tarantula. Not strength, but skill helps her beat Mr. Tarantula. . . .
> Then the hawk and the snake. Our other heavy is the snake. . . . With wasp

and tarantula it's a ballet—or more like a couple of wrestlers. The hawk should follow. Tarantula gets his and then Mr. Snake gets his. . . . *Pepsis* wasp doesn't use brute strength, but science and skill. Should be ballet music. Hawk uses force and violence. One could follow the other and have a different musical theme as contrast.[98]

Smith followed Disney's instructions all too well: his tightly synchronized music, like Winston Hibler's jocular narration, gives *The Living Desert* a frivolous tone at odds with the grimness of much of what is on the screen. That incongruity was a nagging problem in the *True-Life Adventures,* but the frequent manipulation of both animals and film—the *Seal Island* pattern, imposing a story on the material whenever possible—was even more troublesome. And yet if Disney were to be more scrupulous, the result on-screen would inevitably be a harsher view of nature. That is pretty much what happens in *The African Lion,* the third *True-Life* feature, released in September 1955 and made when Disney was preoccupied with the construction of Disneyland. Manipulation is minimal, at least compared with earlier films in the series, and there is a straightforward emphasis on just how much killing the big cats do (swaddled in reassuring narration about "nature's way").

Although Disney made three more *True-Life* features, this was not an avenue that he could pursue very far, and so he began to turn toward live-action animal stories—that is, fiction films with real animals. He was speaking of making such films in early 1953,[99] and in 1957 he finally completed one: *Perri,* based on a story about a squirrel by Felix Salten, author of *Bambi.* Disney called *Perri* a "True-Life Fantasy"—the only time he used that designation for a live-action animal story—and the film is an unsettling mix of sugary sentiment and real death, as when a marten chases and kills the squirrel that is supposedly the heroine's father. As to how many squirrels died in the filming, that was a subject that the film's producer, Winston Hibler, preferred to avoid.[100]

Real life was a stubbornly resistant subject for Disney films. The *People and Places* series of half-hour short subjects, which Disney launched in 1953 as a companion to the *True-Life Adventures,* boasted on a title card that "All scenes are authentic and the stories are factual," but the air of contrivance was even stronger than in the animal films. In *Switzerland* (1955), a goatherd tracks down and retrieves a lost kid in staged action, but what is ultimately most disturbing about the film is the pretense that it is eavesdropping (with CinemaScope cameras!) on unspoiled village life—making cheese, plowing a field with horses, practicing traditional crafts at Christmas. Not just in

Switzerland, but in *People and Places* shorts made in Germany, Austria, Italy, and Japan, the sense is not that traditional ways have survived World War II, but that World War II never happened.

Perri was released in August 1957, just before Walt and Lillian Disney left for a two-month trip to Europe.[101] It was their first trip there in four years, since Walt had immersed himself in the planning and construction of Disneyland. In contrast to their earlier trips, this was a true vacation. They drove most of the time, visiting England, Germany, France, Spain, and Italy. It was "just too much all at once," Disney wrote to his sister,[102] but his appetite for Europe—and for filming there—had been whetted. Earlier in the year he had bought the rights to *Banner in the Sky,* a James Ramsey Ullman novel about the first ascent of the Matterhorn, as a vehicle for his new young star James MacArthur.[103] His production manager, Bill Anderson, hired Ken Annakin to direct and scouted locations on a trip to Europe. Annakin then came to Burbank for several months of preproduction work with Disney and Anderson.

"This time," Annakin wrote in his autobiography, "Walt seemed to have such confidence in me that so long as he was convinced that I knew exactly his approach to the story and how he envisioned the characters and scenes, he was not demanding the whole script should be storyboarded. He allocated three of his sketch artists to work with me, but we only sketched out the key scenes."[104]

Most of the film was shot in the summer of 1958, in and around the ancient Swiss village of Zermatt at the foot of the Matterhorn. Disney himself had visited Zermatt—a picturesque place from which most motorized vehicles are barred—on earlier trips to Europe, the first time probably in 1952. He and Lillian spent several weeks on location in 1958, lodging at the town's oldest and most distinguished hotel, the Zermatterhof (he conceived the Matterhorn ride for Disneyland on that visit). In September, the cast and crew moved to London for a few weeks of soundstage filming.[105]

The film, released in November 1959 as *Third Man on the Mountain,* was a startling anomaly in a Disney theatrical program dominated increasingly by shallow, mechanical films. The scenery and the climbing scenes (many of these the actors themselves performed; others made artful use of doubles) were spectacular, but what really set the film apart was Annakin's direction. His skill with actors was here at its peak, so that the cast forms a true ensemble in a way that the actors do in no other Disney film; only a couple of Annakin's other Disney films come close. As Annakin's direction—along with the excellent screenplay, credited to Eleanore Griffin—makes clear, there are no villains in this story, only a group of fundamentally good people, bumping into one another as real people do.

Third Man on the Mountain was a Disney live-action film that bore comparison with some of the better Disney animated features. Unfortunately, it did not do particularly well at the box office, with gross rentals of $2.4 million versus a cost of $1.6 million. Eight months earlier, in March 1959, *The Shaggy Dog,* produced at a cost of a little over a million dollars, had become Disney's highest-grossing picture ever in the United States and Canada, with gross rentals of more than nine million dollars. The animated feature *Sleeping Beauty,* released in January 1959 in a seventy-millimeter widescreen process called Technirama, and with much ballyhoo, cost much more—roughly six million dollars—and was weaker at the box office, returning $7.7 million in gross rentals.

The combined effect of *Shaggy Dog's* spectacular success and the relatively poor performance of the other two features was to cement into place Disney's reliance on television-flavored films and on people whose experience was mostly in TV. Disney had conceived of *The Shaggy Dog* as a television series—what Bill Walsh called "a modernized teenage thing"—and he made it as a feature only after ABC turned it down.[106] (It was based on *The Hound of Florence,* the Felix Salten story that Disney had considered filming in live action almost twenty years earlier.) "I was mad," Disney said in 1964, "so I went back to the studio and called in Bill Walsh and said, 'Let's make a feature of this.' He said, 'That's what I've been telling you all the time.' 'Let's go.'"[107] As a black-and-white theatrical release directed by Charles Barton—who was, like Bill Beaudine, a veteran of decades of work in low-budget movies and TV—*The Shaggy Dog* is powerfully reminiscent of the popular TV situation comedies of the late 1950s. That association presumably encouraged audiences to forgive its slack pacing and flatly played scenes. Disney recalled that its star, the veteran actor Fred MacMurray, complained that a policeman in an incidental comic role had a better part than he did; MacMurray had a point.

Disney had entered television in 1954 thinking that he could bend it to his purposes, but five years later it was he who was bowing to TV's demands. He may have underestimated just how voracious TV would be. By 1957, after only three years on the air, the weekly Disney TV show had already consumed most of the usable inventory of animated shorts. (*Mickey Mouse Club* was showing a cartoon almost every day, but many of those, particularly the black-and-white cartoons from the early 1930s, had always been deemed too antiquated for use on the weekly show.) As Harry Tytle wrote, "Walt was caught in a bind."[108] If fewer of the old shorts were used, the difference had to be made up with new animation—a very costly alternative, in TV terms, if it was to resemble the old animation—or with live action that might be an awkward fit with the cartoons. Disney's freedom of action was thus severely limited, exactly the sort of situation that he disliked.

As it happened, television's imperatives forced him to scale back his shows with animation, old or new, and rely more heavily on live action instead. In the 1957–58 season, NBC scheduled a star-heavy western called *Wagon Train* on Wednesday nights against *Disneyland,* whose ratings suffered. Such westerns were the most popular shows on TV, and Disney loaded his schedule with westerns in the 1958–59 season because, he said, "I had to," at the insistence of ABC and a sponsor. His preoccupation with "control" did not inoculate him from such pressures, certainly not when his ratings were affected.

The Disneys' relations with ABC soured early in 1959, when, Roy Disney wrote, "ABC insisted on terms and conditions for the Mickey Mouse Club and Zorro shows which were totally unacceptable to us," then refused to let Disney take the shows to other networks.[109] (For his part, ABC's Leonard Goldenson dismissed the Disneys as "terrible business partners" because they preferred to reinvest Disneyland's profits.)[110]

Consumed by his roles as proprietor of an amusement park and overseer of a studio churning out mediocre live-action movies, Walt Disney had surrendered his role as artist. There is sometimes the sense, in the recollections of people who worked with him on his best films and were still on his staff in the 1950s, that their presence could be an annoying reminder of what he had left behind.

"When he got off on the park," Ward Kimball said, "there was no stopping him; you couldn't get him in to look at something. He'd just say, 'Go ahead and do it.'" Kimball himself benefited from Disney's inattention when he made several *Tomorrowland* shows about space travel for *Disneyland.* Kimball's shows were inventive and mostly serious in their approach to the subject, but they departed sharply from the mid-1950s Disney norm in their knowing use of modern design and their occasionally flippant tone.

Kimball was aware of how unusual—and how hazardous—his situation was: "This was a risk you never ran before; you never dared go ahead on your own, without the OK. What could you do? He was interested in something else."[111]

CHAPTER 9

"Where I Am *Happy*"

Restless in the Magic Kingdom

1959–1965

In the 1960s, Walt Disney drove himself to work from Holmby Hills to Burbank, first in a Ford Thunderbird and then, from 1964 on, in a Mercedes-Benz 230 SL. His normal route took him right onto Carolwood Drive from his driveway, then left onto Sunset Boulevard, east toward Beverly Hills. He turned left onto Beverly Drive, soon bearing right at a V onto Coldwater Canyon Boulevard. From Coldwater he turned right onto the Ventura Freeway, recently completed across the San Fernando Valley, and headed east toward the Buena Vista Street exit in Burbank.[1]

He usually arrived at his studio by 8:30 A.M. and parked in a double slot under a parking shed that he shared with Roy (Walt's slot was on the left, where it was easier for him to get in and out of his car). "I don't think I ever got down ahead of Walt," Roy Disney said. "Walt's car was always in the stall next to mine and he was there when I came in the morning, and his car was there when I left at night. He was a bear for work."[2]

The Disney brothers presided over a studio that had undergone a dramatic transformation in the previous decade. As Walt Disney remarked in 1961, "in the last ten years we've gone into three big businesses—the [live-action] feature field, the amusement park field,* and TV. If it were just animated cartoons, it'd be a cinch."[3]

Sleeping Beauty's poor box-office returns had proved, of course, that car-

* To set Disneyland apart from the tawdry amusement parks of the past, the official Disney position has always been that it is a "theme park," and that its rides are "attractions." Walt Disney often ignored such distinctions.

toons were anything but a cinch. For fiscal 1960, Walt Disney Productions showed a loss of $1,342,037, after a $6 million write-down of inventories. Gross income, which had shot up since the opening of Disneyland, fell to around $46.4 million from $58.4 million the previous year. Film revenue fell by more than $7 million, largely a reflection of *Sleeping Beauty*'s performance, and television revenue by $4.6 million, thanks to ABC's cancellation of *Zorro* and *Mickey Mouse Club*. Only Disneyland's revenue was up.[4]

In one respect, the opening of the Disneyland park—and its almost immediate success—had been a great boon to the people working on Disney's feature cartoons. "It took the pressure off," Ollie Johnston said. "It was a big relief, because before Disneyland we'd always wonder if we would make another film, and that can be a tough way to have to live." But the TV show and the park not only diverted Walt Disney himself from *Sleeping Beauty*, they also took away talented people who would otherwise have been available for the feature. Said Rolly Crump, who was an assistant animator in the late 1950s when he was recruited to work at WED: "One guy in particular used to refer to WED as 'cannibal island' because of the way it would eat up studio employees."[5]

During work on *Sleeping Beauty*, Frank Thomas said, "Walt was not supporting us. And you couldn't figure out what he didn't like. Why he said the things he did. And we didn't feel it was personal condemnation, it was more that there was something in the way he saw the picture that he couldn't get over to us. Now, this happened many times. . . . Fergy [Norm Ferguson] said, when [I] first came here, 'Don't do what Walt says, do what Walt means.' And I said, 'How are you supposed to know?' And he said, 'Well, you'll find out in a hurry.'"[6]

That worrisome lack of specificity is not something that turns up in the memories of people whose time then was devoted to Disneyland. For that matter, Disney's critiques in the middle to late 1930s were always clear enough in their intent. It was all a matter of where his interest was keenest at the time. He was vaguer the further he got from that center—but since his control did not slacken even as his interest did, he generated problems for his animators in particular. *Sleeping Beauty* is full of lapses of a kind that Disney would not have tolerated twenty years earlier. In one scene, to cite a small example, Prince Phillip picks up his father, King Hubert, and swings him through the air in a circle, effortlessly. Live action was no aid here—as Frank Thomas said, "Who's strong enough to pick up a man who weighs 250 pounds and dance with him?"[7] The scene had to be convincing on other terms, but it is not; instead, the king becomes, temporarily, a sort of human beach ball.

"We were on that for five years," Ollie Johnston said of *Sleeping Beauty*, "and that was all because we couldn't get Walt to come into any of the meetings. You'd eventually get him, but you couldn't move anything."[8] But if there was one thing worse than Walt Disney's not paying enough attention to his animated features, it was his paying too much of the wrong kind of attention. Disney damaged the film most not by neglecting it but by insisting that it adhere to a certain kind of design. That design was set by the background painter Eyvind Earle, whose early sketches showed that he wanted the film to echo medieval tapestries and miniatures in its general feeling (one sketch was modeled on a unicorn tapestry at the Cloisters, the Metropolitan Museum of Art's medieval galleries in upper Manhattan, another on a page from the book of hours of the duc de Berry).

Sleeping Beauty resembled *Snow White* in its general shape, and in some particulars it recalled ideas that Disney had considered for *Snow White* and then rejected. The early story outlines for *Snow White* placed great emphasis on the prince ("Doug Fairbanks type") and his highly intelligent horse ("Like Tom Mix's Horse Tony"); they were to be "great pals."[9] The prince and his horse in *Sleeping Beauty* matched those descriptions precisely. As with *Cinderella* ten years earlier, Disney sought a safe haven, in effect, by remaking *Snow White*. But Disney's intention to make yet another version of *Snow White* could not be reconciled with his embrace of Earle's background paintings.

Those paintings have, at their strongest, a hallucinatory clarity, but they have no emotional content—they never reflect or reinforce the emotions the characters are supposed to be feeling. The practical problem the backgrounds posed for the animators, Frank Thomas wrote more than thirty years later, was that "we had to find designs that enabled us to get some kind of life in the characters, but still recognize that they would have to 'work' against the busy detail of the backgrounds and hold their own graphically regardless of the choices Eyvind made for the colors on the costumes."[10]

Earle was a particularly striking specimen of the kind of artist who has a splendid technique but nothing much to say. Such artists are highly useful to someone who does have something to say but must rely on others' skills. By the late 1950s, the Disney studio employed many accomplished artists of the same general kind. Under other circumstances, Disney might have found some way to bend Earle's designs to broader purposes; but what recommended Earle's work to him now was simply its forwardness.

Of the artists with strong personalities still left on the staff, the most important was probably the writer Bill Peet, who was skillful not only at constructing narratives but at drawing cartoon characters as well. Although Disney allowed himself one burst of enthusiasm for his storyboards, Peet recalled, "after a few months Walt lost touch with the project and also seemed to resent spending time to discuss *Sleeping Beauty. . . .* He kicked me downstairs to work on TV commercials." Eyvind Earle remembered Peet's storyboards as "extraordinarily funny, wonderful stuff," all of it thrown out by Disney, "without a trace of it left. Because Walt was too busy; and in story, Walt wanted to have a part of it or he wouldn't accept it. It had nothing to do with whether it was good or not."[11]

Harry Tytle recorded what he said was the "only . . . mention [in his diary] of Walt not *meticulously* working on the product that he was doing": a *Sleeping Beauty* meeting at 10 A.M. on August 22, 1957, "showing the whole picture." This meeting took place just before Disney left on his long driving vacation in Europe. Tytle wrote that Disney "seems to be tired, has so much on his mind; he didn't give this the treatment he would have in years past, where he'd go in for a couple of days and fine-tooth comb the whole picture. . . . He hit more from a broad aspect than from small specifics, like he used to."[12]

Disney complained constantly about the cost of his cartoon features. The problem was, as Tytle said, that where the features were concerned, "Walt alone could determine how much to spend and where to spend it." Disney's complaints were in fact directed at himself. Anyone who took his complaints seriously and tried to act on them risked being handed his head. "Sooner or later," Tytle wrote, "the suggestions you would make for simplification or cost savings were going to interfere with Walt's efforts in building a cartoon feature, and you'd be switched, in Walt's eyes, from the role of lovable Jiminy Cricket to an evil Stromboli. The cost-savings approach would only work if it was *your* picture being produced and *Walt* was calling for changes. The reverse was a no-win deal."[13]

In other words, *Sleeping Beauty* was doomed from the start. It was a hapless relic from what now seemed like a very distant period in the Disney studio's history.

Disney read *Sleeping Beauty*'s failure not as owing to his own distracted role in its production but as evidence that animation should play an even smaller role in the company. He had been gradually turning away from animation since World War II; now he did so decisively. He reduced the animation staff sharply, dismissing studio veterans with twenty or thirty years of service.

It was, ironically, around this time that the members of Disney's animation board began to acquire a modest celebrity.[14] By 1950, Frank Thomas and Ollie Johnston have written, "the board had settled down to a permanent group of nine supervising animators"—the "nine old men," as Disney called them, a joking reference to Franklin D. Roosevelt's denigration of the Supreme Court in the 1930s. The nine were, in addition to Thomas and Johnston, Les Clark, Woolie Reitherman, Eric Larson, Ward Kimball, Milt Kahl, John Lounsbery, and Marc Davis.[15] By late in the decade, most of the "nine old men" had moved on to direction or Disneyland or other projects at the studio (and they were all well into middle age), but they remained the ultimate authorities where animation was concerned. Their continuing preeminence was a sign of animation's diminished status: there were no longer any younger men rising in the ranks who could be considered likely successors to some of the nine.

Not that membership in the "nine old men" was any sort of guarantee. Around 1960, Marc Davis recalled, "Ken Anderson, myself, and a couple of others worked on some cartoon stories, and I don't think we could have sold anything, no matter how good. We put together a story on Chanticleer, and when we had a meeting, the answer was no! The excuse was that you can't make a personality out of a chicken." Disney's dismissal of "Chanticleer" was actually not that abrupt. In the August 24, 1960, meeting that Davis was probably remembering, Disney remarked that the problem with making a rooster a leading character was that "[you] don't feel like picking a rooster up and petting it." Disney took "Chanticleer" seriously as a feature possibility—the August 24 meeting followed other "Chanticleer" meetings in 1960—but the eventual outcome was as Davis said.[16]

One Hundred and One Dalmatians had already been in production for a couple of years by then, and it was turning out to be radically different from *Sleeping Beauty.* For one thing, the writing was entirely in Bill Peet's hands— he wrote the screenplay and then developed and sketched all the storyboards (he also directed the recording of the voices).[17] But *Dalmatians* promised to be most different in how it looked on the screen.

Ken Peterson, the head of the animation department, wrote to Walt Disney on May 21, 1958: "Ken Anderson is making some very interesting experiments on a new style of background and layout handling for this picture. Everyone is very enthusiastic over the possibilities."[18] Anderson, who was principally responsible for *Dalmatians'* design, remembered that "I got to fooling around with the cost people, and asking them various things about the cost of the pictures, and it turned out that if we were to eliminate the ink and paint process, we would save over half the cost of a picture. I thought, gee, that's attractive, and I went to Walt with it, and he said, 'Ah, yeah, yeah, you can fool around all you want to.'" Anderson was thinking about using the Xerox process to transfer the animators' drawings directly from paper to celluloid—a technique used only sparingly in *Sleeping Beauty,* in the animation of a thorn forest—but he wanted to do more than that, by unifying the drawing styles of the animation and the backgrounds. He had in mind a reversal of what had happened on *Sleeping Beauty,* where Eyvind Earle's bejeweled background paintings dominated the animation. In *Dalmatians,* the animators' pencil lines would be echoed in the backgrounds.

"I had the idea that we could do a whole damned picture without ever painting a background," Anderson said.

> My idea was that it would all be one style. You'd have drawings in the background, and you'd see the animators' drawings—which they liked. . . . I thought Walt knew about it; he'd always butt in if he could. I had him lined up [for meetings], but he kept ducking me. . . .
>
> There was no attempt to disguise the lines; I knew they were going to be a half foot across on a big screen, but they were good-looking lines, and [because] they were animators' lines they always had more life than tracings. The animators were high on it; everybody was high on the thing. Except Walt never would see this thing; he wouldn't believe that I was doing that. So I showed him [a pilot scene, evidently]—I had done the animation, too, so the animators wouldn't have to be responsible for it. He objected to [putting the drawings for the] backgrounds on cels; I went along with him but put the backgrounds on cels anyway.[19]

Jack Cutting, who had worked for Disney since 1929 in various capacities, could have had such a situation in mind when he said: "Walt would sometimes say . . . 'I'm busy, go ahead and take care of that, do that.' Well, if you were going to be a survivor, you had to stop and think, just what does he mean? . . . With Walt, if you went too far, that was too far. Even if he had opened the way for you to do it."[20]

That is exactly what happened to Anderson. "After [*Dalmatians*] came out [in January 1961], he went to Europe," Anderson said. "When he came back, he seemed rather strange. Everybody loved [the film] but Walt. He really hurt me; I was in a meeting with the animators and Walt, and he said, 'We're never gonna do another one of those *goddamned* things like Ken did.' This was in front of me, and in front of my friends. It couldn't have been any worse. And he didn't talk to me for about a year."[21] Anderson received screen credit for art direction on the next Disney animated feature, *The Sword in the Stone* (1963), but there is no sense, as in *Dalmatians,* that the boundary between characters and backgrounds has been erased.

Disney had always divided his animated features among several directors, but after *Dalmatians* he put one of them, Woolie Reitherman, completely in charge of *The Sword in the Stone*. As to why Disney would have delegated so much authority over the animated features to Reitherman, whose forte for years had been the broadest sort of comedy (his segments in *Dalmatians* are heavy-handed compared with the rest of the film), the animator Bob Carlson offered this clue: "I was in a room once when Walt was discussing certain things, and in the course of the conversation he started talking about Woolie. He said, 'Whenever I want to know what the public thinks about a film I'm making, I ask Woolie, because in a way he's the All-American boy. . . . If Woolie approves of a certain thing, or makes a suggestion, I consider it very favorably.'"[22]

Bill Peet remembered that Disney now came to story meetings cold—he had not already seen the boards on one of his nighttime rambles through the studio, as he would have in earlier years—and would not take into account how his increasingly troubled physical state affected his response to stories. On one occasion, he came into a meeting saying, in Peet's recollection, "My head feels like it's full of cement. Now, what the hell ya got here?"[23] Peet's exasperation mirrored the way others on the staff felt. "No one had an easy time with Walt or found him particularly comfortable to be around," Frank Thomas and Ollie Johnston wrote, "and anyone as argumentative as Bill [Peet] was bound to compound the problem. . . . Walt's passing moods had a profound effect on both his judgment and his behavior, and on his dark days he was apt to rip a storyboard apart for no apparent reason."[24]

In the years just before he left the staff, Peet said—he quit on January 29, 1964, in the midst of the writing of *The Jungle Book*—"Walt was involved in so many varieties of projects he couldn't concentrate on any one thing. I didn't expect him to put much thought into the cartoon features and I felt many of his suggestions were wrong—so I disagreed quite often. . . . How could he be sharp in a story meeting with his head full of all the other stuff. Such was Walt's ego, he often said, 'I'm the little honeybee who goes flying around sprinkling pollen here and there to keep everything going.' And so he believed his snap judgment was not to be questioned. If the little bee gave you a bum steer, then went buzzing off to bigger things, you were stuck with it."[25]

Floyd Norman, who helped write *The Jungle Book* as a young member of the Disney staff, remembered that Disney shrugged off Peet's departure. "Walt said the movie was too dark anyway. He didn't like Bill's vision of the film. He said, 'I want to have some fun stuff. Make the film fun. It's just too dark.' . . . He was very much against the film being too serious. He said, 'I just want to have fun. Make it fun. More laughs, more personality stuff.'"

Always, Norman said, Disney had to sign off on whatever was done, even if that meant the writers marked time for weeks. "Nothing got past him. If he hadn't seen it yet, it wasn't going to go anywhere. We would simply have to wait until he had time to give it his OK. It truly was a one-man studio. Everything had Walt's touch."[26]

By the middle 1960s, Disney had turned his back on serious retellings of classic stories. "We do better with our own stories where we have greater latitude," he said in 1965. "People keep urging us to do *Don Quixote*"—a story that Disney had contemplated making as early as 1940, when Bill Tytla was anxious to work on it.[27] "We'd be crucified if that didn't turn out just right—especially in the Latin countries. I got trapped into making *Alice in Wonderland* against my better judgment and it was a terrible disappointment. Frankly, I always liked the Tenniel illustrations in *Alice* but I never exactly died laughing over the story. It's terribly tough to transfer whimsy to the screen."[28]

Woolie Reitherman's boisterous, careless kind of comedy bore a general resemblance to much of what passed for comedy on television at the time, and the thinking behind the Disney feature cartoons and the occasional short subject now resembled the thought that went into TV situation comedies. But there was no mistaking one of those films for a television product; in the 1960s, as in earlier decades, the level of craftsmanship remained stubbornly high. That was not the case where Disney's live-action films were concerned.

By the early 1960s, Disney was no longer speaking of television as a means of promoting his theatrical films. Instead, he had begun to regard most of the films he made as interchangeable, suitable for either venue, as the need arose, the *Johnny Tremain* precedent expanded to encompass most of the studio's output. "Some of our pictures will be for theaters and others for TV," he said in 1960. "I'll make up my mind about that later."[29] The decisive step came in 1961, when Disney switched networks, from ABC to NBC. It is not clear who courted whom, but Disney and NBC were a good match, in any case. NBC was the network most aggressively programming in color, and Disney, after seven years in black and white on ABC, badly wanted color. The NBC show, telecast on Sunday evening as *Walt Disney's Wonderful World of Color*, was devoted largely to multipart live-action films that were at least barely imaginable as theatrical releases and were often released theatrically overseas.

The *New York Times* explained the strategy: "By parlaying television into movies—[and] the other way around—Mr. Disney believes he has found the most sensible way to make television shows of quality and still earn a profit." Disney himself told the *Times:* "Once you are in television, it's like operating a slaughter house. Nothing must go to waste. You have to figure ways to make glue out of the hoofs."[30] Animation survived on the NBC show mainly through the presence of a hyperactive, Viennese-accented character called Ludwig Von Drake, who was presented as Donald Duck's uncle. (Donald was named Duck, rather than Drake, Disney explained in 1961—not on TV—because "he was a little bastard and he took his mother's name.") Von Drake, a self-proclaimed expert on almost everything, served as the guest host for programs pieced together from short films like those in the *People and Places* series. He filled a role that might otherwise have demanded more of Disney's time than the very brief introductions he filmed for most of the shows.

ABC had been a part owner of the Disneyland park, but the Disneys severed that tie before the ABC show ran its course. Disneyland became a wholly owned subsidiary of Walt Disney Productions during the 1960 fiscal year, with the purchase of ABC's 34.48 percent share for $7.5 million. Walt Disney Productions had already exercised options to buy the ownership interests of Western Printing and Lithographing Company and Walt himself, for much less than they were worth by the time of the sales, in 1957. It had no such option to buy ABC's share, and so Roy Disney had no choice but to haggle with the network. In May 1961, Disneyland, Incorporated, was merged into the parent company.[31]

ABC's part ownership of Disneyland disturbed Roy more than it did him, Walt said in 1961: "It was an obsession with him to get them out." Roy said a few years later: "They were not likeable, workable people."[32] Such judgments carried extra weight because Walt Disney Productions' personal flavor was still so strong: as late as 1966, Walt and Lillian Disney still owned more than 16 percent of the company's common stock, Roy and Edna Disney almost 8 percent.[33]

After the shooting of *Third Man on the Mountain,* Disney warmed to the idea of much more filming in Europe, and by the fall of 1959 a half dozen projects were under way. Over the next few years, he made several dozen films in Europe, most of them bearing the marks of the relatively short shooting schedules—and relatively low costs—that made it possible to think of theatrical and TV films as interchangeable. Thanks to jets, which halved the flight time to Europe starting in 1959, his overseas visits were now more frequent. He and Lillian visited Europe four times in 1960, stopping in London each time. They were in Vienna twice that year and were there again in 1961, when they also visited London (three times) and Paris. In August 1962 they visited Lisbon, and then London in September.[34] Disney found ocean voyages to Europe tedious, his daughter Diane said in 1956—"Daddy when he gets away from the studio, and has nothing to do except sightsee and walk around and talk to people, he gets bored"[35]—so the greater speed of air travel was made to order for him.

More and more of the films made in the United States were television-flavored, too, not just in their obvious back-lot shooting, flat lighting, ham-fisted music, and reliance on TV-bred actors, but in their tendency to instruct the audience how to respond to what was happening on the screen, through reaction shots at supposedly funny or touching moments. Movies like *Toby Tyler* (1960) are as curiously airless as many TV shows of the time; there is little or no sense that the movie's events are part of life going on outside the screen. Disney was pleased, though, with the hack TV directors he hired to direct more and more of his theatrical features. "I like young talent," he said in 1963. "When people get to be institutions, they direct pictures with their left hand and do something else with their right."[36] Those reaction shots in *Toby Tyler* were probably his editing choices.

In live action, as in animation, Disney was spread thinner than ever before, and in consequence he made careless, self-indulgent decisions that undermined films he cared about. *Pollyanna* (1960) may have been fatally hobbled by its title, as Disney himself believed; but it is also much too long, and according to its director, David Swift, Disney rejected his efforts to trim twenty minutes from the film and restructure a sequence devoted to a turn-of-the-century bazaar. The effect would have been to strengthen the film's narrative line and make it less of a nostalgic bath, but Disney insisted that it be the latter.[37]

Pollyanna was Disney's first film with Hayley Mills, a young (thirteen at the time of filming) British actress who all but rescues it. The illusion of spontaneity in her performance is complete—and vital, because any sense of calculation, whether originating with the actor or imposed by the director, would be deadly. Instead, Pollyanna's goodness (which is most emphatically *not* the same as sweetness) seems natural and unforced, and is thus wholly winning. It was no wonder that Disney signed her to a multipicture contract.

Mills and her parents, the actor John Mills and writer Mary Hayley Bell, were British film people who, like Richard Todd and Ken Annakin, were guests in Disney's home. (Fess Parker and James MacArthur, the two young American actors who succeeded Todd as the principal leading man in Disney films, both spoke warmly of Disney, but neither was ever invited to Holmby Hills.) "I loved going to his home in Hollywood *[sic]*," Hayley Mills said in an interview published in 1968. "In most Hollywood houses, there are those private viewing theaters for the latest films, and you sit back in those comfortable chairs with a drink in your hand, and the Renoirs disappear, and the screen comes down. But at his house, he didn't have a bar in his screening room. He had a soda fountain, and all through a movie, you'd hear pshissh, squirt, bubble bubble—he was behind there concocting all those wonderful sodas and sundaes."[38]

Ken Annakin was ultimately undone, as a Disney director, by the same sort of warm social relationship with Disney.

After directing *Third Man on the Mountain,* Annakin directed *Swiss Family Robinson,* a difficult and, for Disney, unusually expensive film (shot entirely on the Caribbean island of Tobago, at a cost of $4.5 million) that was extremely popular when it was released just before Christmas 1960. Although Annakin worked on the script and storyboards with Disney at Burbank before shooting began early in 1959, Disney never visited Tobago during filming, and the film's most distinctive characteristics are clearly Annakin's. As different as the film's actors are in accents and acting styles, it is possible to believe they are a family, thanks to the way they respond to one another. There is real tenderness between John Mills and Dorothy McGuire, as the parents, and the sibling rivalry between James MacArthur and Tommy Kirk is strong but never overplayed. Because these characters form a believable family, *Swiss Family's* knockabout qualities—this is a film about a family stranded on a desert island and besieged by pirates—never quite get out of hand.

Not long after *Swiss Family's* release, on one of Walt and Lillian's visits to London in the early 1960s—the date is uncertain—they had dinner with Annakin and his wife, Pauline, at their London apartment. Disney and Annakin talked warmly about a new project, a film based on the life of Sir Francis Drake. "Over dinner," Annakin wrote in his autobiography, "Pauline talked mainly to Lillian, whose glass I seemed to be refilling more often than usual." (Pauline, who had met Lillian during the filming of *Third Man on the Mountain,* described her as "pleasant" but "tricky" compared with Walt, meaning that she was not as forthright; in Pauline's eyes, Lillian lacked Walt's openness and enthusiasm.)[39]

When the Disneys' limousine arrived at the end of the evening, Ken Annakin wrote, Lillian "began descending the six stone steps onto Onslow Square, teetered and fell, sprawling on the ground. I rushed down to help her and was raising her to her feet when Walt took over. Brusquely, he pushed me aside and led her limping to the car. As we waved them away and closed the door, Pauline said, 'You'll never work for Walt, again.'"[40]

Such was the case. Annakin said in 2005: "I'd made Walt four very successful pictures, and I never heard from him again."[41] The Annakins had known the Disneys for years, but given the limited importance that Disney assigned to a director's part in making his films, there was no way that a record as successful as Annakin's could outweigh a moment of embarrassment, a lapse in control.

Even as Disney's grip weakened on each film as a whole, his intimidating awareness of details did not. Dee Vaughan, who helped ensure consistency from shot to shot, as an "assistant continuity," remembered a Disney visit to the set when *In Search of the Castaways* (starring Hayley Mills) was made in London in the last half of 1961. He was "charming, absolutely sweet. Shook all of our hands and spoke to us, and watched us while we were working." Disney "let us come to rushes, which was exceptional, really, because he could have had a private screening himself, couldn't he? But he came when we all went. We were sitting in the theater watching rushes, and . . . he turned to Robert [Stevenson, the director] and he said there was a line missing in the dialogue. He was absolutely right. Robert had changed it, because somebody had difficulty saying it or something. [Disney] picked up on it immediately. He was not unpleasant, just matter-of-fact. He let us know that the finger was totally on the pulse. Afterward, I said to [Stevenson], 'How many pictures has he got on the floor at the moment?' 'Oh, about five.' One line!"[42]

The same was true in Burbank. Floyd Norman remembered watching the rushes for the live-action films in a screening room there. "I probably wasn't supposed to be there, but it didn't matter, because it was a screening room, and it's dark, and they can't see you. . . . It gave me the opportunity to see how Walt was handling his producers and directors. As they would be showing the previous day's filming, the rushes, Walt would be making comments, like, 'Why wasn't that lit better?' or 'Why didn't that work?' or 'Why is that monkey doing that?' And, of course, the poor director is making excuses— you know, 'Well, we had trouble, Walt, we couldn't get the animal to sit still,' and this happened and that happened, we're sorry, we'll do better."[43] Disney was not cruel, but to be subject constantly to such scrutiny could not have been pleasant.

For years, Disney walked the studio lot, looking into every corner, but in the 1960s, with the lot busier and Disney himself older, he began riding from place to place in an electric cart. Card Walker remembered that Disney toured the lot every day after lunch, going "from one shop to another. And if you ever made those trips with him, it was fantastic. He really knew what was going on." If a set was under construction, Walker said, he would check it carefully to make sure he approved of it. "The guy was just that interested in every damn detail of production."[44]

(There was something of the small businessman in those tours of the lot, too. Frank Thomas remembered a time when Disney entered a sound stage and found nothing going on, then said, "Look at everybody standing around with their hands in my pocket.")[45]

By the 1960s, scorn for Disney's live-action films was a reflex among most critics, and for good reason. *In Search of the Castaways,* the studio's big Christmas release for 1962, is shockingly bad, not just because its special effects are cheesy but because the characters behave in such arbitrary fashion, doing whatever is required to move the plot from point A to point B, with scant regard for plausibility. Disney would have countenanced nothing so crude when he was making his best animated features. For all the Oscars he had won—more than any other filmmaker, mostly for animated and documentary short subjects—he was not taken seriously as a live-action filmmaker, in Hollywood or elsewhere. None of his live-action features had ever been nominated as best picture; none of the actors in those films had ever been nominated for anything (although Hayley Mills did receive an honorary Oscar).

As he had ten years earlier, when he made the uncharacteristically lavish *20,000 Leagues Under the Sea* to establish his live-action bona fides, Disney now invested far more money and effort in a film than he usually did. The film was *Mary Poppins.* He had pursued the rights to the P. L. Travers stories for almost twenty years before finally persuading the author to sell them in 1960, and he was deeply involved in the writing of the script and the negotiations with the lead actors—Julie Andrews and Dick Van Dyke—for the next two years. (Andrews was a Broadway star, Van Dyke a television star. Disney signed no true Hollywood film stars like those in *20,000 Leagues.*)

Although set in London, *Poppins* was a defiantly old-fashioned musical filmed entirely on Disney soundstages. It was exceptional mostly in its extensive combination of animation and live action, which was in its effect, if not in the technology used to achieve it, all but identical with the combination work in *Song of the South,* almost twenty years earlier. The filming occupied much of 1963, but by all accounts it went smoothly, and by the time of the premiere—an extravagant affair at Grauman's Chinese Theatre in Hollywood, on August 27, 1964—there was little question but that *Poppins* would be a great success. The film ultimately grossed around forty-four million dollars and won five Academy Awards (*20,000 Leagues* received two, for art direction and special effects). It lost the Oscar for best picture to *My Fair Lady,* but Julie Andrews's Oscar for best actress amounted almost to a sharing of that award because Andrews, who had played Eliza Doolittle on the stage, was so conspicuously denied the opportunity to play the same part in the film version of *Fair Lady.*

Given the attention that Walt Disney himself lavished on *Mary Poppins*, it should have been his triumph, and it certainly was such as measured by the box office. Beneath its bright surface and cheerful songs, however, there was lurking a failure that was Disney's in his once strong role as story editor. *Poppins* had no story apart from the transformation of Mister Banks, the father of the children whom Mary Poppins, the magical nanny, takes under her care; but David Tomlinson, who played the role, was a supporting actor, nothing more, too clearly confined by mannerisms and temperament to roles calling for a stuffy, easily ruffled Englishman. Disney wanted Mary Poppins herself at the center of the film, and so putting a strong actor—much less a difficult actor, someone like Rex Harrison—in Tomlinson's place was unthinkable; but without such an actor, the film could be only a succession of musical numbers held together by a very slim narrative thread. Mister Banks's transformation has no weight, a fact underlined by the very casual (and wholly unbelievable) manner in which he regains his job at a bank after he has been liberated by losing it. A centerpiece dance number on the rooftops has no strong dancer leading it; Dick Van Dyke hardly fills that role.

Everywhere that Disney's hand is most evident, as in some of the casting and incidental "business," *Mary Poppins* suffers from debilitating weaknesses. At the least, a question mark hangs over the casting of Van Dyke as Bert the chimney sweep—the role would have benefited from an actor such as Tommy Steele, who, like Andrews, had roots in British music-hall comedy. Bob Thomas told how Disney "made a habit of 'walking through' the sets after they had been built, searching for ways to use them. Bill Walsh [the film's principal writer and co-producer] described a visit by Walt to the Bankses' living room in search of reaction to the firing of Admiral Boom's cannon: 'Walt got vibes off the props. As he walked around the set he said, 'How about having the vase fall off and the maid catches it with her toe?' or, 'Let's have the grand piano roll across the room and the mother catches it as she straightens the picture frame.'"[46] But the havoc supposedly caused by Admiral Boom's cannon—on a regular schedule!—is simply ridiculous. There is no reason to believe it would be tolerated in a well-ordered London neighborhood. Here, as elsewhere, *Poppins* is the sort of shallow fantasy that undermines its own premises.

Although *Mary Poppins* received better press than most Disney films—some critics were skeptical, but many more were genuinely enthusiastic—Disney enjoyed no more than a truce in his long-running war with reviewers. He was in return often belligerent and defensive, dismissing his critics as "smarty-pants, wisecracking guys."[47] In an interview published early in 1964, he said:

"I am not a literary person. As far as realism is concerned, you can find dirt anyplace you look for it. I'm one of those optimists. There's always a rainbow. The great masses like happy endings. If you can pull a tear out of them, they'll remember your picture. That little bit of pathos was Chaplin's secret. Some directors in Hollywood are embarrassed by sentimentality. As for me, I like a good cry."[48] He sounded the same theme in other interviews published later that year, in the wake of *Poppins's* success. "I like perfection, but I also like corn," he said. "I don't make pictures for sophisticates. Styles may change on the surface, but at bottom the big audience taste doesn't change. They like sympathetic characters and life-like action. And that's what I like, too, whether it's cartoons, live action or all those creatures at Disneyland."[49]

One problem was that the Disney who did not make pictures for sophisticates had become in many respects a sophisticate himself. After he went into television and opened Disneyland, his daughter Diane said, "Dad had a tremendous amount of growth. . . . I think this happens to people—as you become a figure of some prominence and all that, you find yourself a bit. You feel the weight, the importance of your public image."[50] Disney's simplicity and directness, so important to the success of the shorts of the 1930s and *Snow White,* could not be maintained in the same form in later years without falsification. Bill Davidson, interviewing Disney for *TV Guide* in 1961, was struck by this incongruity:

"While the public thinks of Disney as playing with trains and exchanging pleasantries with juvenile alumni of the now-defunct *Mickey Mouse Club,* he actually is one of the most widely read, most widely traveled, most articulate men in Hollywood. I became acutely aware of this when I spoke with him recently at lunch in the private dining room of his . . . studio. While he devoured a dietetic meal of lean hamburger and sliced tomatoes he spouted rustic witticisms with the aplomb of a modern-day Bob Burns. But every once in a while his eyes would narrow, the rural twang would disappear from his voice and he'd discuss financial projections for 1962, the modern art of Picasso and Diego Rivera, and Freudian psychiatry. In a few moments, however, he'd catch himself" and revert to homespun stories.[51]

By the early 1960s, Disney had lived in Los Angeles and been part of its film industry for forty years. The industry and Los Angeles itself had changed dramatically in those years. The industry and its attendant glamour and cynicism were far more dominant in the city's culture than in the 1920s, when Disney's journey from Kansas City to Los Angeles was in effect a move from one midwestern city to another, the California version distinguished mainly by its better climate. To the extent that Disney had real friends in the 1960s, they held high places in the film industry or in industries that were in some ways comparable to it, like architecture (he and Lillian traveled with the celebrity architect Welton Becket and his wife, who were neighbors in Holmby Hills). Disney could have remained a "country boy" under such circumstances only through a calculated exercise of the will in itself hard to reconcile with warmth and spontaneity. Repeatedly, the magazine writers who spoke with Disney in the 1960s found him a different man than they expected, or thought they had seen on television, and so they observed him intently. They may have borrowed from one another to some extent, but for the most part their descriptions seem drawn from life.

"Before I met him," Aubrey Menen wrote in *Holiday* in 1963, "every effort was made by his aides to impress me that Walt Disney was, in fact, avuncular. He was open and affable, they said, and easy to talk to. Instead I met a tall, somber man who appeared to be under the lash of some private demon. Mr. Disney's face and figure are familiar to all the world. In private he smiles less—I remember him smiling only once—and he is not at ease. He speaks in short sentences with pauses in which he looks at, or rather through, his listener. . . . Mr. Disney's hands move restlessly all the while he talks, picking up things from his desk or the restaurant table, playing with them and casting them aside with a sharp gesture, as though they had failed to come up to his standards."[52]

In 1964, Stephen Birmingham, writing for *McCall's*, described Disney in similar terms, as "a haggard, driven-looking man with a long, mournful face and dark, heavy-lidded eyes. The man who is almost always photographed grinning actually grins seldom, and when he does grin, it is with an almost bitter curl of the lip. Sometimes his eyes seem to withdraw and to focus on remote, secret places. 'You can always tell when Walt's bored or dissatisfied with something,' an associate says. 'He gets that glassy look, as though he's just noticed something very small and ugly at the back of your skull.' His big hands move restlessly and incessantly, as though his body, even in repose, knew no peace—pawing at the package of French Gitanes cigarettes that is never far from his reach or, at a dinner table, playing noisily and endlessly with the silverware. Sometimes his fingers begin to rap out a sharp staccato rhythm on the desk top or chair arm—a storm warning, almost invariably. . . . His dress is casual, to put it mildly. Usually, his clothes have a look of having been tossed on in great haste that morning from the chair where they were hurled the night before. Despite the benign Southern California sunshine, Disney tends to bundle up—in a shapeless cardigan, a baggy tweed coat, or a wind-breaker."[53] The natty young dresser of the early 1930s had disappeared along with the enthusiastic young cartoon maker.

"He is shy with reporters," Edith Efron wrote for *TV Guide* in 1965. "His eyes are dull and preoccupied, his affability mechanical and heavy-handed. He gabs away slowly and randomly in inarticulate, Midwestern speech that would be appropriate to a rural general store. His shirt is open, his tie crooked. One almost expects to see over-all straps on his shoulders and wisps of hay in his hair. . . . If one has the patience to persist, however, tossing questions like yellow flares into the folksy fog, the fog lifts, a remote twinkle appears in the preoccupied eyes, and the man emerges."

Here again, as in other interviews from the 1960s, Disney permitted himself to sound bitter and resentful when he said anything of substance: "These avant-garde artists are adolescents. It's only a little noisy element that's going that way, that's creating this sick art. . . . There is no cynicism in me and there is none allowed in our work. . . . I don't like snobs. You find some of intelligentsia, they become snobs. They think they're above everybody else. They're not. More education doesn't mean more common sense. These ideas they have about art are crazy. . . . I don't *care* about critics. Critics take themselves too seriously. They think the only way to be noticed and to be the smart guy is to pick and find fault with things. It's the *public* I'm making pictures for."[54]

It is at this point in his life that anecdotes about Disney's drinking become more numerous. No one ever suggests that he was an alcoholic, but his consumption—perhaps stimulated by his increasing physical discomfort, from his old polo injury and nagging sinus trouble—was undoubtedly higher than average. One of Disney's luncheon companions in the early 1960s remembered him, in a hurry, start their meal by telling the waiter, "We'll have two martinis each and bring them both at the same time." More drinks followed.[55]

Alcohol was taken for granted in the Disney household. Disney taught one of his daughters, presumably Diane, how to mix drinks when she was twelve, although, he said, neither girl drank as an adult.[56] A five o'clock drink, preceding a massage by the studio nurse, Hazel George, was part of his office routine, but frequently that single drink became several, because Disney often stayed at the office until 7 or 7:30 at night. His secretary Tommie Wilck, concerned about his drive home, tried to limit his consumption by serving him a scotch mist, a drink made up mostly of ice and water.[57]

There was no such constraint operating when Disney was on the road, as one of his traveling companions remembered. "I think he was meaner than hell when he had five scotches," Buzz Price said, "but who isn't? . . . Walt would work all day, intense, intense, intense, and he would unwind in the evening with a few glasses of scotch. My experience, in traveling, was that his intensity began to transition into irritation."[58]

Disney's absorption in his own thoughts, always a distinct characteristic, was, if anything, more pronounced now than ever before. *Newsweek* suggested in 1962 that "his only conspicuous trait" might be "his capacity for total preoccupation. One associate recalls him considering a problem and absently dipping a doughnut in his Scotch." The magazine quoted Fred MacMurray: "He's never quite listening to what you say."[59]

Tommie Wilck remembered a Disney who "had tremendous powers of concentration. Sometimes he'd be sitting in his office and I'd go in and talk to him and he wouldn't even hear me. He could shut himself off with all sorts of noise, phones ringing, and think." A common experience, the animator Milt Kahl said, was "to lose him while you were talking to him. This didn't happen just to me. . . . And it could be quite annoying sometimes if you didn't realize what he was doing. . . . You didn't [bring him back]. You just [had] to pick another time, or wait till he's in a frame of mind to start listening again."[60]

When Disney thought out loud, he wanted only an audience, not a response—someone to talk at, not with. Lillian regularly played that role, hearing without really listening, but other people, like Ward Kimball and Bill Peet, were on occasion recruited into it, too. Disney might reminisce or speculate for many minutes, but then, if his auditor tried to respond in kind, he would end the conversation abruptly.

In the memories of his employees, Disney was variously considerate or irritable, kind or petty, depending on the circumstances and his state of mind— a perfectly ordinary man in many respects, and more decent and likable than most—but he rarely showed real interest in other people. In this he was indistinguishable from entrepreneurs generally, who are almost by definition people engrossed in their businesses. Said Price: "He had no patience with people who weren't on the same wavelength with him, or people who couldn't help him, or people who were trying to finesse him. If you could help him, everything was rosy."[61] Joyce Carlson told Jim Korkis about Disney's visits to WED's Christmas parties: "He'd always show up! He'd talk to the traffic boys [studio messengers] and tell which project, like the Haunted Mansion, was coming up and they'd stand there listening to Walt. He used to be so excited telling them about all the new projects. He was wonderful and the boys were just so thrilled."[62] But the boys were, of course, an audience.

When Disney got carried away with an idea while he was talking to an employee about it, noted Jack Cutting, "if you did say, 'Well, now, wait a minute, Walt, you said so-and-so . . . ,' a cloud would come over his face. It was like you'd dumped a bucket of cold water on him. . . . He might later think it over and take that into consideration, but if you did that at a time like that, you were somebody he couldn't work with."[63]

The Disney of the 1960s was still capable of enthusiasms, as some of his interviewers discovered. "His heavy-lidded and rather mournful eyes grow dim with ennui when a subordinate or friend tries to slip in a compliment," Peter Bart wrote in the *New York Times*. "Disney's dry Midwestern voice trails off into inaudibility when he is asked to discuss some question that does not interest him—and a formidable list of things fit into this category." But Disney came to life, Bart wrote, when he talked about the Christmas parade at Disneyland: "Disney's voice booms, his face crinkles into an exuberant smile. 'We'll have these giant mushrooms and dolls,' he enthuses. 'Inside the figures will be men riding little motor scooters. The parade may set us back $250,000 but it will be the best we've ever had.'"[64]

In the 1960s, as his park neared the end of its first decade, he still spoke of Disneyland with a lover's fierce passion. "You need the sharp-pencil boys, but you can't let them run the joint," he said in a *Look* interview published early in 1964. "Since Disneyland opened, I've poured another $25 million into it. To me, it's a piece of clay. I can knock it down and reshape it to keep it fresh and attractive. That place is my baby, and I would prostitute myself for it."[65]

That intensity, never visible to viewers of Disney's television show, showed itself in his behavior when he was in the park. "He would never walk past a piece of litter," said Michael Broggie, a ride operator in the early 1960s. "He would reach down and grab it, and everyone was expected to do that." Disney employees observed him as intently as he scrutinized the park. He followed a routine when he was escorting an important guest around the park, Broggie told *The "E" Ticket.* "He would go to the Golden Horseshoe Saloon, and if he came out and turned right, it meant he was to go to the Mine Train. If he turned left, it meant he was going [toward New Orleans Square] or back to his apartment. His route was monitored, and with two-way radios they would report on Walt's location. This went on whenever he was in the park, unbeknownst to Walt, because everyone wanted to be on their toes when the boss was in the area."[66]

Disneyland was malleable, and—much like the Disney studio in the late 1930s—it was staffed by hundreds of people eager to carry out their patron's wishes. The challenge was to find ways to change the park that went beyond simply adding new rides that would inevitably echo rides in older amusement parks or at Disneyland itself. One way was to make the place funnier.

When Marc Davis finished his work on *One Hundred and One Dalmatians,* Disney sent him to Disneyland to look at a train ride through the landscaped area called Nature's Wonderland, because it was full of mechanical animals and, Davis said, "he knew I knew a lot about animals. I did a flock of drawings on it."[67] As it turned out, Davis said, "he just wanted me to look it over and tell him how great it was, [but] I looked at it quite critically and came up with a lot of opinions."[68] Davis had not been an admirer of the park. "When I went down to Disneyland the first time," he said, "I felt from the very beginning that there was very little that was entertaining or funny to me. There was just a lot of stuff, like a World's Fair. . . . As soon as I started to work on this stuff, I tried to find ways to add something that people could get a laugh out of."

Davis provided what he called "storytelling tableaus." "Here's a prime example of the humor, the storytelling that was missing: He had a couple of 'kit foxes' . . . one was looking at the train over here, and its head went up and down, and there was another one maybe a hundred feet away, and its head went side to side. Well, I took the two of them and put them face-to-face . . . so one nods like this and the other one does this . . . and you immediately have an idea. That's what I started doing on the rides."[69]

There were limits to what could be done along those lines, though, and Davis acknowledged them on other occasions when he contradicted his own use of "storytelling." An amusement park's rides "should be what people don't expect them to be," he said, "and it doesn't have a lot to do with continuity of story. It does have to do with the entertainment value of surprise and seeing things that you can't see anyplace else."[70] He and Disney were in agreement on that, he said: "Walt knew that we were not telling stories . . . he and I discussed it many times. And he said very definitely, 'You can't tell a story in this medium.'"[71] By the early 1960s, preliminary work on a Haunted Mansion was under way, but that work was wedded to the idea of telling a gruesome story as visitors walked through. And that story line, Davis believed, was the reason "Walt never bought the Haunted Mansion in his time."[72]

If storytelling was not possible, the experiences that Disneyland could provide otherwise were constrained by the extremely limited movement that was possible for its mechanical creatures. As *The "E" Ticket* explained, the Jungle Cruise's mechanized animals "moved without really moving. These animal replicas . . . were very realistic in appearance but were mostly limited to lateral motion and a few hydraulic mechanical functions." The animals included "crocodiles with hinged jaws, a gorilla that rocked up and down, giraffes whose necks would sway and rhinos which circled on tracks in the dry grass."

Their actions "consisted mostly of charging and trumpeting, surfacing and submerging, and sliding around on underwater runways." (In the early days of the park, these simple mechanical movements were called "gags.")[73]

Disneyland's vaunted malleability was thus something of an illusion. Finding some way to make his mechanical animals more lifelike was for Disney a necessity if the park was not to become an increasingly ordinary place, for him and for its visitors.

As with so many other things, Disney had nursed an interest in mechanical movement for years before he put it to use at Disneyland. At least since his 1935 trip to Europe, he had been intrigued by mechanical toys and had brought them back to the studio. "When we went to Paris," Diane Disney Miller said—that was probably in 1949—"Dad went off on his own and came back with boxes and boxes of these little windup toys. He wound them all up and put them on the floor of the room and just sat and watched them. You know, the dog that rolls over and stuff like that. He said, 'Look at that movement with just a simple mechanism.' He was studying. . . . We thought he was crazy."[74]

Even before that, probably in New Orleans on his 1946 train trip to the Atlanta premiere of *Song of the South,* Disney had bought what Wathel Rogers called "this little mechanical bird in a cage. . . . One of those that you could wind up and it would whistle." Years later, when Disneyland was open and Rogers was on the WED staff, "Walt gave it to me and asked me to look inside it. I was supposed to take it apart, and it was like taking apart a piece of jewelry. When I finally got it all apart and laid everything out I found a little bellows made of canvas, and some little cams and other parts."[75]

To an extent now hard to determine, Disney's interest in such mechanical toys figured into his plans in the early 1950s for his Americana in miniature, but it was for Disneyland that his WED employees seriously investigated such mechanisms and began applying what they learned to animated figures. By the fall of 1960, Disney was demonstrating to reporters the animated heads of what one writer called "his new waxworks figures."[76] In 1963, it was when his glum luncheon conversation with Aubrey Menen turned to the robotic technology he now called "Audio-Animatronics" that Disney finally brightened: "'Now *there,*' he said, smiling at last. 'There is where I am *happy.*'"[77]

That interview was published when Disneyland was about to open the Enchanted Tiki Room, the first true Audio-Animatronics attraction. As *The "E" Ticket* explained, "The mechanized figures developed after 1963 were a complete departure from those installed in the park in its first years of operation. . . . Access to space-age fabrics, plastics and metals, miniaturized sole-noids and other electronic components made new degrees of animation pos-sible. With hydraulic movements (for strength) and pneumatic movements (for low-pressure delicacy), and with ever smaller servo-mechanisms, Disney began creating improved, more believable animals and humans. . . . For the first time (with the help of Marc Davis and other new designers) they could individually perform for the audience. The complex control systems devised for the Enchanted Tiki Room and other shows began as notched platters and light-sensitive photo cells," were succeeded by magnetic tape and ultimately were computerized, long after Disney's time.

"With these methods, Disney was able to dictate and sequence great num-bers of actions for one or more figures, from a distance. It became possible to program specific movements of face and head, limbs and body, the char-acter's words and music, and even coordinate the actions of many perform-ers within an entire attraction or show."[78]

The Tiki Room aside, the initial showcases for the new technology were not at Disneyland, but at the New York World's Fair of 1964–65.[79] He un-dertook the world's fair projects "to benefit Disneyland," Disney said in 1963. "We won't lose money on the work, but we don't expect to make much, ei-ther. We expect these exhibits, or part of them, to end up at the park, where they will add to our free attractions. Or, if the corporations do not decide to exhibit them at Disneyland, they will pay a penalty which will amount to our profit in creating them."[80]

Said Bob Gurr, a member of the WED staff: "One big thrust behind our design work for the World's Fair was the fact that we were going to own all the equipment. In other words, somebody else would build the pavilion, on somebody else's property, but the show equipment that went in there was Disney's, and he had a ready-made location waiting for it. The fact that the Fair was going to run two years meant he could build more expensively, and Disney priced these projects in a way that the sponsors were paying for every-thing for a two-year use."[81]

Disney approached the fair with a certain skepticism, even so. "You don't like to do those things unless you have fun doing 'em," he said in 1961, when work on the exhibits was just getting under way. "You don't do 'em for money." Robert Moses, the imperious road builder who was in command of the fair, "wanted us to develop the amusement area and we looked at it," Disney said, "but it just wasn't for us. I wouldn't want to try to do anything in New York. I'm not close enough. . . . On top of that, I mean I don't know whether I want to do any outside of Disneyland because you don't want to spread yourself thin."

By the time the fair opened, Disney had banished any such reservations and was planning a new amusement park in central Florida. His world's fair exhibits would allow him to learn just how receptive East Coast audiences— especially tough New York audiences—would be to the Disneyland-style entertainment he expected to offer in Florida, although by 1964 he had scant reason for doubt on that score.

All four exhibits were, however, a reversion to the kind of sponsored shows that Disney had abandoned almost twenty years earlier when he stopped making industrial films. (Dick Irvine referred to General Electric's Progressland Pavilion, which housed the Disney-designed Carousel of Progress, as "a refrigerator show.")[82] When he was desperate to fill Tomorrowland's empty spaces before Disneyland opened, Disney let several companies open static exhibits— including what the official guidebooks called "the modernistic Bathroom of the Future"—that were nothing more than displays of their products. In general, Disney had not had happy experiences with such sponsors, except when his position was strong enough that he could tell them what to do.

But the fair was appealing to Disney because with the help of subsidies from the four sponsors, he could use all the exhibits to refine Audio-Animatronics. That technology was now central to his continuing enthusiasm for Disneyland.

Two of the exhibits, Great Moments with Mr. Lincoln (for the state of Illinois) and the Carousel of Progress, revived ideas for unrealized attractions in Disneyland itself. "As usual," Randy Bright wrote, "Disney kept closely involved in the [carousel's] design. When his staff worked on a comical 1920s scene in which lazy, beer-drinking 'Cousin Orville' was to sit in a bathtub with his back to the audience, Walt questioned the staging. He turned the tub around to face the audience, took off his shoes and socks, and jumped in. 'He'd wiggle his toes, don't you think?' was Disney's conclusion. It was another of the subliminal touches that had become a Disney trademark."[83]

Audiences at the Carousel of Progress rotated around four central stages, each depicting a home that became increasingly electrified over the course of the century. The carousel, populated by Audio-Animatronics figures, was optimistic about the future in a way that brooked no dissent, highly sentimental in its depiction of changing family life, and curiously ambiguous about the family itself (it seemed as if no one in it ever died). Like the carousel, two other Disney-designed exhibits were technologically ingenious but vulnerable to criticism on other grounds. Pepsi-Cola's exhibit, It's a Small World, combined an insistently repetitive song by Disney's house composers, the brothers Richard and Robert Sherman, with animated displays designed by

Mary Blair to represent the world's children. Blair, who made preliminary color sketches for many of the animated features of the 1940s and early 1950s, embraced emphatically modern ideas about color and form but applied them to figures that could only be called "cute" (and without a trace of irony). The Audio-Animatronics Abraham Lincoln for the Illinois pavilion provoked especially intense criticism—it seemed to the novelist John Gardner that what made the "obviously dead" figure "horrible . . . was the ghastly suggestion, which had never occurred to Disney and his people, that all religion and patriotism are a sham and a delusion, an affair for monstrous automatons."[84] All three exhibits invited aesthetic and intellectual objections that could not be applied seriously to the earlier rides at Disneyland.

The Ford exhibit, called Magic Skyway, was more conventional, with less-advanced animated figures. Disney's friend Welton Becket was the architect for the pavilion that housed the Magic Skyway exhibit, and he remembered the intense interest Disney took not just in the exhibit itself but in its surroundings. "He wanted the toilets in the right positions," Becket said, and he wanted the people waiting in line to have something to look at. "I've never seen a great executive get down and take his coat off and really direct and work as he did on those exhibits."[85]

Disney emerged from his experience with the New York fair skeptical of world's fairs in general. They were out of date, he said, and of benefit only to hotels and restaurants.[86] Neither had his skepticism about working with big corporations been much eased. Ford decided not to come into Disneyland as the sponsor of an exhibit, despite what Marty Sklar, who had been writing promotional material of various kinds since Disneyland opened, called "a major effort" by Disney himself. "I went back with Walt for the Ford presentation. . . . Walt had Bob and Dick Sherman write a song, called 'Get the Feel of the Wheel of a Ford.' . . . It was a fabulous piece, and it would have been the greatest commercial for Ford. We went back there, and we made this pitch, and the end of the presentation was this song. And they turned us down. Walt couldn't understand, and he was really upset on the plane going back to New York. When Walt got involved with somebody, he did it all the way."[87]

Once the fair was out of the way, Disney shifted his attention back to how the technology the fair had nurtured could improve Disneyland. Walt Disney Productions purchased its first aircraft, a Beechcraft Queen Air, in January 1963, and took delivery of second plane, a Grumman Gulfstream, in March 1964.[88] Disney used the Gulfstream for short trips inside California and the Queen Air for longer trips out of state (it was replaced in July 1965 by a Beechcraft King Air). By mid-1965, according to *Business Week,* Disney was flying south to Disneyland about once a week. But he was driving several times a week to WED in Glendale to keep tabs on the development of Audio-Animatronics figures.[89]

Audio-Animatronics, based on Marc Davis's designs, transformed the Jungle Cruise in particular. The elephants bathing in the river were sly comedians now, as were the hyenas laughing at the five members of a safari trapped atop a pole by a rhinoceros.

Davis recalled designing a walk-through attraction on a pirate theme after talking about one with Disney, evidently in the early 1960s. "But the funny thing was, Walt was never quite ready to look at these drawings. He'd come into my room and not look at the walls and boards. He'd come in and he'd talk to me about pirates, but he would deliberately not look at the storyboards. It was annoying as hell to me, because I knew I had some work that I thought was pretty good, and also, I wanted to know what he thought about them. This went on until we went back to New York . . . and I think when we came back from there, Walt knew what he wanted to do"—not a walk-through attraction under New Orleans Square but a much more elaborate ride.[90]

The idea at that time, the designer Claude Coats said in 1991, was to confine the new ride within an underground space inside the park. "A big hole in the ground was there, and the steel was up for two or three years while we did the World's Fair shows. Then, when we came back and I started working on what might be in that space," after Disney had decided on a ride, "it was very, very small and very tight. We had a model going on it and Walt came around and looked at it one day, and then finally said, 'We're just going to go under the railroad track and into a big building outside the berm. There are too many ideas happening that are too confined in this small space.'"[91]

This was the ride eventually known as Pirates of the Caribbean, a dazzling display of how rapidly Disney's "Imagineers," as he called the designers at WED, had mastered their new technological opportunities. A total of sixty-five animated figures—pirates, townspeople, animals—made up the cast, moving more or less freely. *The "E" Ticket* explained some of what was involved in generating that movement:

> In developing and programming figural movement for the original Pirates ride, Imagineers used a coded reference system to plan and track the animation of each figure, and the [pirates'] captain has eleven of the functions. These codes represent broad motions like "left arm swing" and "right arm forward," "torso twist," "body side sway" and "body foresway." The function codes range up

to 37 movements for the body (including ten codes for the fingers) and another 13 codes for the head. Examples of the "head functions" include "eye blink," "mouth pinch right" and "smile left." Another group of 37 codes is used for the animals, birds and sea creatures within the ride. Some of the pirates have as few as three or four motions, while most have about seven or eight. When Pirates of the Caribbean opened, there were twelve pirates and villagers with ten or more of these animation functions.[92]

The central episode of the many that spectators see, as they pass through Pirates of the Caribbean in boats, is one in which the pirate captain auctions off the women of the town. The "audio" half of Audio-Animatronics comes very much into play as pirate voices call for "the redhead," a voluptuous young woman who is to be next on the auction block. "Walt added the auctioneer scene kind of late," Claude Coats said. "He came in one time and even said, 'This will be all right, won't it?' He was just a little doubtful of auctioning off the girls. Was that quite 'Disney' or not? We added some other signs around, *buy a bride* or something like that, that augmented the auction scene as though it was a special big event. . . . The way the girls were done it's not an offensive scene at all, but it probably could have been if it hadn't been handled in a very interesting way."[93]

As it is, there is an undertone of rape, but the sheer lavishness of the scene encourages the squeamish spectator to put such doubts aside. "We had made the auctioneer pirate so sophisticated that you could watch him move and it was as good as watching Lincoln," Marc Davis said. "He had all the little mouth movements and all that, and I mentioned to Walt that I thought it was a 'hell of a waste.' Walt said, 'No, Marc, it's not a waste . . . we do so much return business down here, and the next time people come in they'll see something they hadn't noticed before.'"[94]

There was, however, an intractable problem with Audio-Animatronics, even when its figures were as sophisticated—that is, programmed with as many movements—as the pirate captain and the robot Lincoln. The problem, the sculptor Blaine Gibson said, was "just how crude our medium is, relative to the human figure. There are a whole lot of muscles that allow a human actor to go from one expression to the other with extreme ease. You can't program this into a machine, and we don't have a material that can handle that."[95]

In short, the Audio-Animatronics figures were not really lifelike, and they could not be. As clever and intricate as it was, Pirates of the Caribbean was different only in degree, not in kind, from the tableaux that made up the rides in Fantasyland. As in the 1930s, Disney had forced the growth of a kind of animation, bringing to the movement of robotic figures a subtlety that had not existed before. In the 1930s, what he had achieved by the time he made *Snow White and the Seven Dwarfs* had opened up all kinds of possibilities for his medium—but in the middle 1960s, he was about to hit a brick wall. Audio-Animatronics was never going to make anyone weep. It was a kind of animation that could only remind Disney, as it became more sophisticated technologically, of what he had given up, a quarter century before, when he faltered in the face of the challenges and opportunities that the character animation in *Snow White* represented.

"For years afterward," Disney said in 1956, "I hated *Snow White* because every time I'd make a feature after that, they'd always compare it with *Snow White,* and it wasn't as good as *Snow White.*"

Wilfred Jackson, who was the most sympathetic and observant of Disney's cartoon directors, confirmed that "*Snow White* was a source of great trouble to Walt in later years. . . . Years and years after he made *Snow White,* we were discussing some footage to go on TV. He said then that it didn't seem possible to make a better picture than *Snow White.* I'm not sure it gave him a lot of pleasure to make that picture. He had a hard time trying to make a better one later on. . . . Other pictures have had better animation or better dialogue or better techniques in recording. These were not Walt's criteria for a better picture. His criterion was the impact it had on the public. And that film was *Snow White.*"[96]

Audio-Animatronics attractions were complex and challenging, but they—and by extension theme parks themselves—were a dead end for someone whose ambitions were more than entrepreneurial, as Disney's clearly were. As he had demonstrated repeatedly in work on *Snow White* and his other early films, he was a deeply serious man, but his life had run in reverse—Disneyland, for all its virtues, was simply not as serious an undertaking as his early features, and there was no way Audio-Animatronics could make it so. To wind up, in his sixties, "playing with his toys" was not where Walt Disney wanted to be.

On the evening of July 17, 1965, exactly ten years after Disneyland opened, Walt and Roy Disney and their wives joined in a celebration with those employees who had been with the park since the beginning. Walt spoke to the group, characteristically blunt and profane, but his words conveyed none of the giddy happiness of ten years earlier. He was more like the truculent tycoon reporters had been surprised to encounter:

> Well, we had a lot of problems putting this thing together. There was pressure for money. A lot of people didn't believe in what we were doing. And we

were putting the squeeze play where we could. I remember we were dealing with all three networks, they wanted our television show. And I kept insisting I wanted an amusement park. And everybody said, "What the hell's he want that damn amusement park for?" I couldn't think of a good reason except, I don't know, I wanted it. ABC needed the television show so damned bad that they bought the amusement park. . . . I just want to leave you with this thought, that it's just been sort of a dress rehearsal and we're just getting [started]. So if any of you start to rest on your laurels, I mean, just forget it.[97]

There was no retracing his steps to become the artist he once was; and so Disney began devoting more and more of his time to projects that bore little resemblance to either his films or his park.

One of those projects had its genesis in the mid-1950s, when Marc Davis, who had been teaching at the Chouinard Art Institute since 1947, received a phone call from its founder, Nelbert Chouinard. As a result of her call, Walt Disney sent two members of his financial staff, Royal Clark and Chuck Romero, to the school to, as Davis said, "kind of take a look at her financial problems," which were severe. When Clark and Romero inspected the school's books, they soon concluded that it had been swindled out of tens of thousands of dollars by its bookkeeper. Disney—perhaps energized by the honorary degree Chouinard gave him in May 1956—began taking a hand in the school's messy business affairs that year. Even with honest books, Chouinard was losing money, and so, in 1957, Walt Disney Productions began subsidizing the school—and, in effect, took control of it.[98] "Walt always said she had been wonderful to him," Davis said. "This was the basis of him getting into that."[99]

By the late 1950s, Disney had seized on the idea of transforming Chouinard into what one alumnus, Robert Perine, called "a multi-disciplined school of the arts where the graphic arts, music, drama, and film could all be gathered under one roof and offered to especially talented students who wanted to partake of this unique cross-breeding of activities."[100] Millard Sheets, a highly respected watercolorist and a Chouinard instructor, explained Disney's thinking to Perine, as Disney had explained it to him around 1960:

Walt felt that a new art would be born, a new concept of motion pictures. This was his whole dream. This is what very few people seem to understand, that a new form would come out of it, *if* a school was designed where there was a school of dance, cinemaphotography *[sic]*, drama, art, music, and eventually literature where they could develop writers. He felt that if all these things could be, as he used to say, "under one roof"—meaning they were really tied together *physically*—there'd be a cross-fertilization in the activities of the school and in the dormitories. . . . He felt that for a six-year program, which he envisaged, there'd be a totally new synthesis in the sense of mutual respect and understanding, and that it would make the motion picture art a *new art*.[101]

In 1961, a study by Economic Research Associates—a new consulting firm that Price had established with Disney's support—pinpointed the most desirable location for the new "university of the arts" as in the vicinity of the Hollywood Bowl. Disney "gave the green light to the design of a master plan," Perine has written, "the eventual renderings for which showed the school nestled in a small valley just across the Hollywood Freeway from the Bowl." By early 1962, the plan's substance still amounted to no more than pulling together Chouinard and the Los Angeles Conservatory of Music—another struggling institution—on one campus, with neither school's name subsumed in the name of the other.[102] In September 1962, though, they were merged into a new institution, the California Institute of the Arts, or CalArts.

By the fall of 1964, with his all-consuming work on the world's fair behind him, Disney was speaking expansively and publicly about his hopes for the new school. "This is a really new, exciting idea—all the arts taught on one spread-out campus, the students of each getting together to broaden their knowledge and stimulate their creative powers," he told an interviewer. "It grew out of our experience in the studio where a person might come in as an artist but wind up as a writer, a musician or an actor. This is something I've set my heart on and we have high-powered people ready to help it become reality. But it's too good to go off half-cocked. We'll hold our fire until some of these other big cultural projects here [he was referring to the Music Center and the Dorothy Chandler Pavilion in downtown Los Angeles] are completed. Then watch us go."[103]

When Millard Sheets had lunch with Disney in 1964, he was taken aback by the scale of the architectural drawings Disney showed him: "I looked and said, 'My God, this is a big university, not an art school! It's a nice design, but . . .' [Disney] said, 'Well, this is what we'll grow into. We'll start simply, but this is the master plan.'" Marc Davis was also startled by the architectural drawings: "He told me a number of times . . . 'I don't want to see this as an ivory tower type of school. I want to see this as a real practical thing.' He talked the same about the buildings. . . . I made a comment after seeing the drawings on this and I said, 'God, Walt, it would be marvelous if this had some one unique thing about it'" to give the school a distinct architectural identity. Disney responded more impatiently this time: "Oh, for Christ's sake, goddamn it, Marc."[104]

Consistent with Sheets's and Davis's memories, the promotional material for CalArts emphasized its practical, even commercial side—there was a hint in it of Walt Disney's earliest job as an artist, when he learned what he called "tricks." A lavish, full-color, spiral-bound fundraising booklet for CalArts titled "To enrich the lives of all people . . . " included a preface by Disney, who was chairman of the board of trustees. He said in part:

> The remarkable thing that's taking place in almost every field of endeavor is an accelerating rate of dynamic growth and change. The arts, which have historically symbolized the advance of human progress, must match this growth if they are going to maintain their value in, and influence on, society.
>
> The talents of musicians, the self expression of the actor, and the techniques and applications of fine and commercial artists are being used more and more in today's business, industry, entertainment and communications—not by themselves, but rather, in close association with each other.
>
> So artists who can operate in only one field are finding themselves limited and ill-equipped to meet the challenges and opportunities that come their way.
>
> What we must have, then, is a completely new approach to training in the arts—an entirely new educational concept which will properly prepare artists and give them the vital tools so necessary for working in, and drawing from, every field of creativity and performance.[105]

On August 16, 1966, Disney called James Algar, once a cartoon director but now one of his live-action producers. He wanted to talk about a promotional film for CalArts, and about his doing an introduction for it like those he did for the weekly TV show. His ideas, as Algar summarized them, again emphasized the arts' practical applications:

> Everyone says do we need artists? Let's make the point that we need *all* the arts; in medical research, in space travel, we need artists to help *visualize* things. Notice how much of the moon story in the papers is visualized through artist's renderings. . . .
>
> Walt would tell the need for artists, how important they are, the CalArts theory of education, his own experience at the studio in working with all the arts, never dreamed at the start he'd be this involved with all the arts; problems today in this complex world of communication, educational TV, world problems of illiteracy—pictures communicate instantaneously—the CalArts approach to professional competency, the training of teachers, professionals as practitioners, a College of Arts for tomorrow, heart of it talent.[106]

Buzz Price, from the beginning a member of CalArts' board, wrote of a Disney "whose personal art preference was representational and whose social values were essentially conservative, launching a complex inter-art school the stated intent of which was to be out-front in innovation, combination and presentation of art forms."[107] On the evidence of Disney's own words, though, he envisioned not such a school but rather one that could produce people like those who had been so useful to him at Disneyland; that is, exceptionally versatile and flexible commercial artists whose skills extended across a range of disciplines.

As for the school itself, ideas resembling Disney's were in the air in the late 1950s and early 1960s, when performing-arts complexes like Lincoln Center in New York (with its Juilliard School component) and the Kennedy Center in Washington were being planned and built. Even earlier, the composer Richard Rodgers had pressed for an arts complex in New York.[108] It was a given, in the demented city planning of the period, that it was desirable to segregate such functions into their own precinct, just as it was desirable to separate and isolate all the other strands of urban life—residential, commercial, governmental, and so on. It made sense, on such terms, not just to combine two schools that had very little in common but to seal them off from their surroundings.

In 1965, Walt Disney Productions—and presumably Walt Disney himself—took the logical next step and decided to take the school out of the city altogether and build it on a thirty-eight-acre tract cut out of the studio's 728-acre Golden Oaks Ranch at Newhall, northwest of Los Angeles. That would, at the least, be simpler than trying to raise the millions of dollars that would be required to build near the Hollywood Bowl.[109] Whether students would really benefit from such isolation, or from enforced exposure to one another's disciplines, was another matter, but Walt Disney took such gains for granted. In his planning for the school there were echoes of his planning in the late 1930s for the Burbank studio, a facility that he also expected to be an ideal environment for artists of various kinds.

The same impulse—to plan comprehensively and impose order—was at work in the mid-1960s as Disney approached the development of a much larger project.

CHAPTER 10

"He Drove Himself Right Up to the End"

Dreaming of a Nightmare City

1965–1966

Even before Disneyland opened, Walt Disney identified Florida as the only possible location for a second version of the park. "You have to have a year-round business to make money from such a large investment," he told Bob Thomas in the spring of 1955. "The only other place it would be possible is Florida. In the East, you could get only three or four profitable months."[1]

Late in 1959, Disney's WED Enterprises and Buzz Price's Economic Research Associates prepared what Price later described as "an economic and physical master plan for the City of Tomorrow at Palm Beach, Florida, on 12,000 acres owned by John McArthur, the billionaire insurance man." This would have been, Price said, "a four-way deal" involving Disney, RCA, NBC, and McArthur. "We put our effort together with WED in determining what kind of an interrelated park and city could be developed on that site. Walt wanted to emphasize future development in urban living. . . . The park would take up some 400 acres. A town base of 70,000 people would take up the rest." The deal fell through. "At the presentation, no one seemed to rally to what Walt was talking about."[2]

Price's report, titled "The Economic Setting of the City of Tomorrow" and dated December 14, 1959, suggests that Disney actually had narrower concerns at that time (and it puts the total acreage involved at five thousand to six thousand, not twelve thousand). One question the report addressed was whether "the local and tourist populations in Florida will provide adequate support for a major park development." Another was whether a new Florida park would cannibalize Disneyland's business. (Both answers favored a Florida park.) As far as the City of Tomorrow was concerned, the idea was to incorporate "advanced concepts of architectural design and technological improvement . . . in all phases of the town development," but there is no hint that Disney would have been deeply involved in that aspect of the development.[3]

The City of Tomorrow fizzled, evidently when RCA backed away, but Walt Disney's interest in such a city had been piqued. With Disneyland a huge success and an eastern version clearly practicable, Disney was now contemplating Florida as the setting not just for a second theme park, but also for a sort of large-scale, working version of Tomorrowland. In particular, his success in manipulating people's movements at Disneyland may have encouraged him to believe that he could do the same thing in an entire city. Although cars and the adjacent freeway were both critical to the success of Disneyland, the park itself, as Karal Ann Marling has pointed out, "offered a utopian alternative to the ongoing erosion of city centers by cars."[4] Public transportation of a sort—the monorail, for instance, and the PeopleMover, small, constantly moving vehicles propelled by the electricity in their track— was the rule at Disneyland.

Disney asked Price to study Florida locations in 1961 and then again in late 1963, when Disney's work for the New York World's Fair was almost done. The second study, Price wrote, identified "Orlando, centrally located, [as] the point of maximum access to the southerly flows of Florida tourism from both the east and west shores of the state."[5] In 1964, Walt Disney Productions began quietly assembling thousands of acres southwest of Orlando. The eventual total was around twenty-seven thousand acres, a much larger tract than would be needed for a theme park alone.

In 1965, his interest in a city of the future quickening, Disney flew east for a week to meet with the developer James Rouse and tour Reston, Virginia, and Columbia, Maryland, two "new towns" that Rouse had developed.[6] Disney had been praised by Rouse, who famously said at a 1963 urban design conference at Harvard University that "the greatest piece of urban design in the United States today is Disneyland. If you think about Disneyland and think about its performance in relation to its purpose; its meaning to people—more than that, its meaning to the process of development— you will find it the outstanding piece of urban design in the United States."[7]

By November 15, 1965, when Walt and Roy Disney and Governor Haydon Burns announced plans for the Florida development, Walt Disney was thinking in more specific terms about his City of Tomorrow. He was deliberately vague, though, when asked at that press conference whether such a city was in his plans. "Well," he said, "that's been the thing that's been going around in our mind for a long time and there's a lot of industrial concerns that would like to work on a project of that sort. The only problem with anything of tomorrow is at the pace we're going right now, tomorrow would catch up to us before we got it built."

In the same news conference, Disney said that his new amusement park would not be "another Disneyland" but rather "the equivalent of Disneyland. . . . This concept here will have to be something that is unique, and so that there is a distinction between Disneyland in California and whatever Disney does—and notice I didn't say Disneyland in Florida—whatever Disney does in Florida."[8]

In fact, a second Disneyland—or something immediately recognizable as Disneyland's very close kin—was essential to Disney's plans for his city of the future. "Walt was so smart," said Richard Nunis, by then one of Disney's theme-park executives, of the planning for what was to be called Disney World. "He said, 'We've got to put Disneyland, which everybody will know, at the very upper end of the property because that will be the weenie"—the term Disney liked to use for conspicuous landmarks that drew people toward them, like Sleeping Beauty Castle at the end of Disneyland's Main Street. "Then whatever we build after that, the public will have to drive by to get to the Park."[9]

The scale of the Florida development, and the nature of its city-of-the-future component in particular, made it highly desirable that Walt Disney Productions have quasi-governmental powers over the property, so that local governments could not throw up roadblocks. The Disneys thus had to bargain with state government to a much greater extent than they had in California. By the middle 1960s, the brothers had settled into a good cop–bad cop routine both within the studio—where Roy was the affable, sympathetic one—and outside it, where Roy assumed a more forbidding role. Once the Florida project was public knowledge, they played those parts in dealings with Florida officials. As *Fortune* reported in the spring of 1966:

> A Florida state delegation sent to California to talk to the Disneys came back awed by the brothers as negotiators. "I think those two men offer as effective a combination as I've ever worked with," says one member of the delegation. "It is more effective than any I have seen in Wall Street, Miami, anywhere. Roy Disney is the hard shell, the tightfisted conservative businessman, the financier. He'll keep asking when are you going to be specific. And Walt is the best politician I ever saw. The night we said goodby, he came in and said, 'Let me show you what we can do with a mallard duck.' He had some plastic ones. We have a lot of mallards in Florida. He said, 'How do you think 500 of these would look on the lake near Kissimmee?' He described how he would put lights

on the lake so it would be pretty at night. Then, later, when Walt was not there, Roy was back in business asking, 'What about those tax liabilities?' Walt keeps giving you confidence that they are going to be there and Roy keeps sharpening the pencil."[10]

Walt Disney had by this time become something like a highly unusual real estate developer, one who specialized in unique projects, and the Florida project was only the largest such.

Disney had been a skier since the 1930s, when he helped finance the Sugar Bowl resort, and he had been delighted with Zermatt, the Swiss ski town he visited several times in the 1950s, starting in 1952 and culminating in his filming there of *Third Man on the Mountain* in 1958. Buzz Price wrote: "The things he liked about Zermatt were simple: a great mountain, no autos, entry by shuttle train, and dual season operation with a base development full of charm and activity in both summer and winter. The village at Zermatt reflected the qualities of a Disney style and ambience."[11] Disneyland's success had confirmed, in the most emphatic fashion, Disney's good judgment about what would draw visitors. Now he decided to transform the ski business by creating a resort that would mimic Zermatt.

Through his own company, WED Enterprises, Disney commissioned Price to study the ski-resort potential at several locations, over a five-year span beginning in 1960. One of the earliest of those studies, in 1960, concerned the Mineral King Valley in the Sierra Nevada Mountains, but it was not until 1962, Price wrote, that Disney began the "serious final quest for Mineral King . . . after a fruitless search throughout the rest of the U.S. for a comparable resort site." In Price's account, the United States Forest Service (part of the Agriculture Department and committed to the productive use of the national forests under its control) encouraged Disney to pursue development of Mineral King. "Late in 1964, under Walt's instruction, we began the assembly of the private acreage holdings on the floor of the Mineral King valley, a 26-acre site essential for the project base village. One of our group . . . succeeded in buying out the Forest Service leasehold positions of 18 families."[12]

On December 17, 1965, after competitive bidding, the Forest Service designated Walt Disney Productions to develop Mineral King Valley and the surrounding slopes. The Disney proposal called for spending thirty-five million dollars. In a brochure published the next year, the company laid out plans for a development that would resemble Zermatt. "Mineral King is perhaps more similar to the European Alps than any other area in the western United

States," the brochure said, and, accordingly, all structures would be "styled along the lines of the Swiss chalet." As at Zermatt, automobiles would be barred from the valley.

"Plans called for a facility that would handle a wintertime daily throng of 20,000 skiers in six great areas," Price wrote many years later. In the summer, the Disney development at Mineral King would gear up "to handle a demand comparable to Yosemite."[13]

Disney himself was quoted in the brochure in terms that echoed what he had often said about Disneyland: "When we go into a new project, we believe in it all the way. That's the way we feel about Mineral King. We have every faith that our plans will provide recreational opportunities for everyone. All of us promise that our efforts now and in the future will be dedicated to making Mineral King grow to meet the ever-increasing public need. I guess you might say that it won't ever be finished."[14]

As he approached a normal retirement age, Disney was pushing himself perhaps harder than ever before. "He worked seven days a week, he established a pace that he could never get rid of," his son-in-law Ronald Miller Jr. told Richard Hubler. Disney read scripts on Saturday and Sunday, whether he was at the Holmby Hills house or at his weekend home in Palm Springs (he built a second home at Smoke Tree Ranch in 1957 to replace the one he had sold to finance Disneyland). "He would get up in the morning and start reading," Miller said, taking a break only for the lawn bowling that had become a late-life passion. After bowling on the green—there was one both at Smoke Tree and in Roxbury Park, near his home in Holmby Hills—he returned to reading scripts. "Seven days a week," Miller said. "If he wasn't working here, he worked there."[15]

There are hints in some memories that Disney's marriage had come under strain by the 1960s. It had certainly changed, as marriages do after thirty or forty years. Lillian Disney had lost interest in her husband's business years before, her energies absorbed by redecorating her home and scouting for antiques. Marc Davis, who had become increasingly important to Disney as an animator and then as a designer for Disneyland, said in 1968: "I have met Mrs. Disney maybe 25–30 times and, finally, I reached the point where I permitted myself always to be reintroduced."[16] By the middle 1950s, when Disney was starting to accumulate a new batch of Oscars, Lillian had stopped going to the ceremonies with him, troubled by the "commotion" surrounding them.[17]

"I come home at night and eat in the front of the TV set," Disney said around the time he turned sixty-one, in December 1962. "It's either that or eat alone, my wife says."[18] By then, Lillian had long since stopped cooking for her husband. She had learned to be a very good cook, she said, but "I never did like it,"[19] and so the Disneys' meals were cooked for them by Thelma Howard, their housekeeper and cook after they moved to Holmby Hills. Walt Disney was, in his family's description, a fussy eater who always preferred "hash house" food—a typical middle-aged husband of the time, in other words. As his daughter Diane said, "You can generally satisfy him with something out of a can."[20]

By the mid-1960s, Disney was working exceptionally long hours and on at least one occasion he spent several nights in his office suite at the studio after quarreling with Lillian.[21] Disney was in his sixties, his health was failing, and he was working very hard at a time in his life when many others, sensing their mortality, might scale back professional concerns and spend more time with family members. Little wonder that Walt and Lillian might sometimes have words.

(Diane, who married Ron Miller on May 9, 1954, had six children by 1966; Sharon, who married Robert Brown on May 10, 1959, had one. Disney had successfully urged both new husbands to go to work for him—Miller in live-action film production, Brown at WED—within a few years of their marriages.)

Disney also quarreled heatedly with the other person closest to him, his brother Roy. The cause was Walt's continued ownership of WED Enterprises, the company he had set up in 1952 to design Disneyland and its attractions. In the early 1960s, after Disneyland itself became a wholly owned subsidiary of Walt Disney Productions, WED remained Walt Disney's personal corporation. Roy Disney had always seen legal perils in this arrangement, smacking as it did of self-dealing and conflicts of interest, and WED's prominent role in designing the Disney attractions at the 1964–65 world's fair may have brought his fears to a head. It was only after months of turmoil and argument and pained silences, ending late in 1964, that Walt Disney finally agreed to sell most of WED.[22] The purchase agreement, dated November 20, 1964, and approved by the company's shareholders the following February, provided for a payment of $3.75 million for WED's rights in the world's fair exhibits and other assets. WED's design, architectural, and engineering staff, about a hundred employees in all, became employees of Walt Disney Productions.[23]

Walt Disney was possessive about his private company, the source of most of his pleasure in his business for the previous ten years. Marvin Davis remembered the time—this would have been in the mid-1960s, most likely when the brothers were still at odds—when Roy Disney asked him and another WED executive, Dick Irvine, to have lunch with him at the studio. Dick and I didn't know what the heck was going on, but we couldn't turn down an invitation to have lunch with Roy Disney. On that day, Walt was sitting at this table over in the corner of the commissary. So we're there having a nice lunch, and Roy asked us about something down at Disney World . . . I've forgotten exactly what it was. When we finished eating, Dick and I were going to go back to WED. We got in my car, drove back to Glendale, and parked right by the door to my office. I went to unlock the door, and was just putting the key in the lock, when somebody tapped me on the shoulder. I turned and . . . God . . . Walt was standing right behind me. And I had just left him back at the studio having lunch. He must have gotten right up and followed us. He came in and sat down and asked, "What did Roy want? What was he talking about?" And I said, "Geez, Walt, he just asked us to lunch." And Walt said, "Well, I just wondered what's going on." It just shows how intense he was about everything, especially his brother, who he didn't want to get ahead of him on anything.[24]

After the sale of most of WED to Walt Disney Productions was completed in 1965, what was left continued under a new name, Retlaw (Walter spelled backwards).[25] Retlaw kept ownership of the Disneyland trains and monorail.

Disney traveled extensively in 1966. He began trying to sell his city of the future—what he called EPCOT, for "experimental prototype community of tomorrow"—to American industry, starting with a presentation to Westinghouse in January.[26] On what Bob Gurr remembered as "a turbulent, low-level flight" to Pittsburgh, Disney spread out brown-line drawings of the center of EPCOT on a conference table that unfolded in the middle of a company plane.[27] Even more than when he sought corporate sponsors for Disneyland attractions—and in sharp contrast to his recoil from such sponsors' interference after the war—Disney was now courting industry and seeking its involvement in his new project.

He knew that his name alone could open doors. His awards had piled up steadily; he was, as Peter Bart wrote in the *New York Times,* a man "revered and honored almost to the point of absurdity."[28] In September 1964, he received the Medal of Freedom, the highest civilian honor a president can bestow, from President Lyndon Johnson, sharing the moment with former secretary of state Dean Acheson, the composer Aaron Copland, Helen Keller, and two dozen other familiar names. After the world's fair, he hired a chief aide of Robert Moses, retired General William E. "Joe" Potter, to help find sponsors for EPCOT. "When I first started out," Potter told an interviewer a few years after Disney's death, "I said, Walt, how am I going to get in? And he said—Tell them I sent you! And I wrote to all these industries saying what we were going to do, and I would like to come and talk to them . . . and I never got turned down once."[29]

Disney's celebrity by the early 1960s was such that it colored his dealings with the heads of corporations much larger than Walt Disney Productions. Said Bob Gurr: "When Don Burnham, the [president and chief executive officer] of Westinghouse, got close to Walt, his bottom lip would start quivering and it was hard for him to speak. When some people got too close to Walt, they got spooked because they idolized Walt Disney. Walt was aware of this and he would deliberately dress down by undoing a button or slopping up his tie so it was askew. He tried to send a signal, 'I'm okay.' . . . He knew he scared the daylights out of people and didn't want to let that get in the way of being able to work with him. Otherwise all he'd have is a bunch of people agreeing with him and their expertise wouldn't show."[30]

For the most part, Disney used a company plane not to sell his ideas to industry but for visits to shopping centers, hotels, and schools while he trawled for ideas he could put to use at EPCOT and CalArts. As Disney's ideas for EPCOT took shape, he determined that the hub-and-spoke plan he had adopted for Disneyland would be the central element of EPCOT, too. As Disneyland's planner Marvin Davis said, Disney "wanted to solve everything with the radial idea."[31]

He turned for ideas to two books on city planning, both then recently published. Victor Gruen's *The Heart of Our Cities* (1964) was a persuasive diagnosis of city ills, which Gruen traced to a never-ending, ultimately futile catering to the automobile. Gruen's own career was a bundle of contradictions, however. This severe critic of an auto-centered society was also the foremost designer of enclosed suburban malls, those magnets for auto traffic, and his solutions for inner-city ills amounted to little more than transplanting suburban features—including enclosed malls—to downtowns. For some cities he proposed a ring road around downtown that was inevitably reminiscent of Gruen's native Vienna and its Ringstrasse (although in Gruen's new version the road was more an expressway than a broad avenue).[32]

Gruen was also an advocate of "the radial idea," and he admired Ebenezer Howard, whose 1902 book *Garden Cities of To-morrow*, reissued in 1965, was the earliest and most forceful statement of that idea. Howard's book was probably the strongest single influence on Walt Disney's thinking. Howard, an Englishman, was a city planner who did not care for cities—he called them "ulcers on the very face of our beautiful island"[33]—and there was a similar strain in Disney's thinking. Although he spent months at a time in New York in the late 1920s, he never warmed to that city, referring to it in his letters as "this DAMN TOWN,"[34] grumbling about having to walk so much, complaining about the weather and how bored he was, and wishing aloud that he was back home in Los Angeles. He mentioned in one 1928 letter seeing a Broadway show, *Gentlemen Prefer Blondes*, but he seems never to have made much effort to enjoy what was then America's most dynamic and exciting city. Europe was another matter—Disney liked London a lot more than Howard did—but his plans for EPCOT owed little or nothing to European models.

Planning for Disney World, and for EPCOT in particular, took place in a "war room" at WED Enterprises' offices in Glendale. On October 27, 1966, when Disney went before the cameras for segments of a twenty-four-minute film promoting EPCOT, it was not in the actual war room, with what Anthony Haden-Guest called its "urgent display of maps, blueprints, aerial photographs and projection screens," but in a re-creation of that room on a studio sound stage.[35] Disney rehearsed his pitch for EPCOT before select groups of friends—the actor Walter Pidgeon, the television personality Art Linkletter, Welton Becket and his two young sons.[36]

The film was completed in two slightly different versions, one aimed at the Florida legislature and the other at the large corporations Disney hoped would sponsor much of EPCOT. The film, known as *Walt Disney's EPCOT '66*, was to be the most important tool in Disney's effort to recruit corporate sponsors. It is the fullest expression of Disney's vision—for once the word, applied so often to Disney's ideas, is appropriate—for his utopian city.

In the film, a narrator describes EPCOT's "dynamic urban center," home to a "cosmopolitan hotel and convention center towering thirty or more stories," as well as "shopping areas where stores and whole streets re-create the character and adventure of places 'round the world," restaurants, theaters, and, of course, "office buildings . . . most of them designed especially to suit local and regional needs of major corporations."[37] Most remarkably, "this entire fifty acres of city streets and buildings will be completely enclosed," the narration continues. "In this climate-controlled environment, shoppers, theatergoers, and people just out for a stroll will enjoy ideal weather conditions, protected day and night from rain, heat and cold, and humidity."

This plan was an extreme expression of the idea advocated most eloquently in Gruen's book, that the cure for the ills of city centers was to increase their resemblance to suburban malls. (Enclosed shopping malls were still a recent phenomenon in 1966—the first one, Southdale, designed by Gruen, had opened outside Minneapolis in October 1956, a little over a year after Disneyland's opening and exactly ten years before Disney's EPCOT filming.) Raising such a huge dome would have been technologically difficult, if not impossible, and wildly expensive.

Moving out from the domed downtown, Disney's EPCOT, as visualized in the film, was very much in the Ebenezer Howard vein. High-density apartments were to be succeeded by a "greenbelt" and then by "radial neighborhoods" of single-family homes. Residences were to be rigidly separated from commercial uses (and, for that matter, from churches and schools, which would be confined to the "greenbelt"). Since the idea was that EPCOT would be "a working community with employment for all," one inevitable effect of such segregation would have been to leave vast stretches of the new city dull and empty throughout the day—making EPCOT indistinguishable from many existing suburbs, except in the greater tidiness and regularity of its design

Disney, the man who commuted to work on an increasingly crowded California freeway, was most concerned with taming auto traffic, and his plan for EPCOT entailed an elaborate transportation system with only a subordinate role for the private auto. Two electrically powered systems—the monorail and, in modified form, the PeopleMover already in use in Disneyland—were to be what the narration called the "transportation heartbeat of EPCOT," while residents typically drove their cars "only on weekend pleasure trips." The film showed most employees commuting to jobs not in EPCOT's city center, but at the new version of Disneyland or in a thousand-acre industrial park that would be "a showcase of industry at work." It also showed most of them making two transfers, from a PeopleMover to the monorail, and from the monorail to another PeopleMover—exactly the sort of inconvenience, however minor, that motorists have always used to justify driving rather than using public transportation.

This was the canker at the heart of Disney's vision of EPCOT: his failure to enter as imaginatively into the minds of suburban motorists as he had into the minds of his guests at Disneyland. He wanted people to drive when he wanted them to—he said in the EPCOT film that he had chosen the Florida site "because it's so easy for tourists and Florida residents to get here by automobile"—and to use his mass transit system when he wanted them to. Day visitors at Disneyland might accept such direction willingly, but there was no reason to believe that long-term residents of EPCOT would be so accommodating. It is all too easy to imagine Disney's commuters finding ways to drive to their jobs in air-conditioned cars on humid summer mornings, rather than walk from home to a PeopleMover station, make two transfers, and walk from another station to work.

Disney's narrator spoke of the radial plan as "an idea new among cities built since the birth of the automobile," even though Ebenezer Howard's book, first published under a different title in 1895, predated automobile traffic and held no solutions to the problems such traffic created. The radial plan offered only the promise of a superficial order. It did not address the bundle of hopes and fears—racial fears, especially—that had put so many Americans behind the wheels of cars and had encouraged them to leave the central city behind in favor of single-family homes on large suburban lots.

Only once did Disney flirt seriously with a possible inner-city project, a sort of pocket Disneyland covering two city blocks that would have been a key element in the planned revival of downtown Saint Louis. But after circling the idea for more than two years, from March 1963 to July 1965, he backed away from it, for reasons that appear to have been mostly if not entirely financial. Disney wanted the city of Saint Louis to pay the building costs and recoup its money from the project's net profits—if there were any—while city officials had assumed that Walt Disney Productions would pick up the tab.[38]

Disney said in the film, "I don't believe there is a challenge anywhere in the world that's more important to people everywhere than finding solutions to the problems of our cities," but he added that "the need is not just for curing the old ills of old cities. We think the need is for starting from scratch on virgin land and building a special kind of new community." The "need" involved, a need expressed so often, was Disney's own need for control of whatever project commanded his attention. There would have been no way for him to exercise such control were he to try to cure "the old ills of old cities," but "a special kind of new community" was another matter.

As Disney's ideas about EPCOT's governance took shape in late 1966, he leaned more and more toward the sort of control he had exercised over Disneyland. Not only would everyone be employed, but, he said, no residents would own property. There would be no slums "because we won't let them develop."[39] EPCOT's value as a living laboratory—a place where ideas would be tried, to be adapted for other towns—would be reduced accordingly.

An inherent conflict in Disney's ideas—that EPCOT could be both "an experimental prototype" and a true "community"—had been resolved in favor of the "experimental prototype." Marvin Davis told Anthony Haden-Guest: "Walt's thought was that in order to maintain the original philosophy of keeping this an experimental prototype, it would have to be something that was pretty much controlled by the company. . . . This is something we never really discuss very much publicly. . . . In order to have the control that is necessary there, you would just about eliminate the possibility of having a *vot-*

ing community. Because the minute they start voting, then you lose control, and that's the end of the possibility of experimental development!"[40]

Disneyland was self-contained and centrally directed—and, above all, orderly—in a way no real city could be. However successful the park's design, there was no reason to believe that its essential elements could be enlarged and applied to a whole city. Disneyland could be an exemplar only for self-contained developments of the same general kind. That was, increasingly, what Disney envisioned EPCOT as being.

Disney was by the middle 1960s more than ever a conservative Republican. He and former president Eisenhower saw each other socially at Palm Springs, and they were photographed together at the 1964 Republican national convention in San Francisco. Also in 1964, Disney lent his name and picture to a campaign mailing and full-page newspaper advertisement in support of his friend George Murphy's successful campaign for the United States Senate.[41] But this conservative man had become an advocate for a city of the future that could function only as a totalitarian enterprise.

EPCOT was not the only questionable project that absorbed Disney's time in 1966. Another was the Mineral King ski development, which was, beneath the glitter, a highly dubious use of a fragile valley. Disney had said of Mineral King in 1965 that it was "a natural extension of what I've been doing all my life," and "a recreation project, not an entertainment center,"[42] but Peter Browning, writing a few years later, identified a fatal flaw:

> Disney estimates that 60 per cent of the visitors to Mineral King will come in the summer. Many of them will make the trip simply because it is there to be made; it will be a nice one-day jaunt. But many would *not* make the drive if there were nothing at the end of the road—such as an excursion train, cafeterias, shops, and an audio-visual presentation to provide entertainment. . . . The Disney development itself would be the major attraction at Mineral King. For all that some visitors might care about the surroundings, it could just as well be located in the Mojave Desert or Los Angeles.[43]

In other words, the distinction between "entertainment" and "recreation" was much more significant than Disney thought, at least in this case. He understood entertainment—"That's our business," as he said at his 1965 Florida press conference—but recreation's complexities had eluded him. Measured against the damage to the Mineral King Valley that would inevitably accompany growth to meet what Disney called "the ever-increasing public need," his statement that "it won't ever be finished" had a far more ominous coloration than when he made such a vow about Disneyland.

Walt Disney had committed himself to two ambitious but badly flawed ideas. Perhaps he could have salvaged one or the other, with time, but as it happened, he had only a little time left for Mineral King, or EPCOT, or anything else.

On June 23, 1966, Disney wrote to his friend Eisenhower: "Grandma and Grandpa Disney and all of the Disney clan (including our seven grandchildren) have chartered a yacht out of Vancouver for two weeks to cruise the inlets of British Columbia. Our trip will end on the 13th of July which happens to be the 41st anniversary for Grandma and Grandpa."[44] As always, Disney took work along. "I don't know how many things he took on the boat to Vancouver, read 'em all," Ron Miller told Richard Hubler. "He even took one book on how to select faculty for colleges, because he had CalArts, which was of great interest to him." At that time, Miller said, Disney was already scheduled to "go into the hospital and have his back looked into. I noticed he was having a helluva time with his leg. [The pain] came down and it bothered his hip. Whenever he would get in a rowboat or anything, he would have to literally do this to his leg [indicating "lifting" his leg, as though stepping over a low fence]. It was the damnedest thing. And that's as far as the whole family, or anyone, knew was the extent of his illness."[45]

Later that month, Disney underwent hospital tests that indicated that surgery might relieve the nagging aftereffects of the polo injury to his neck almost thirty years before, but he held off scheduling any such operation. Over the next few weeks, other people were struck by the signs of his poor health.

On September 19, 1966, Disney and Governor Edmund G. "Pat" Brown of California held a news conference at Mineral King so that the governor could declare publicly his commitment (backed by three million dollars in federal funds) to the new all-weather road that was one of the Forest Service's conditions for letting Walt Disney Productions develop the valley. The press conference was scheduled for noon, but it was delayed when both Brown and the press buses ran late. It was unseasonably cold, with cloudy skies, intermittent rain, and a temperature around 20 degrees. Disney and the rest of his party flew into the Visalia airport in a company plane and then drove to Mineral King in a motorcade.

Robert Jackson, a Disney publicist, wrote later in a brief memoir of the occasion:

By mid-September, it was known within and outside the organization that Walt would enter the hospital in November for "a check up and for therapeutic measures." It was no surprise, then, that Walt's appearance drew comment of concern from two members of the press, both of whom mentioned to me that he did not look well. I attributed his fatigue and pallor to the high altitude and cold.

Following the official press conference, Walt excused himself and went into . . . a combination café and general store operated by . . . long-time residents of Mineral King. Walt was warming himself in front of a wood-burning stove when I entered to tell him that members of the press requested his return outside. They wanted photos with Governor Brown taken against the scenic beauty of Mineral King's southern area.

Walt's complexion was ashen, and this is the first time that I became truly worried about his well-being. . . . In a very quiet manner, Walt asked me to delay the photos for a few minutes "until I catch my breath and can rest a while." . . . Walt came out a few minutes later and posed with Governor Brown. The entire group then ate box lunches embellished by hot baked beans and plenty of coffee, which helped only temporarily to neutralize the cold.[46]

On October 9, 1966, Mark Kausler, a freshman art student at the Kansas City Art Institute—the school whose classes Disney attended fifty years before—heard a rumor that "Walt Disney's coming to visit the dean!" Disney had flown to Kansas City the day before to accept an award presented by Eisenhower at a People to People banquet (that international goodwill organization was head-quartered in Kansas City). He had added a visit to the art institute, un-doubtedly as part of his informal research for CalArts. Kausler was skeptical until "a car drove on to the campus, and from my dorm room I could see Walt Disney getting out of the passenger seat and walking into the main building on campus where the dean's office was." A crowd of autograph seekers gath-ered. "After what seemed like years, Walt, the dean and some staffers came out of the ivy covered building. Trembling like the true fan-boy I was, I stam-mered, 'Mr. Disney, would you sign my book [Bob Thomas's *Walt Disney, the Art of Animation*] for me, please?' . . . He dutifully autographed the book and I managed to tell him that I 'always wanted to get into the business.' He said, 'You want some advice from me, kid?' Of course I said yes. Walt paused a sec-ond and then said quietly, 'Learn to draw.' Everybody cracked up laughing, but it was good advice." What most stayed in Kausler's mind, though, was "how drawn, tired and old he looked, compared with his TV image."[47]

Disney's health was now deteriorating rapidly. No one yet suspected that he was suffering from more than the cumulative effects of his old polo injury, but he was about to pay a penalty for decades of very heavy cigarette smoking.

He smoked cigarettes until they burned so far down that he could barely hold them, his daughter Diane said in 1956—not to be economical, but because in his preoccupation he would forget about them until they practically burned his fingertips.[48] Fulton Burley, a performer in the Golden Horseshoe Revue at Disneyland, remembered having lunch with Disney when he "picked up a cigarette with a filter on it, broke the filter off, lit it and took a puff. He caught me watching him and said, 'You're looking at me quizzically, Fulton. . . . My daughter gave me these cigarettes. She gave me two cartons of them at Christmas. She said, "Dad, the way you're coughing, please use these cigarettes instead." I promised her I would, but as you've noticed, I didn't tell her *how* I would use them.'"[49]

Disney had coughed so long and so loudly, even in his early twenties, that it was always tempting to some people who knew him to shrug off his coughing. In later years, though, Ollie Johnston said, Disney coughed more, "that nervous cigarette cough. It seemed he'd get into this hacking awfully quickly if anything worried him a lot."[50]

Disney entered Saint Joseph's Hospital, across Buena Vista Street from the studio, on November 2, 1966, a week after appearing before the cameras for the EPCOT film. (He had in the meantime flown to Williamsburg, Virginia, to accept an award from the American Forestry Association.)[51] X rays showed a spot the size of a walnut on his left lung. He underwent surgery the following Monday, November 7.

On Tuesday, November 22, Walt Disney Productions announced that Disney had returned to work the previous day and for the first time acknowledged the seriousness of his illness:

> Walt Disney initially was admitted to the hospital on Wednesday Nov. 2, for treatment and preliminary examination of an old polo injury. During the preliminary examination a lesion was discovered on the left lung. Surgery was decided upon by the doctors in charge and was performed the next week. A tumor was found to have caused an abscess which in the opinion of the doctors required a pneumonectomy [removal of the lung]. Within four to six weeks Mr. Disney should be back on a full schedule and there is no reason to predict any recurrence of the problem or curtailment of Mr. Disney's future activities.[52]

An unidentified studio spokesman would not tell the *Los Angeles Times* if there was a malignancy.[53] But Disney's surgeon had told his family that the lung was cancerous and Disney had only two years at most to live.

Ron Miller spoke of his father-in-law's state of mind after his lung was removed: "Scared. Couldn't believe that it could happen to him. . . . [But he] thought he had it licked. He was full of confidence. I think the thing that really helped him a great deal was a telegram that John Wayne had sent him when he heard that Walt had had his lung removed, saying, 'Welcome to the club. The only problem is height' [that is, altitude]. . . . That really meant a lot to him. It really did."

Even when he was deathly ill, Disney's mind was on work, Miller said. "Up there [in the hospital after his surgery] he said, 'Okay, I think you guys [the film producers, including Miller, who answered directly to him] can work as a team, 'cause you've shown it in the past three years.' He said, 'I'm gonna stick with Disney World and EPCOT. I'll read the scripts, and I'll just tell you whether to go or not. I just can't become as active as I used to be.'"[54]

When Disney was back at the studio on the three days before Thanksgiving, his precarious health was unmistakably visible to his employees. Milton Gray, a Disney inbetweener, remembered walking rapidly down the central hall on the third floor of the Disney animation building—the floor that housed Disney's office—when he passed "some real old man, walking slowly northward (with his back to me), all slouched over, wearing a blue sweater. I had no idea who that would be, and it was quite unusual to see someone looking that decrepit in the studio. . . . I just went around this old man at my brisk pace. Just as I did, though, a couple other men in the hallway ahead of me turned toward the old man and said, 'Oh, hi, Walt.'"[55]

Disney had Thanksgiving dinner with the Millers and watched film that Ron Miller had taken on the Vancouver trip. The next day, he flew to Palm Springs. Kelvin Bailey, Disney's pilot, remembered his boss's last visit to his weekend home:

> While flying to Palm Springs, which took only twenty minutes, he came up to the cockpit and said, "Kel, I've been at old Saint Joe's Hospital for some time. I'm a sick boy. But I'm going to Palm Springs and stay there until I get better. I'll call you then. I don't know when, but stand by for the call."
>
> I assumed it would be weeks or months. Two or three days later, the phone rang. "Kel? This is Wa-a-a-l-t." His voice was so fragile, so dilapidated, I hardly recognized him. "Come and get me." At Palm Springs airport, the car drove up. Lilly got out and had to help Walt out. He couldn't do it alone. There was a stairway leading up to the plane and he had to put his hands on both rails. He went straight to Saint Joseph's from the Burbank airport.[56]

Disney turned sixty-five in room 529 at the hospital. Private nurses assigned to "Mr. John Smith" were staying with him around the clock.[57] In his last days, his daughter Diane told Richard Hubler, "when he had moments of great pain or felt something happen that he couldn't control, he'd get very upset and you knew that he'd rather be alone then. . . . So we would just come and go."[58]

Disney died at Saint Joseph's the morning of December 15, 1966. Lillian and the Millers arrived at the hospital minutes after his death. "As we got off the elevator on the floor," Diane Miller said in an interview for a book and film about her father, "I turned and saw Ron go striding right into Dad's room and then come out with his arms up as though someone had pushed him back. When we went into the room Dad's hands were on his chest and he was gone. Uncle Roy was standing at the foot of his bed, massaging one of Dad's feet. Just kind of caressing it. And he was talking to him. It sounded something like, 'Well, kid, this is the end, I guess.' You know, that sort of thing. And I saw his love as I'd never seen it before."[59]

As word spread at the studio, which had been so personal an instrument for Walt Disney, some of his employees wept as if they had lost a parent. The studio closed for the day, but Disneyland remained open. Disney's body was cremated, and only his immediate family attended a brief memorial service at Forest Lawn on December 16.

A few weeks later, after the flood of public tributes had ebbed, Roy Disney spoke to the Associated Press reporter Bob Thomas about his brother's death. "On the day before he died," Roy said, "Walt lay on the hospital bed staring at the ceiling. It was squares of perforated acoustical tile, and Walt pictured them as a grid map for Disney World, which he planned to build in Florida. Every four tiles represented a square mile, and he said, 'Now there is where the highway will run. There is the route for the monorail.'

"He drove himself right up to the end."[60]

"Let's Never Not Be a Silly Company"

When the Carousel of Progress was installed at Disneyland a few months after Walt Disney's death, visitors who had just watched that revolving Audio-Animatronics show were directed next to an upper floor, where they saw a huge model of "Progress City"—Walt Disney's EPCOT. The model, built to a scale of one-eighth inch to the foot, filled 6,900 square feet, held 20,000 miniature trees, 4,500 structures lit from within, and 1,400 working street lights, each about an inch tall.[1]

That was as close as EPCOT ever came to being built. Not long after Disney's death, Marvin Davis recalled, "there was a big meeting that included Card Walker, Bill Anderson, and Roy Disney. . . . Walt had been working with me on the Florida plan. Walt just let me do it. This meeting was in a big room, and to the best of my ability I represented Walt's concepts. I had all this material showing what EPCOT was going to be, and what Walt's ideas were. I got through, and sat down, and Roy turned around and looked at me and he said, 'Marvin . . . Walt's gone.' By this he meant forget what Walt was doing and start over. . . . The original plan didn't fit very well with entertainment. Roy had figured in these difficulties in his decision, and he knew that Walt's EPCOT wouldn't have a lot of entertainment value."[2]

When Walt Disney died, Van Arsdale France wrote, in words that inevitably call Elias Disney as well as his son to mind, "it was a bit like a family losing a lovable yet domineering father."[3] As in most such cases, the family's response was a sort of paralysis at first, followed by a halting effort to carry out his wishes, and then, gradually, by a questioning of the parent's commands.

Some projects were so near completion that adhering to the father's wishes was the simplest course of action. That was true of Pirates of the Caribbean, which opened at Disneyland in the spring of 1967, a few months after Disney's death. Where *EPCOT '66* was concerned, finishing it quickly was essential because it had to be shown early in 1967 to Florida legislators.

Once the EPCOT film had served its immediate purpose, however—the Florida legislature approved the legal status for the Disney property that Walt Disney Productions wanted—EPCOT began to look like a much more questionable project. "It was a great idea, but it was Walt's vision," Marty Sklar said, "and only Walt Disney could have convinced industry to support it. What we were left with was 27,000 acres of land in Florida, and a corporate management that didn't know the talent at WED."

WED was alien territory as far as most Disney executives were concerned. "Roy Disney had been in our building once," Sklar said, "and Card Walker and Donn Tatum, who ran [Walt Disney Productions], had been in the building once or twice. I mean, this was Walt's place." Even though Disney had agreed to sell WED to Walt Disney Productions two years before his death, it remained his private preserve, and EPCOT his private project. "It was clear pretty early that no one in the company knew how to get hold of that EPCOT idea," Sklar said. "But everybody knew how to do . . . another Disneyland in Florida with hotels where people could stay."[4]

Construction of a second Disneyland—called not that but the Magic Kingdom, the sobriquet attached to Disneyland by its publicists from the beginning—at what was now to be called Walt Disney World began in May 1969. It opened in 1971. By the time a theme park called Epcot Center opened eleven years later, it bore no resemblance to Walt Disney's city of the future. This new Epcot was, ironically—given Walt Disney's own cool remarks about the New York World's Fair—a sort of permanent world's fair, a hodgepodge of international pavilions and industrial exhibits. It was as if the name had been kept only to placate Disney's ghost.

Another of Disney's last few large-scale projects disappeared without a trace. His plans for Mineral King were always vulnerable because they required the support of both the state and federal governments, and that support slowly evaporated after Disney's plans for the valley were attacked in a lawsuit by the Sierra Club. Disney's successors—unhappy with the controversy, lacking Walt Disney's personal interest, and dubious about the financial prospects—eventually backed away from Mineral King. The valley was incorporated into Sequoia National Park in 1978.

Only the California Institute of the Arts, among Disney's late-life passions, survived his death. He left 45 percent of his estate after taxes to charity, and 95 percent was designated for CalArts. The school eventually received about fifteen million dollars. The problem was, he also left only the vaguest guidance as to how that money should be spent and what he expected the school to be like. As a result, the school's administrators could invoke his name even as they dismantled Chouinard and turned CalArts into a radically different sort of institution, one that attached little value to the traditional skills that Chouinard's teachers had encouraged their students to develop.[5]

When CalArts officially opened its doors in temporary quarters in 1970, it was fertile ground for the sort of radical posturing and student unrest that had spread to colleges across the country. Roy Disney and other members of the family, active overseers of the school to which Walt attached so much importance, all but despaired of taming it, at one point even trying to foist it off on the University of Southern California or some other large institution. Roy Disney's wife, Edna, believed that the stress of dealing with CalArts hastened her husband's death in December 1971. But CalArts, like other colleges, cooled later in the decade.

The site for CalArts' permanent quarters had changed once again in April 1966, this time to a rural "new town," Valencia, north of Los Angeles.[6] A huge structure like the one whose plans startled Millard Sheets and Marc Davis opened there in 1971. CalArts survives today, from all appearances as a collection of art schools whose twelve hundred students happen to share a roof. Although CalArts boasts any number of distinguished alumni, there is little evidence that bringing the arts together has resulted in unique accomplishments, whether measured in fine-arts terms or by the standards of Imagineering.

Within Walt Disney Productions itself, Walt Disney's influence lingered in wholly predictable ways, as in the studio's continuing output of clumsy and obvious "family" comedies. Those films' producers clearly felt Disney's inhibiting presence at their shoulders, almost as much as they had when he was alive.

Winston Hibler, who advanced from writing and narrating *True-Life Adventures* to producing live-action features, remembered approaching Disney about a problem that arose during production of a comedy called *The Ugly Dachshund* (1966) after Disney had approved a shooting script. "Walt said, 'Look I'm busy—are you producing this or aren't you?' Later that day, Walt called and asked what we were doing in the back lot. I said, 'That's where the dog picture is going to be shot.' Walt said, 'I think it should be shot inside'—and mentioned the time of year, etc. So that's where we shot it. On the first day of shooting I was on the set and Walt came up, tapped me on the shoulder and asked, 'What's it doing out there?' Sure enough, it was raining. Walt just had good common sense judgment about everything."[7]

Except, Hibler might have added, about *The Ugly Dachshund* itself, a film that comes to life only during three episodes of canine destruction. In one of those episodes a Great Dane and a supporting cast of dachshunds wreck an artist's studio—and the artist is not a pretentious comic figure but the film's leading man, an earnest and amiable sort played by Dean Jones. Disney would no doubt have found such a disaster heartrending rather than amusing if it had happened to an artist on his staff, but in his later years he let his movies fill up with well-trained animals whose destructiveness is supposed to be funny. Hibler and the other Disney live-action producers could not break themselves of the habit of reaching for such easy answers, and so their films made after Walt Disney's death are like his own most unfortunate productions, only worse.

Thanks largely to the dreariness of the studio's live-action output—and its increasingly poor reception in theaters—Walt Disney Productions passed through a traumatic change in management in 1984. That change resulted in the ouster of Disney's son-in-law Ron Miller, who had succeeded him as executive producer, the ultimate decision maker where films were concerned, and had then become the company's president. Michael D. Eisner became chairman and chief executive officer. He was at the center of similar turmoil before the ascension of Robert Iger to the CEO's job in 2005. Roy Disney's son, Roy Edward Disney, rallied opposition to the incumbent in both episodes.

The Walt Disney Company, as it now exists, is huge compared with the Walt Disney Productions that Walt and Roy Disney knew, and it has changed in countless ways (who could have guessed in 1954 that the ABC television network would become a Disney property?). And yet, remarkably, its foundations are still those that Walt Disney laid. The company that bears his name is still strongest at the points where Disney's own interest was keenest. In that respect, the noisy changes at the top of the company have simply not made much difference.

Forty years after Walt Disney's death, when Disney parks have spread not just to Florida but to Europe and East Asia, the original Disneyland remains the template for each new version of the Magic Kingdom. All those parks make sense only when they seem to be striving for perfection on Walt Disney's terms. Poorly conceived rides, indifferent employees, unkempt restrooms—consciously or not, park visitors experience such things not just as annoyances but as defiance of Walt Disney's clearly expressed wishes.

It is, however, through his animated films that Walt Disney retains his firmest grip on the company he founded. In the parks not just rides but costumed employees evoke the cartoon characters, and they are otherwise everywhere that Disney's writ extends. More than anything else, "Disney" means characters like Mickey Mouse and Donald Duck, and feature films like *Snow White* and *Dumbo*. The Disney animated features made since Walt Disney's death have always competed—sometimes successfully, more often not—against memories of the films he produced himself, and their makers have squirmed inside the luxurious prison that Walt constructed, the one built of expectations that animated features will always be, if not films made especially for children, then films readily accessible to them. That prison confines even the makers of today's best animated features, the computer-animated films made by the Pixar studio and released by the Walt Disney Company.

The power of Disney's art was harnessed to commerce first by Disney himself and then by his successors. Transforming his best films into durable commercial properties has meant the loss of their emotional immediacy—thus the heavy-handed repetition of words like "happy" and "magic" in selling them, to make up for what is missing. Distinguishing what is genuine and valuable, among the many things that bear the Disney name, from what is flimsy and synthetic has been a task building since long before Disney's death. That task is extraordinarily difficult now because so many people—whether they are critics or apologists—have acquired a vested interest in conflating everything "Disney."

Walt Disney has since his death become a sort of Disney character himself. In 1981, Walt Disney Productions exchanged $46.2 million in its stock for all the stock of Retlaw Enterprises, the family company that owned not just Disneyland's narrow-gauge railroad and monorail but also the rights to Disney's name.[8] There was never any question about the use of Disney's name in the name of the company itself, or on those films and TV shows that he produced, but Retlaw got a 5 percent share of Walt Disney Productions' royalties on licensed products that bore Walt Disney's name.

Walt Disney, as a name and a person, is a far more visible part of his company's activities than, say, Henry Ford is at the company that bears his name. "Disney" has not become as generic as "Ford," or, for that matter, the names of many other company founders, and appropriately so, considering that Walt Disney's presence in his company's products is still so large. His name is routinely invoked in ways that would be unusual at other large corporations. Said CEO Michael Eisner in 2001: "You ask what is the soul of the company and what is our direction? I'm trying to be the bridge from what Walt Disney made and created to whoever will be the next person after me that maintains that same philosophy of 'Let's put on a show.' Let's be silly. We're a silly company. Let's never not be a silly company."[9]

Curiously, those repeated invocations of Walt Disney's name, and incessant praise for his "dreams" and his "vision," have made him seem less like a real person. "When I talk to school groups," Michael Broggie said in 2003, "I'll ask for a show of hands . . . who was Walt Disney? Was he real? Was he fictional? They answer overwhelmingly that he was a fictional character, and that he never really lived."[10] The Disney family, in voicing its loyalty to Walt Disney's memory, has contributed to the sense that he is as much a fabrication as Betty Crocker. Disney's surviving daughter, Diane Disney Miller, has sponsored a film, a book, a CD-ROM, and a Web site about her father that are occasionally illuminating but more often devotional; Roy Disney's son, Roy Edward Disney, has glorified his uncle ("The Great One") as one means of denigrating Walt's successors at the head of the Disney company, including his cousin's husband.*

Disney seems no more real in the growing body of academic critiques of the man and the company that bears his name. Many of these critiques are vaguely if not specifically Marxist in their methodology, and they display the usual Marxist tendency to bulldoze the complexities of human behavior in the pursuit of an all-embracing interpretation of Disney's life and work. What fatally cripples most academic writing about Walt Disney is simple failure to examine its supposed subject. Disney scholarship, like many other kinds of scholarship in today's academy, feeds on itself. The common tendency is for scholars to rush past the facts of Disney's life and career, frequently getting a lot of them wrong, in order to write about what really interests them, which is what other scholars have already written. It is this incestuous quality, even more than such commonly cited sins as a reliance on jargon, that makes so much academic writing, on Disney as on other subjects, claustrophobically difficult to read.

Disney has attracted other writers whose unsupportable claims and speculations sometimes win approval of scholars all too eager to believe the worst of the man. The persistent accusations of anti-Semitism are only the mildest examples of an array whose cumulative effect is to portray a Disney who was, among other vile things, racist, misogynist, imperialist, sexually warped, a spy for J. Edgar Hoover, desperate to conceal his illegitimate Spanish birth,

---

* Diane Disney Miller and Roy Edward Disney are the only surviving blood relatives who can claim to have known Walt Disney intimately. Lillian Disney married John L. Truyens in 1969, was widowed again in 1981, and died in 1997, at the age of ninety-eight. Sharon Disney Brown was widowed in 1967, remarried in 1969—her second husband was William Lund— divorced in 1975, and died in 1993, at the age of fifty-six.

and so terrified of death that he had his body cryogenically frozen. Pathologies are undoubtedly at work here, none of them Disney's.

The real Disney may yet elude his most fervent admirers' and detractors' suffocating grasp. When he was young, he was a sort of human Brer Rabbit, constantly wriggling out of the snares set for him by the likes of Charles Mintz and Pat Powers (not to mention Laugh-O-gram's creditors). He emerged finally, and unexpectedly, as the creator of a new art form, one whose potential has still scarcely been tapped, by him or anyone else. It is hard to imagine that man—the passionate young artist, the intense "coordinator," the man who scrutinized every frame of *Snow White and the Seven Dwarfs* with a lover's zeal—trapped forever in anyone's briar patch.

NOTES

Corporate Archives

RKO: RKO Radio Pictures Corporate Archives, Turner Entertainment Company, Culver City, California (as of 1988)
WDA: Walt Disney Archives, Burbank

Court Cases

Laugh-O-gram bankruptcy papers: Bankruptcy Case 4457, Laugh-O-Gram Films, Inc., filed October 4, 1923, in the U.S. District Court for the Western District of Missouri, Kansas City. National Archives, Central Plains Region, Kansas City.

Government Archives

NLRB/Babbitt: In the Matter of Walt Disney Productions, Inc., and Arthur Babbitt; Office of the Executive Secretary, Transcripts, Briefs, and Exhibits 4712, 8 October 1942. Records of the National Labor Relations Board, Record Group 25, National Archives, Washington, D.C. Except as noted, all NLRB/Babbitt citations are to pages in the hearing transcript.
References to published NLRB decisions are in standard legal form, e.g., 13 NLRB 873.

Libraries

AMPAS: Margaret Herrick Library, Academy of Motion Picture Arts and Sciences, Beverly Hills. Magazine and newspaper articles identified this way have been copied from the Herrick Library's microfiche files, which typically do not include page numbers.

Baker: Baker Library, Harvard Business School, Cambridge

BU/RH: Richard G. Hubler Collection, Howard Gotlieb Archival Research Center, Boston University

CSUN/SCG: Screen Cartoonists Guild Collection, Local 839, AFL-CIO, 1937–1951, Urban Archives Center, California State University, Northridge

NYU/JC: John Canemaker Animation Collection, Fales Library/Special Collections in the Elmer Holmes Bobst Library, New York University

RAC: Rockefeller Archive Center, Sleepy Hollow. All references are to Nelson A. Rockefeller, Personal, Record Group 111, Series 4.

Wisconsin/UA: United Artists Collection, Wisconsin Center for Film and Theater Research, State Historical Society of Wisconsin, Madison

Oral Histories

Adamson/Freleng, Adamson/Huemer: These oral histories were conducted by Joe Adamson with Friz Freleng and Richard Huemer, respectively, for the University of California, Los Angeles, Department of Theater Arts in 1968–69 as part of "An Oral History of the Motion Picture in America."

Personal Papers

AC	author's collection
BS	Ben Sharpsteen
CGM	Carman G. Maxwell
DH	David Hand
FN	Fred Niemann
HH	Hugh Harman
RH	Richard Huemer
RI	Rudolph Ising
SB	Stephen Bosustow

Disney cost and box-office figures were provided by the Walt Disney Archives for films completed after 1947. The figures cited as grosses include both domestic and foreign revenue and are the combined rentals received by the Disney studio and its distributors. The pre-1947 figures are, as noted, from a balance sheet prepared by the studio for negotiations with RKO and are the actual rentals that Disney itself received.

Employment dates are also from the Walt Disney Archives.

The Disney "meeting notes" are ordinarily—although not invariably—transcripts; the term "meeting notes" is one used at the Disney studio itself. Meeting notes were usually distributed as typescripts, in multiple carbon copies, or sometimes hectographed, although at the height of the studio's prosperity, during the production of *Pinocchio* and *Fantasia,* notes were frequently mimeographed. The cited lecture transcripts and memoranda were also variously distributed in mimeographed or carbon copy form.

Complete runs of the studio and union newsletters mentioned in these notes are rare or nonexistent. The Walt Disney Archives does not have a complete set of that studio's *Bulletin,* for instance.

Although it would be normal to identify the city where each interview occurred, that has not been done here, both to save the space that would otherwise be devoted to essentially redundant information—most of the interviews took place in the Los Angeles area—and, in a few cases, to protect the privacy of the people involved. Except as specified, all interviews were conducted by the author (in many cases with Milton Gray as a participant).

My standard procedure was to make a transcript, or in some cases summary notes, of each interview, and to give the interviewee the opportunity to revise that transcript; usually, but not always, the interviewee took that opportunity. (A few people died before an interview was transcribed, or before they returned a transcript.) I have quoted from the revised transcript whenever there is one.

PREFACE

1. Diane Disney Miller, foreword to *Inside the Dream: The Personal Story of Walt Disney,* by Katherine Greene and Richard Greene (New York, 2001), 9–10. *The Story of Walt Disney* was reissued by Disney Editions in 2005, for sale at Disneyland as part of the observance of the park's fiftieth anniversary, with a new introductory note by Miller and corrections of factual and typographical errors by David R. Smith of the Walt Disney Archives. In her note, Miller says that the *Post* offered Disney $150,000 for his autobiography and paid Miller and her sister, Sharon, half that amount. Curiously, the version of *The Story of Walt Disney* published in the *Post* differs from the version published as a book. Disney is "Dad" in the magazine— as he was to his daughters in real life—but he is "Father" in the book.

2. Richard Hubler to author, July 29, 1969.

INTRODUCTION "It's All Me"

1. Anthony Bower, "Snow White and the 1,200 Dwarfs," *Nation,* May 10, 1941, 565.

2. "'Snow White' Sets Mark with $6,740,000 Gross," *New York Times,* May 2, 1939, 29.

3. "Drive on Walt Disney by Cartoonists Guild," *Variety,* January 15, 1941, 16.

4. George Goepper to Walt Disney, memorandum, February 4, 1941, WDA.

5. Adelquist exhibit 11, NLRB/Babbitt. A copy of the memorandum is also at CSUN/SCG.

6. George Goepper, interview with Milton Gray, March 23, 1977.

7. Disney's speech exists in three versions. The version delivered on February 10, 1941, in manuscript and on discs at WDA, includes remarks directed specifically to the animators. The version of February 11, which is Lessing exhibit 29, NLRB/Babbitt, was delivered to lower-ranking employees at the studio, particularly the women who inked and painted the cels. An abbreviated version of the February 10 speech, with Disney's profanity removed, is part of CSUN/SCG. Memos listing the departments summoned to each of the two speeches are also part of that collection.

8. "Labor Fantasia," *Business Week,* May 17, 1941, 50.

CHAPTER 1 "The Pet in the Family"

1. A "History of Marceline," first published in the 1938 Golden Jubilee edition of the *Marceline News,* was reprinted in *The Magic City, Marceline, Missouri, Diamond Jubilee Celebration,* a program book published by the Marceline-based Walsworth Publishing Company for the celebration of Marceline's seventy-fifth anniversary, June 29–July 4, 1963.

2. Census records show only eight siblings, but all ten are listed in the most thoroughly researched genealogical examination of the Disney family, Edward Disney, *A Story of Disneys: Some Myths Exploded* (Bristol, England, 1997), 166.

3. Elias Disney's visit was reported in the *Marceline Mirror,* February 9, 1906 (this citation and other Marceline newspaper citations are from clippings compiled by May Bartee Couch). His sale of his Chicago house to Walter Chamberlain on February 10, 1906, is recorded in Torrens Book 221-A, p. 302, Cook County Recorder of Deeds.

4. *Marceline Mirror,* December 1, 1905.

5. From records of those transactions at the Linn County Abstract Company, Brookfield, Missouri.

6. The house number was changed to 2156 in 1909 as part of a citywide rationalization of Chicago house numbers.

7. 3515 Vernon Avenue is the address on the "Return of a Birth," or birth certificate, for Raymond Arnold Disney (misidentified on the certificate as "Walter") and in Elias Disney's city directory listing.

8. Elias Disney's purchase of the lot from James E. McCabe is recorded in Torrens Book 221-A, p. 302. The 1892 date was assigned to the house during a Historic Resources Survey by the Chicago Landmarks Commission in 1983–95.

9. On Hermosa, see the *Encyclopedia of Chicago,* online edition, www.encyclopedia.chicagohistory.org/pages/578/html.

10. Roy Disney, interview with Richard Hubler, November 17, 1967, BU/RH.

The incomplete transcript at Boston is a preliminary version of a complete transcript bearing that date at the Walt Disney Archives.

11. Roy Disney, 1967 interview. Roy seems to say that Elias and the older boys left first, but Bob Thomas, *Building a Company: Roy O. Disney and the Creation of an Entertainment Empire* (New York, 1998), 18, says that Flora and the younger children moved to Marceline ahead of Elias and the two older boys, as Walt Disney's memory of the event suggests.

12. "Walt Disney Recalls Some Pleasant Childhood Memories," *Marceline News,* October 13, 1960. The newspaper marked a Disney visit (to dedicate an elementary school named for him) by reprinting a letter he wrote more than twenty years earlier on the occasion of Marceline's fiftieth anniversary.

13. Roy Disney, 1967 interview.

14. Walt Disney, interview with Pete Martin, May or June 1956. Except as noted otherwise, all quotations from Walt Disney throughout the book are from the Martin transcripts, copies of which are housed at both WDA and BU/RH. Lillian Disney and her two daughters, Diane and Sharon, were interviewed by Martin at intervals during the marathon taping sessions with Walt Disney when he was unavailable, and their comments are part of the Martin transcripts.

15. A recording of Disney's brief speech at Marceline is included on a compact disc accompanying Robert Tieman, *Walt Disney Treasures* (New York, 2003). He also spoke of being a "champion hog rider" in the 1956 Martin interview.

16. Roy Disney, interview with Hubler, June 18, 1968, BU/RH.

17. In the 1900 census, almost 46 million Americans lived in "rural" places with a population of fewer than 2,500; about 30 million lived in larger towns.

18. The telephone directory was published in a newspaper, the *Marceline Mirror* for February 22, 1907.

19. *Lady and the Tramp* meeting notes, May 15, 1952, WDA.

20. Roy Disney, 1967 interview.

21. Disney, *Some Myths Exploded,* 154.

22. Disney, *Some Myths Exploded,* 169.

23. The Chicago Historical Society maintains a database with information from building permits cited in *American Contractor* from 1898 to 1912. Elias is listed as the owner of four properties for which permits were issued between 1898 and 1901. Contractors were not listed on building permits at the time, so Elias could have been, and probably was, the contractor for many other properties he did not own.

24. Roy Disney, June 1968 interview.

25. Saint Paul Congregational Church (Chicago) record books, now housed at Chicago Theological Seminary.

26. Roy Disney, 1967 interview.

27. Saint Paul record books. The name "Walter" was one that Elias and Flora had in mind for some time. When their second son, Raymond, was born in 1890, his birth certificate (filled out on January 8, 1891) showed his name as "Walter Dis-

ney." There is also a birth certificate for Roy Disney, but none for either Walt Disney or his sister, Ruth, both of them also born in Chicago; there was no requirement that births be registered with the Cook County clerk until 1916. Walt's birth date is noted, however, in the Saint Paul baptismal record.

28. Roy Disney, June 1968 interview.

29. Roy Disney, 1967 interview. Thomas, *Building a Company,* 24, says the trigger for the two boys' break with their father was his insistence that they give him the money they had earned by farming land Elias leased from Robert Disney.

30. Roy Disney, June 1968 interview.

31. Roy Disney, June 1968 interview.

32. Diane Disney Miller, Martin interview.

33. Don Taylor, "The Disney Family as I Remember Them," in *Our Marceline Heritage, Part 1* (Marceline, 1974), 16.

34. Roy Disney, June 1968 interview.

35. Roy Disney, June 1968 interview.

36. Mary Richardson Disney died on March 10, 1909, at Ellis, Kansas. Her husband had died in 1891.

37. Roy Disney remembered Margaret Disney as "a wonderful character with an infectious laugh . . . and she was always enamored with Walt from the time he was a little fellow. She was the one used to bring him tablets and pencils, you remember the Big Chief Indian red tablet that we used to buy as kids? She used to keep him supplied with those." June 1968 interview.

38. Roy Disney, June 1968 interview.

39. Taylor, "Disney Family as I Remember Them."

40. Bob Thomas, *Walt Disney: An American Original* (New York, 1976), 31.

41. Roy Disney, 1967 interview.

42. Walt and Roy Disney identified the house to their Marceline hosts on their 1956 visit, but there is no documentary record the Disneys lived there.

43. *Marceline Mirror,* May 18, 1911. A brief notice: "Elias Disney and family left Wednesday morning for Kansas City to make their future home."

44. That is the address for Elias Disney shown in Kansas City city directories for 1912–14.

45. Elias and Flora Disney purchased the house at 3028 Bellefontaine Street from Florence E. and James R. Scherrer on September 4, 1914, and executed a deed of trust to J. P. Crump on the same day. Jackson County (MO) Records Office, KCWPA 1900–1920 Grantee Index COO-FZ, Grantor Index CA-DZ, Deeds 1002149 and 1002150.

46. Brian Burnes, Robert W. Butler, and Dan Viets, *Walt Disney's Missouri: The Roots of a Creative Genius* (Kansas City, 2002), 53, cites an internal *Star* memorandum from 1955 in identifying Roy as the route's official owner and as the source of these circulation figures: morning *Times,* 680; afternoon and Sunday *Star,* 635. By the time the Disney family sold the route, on March 17, 1917, they served 925 sub-

scribers to the *Times,* 840 to the daily *Star,* and 876 to the Sunday paper. The $2,100 sales price is from Thomas, *Building a Company,* 29.

47. Roy Disney, 1967 interview.

48. "Walt Disney, Showman and Educator, Remembers Daisy," *CTA* [California Teachers Association] *Journal,* December 1955, 4. The Daisy of the article's title was Daisy Beck, Disney's seventh-grade homeroom teacher, whom he remembered fondly.

49. The 1912 graduation date comes from David R. Smith of the Walt Disney Archives. The Kansas City (MO) School District has no record that Roy Disney ever attended school there, but its records from that period are fragmentary. Even Walt Disney's attendance at Benton School is reflected only in a single school census.

50. Meyer Minda, undated interview posted on the Walt Disney Family Museum Web site, February 2004.

51. Minda interview.

52. City directories show Herbert A. Hudson's Benton Barber Shop at 2914 East Thirty-first Street in 1915–17.

53. The date, 1917, is in what David R. Smith of the Walt Disney Archives calls "Ruth's graduation book." Smith to author, e-mail, May 1, 2006.

54. David R. Smith of the Walt Disney Archives provided a list of O-Zell-related items stolen from Ruth Disney Beecher's former home in Portland in 1974 and later found in the possession of an antiques dealer. The archives has copies of none of the items, which are described on Smith's list mainly as stock certificates, receipts for the purchase of stock, and the like, but also include "6 [undated] IOUs signed by Elias Disney for O-Zell." The earliest stock certificates—a hundred shares in Flora's name and two thousand in Elias's—were dated in April 1912. Smith to author, e-mail, November 3, 2005.

55. Thomas, *Walt Disney,* 40. Walt Disney, in the 1956 interview, identified Fred Harvey as Roy's employer but remembered Roy's working as a news butcher only one summer.

56. Roy Disney, June 1968 interview.

57. The Disneys' address and their renter status are reflected in the 1920 federal census, which incorrectly listed Elias as "Charles Disney."

58. The O-Zell Company's address appears in want ads and Yellow Pages listings from that period.

59. Not to be confused with the Art Institute of Chicago. The Art Institute was originally called the Chicago Academy of Fine Arts, but it changed its name in the 1880s. The academy where Disney studied was an entirely separate school, founded around 1903—as a rival to the Art Institute's school, in fact.

60. Thomas, *Walt Disney,* 331. The school was later renamed the Kansas City Art Institute.

61. Five examples of Disney's *Voice* cartoons, including several showing the strong McManus influence, were published in *Chicago's American,* April 27, 1967.

62. Disney's "roster card" from the Chicago Post Office shows he was appointed a "sub carrier" June 25, 1918; his appointment was approved July 5 and ended September 24. National Personnel Records Center, Saint Louis.

63. Thomas, *Building a Company*, 35, has Roy proceeding immediately to Great Lakes after he enlisted, but that version of events is at odds with Walt's account of meeting his brother at the Chicago terminal, since Walt was not in Chicago until the fall.

64. As reflected in Kansas City city directories and the 1920 federal census. Herbert apparently moved into the family home shortly before Elias, Flora, Walt, and Ruth moved to Chicago in 1917.

65. The name Pesmen-Rubin Commercial Art Studio appears in a brief memoir written by Louis Pesmen in 1971, at the invitation of David R. Smith of the Walt Disney Archives, but there is no comparable listing in city directories for 1920 or 1921. (Pesmen and Rubin had separate listings as commercial artists in 1920, and Pesmen shared a listing with another artist in 1921.) Pesmen's memoir is regrettably dubious in most respects, his memories of the young Disney's employment far too precise to be credible.

66. Kansas City Slide advertised for a "first class man . . . steady" to make "cartoon and wash drawings."

67. In a July 27, 1959, letter to William Beaudine, congratulating him on fifty years in the movies, Disney said: "I want you to know that I am not far behind you—next February will make my 40th year as part of the motion picture business!" William Beaudine Collection, AMPAS.

68. Although Iwerks returned to the Disney studio as an employee in 1940, he filled out an application for employment on January 7, 1943, probably for reasons related to the studio's wartime work. On the application, he stated that he had worked for "Pessman [*sic*] & Rubin Gray Advertising Agency" from September 1919 to January 1920 and for United Film Ad (the eventual name of the company earlier known as Kansas City Slide and Kansas City Film Ad) from March 1920 to June 1924, ignoring his few months at Laugh-O-gram. WDA.

69. Hugh Harman, interview, December 3, 1973.

70. Michael Barrier, *Hollywood Cartoons: American Animation in Its Golden Age* (New York, 1999), 20–21.

71. Walt Disney to Irene Gentry, August 17, 1937, WDA.

72. Roy Disney, June 1968 interview.

73. "Shake-up in Police Jobs," *Kansas City Star,* February 6, 1921, 1; courtesy of J. B. Kaufman.

74. Russell Merritt and J. B. Kaufman, *Walt in Wonderland: The Silent Films of Walt Disney* (Baltimore, 1993), 125.

75. David R. Smith to author, e-mail, July 17, 2006.

76. Merritt and Kaufman, *Walt in Wonderland,* 125, identifies March 20, 1921,

as the date of the first showing. An advertisement in the *Kansas City Star* for that date (on page 2B) lists "Newman Laugh-a-Grams" as among the components of a newsreel compilation called "News and Views"; courtesy of J. B. Kaufman.

77. Herbert Disney's folder at the National Personnel Records Center, Saint Louis, shows that he worked as a carrier in the Kansas City post office until July 15, 1921, when he transferred to Portland. Some sources say that Elias, Flora, and Ruth followed him there in November 1922, but 1921 fits better with what is known of Walt Disney's own activities in 1921 and 1922.

78. Hugh Harman, 1973 interview.

79. Hugh Harman, 1973 interview.

80. Fred Harman, "New Tracks in Old Trails," *True West,* October 1968, 10–11.

81. Fred Harman to Walt Disney, May 10, 1932, WDA. Disney replied—in the same warm, friendly tone—on May 23.

82. Roy Disney, June 1968 interview.

83. Rudolph Ising to author, December 20, 1979; Hugh Harman, 1973 interview. The name of Peiser's restaurant is from the Laugh-O-gram bankruptcy papers and a 1923 Kansas City city directory.

84. Ising, interviewed by J. B. Kaufman on August 14, 1988, in Didier Ghez, ed., *Walt's People: Talking Disney with the Artists Who Knew Him* (2005), 1:20–21.

85. Incorporation papers, Laugh O Gram Corporation, Corporation Division, Office of the Secretary of State, Jefferson City, MO. Although the incorporation papers show the company's name as "Laugh O Gram," the more common form was "Laugh-O-gram."

86. "Laugh-O-Gram *[sic]* Cartoons Announced," *Motion Picture News,* June 17, 1922, 3257; "Plan Distribution of Laugh-O-Grams," *Motion Picture News,* August 26, 1922, 1055.

87. C. G. Maxwell, interview with Gray, April 6, 1977.

88. Hugh Harman, 1973 interview.

89. Ising, interview, June 2, 1971.

90. Hugh Harman, 1973 interview.

91. The record of Laugh-O-gram's bankruptcy shows the purchase in November and December 1922 and January 1923 of sheets of celluloid measuring 20 inches by 50 inches from E. I. du Pont de Nemours & Company.

92. Maxwell to Bob Thomas, August 20, 1973. Maxwell gave a copy of that letter to the author in 1986.

93. The contract's terms and its subsequent history are reflected in various documents filed during Laugh-O-gram's bankruptcy proceedings.

94. David R. Smith, "Up to Date in Kansas City," *Funnyworld* 19 (Fall 1978): 23–24.

95. "Recording the Baby's Life in Films," *Kansas City Star,* October 29, 1922, 3D; courtesy of J. B. Kaufman.

96. Maxwell interview.

97. Copies of the promotional piece and a newspaper advertisement for the course were in Ising's papers.

98. After Laugh-O-gram was declared bankrupt, a bankruptcy referee rejected as transparent dodges Schmeltz's chattel mortgages and the assignment of the Pictorial Clubs contract to him, denying his claim that the debts covered by those instruments should take priority over those of unsecured creditors.

99. Edna Francis Disney, interview with Richard Hubler, August 20, 1968, BU/RH.

100. A photocopy of the contract is in a private collection.

101. Hugh Harman, 1973 interview. As reflected in the Laugh-O-gram bankruptcy proceedings, Harman, Ising, and Maxwell worked for Laugh-O-gram much later in its life than most employees. Harman and Maxwell were Laugh-O-gram employees through the end of June 1923, Ising almost as long. Ub Iwerks's Laugh-O-gram employment ended on May 5, 1923.

102. Ising, December 20, 1979. Documents in the Laugh-O-gram bankruptcy case indicate that Fred Schmeltz paid the back rent in late July. Some sources say that Laugh-O-gram moved to the Wirthman Building, but that building was at Thirty-first and Troost, more than a block away from the space above Peiser's. Laugh-O-gram was never housed at the Wirthman Building, but Hugh Harman, Ising, and Maxwell made *Sinbad the Sailor,* their single *Arabian Nights* cartoon, in two offices there in 1924.

103. Maxwell, August 20, 1973.

104. M. J. Winkler to Walt Disney, May 16, 1923, photocopy, WDA.

105. Walt Disney to Winkler, June 18, 1923, photocopy, WDA.

106. Winkler to Walt Disney, June 25, 1923, photocopy, WDA.

107. Hugh Harman and Ising, joint interview, October 31, 1976. Harman and Ising both remembered the damage to the emulsion, but only Ising remembered the film's being reshot. The film was definitely reshot, though, since the surviving version shows none of the damage that both men remembered.

108. Ising, note to transcript of October 31, 1976, joint interview with Hugh Harman.

109. Walt Disney to Winkler, May 14, 1923, photocopy, WDA. The letter is reproduced in Smith, "Up to Date in Kansas City," 33.

110. Pictorial Clubs ultimately paid for the films as part of Laugh-O-gram's bankruptcy proceedings, but the creditors' representatives had great difficulty collecting the money.

111. Ising, December 20, 1979.

112. Lowell Lawrance, "'Mickey Mouse'—Inspiration from Mouse in K.C. Studio," *Kansas City Journal Post,* September 8, 1935, clipping, Kansas City Public Library.

1. "Walt Disney's Kin and Backer Taken by Death," *Los Angeles Times,* July 31, 1953, AMPAS. Robert Disney died at the age of ninety-one. His wife Margaret, who encouraged the young Walt Disney to draw, died in 1920; Robert remarried in 1921.

2. Walt Disney, interview with Pete Martin, early 1961. This transcript accompanies the transcripts of the 1956 interviews but its internal references are clearly to the later date. References in the text to statements Disney made in 1961 are references to this transcript unless noted otherwise.

3. Roy Disney, 1967 interview.

4. Robert De Roos, "The Magic Worlds of Walt Disney," *National Geographic,* August 1963, 173.

5. Walt Disney to Winkler, August 25, 1923, photocopy, WDA.

6. Winkler to Walt Disney, September 7, 1923, photocopy, WDA.

7. Winkler to Walt Disney, telegram, October 15, 1923, WDA.

8. Walt Disney to Winkler, October 24, 1923, photocopy, WDA.

9. Walt Disney to Winkler, January 21, 1924, photocopy, WDA.

10. Roy Disney, 1967 interview.

11. David R. Smith, "Disney Before Burbank," *Funnyworld* 20 (Summer 1979): 33.

12. Wilfred Jackson, interview, December 2, 1973.

13. Roy Disney, June 1968 interview. In this interview, Roy put the total loan from Robert Disney at seven hundred dollars, but an early account book, cited in Thomas, *Building a Company,* 48–49, showed a loan in five installments totaling $500 between November 14 and December 14, 1923. The loan was repaid with interest—the total was $528.66—on January 12, 1924.

14. Roy Disney, 1967 interview.

15. Roy Disney, 1967 interview.

16. Walt Disney to Margaret J. Davis, October 16, 1923, photocopy, private collection.

17. Lowell E. Redelings, "The Hollywood Scene," *Hollywood Citizen-News,* February 18, 1957, AMPAS.

18. Lillian Disney, 1986 interview posted on the Walt Disney Family Museum Web site in 2001.

19. Smith, "Disney Before Burbank," 34.

20. Iwerks's letter has apparently not survived, but Disney's reply, dated June 1, 1924, says in part, "I'll say I was surprised to hear from you and also glad to hear from you. . . . Am glad you have made up your mind to come out," photocopy, WDA.

21. Smith, "Disney Before Burbank," 34.

22. Roy Disney, interview with Hubler, February 20, 1968, BU/RH.

23. Lillian Disney, Martin interview.

24. Lillian Disney, interview with Hubler, April 16, 1968, BU/RH. This inter-

view was apparently not recorded, the transcript based instead on notes taken by Marty Sklar of the Disney staff.

25. Lillian Disney, Hubler interview.

26. Disney was apparently mentioned only once in the *Los Angeles Times* before 1929, in a one-paragraph item, "Actors Mix With Cartoons," *Los Angeles Times,* July 6, 1924, B3.

27. Lillian Disney ("Mrs. Walt Disney"), as told to Isabella Taves, "I Live with a Genius," *McCall's,* February 1953, 105, AMPAS.

28. Lillian Disney, Hubler interview. Lillian spoke of the bet as involving Hugh and Walker Harman and Rudolph Ising, as well as Ub Iwerks, but the Harmans and Ising did not join the Disney staff until just before the Disneys' wedding, and Walt Disney has a mustache in photos taken before then.

29. Lillian Disney, Martin interview.

30. "General Expense Account 1925–1926–1927 by Roy O. Disney," WDA.

31. Lillian Disney, 1986 interview.

32. "General Expense Account 1925–1926–1927."

33. Lillian Disney, Martin interview.

34. The Disneys' addresses from before their purchase of a home in 1926 are from "family and archival sources." David R. Smith to author, e-mail, April 24, 2006.

35. Lillian Disney, Martin interview.

36. Ising, 1971 interview.

37. Walt Disney to M. J. Winkler, May 29, 1924, WDA.

38. Hugh Harman, 1973 interview.

39. Ising, 1971 interview.

40. Smith, "Disney Before Burbank," 34.

41. Hugh Harman, 1973 interview.

42. Hugh Harman, 1973 interview.

43. Hugh Harman, 1976 joint interview with Ising.

44. Ising, 1971 interview.

45. Hugh Harman and Ising, 1976 joint interview.

46. Ising, 1973 interview.

47. Ising, 1971 interview.

48. Hugh Harman, 1973 interview.

49. Ising, 1976 joint interview with Hugh Harman.

50. Ising, 1971 interview.

51. Hugh Harman, 1973 interview; Hugh Harman and Ising, 1976 joint interview.

52. Smith, "Disney Before Burbank," 34.

53. Hugh Harman, 1973 interview.

54. Ising to Maxwell, February 28, 1926, RI.

55. Ising, 1976 joint interview with Hugh Harman.

56. Ising to family members, April 13, 1926, RI.

57. David R. Smith to author, e-mail, October 31, 2005.

58. Roy Disney, June 1968 interview.

59. Winkler to Walt Disney, April 7, 1924, WDA.

60. Charles Mintz to Walt Disney, October 24, 1924; Walt Disney to Mintz, November 3, 1924, WDA.

61. Mintz to Walt Disney, October 6, 1925, WDA.

62. Mintz to Walt Disney, November 17, 1925, WDA.

63. Mintz to Walt Disney, November 24, 1925, WDA.

64. Mintz to Walt Disney, January 31, 1927, WDA.

65. "'U' Will Release Animated Cartoon Comedies," *Motion Picture News,* March 25, 1927, 1052; "General Expense Account, 1925–1926–1927."

66. Hugh Harman, 1973 interview.

67. Dick Huemer, interview, November 27, 1973.

68. Paul Smith, interview with Gray, March 22, 1978.

69. Maxwell, August 20, 1973.

70. Paul Smith interview.

71. Hugh Harman, 1973 interview.

72. Paul Smith interview.

73. Ising to Adele Ising, January 29, 1927, RI.

74. Maxwell, August 20, 1973.

75. Maxwell interview.

76. Adamson/Freleng.

77. Friz Freleng, tape-recorded letter to author, circa July 1976.

78. Ising to Ray Friedman, circa August 27, 1927, RI.

79. Ising to Freleng, November 15, 1927, RI.

80. Paul Smith interview.

81. Ising to Freleng, February 10, 1928, RI.

82. Walt Disney to Roy Disney, March 7, 1928, WDA.

83. Walt Disney to Roy Disney, February 28, 1928, WDA.

84. Walt Disney, February 28, 1928.

85. Walt Disney to Roy Disney, March 2, 1928, WDA.

86. Walt Disney to Roy Disney, March 5, 1928, WDA.

87. Lillian Disney, Martin interview.

88. Lawrance, "'Mickey Mouse'—Inspiration from Mouse in K.C. Studio."

89. Lillian Disney, "I Live with a Genius," 104.

90. Hugh Harman, 1973 interview.

91. Paul Smith interview.

92. There is an entry under that date for "2 Previews & Express" in "General Expense Account 1925–1926–1927." The "express" portion of that charge was for shipping a print of *Plane Crazy* to a film storage company in New York.

93. Diane Kirkpatrick, "Animation Gold: An Interview of Pioneer Animator Frank Goldman," *Cinegram* 2, no. 1 (1977): 39.

94. Jackson to author, November 13, 1975.

95. Jackson, 1973 interview.

96. Jackson to author, February 22, 1977. Many of the exposure sheets, discarded by the Disney studio years ago, have survived in a private collection.

97. The first page of the sketches and synopses is reproduced in Christopher Finch, *The Art of Walt Disney: From Mickey Mouse to the Magic Kingdoms* (New York, 1973), 51.

98. That was a standard figure—the amount paid to the projectionist—recorded in Roy Disney's account book for theatrical previews, but it seems unlikely that the unfinished *Steamboat Willie* would have been previewed in a theater, even in silent form. The two dollars may have paid for something else, perhaps refreshments.

99. Walt Disney, "Growing Pains," *Journal of the Society of Motion Picture Engineers*, January 1941, 33–34.

100. Jackson, 1973 interview.

101. Michael Barrier, Milton Gray, and Bill Spicer, "An Interview with Carl Stalling," *Funnyworld* 13 (Spring 1971): 21. The interviews on which the published interview was based were conducted on June 4 and November 25, 1969.

102. Walt Disney to Roy Disney and Iwerks, September 7, 1928, WDA.

103. Walt Disney to Roy Disney and Iwerks, September 14, 1928, WDA.

104. Walt Disney to Roy Disney and Iwerks, undated but probably written September 6, 1928, WDA.

105. Walt Disney, September 7, 1928.

106. Walt Disney to Roy Disney and Iwerks, September 20, 1928, WDA.

107. Walt Disney to Roy Disney and Iwerks, September 23, 1928, WDA.

108. Walt Disney to Roy Disney, September 25, 1928, WDA.

109. Walt Disney to Roy Disney and Iwerks, September 28, 1928, WDA.

110. Walt Disney, September 23, 1928.

111. Walt Disney to Roy Disney and Iwerks, October 6, 1928, WDA.

112. Walt Disney to "gang," September 30, 1928, WDA.

113. Walt Disney, September 23, 1928.

114. According to David R. Smith of the Walt Disney Archives, Columbia Pictures—by then Disney's distributor—paid a license fee of $150 on April 25, 1931. Smith to author, e-mail, March 28, 2006.

115. Walt Disney to Roy Disney and Iwerks, October 1, 1928, WDA.

116. Walt Disney, October 6, 1928.

117. Walt Disney to Roy Disney and Iwerks, October 22, 1928, WDA.

118. Walt Disney to Lillian Disney, October 20, 1928, WDA.

119. Walt Disney to Lillian Disney, October 26, 1928, WDA.

120. Barrier, Gray, and Spicer, "Interview with Carl Stalling," 21.

121. Walt Disney to Lillian Disney, October 27, 1928, WDA.

122. Even in the early 1930s, when Mickey Mouse was wildly popular, New York theaters were paying considerably less than a thousand dollars for a Disney cartoon's

two-week run. The Rivoli Theatre was paying $250 for the first week of each of seventeen *Mickeys*, and $150 for the second week; the Roxy was paying $500 for the first week and $300 for each additional week. Henry W. "Hank" Peters to Roy Disney, August 29, 1932, WDA.

123. From a speech Disney gave on October 1, 1966, to the National Association of Theatre Owners. The speech was published in *Motion Picture Exhibitor,* October 19, 1966, AMPAS. Disney's speech has also been published in Kathy Merlock Jackson, *Walt Disney: A Bio-Bibliography* (Westport, 1993), 139–44.

124. "Report Universal Seeks to Be Rid of Colony Lease," *Motion Picture News,* January 12, 1929, 78.

125. Walt Disney, October 20, 1928.

126. Walt Disney, October 27, 1928.

127. Walt Disney to Iwerks, November 11, 1928, WDA.

128. Advertisement, *New York Times,* November 18, 1928, sec. 9, 5.

129. Barrier, Gray, and Spicer, "Interview with Carl Stalling," 22.

130. *Film Daily*'s review and other laudatory reviews from the Colony Theatre run were reproduced in a promotional sheet issued by Pat Powers, doing business as "Disney Cartoons," around the end of 1928. The sheet itself is reproduced in the spring 1971 *Funnyworld,* 28–29.

131. As summarized in a letter to Charles J. Giegerich from Roy Disney, September 2, 1929, WDA. Giegerich, who worked for Powers, was trying to go behind his boss's back and make his own deal with the Disneys; Roy politely turned him aside.

132. Giegerich to Walt Disney, December 19, 1928, WDA.

133. Giegerich to Walt Disney, December 31, 1928, WDA.

134. Jackson to author, July 28, 1975.

135. Jackson, July 28, 1975.

136. Walt Disney, "Growing Pains," 32.

CHAPTER 3 "You've Got to Really Be Minnie"

1. Jackson, February 22, 1977.

2. Jackson, interview, November 5, 1976.

3. Walt Disney, "Growing Pains," 35.

4. Walt Disney, September 20, 1928.

5. Walt Disney, September 25, 1928, WDA.

6. The scenario is titled "The Spook Dance," WDA.

7. Iwerks described the disagreement in an interview represented by notes in the Walt Disney Archives. The interview was probably conducted by Bob Thomas as part of his research for *Walt Disney, the Art of Animation* (New York, 1958).

8. Walt Disney to Giegerich, June 12, 1929, WDA.

9. Giegerich to Walt Disney, night letter, August 12, 1929, WDA.

10. Walt Disney to Giegerich, July 26, 1929, WDA.

11. Walt Disney to Roy Disney and Iwerks, February 9, 1929, WDA. In a letter to his Laugh-O-gram investor J. V. Cowles on December 28, 1928, Disney described his plans and invited Cowles to invest in the "series of one reel talking comedies." Cowles evidently met with Disney and Stalling in Kansas City on January 27, 1929, when they were on their way to New York, but nothing indicates that he ever invested in Disney's separate sound recording company.

12. Jackson, 1973 interview.

13. Al Eugster, interview, March 17, 1978.

14. Jackson, November 13, 1975.

15. Jackson to author, October 28, 1975.

16. Ben Sharpsteen, interview, October 23, 1976.

17. Jackson, November 13, 1975.

18. Jackson to author, December 23, 1978.

19. Sharpsteen, 1976 interview.

20. Dick Lundy, interview, November 26, 1973.

21. Jackson to author, June 3, 1985.

22. Walt Disney to Giegerich, December 23, 1929, WDA.

23. Jackson to author, September 10, 1977.

24. Jackson, 1973 interview.

25. Jackson to author, May 3, 1977.

26. Lundy, 1973 interview.

27. Jackson, 1973 interview.

28. Jackson, November 13, 1975.

29. Jack Zander, interview, March 24, 1982. The California Institute of the Arts, Chouinard's successor institution, has no student records from that period.

30. P. A. Powers to Walt Disney, December 26, 1929, WDA.

31. Walt Disney Productions was a partnership until December 16, 1929, when the company was incorporated. The corporation acquired the partnership's assets on June 30, 1930.

32. Roy Disney to Walt Disney, January 24, 1930, WDA.

33. Copies of the release and the promissory note are held by the Walt Disney Archives.

34. Roy Disney to Walt Disney, February 1, 1930, WDA.

35. Roy Disney to Walt Disney, January 25, 1930, WDA.

36. Sharpsteen, 1976 interview.

37. Roy Disney, January 25, 1930.

38. Barrier, Gray, and Spicer, "An Interview with Carl Stalling," 24.

39. Carl Stalling to author, September 23, 1970, and February 21 and March 16, 1971.

40. Roy Disney, January 25, 1930.

41. Al Lichtman, United Artists' vice president and general manager for distribution, expressed regret to Roy Disney on June 3, 1932, that "the deal I worked on for so long for the purchase of an interest in your business fell through." Joseph Schenck, UA's chairman, had discussed the idea of investing in the Disney company with his brother, Nicholas, the head of Loew's, Metro-Goldwyn-Mayer's parent company, and had concluded that in the weak economy, "the investment was too large at this time." Roy, in a June 10 reply to Lichtman, found "a source of satisfaction that men of the calibre of Mr. Schenck and yourself have thought well enough of us to wish to be associated with us," WDA.

42. David Hand, interview, November 21, 1973.

43. Roy Disney to Walt Disney, January 24, 1930, WDA.

44. Lillian Disney to Roy and Edna Disney, January 30, 1930, WDA.

45. Walt Disney to Roy Disney, typescript for night letter, February 7, 1930, WDA.

46. Roy Disney to Walt Disney, April 24, 1930, WDA.

47. Roy Disney to Walt Disney, night letter, May 6, 1930, WDA.

48. Walt Disney, "Color and Wide Screen in Cartoon Field," *Film Daily,* April 6, 1930, 17.

49. Harry Carr, "The Only Unpaid Movie Star," *American Magazine,* March 1931, 125.

50. David Hand, October 29, 1946, lecture at Rank animation studio, DH.

51. Carr, "Only Unpaid Movie Star," 57.

52. Sharpsteen, 1976 interview.

53. Les Clark, telephone interview, August 19, 1976.

54. Jackson, July 28, 1975.

55. Jackson, 1973 interview.

56. Hand, 1973 interview.

57. Ed Benedict, interview with Gray, January 31, 1977.

58. Jackson, 1973 interview.

59. Jackson, May 3, 1977.

60. Arthur Mann, "Mickey Mouse's Financial Career," *Harper's,* May 1934, 719.

61. Walt Disney to Giegerich, July 30, 1929, WDA.

62. Cecil Munsey, *Disneyana: Walt Disney Collectibles* (New York, 1974), 16–17; Gunther Lessing to Art Arthur, Motion Picture Industry Council, November 18, 1949, AMPAS. According to Munsey, Roy Disney verified the accuracy of Walt Disney's account of the writing-tablet deal.

63. For example, Disney wrote to Gottfredson on February 1, 1935: "This first week's strip gives indications of a very interesting continuity. The characters you are using are interesting types and I especially like the old man from whom Mickey bought the paper—he's very funny looking." Walt Disney to Floyd Gottfredson and "Merle" (probably Merrill de Maris), memorandum, February 1, 1935, WDA.

64. Ed Love, interview with Gray, January 18, 1977.

65. Love, 1977 interview.

66. Jackson, 1976 interview.

67. Dana Larrabee, "Ed Benedict on Animation: The Facts of Life," *Film Collector's World*, May 1, 1977, 32.

68. Hand, telephone interview, June 29, 1976.

69. Aubrey Menen, "Dazzled in Disneyland," *Holiday*, July 1963, 106.

70. Clark, interview, December 1, 1973.

71. Thomas, *Building a Company*, 71–72.

72. Love, interview, September 25, 1990.

73. Dick Hall, interview, September 8, 1978.

74. Jackson, 1976 interview.

75. Mark Langer, "Designing *Dumbo:* An Annotated Interview with A. Kendall O'Connor," *Animation Journal*, Fall 1993, 48.

76. Jackson, May 3, 1977.

77. Jackson, June 3, 1985.

78. Clark, telephone interview.

79. Lundy, 1973 interview.

80. Chuck Couch, interview with Gray, March 22, 1977.

81. Lundy, 1973 interview.

82. Jackson, 1976 interview.

83. Clark, 1976 interview.

84. Al Lichtman to Roy Disney, February 15, 1932, WDA.

85. Lichtman to Roy Disney, June 3, 1932, WDA.

86. Roy Disney to Lichtman, July 28, 1932, WDA.

87. Roy Disney to Lichtman, November 10, 1932, WDA.

88. Jackson, 1976 interview.

89. Don Patterson, interview, February 19, 1991.

90. "Hollywood Man Builds Fine Home," *Los Angeles Times*, June 16, 1932, AMPAS.

91. Roy Disney, June 1968 interview.

92. Notes from Hedda Hopper's November 9, 1964, interview with Walt Disney, AMPAS.

93. From a copy of the outline in Sharpsteen's papers.

94. From a copy of the outline in Sharpsteen's papers.

95. From a copy of the outline in Sharpsteen's papers.

96. From a copy of the outline in Sharpsteen's papers.

97. Thomas, *Art of Animation*, 19. According to an unpublished manuscript by Don Graham, the first such storyboard was put together for *Babes in the Woods*, released in November 1932. The Graham manuscript, titled "The Art of Animation," was commissioned by the Disney studio in the 1950s, but it was superseded by the book with a similar title by Bob Thomas; the title page of the Thomas book credits Graham for "research." Dick Huemer, Ted Sears's colleague at the Fleischer studio

and, from 1933 on, the Disney studio, credited Sears with devising the first story-board while he was "story coordinator" at Fleischer's, but there is no evidence that Sears brought that idea with him to Disney's. "Huemeresque," *Funnyworld* 18 (Summer 1978): 15.

98. Jackson, November 13, 1975.

99. Arthur Babbitt, interview, December 2, 1973.

100. Donald W. Graham to Christopher Finch, July 25, 1972, WDA.

101. Phil Dike, interview with Gray, March 29, 1977.

102. Bill Hurtz, interview with Gray, January 15, 1977.

103. Lundy, 1973 interview.

104. Walt Disney, "Growing Pains," 36.

105. From a copy of the outline in Sharpsteen's papers.

106. Frank Thomas and Ollie Johnston, *Disney Animation: The Illusion of Life* (New York, 1982), 120.

107. Ross Care, "Symphonists for the Sillies: The Composers for Disney's Shorts," *Funnyworld* 18 (Summer 1978): 42.

108. Sharpsteen, 1976 interview.

109. Jackson to author, August 22, 1975.

110. Huemer, 1973 interview.

111. Lillian Disney, Hubler interview.

112. E. H. Gombrich, *The Story of Art* (Englewood Cliffs, NJ, 1983), 61.

113. Paul Fennell, interview with Gray, December 7, 1977. According to the records for *Mickey's Mechanical Man,* Fennell animated a scene in which Mickey—not Minnie, as he remembered it—is pounding the mat.

114. Jackson, September 10, 1977.

CHAPTER 4 "This Character Was a Live Person"

1. Letter to the editor, *Hollywood Citizen-News,* March 19, 1934, AMPAS.

2. Ruth Waterbury, "What Snow White's Father Is Doing Now," *Liberty,* November 26, 1938, AMPAS.

3. Art Babbitt to Bill Tytla, circa November 27, 1933 (the postmark on the envelope), JC/NYU.

4. "'Snow White' to 31,000!" *Kansas City Star,* January 27, 1917, 1; "They Came in Thousands," *Kansas City Star,* January 28, 1917, 1; "'Snow White' Set Record," *Kansas City Times,* January 29, 1917, 1. Walt Disney to Frank L. Newman Sr., January 21, 1938, WDA.

5. Walt Disney, January 21, 1938.

6. "Snowhite Suggestions," whose cover sheet is actually titled "Manuscript," exists in the Walt Disney Archives in two copies, including one with Walt Disney's

annotations. He marked "OK" by the descriptions and suggested names of four of the dwarfs: Sleepy, Hoppy-Jumpy, Bashful, and Sneezy-Wheezy.

7. Lawrance, "'Mickey Mouse'—Inspiration from Mouse in K.C. Studio."

8. Shamus Culhane, *Talking Animals and Other People* (New York, 1986), 113.

9. Adamson/Huemer.

10. Grim Natwick, interview, November 4, 1976.

11. McLaren Stewart, interview with Gray, March 31, 1977; Eric Larson, interview, October 27, 1976; David R. Smith, "Ben Sharpsteen," *Millimeter,* April 1975, 39; Jack Bradbury, interview with Gray, March 23, 1977.

12. Goepper, 1977 interview.

13. Larson interview.

14. Sharpsteen to author, November 12, 1980.

15. Ollie Johnston, joint interview with Frank Thomas, July 13, 1987.

16. Douglas W. Churchill, "Now Mickey Mouse Enters Art's Temple," *New York Times Magazine,* June 3, 1934, 12–13.

17. A mimeographed syllabus for the lecture series and a two-page critique of *The Steeplechase* are part of the Burt Gillett collection in the Walt Disney Archives.

18. From the preview dates as noted on Sharpsteen's copies of the story outlines for those cartoons.

19. "Notes to Members of the Staff," WDA.

20. A typescript of the continuity is in the Bill Cottrell files at the Walt Disney Archives. Although undated, it appears to antedate the three versions of the continuity that Cottrell dictated himself.

21. "The *Golden Touch* treatment," an undated typescript, is in the Walt Disney Archives.

22. Dick Creedon, "Snow White (tentative outline)," October 22, 1934, WDA. Creedon's authorship is reflected in a draft of the outline accompanied by his instructions to "Frances" to make fifty numbered copies. Creedon's pages of radio-flavored dialogue are part of the same file at the Walt Disney Archives but were apparently not widely distributed.

23. Walt Disney, "'Snow White and the Seven Dwarfs' Skeleton Continuity," December 26, 1934, WDA.

24. *Walt Disney Studio Bulletin* 6, November 19, 1934, WDA.

25. "Request for Original Gag Situations," undated but probably distributed in mid-1935, WDA.

26. Babbitt, 1973 interview.

27. Sharpsteen to Tytla, December 2 and 23, 1933, NYU/JC.

28. Marge Champion, telephone interview, December 2, 1993.

29. Johnston, telephone interview, May 24, 1994.

30. Graham to Finch, July 28, 1972, WDA.

31. Larson interview.

32. Campbell Grant, interview with Gray, February 2, 1977.

33. Thor Putnam, interview, December 1, 1990.

34. Homer Brightman, interview with Gray, February 14, 1977.

35. Joe Grant, interview, October 14, 1988.

36. Jackson, 1973 interview.

37. Natwick interview.

38. Adamson/Huemer.

39. Adamson/Huemer.

40. Cannon's memo is dated March 1, but it was typed by a stenographer on March 4; Disney replied on March 5, WDA. Cannon, who joined the Disney staff in 1927, left in 1940.

41. Ken Anderson, interview, December 7, 1990.

42. Walt Disney to Bob Wickersham, memorandum, June 1, 1935, WDA.

43. Walt Disney to Babbitt, memorandum, June 1, 1935, WDA.

44. "British Crowd Mobs Disneys," *Los Angeles Times,* June 13, 1935, AMPAS.

45. "Disney and Wife to Meet Notables," *Hollywood Citizen-News,* July 20, 1935, AMPAS.

46. Roy Disney, February 1968 interview.

47. "Mickey Mouse Creator Returns in Triumph," *Los Angeles Examiner,* August 2, 1935, AMPAS.

48. "Walt Disney and Wife Home from Europe," *Los Angeles Examiner,* August 6, 1935, AMPAS.

49. Tytla to "Anna," September 9, 1935, JC/NYU.

50. Louella O. Parsons, "Walt Disney's Elaborate Plans; Will Spend Fifteen Months Making First Full Length Cartoon," *Los Angeles Examiner,* August 11, 1935, AMPAS.

51. Walt Disney, memorandum, "Action Analysis," October 17, 1935, WDA. The memo was addressed to all the studio's directors, animators, writers, assistant directors, assistant animators, and layout men.

52. Ham Luske, "General Outline of Animation Theory and Practice," December 31, 1935, mimeographed, Kerlan Collection, University of Minnesota Library.

53. "Production Notes—Shorts," mimeographed, WDA.

54. Walt Disney and Paul Hopkins to Tytla, memorandum, "Credit Rating 'Cock o' the Walk,'" December 20, 1935, WDA.

55. Walt Disney to Graham, memorandum, December 23, 1935, WDA.

56. Jackson, 1973 interview.

57. Churchill, "Mickey Mouse Enters Art's Temple," 13.

58. Ward Kimball, interview, November 2, 1976.

59. Keith Scott provided the author with a tape recording of this program. According to Scott, *Hind's Hall of Fame,* sponsored by Hind's Honey and Almond Cream, was broadcast only in 1934.

60. Dolores Voght, undated interview with Hubler, BU/RH.

61. Marcellite Garner Lincoln to author, March 15, 1978.

62. Walt Disney, "Mickey Mouse Presents," in *We Make the Movies,* ed. Nancy Naumberg (New York, 1937), 260; Sharpsteen, 1976 interview.

63. "Production Notes—Shorts."

64. Walt Disney to Hopkins and others, memorandum, "Production Notes on Snow White," November 25, 1935, WDA.

65. Maurice Noble, interview, December 3, 1990.

66. "Routine Procedure on Feature Production," undated, photocopy, WDA.

67. Champion, telephone interview.

68. *Bambi* sweatbox notes, September 1, 1939, WDA.

69. Frank Thomas and Ollie Johnston, *Disney Animation: The Illusion of Life* (New York, 1982), 320.

70. Perce Pearce, lecture, "Acting and Pantomime," March 9, 1939, WDA.

71. Graham, action-analysis lecture, July 26, 1937, mimeographed, WDA.

72. *Snow White* meeting notes, dwarfs personality meeting, December 22, 1936, WDA. Disney's continuity was extracted from these notes and hectographed for general distribution in the studio.

73. Creedon, memorandum, "The Meeting and the Bed," November 15, 1936, WDA.

74. *Snow White* story meeting notes, sequence 6B, soup sequence, November 30, 1936, WDA.

75. *Snow White* story meeting notes, sequences 11A and 11B, meeting and bed building, February 23, 1937, WDA.

76. *Snow White* layout meeting notes, January 25, 1937, WDA.

77. Lundy, 1973 interview.

78. Robert Stokes, interview with Gray, March 9, 1977.

79. Huemer, 1973 interview.

80. Jackson, 1973 interview.

81. Tom Codrick, lecture, January 19, 1939, WDA.

82. *Snow White* meeting notes, "Layout Meeting—Discussion of Sequence Problems," February 22, 1937, WDA.

83. *Snow White* meeting notes, sequence 3B, Snow White and animals in the woods, September 3, 1936, WDA.

84. *Snow White* meeting notes, sequence 4A, dwarfs at the mine, October 2, 1936, WDA.

85. Hand, "'Staging' as Applied to Presentation of Story and Gag Ideas," class conducted October 13, 1938. The transcript of this class, part of the Disney studio's "development program," comes from a 1939 compilation called "Story Department Reference Material," photocopy, AC.

86. *Snow White* story meeting notes, Sequences 15A and 16A (SW dead to end of picture), May 6, 1937.

87. *Fantasia* meeting notes ["Clair de Lune"], December 8, 1938, WDA.

88. Thomas and Johnston, *Illusion of Life,* 471.

89. Graham, action-analysis lecture, April 26, 1937, mimeographed, WDA.

90. Pearce, "Acting and Pantomime."

91. Marceil Clark Ferguson, interview, October 10, 1987.

92. Mary Eastman, interview, May 29, 1983.

93. Margaret Smith, interview, December 2, 1990.

94. Dodie Monahan, interview with Gray, March 28, 1977.

95. *An Introduction to the Walt Disney Studios* (Los Angeles, 1938), 18, AC. This thirty-one-page booklet was "a brief outline of the studio's principal departments and an explanation to artists of its employment policies."

96. The exact figure is $1,488,422.74 in a March 29, 1947, balance sheet that Walt Disney Productions submitted to RKO during negotiations for a merger of some kind, RKO.

97. Walt Disney, "Growing Pains," *Journal of the Society of Motion Picture Engineers,* January 1941, 35.

98. Roy Disney to Walt Disney, memorandum, September 10, 1937, WDA.

99. Jackson, 1973 interview. Jackson spoke of the preview as having taken place at the Carthay Circle Theatre, where *Snow White* had its premiere, but he was evidently confusing the two occasions.

100. Dorothy Ducas, "The Father of Snow White," *This Week Magazine,* June 19, 1938, AMPAS.

101. Walt Disney Productions, Prospectus, April 2, 1940, 25, Baker.

102. "Walt Disney Honored by Degree from Yale," *Los Angeles Herald,* June 22, 1938; "Harvard Confers Degree on Disney," *Los Angeles Times,* June 24, 1938, AMPAS.

103. "Disney Honored, Wishes He Had Gone to College," *New York Herald-Tribune,* June 24, 1938, AMPAS.

104. Walt Disney, "Mickey Mouse Presents," 271.

105. Douglas W. Churchill, "Disney's 'Philosophy,'" *New York Times Magazine,* March 6, 1938, 9, 23.

106. Robert Wilson, ed., *The Film Criticism of Otis Ferguson* (Philadelphia, 1971), 209. Ferguson's review was published in the *New Republic'*s issue of January 26, 1938.

CHAPTER 5 "A Drawing Factory"

1. Michael Broggie, *Walt Disney's Railroad Story* (Pasadena, 1997), 43. Disney's association with Sugar Bowl has been chronicled on a number of Web sites, including the "When Skiing Was!" section of the "First Tracks!" online ski magazine (www.firsttracksonline.com). *The Art of Skiing* (1941), a *Goofy* cartoon, shows a lodge supposedly based on the one at Sugar Bowl, as well as a peak modeled on Sugar Bowl's "Mount Disney." Disney's involvement with Hollywood Park is noted at the track's Web site (www.hollywoodpark.com). He still owned shares in both Sugar Bowl and the Hollywood Turf Club, the track's owner, at the time of his death.

2. That is the figure in two family-authorized books, Broggie, *Walt Disney's Railroad Story,* 43; and Greene and Greene, *Inside the Dream,* 45 (see Preface, n. 1).

3. Robert Stack, undated interview posted on the Walt Disney Family Museum Web site in 2006.

4. Dorothy Ducas, "The Father of Snow White," *This Week Magazine,* June 19, 1938, AMPAS. This may be the only reference in print to Disney's injury from around the time the injury occurred. Broggie, *Walt Disney's Railroad Story,* 44, says that "a ball hit Walt on the back of his neck," fracturing several vertebrae. His injury was probably painful but must not have interfered seriously with his work. As with his 1931 breakdown, it seems to have made little or no impact on the studio. It is at least possible that Disney, with his tendency to self-dramatize, used his injury as an excuse to cut back on a hazardous sport he was growing tired of.

5. Frank Bogert, telephone interview, August 5, 2005.

6. Hand, 1973 interview. According to an entry in Disney's desk diary, he rode with the Rancheros as late as May 7, 1942, WDA.

7. Garity's typewritten "Daily Reports" (as each sheet is headed), in two loose-leaf binders, cover the period from August 1937 through August 1938 (in vol. 1)—although there are actually only two pages from 1937—and September through December 1938 (in vol. 2, which also holds a few stray pages from later years), WDA.

8. A full account of this sad episode is in Thomas, *Building a Company,* 25–26, although Thomas incorrectly gives the date of Flora's death as November 28.

9. Tino Balio, *United Artists: The Company Built by the Stars* (Madison, 1976), 131.

10. Balio, *United Artists,* 136–37.

11. From copies of both contracts in the RKO files, RKO.

12. 13 NLRB 873.

13. Sharpsteen, 1976 interview.

14. Hand to author, December 4, 1976.

15. Luske, lecture, "Character Handling," October 6, 1938, WDA.

16. *Pinocchio* story meeting notes, December 3, 1937, AC.

17. *Pinocchio* story meeting notes, December 11, 1937, AC.

18. *Pinocchio* story meeting notes, December 11, 1937; *Pinocchio* story meeting notes, sequence 1, January 6, 1938, AC.

19. Hand lecture at the Rank studio, undated but numbered as the fourth lecture in the second series, DH.

20. Thomas and Johnston, *The Illusion of Life,* 221.

21. Frank Thomas, 1987 joint interview with Johnston.

22. Steve Hulett, "The Making of 'Pinocchio,' Walt Disney Style," *San Francisco Chronicle,* Datebook sec., December 24, 1978.

23. *Pinocchio* story meeting notes, Boobyland and escape, December 8, 1938, WDA.

24. Leopold Stokowski to Hubler, December 5, 1967, photocopy, WDA.

25. Gregory Dickson to Walt Disney, October 18, 1937, WDA.

26. Walt Disney to Dickson, October 26, 1937, WDA.

27. Garity, "Daily Report" for January 9, 1938. The recording began at midnight, and Garity's report is largely concerned with his preparations on January 9 (a Sunday) for the recording that night.

28. A "Tabulation of Answers to Questionnaires—Sorcerer's Apprentice" mentions that a "rough preview" was held for studio employees on that date, WDA.

29. Jackson, 1973 interview.

30. *Fantasia* story meeting notes, September 14, 1938, WDA.

31. *Fantasia* story meeting notes ["Nutcracker Suite"], September 28, 1938, WDA.

32. *Fantasia* story meeting notes ["Rite of Spring"], October 19, 1938, WDA.

33. *Alice in Wonderland* story meeting notes, January 14, 1939, WDA.

34. *Pinocchio* meeting notes, contemplated changes in sequences 1.5, 1.6, and 1.7, January 12, 1939, WDA.

35. Walt Disney to Sharpsteen, memorandum, June 20, 1938, BS; *Pinocchio* story meeting notes, sequences 7–12, February 16, 1938, photocopy, WDA.

36. Gordon Legg, interview with Gray, December 5, 1976.

37. Lincoln, March 15, 1978.

38. Sharpsteen to author, November 12, 1980.

39. Hugh Fraser, interview with Gray, March 31, 1977. Fraser's scene is identified in the *Pinocchio* draft—the scene-by-scene breakdown of who animated what—as scene 30 in sequence 7.

40. *Bambi* sweatbox notes, September 1, 1939, WDA.

41. *Fantasia* story meeting notes ["Pastoral Symphony"], August 8, 1939, WDA.

42. *Fantasia* meeting notes, July 14, 1939, WDA.

43. *Fantasia* story meeting notes, September 26, 1938, WDA.

44. Prospectus.

45. "Disney to Give Staff 20 Pct. of Profit on 'Snow White,'" *Los Angeles Evening Herald and Express*, June 28, 1938, B8. As Disney said in January 1940, when discussing a profit-sharing plan with some of his key employees, "the *Snow White* profits are back in *Pinocchio*." Transcript of meeting, "Studio Profit-Sharing Plan," January 30, 1940, WDA.

46. Sharpsteen, interview, January 3, 1979; Frank Thomas to author, August 12, 1992.

47. Lincoln, March 15, 1978.

48. Cornett Wood, telephone interview with Gray, March 16, 1977.

49. For an account of what may be the only extant example of such a personal reference, see John Canemaker, "Secrets of Disney's Visual Effects: The Schultheis Notebooks," *Print*, March–April 1996, 66–73, 118. Herman Schultheis, who compiled notebooks illustrated with his own photographs that showed how various effects were achieved, worked in the department called the Process Lab from February 1938 to June 1940, and again from December 1940 to January 1941.

50. George Rowley, interview, February 11, 1990.

51. Al Perkins, "Analysis of the Book 'Alice in Wonderland,'" September 6, 1938, WDA.

52. *Alice in Wonderland* story meeting notes, September 20, 1939, WDA.

53. Ducas, "The Father of Snow White."

54. Waterbury, "What Snow White's Father Is Doing Now."

55. Graham to Finch, July 25, 1972, WDA.

56. Carl Fallberg, interview with Gray, April 1, 1978; Douglas W. Churchill, "The Hollywood Boys Commune with Nature," *New York Times,* August 14, 1938, sec. 9, 3.

57. Fallberg interview.

58. Marc Davis, interview, November 3, 1976.

59. Clair Weeks, interview with Gray, May 13, 1978.

60. Thomas and Johnston, *Illusion of Life,* 372.

61. *Bambi* sweatbox notes, first four reels, September 9, 1939, WDA.

62. *Bambi* story meeting notes, December 11, 1939, WDA.

63. Thomas and Johnston, *Illusion of Life,* 164.

64. *Bambi* story meeting notes, sequence 10.1–10.3, Spring, February 3, 1940, WDA.

65. *Bambi* story meeting notes, sequence 10.1–10.3, Spring, April 19, 1940, WDA.

66. Wood, interview with Gray, November 30, 1976.

67. David Hilberman, interview, October 24, 1976.

68. "Center Theatre to Revert to Films for 'Pinocchio,'" *New York Times,* January 12, 1940, 12.

69. Walt Disney Productions, 1940 annual report, 2, AC. The Disney Archives holds three pages of undated typewritten notes from an interview with Luske, probably conducted around 1956 by Bob Thomas.

70. Arthur Millier, "Walter in Wonderland," *Los Angeles Times Sunday Magazine,* December 4, 1938, 20, AMPAS.

71. "Studio Profit-Sharing Plan."

72. "Walt Disney Issue Offered to Public," *New York Times,* April 2, 1940, 37.

73. Walt Disney to publicity department, memorandum, July 1, 1940, BU/RH.

74. Dan Noonan, interview with Gray, December 12, 1977; Davis, 1976 interview.

75. Prospectus, 3; 1940 annual report, 7, puts the total at 1,179 as of September 28, 1940.

76. Norman Tate, interview, August 9, 2004.

77. *An Introduction to the Walt Disney Studios,* 26; Howard Swift, tape-recorded letter to author, November 10, 1976.

78. Martin Provensen, interview, July 4, 1983.

79. Herbert Ryman, interview, July 17, 1987.

80. A. Eisen, "Two Disney Artists," *Crimmer's,* Winter 1975, 40–41.

81. Adrian Woolery, interview with Gray, January 13, 1977.

82. Joe Grant, 1988 interview.

83. John P. Miller, interview, October 6, 1991; Provensen interview.

84. Jim Bodrero, interview with Gray, January 29, 1977.

85. Carl Barks, interview, May 30, 1971.

86. *Donald's Roadside Market* story meeting notes, August 8, 1939, AC.

87. Legg, interview with Gray, March 13, 1976.

88. *The Practical Pig* story meeting notes, October 15, 1937, WDA.

89. *The Fox Hunt* story meeting notes, August 3, 1937, AC.

90. Walt Disney to Chester Cobb, memorandum, July 12, 1937, WDA.

91. Jack Cutting, interview, December 11, 1986.

92. Jackson to author, August 3, 1980.

93. Campbell Grant interview.

94. T. Hee, interview with Gray, April 13, 1977.

95. Hand interview.

96. Campbell Grant interview.

97. Couch, 1977 interview.

98. Jack Hannah, interview, November 3, 1976

99. Leo Salkin, speaking during a conference on writing for animation at the University of Southern California, 1978 (Salkin's comments were recorded but the date is uncertain).

100. Hee interview.

101. Bill Peet to author, January 20, 1988.

102. Lundy, 1973 interview.

103. Ken Anderson, interviewed by Paul F. Anderson in 1992, in Didier Ghez, ed., *Walt's People: Talking Disney with the Artists Who Knew Him* (2005), 1:119.

104. W. E. Garity and J. L. Ledeen, "The New Walt Disney Studio," *Journal of the Society of Motion Picture Engineers,* January 1941, 4.

105. The details of this transaction are set out in documents filed by Walt Disney Productions in connection with *City of Los Angeles v. City of San Fernando, Walt Disney Productions, et al.,* Superior Court, Los Angeles County, no. C650079 (1956).

106. "Studio Profit-Sharing Plan."

107. *Bulletin* (Disney in-house newsletter), September 1, 1939; prospectus, 4.

108. Garity and Ledeen, "New Walt Disney Studio," 12.

109. Fred Kopietz, interview, April 30, 1991.

110. Bradbury interview; Stephen Bosustow, interview, November 30, 1973.

111. Kimball, interview, June 6, 1969; Kimball, 1976 interview.

112. Van Kaufman, interview, February 23, 1991; Hawley Pratt, interview with Gray, December 15, 1977.

113. Barks to author, May 8, 1975.

114. Jim Korkis, "Jack Hannah, Another Interview," *Animania* 23 (March 5, 1982): 19.

115. Testimony of Walter Elias Disney, NLRB/Babbitt, 942.

116. Robert Benchley to Gertrude Darling Benchley, November 3, 1940, Robert Benchley Collection, Howard Gotlieb Archival Research Center, Boston University.

117. *Pinocchio* story meeting notes, Boobyland and escape, December 8, 1938, WDA.

118. "Theatre Taken Here for Disney 'Fantasia,'" *New York Times,* September 25, 1940, 35.

119. Franz Hoellering, "Films," *Nation,* November 23, 1940, 513.

120. Hermine Rich Isaacs, "New Horizons: *Fantasia* and Fantasound," *Theatre Arts,* January 1941, 58.

121. Walt Disney Productions, 1941 annual report, 13, Baker.

122. Walt Disney, "Growing Pains," 39.

123. Herb Lamb to Walt Disney, memorandum, February 8, 1941, WDA.

124. *Fantasia* sequel story meeting notes, January 27, 1941, WDA.

125. *Invitation to the Dance* story meeting notes, April 24, 1941, WDA.

126. Walt Disney to George J. Schaefer, March 27, 1941, WDA. *The Hound of Florence* was the source of *The Shaggy Dog,* a Disney live-action comedy made almost twenty years later.

127. 13 NLRB 873, 875.

128. Johnston, interview with Bob Thomas, May 17, 1973, WDA; Hannah, 1976 interview.

129. Legg, December 1976 interview.

130. Legg, March 1976 interview.

131. Hal Adelquist to Walt Disney, memorandum, December 23, 1940, WDA. The first members of the animation board were Eric Larson, Fred Moore, Ward Kimball, Dick Lundy, Charles Nichols, John Lounsbery, Milt Kahl, Frank Thomas, Ollie Johnston, and Norm Ferguson.

132. Lundy, interview with Gray, December 5, 1977.

133. Douglas W. Churchill, "Disney's 'Philosophy,'" 23.

134. Kimball, 1976 interview.

135. The union was variously known in its early days as the Screen Cartoonists Guild and the Screen Cartoon Guild.

136. Testimony by Arthur Babbitt, 125, NLRB/Babbitt.

137. Babbitt exhibit F, NLRB/Babbitt.

138. Babbitt, 1973 interview.

139. Babbitt exhibit F.

CHAPTER 6 "A Queer, Quick, Delightful Gink"

1. Lessing exhibit 23A, 943–45, NLRB/Babbitt.

2. Lessing exhibit 23, NLRB/Babbitt.

3. Testimony by Hal Adelquist, 903, NLRB/Babbitt.

4. "Who Started the Guild?" CSUN/SCG.

5. Lessing exhibit 23.

6. Bradbury interview.

7. *The Exposure Sheet* (newsletter of the Disney unit of the Screen Cartoonists Guild), undated but published late in February 1941, reported that Babbitt was elected chairman at the February 18 meeting, AC. Babbitt's own testimony in his NLRB case placed his election in March, however.

8. House Committee on Un-American Activities, *Hearings Regarding the Communist Infiltration of the Motion Picture Industry,* 80th Congress, 1st sess., 1947, 284. Disney testified on October 24, 1947.

9. Walt Disney to Bosustow, memorandum, May 20, 1941, SB; Bosustow interview.

10. Lessing exhibit 23A, NLRB/Babbitt; Hilberman, 1976 interview.

11. Adelquist exhibit 12B, NLRB/Babbitt.

12. Lessing exhibit 23.

13. Hilberman, 1976 interview.

14. Jack Boyd, interview with Gray, March 14, 1977.

15. Thomas Brady, "Whimsy on Strike," *New York Times,* June 29, 1941, sec. 9, 3; Babbitt, 1973 interview.

16. Preston Blair to author, October 3, 1978.

17. Schaefer to N. Peter Rathvon, June 27, 1941, RKO.

18. Arthur W. Kelly to E. C. Raftery, June 24, 1941, Wisconsin/UA.

19. Testimony by Phyllis Lambertson, 364, NLRB/Babbitt.

20. George Morris to Roy Disney, memorandum, October 16, 1941, WDA.

21. "Disney Strike Washup Near," *Daily Variety,* July 1, 1941, 1.

22. "AF of L Quits Disney Strikers," *Daily Variety,* July 9, 1941, 1.

23. Roy Disney, June 1968 interview.

24. Hilberman, interview, November 24, 1986.

25. Stanley White to J. R. Steelman, telegram, July 4, 1941, Case File 196/2188, Subject and Dispute Files, records of the Federal Mediation and Conciliation Service, Record Group 280, National Archives, Washington, D.C. Other documents related to the Disney strike—including the arbitrators' "final report"—are part of the same file.

26. "Disney Strikers Return to Jobs," *Los Angeles Times,* July 30, 1941.

27. "Disney Closed Shop Okayed," *Daily Variety,* July 31, 1941, 1.

28. Harry Teitel to Walt Disney, memorandum, October 14, 1941, WDA. Teitel later changed the spelling of his name to Tytle.

29. Hilberman, 1976 interview.

30. Testimony by Adelquist, 893, NLRB/Babbitt.

31. Walt Disney to Westbrook Pegler, August 11, 1941, WDA.

32. Roy Disney to Walt Disney, memorandum, "Visit of Jock Whitney," October 31, 1940, WDA.

33. Roy Disney to Francis Alstock, June 9, 1941, RAC.

34. Roy Disney, memorandum, "South American Short Subjects," October 7, 1941, WDA.

35. "Report on the Walt Disney South American Field Survey," records of the Department of Information, Motion Picture Division, Office of Inter-American Affairs, Record Group 229, National Archives, Washington, D.C. (hereafter cited as Department of Information records).

36. Alstock to Nelson A. Rockefeller, memorandum, "Report of John Hay Whitney from Rio de Janeiro, August 29, 1941," September 8, 1941, RAC.

37. "Report on the Walt Disney South American Field Survey."

38. "Pollen Man," *New Yorker*, November 1, 1941, 14–15.

39. 1940 annual report, 4.

40. As reflected in Disney's remarks in the *Bambi* story meeting notes from February 27, 1940, WDA.

41. George Morris to Roy Disney, memorandum, "Resume of Events," October 16, 1941, WDA.

42. March 29, 1947, balance sheet. The Walt Disney Company's more recent negative-cost figure is more than $25,000 higher, perhaps reflecting costs related to early reissues.

43. Huemer, 1973 interview.

44. Thomas and Johnston, *The Illusion of Life*, 94–95.

45. Larson interview.

46. Thomas and Johnston, *Illusion of Life*, 475.

47. "Mammal of the Year," *Time*, December 29, 1941, 27.

48. Adelquist exhibit 9, NLRB/Babbitt. Luske was briefly classified as an animator after the strike, although he had directed parts of *Pinocchio* and *The Reluctant Dragon*. Tytla quit the Disney staff in February, 1943.

49. Frank Tashlin, in a December 4, 1939, letter to Fred Niemann, FN; Tashlin wrote that Disney had given him "a feature to do—with Mickey, Donald, and Goofy in it—I'm writing the screen adaptation now—am working for Walt directly with no in between bosses." His involvement receded rapidly over the next six months, as other writers prepared storyboards for different sequences.

50. *Bambi* story meeting notes, February 27, 1940, WDA.

51. *Alice in Wonderland* meeting notes, April 2, 1940, WDA.

52. "Jack and the Beanstalk" story meeting notes, May 14, 1940, WDA.

53. March 29, 1947, balance sheet.

54. March 29, 1947, balance sheet. The Walt Disney Company's more recent negative-cost figure for *Bambi* is about $40,000 higher, perhaps reflecting costs related to early reissues.

55. Roy Disney to Walt Disney, memorandum, "Studio Situation," October 18, 1941, WDA.

56. Walt Disney to Jackson, memorandum, March 3, 1941, WDA.

57. Testimony by Arthur Babbitt, 153–55, NLRB/Babbitt. This episode, which Babbitt placed around April 15, 1941, is curiously similar to a presumably different incident that he described in a personal letter written more than six months earlier; internal references suggest that it was written in late September 1940. "A month ago," Babbitt wrote, "I tried to get a raise for a chap doing inbetweens for me. He was as capable and as speedy as any of the other boys—but still was receiving $18.00 a week—same as he had been paid in the traffic dept. Knowing full well that the 'proper officials' wouldn't do a damn thing—I wrote a note to Walt asking him to consider this particular case and if necessary set aside his rules about raises. He called me on the phone and for ten minutes blistered my ears. It seems that I don't mind my own business, that I'm a 'Bolshevik in a corner uninformed about the rest of the studio'— a 'sourpuss with a chip on my shoulder' and 'someday someone would knock the chip off and me out from under it' and on and on. I won't go into details but I had the doubtful pleasure of telling Mr. Disney what I've wanted to say for years—fully expecting to get fired for it. But instead of getting angrier—he started to laugh and assured me many times that there were no hard feelings and that he was glad I had brought the matter to his attention. Still reeling from all the unexpected turns my little note had brought about I sat down for a breather—when his secretary came down to tell me—that 'I don't know what you said to Walt—but when he finished talking with you—he called Herb Lamb and Hal Adelquist [two Disney executives concerned with personnel and financial matters] and gave them hell about something.' It seems that not only my inbetweener but 12 more got $4.00 raises. You try to figure it out. Walt has smiled charmingly at me ever since but nary a word has been mentioned—maybe *I'm* crazy." Babbitt to Robert Durant Feild, Feild Papers, Archives of American Art, Smithsonian Institution, Washington, D.C.

58. Testimony by Babbitt, 159, NLRB/Babbitt.

59. Testimony by Babbitt, 201, NLRB/Babbitt.

60. Babbitt to Feild, undated letter written in late fall of 1942, Feild Papers.

61. Roy Disney, 1967 interview.

62. "Production Shift at Disney Plant Lays Off 200," *Daily Variety,* November 25, 1941, 6.

63. "Disney Turns Over Studio Bldg. to Army Detachment," *Variety,* December 17, 1941, 145.

64. Dick Pfahler to "Those Listed," memorandum, July 29, 1941; Carl Nater to "Those Concerned," memorandum, January 22, 1942, WDA.

65. Robert Perine, *Chouinard: An Art Vision Betrayed* (Encinitas, 1985), 99.

66. "Walt Disney Weeps as He Gets Oscar," *Daily Variety,* February 27, 1942, AMPAS.

67. J. R. Josephs, Motion Picture Sub-Committee, to Coordination Committee for Mr. Francis Alstock, memorandum, "Argentine Opening of Walt Disney's *Saludo,*" Department of Information records.

68. March 29, 1947, balance sheet.

69. "Walt Disney: Great Teacher," *Fortune,* August 1942, 156; "Walt Disney Goes to War," *Life,* August 31, 1942, 61.

70. As reported in *Dispatch from Disney's,* a booklet intended for former Disney staff members in the armed services and published in June 1943.

71. Herbert Ryman, as interviewed by Robin Allan on July 7, 1985, in Didier Ghez, ed., *Walt's People: Talking Disney with the Artists Who Knew Him* (2006), 2:199.

72. March 29, 1947, balance sheet.

73. Joe Grant, interview, December 6, 1986. Grant's comparison actually fits George Pullman better than Henry Ford.

74. David Culbert, "'A Quick, Delightful Gink': Eric Knight at the Walt Disney Studio," *Funnyworld* 19 (Fall 1978): 13.

75. Johnston to author, August 8, 1977.

76. "Corn & Corn Products" and "The Soy Bean," story meeting notes, April 15, 1942, WDA.

77. Production Management to "Those Concerned," memorandum, Prod. 2016, June 9, 1942, AC. This memorandum reported that story work had been authorized on June 5, 1942, for the interstitial material in the second Latin American compilation feature.

78. Alstock to Roy O. Disney, December 8, 1942, Department of Information records.

79. From a translation of an article in *Poblicaciòn,* February 1943, Department of Information records.

80. Edwin Schallert, "Busy Future Outlined by Disney as Mickey Mouse Turns 25 Years," *Los Angeles Times,* February 22, 1953, AMPAS.

81. Roy Disney, June 1968 interview. For a brief summary of how Eyssel made his way from Kansas City to New York, see David Loth, *The City Within a City: The Romance of Rockefeller Center* (New York, 1966), 84.

82. G. S. Eyssell to Rockefeller, November 29, 1944, RAC.

83. March 29, 1947, balance sheet.

84. *Dispatch from Disney's.*

85. "Disney's Speed-up," *Variety,* June 30, 1943, 20.

86. W. H. Clark to Rathvon et al., memorandum, May 24, 1943, RKO. The memorandum says that the contract was canceled by a letter agreement dated May 19, 1943.

87. Walt Disney Productions, 1945 annual report, 3, RKO.

88. "Walt Disney—Teacher of Tomorrow," *Look,* April 17, 1945, 26, AMPAS.

89. "Walt Disney Plans Cartoon Movies for Industrial Use," *Wall Street Journal,* December 1, 1943, 4.

90. J. V. Sheehan to Walt Disney and Roy Disney, memorandum, November 9, 1944, WDA.

91. "Realign Disney Organization Top Personnel," *Motion Picture Herald,* September 15, 1945, AMPAS.

92. Harry Tytle, *One of "Walt's Boys"* (Mission Viejo, 1997), 99.

93. Tytle, *One of "Walt's Boys,"* 51.

94. Joe Grant, 1986 interview.

95. Jackson, 1973 interview; Jackson, July 28, 1975.

96. Roy Disney to Flora Disney, August 18, 1938, photocopy, private collection.

97. Diane Disney Miller, interview with Hubler, June 11, 1968, BU/RH.

98. Sharon Disney Brown, interview with Hubler, July 9, 1968, BU/RH.

99. Sharon Disney Brown, Hubler interview.

100. Diane Disney Miller, Hubler interview.

101. Diane Disney Miller, Hubler interview.

102. Diane Disney Miller, Hubler interview.

103. Disney was interviewed on the *Vox Pop* program on November 12, 1946, from the premiere of *Song of the South* at the Fox Theater in Atlanta. Recording courtesy of Keith Scott.

104. "Background on the Uncle Remus Tales," April 8, 1938; "The Uncle Remus Stories," April 11, 1938, WDA.

105. Hee interview.

106. From "About the Author" on the dust jacket of Dalton Reymond's only novel, *Earthbound* (Chicago, 1948).

107. Hedda Hopper, "Looking at Hollywood," *Los Angeles Times,* January 24, 1945, 9; "Potter Sues Disney, Asks $11,000 Salary," *Hollywood Reporter,* May 2, 1945, 3.

108. Jackson, 1973 interview.

109. Jackson, 1976 interview. Jackson spoke of the shooting as taking place at MGM, but that was probably a slip of the tongue: the Disney studio's records show that it took place at the Goldwyn Studio. David R. Smith to author, e-mail, July 17, 2006.

110. Jackson, 1976 interview.

111. Roy Disney to Ned E. Depinet, March 29, 1946, RKO.

112. Depinet to Rathvon, April 25, 1946, RKO.

113. Tytle, *One of "Walt's Boys,"* 57–58.

114. Walt Disney Productions, 1946 annual report, 9, photocopy, AC. RKO's loan was paid off by 1949, liquidated, as Roy Disney wrote, "entirely from the conversion into dollars of motion picture earnings from twenty-four blocked currency countries." Walt Disney Productions, 1949 annual report, 5, Jackson Library, Stanford University, Stanford, CA.

115. Tytle, *One of "Walt's Boys,"* 74, 83.

116. Tytle, *One of "Walt's Boys,"* 58.

117. Joe Grant, 1988 interview.

118. Jack Kinney, interviews, November 3, 1976, and December 8, 1986.

119. Eldon Dedini, interview with Gray, January 31, 1977.

120. Davis, 1976 interview.

121. Ralph Wright, interview with Gray, February 1, 1977.

122. Brightman interview.

123. Hedda Hopper, "Walt Disney Back in Stride," *Los Angeles Times,* June 30, 1946, AMPAS.

124. "Disney to Go to Ireland," *New York Times,* November 20, 1946, 43.

CHAPTER 7 "Caprices and Spurts of Childishness"

1. The alliance's "statement of principles" was published as a full-page advertisement in both *Daily Variety* and *Hollywood Reporter* on February 7, 1944.

2. "Leaders of Film Industry Form Anti-Red Group," *Los Angeles Times,* February 5, 1944, 1; "Film Leaders Form Alliance Against Communism, Fascism," *Los Angeles Herald-Express,* February 5, 1944, B1; and "The Battle of Hollywood," *Time,* February 14, 1944, 23.

3. Maurice Rapf, *Back Lot: Growing Up with the Movies* (Lanham, 1999), 131.

4. Rapf, *Back Lot,* 140.

5. Hilberman, 1976 interview.

6. House Committee on Un-American Activities, *Hearings Regarding the Communist Infiltration of the Motion Picture Industry,* 80th Congress, 1st sess., 1947, 284–85.

7. Tytle, *One of "Walt's Boys,"* 14.

8. Lillian Disney, Hubler interview.

9. Sharon Disney Brown, Hubler interview.

10. Hal Adelquist, story inventory report, May 28, 1947, RKO.

11. Roy Disney to Rathvon, May 29, 1947, RKO.

12. Thomas F. Brady, "Hollywood's Mr. Disney," *New York Times,* July 14, 1946, sec. 2, 1. Hedda Hopper, "Walt Disney Back in Stride," *Los Angeles Times,* June 30, 1946, said that *How Dear to My Heart* would be "about 90 per cent live action. In that one, Walt will resort to cartoons only when nature can't provide his needs," AMPAS. According to David R. Smith of the Walt Disney Archives, a script dated December 28, 1945, seems not to allow for animation, but other scripts, from October 1945 and March 9, 1946, clearly do provide for animated inserts, and a budget for the film dated February 25, 1946, includes cartoon sequences. Smith to author, e-mail, October 25, 2005.

13. The contract, dated June 24, 1946, does not mention *So Dear to My Heart* by name, referring only to "four (4) feature length, colored motion pictures," but it is clear from 1946 correspondence between RKO and Roy Disney that *So Dear to My Heart* was always envisioned as one of the four, RKO.

14. Card Walker, interview with Hubler, July 2, 1968, BU/RH.

15. Leonard Maltin, *The Disney Films* (New York, 1973), 89. Live-action filming for *So Dear to My Heart* began on April 30, 1946, and continued until August 23, 1946. It resumed on February 5, 1947, and continued until March 28, 1947. Filming was at the studio April 30–May 23 and August 6–23, 1946, and in 1947. The rest of

the film was shot on location, primarily at Porterville. David R. Smith to author, e-mail, July 26, 2006.

16. Bob Thomas, "Disney Talks of Plans," *Los Angeles Herald-Express,* September 16, 1955, AMPAS.

17. Those negotiations were reflected in the RKO file labeled "Disney/Special Negotiations" as of 1988, RKO. Bob Thomas, *Walt Disney,* 239 (see ch. 1, n. 40), says that "Hughes tired of running the film company and offered to give it outright to the Disneys, along with a $10,000,000 bank-credit line, but there was a catch: RKO had incurred heavy liabilities during its decline. After a meeting with Hughes to discuss the offer, Walt told Roy, 'We've already got a studio—why do we need another one?'" There was no record of such an offer in RKO's Disney-related files in 1988.

18. Walt Disney Productions, 1947 annual report, 5, RKO.

19. "Atlas Buys 25,000 Shares of Disney Productions," *New York Times,* June 16, 1945, 22. In August 1945, preferred shareholders got the opportunity to exchange their shares for debentures and common stock, and most did so. Several years later, though, the Disneys still owned more than half the common stock. Walt Disney Productions, 1951 annual report, 6, Baker.

20. Roy Disney, June 1968 interview.

21. A fourteen-page outline by Al Perkins, dated April 20, 1938, is titled "CINDERELLA—Outline of a proposed Walt Disney Storybook Version of the Fairy Tale—Story to Be Used as a Basis for a Feature Motion Picture Production," WDA.

22. Tytle, *One of "Walt's Boys,"* 150.

23. Adelquist, story inventory report.

24. Thomas F. Brady, "Walt Disney to Do a Film on Alaska," *New York Times,* August 12, 1947, 27.

25. Sharon Disney Brown, Hubler interview.

26. A. H. Weiler, "By Way of Report," *New York Times,* April 18, 1948, sec. 2, 5; "Documentary Series of Travelogs for Disney," *Variety,* April 21, 1948.

27. Thomas F. Brady, "Hollywood Arms," *New York Times,* June 6, 1948, sec. 2, 5.

28. William H. Clark to Gordon E. Youngman, May 13, 1949, RKO.

29. James Algar, "The Animated Film: Fantasy and Fact," *The Pacific Spectator,* Winter 1950, 18–19.

30. Hedda Hopper, "Disney Marches On," *Chicago Sunday Tribune,* December 26, 1948, AMPAS.

31. Walt Disney Productions, 1950 annual report, 3, Baker.

32. Winston Hibler, interview with Hubler, April 30, 1968, WDA.

33. Thomas, *Walt Disney,* 213.

34. Johnston, interview with Finch, June 2, 1972, WDA

35. Michael Broggie, *Walt Disney's Railroad Story* (Pasadena, 1997), 45.

36. Roger Broggie, interview with Hubler, July 16, 1968, BU/RH.

37. Lillian Disney, Hubler interview. Disney's deed to the lot, purchased from

Janus Investment Corporation, is recorded in book 27503, p. 279, of Los Angeles County's real estate records. Broggie, *Walt Disney's Railroad Story,* 109, dates the purchase one year later, on June 1, 1949—a particularly unfortunate error, since it throws off the chronology of Disney's rapidly growing interest in railroads in other respects.

38. Karal Ann Marling, "Imagineering the Disney Theme Parks," in *Designing Disney's Theme Parks: The Architecture of Reassurance,* ed. Karal Ann Marling (Paris, 1997), 43.

39. Patrick A. Devlin, who is listed in the program for the pageant as Pat Devlin, in a letter published in the *Arkansas Gazette* (Little Rock), December 31, 1966.

40. Marling, "Imagineering the Disney Theme Parks," 43.

41. *Official Guide Book and Program for the Pageant, "Wheels a-Rolling,"* Chicago Railroad Fair, 1948; the Santa Fe published a thirty-six-page souvenir booklet describing its Indian village, AC.

42. An extensive excerpt from the memo is reproduced in Broggie, *Walt Disney's Railroad Story,* 88–91.

43. Roger Broggie, "Walt Disney's The Carolwood-Pacific Railroad," *The Miniature Locomotive: The Live Steamers Magazine,* May–June 1952, 15; courtesy of Hans Perk.

44. Diane Disney Miller, Martin interview.

45. Lloyd Settle, "Railroading with Walt Disney," *Electric Trains,* December 1951, 18, AC.

46. Roger Broggie, Hubler interview.

47. Davis, interview with Hubler, May 21, 1968, BU/RH.

48. Amy Boothe Green and Howard Green, *Remembering Walt: Favorite Memories of Walt Disney* (New York, 1999), 183.

49. Sharon Disney Brown, Hubler interview.

50. Diane Disney Miller, Martin interview.

51. Johnston, Bob Thomas interview.

52. Diane Disney Miller, Hubler interview.

53. Hedda Hopper, "Disney Lives in World of Ageless Fantasy," *Los Angeles Times,* July 29, 1953, AMPAS.

54. Broggie, "Walt Disney's The Carolwood-Pacific," 15.

55. Lillian Disney, "I Live with a Genius," 103 (see ch. 2, n. 27).

56. David R. Smith to author, e-mail, October 31, 2005.

57. Broggie, "Walt Disney's The Carolwood-Pacific," 16.

58. Broggie, *Walt Disney's Railroad Story,* 173.

59. Starting in its May–June 1953 issue, *Miniature Locomotive* offered (for 35 cents) a catalog that included "everything needed to complete" a copy of Disney's *Lilly Belle.*

60. Lillian Disney, "I Live with a Genius," 103. "Walt Disney's Barn" was eventually moved to Griffith Park in Los Angeles, where it is open to tourists once a month.

61. Roger Broggie, Hubler interview.

62. Green and Green, *Remembering Walt,* 33.

63. Roger Broggie, Hubler interview.

64. Lillian Disney, "I Live with a Genius," 103.

65. Roger Broggie, Hubler interview.

66. Johnston, interview with Finch and Linda Rosenkrantz, June 2, 1972, WDA.

67. Transcript of meeting, "Discussion of New Studio Unit Set-Up," October 24, 1938, WDA.

68. Frank Thomas, interview with Bob Thomas, May 19, 1973, WDA.

69. Thomas and Johnston, *The Illusion of Life,* 331.

70. *Cinderella* meeting notes, December 13, 1948, WDA.

71. Davis, 1976 interview.

72. Frank Thomas, 1987 joint interview with Johnston.

73. *Cinderella* story meeting notes, January 15, 1948, WDA.

74. *Cinderella* meeting notes, February 28, 1949, sequences 01.2, 01.4, 01.5—review of cuts; timing according to a "Revised Cinderella Sequence Breakdown," dated September 28, 1948, WDA.

75. Frank Thomas, interview with Bob Thomas, May 17, 1973, WDA.

76. Larson, 1976 interview.

77. Jackson to author, September 30, 1975.

78. Johnston, 1987 joint interview with Frank Thomas.

79. Jackson, September 30, 1975.

80. Jackson, May 3, 1977.

81. Edwin Parks, interview with Gray, January 30, 1977.

82. John Mason Brown, "Recessional," *Saturday Review,* June 3, 1950, 29.

83. "Disney Home After Making British Film," *Los Angeles Times,* August 29, 1949, AMPAS.

84. *Cinderella* meeting notes, "Sweatboxed Ham's sequences with Walt upon his return from England," August 29, 1949, WDA.

85. "British Court Upholds Bobby Driscoll Fine," *Los Angeles Times,* September 28, 1949; "'Treasure Island' Started in England," *Hollywood Reporter,* July 20, 1949, 4, AMPAS.

86. Joe Adamson, *Byron Haskin* (Metuchen, NJ, 1984), 177.

87. Gus Walker, interview, June 23, 2004.

88. Sharon Disney Brown, Hubler interview.

89. Walt Disney Productions, press release, January 13, 1950, RKO.

90. "Disney Execs to Britain on 'Robin Hood' Pic," *Variety,* January 10, 1951, AMPAS.

91. Hedda Hopper, "Disney Data Up to Date," *Chicago Sunday Tribune,* May 11, 1952, AMPAS.

92. "British Court Upholds Bobby Driscoll Fine."

93. Richard Todd, interview, June 22, 2004.

94. Richard Todd, *Caught in the Act* (London, 1986), 282.

95. Ken Annakin, *So You Wanna Be a Director?* (Sheffield, England, 2001), 46.

96. Walt Disney to Perce Pearce and Fred Leahy, memorandum, March 6, 1951, WDA.

97. Todd interview. The timing of Disney's trip was dictated in part by the world premiere of *Alice in Wonderland,* which took place in London in July 1951.

98. "Walt Disney Net Dips to 196," *Daily Variety,* May 20, 1952, 1. Walt Disney Productions, 1952 annual report, 4, AC; and 1953 annual report, 4, Jackson Library, Stanford University, Stanford, CA.

99. "Disney to London," *Daily Variety,* June 24, 1952, 11; "Walt Disney Debarks," September 4, 1952, 15.

100. "Words of Encouragement from Our Foreign Friends," *The Miniature Locomotive: The Live Steamers' Magazine,* September–October 1952, 23, AC; "Walt Disney Discovers Live Steam in the Alps," *The Miniature Locomotive: The Live Steamers' Magazine,* September–October 1953, 12–13, AC.

101. Annakin, *So You Wanna Be a Director?* 57; Richard Todd, *In Camera* (London, 1989), 22.

102. Todd, *In Camera,* 28.

103. Ken Annakin, interview, June 25, 2005.

104. Todd interview.

105. "An Interview with Harper Goff," *The "E" Ticket* 14 (Winter 1992–93): 4–5.

106. Copies of the relevant correspondence are part of the Wilbur G. Kurtz Collection, AMPAS.

107. Walt Disney Productions, 1951 annual report, 3, Baker.

108. "$20,000,000 Disney Three-Year Slate," *Daily Variety,* June 20, 1952, 1.

109. Edwin Schallert, "Busy Future Outlined by Disney as Mickey Mouse Turns 25 Years," *Los Angeles Times,* February 22, 1953, AMPAS.

110. "Walt Disney Building 3d Stage at Studio," *Daily Variety,* April 24, 1953, 3.

111. Joel Frazer and Harry Hathorne, "*20,000 Leagues Under the Sea:* The Filming of Jules Verne's Classic Science Fiction Novel," *Cinefantastique,* May 1984, 35–36.

112. "Disney Cancels Annual Live Prod'n in Britain," *Daily Variety,* September 1, 1953, 1.

113. A. H. Weiler, "By Way of Report," *New York Times,* October 14, 1945, AMPAS.

114. Tytle, *One of "Walt's Boys,"* 113.

115. Bill Walsh, interview with Hubler, April 30, 1968, BU/RH.

116. Walt Disney Productions, 1950 annual report, 2, Baker.

117. Tytle, *One of "Walt's Boys,"* 114.

118. Walt Disney Productions, 1951 annual report, 7, Baker.

119. "Disney Producing Spot Telepix Blurbs," *Daily Variety,* September 22, 1952, 1.

120. Hopper, "Disney Data Up to Date."

121. Tytle, *One of "Walt's Boys,"* 115–16.

122. Thomas, *Walt Disney,* 248.

123. "Call sheets" for the live-action shooting are part of the *Alice* files at the Walt Disney Archives.

124. Stephen Birmingham, "Once Upon a Time . . . ," *McCall's,* July 1964, 121.

125. Frank Thomas, joint interview with Johnston, October 28, 1976.

126. Frank Thomas, interviewed by Christian Renaut in 1987 and 1998, in Didier Ghez, ed., *Walt's People: Talking Disney with the Artists Who Knew Him* (2006), 2:209.

127. Those dates are part of the extensive correspondence in the George Cukor Collection, AMPAS, in regard to a never-made live-action version of *Peter Pan* that would have starred Audrey Hepburn.

128. *Peter Pan* story meeting notes, May 20, 1939, WDA.

129. Roger Broggie, Hubler interview.

130. "Disney to Unveil Feature at California Living Fete," *Los Angeles Times,* November 28, 1952, 25.

131. Tytle, *One of "Walt's Boys,"* 128. Photographs of Disney's collection accompany "The Story of Walt Disney's Private Collection," *Small Talk: All about the Exciting World of Miniatures,* February 1978, 4–13, AC.

132. Bruce Gordon and David Mumford, *Disneyland: The Nickel Tour* (Santa Clarita, 2000), 12.

133. "Interview with Harper Goff," 5.

134. "Walt Disney Builds Half-Pint History," *Popular Science,* February 1953, 119.

135. Walt Disney to Ruth Disney Beecher, December 4, 1952, posted on the Walt Disney Family Museum Web site in 2003.

136. Blair Howell, "Harper Goff," *StoryboarD,* September–October 1988, 10.

137. "Interview with Harper Goff," 5–6.

138. Broggie, *Walt Disney's Railroad Story,* 195.

139. "Walt Disney Make-Believe Land Project Planned Here," *Burbank Daily Review,* March 27, 1952, 1; courtesy Burbank Public Library. There is scant evidence of any movement toward making the park a reality. A September 2, 1952, article, "Disneyland to Be Discussed at P-R Board," says that Disneyland is to be discussed at a meeting of the Board of Parks and Recreation and quotes a board member as saying the project is "very much in the planning stage. No commitments have been made."

140. "Rare Sardinian Donkeys Imported by Walt Disney," *Los Angeles Times,* December 3, 1951, AMPAS.

CHAPTER 8 "He Was Interested in Something Else"

1. Chris Merritt, "60 Years in the Amusement Business . . . Bud Hurlbut," *The "E" Ticket* 35 (Spring 2001): 20.

2. Charles Luckman, *Twice in a Lifetime: From Soap to Skyscrapers* (New York,

1988), 109. It is most unlikely that Disney was talking about a monorail in 1952; what Luckman was probably remembering was a reference by Disney to a miniature train of the kind that was always part of his plans for a park.

3. Sheilah Graham, "Just for Variety," *Daily Variety,* October 27, 1952, 2.

4. "Stockholder's Suit Attacks Salary Paid Walt Disney," *Daily Variety*, June 18, 1953, 3; "Disney Contract Is Target of Suit," *New York Times*, June 18, 1953, 38.

5. From the articles of incorporation filed with the California secretary of state.

6. Richard Irvine, interview with Hubler, May 14, 1968, BU/RH.

7. "Disneyland Art Director . . . Bill Martin," *The "E" Ticket* 20 (Winter 1994–95): 10. Winecoff, in Harrison Price's words, "was a movie guy at Fox who was hanging around Walt to help him with this idea of the park. . . . He went on the staff. But he was like an independent contractor; he was a guy that Walt was using for ideas, for a while. He was there to worry about the doing of the park, but he had no line function." Price, interview, September 24, 2003. Winecoff signed corporate documents as the secretary of Walt Disney Incorporated (later WED Enterprises) in November 1953. There is apparently no way to confirm the exact dates when the earliest WED employees were hired, since the company was separate from Walt Disney Productions at the time.

8. "Planning the First Disney Parks . . . A Talk with Marvin Davis," *The "E" Ticket* 28 (Winter 1997): 9–10.

9. Karal Ann Marling, "Imagineering the Disney Theme Parks," in *Designing Disney's Theme Parks: The Architecture of Reassurance,* ed. Karal Ann Marling (Paris, 1997), 149.

10. "A Talk with Marvin Davis," 8–9.

11. "Disneyland Art Director . . . Bill Martin," 15.

12. Irvine, Hubler interview.

13. Charles E. Davis Jr., "Disneyland Schedules Two Major Projects," *Los Angeles Times,* March 1, 1965, 3.

14. Thomas, *Walt Disney,* 228.

15. Lillian Disney, Martin interview.

16. Price interview.

17. June 3, 1953, is the date in Disney's desk diary, Robert Tieman (Disney archivist) to author, e-mail, April 20, 2006. Harrison "Buzz" Price, *Walt's Revolution! By the Numbers* (Orlando, 2003), 26, places the meeting in July—clearly too late, especially since Disney left for Europe on July 1 and spent the rest of the month away from the studio—whereas Bob Thomas, in *Building a Company,* 186, places it in April— clearly too early, again because Disney was away from the studio, this time for all but the first few days of the month.

18. Price, *Walt's Revolution!* 26–27.

19. Price interview.

20. The Disney legal department holds a copy of the June 5, 1953, proposal. David R. Smith to author, e-mail, November 1, 2005.

21. Thomas, *Building a Company*, 186; Price, *Walt's Revolution!* 26, says: "I drafted two proposals, one on site location and one on economic planning, involving 12 weeks of work with a budget of $25,000, a big fee for 1953." Since the feasibility study extended into the fall of 1953 (it was essentially irrelevant by the time it was completed), the two figures are not necessarily inconsistent.

22. Harrison A. Price, William M. Stewart, and Redford C. Rollins, "Final Report: An Analysis of Location Factors for Disneyland," August 28, 1953. A copy of the report is in the Earnest W. Moeller Collection in the Anaheim History Room at the Anaheim Public Library.

23. Price interview.

24. Howell, "Harper Goff," 10.

25. *Kirk Douglas v. Walt E. Disney*, Superior Court, Los Angeles County, no. C664346 (1956). Douglas sued Disney over unauthorized use on the *Disneyland* show of film showing Douglas and his sons riding the miniature train at Disney's home. Disney contended successfully that his use of the film was acceptable as publicity for *20,000 Leagues Under the Sea*.

26. "Interview with Harper Goff," 5.

27. "Peter Pan, Captain Hook and . . . Frank Thomas," *The "E" Ticket* 26 (Spring 1997): 39.

28. Todd interview.

29. Todd, *In Camera*, 52.

30. Disney attended a board meeting regarding Disneyland on that date. David R. Smith to author, e-mail, October 25, 2005. Thomas, *Walt Disney*, 245, reproduces what appear to be quotations from a transcript of that meeting.

31. Irvine, Hubler interview.

32. David R. Smith of the Walt Disney Archives provided the dimensions, Smith to author, e-mail, November 16, 2005. One of the best reproductions of this often-reproduced map is in Bruce Gordon and David Mumford, eds., *A Brush with Disney: An Artist's Journey, Told through the Words and Works of Herbert Dickens Ryman* (Santa Clarita, 2000).

33. From a photocopy of the "pitch kit" that originated in the "Info. Research Center" at WED Enterprises, AC.

34. "Disney to Use 'Scope Widely on New Films," *Motion Picture Daily*, November 23, 1953, 1.

35. Thomas, *Building a Company*, 184.

36. Leonard H. Goldenson with Marvin J. Wolf, *Beating the Odds: The Untold Story Behind the Rise of ABC: The Stars, Struggles, and Ego That Transformed Network Television by the Man Who Made It Happen* (New York, 1991), 122–23.

37. "Its Deal with Disney Precludes ABC Tapping Theatrical Film Lode," *Daily Variety*, April 6, 1954, 1.

38. "Disney Warns Major Studios Entering TV Not to Give Medium Stepchild Treatment," *Daily Variety*, May 11, 1955, AMPAS.

39. A request to the California secretary of state produced only Disneyland incorporation papers of later date, but according to David R. Smith of the Walt Disney Archives, "It was in business on August 17, 1953, when the Division of Corporations issued a permit to authorize the sale of securities." Smith to author, e-mail, January 13, 2006. By October 1953, Disneyland, Incorporated, was officially housed in the downtown Los Angeles law offices of Lloyd Wright, who was Disneyland's president.

40. Walt Disney Productions, proxy statement, December 30, 1964, BU/RH.

41. "Disney Chosen Chief of $9,000,000 Project," *Los Angeles Times,* May 14, 1954, AMPAS.

42. Price, *Walt's Revolution!* 29.

43. Randy Bright, *Disneyland Inside Story* (New York, 1987), 52.

44. "Interview with Harper Goff," 6–7.

45. Roger Broggie, 1968 Hubler interview.

46. Broggie, *Walt Disney's Railroad Story,* 222. According to David R. Smith of the Walt Disney Archives, the Disneys "apparently vacationed in rented cottages at Smoke Tree Ranch beginning as early as 1941. They agreed to buy lot 39, unit 2 on Sept. 19, 1946, with the deed dated Jan. 10, 1949, and the architect hired Apr. 8, 1950." Smith to author, e-mail, November 8, 2005.

47. Hal Adelquist, story inventory report, May 28, 1947, RKO. According to David R. Smith of the Walt Disney Archives, Benton was never a Disney employee. "He did prepare a rough outline for us in March, 1946, of a Davy Crockett-themed musical production subtitled 'Hunter of Kaintucky.' Nothing ever came of this . . . and it was totally different from our later TV production (whose production number was opened in July 1954)." Smith to author, e-mail, October 25, 2005.

48. Hedda Hopper, "Disney's Dreams Come True," *Chicago Sunday Tribune,* May 9, 1948, AMPAS.

49. Peter Ellenshaw, *Ellenshaw Under Glass* (Santa Clarita, 2003), 127.

50. "Showman of the World Speaks," *Motion Picture Exhibitor,* October 19, 1966, AMPAS.

51. Bob Greene, *American Beat* (New York, 1983), 233.

52. Dave Kaufman, "On All Channels," *Daily Variety,* May 13, 1955, AMPAS; "Disney Warns Major Studios."

53. *Hollywood Bowl Magazine* (concert program), July 12–16, 1955.

54. Bright, *Disneyland Inside Story,* 68. For an anecdote similar in substance but different in detail, see Broggie, *Walt Disney's Railroad Story,* 200.

55. Bright, *Disneyland Inside Story,* 76.

56. Bright, *Disneyland Inside Story,* 92.

57. "Disney's Live-Action Profits," *Business Week,* July 24, 1965, 82.

58. "Interview with Harper Goff," 7–8.

59. "Creating the Disney Landscape: An Interview with Bill Evans," *The "E" Ticket* 23 (Spring 1996): 9.

60. Roger Broggie, Hubler interview.

61. Leon J. Janzen, "Walt Disney and Ward Kimball . . . On Track to Disneyland," *The "E" Ticket* 12 (Winter 1991–92): 29.

62. Cash Shockey to Marty Sklar, memorandum, July 26, 1968, BU/RH. Shockey's was one of many anecdotes submitted to Sklar by Disney employees in response to Roy Disney's request in a July 10, 1968, memorandum for material that Hubler might use in his biography.

63. "Creating the Disney Landscape: An Interview with Bill Evans," 9.

64. Bright, *Disneyland Inside Story,* 99.

65. "Disney, Disneyland and Davy Crockett . . . A Talk with Fess Parker," *The "E" Ticket* 33 (Spring 2000): 12.

66. "'Walt's Happy Place': An Interview with Michael Broggie," *The "E" Ticket* 39 (Spring 2003): 10.

67. "A World Walt Disney Created," *New York Times*, July 31, 1955, sec. 2, 17.

68. Menen, "Dazzled in Disneyland," 70 (see ch. 3, n. 69).

69. Price interview.

70. "Walt Disney Speaks at Dane Festival," *Los Angeles Times,* July 5, 1961, AMPAS.

71. Menen, "Dazzled in Disneyland," 106.

72. Gladwin Hill, "The Never-Never Land Khrushchev Never Saw," *New York Times*, October 4, 1959, sec. 2, 11.

73. Price interview.

74. Thomas, *Walt Disney,* 274.

75. The Moeller Collection at the Anaheim Public Library includes two 1980 letters from Wood to Moeller describing in detail what was involved in acquiring the Anaheim property. On Wood's career and personality, see Price, *Walt's Revolution!* 129–39. On Wood's last days at Disneyland, see Van Arsdale France, *Window on Main Street: 35 Years of Creating Happiness at Disneyland Park* (Nashua, 1991), 49–50.

76. France, *Window on Main Street,* 116.

77. Jack E. Janzen, "The Original Snow White Dark Ride," *The "E" Ticket* 13 (Summer 1992): 24–25.

78. Bright, *Disneyland Inside Story,* 111.

79. John Hench, *Designing Disney: Imagineering and the Art of the Show* (New York, 2003), 21.

80. "Disneyland Art Director . . . Bill Martin," 17–19.

81. France, *Window on Main Street,* 44–45. For a slightly different version, see Bright, *Disneyland Inside Story,* 115. Nunis's own version, exactly the same in substance but briefer and considerably drier, is in Greene and Greene, *Inside the Dream,* 126–27. France's version has a stronger flavor of what it must have been like to get a Disney tongue-lashing.

82. France, *Window on Main Street,* 69.

83. Walt Disney Productions, 1955 annual report, 5, RKO.

84. Those notes are reproduced in Keith Keller, *Mickey Mouse Club Scrapbook* (New York, 1975), 21.

85. Murray Horowitz, "Disney Finds TV, Alone, Is Not Profitable," *Motion Picture Daily,* November 16, 1955, AMPAS.

86. Walt Disney Productions, 1956 annual report, 4, Baker.

87. Paul Jones, "Disney Camera Crews Begin Clayton Shooting," *Atlanta Constitution,* September 27, 1955, photocopy, Kurtz Collection, AMPAS.

88. The William Beaudine Collection, AMPAS, includes a budget breakdown and daily production reports for *Westward Ho the Wagons!* The film was based on *Children of the Covered Wagon,* the book proposed to RKO as an all-live-action feature in 1947.

89. "Decree Led Disney into Distribution of 'Desert,' 'Ben and Me' Package," *Motion Picture Daily,* November 23, 1953, 1.

90. "Disney to Sell Pix Package Independently of RKO Deal," *Daily Variety,* July 1, 1953, 11.

91. Roy Disney to J. R. Grainger (RKO's president), September 17, 1954, RKO; Grainger to Tom O'Neil and Dan O'Shea, memorandum, September 20, 1955, RKO. O'Neil had bought RKO from Hughes earlier in 1955.

92. Lillian Disney, Martin interview.

93. Robert Stevenson, interview with Hubler, August 20, 1968, BU/RH.

94. Walt Disney to Fred Gipson, January 8, 1957 (misdated 1956), Fred Gipson Collection, Harry Ransom Humanities Research Center, University of Texas at Austin.

95. Harry Tytle, *One of "Walt's Boys"* (Mission Viejo, 1997), 151.

96. Fess Parker, interview, September 26, 2003.

97. Michael McFadden, "Bill Beaudine and 'the Business,'" *TV Guide,* December 21, 1963, 14. Disney had written a warm letter to "Bill" on July 27, 1959 (Beaudine Collection, AMPAS):

> I see by the Trades you are celebrating your 50th Anniversary in the film business having started as a general helper, set sweeper, etc., and now you are completing the cycle by sweeping up the bits and pieces at the Disney Lot and making them into one hour shows!
>
> However, if it's any consolation, I want you to know that I am not far behind you—next February will make my 40th year as part of the motion picture business! I know you're not that much older than I am—you just got started earlier!
>
> Anyway, my congratulations and best wishes for whatever in hell you want in the future.
>
> Love,
>
> [Walt]
>
> P.S.—Please don't let this go to your head!

98. De Roos, "The Magic Worlds of Walt Disney," 185 (see ch. 2, n. 4).

99. "*Peter Pan:* Real Disney Magic; Real Animals Also Make Money," *Newsweek,* February 16, 1953, 99.

100. Winston Hibler, interview with Hubler, May 7, 1968, BU/RH. Hibler said:

"If squirrels died, they died, I know, from disease. But I think that the deaths were not anything more unusual than any zoo animals that would be confined."

101. Tytle, *One of "Walt's Boys,"* 144.

102. Walt Disney to Ruth Disney Beecher, December 4, 1957, posted on the Walt Disney Family Museum Web site in 2003.

103. "Disney to Film 'Banner,'" *Variety*, July 22, 1957, AMPAS.

104. Annakin, *So You Wanna Be a Director?* 97–98.

105. "Disney's '3d Man' Ends Swiss Filming," *Daily Variety*, September 24, 1958, AMPAS.

106. Walsh, Hubler interview.

107. November 9, 1964, Hopper interview notes.

108. Tytle, *One of "Walt's Boys,"* 122.

109. Walt Disney Productions, 1959 annual report, 5, AC.

110. Goldenson, *Beating the Odds*, 124.

111. Kimball, 1976 interview.

CHAPTER 9 "Where I Am *Happy*"

1. A sheet dated December 7, 1967, and headed "Remarks made by Tommie Wilck" includes notes about Disney's cars and his commuting route added by George Sherman of the Disney publications department, BU/RH.

2. Roy Disney, 1967 interview.

3. Peter Barnes, "Who Will Take Disney's Place?" *Los Angeles Times*, December 24, 1961, AMPAS.

4. Walt Disney Productions, 1960 annual report, 3, AC.

5. "A Conversation with . . . Ollie Johnston," *The "E" Ticket* 19 (Summer 1994): 13; "Early Illusions for the Haunted Mansion: An Interview with Rolly Crump," *The "E" Ticket* 9 (Summer 1990): 28.

6. Frank Thomas, Bob Thomas interview (see ch. 7, n. 28).

7. Frank Thomas, Bob Thomas interview.

8. Johnston, 1987 joint interview with Frank Thomas.

9. October 22, 1934, outline and December 26, 1934, continuity.

10. Frank Thomas to author, October 11, 1989.

11. Peet to author, January 20, 1988; Eyvind Earle, interview, May 30, 1983.

12. Tytle, *One of "Walt's Boys,"* 219.

13. Tytle, *One of "Walt's Boys,"* 41–42.

14. The members of the board were the subjects of a two-page spread in Thomas, *Art of Animation*, 134–35 (see ch. 3, n. 7).

15. Thomas and Johnston, *The Illusion of Life*, 159–60.

16. Davis, 1976 interview; "Chantecler" Storyboard Meeting with Walt— Opening Seq., August 24, 1960, photocopy, AC.

17. Peet to author, circa April 1979. This was not unusual; Winston Hibler, a writer on *Alice in Wonderland,* directed Kathryn Beaumont's recording sessions for Alice's voice, for instance.

18. Ken Peterson to Walt Disney, memorandum, May 21, 1958, WDA.

19. Anderson, 1990 interview.

20. Cutting, 1986 interview.

21. Anderson interview.

22. Bob Carlson, interview, November 25, 1986.

23. Peet, interview, August 15, 1978.

24. Thomas and Johnston, *The Illusion of Life,* 379.

25. Peet, January 20, 1988.

26. Floyd Norman, telephone interview, December 8, 2003.

27. Don Graham to John Rose, memorandum, April 1, 1940, WDA. A staff member named Diana March assembled hundreds of pages of "research material" in June 1939, RH.

28. Peter Bart, "The Golden Stuff of Disney Dreams," *New York Times,* December 5, 1965, sec. 2, 13.

29. Philip K. Scheuer, "Realist Disney Kept His Dreams," *Los Angeles Times,* June 26, 1960, AMPAS.

30. Murray Schumach, "Films by Disney Work Two Ways," *New York Times,* November 13, 1961, 40.

31. Walt Disney Productions, 1960 annual report, 3, AC; 1957 annual report, 3, Baker; and 1961 annual report, 4, Baker.

32. Cleveland Amory, "Cleveland Amory's Headliners," *This Week,* June 18, 1967, 2.

33. Walt Disney Productions, Notice of Annual Meeting of Stockholders, January 15, 1966, BU/RH.

34. Tytle, *One of "Walt's Boys,"* 159, 169, 172, 183, 226.

35. Diane Disney Miller, Martin interview.

36. Hedda Hopper, "Walt Disney Studio Enchanted Kingdom," *Los Angeles Times,* June 18, 1963, AMPAS.

37. Swift's comments are part of his audio commentary (shared with Hayley Mills) for the DVD release of *Pollyanna* in 2002.

38. Jack Hamilton, "Hayley Mills," *Look,* May 28, 1968, 102.

39. Pauline Annakin made those comments after joining her husband toward the end of the 2005 interview, during discussion of Lillian Disney's fall and its consequences.

40. Annakin, *So You Wanna Be a Director?* 123.

41. Annakin interview.

42. Dee Vaughan Taylor, telephone interview, June 1, 2004.

43. Norman interview.

44. Card Walker, 1968 Hubler interview.

45. Frank Thomas, Bob Thomas interview.

46. Thomas, *Walt Disney*, 321.

47. John E. Fitzgerald, "The Controversial Kingdom of Walt Disney," *U.S. Catholic*, August 1964, 18, AMPAS.

48. Gereon Zimmerman, "Walt Disney, Giant at the Fair," *Look*, February 11, 1964, 32.

49. Arthur Millier, "Citizen Disney," *Los Angeles Magazine*, November 1964, 34, AMPAS.

50. Diane Disney Miller, Hubler interview.

51. Bill Davidson, "The Latter-Day Aesop," *TV Guide*, May 13, 1961, 9, AMPAS.

52. Menen, "Dazzled in Disneyland," 75.

53. Birmingham, "Once Upon a Time . . . ," 100 (see ch. 7, n. 124).

54. Edith Efron, "Still Attacking His Ancient Enemy—Conformity," *TV Guide*, July 17, 1965, 10.

55. Dwain Houser, quoted in Perine, *Chouinard*, 165 (see ch. 6, n. 65).

56. Wade H. Mosby, "Everything Works for Walt," *Milwaukee Journal*, February 10, 1963, AMPAS.

57. Tommie Wilck, interview with Hubler, August 13, 1968, BU/RH.

58. Price interview.

59. "The Wide World of Walt Disney," *Newsweek*, December 31, 1962, 51, AMPAS.

60. "Remarks Made by Tommie Wilck"; Milt Kahl, interview with Hubler, February 27, 1968, BU/RH.

61. Price interview.

62. Joyce Carlson, interviewed by Jim Korkis in 1998 and 2000, in Didier Ghez, ed., *Walt's People: Talking Disney with the Artists Who Knew Him* (2005), 1:242.

63. Cutting interview.

64. Bart, "Golden Stuff."

65. Zimmerman, "Walt Disney, Giant at the Fair," 32.

66. "'Walt's Happy Place': An Interview with Michael Broggie," 5. Broggie spoke of Disney's "going to Club 33 or back to his apartment"—Club 33 is a private restaurant at Disneyland's New Orleans Square—but Club 33 did not open until 1967, after Disney's death.

67. "Designing Disneyland with Marc Davis," *The "E" Ticket* 7 (Summer 1989): 8.

68. Davis, interviewed by John Province in 1991 and 1992, in *Walt's People*, 1:197.

69. "Designing Disneyland with Marc Davis," 8.

70. "Marc Davis and the Haunted Mansion," *The "E" Ticket* 16 (Summer 1993): 27.

71. Davis, interview with Bob Thomas, May 25, 1973, WDA.

72. "Designing Disneyland with Marc Davis," 12.

73. "Jungle Cruise Journeys," *The "E" Ticket* 23 (Spring 1996): 32; "Alice in Wonderland," *The "E" Ticket* 31 (Spring 1999): 27.

74. Green and Green, *Remembering Walt*, 165 (see ch. 7, n. 48).

75. "Wathel Rogers and Audio-Animatronics," *The "E" Ticket* 25 (Winter 1996): 27.

76. Norris Leap, "Disney Has One Success Secret: He Makes Daydreams Come True," *Los Angeles Times,* September 25, 1960, AMPAS.

77. Menen, "Dazzled in Disneyland," 106.

78. "Disney's Mechanized Magic," *The "E" Ticket* 25 (Winter 1996): 16–18.

79. For a book-length account of Disney's involvement in the fair, see Paul F. Anderson, "A Great Big Beautiful Tomorrow," *Persistence of Vision* 6–7 (1995): 27–130.

80. Bob Thomas, "Walt Disney Tries a New One: Action Animatronics," *Arkansas Gazette* (Little Rock), May 19, 1963, 8E.

81. "Disneyland on Wheels . . . An Interview with Bob Gurr," *The "E" Ticket* 27 (Summer 1997): 34.

82. Bright, *Disneyland Inside Story,* 176.

83. Bright, *Disneyland Inside Story,* 175.

84. John Gardner, "Saint Walt: The Greatest Artist the World has Ever Known, Except for, Possibly, Apollonius of Rhodes," *New York,* November 17, 1973, 70.

85. Welton Becket, interview with Hubler, July 30, 1968, BU/RH.

86. Millier, "Citizen Disney," 34.

87. "Imagineering and the Disney Image . . . An Interview with Marty Sklar," *The "E" Ticket* 30 (Fall 1998): 9.

88. Sklar to Hubler, June 13, 1968, BU/RH.

89. "Disney's Live-Action Profits," *Business Week,* July 24, 1965, 81.

90. "Designing Disneyland with Marc Davis," 14.

91. "Pirates of the Caribbean . . . More Gems from This Disney Treasure," *The "E" Ticket* 32 (Fall 1999): 26–27.

92. "Sign on & Set Sail with the . . . Pirates of the Caribbean," *The "E" Ticket* 21 (Spring 1995): 32–33.

93. "Pirates of the Caribbean . . . More Gems," 33.

94. "A Marc Davis Pirates Sketchbook," *The "E" Ticket* 32 (Fall 1999): 14.

95. "Walt Disney's Sculptor Blaine Gibson," *The "E" Ticket* 21 (Spring 1995): 24.

96. These comments are from an undated sheet headed only "Jackson," but its content identifies Wilfred Jackson as the source, BU/RH.

97. France, *Window on Main Street,* 79. A somewhat different version of that speech, apparently edited from a transcript similar to France's, is in Thomas, *Walt Disney,* 326–27.

98. Perine, *Chouinard,* 155–58.

99. Davis, 1968 Hubler interview.

100. Perine, *Chouinard,* 161.

101. Perine, *Chouinard,* 194.

102. Perine, *Chouinard,* 167.

103. Millier, "Citizen Disney," 62, AMPAS.

104. Davis, Hubler interview.

105. Walt Disney, preface of "To enrich the lives of all people," California Institute of the Arts, undated, BU/RH.

106. "Jim Algar's notes of call from Walt," August 16, 1966, BU/RH.

107. Price, *Walt's Revolution!* 61.

108. Richard Rodgers, *Musical Stages: An Autobiography* (New York, 1975), 256.

109. Perine, *Chouinard*, 195.

CHAPTER 10: "He Drove Himself Right Up to the End"

1. From a teletype copy of a Bob Thomas article the Associated Press distributed for publication on May 8, 1955, AC.

2. Price, *Walt's Revolution!* 36, 39–40.

3. A copy of the report is part of the Harrison Price Collection, Special Collections Department, University of Central Florida Libraries, Orlando.

4. Marling, "Imagineering the Disney Theme Parks," 87.

5. Price, *Walt's Revolution!* 41.

6. Price, *Walt's Revolution!* 42.

7. As quoted in Bright, *Disneyland Inside Story*, 29.

8. Excerpts from a transcript of the news conference were published on the Walt Disney Family Museum Web site in 2005.

9. Green and Green, *Remembering Walt*, 179.

10. John McDonald, "Now the Bankers Come to Disney," *Fortune*, May 1966, 230.

11. Price, *Walt's Revolution!* 46.

12. Price, *Walt's Revolution!* 49.

13. Price, *Walt's Revolution!* 50.

14. Brochure, "Walt Disney Plans for Mineral King," 1966, BU/RH.

15. Ron Miller, interview with Hubler, May 28, 1968, BU/RH.

16. Davis, Hubler interview.

17. Lillian Disney, Martin interview.

18. "Disney Studio Sets Busy TV Schedule," TV Key feature by Charles Whitbeck for release February 9–10, 1963, AC.

19. Lillian Disney, Martin interview.

20. Diane Disney Miller, Martin interview.

21. Wilck, Hubler interview.

22. Thomas, *Building a Company*, 253–62.

23. December 30, 1964, proxy statement (see ch. 8, n. 40).

24. "Planning the First Disney Parks . . . A Talk with Marvin Davis," *The "E" Ticket* 28 (Winter 1997): 15–16.

25. WED's directors approved the name change on November 20, 1964. An amendment to the articles of incorporation was filed with the California secretary of state on February 5, 1965.

26. Steve Mannheim, *Walt Disney and the Quest for Community* (Burlington, 2003), 93.

27. "Disneyland on Wheels . . . An Interview with Bob Gurr," *The "E" Ticket* 27 (Summer 1997): 37–38.

28. Peter Bart, "The Golden Stuff of Disney Dreams," *New York Times*, December 5, 1965, sec. 2, 13.

29. Anthony Haden-Guest, *The Paradise Program* (New York, 1973), 297.

30. Green and Green, *Remembering Walt*, 90–91.

31. Mannheim, *Quest for Community*, 11.

32. Victor Gruen, *The Heart of Our Cities* (New York, 1964). Gruen's career and ideas are the subject of a harsh book-length critique by M. Jeffrey Hardwick, *Mall Maker: Victor Gruen, Architect of an American Dream* (Philadelphia, 2004).

33. Ebenezer Howard, *Garden Cities of To-morrow* (1902; reprint, Cambridge, 1965), 145.

34. Walt Disney to Roy Disney and Iwerks, September 11, 1928, WDA.

35. Haden-Guest, *Paradise Program*, 306.

36. Marling, "Imagineering the Disney Theme Parks," 150.

37. The film itself was released on DVD in 2004, as part of a "Walt Disney Treasures" set called "Tomorrowland." A complete transcript was published in 2003 on the Web site called Waltopia.

38. "Disneyland-Type Center for St. Louis Planned by Disney Productions," *Wall Street Journal*, June 19, 1964, 18; "Plan for a Disneyland in Downtown St. Louis Is Said to Be Canceled," *Wall Street Journal*, July 9, 1965, 13.

39. Mannheim, *Quest for Community*, 113.

40. Haden-Guest, *Paradise Program*, 309.

41. Correspondence between Disney and Eisenhower, much of it warm and personal, is part of the 1963–66 Principal Files, Post-Presidential Papers, Dwight D. Eisenhower Library, Abilene. Disney's activity on Murphy's behalf is described in Herbert Gold, "Nobody's Mad at Murphy," *New York Times Magazine*, December 13, 1964, 52, 55–56.

42. Vernon Scott, "Walt Disney Has a Project—a Huge New Ski Resort," *Arkansas Gazette* (Little Rock), September 26, 1965, 12E.

43. Peter Browning, "Mickey Mouse in the Mountains," *Harper's*, May 1972, 70.

44. 1966 Principal File, Post-Presidential Papers, Eisenhower Library.

45. Ron Miller, Hubler interview.

46. Robert Jackson, writing in response to Roy Disney's request for anecdotes about Walt Disney for the Hubler biography, submitted several long and detailed accounts of incidents including his last press conference (on Mineral King) and the failure of the Lincoln robot to work when the New York World's Fair opened, BU/RH.

47. Mark Kausler to author, e-mail, July 11, 2005.

48. Diane Disney Miller, Martin interview.

49. Green and Green, *Remembering Walt*, 200–201.

50. Johnston, 1973 Bob Thomas interview.

51. Thomas, *Walt Disney*, 349.

52. "Disney Gets Clean Bill from Doctors," *Daily Variety*, November 23, 1966, AMPAS.

53. "Disney Undergoes Surgery on Lung," *Los Angeles Times*, November 23, 1966, AMPAS.

54. Ron Miller, Hubler interview.

55. Milton Gray, "The Death of Walt Disney," *Well, Hallelujah*, no. 57, privately published in *APAtoons* 114 (May–June 2001).

56. Green and Green, *Remembering Walt*, 196–97.

57. Probate File P516859, Walter E. Disney, Los Angeles Superior Court (1966).

58. Diane Disney Miller, 1968 Hubler interview.

59. Greene and Greene, *Inside the Dream*, 179–80 (see Preface, n. 1).

60. Bob Thomas, "Disney's Brother Has Plans for Future," *Arkansas Democrat* (Little Rock), January 9, 1967, 7.

AFTERWORD "Let's Never Not Be a Silly Company"

1. "Walt Disney's Carousel of Progress," *The "E" Ticket* 22 (Winter 1995): 36.

2. "Planning the First Disney Parks . . . A Talk with Marvin Davis," *The "E" Ticket* 28 (Winter 1997): 17.

3. France, *Window on Main Street*, 83.

4. "Imagineering and the Disney Image . . . An Interview with Marty Sklar," *The "E" Ticket* 30 (Fall 1998): 12.

5. Perine, *Chouinard*, 214; Herbert Gold, "Walt Disney Presents: Adventures in Collegeland!" *Atlantic*, November 1972, 49.

6. Peter Bart, "Art School Aims for New Campus," *New York Times*, April 6, 1966, 40.

7. Winston Hibler, April 1968 interview.

8. Pamela Moreland, "Family Selling Rights to Walt Disney Firm," *Los Angeles Times*, July 9, 1981, AMPAS.

9. Seth Schiesel, "For Disney's Eisner, the Business Is Content, Not Conduits," *New York Times* (online edition), July 2, 2001.

10. "'Walt's Happy Place': An Interview with Michael Broggie," 14 (see ch. 8, n. 66).

INDEX

ABC of Hand Tools, The, 189
Academy Awards, 111, 183, 208, 282, 305
Academy of Motion Picture Arts and
  Sciences, 111
Acting: The First Six Lessons (Boleslavsky), 128
Adamson, Joe, 54, 103, 112, 222
Adelquist, Hal, 168, 170
Adventures of Ichabod and Mr. Toad, The,
  204
Aesop's Fables (series), 33, 61, 63, 67, 81
African Lion, The, 266
Aircraft Production Methods (series), 184
Alaska, filming in, 206
Algar, James, 181, 199, 208, 209, 299
Alice Comedies (series), 40, 42, 47–51, 66,
  67, 107
Alice in Wonderland (feature), 188, 214–15,
  228, 248, 277; difficulties in produc-
  tion of, 229–30; in postwar plans,
  199, 206, 249; prewar work on, 143,
  147–48, 218
Alice Picks the Champ, 48
Alice's Balloon Race, 48
Alice's Brown Derby, 50–51, 79
Alice's Day at Sea, 41
Alice's Fishy Story, 79
Alice's Orphan, 79
Alice's Wonderland, 36–37, 41
All in Fun. See *Melody Time*
American Ambulance Corps, 22
American Broadcasting Company (ABC),
  243–45, 249, 251, 269, 277, 278, 297,
  322

Amos 'n Andy (radio program), 108
Anderson, Bill, 267, 319
Anderson, Kenneth, 112, 127, 158, 195, 198,
  231, 258, 274–75
Andrews, Julie, 282
*Animated Cartoons: How They Are Made,
  Their Origins and Development*
  (Lutz), 26, 33
Annakin, Ken, 224, 225–26, 267, 279,
  280–81
Annakin, Pauline, 280
Appeal to Reason (newspaper), 13
Arness, Jim, 249
Atchison, Topeka and Santa Fe Railroad
  Company (the Santa Fe), 9, 20,
  211–12
Atlas Corporation, 205
Atwell, Roy, 123
Audio-Animatronics, 290–91, 292, 294–
  96, 319
Autumn, 76
"Ave Maria" (segment of *Fantasia*), 143

Babbitt, Art, 101, 109, 113, 115, 118; as
  leader of Disney unions, 165, 169,
  170, 181–82, 200, 357n57; and life
  classes, 92–93; as *Pied Piper* animator,
  98; after strike, 173, 182
Babes in the Woods, 92
Baggage Buster, 181
Bailey, Kelvin, 316
"Ballad of Davy Crockett, The" (song),
  251

Bambi, 153, 155, 178, 179, 181, 182, 184, 190, 206; as feature subject, 136, 138; loss on initial release, 180; production of, 148–51, 171

Bambi: A Life in the Woods (Salten), 136, 138, 266

Band Concert, The, 141

Banner in the Sky (James Ramsey Ullman), 267

Bank of America, 130, 136, 163, 168, 252

Barks, Carl, 155, 160

Barn Dance, The, 63–64, 65

Barnyard Olympics, 86

bar sheet, 59

Bart, Peter, 288, 307

Barton, Charles, 268

Baskett, James, 194–95

Beaudine, William, 265, 268

Beaumont, Kathryn, 228, 229, 231

Beaver Valley, 208

Becket, Welton, 239, 285, 293, 309

Beecher, Ruth Disney, 10, 11, 15, 16, 20, 209, 232

Belcher, Marjorie. *See* Champion, Marge

Bell, Mary Hayley, 279

Benchley, Robert, 161

Benedict, Ed, 81, 84

Benton, Thomas Hart, 249

Benton School (Kansas City), 17

Bergen, Edgar, 204

"biff-sniff" (animation technique), 35

Big Bad Wolf, The, 105

Bioff, Willie, 171–72

Birds in the Spring, 94

Birmingham, Steven, 285

Blackburn, Tom, 249

Blair, Lee, 161

Blair, Mary, 293

Blair, Preston, 170

Blank, Dorothy Ann, 130

Bodrero, James, 154

Bogert, Frank, 134–35

Boleslavsky, Richard, 128

Bondi, Beulah, 231

"Bongo" (segment of *Fun and Fancy Free*), 204

Bongo (unmade feature), 171

Borgfeldt, Geo., & Co., 83

Bosustow, Stephen, 159, 169

Bounds, Lillian (wife). *See* Disney, Lillian Bounds

Bounds, Phyllis (niece), 229

Boyd, Jack, 170

Bradbury, Jack, 159, 169

Bray, John R., 26, 58, 73

Bressman, Earl, 186

Bright, Randy, 246, 251, 252, 258, 292

Bright Lights, 52, 57

Brightman, Homer, 111, 198–99

Bringing Up Father (comic strip), 21

Broadway Theatre (New York), 161

Broggie, Michael, 212, 254, 288, 324

Broggie, Roger, 210, 212–13, 216, 217, 230, 231, 246, 253

Broken Toys, 118–19

Brown, Clarence, 200

Brown, Governor Edmund G. "Pat," 313–14

Brown, John Mason, 221

Brown, Robert (son-in-law), 306

Brown, Sharon Disney (daughter), 131, 191–92, 202, 207, 214, 223, 324n

Browne, George E., 171

Bruns, George, 249

Buena Vista Distribution, 262

Building a Building, 91

Burbank studio. *See* Disney, Walt, Productions

Burley, Fulton, 315

Burnham, Don, 308

Burns, Governor Haydon, 302

California Institute of the Arts (CalArts), 298–300, 307, 313, 320–21

Call, Flora (mother). *See* Disney, Flora Call

Campbell, Jack, 103

Cannon, Johnny, 58, 71, 112

Capra, Frank, 177, 186

Care, Ross, 96

Carlson, Bob, 276

Carlson, Joyce, 287

Carolwood Pacific (miniature railroad), 216, 237, 247, 254

Carr, Jack, 78

Carthay Circle Theatre (Los Angeles), 70, 131
casting by character, 118–19, 141, 177–78,
    219–20
Cauger, A. Verne, 25, 26, 29, 30, 31
cels, 33
Center Theatre (New York), 151–52
Champion, Marge (Marjorie Belcher), 110,
    120
"Chanticleer" (proposed feature), 274
Chaplin, Charlie, 79, 101, 128, 131, 135–36,
    170
Chicago, Disney homes at, 10, 21
Chicago Academy of Fine Arts, 21
Chicago Railroad Fair of 1948, 211–12
Children of the Covered Wagon, 202
China Plate, The, 84
Chouinard, Nelbert, 297
Chouinard Art Institute (Los Angeles),
    74–75, 92, 93, 297–98, 321
Churchill, Douglas, 104, 114, 117, 132,
    164–65, 297
Churchill, Frank, 95
Cinderella (feature), 188, 206, 217–21, 272
Cinderella (Laugh-O-gram), 35
City of Tomorrow (Palm Beach, Florida),
    301–2
Clark, Les, 58, 71, 80, 85, 87, 88, 118, 274
Clark, Marceil, 129
Clark, Marguerite, 101, 121
Clark, Royal, 297
Clopton, Ben, 57
Coats, Claude, 294, 295
Cock o' the Walk, 115, 116
Codrick, Tom, 126
Collins, Eddie, 122
Collodi, Carlo, 136
Colony Theatre (New York), 65–66
Columbia Broadcasting System (CBS),
    243, 249
Columbia Pictures Corporation, 70,
    78–79, 83, 89
Colvig, Pinto, 117
commercial films, 188–89
Conciliation Service, 172–73
Conried, Hans, 230
coordinator of inter-American affairs,
    office of the, 175, 186

Cottrell, Bill, 106, 173, 237, 245
Couch, Chuck, 88, 157
Cowles, J. V., 32, 35
Crane, William E., 10
Creedon, Dick, 107–8, 124
Crump, Rolly, 271
Cuban Carnival (unfinished feature), 188
Culhane, James, 103, 121
Cutting, Jack, 85, 156, 275, 287–88

DaGradi, Don, 197
Dali, Salvador, 249
"Dance of the Hours" (segment of
    Fantasia), 162
Darby O'Gill and the Little People, 14n
Davidson, Bill, 284
Davis, Marc, 153, 154, 198, 213, 218, 220,
    274, 305; and CalArts, 297, 298, 321;
    and Disneyland, 289, 294, 295
Davis, Margaret, 42
Davis, Marjorie (niece), 210
Davis, Marvin, 237–38, 306–7, 308, 311,
    319
Davis, Virginia, 36, 42, 47
"Davy Crockett, Indian Fighter" (*Frontier-
    land* episode of *Disneyland*), 249
Davy Crockett, King of the Wild Frontier,
    250
Dawn of Better Living, The, 189
Debs, Eugene V., 13
Dedini, Eldon, 198
Depinet, Ned E., 196
"Destino" (unfinished film), 249
Devlin, Pat, 211
Dewey, James F., 172–73
Dickson, Gregory, 142
Dike, Phil, 93
Dinner Time, 61
Disney, Diane Marie (daughter). *See*
    Miller, Diane Disney
Disney, Edna Francis (Mrs. Roy), 36, 43,
    49, 57, 113, 321
Disney, Elias (father), 9–10, 12–13, 15, 16–
    17, 22, 29; accidental gas poisoning
    in new home, 135; death of, 174; as
    disciplinarian, 14–15, 20; loan to Walt

Disney, Elias (father) *(continued)*
and Roy, 41; move back to Chicago,
20; move to Portland, Oregon, 30;
as newspaper route owner in Kansas
City, 18–19; return to Kansas City
from Chicago, 27–28; socialist and
Christian beliefs of, 13–14
Disney, Flora Call (mother), 9, 10, 11, 12–
13, 15, 20, 22, 30, 191; accidental death
in new home, 135
Disney, Herbert Arthur (brother), 9, 10, 13,
14, 20, 23, 29, 210
Disney, Kepple (grandfather), 12
Disney, Lillian Bounds (wife), 42, 78, 97,
191–92, 201–2, 242, 253, 317; birth
of daughter, 102; courtship and marriage, 43–45; death, 324n; dinners in
front of TV set, 263, 305; fall outside
Annakin home, 280; financial inse-
curity of, 239; miscarriages, 102, 131;
on origin of Mickey Mouse, 56–57;
possible strains in marriage, 306–7;
travels with Walt, 75, 85, 111, 113, 173,
267, 278, 285; and Walt's miniature
railroad, 215–16, 217
Disney, Margaret (aunt), 16
Disney, Mary Richardson (grandmother),
12, 16
Disney, Raymond Arnold (brother), 9, 10, 14
Disney, Robert (uncle), 10, 16, 17, 39, 40,
41, 43
Disney, Roy Edward (nephew), 191, 322, 324
Disney, Roy Oliver (brother), 2, 5, 29, 31,
39–40, 60, 191, 228, 248; ABC,
conflicts with, 269, 278; attitude
toward employees, 201; Chicago,
memories of life in, 10, 14; conflict
with Walt over WED, 306–7; death,
321; disagreement with Walt over
features, 205–6; Disney Brothers
Studio, 41–42, 46, 50; Disneyland,
initial skepticism about, 236; Florida
project, 302, 303; hospitalization with
tuberculosis, 35; Iwerks and Stalling,
break with, 75–77, 78; in Kansas
City, 19, 20, 23, 28; Marceline, memories of life in, 11, 12, 16–17; marriage

to Edna Francis, 43; move to home
on Lyric Avenue, 49; in navy, 22; on
1935 European trip, 113–14; Powers
settlement, 78–79; search for financial aid, 196; on *Snow White* screening
for banker, 130; during strike and
aftermath, 171, 172, 173, 181; Technicolor for Silly Symphonies, 89–90;
TV networks, meetings with, 243;
unions, hostility toward, 165; on Walt
as "bear for work," 270; on Walt's
attire, 102; Walt's death, 317; on Walt's
home on Woking Way, 90; Walt's
1931 "breakdown," 85
Disney, Ruth Flora (sister). *See* Beecher,
Ruth Disney
Disney, Sharon Mae (daughter). *See*
Brown, Sharon Disney
Disney, Walt (Walter Elias Disney):
acceptance of conflict at studio,
198–99; addenda to story outlines,
91–92; *Alice in Wonderland,* frustration with, 148; as amateur performer,
21; anger at Iwerks, 78; as animator
for Kansas City Film Ad, 25–28,
29; anti-Semitism, charges of, 182;
arrangement of life classes for staff,
74–75; attire, 103, 286; awareness of
details, 281–82; *Bambi,* role in production, 148–49, 151; birth, 10; break
with Powers and Iwerks, 75; "caricature of life," emphasis on, 116, 128,
132, 178; changing role in production,
71; *Cinderella,* role in production,
218–20; comedy, ideas about, 52, 73,
79, 105, 156; as commercial artist,
24–25; communism, opposition to,
200–201; concerns with cost and
appearance of animation, 144, 147,
154; conflicts with Bill Peet, 276;
conflict with Roy over WED, 306;
control of postwar short cartoons,
198; courtship and marriage to Lillian
Bounds, 43–45; cremation and memorial service, 317; crisis in spring
of 1940, 160; critiques of animators'
work, 112–13; diminishing role in

animated features, 229–30; disagreement with Roy over features, 205–6; dislike of world's fairs, 293; at Disney Brothers Studio, 41–50; Disneyland, anxiety during construction, 251; Disneyland, conception of, 238–39; Disneyland, passion for, 288; Disneyland, scrutiny of operations, 258–60, 288; Disneyland's limits as source of satisfaction, 296; drinking, 286–87; *Dumbo*, role in production, 177, 179; early ambitions for studio, 67; eating habits, 306; as editor of ideas, 155; Elias Disney, memories of, 14–15, 19–20; enthusiasm for CalArts, 297–300; EPCOT, promotion of, 307–8, 309–11; European filming and travel, 278–79; exceptional memory, 213; *Fantasia*, role in production, 141–43; as father, 102, 131, 191–92; February 10, 1941, speech to employees, 1, 4–8, 166–67; filming in Britain, 220–26; on films as interchangeable for TV, theaters, 277–78; final illness and death, 313–17; first new car, 102; flying trip to Alaska, 207; in France as ambulance driver, 22–23; habits of command, 197; heavy smoking and cigarette cough of, 42, 45, 111, 314–15; home in Holmby Hills, 210; home on Woking Way, 90–91; honorary degrees from Harvard and Yale, 131; as host of television show, 247; interest in licensing merchandise, 83; interviews with, 284–86; at Kaycee Studios, 30–31; at Laugh-O-gram Films, 31–38; lawn bowling, 305; limited role in studio's early advances, 82; "live steam" backyard railroad, 210–13, 214–17; Marceline, Missouri, memories of, 11–12; Medal of Freedom, 307; move to home on Lyric Avenue, 49; move to Los Angeles, 39–40; negotiations with Charles Mintz, 55–56; Newman Laugh-O-grams, 29; as news butcher, 20–21; as newspaper delivery boy in Kansas City, Missouri, 18–20; nighttime visits to studio, 84; 1931 "breakdown," 84–85; 1935 European trip, 113–14; 1957 commuting route, 270; and *One Hundred and One Dalmatians*, 274–75; on origin of Mickey Mouse, 56; passion for miniatures, 230–33; personal financial status in early 1950s, 239, 240–41; personal identification with studio, 136–37; *Pinocchio*, regrets about, 145, 152; *Pinocchio*, role in production, 138–40; on plans for Florida park, 302–3; playacting, value of, 117; pleasure in True-Life Adventures, 208–9; political involvement, 312; possible strains in marriage, 305–6; profanity, 155–56; return to Kansas City, 23–24; role in live-action filming, 203–4; self-absorption, 287–88; Silly Symphonies, 68–70; *Sleeping Beauty*, role in production, 272–73; *Snow White and the Seven Dwarfs*, role in production, 118, 122, 123–29; *Song of the South*, role in production, 193–95; sports, participation in, 85, 104, 134; and *Steamboat Willie*, 58–66; story, ideas about, 106; strike's effect on, 170, 173–74, 181–82; as studio's coordinator, 86, 89, 92, 97, 100–101, 104, 175; television, interest in, 228; trains, love for, 21; turn away from animation, 273; vacation in Europe, 267; work habits, 305; work on Carousel of Progress, 292; work on Pirates of the Caribbean ride, 294–95; during World War II, 182–88; writers' attempts at manipulation, 156–58; "writing" of live-action films, 263–64

Disney, Walt, British Films Limited, 225
Disney, Walt, Company, 322
Disney, Walt, Enterprises, 236
Disney, Walt, Incorporated, 236
Disney, Walt, Productions, 136, 271, 308, 311, 320; acquisition of most of WED, 306; aircraft, 293; announcement of Disney's surgery, 315; application for

Disney, Walt, Productions (continued)
   television license, 228; Burbank
   studio, 1, 2, 146, 149, 158–60; buyout
   of other Disneyland owners, 278; cuts
   to production costs, 168; Disneyland,
   part ownership of, 245, 246; after
   Disney's death, 321–23; Florida park,
   302, 303; name adopted, 50; negotiations for RKO merger, 204–5; stock
   offerings, 152, 205; subsidy to arts
   schools, 297, 300
Disney Brothers Studio, 41–50; move to
   Hyperion Avenue, 48–49
Disney Film Recording Company, 71, 77
Disneyland, 8, 263, 271, 274, 284, 293,
   301, 315, 322; Audio-Animatronics
   at Enchanted Tiki Room, 290–91;
   choice of location, 239–40; construction, 247, 251–53; and death of
   Disney, 317; Disney's speech at tenth
   anniversary celebration, 296–97;
   early plans, 232, 233–34, 235–39; end
   of shared ownership, 278; Fantasyland, 255; Jungle Cruise ride, 259,
   294; limits on storytelling and movement, 288–90; Main Street, 256;
   Matterhorn ride, 260, 267; opening
   day, 253–54; operating problems,
   256–58; other "themed" attractions,
   255–56; Pirates of the Caribbean ride,
   294–95, 319; search for television
   partner, 242–45; transportation in,
   302, 310
Disneyland (television series), 247–51,
   260–61, 269
Disneyland, Incorporated, 245, 246, 278
"Disneylandia" (proposed traveling exhibit),
   232–33
Disney World (Florida), 303, 307, 309, 316,
   317, 320. Also see Florida, as location
   for second park
division of labor at Disney studio, 81–82,
   109
Dollard, Kathleen, 42
Donald's Roadside Market. See Old
   MacDonald Duck
Don Juan, 58

Don Quixote, 277
D'Orsi, Ugo, 144
Douglas, Kirk, 241, 262
Drake, George, 103–4
Driscoll, Bobby, 202, 222, 223
Dumbo, 176–81, 182, 188, 190, 323
DuMont network, 243, 249

Earle, Eyvind, 272, 273, 275
Eastman, Mary, 129
Ebsen, Buddy, 231, 251, 254
Economic Research Associates, 298, 301
Edouarde, Carl, 62
Efron, Edith, 286
Eisenhower, Dwight, 312, 313, 314
Eisner, Michael, 322, 323
Ellenshaw, Peter, 249
Elmer Elephant, 119
Englander, Otto, 124, 138
EPCOT (Experimental Prototype Com-
   munity Of Tomorrow), 307–12, 316,
   319, 320
Epcot Center, 320
"E" Ticket, The, 231, 294–95
Eugster, Al, 72
Evans, Morgan "Bill," 252–53, 254, 256
Evans, W. L., School of Cartooning, 33
exposure sheets, 47, 59
extremes (key drawings), 69
Eyssel, G. S., 187

Fairbanks, Douglas, 57
Fallberg, Carl, 149
Fantasia, 2, 4, 141–43, 146, 147, 149, 154,
   161–62, 163, 168, 175–76, 218
Fantasound, 161, 162
Farwell, Captain Raymond F., 183
Father Noah's Ark, 92, 94
Federation of Screen Cartoonists, 163, 165,
   169
Feld, Milton, 29
Felix the Cat (series), 38, 40, 48, 71–72
Felton, Earl, 262
Fennell, Paul, 98–99
Ferguson, Norman, 81, 83, 85, 87, 95, 97,
   105–6, 107, 115, 140, 145, 150, 178,
   230, 271

Ferguson, Otis, 133
Festival of California Living at Pan-Pacific
    Auditorium, 231, 232, 233
Film Booking Offices (FBO), 51
Fine Arts Institute. *See* Kansas City Art
    Institute
Fleischer, Max, 36, 40, 58, 71, 103, 110, 120
Fleischer, Richard, 262
Flohri, Emil, 90
Florida, as location for second park, 292,
    301, 302–4. *See also* Disney World
Flowers and Trees, 88, 89–90
Flying Jalopy, The, 173
Flying Mouse, The, 105
Ford, Henry, 152, 212, 323
Ford, John, 2, 136, 177
Ford Motor Company, 152, 293
Forest Inn Café (Kansas City), 36
Forest Service, U.S., 304
Forsythe, Clyde, 134–35
Foster, Harve, 193
Foster, Norman, 261
Four Musicians [of Bremen], The (Laugh-
    O-gram), 32
Fowler, Joe, 251, 252
Fox Hunt, The, 156
France, Van Arsdale, 259–60, 319
Francis, Edna. *See* Disney, Edna Francis
Fraser, Hugh, 145
Freleng, Isadore "Friz," 54, 55
Friedman, Ray, 34, 54, 55
Frolicking Fish, 81, 83
Frontierland (episodes of *Disneyland*), 249
Fuller, William, 227
Fun and Fancy Free, 204, 205

Gallopin' Gaucho, The, 57, 64, 65
Garbutt, Bernard, 149
Garden Cities of To-morrow (Howard),
    308–9
Gardner, John, 293
Garity, Bill, 135, 142, 165, 172
Garner, Marcellite, 117–18, 144, 147
Gaucho, The, 57
General, The, 226
General Electric, 292
General Motors, 189

George, Hazel, 286
Gibson, Blaine, 295
Giegerich, Charles J., 66–67, 75, 76, 83
Gillett, Burt, 72, 74, 78, 96–97, 118
Gipson, Fred, 263–64
Goddess of Spring, The, 108, 120
Goepper, George, 3–4, 6, 104
Goff, Harper, 226–27, 231–33, 238, 240–
    41, 246, 252
Gold Diggers of 1935, 115
Golden Oaks Ranch, 300
Goldenson, Leonard, 244, 269
Golden Touch, The, 101, 105, 107, 108, 112
Goldman, Frank, 58
Gombrich, E. H., 98
Gone With the Wind, 1
Gottfredson, Floyd, 83
Graham, Donald W., 93, 110, 114–15, 123,
    128, 129
Grain That Built a Hemisphere, The, 186
"Granny's Cabin," 231
Grant, Campbell, 111, 157
Grant, Joe, 111, 154, 157, 176, 177, 185, 190,
    197
Grant, Morton, 193
Grauman's Chinese Theatre, 89, 282
Gray, Milton, 316
Great Locomotive Chase, The, 226–27, 261,
    265
Greene, Bob, 250
Greenfield Village, 212
Griffin, Eleanore, 267
Grimes, Steven, 225
Gruen, Victor, 308, 309
Gurr, Bob, 291, 307, 308

Haden-Guest, Anthony, 309, 311
Hall, Dick. *See* Marion, Dick
Hamilton, Rollin, 42, 53, 55, 57
Hand, David, 77–78, 79, 81, 83, 84, 87,
    135, 140, 157, 198, 222; as *Bambi*
    supervising director, 149; in charge
    of short subjects, 137, 155; as *Snow
    White* supervising director, 122, 124,
    126, 127, 145
Hannah, Jack, 157, 160, 164
Harline, Leigh, 95

Harman, Fred, 30–31, 77
Harman, Hugh, 30, 97, 99, 148; at Disney Brothers Studio, 46, 47; at Laugh-O-gram, 33, 36; at Walt Disney Productions, 51, 53, 54, 55, 57
Harman, Walker, 46
Haskin, Byron, 222
Havenstrite, Russell, 207
Hawks, Howard, 2, 177
Heart of Our Cities, The (Gruen), 308
Hee, Thornton, 145, 157, 158, 192–93
Helvenston, Harold, 120
Hench, John, 258
Hermosa neighborhood (Chicago), 10
Hibler, Winston, 209, 266, 321–22
Hilberman, Dave, 151, 169, 170, 172, 173, 182, 200, 201
Hind's Hall of Fame (radio program), 117
Hollywood Bowl "Tribute to Walt Disney," 251
Hopper, Hedda, 193, 199, 215, 249
Hound of Florence, The (Salten), 163, 268
House Committee on Un-American Activities, 200–201
Howard, Ebenezer, 308–9, 310, 311
Howard, Thelma, 306
Hubler, Richard, 10, 41, 44, 182, 192, 213, 223, 237, 263, 305, 313, 316
Hudson, Bert, 19
Huemer, Dick, 51, 78, 96, 103, 111, 112, 113, 118, 125, 156, 176, 177
Hughes, Howard, 204, 205, 263
Hurlburt, Bud, 235
Hurrell, George, 229
Hurrell Productions, 229
Hurter, Albert, 95, 107
Hurtz, William, 93
Huxley, Aldous, 249

Iger, Robert, 322
inbetweeners, 69
inbetweens, 69, 81
In Search of the Castaways, 281, 282
Invitation to the Dance (unfinished film), 163
Irvine, Richard, 237, 238, 243, 245, 251, 252, 292, 306–7

Isaacs, Hermine Rich, 162
Ising, Adele, 53
Ising, Rudolph, 29, 31, 52, 53, 54, 55, 148; at Disney Brothers Studio, 46, 47, 49; at Laugh-O-gram Films, 35, 37–38
Isis Theatre (Kansas City), 46, 60
Iwerks, Ub (Ubbe Iwwerks), 24–25, 27, 73, 80, 99; break with Disneys, 75–78; as director of *Silly Symphonies,* 74; disagreements with Walt Disney, 69–70, 77; at Disney Brothers Studio, 42–43, 47; at Laugh-O-gram Films, 34–35; as *Mickey Mouse* animator, 57, 58, 60, 61, 63, 66, 72; and *Mickey Mouse* comic strip, 83; as *Oswald* animator, 52–53, 55; as *Skeleton Dance* animator, 69
Iwerks-Disney (commercial art partnership), 25, 31

"Jack and the Beanstalk" (unfinished feature), 179–80, 188, 204
Jackson, Robert, 313
Jackson, Wilfred, 41, 67, 68, 71, 73–74, 82, 84, 87, 88, 90, 111, 157, 181; as cartoon director of *Song of the South,* 193–95; as *Cinderella* director, 220; as director of *Lullaby Land,* 96–97; as director of *The Goddess of Spring,* 108; as director of *The Old Mill,* 143; as director of *The Pied Piper,* 98; on Disney as inspirational boss, 99; on Disney's attitude toward studio, 116; on Disney's disengagement from animation, 190; on Disney's "fast eye," 80–81; on *Father Noah's Ark* and storyboard, 92; on *Snow White* as "source of great trouble" to Disney, 296; as *Snow White* director, 122, 125–26, 130; and *Steamboat Willie,* 58–60
Janzen, Leon, 253
Johnny Tremain, 263, 264, 277
Johns, Glynis, 225
Johnston, Ollie, 95, 104, 122, 128, 150, 163, 178, 186, 213, 271, 273–74, 276, 315; as backyard railroad enthusiast, 209–10, 217; as *Cinderella* animator, 218, 219,

220; as *Pinocchio* animator, 140, 145, 147; as *Sleeping Beauty* animator, 272

Jones, Dean, 322

Jungle Book, The, 276

Justice, James Robertson, 225

Kahl, Milt, 274, 287; as *Bambi* animator, 149, 150, 151, 178, 179; as *Cinderella* animator, 219; as *Pinocchio* animator, 140–41, 147

Kansas City, Missouri, 17–18

Kansas City Art Institute, 21, 314

Kansas City Film Ad Company, 25–27, 29, 30, 36, 54, 77

Kansas City Slide Company, 25

Kaufman, J. B., 28, 31

Kaufman, Van, 160

Kausler, Mark, 314

Kaycee Studios, 30–31, 36

Keaton, Buster, 101, 226

Kelley, W. R., 37

Kelly, Arthur W., 171

Kennedy Center, 300

Kimball, Ward, 117, 141, 159, 165, 177, 200, 219, 253, 269, 274, 287; as train enthusiast, 209, 211–12, 216

King, Jack, 87, 88

King Features Syndicate, 83

King Neptune, 95

Kinney, Jack, 197

Kirk, Tommy, 280

Knight, Eric, 185–86

Kopietz, Fred, 159

Korkis, Jim, 160, 287

Krazy Kat (series), 61

Kurtz, Wilbur, 227

Lady and the Tramp, 12, 248, 263

Laemmle, Carl, 61

Lafflets, 32, 35

Langer, Mark, 87

Lantz, Walter, studio, 159

Larson, Eric, 104, 110–11, 150, 178, 220, 274

Laugh-O-gram Films, 31–38, 39, 46, 325

Leahy, Fred, 189, 223, 224

Legg, Gordon, 156, 164

Leica reels, 144, 148

Lessing, Gunther, 75, 83, 85, 168, 169, 170, 172

Lewis, Bert, 95

licensing of Disney merchandise, 83

Lichtman, Al, 89–90

Light in the Forest, The, 261–62

Lights of New York, 58

Lilly Belle (miniature locomotive), 215, 216, 228, 239, 246

Lincoln Center, 300

Lindbergh, Charles, 57

Linkletter, Art, 309

Little Hiawatha, 144

Little People, The, 199. See also *Darby O'Gill and the Little People*

Little Red Riding Hood (Laugh-O-gram), 29, 32

Living Desert, The, 262–63, 265–66

Lloyd, Harold, 101

Lockheed Aircraft, 182, 183

Los Angeles Conservatory of Music, 298

Los Rancheros Visitadores, 134–35

Lounsbery, John, 219, 274

Love, Ed, 83–84, 88–89

Lovelace, Jonathan Bell, 204

Luckman, Charles, 235–36, 239

Lullaby Land, 96

Lundy, Dick, 73, 74, 85, 88, 93, 95, 106, 113, 158, 164; as *Snow White* animator, 118, 125

Luske, Hamilton, 113, 115, 138, 139, 143–44, 152, 179, 221; as *Pied Piper* animator, 98; as *Snow White* animator, 118, 120, 122, 124, 178, 219; as *Tortoise and the Hare* animator, 109

Lutz, Edwin G., 26, 33

Lyon, Francis, 265

Lyon, Red, 31, 34

MacArthur, James, 262, 267, 279, 280

Mace, Leslie, 32

Mack, Brice, 165

MacMurray, Fred, 268, 287

Make Mine Music, 189–90, 197, 199, 204, 205

Maltin, Leonard, 203

Mamma's Affair, 29
Manriquez, Carlos, 72
Marceline, Missouri, 9–12, 16–17, 52
Marion, Dick, 87
Marling, Karal Ann, 211, 302
Martha ("Song-O-Reel"), 35, 61
Martin, Alice (aunt), 12
Martin, Bill, 237, 238, 259
Martin, Mike (uncle), 12
Martin, Pete, 18
Mary Poppins, 282–84
Mason, James, 241, 262
Maxwell, C. G. "Max," 32–33, 34, 35, 36,
    46, 52, 54, 55
Mayer, Hy, 28
McArthur, John, 301
McConahy Building (Kansas City), 32, 34,
    36, 38
McGuire, Dorothy, 280
McKinley High School (Chicago), 21
Melody Time, 204, 249, 255
Menen, Aubrey, 256, 257, 285, 290
Merritt, Chris, 235
Merritt, Russell, 28
Messmer, Otto, 72
Metro-Goldwyn-Mayer (MGM), 52, 135,
    198
Mickey Mouse (character), 5, 56–57, 73,
    101, 140, 141
Mickey Mouse (series), 57, 58, 60, 70, 72,
    74, 75, 105
Mickey Mouse Club, 260–61, 265, 268, 270,
    284
"Mickey Mouse park," 212
Mickey Plays Papa, 105–6
Mickey's Circus, 177
Mickey's Good Deed, 91
Mickey's Mechanical Man, 91, 98–99
Mickey's Steamroller, 106
Midnight and Jeremiah (Sterling North), 202
Midnight in a Toy Shop, 82–83
Miller, Diane Disney (daughter), 15, 102,
    191–92, 213, 214, 278–79, 290, 306,
    314–15, 316, 324
Miller, John P., 154
Miller, Ronald P., Jr. (son-in-law), 305,
    306, 313, 315–16, 317, 322

Mills, Hayley, 279–80, 281
Mills, John, 279
Milotte, Alfred and Elma, 208
Minda, Meyer, 19
Mineo, Sal, 262
Mineral King project, 304–5, 312, 313–14,
    320
Miniature Locomotive (magazine), 216
Mintz, Charles, 49–51, 54–56, 71, 90, 110,
    164, 325
model department, 154–55
Modern Times, 136
Monahan, Dodie, 130
Moore, Fred, 109, 110, 179, 230; as *Dumbo*
    animator, 177–78; as *Golden Touch*
    animator, 107; and *Pinocchio,* 139–
    40, 150; as *Snow White* animator,
    118, 119, 121, 122, 125, 129, 139, 219;
    as *Three Little Pigs* animator, 95, 97,
    105
Morkovin, Boris V., 105
Moses, Robert, 291, 307
Motion Picture Alliance for the Preserva-
    tion of American Ideals, 200
Moving Day, 177
multiplane camera, 126, 143
Murphy, George, 217, 312
Music Land, 115
Mussolini, Benito, 114
Muybridge, Eadweard, 26
My Fair Lady, 282
My Friend Flicka, 203

Nash, Clarence, 117
National Broadcasting Company (NBC),
    228, 243, 249, 277, 301
National Film Board of Canada, 183
National Labor Relations Board (NLRB),
    3, 160, 163, 168, 182
Natwick, Grim, 103, 111, 113, 118–19, 120
Newman Laugh-O-grams, 29
Newman Theatre, 29
Newton, Robert, 222
New York World's Fair of 1964–65, 291–
    93, 298, 302, 307, 320; Carousel of
    Progress, 292, 319; Great Moments
    with Mr. Lincoln, 292, 293; It's a

Small World, 292–93; Magic Skyway, 293

"Night on Bald Mountain" (segment of *Fantasia*), 178

"nine old men" (supervising animators), 274

Noble, Maurice, 119

Nolan, Bill, 33

Nolley, Lance, 197

Noonan, Dan, 153

Norman, Floyd, 276–77, 281

Nunis, Richard, 259, 303

"Nutcracker Suite" (segment of *Fantasia*), 143, 175

Nutcracker Suite (Tchaikovsky), 143

O'Connor, Kendall, 87

Odlum, Floyd, 205

Old MacDonald Duck, 155

Old Mill, The, 143

Old Yeller, 261, 264

"One Hour in Wonderland," 228

One Hundred and One Dalmatians, 274–75, 276, 289

ones and *twos* (animation techniques), 86–87

On Ice, 110, 150, 177

Opry House, The, 65, 68, 71

Oreb, Tom, 197

Oswald the Lucky Rabbit (character), 51, 52

Oswald the Lucky Rabbit (series), 51–53, 55, 57, 65, 66, 71, 107

Our Gang (series), 42

Out of the Inkwell (series), 48

Owens-Illinois Glass Company, 188

O-Zell Company, 20, 28

Pacific Ready-Cut Homes, 49

Palm Springs, California, 134, 246, 305, 312

Pantages theater chain, 40

Papineau, Grace, 192

Parker, Fess, 249–51, 254, 261–62, 265, 279

Parks, Edwin, 221

Park School (Marceline), 16

Parr, Walter Robinson, 13

Parsons, Louella, 114

Patten, Luana, 199, 202, 204

Patterson, Don, 90

Pearce, Perce: as *Bambi* supervisor, 148, 157; as *Snow White* writer and director, 123, 129; as *Song of the South* associate producer, 194; as *Story of Robin Hood* producer, 223, 224; as *Sword and the Rose* producer, 225; as *Treasure Island* producer, 222

Pease, Paul, 196, 245

Peculiar Penguins, 106

Peet, Bill, 158, 219, 272–73, 274, 276, 287

Pegler, Westbrook, 173–74

Peiser's restaurant (Kansas City), 31, 36

pencil tests, 74, 82, 87–88

Penner, Ed, 192

People and Places (series), 266–67

Pereira, William, 239

Pereira and Luckman (architectural firm), 235, 237

Perine, Robert, 183, 297, 298

Perkins, Al, 147–48

Perri, 266, 267

Pesmen, Louis A., 24

Pesmen-Rubin Commercial Art Studio, 24

Peter Pan, 171, 188, 206, 218, 229, 230, 231

Peterson, Ken, 274

Pfeiffer, Walt, 21

Pictorial Clubs, 34, 35, 37

Pidgeon, Walter, 309

Pied Piper, The, 98

Pinocchio, 2, 136, 138, 149, 154, 155, 161, 168, 196, 220, 229; animation of title character, 140–41, 147; failure at box office, 151–52, 176; live action, use of in animation, 145, 218; writing of, 138–39, 143, 144, 145, 153–54

Pinocchio (Collodi), 136, 138

Pixar studio, 323

Plane Crazy, 57, 64, 65

Playful Pluto, 105

Plowboy, The, 73

Pollyanna, 279

Poor Papa, 51

Potter, General William E. "Joe," 307–8

Potter, H. C., 193

Powers, Patrick A., 61, 62, 64, 66, 75, 76, 83, 164, 325

Powers Cinephone, 61, 66
Practical Pig, The, 156
Pratt, Hawley, 160
Price, Harrison "Buzz": and CalArts, 298, 300; on choosing site for Disneyland, 239–40, 366n17; and City of Tomorrow, 301, 302; on Disneyland's success, 257; on Disney's attitude toward other people, 287; on Disney's drinking, 286–87; and Mineral King, 304; on planning for Disneyland, 245–46, 256
Principles of Scientific Management (Taylor), 81
Provensen, Martin, 153, 154
Pullman strike, 13
Puss in Boots (Laugh-O-gram), 34
Putnam, Thor, 111

Radio City Music Hall (New York), 97, 151, 187
Radio Corporation of America (RCA), 61, 301–2
Rapf, Maurice, 193, 200
Rathvon, N. Peter, 196
Red Cross, 22
Reeder, John F., 189–90
Reichenbach, Harry, 65
Reitherman, Wolfgang "Woolie," 177, 274, 276, 277
religion, in Disney family life, 13–14, 18, 191
Reluctant Dragon, The, 153, 161, 180
Renaut, Christian, 230
Retlaw Enterprises, 307, 323
Reymond, Dalton S., 193
Rice, Joan, 224
"Ride of the Valkyries, The" (Wagner), 163
"Rite of Spring, The" (segment of *Fantasia*), 147, 162
Rite of Spring, The (Stravinsky), 143, 162
RKO Radio Pictures, 130, 136, 171, 183, 196, 204–5, 263
Roberts, Bill, 118, 165, 180
Rob Roy, the Highland Rogue, 226
Rockefeller, Nelson, 175, 187
Rodgers, Richard, 300

Rogers, Wathel, 231, 290
Romero, Chuck, 297
Rose, David, 214
Rose, John, 175
Rouse, James, 302
Rowley, George, 147
Rub, Christian, 145
rubber-hose animation, 84, 86
Rubin, Bill, 24
Rules of the Nautical Road (Farwell), 183
Ryman, Herbert, 153–54, 184–85, 242–43

Saint Joseph's hospital (Burbank), 315, 316–17
Saint Louis project, 311
Saint Paul Congregational Church (Chicago), 13
Salkin, Leo, 158
Salten, Felix, 136, 163, 266
Saludos Amigos, 183–84, 186–87, 190, 206
Santa's Workshop, 94, 124
Sargeant, Eddie, 210, 212
Schaefer, George, 171
Schmeltz, Fred, 35, 36, 46
Schneider, Charles and Nettie, 43
Schuster, Harold D., 203
Screen Cartoonists Guild, 3, 165–66, 169, 170, 171, 196
Seal Island, 207–8, 209, 266
Sears, Ted, 86, 115, 214
Seversky, Alexander de, 184, 185, 193
Sewell, Hazel, 57, 173, 192
Shaggy Dog, The, 268
Sharpsteen, Ben, 71, 72–73, 80, 88, 89, 96, 111, 118, 122, 137; as *Dumbo* supervisor, 177; on George Drake, 104; as *Pinocchio* supervisor, 144, 147, 152; on Ub Iwerks, 77, 78
Shaw, Chuck, 181
Sheets, Millard, 297–98, 321
Sherman, Richard and Robert, 292, 293
Sherwood, Leighton I. ("Doc Sherwood"), 16
Shockey, Cash, 253
Silly Symphonies (series), 68–70, 74, 75, 77, 78, 89, 101, 102
Simpson, Nadine, 33

Sinbad the Sailor, 46
Skeleton Dance, The, 68–70, 80
Sklar, Marty, 293, 319
Sleeping Beauty, 268, 270, 271–73, 275
Smith, Margaret, 130
Smith, Paul (animator), 52, 53, 55, 57
Smith, Paul (composer), 265, 266
Smith, Webb, 86, 92
Smoke Tree Ranch (Palm Springs), 246, 305
"Snow White" (Brothers Grimm), 102, 138
Snow White (silent feature), 101–2
Snow White and the Seven Dwarfs, 4, 6, 101, 114, 116, 139, 142–43, 148, 169, 176, 178, 196, 221, 229, 248, 284, 323, 325; difficulties with animation of dwarfs, 121–22, 125; difficulties with layouts, 126; difficulties with story, 121, 123–24; Disney's role, 118, 122, 123–29; early story work, 102, 107–8; influence on *Sleeping Beauty,* 272; live action, use of in animation, 120, 122–23, 218; music's role in, 146; premiere, 131, 136; preview, 130–31; proposed bonus from profits, 146; RKO distribution contract, 136; rush to finish inking and painting of cels, 129–30; as "source of great trouble" to Disney, 296; success, 1, 131–32
So Dear to My Heart, 202–4, 231, 248
Song of the South, 171, 192–95, 199, 202, 203, 205, 219, 282, 290
Sorcerer's Apprentice, The (Dukas), 141–42
"Sorcerer's Apprentice, The" (segment of *Fantasia*), 142, 148, 149, 162, 181
Sorrell, Herbert, 172
sound, synchronization of cartoon with, 59
South American trip, 173, 174–75
Southdale mall (Minneapolis), 309
Soy Bean, The (unfinished film), 186
Stack, Robert, 134
Stalling, Carl: break with Disneys, 77, 99; with Disney in Los Angeles, 71, 74; with Disney in New York, 63, 64, 65, 66, 69; in Kansas City, 60–61; as pianist for *Three Little Pigs,* 96; and Silly Symphonies, 68–69

Stalmaster, Hal, 264
Stanford Research Institute (SRI), 239, 257
Stanford University, as source of Disney artists, 103, 104, 140
Stanislavsky, Konstantin, 128, 154
Stanley Fabian Warner theater chain, 66
"Steamboat Bill" (song), 58, 59, 63
Steamboat Willie: New York premiere, 65–66; New York recording sessions, 62–63; planning for sound, 58–60; preview at Disney studio, 60
Steeplechase, The, 105
Stein, Jules, 216
Stevenson, Robert, 263, 281
Stokes, Robert, 125
Stokowski, Leopold, 142, 146
storyboard, 92
Storyland, 254
Story of Robin Hood and His Merrie Men, The, 223–25, 226, 233
Strange Interlude, 89
stretch and squash (animation technique), 95
Strickland, Eddie, 118
strike at Disney studio, 170–73
Sugar Bowl (ski resort), 134
Sullivan, Pat, 40, 71–72
Swan of Tuonela, The (Sibelius), 163
sweatbox, 88
Swift, David, 279
Swift, Howard, 153
Swiss Family Robinson, 280
Switzerland, 266
Sword and the Rose, The, 225–26, 242
Sword in the Stone, The, 275, 276

Talmadge, Constance, 29
Tate, Norman, 153
Tatum, Donn, 320
Taurog, Norman, 200
Taylor, Deems, 161
Taylor, Don, 15, 17
Taylor, E. H. ("Grandpa Taylor"), 16
Taylor, Frederick W., 81–82
Technicolor, 89–90, 92
Technirama, 268

television, Disney's early involvement with, 228–29

television commercials, 229

Tempo studio, 201

Terry, Paul, 30, 33, 56, 63, 67, 81, 92

Terrytoons studio, 92, 109

Them! 249

Third Man on the Mountain, 267–68, 278, 280, 304

Thomas, Bob, 91, 163, 229, 239, 283, 301, 317

Thomas, Frank, 95, 128, 149, 199, 241, 273–74, 276, 282; as *Alice in Wonderland* animator, 229–30; as *Bambi* animator, 149, 150–51, 178, 179; as *Cinderella* animator, 218–19; as *Pinocchio* animator, 140–41, 145, 147; as *Sleeping Beauty* animator, 271, 272; as *Snow White* animator, 122, 123

Three Caballeros, The, 187–88, 190, 237

Three Little Pigs, 94–98, 101, 105, 106, 118, 119

Tivoli Gardens (Copenhagen), 245, 256–57

Toby Tyler, 279

Toccata and Fugue in D Minor (Bach), 161

Todd, Richard, 223–24, 225, 226, 242, 279

Toland, Gregg, 194–95

Tomlinson, David, 283

Tommy Tucker's Tooth, 35

Tomorrowland (episodes of *Disneyland*), 269

Tonka, 262

Tortoise and the Hare, The, 109

Travers, P. L., 282

Treasure Island, 202, 221–23, 229

True-Life Adventures (series), 208–9, 248, 262, 265, 266, 321

"True-Life Fantasy," 266

Tunberg, William, 264

20,000 Leagues Under the Sea, 227, 241, 248, 255, 262, 263, 282

Two Fabulous Characters. See *Adventures of Ichabod and Mr. Toad, The*

Tytla, Vladimir "Bill," 101, 109–10, 113, 114, 116, 118, 230, 277, 356n48; as *Dumbo* animator, 177–79; as *Snow White* animator, 118, 119, 122, 125, 128, 139, 219

Tytle, Harry, 189, 196, 197, 201, 228, 264, 268, 273

Ugly Dachshund, The, 321–22

Uncle Remus. See *Song of the South*

United Artists (UA), 89, 94, 136, 171, 185

Universal studio, 51, 56, 65

Van Beuren studio, 103

Van Dyke, Dick, 282, 283

Van Noy Interstate Company, 20

Vaughan, Dee, 281

Victory Through Air Power, 184–85, 188, 193, 237

Voght, Dolores, 117

Wagon Train, 269

Walker, Card, 202–3, 281, 319, 320

Walker, Gus, 222

Walker, Ryan, 13

Wallace, Ollie, 220

Walsh, Bill, 228, 268, 283

Walt Disney, Incorporated. *See* Disney, Walt, Incorporated

Walt Disney, the Art of Animation (Thomas), 314

Walt Disney Company. *See* Disney, Walt, Company

Walt Disney Productions. *See* Disney, Walt, Productions

Walt Disney World. *See* Disney World

Walt Disney's EPCOT '66 (film), 309–10, 319

Walt Disney's Wonderful World of Color (television series), 277–78

Warner Brothers, 52, 54, 135, 193, 198

Water Birds, 209

Watkin, Lawrence Edward, 222, 223, 224, 225, 261

Wayne, John, 315–16

WED Enterprises, 271, 287, 309; and Audio-Animatronics, 290, 291, 294; and City of Tomorrow, 301; as Disney's private company, 236, 245; and Mineral King project, 304; as owner of Disneyland railroad, 246; sale to Walt Disney Productions, 306

Weeks, Clair, 149

Western Printing and Lithographing
	Company, 245, 278
Westinghouse Electric, 189, 307, 308
Westward Ho the Wagons! 261, 265
"Wheels a-Rolling" pageant, 211
White, Stanley, 172
Whitney, John Hay, 174, 175
"Who's Afraid of the Big Bad Wolf?"
	(song), 96, 97
Why We Fight (series), 186
Wickersham, Bob, 113
Wilck, Tommie, 286, 287
Wind in the Willows, The (unfinished
	feature), 171, 180, 181, 199
Winecoff, Nat, 237, 245, 366n7
Winkler, George, 49, 55
Winkler, Margaret J., 36–37, 40–41, 49
Winkler Pictures, 49, 50, 55
women at Disney studio, restricted roles
	of, 130

Wood, C. V., 257
Wood, Cornett, 147, 151
Wood, Sam, 200
Woodward, Marvin, 121
Woolery, Adrian, 154
World's Columbia Exposition of 1893,
	13
Wright, Ralph, 198
Wynn, Ed, 229

Ye Olden Days, 91–92
York, Jeff, 261, 264

Zamora, Rudy, 84
Zander, Jack, 74–75, 92
Zanuck, Darryl, 136
Zermatt, Switzerland, 267, 304
"Zip-A-Dee-Doo-Dah" (song), 194
Zorro (television series), 261n, 269, 271
Zorro building, 237, 238

Text:	11/14 Adobe Garamond
Display:	Bodoni Poster Compressed, Adobe Garamond
Compositor:	Integrated Composition Systems
Printer and binder:	Thomson-Shore, Inc.